THE BIBLE CONCORDANCE

Index to the
King James Bible
Old and New
Testament entries

Easily locate thousands of words in your Bible

BARBOUR BOOKS
Westwood, New Jersey

Barbour and Company, Inc.
P.O. Box 1219
Westwood, New Jersey 07675

Printed in the United States of America

ISBN 1-55748-227-6

A NEW PRACTICAL, COMPARATIVE CONCORDANCE

TO THE

OLD AND NEW TESTAMENTS

Arranged in a simplified form for easy reference. It embraces the salient and ready-working features of the larger Concordances. In its Comparative feature it notes the word-changes made in the Revised Version, wherever such are of moment. Words omitted in the Revised Version are indicated by a —— (dash). The Subject Words are set in BLACK FACE CAPITALS, and those derived from them are shown in *italic* type. Plural Nouns are referred to under their singulars. Past tenses of Verbs and their Participles, as a rule, follow their present tenses.

ABASE, make low, &c.
Job 40. 11. every one proud *a.*
Isa. 31. 4. lion will not *a.* himself
Ezek. 21. 26. exalt him that is low and *a.* him that is high
Dan. 4. 37. those that walk in pride he is able to *a.*
Matt. 23. 12. whosoever shall exalt himself shall be *abased*
Phil. 4. 12. how to be *a.* and how to
2 Cor. 11. 7. offence in *abasing* myself
R. V. Matt. 23. 12; Luke 14. 11; 18. 14. humbled
ABATED, waters were, Gen. 8. 3.
Gen. 8. 11. so Noah knew that the waters were *a.*
Lev. 27. 18. it shall be *a.* from thy
Deut. 34. 7. his eye was not dim, nor his natural force *a.*
Judg. 8. 3. then their anger was *a.*
R. V. Gen. 8. 3. decreased
ABBA, *father*, Mark 14. 36. Rom. 8. 15. Gal. 4. 6.
ABHOR, greatly hate and loathe
Lev. 26. 11. my soul shall not *a.* you
15. if your soul *a.* my judgments
30. my soul shall *a.* you
Deut. 7. 26. utterly *a.* it
1 Sam. 27. 12. made his people to *a.* him
Job 30. 10. they *a.* me, they flee
42. 6. I *a.* myself and repent
Ps. 5. 6. Lord will *a.* the bloody
119. 163. I hate and *a.* lying
Jer. 14. 21. do not *a.* us for thy name's sake
Amos 5. 10. they *a.* him that speak.
6. 8. I *a.* the excellency of Jacob
Mic. 3. 9. ye that *a.* judgment
Rom. 12. 9. *a.* that which is evil
Ex. 5. 21. made our savour *abhorred*
Lev. 26. 43. their soul *a.* my statutes
Deut. 32. 19. when the Lord saw it he *a.*
1 Sam. 2. 17. men *a.* the offering of
Job 19. 19. all my inward friends *a.*
Ps. 22. 24. nor *a.* affliction of afflict.
78. 59. wroth and greatly *a.* Israel
89. 38. hath cast off and *a.* anoint.
106. 40. he *a.* his own inheritance
Prov. 22. 14. *a.* of the Lord shall fall
Lam. 2. 7. Lord hath *a.* his sanctuary
Ezek. 16. 25. made thy beauty to be *a.*
Rom. 2. 22. thou that *abhorrest* idols
Zech. 11. 8. their soul *abhorreth* me
Job 33. 20. his life *a.* bread
Ps. 10. 3. covetous whom the Lord *a.*
107. 18. their soul *a.* all manner of
Isa. 49. 7. him whom the nation *a.*
66. 24. be an *abhorring* to all flesh
R. V. Ps. 89. 38. rejected; Ezek. 16. 25. an abomination
ABIDE, continue, bear
Ex. 16. 29. *a.* ye every man in his
Num. 35. 25. *a.* in it unto the death
2 Sam. 11. 11. ark and Israel *a.* in tents
Ps. 15. 1. who shall *a.* in thy tabernacle
7. he shall *a.* before God for ever
Prov. 7. 11. her feet *a.* not in her house
Hos. 3. 3. shall *a.* for me many days
4. Israel shall *a.* without a king
Joel 2. 11. day of the Lord is great and very terrible; who can *a.* it
Mal. 3. 2. who may *a.* the day of his coming
Matt. 10. 11. there *a.* till ye go thence
Luke 19. 5. to-day I must *a.* at thy
John 12. 46. should not *a.* in dark.
15. 4. *a.* in me and I in you, 7.
Acts 20. 23. afflictions *a.* me.
1 Cor. 3. 14. if any man's work *a.*
7. 8. it is good for them if they *a.* even as I
20. let every man *a.* in the same calling wherein he was called
24. is called therein *a.* with God
Phil. 1. 24. to *a.* in the flesh is needful
25. know that I shall *a.* with you
1 John 2. 24. let that therefore *a.* in you
27, 28. ye shall *a.* in him
Ps. 49. 12. man in honor *abideth* not
Eccl. 1. 4. the earth *a.* for ever
John 3. 36. wrath of God *a.* on him
8. 35. servant *a.* not but the Son *a.* ever
12. 24. except it die it *a.* alone
1 Cor. 13. 13. now *a.* faith, hope
2 Tim. 2. 13. yet he *a.* faithful
1 Pet. 1. 23. word of God *a.* for ever
1 John 3. 6. whoso *a.* in him sinneth not
24. hereby we know he *a.* in us
John 5. 38. not his word *abiding* in you
1 John 3. 15. no murderer hath eternal life *a.*
John 14. 23. make our *abode* with him
R. V. Ps. 15. 1. sojourn; Hos. 11. 6. fall upon; Rom. 11. 23. continue
ABILITY, in strength, wealth, &c.
Lev. 27. 8. Ezra 2. 69. Neh. 5. 8. Dan. 1. 4.
Matt. 25. 15. to every man according to his *a.*, Acts 11. 29.
1 Pet. 4. 11. as of the *a.* God giveth
R. V. 1 Pet. 4. 11. strength
ABJECTS, *base men*, Ps. 35. 15.
ABLE men, such as fear God, Ex. 18. 21.
Lev. 14. 22. such as he is *a.* to get
Deut. 16. 17. every man give as he is *a.*
2 Chron. 20. 6. none is *a.* to withstand
Prov. 27. 4. who is *a.* to stand
Ezek. 46. 11. as he is *a.* to give
Dan. 3. 17. our God is *a.* to deliver
4. 37. walk in pride he is *a.* to abase
Matt. 3. 9. God is *a.* of these stones to raise up children, Luke 3. 8.
9. 28. believe ye that I am *a.* to
20. 22. are ye *a.* to drink of cup
Mark 4. 33. as they were *a.* to hear
John 10. 29. no man *a.* to pluck
Rom. 4. 21. promised he was *a.* to perform
14. 4. God is *a.* to make him stand
1 Cor. 3. 2. neither yet now are ye *a*
10. 13. tempted above that ye are *a.*
2 Cor. 9. 8. *a.* to make all grace abound
Eph. 3. 20. *a.* to do exceeding
2 Tim. 1. 12. *a.* to keep that committed
Heb. 2. 18. *a.* to succor the tempt.
5. 7. *a.* to save him from death
7. 25. *a.* to save to the uttermost
James 1. 21. *a.* to save your souls
4. 12. *a.* to save and to destroy
Jude 24. *a.* to keep you from fall.
R. V. Lev. 25. 26. waxen rich; Josh. 23. 9 ——; Acts 25. 5. are of power; 2 Cor. 3. 6. sufficient as; Eph. 3. 18. strong.
ABOLISHED, made to cease
Isa. 2. 18. idols he shall utterly *abolish*
Ezek. 6. 6. your works may be *a.*
2 Cor. 3. 13. to the end of that *a.*
2 Tim. 1. 10. Jesus Christ who hath *a.* death
R. V. Isa. 2. 18. pass away; 2 Cor. 3. 13. passing away.

ABOMINABLE, very hateful. Lev. 7. 21. & 11. 43. & 18. 30. Isa. 14. 19. & 65. 4. Jer. 16. 18.
1 Chron. 21. 6. king's word was *a.* to Joab
Ps. 14. 1. have done *a.* works, 53. 1.
Jer. 44. 4. do not this *a.* thing
Ezek. 16 52. has committed more *a.*
Tit. 1. 16. in works deny him being *a.*
1 Pet. 4. 3. walked in *a.* idolatries
Rev. 21. 8. unbelieving and *a.* shall

ABOMINATION, what is very filthy, hateful, and loathsome as sin, Isa. 66. 3. idols, Ex. 8. 26.
Prov. 6. 16. seven things are an *a.*
11. 1. a false balance is *a.* to the Lord. [Lord
12. 22. lying lips are *a.* to the
15. 8. the sacrifice of the wicked is an *a.* [the Lord, 3. 32.
16. 5. proud in heart is an *a.* to
20. 23. divers weights are an *a* to the Lord.
Isa. 1. 13. incense is an *a.* to me.
Dan. 11. 31. *a.* that maketh desolate. [of desolation
12. 11. Matt. 24. 15. Mark 13. 14. *a.*
Luke 16. 15. is *a.* in the sight of God [*a.*
Rev. 21. 27, whatsoever worketh
2 Kings 21. 2. *abominations* of the
Ezra 9. 14. join with the people of these *a.*
Prov. 26. 25. seven *a.* in his heart
Jer. 7. 10. delivered to do all these *a.*
Ezek. 16. 2. cause Jerusalem to know her *a.* 20. 4. & 23. 36.
18. 13. hath done all these *a.* shall
Dan. 9. 27. for the overspreading of *a.*
Rev. 17. 5. mother of harlots and *a.*

ABOUND, become very full, large, Prov. 8. 24. Rom. 3. 7.
Prov. 28. 20. the faithful shall *a.*
Matt. 24. 12. iniquity shall *a*
Rom. 5. 20. offence might *a.* but where sin *a.* grace did much more *a.*
2 Cor. 9. 8. able to make all gr. *a.*
Phil. 1. 9. that love may *a.* more
4. 12. I know how *a.* [count
17. fruit that may *a.* to your ac-
18. I have all and *a.*
1 Thes. 3. 12. the Lord make you *a.*
2 Pet. 1. 8. if these things be in you and *a.* [us
Eph. 1. 8. hath *abounded* toward
1 Cor. 15. 58, always *abounding*
Col. 2. 7. *a.* with thanksgiving
R. V. Matt. 24. 12. multiplied.

ABOVE, higher, heaven, Ex. 20. 4.
John 3. 31. cometh from *a.* is *a.* all
19. 11. power given thee from *a.*
Gal. 4. 26. Jerusalem, which is *a.* is
Eph. 4. 6. one God who is *a.* all
Col. 3. 1. seek things which are *a.*
James 1. 17. every perfect gift is from *a.*

ABSENT one from another, Gen. 31. 49. 2 Cor. 10. 1. [ent
1 Cor. 5. 3. as *a.* in body but pres-
2 Cor. 5. 6. in body we are *a.* from the Lord
10. 1. being *a.* am bold toward you
Col. 2. 5. though I be *a.* in the flesh

ABSTAIN from idols, Acts 15. 20.
1 Thess. 4. 3. *a.* from fornication.
5. 22. *a.* from all appearance of evil
1 Pet. 2. 11. *a.* from fleshly lusts
Abstinence from meat, Acts 27. 21.

ABUNDANCE, great fulness, and plenty. Job 22. 11. & 38. 24.
Deut. 33. 19. 1 Chron. 22. 3, 4, 14, 15.
Deut. 28. 47. for the *a.* of all things
Eccl. 5. 10. he that loveth *a.* with
12. *a.* of the rich will not suffer him to sleep
Isa. 66. 11. delighted with *a.* of her glory
Matt. 12. 34, out of *a.* of the heart the mouth speaketh, Luke 6. 45.
13. 12. shall have more *a.* 25. 29.
Mark 12. 44. they did cast in of their *a.* [*a.*
Luke 12. 15. life consisteth not in
2 Cor. 8. 2. *a.* of their joy abounded
12. 7. through *a.* of revelations
R. V. 2 Cor. 8. 20 bounty

ABUNDANT in goodness and truth, Ex. 34. 6. 2 Cor. 4. 15. & 9. 12.
2 Cor. 11. 23, in labors more *a.*
1 Tim. 1. 14. grace of Lord exceeding *a.*
Job 12. 6. God bringeth *abundantly*
Ps. 36. 8. shall be *a.* satisfied with fatness
S. of S. 5. 1. yea drink *a.* O beloved
Isa. 55. 7. he will *a.* pardon [*a.*
John 10. 10. might have life more
Eph. 3. 20. able to do exceeding *a.*
Tit. 3. 6. shed on us *a.* thro. Jesus
2 Pet. 1. 11. entrance shall be ministered unto you more *a.*
R. V. 2 Cor. 4. 15. multiplied; 1 Pet. 1. 3. great

ABUSE not my power, 1 Cor. 9. 18. 1 Cor. 7. 31. use the world as not *abusing* it [full
R. V. 1 Cor. 9. 18. not to us to the

ACCEPT, receive kindly in favor, Gen. 32. 20. Acts 24. 3.
Lev. 26. 41. *a.* punishment of iniquity, 43.
Deut. 33. 11. *a.* work of his hands
2 Sam. 24. 23. Lord thy God *a.* thee
Job 13. 8. will ye *a.* his person, 10.
32. 21. let me not *a.* any man's person
42. 8. servant Job, him will I *a.*
Ps. 119. 108. *a.* free-will-off. of my mouth
Ezek. 43. 27. I will *a.* you
Mal. 1. 13. should I *a.* this of your hand
Gen. 4. 7. shalt thou not be *accepted*
Lev. 1. 4, shall be *a.* for atonement
Luke 4. 24. no prophet *a.* in his own country [is *a.*
Acts 10. 35. worketh righteousness
2 Cor. 5. 9. we may be *a.* of him
Eph. 1. 6. made us *a.* in the beloved
Luke 20. 21. neither *acceptest* the person
Job 34. 19. him that *accepteth* not the persons of princes
Eccl. 9. 7. God now *a.* thy works
Hos. 8. 13. Lord *a.* them not
Gal. 2. 6. God *a.* no man's person
Heb. 11. 35. not *accepting* deliverance [58. 5.
Acceptable day of the Lord, Isa.
Ps. 19. 14. let the meditation of my heart be *a.*
Eccl. 12. 10. sought out *a.* words
Dan. 4. 27. let my counsel be *a.*
Rom. 12. 1. sacrifice holy *a.* to God
2. know good and *a.* will of God
Eph. 5. 10. proving what is *a.* unto the Lord [ing.
Phil. 4. 18. sacrifice *a.* well-pleas-
Heb. 12. 28. serve God *acceptably* with fear
1 Tim. 1. 15. worthy of all *acceptation* [respect
R. V. Job 13. 10; 32. 21; Ps. 82. 2.

ACCESS, admission through Christ, Rom. 5. 2. Eph. 2. 18. and 3. 12.

ACCOMPLISH, perform fully, finish, Lev. 22. 21. Job 14. 6.
Ps. 64. 6. *a.* a diligent search
Isa. 55. 11. it shall *a.* that I please
Ezek. 6. 12. thus will I *a.* my fury
Dan. 9. 2. would *a.* seventy years
Luke 9. 31. decease he should *a.* at Jerusalem
2 Chron. 36. 22. word might be *accomplished*
Prov. 13. 19. desire *a.* is sweet to soul
Isa. 40. 2. her warfare is *a.* her sin
Luke 12. 50. how am I straitened till it be *a.*
John 19. 28. all things were now *a.*
Heb. 9. 6. *accomplishing* service of God.
R. V. Jer. 25. 34. fully come; 44. 25. establish; Luke 1. 23; 2. 6, 21, 22. fulfilled

ACCORD, hearty agreement, Acts 1. 14. & 2. 1, 46. & 4. 24. & 15. 25.
Phil. 2. 2. of one *a.* of one mind
R. V. Lev. 25. 5. itself; Acts 2. 1. together

ACCOUNT, reckoning, esteem
Job 33. 13. giv. not *a.* of his matters
Ps. 144. 3. that thou mak. *a* of him
Eccl. 7. 27. one by one to find out the *a.*
Matt. 12. 36. give *a.* in the day of judgment
Luke 16. 2. give *a.* of thy stewardship
Rom. 14. 12. give *a.* of him. to God
Heb. 13. 17. as they that must give *a.*
1 Pet. 4. 5. shall give *a.* to him that is ready to judge the quick and
Ps. 22. 30. *accounted* to the Lord for a generation
Isa. 2. 22. wherein is he to be *a.* of
Luke 20. 35. shall be *a.* worthy to obtain that world
21. 36. *a.* worthy to escape
22. 24. which should be *a.* greatest
Gal. 3. 6. *a.* to him for righteousness
Heb. 11. 19. *a.* God able to raise
R. V. 2 Chr. 26. 11; Matt. 18. 23. reckoning

ACCURSED, devoted to ruin
Deut. 21. 23. hanged is *a.* of God
Josh. 6. 18. keep yourselves from the *a.* thing
Isa. 65. 20. sinner a hundred years old shall be *a.*
Rom. 9. 3. wish myself *a.* from Christ
1 Cor. 12. 3. no man by Spirit calls Jesus *a.*
Gal. 1. 8, 9. preach other gospel be *a.*
R. V. 1 Chr. 2. 7. devoted thing; Rom. 9. 3; 1 Cor. 12. 3; Gal. 1. 8. anathema.

ACCUSATION, Ezra 4. 6. Matt. 27. 37. Luke 6. 7. & 19. 8. John 18. 29. Acts 25. 18.
1 Tim. 5. 19. against an elder receive not an *a.*
2 Pet. 2. 11. bring not railing *a.*, Jude 9.
R. V. 2 Pet. 2. 11; Jude 9. judgment

ACCUSE, charge with crimes
Prov. 30. 10. *a.* not servant to master
Luke 3. 14. neither *a.* any falsely
John 5. 45. that I will *a.* you to the Father
1 Pet. 3. 16. that falsely *a.* your good conversation in Christ
Tit. 1. 6. not *accused* of riot
Rev. 12. 10. *a.* them before our God
Accuser of brethren is cast down
Acts 25. 16. have *a.* face to face
2 Tim. 3. 3. false *a.*, Tit. 2. 3.
John 5. 45. there is one that *accuseth*
Rom. 2. 15. thoughts *accusing* or excusing
R. V. Prov. 30. 10. slander

ACCUSTOMED, Jer. 13. 23.

ACKNOWLEDGE, own, confess
Deut. 33. 9. neither did he *a.* his brethren
Ps. 51. 3. I *a.* my transgression
Prov. 3. 6. in all thy ways *a.* him
Isa. 33. 13. ye that are near *a.* my might
Jer. 3. 13. only *a.* thine iniquity

Hos. 5. 15. until they *a.* their offence
1 Cor. 16. 18. *a.* them that are such
Ps. 32. 5. I *a.* my sin
1 John 2. 23. that *acknowledgeth* the Son
2 Tim. 2. 25. *acknowledging* the truth
Tit. 1. 1. *a.* of the truth which is after godliness
Col. 2. 2. to the *acknowledgment* of the mystery of God
R. V. 1 John 2. 23. confesseth
ACQUAINT thyself with him, Job 22. 21.
Ps. 139. 3. *acquainted* with my ways
Isa. 53. 3. *a.* with grief
Acquaintance, familiar friends or companions, Job 19. 13. & 42. 11. Ps. 31. 11. & 55. 13. & 88. 8, 18.
R. V. Acts 24. 23. friends
ACQUIT, hold innocent, Job 10. 14.
Nah. 1. 3. will not at all *a.* the wicked
ACTS of the Lord, Deut. 11. 3, 7.
Judg. 5. 11. rehearse righteous *a.*
1 Sam. 12. 7. reason of all righteous *a.* of the Lord
Ps. 106. 2. utter mighty *a.* of Lord
145. 6. speak of thy mighty *a.*, 4.
150. 2. praise him for his mighty *a.*
Isa. 28. 21. his *a.* his strange *a.*
John 8. 4. taken in adultery in very *a.*
ACTIONS weighed, 1 Sam. 2. 3.
ACTIVITY, men of, Gen. 47. 6.
ADAMANT, Ezek. 3. 9. Zech. 7. 12.
ADD fifth part, Lev. 5. 16. & 6. 5. & 27. 13, 15, 19, 27, 31.
Deut. 4. 2. shall not *a.* unto the word
1 Kings 12. 11. I will *a.* to your yoke
Ps. 69. 27. *a.* iniquity to their iniquity
Isa. 30. 1. that they may *a.* sin to sin
Matt. 6. 27. can *a.* one cubit, Luke 12. 25.
Phil. 1. 16. to *a.* affliction to my
2 Pet. 1. 5. *a.* to your faith, virtue
Rev. 22. 18. if any man *a.* unto these things, God shall *a.* unto him
Deut. 5. 22. he *added* no more
Jer. 36. 32. were *a.* many like words
Matt. 6. 33. all these things shall be *a.* unto you, Luke 12. 31.
Acts 2. 41. same day were *a.* about three thousand souls
47. Lord *a.* to the church such
5. 14. believers were the more *a.* to
11. 24. much people was *a.* to the Lord
Prov. 10. 22. *addeth* no sorrow with
ADDER, poisonous serpent, Gen. 49. 17. Ps. 58. 4. & 91. 13. & 140. 3. Prov. 23. 32. Isa. 14. 29.
ADDICTED, gave up, 1 Cor. 16. 15.
R. V. 1 Cor. 16. 15. set.
ADJURE, to charge under pain of God's curse, 1 Kings 22. 16. 2 Chron. 18. 15. Matt. 26. 63. Mark 5. 7. Acts 19. 13. Josh. 6. 26. 1 Sam. 14. 24.
ADMINISTRATION, 1 Cor. 12. 5. 2 Cor. 9. 12. & 8. 19, 20. *administered*
ADMIRATION, high esteem, Jude 16. or wonder and amazement, Rev. 17. 6.
2 Thes. 1. 10. *admired* in them that believe
R. V. Rev. 17. 6. wonder; Jude 16. respect of persons.
ADMONISH, warn, reprove
Rom. 15. 14. able to *a.* one another
2 Thes. 3. 15. *a.* him as a brother
Eccl. 12. 12. by these be *admonished*
Jer. 42. 19. know that I have *a.* you
Acts 27. 9. Paul *a.* them
Heb. 8. 5. as Moses was *a.* of God
Col. 3. 16. *admonishing* one another in psalms and hymns
1 Cor. 10. 11. are written for our *admonition*
Tit. 3. 10. after first and second *a.* reject
R. V. Jer. 42. 19. testified unto; Heb. 8. 5. warned.

ADOPTION, putting among God's children, Jer. 3. 19. 2 Cor. 6. 18.
Rom. 8. 15. received spirit of *a.*
23. *a.* redemption of our body
Gal. 4. 5. might receive *a.* of sons
Eph. 1. 5. unto *a.* of children
ADORN, deck out, Isa. 61. 10. Jer. 31. 4.
Tit. 2. 10. *a.* the doctrine of God
Jer. 31. 4. *adorned* with thy tabrets
Luke 21. 5. *a.* with goodly stones
1 Pet. 3. 5. holy women *a.* themselves
Rev. 21. 2. as a bride *a.* for her
Isa. 61. 10. as a bride *adorneth* herself
1 Pet. 3. 3. whose *adorning* let it not
1 Tim. 2. 9. women *a.* themselves in modest apparel
ADULTERER, put to death, Lev. 20. 10.
Job 24. 15. eye of *a.* waits for twilight
Isa. 57. 3. seed of *a.* and whore
Jer. 23. 10. land is full of *adulterers*
9. 2. Hos. 7. 4. be all *a.*
Mal. 3. 5. I will be a swift witness against *a.*
1 Cor. 6. 9. neither *a.* shall inherit the kingdom of God
Heb. 13. 4. whoremongers and *a.* God will judge
James 4. 4. ye *a.* and *adulteresses*
Prov. 6. 26. *adulteress* will hunt for
32. committeth *adultery* lacks
Matt. 5. 28. committeth *a.* in his heart
2 Pet. 2. 14. having eyes full of *a.*
Matt. 15. 19. out of the heart proceed *adulteries*, fornications, Mark 7. 21.
Prov. 30. 20. way of *adulterous* woman
Matt. 12. 39. *a.* generation seeketh a sign, 16. 4. Mark 8. 38.
ADVANTAGE hath Jew, Rom. 3. 1.
2 Cor. 2. 11. lest Satan get an *a.*
Luke 9. 25. what is a man *advantaged*
R. V. Luke 9. 25. profited
ADVERSARY, opposer, enemy
Ex. 23. 22. I will be *a.* to thy *a.*
1 Kings 5. 4. is neither *a.* nor evil
Job 31. 35. my *a.* had written a book
Matt. 5. 25. agree with thine *a.*
Luke 18. 3. avenge me of mine *a.*
1 Pet. 5. 8. your *a.* the devil as a
1 Sam. 2. 10. *adversaries* of the Lord
Lam. 1. 5. her *a.* are the chief
Luke 21. 15. all your *a.* not be able
1 Cor. 16. 9. and there are many *a.*
Heb. 10. 27. shall devour the *a.*
R. V. enemy, in most O. T. texts
ADVERSITY, affliction, misery
2 Sam. 4. 9. redeem my soul from all *a.*
Ps. 10. 6. I shall never be in *a*
35. 15. in my *a.* they rejoiced
94. 13. give rest from days of *a.*
Prov. 17. 17. brother is born for *a.*
Eccl. 7. 14. in the day of *a.* consider
Isa. 30. 20. give you the bread of *a.*
1 Sam. 10. 19. saved you out of all *a.*
ADVICE, Judg. 19. 30. 1 Sam. 25. 33. 2 Sam. 19. 43. Prov. 20. 18.
ADVOCATE with Father, 1 John 2. 1.
AFAR off, Gen. 22. 4. & 37. 18. Ps. 65. 5.
138. 6. proud he knoweth *a.*
Ps. 139. 2. understandest my thoughts *a.* off
Acts 2. 39. promise is to all *a.* and
Eph. 2. 17. preached peace to you *a.*
2 Pet. 1. 9. blind and cannot see *a.*
AFFAIRS, Ps. 112. 5. 2 Tim. 2. 4.
AFFECT, incline, move
Gal. 4. 17. they zealously *a.* you
18. good to be zealously *affected*
Lam. 3. 51. mine eye *affecteth* my heart
Rom. 1. 31. natural *affection*
Col. 3. 5. mortify inordinate *a.*

Rom. 1. 26. them up to vile *affections*
Gal. 5. 24. crucify flesh with *a.*
Rom. 12. 10. be kindly *affectioned*
1 Thes. 2. 8. *affectionately* desirous
R. V. Col. 3. 2. mind; Rom. 1. 26; Gal. 5. 24. passions
AFFINITY, relation by marriage, 1 Kings 3. 1. 2 Chron. 18. 1. Ezra 9. 14.
AFFLICT, grieve, trouble, Gen. 15. 13. Ex. 1. 11. & 22. 22.
Ezra 8. 21. that we might *a.* ourselves
Lev. 16. 29, 31. shall *a.* your souls 23. 27, 32. Num. 29. 7. & 30. 13.
Isa. 58. 5. day for a man to *a.* his soul
Lam. 3. 33. doth not *a.* willingly
2 Sam. 22. 28. *afflicted* people thou wilt save, Ps. 18. 27.
Job 6. 14. to *a.* pity should be
34. 28. heareth the cry of the *a.*
Ps. 18. 27. wilt save the *a.* people
71. it is good that I have been *a.*
107. I am *a.* very much
140. 12. wilt maintain cause of *a.*
Prov. 15. 15. all days of *a.* are evil
Isa. 49. 13. he will have mercy on *a.*
53. 4. smitten of God and *a.*
Mic. 4. 6. gather her I have *a.*
James 5. 13. is any *a.* let him pray
Ex. 3. 7. seen *affliction* of people
2 Kings 14. 26. Lord saw *a.* of
Job 5. 6. *a.* cometh not forth of
Ps. 25. 18. look on my *a.* and pain
107. 10. bound in *a.* and iron
39. brought low through *a.*
119. 50. this is my comfort in *a.*
Isa. 48. 10. chosen thee in the furnace of *a.*
63. 9. in all their *a.* he was
Hos. 5. 15. in their *a.* they will seek
Obad. 13. not have looked on their *a.*
Zech. 1. 15. helped forward the *a.*
2 Cor. 4. 17. our light *a.* which is
Phil. 4. 14. communicate with my *a.*
1 Thes. 1. 6. received word in much *a.*
James 1. 27. to visit fatherless in their *a.*
Ps. 34. 19. many are the *afflictions* of the righteous
132. 1. remember David and all his *a.*
Acts 7. 10. delivered him out of all *a.*
Col. 1. 24. which is behind of *a.* of Christ
1 Thes. 3. 3. no man moved by these *a.*
2 Tim. 1. 8. partaker of *a.* of gospel
Heb. 10. 32. endured great fight of *a.*
1 Pet. 5. 9. the same *a.* accomplished
R. V. Ez. 8. 21. humble; Ps. 55. 19. answer; Job 6. 14. ready to faint; James 5. 13. suffering
AFRAID, Lev. 26. 6. Num. 12. 8. Job 13. 21. Ps. 56. 3. & 119. 120.
Not be *afraid*, Ps. 56. 11. & 112. 7. Isa. 12. 2. Matt. 14. 27. Mark 5. 36. Luke 12. 4. 1 Pet. 3. 6, 14. Heb. 11. 23.
AFRESH, crucify Son of God, Heb. 6. 6.
AGE is as nothing before thee, Ps. 39. 5.
Job 5. 26. come to grave in full *a.*
Heb. 5. 14. strong meat to those of full *a.*
11. 11. Sarah when she was past *a.*
Tit. 2. 2, 3. *aged* men be sober
Ages Eph. 2. 7. & 3. 5, 21.
Col. 1. 26. mystery hid from *a.*
R. V. Josh. 23. 1, 2. years; Job. 11. 17. life; Job 12. 20. elders
AGONY, Christ's, in the garden, Matt. 27. 36; Luke 22. 44, &c.
AGREE, Acts 5. 9.
Matt. 5. 25. *a.* with thine adversary
1 John 5. 8. these three *a.* in one
Amos 3. 3. walk together except *agreed*
Isa. 28. 15. with hell at *agreement*

2 Cor. 6. 16. what *a.* has temple of God
R. V. 2 Kings 18. 31; Isa. 36. 16. your peace
AIR, 1 Cor. 9. 26. & 14. 9. Eph. 2. 2.
1 Thes. 4. 17. Rev. 9. 2. & 16. 17.
R. V. In Gos. and Acts, heaven
ALARM, how sounded, Num. 10. 5.
ALIEN, stranger, Ex. 18. 3. Job 19. 15.
Ps. 69. 8. heathens, Deut. 14. 21. Isa. 61. 5. Lam. 5. 2. Heb. 11. 34.
Eph. 2. 12. *a.* from commonwealth
4. 18. *alienated* from life of God
Col. 1. 21. were sometimes *a.*
R. V. Ex. 18. 3. sojourner; Deut. 14. 21. foreigner.
ALIVE, Gen. 12. 12. Num. 22. 23.
Rom. 6. 11. *a.* to God through Jesus
1 Sam. 2. 6. killeth and maketh *a.*
15. 8. he took Agag *a.*
Luke 15. 24. son was dead and is *a.*
Rom. 6. 13. as those *a.* from the dead
7. 9. I was *a.* without the law once
1 Cor. 15. 22. in Christ shall all be made *a.*
1 Thes. 4. 15, 17. we who are *a.*
Rev. 1. 18. I am *a.* for evermore
2. 8. was dead and is *a.*
R. V. Gen. 7. 23; Lev. 10. 16; 26. 36——; Num. 21. 35. remaining
ALLEGING, Acts 17. 3.
ALLEGORY, Gal. 4. 24.
ALLOW deeds of fathers, Luke 11. 48.
Acts 24. 15. which themselves *a.*
Rom. 7. 15. that which I do I *a.* not
14. 22. in that which he *alloweth.*
1 Thes. 2. 4. as we were *allowed* of God
R. V. Luke 11. 48. consent unto; Acts 24. 15. look for; Rom. 7. 15. know; Rom. 14. 22. approveth; 1 Thes. 2. 4. approved.
ALLURE, Hos. 2. 14. 2 Pet. 2. 18.
R. V. 2 Pet. 2. 18. entice.
ALL THINGS lawful, but not expedient, 1 Cor. 6. 12.
ALMIGHTY GOD, Gen. 17. 1. & 28. 3. & 35. 11. & 43. 14. & 48. 3. Ex. 6. 3. 2 Cor. 6. 18. Rev. 4. 8. & 15. 3. & 16. 14. & 19. 15. & 21. 22.
Job 21. 15. what is the Almighty that we serve
26. shall have delight in Almighty
Ps. 91. 1. under shadow of Almi.
Rev. 1. 8. is to come, the Almighty
ALMOST all things, Heb. 9. 22.
Ex. 17. 4. *a.* ready to stone me
Ps. 73. 2. my feet were *a.* gone
Prov. 5. 14. was *a.* in all evil in cong.
Acts 26. 28. *a.* persuadest me to
R. V. Ps. 94. 17. soon; Prov. 5. 14. well nigh; Acts 26. 28. with but little
ALMS, Acts 3. 2, 3. & 24. 17.
Matt. 6. 1. do not your *a.* before men
Luke 11. 41. give *a.* of such things
12. 33. sell that ye have, give *a.*
Acts 10. 2. gave much *a.* to people
4. thine *a.* are come up for memorial
9. 36. Dorcas full of *a.* deeds
R. V. Matt. 6. 1. righteousness
ALONE, Gen. 32. 24.
Gen. 2. 18. not good for man to be *a.*
Num. 23. 9. peopled well *a.*, Deut. 33. 28.
Deut. 32. 12. Lord *a.* did lead him
Ps. 136. 4. who *a.* doth great wonders
Isa. 5. 8. that they may be placed *a.*
63. 3. I have trodden wine-press *a.*
John 8. 16. I am not *a.*, 16. 32.
17. 20. neither pray I for these *a.*
Ex. 32. 10. *let me a.* that my wrath
Hos. 4. 17. Ephraim is joined to idols, let him *a.*
Matt. 15. 14. let them *a.*
R. V. Mark 4. 34. privately

ALTAR, Deut. 7. 5. & 12. 3.
altar to Lord, Gen. 8. 20. & 12. 7. & 22. 9. & 35. 1, 3. Ex. 30. 27. & 40. 10.
Judg. 6. 25. throw down *a.* of Baal
1 Kings 13. 2. cried against *a.* O *a. a.*
Ps. 26. 6. so will I compass thine *a.*
Matt. 5. 23. if thou bring thy gift to *a.*
24. leave there thy gift before the *a.*
Acts 17. 23. found *a.* with inscription
Heb. 13. 10. we have an *a.* whereof
Rev. 6. 9. saw under the *a.* souls of
8. 3. & 9. 13. the golden *a.*
R. V. Isa. 65. 3.
ALWAY, Deut. 5. 29. Job 7. 16.
Gen. 6. 3. my Spirit not *a.* strive
Deut. 14. 23. learn to fear the Lord *a.*
1 Chron. 16. 15. be mindful *a.* of covenant.
Job 27. 10. will he *a.* call on God
32. 9. great men are not *a.* wise
Ps. 9. 18. needy not *a.* be forgotten
16. 8. I set the Lord *a.* before me
103. 9. he will not *a.* chide
Prov. 5. 19. ravished *a.* with her love
28. 14. happy is the man that feareth *a.*
Isa. 57. 16. neither will I be *a.* wroth
Matt. 26. 11. have poor *a.* with you
28. 20. I am with you *a.* to the end
John 8. 29. I do *a.* things that please
Acts 10. 2. Cornelius prayed God *a.*
2 Cor. 6. 10. yet *a.* rejoicing
Eph. 6. 18. praying *a.* with all prayer
Phil. 4. 4. rejoice in the Lord *a.*
Col. 4. 6. your speech be *a.* with
I AM that I AM, Ex. 3. 14. Rev. 1. 8.
Ambassador, Prov. 13. 17. Isa. 33. 7. 2 Cor. 5. 20. Eph. 6. 20.
R. V. Job 32. 9.
AMBITION reproved, Matt. 18. 1. 20. 25. & 23. 8. Luke 22. 24.
punishment of, Prov. 17. 19. Isa. 14. 12. Ezek. 31. 10.
of Babel, Gen. 11. 4.
of Aaron and Miriam, Num. 12. 10.
Korah, Dathan, and Abiram, Num. 16. 3.
Absalom, 2 Sam. 18. 9.
Adonijah, 1 Kings 1. 5.
Babylon, Jer. 51. 53.
James and John, Matt. 20. 21.
Man of sin, 2 Thes. 2. 4.
Diotrephes, 3 John 9.
AMBUSH, Josh. 8. 4; Judg. 20. 29; 2 Chron. 13. 13; 20. 22.
AMEN, so come Lord Jesus, Rev. 22. 20.
2 Cor. 1. 20. promises in him *a.*
Rev. 3. 14. these things saith the *a.*
R. V. *A.* is omitted in Matt. 6. 13; 28. 20. and many other places in N. T.
AMEND your ways, Jer. 7. 3, 5. & 26. 13. your doings, 35. 15.
R. V. Restitution
AMIABLE thy tabernacles, Ps. 84. 1.
AMISS, 2 Chron. 6. 37. Dan. 3. 29. Luke 23. 41. James 4. 3.
ANCHOR, Acts 27. 30. Heb. 6. 19.
ANCIENT, wisdom is with, Job 12. 12.
Dan. 7. 9. the *a.* of days did sit
Ps. 119. 100. I understand more than *a.*
ANGEL, who redeemed me, Gen. 48. 16.
24. 7. send his *a.* before me
Ex. 23. 23. my *a.* shall go before thee
Angel of the Lord, Ps. 34. 7. Zech. 12. 8. Acts 5. 19. & 12. 7, 23.

Isa. 63. 9. *a.* of his presence saved.
John 5. 4. *a.* went down at a
Acts 6. 15. saw as face of an *a.*
23. 8. Sadducees say neither *a.* nor
Dan. 3. 28. sent his *a.* and delivered
6. 22. sent his *a.* and shut lions' mouths
Ps. 8. 5. a little lower than *a.*
68. 17. chariots of God thousands *a.*
78. 25. man did eat *a.* food
Matt. 4. 11. *a.* came and ministered
13. 39. reapers are the *a.*
18. 10. their *a.* always behold
36. no, not the *a.* of heaven
Mark 12. 25. are as *a.* in heaven, 13. 32.
Luke 20. 36. equal to the *a.*
Acts 7. 53. the law by disposition of *a.*
1 Cor. 6. 3. we shall judge *a.*
Col. 2. 18. beguile worshipping of *a.*
2 Thes. 1. 7. with his mighty *a.*
1 Tim. 3. 16. seen of *a.* preached unto
Heb. 2. 16. took not the nature of *a.*
12. 22. an innumerable company of *a.*
13. 2. entertained *a.* unawares
2 Pet. 2. 4. God spared not *a.* that
11. *a.* greater in power and might
Jude 6. *a.* who kept not their first
Rev. 1. 20. *a.* of seven churches
Angel of God, Gen. 28. 12. & 32. 1. Matt. 22. 30. Luke 12. 8. & 15. 10. John 1. 51.
R. V. Rev. 8. 13. eagle; Rev. 8. 7; 16. 3, 4, 8, 10, 12, 17.
ANGER of the Lord wax hot, Ex. 32. 22.
Deut. 29. 24. meaneth heat of this *a.*
Josh. 7. 26. from fierceness of *a.*
Job 9. 13. if God will not withdraw *a.*
Ps. 27. 9. put not away servant in *a.*
30. 5. his *a.* endureth but a
77. 9. hath he in *a.* shut up
78. 38. turned he his *a.* away
50. he made a way to his *a.*
90. 7. we are consumed by thine *a.*
11. who knoweth power of thine *a.*
Eccl. 7. 9. *a.* resteth in the bosom of fools
Isa. 5. 25. for all this his *a.* is not turned away, 9. 12, 17, 21. & 10. 4.
Hos. 11. 9. not execute fierceness of *a.*
Mic. 7. 18. retaineth not *a.* for ever
Nah. 1. 6. who can abide fierceness of *a.*
Eph. 4. 31. let all *a.* be put away
Col. 3. 8. put off all these; *a.* wrath
Slow to anger, Neh. 9. 17. Ps. 103. 8. Joel 2. 13. Jonah 4. 2. Nah. 1. 3. James 1. 19.
Ps. 106. 32. they *angered* him at
Gen. 18. 30. let not Lord be *angry*
Deut. 1. 37. Lord was *a.* with me
9. 20. Lord was *a.* with Aaron
1 Kings 11. 9. the Lord was *a.* with Solomon
7. 11. God is *a.* with the wicked
76. 7. who may stand when thou art *a.*
Prov. 14. 17. that is soon *a.* dealeth
22. 24. no friendship with an *a.* man
Eccl. 7. 9. be not hasty to be *a.*
S. of S. 1. 6. mother's chil. were *a.*
Isa. 12. 1. though thou wast *a.* with
Jonah 4. 9. I do well to be *a.* even
Matt. 5. 22. whoso is *a.* with brother
Eph. 4. 26. be *a.* and sin not
Tit. 1. 7. bishop must not be soon *a.*
R. V. Ps. 38. 3; 85. 4. indignation; Prov. 22. 8. wrath; Isa. 1. 4.
ANGUISH, excessive pain
Gen. 42. 21. saw the *a.* of his soul
Ex. 6. 9. hearkened not for *a.* of spirit
Ps. 119. 143. trouble and *a.* take hold
John 16. 21. remember not *a.* for joy
Rom. 2. 9. tribulation and *a.* upon
R. V. Gen. 42. 21. distress

ANOINT, rub with oil, appoint, to qualify for office of king, priest, or prophet, Ex. 28. 41.
Dan. 9. 24. to *a.* the most holy
Amos 6. 6. *a.* with chief ointments
Matt. 6. 17. when fastest *a.* thy head
Rev. 3. 18. *a.* eyes with eye salve
1 Sam. 24. 6. *anointed* of the Lord
Ps. 45. 7. *a.* thee with oil of gladness
Zech. 4. 14. two *a.* ones before the Lord
Acts 4. 27. Jesus whom thou hast *a.*
10. 38. how God *a.* Jesus of Nazareth
2 Cor. 1. 21. who hath *a.* us is God
Ps. 2. 2. Lord and his *a.*, 18. 50. 2 Sam. 22. 51. 1 Sam. 2. 10. Ps. 20. 6. & 28. 8.
1 Chron. 16. 22. touch not my *a.*, Ps. 105. 15. & 132. 17.
Ps. 23. 5. *anointest* my head with oil
Isa. 10. 27. because of *anointing*
1 John 2. 27. the *a.* teacheth you of all
Jas. 5. 14. *a.* him with oil

ANSWER, Gen. 41. 16. Deut. 20. 11.
Prov. 15. 1. soft *a.* turneth away
16. 1. *a.* of tongue is from the Lord
Job 19. 16. he gave me no *a.*
S. of S. 5. 6. he gave me no *a.*
Mic. 3. 7. there is no *answering* of God
Rom. 11. 4. what saith the *a.* of God
2 Tim. 4. 16. at my first *a.* no man
1 Pet. 3. 15. ready to give an *a.* to
21. the *a.* of a good conscience
Job 40. 4. what shall I *a.* thee
Ps. 102. 2. *a.* me speedily
143. 1. in thy faithfulness *a.* me
Prov. 26. 4, 5. *a.* fool according to
Isa. 50. 2. I called was none to *a.*
58. 9. shalt call and Lord shall *a.*
66. 4. when I called none did *a.*
Dan. 3. 16. not careful to *a.* thee
Matt. 25. 37. then shall righteous *a.* Lord
Luke 12. 11. what thing ye shall *a.*
13. 25. he shall *a.* I know you not
21. 14. meditate not what to *a.*
2 Cor. 5. 12. have somewhat to *a.*
Col. 4. 6. know how to *a.* every man
Job 14. 15. thou shalt call and I will *a.* & 13. 22. Ps. 91. 15. Isa. 65. 24. Jer. 33. 3. Ezek. 14. 4, 7.
Ps. 18. 41. to Lord but he *answered* not
81. 7. I *a.* thee in secret place
99. 6. called on the Lord and he *a.*
Prov. 18. 23. rich *answereth* roughly
13. he that *a.* matter before hear
27. 19. as in water face *a.* to face
Eccl. 10. 19. money *a.* all things
Gal. 4. 25. *a.* to Jerusalem that now
Tit. 2. 9. not *answering* again
R. V. Acts 25. 16. to make defence; 2 Tim. 4. 16. defence; 1 Pet. 3. 21. interrogation.

ANT, Prov. 6. 6. & 30. 25.

ANTICHRIST, 1 John 2. 18, 22. & 4. 3. 2 John 7.

APART, Ps. 4. 3. Zech. 12. 12. Jas. 1. 21.
R. V. Jas. 1. 21. away

APOSTATES, Deut. 13. 13; Matt. 24. 10; Luke 8. 13; John 6. 66; Heb. 3. 12; 6. 4; 2 Pet. 3. 17; 1 John 2. their doom, Zeph. 1. 4; 2 Thes. 2. 8; 1 Tim. 4. 1; Heb. 10. 25; 2 Pet. 2. 17.

APOSTLE, minister sent by God, or Christ, infallibly to preach the gospel, and found churches, Rom. 1. 1. 1 Cor. 1. 1. & 12. 28.
Rom. 11. 13. I am *a.* of Gentiles.
1 Cor. 9. 1. am I not a free *a.*
2 Cor. 12. 12. signs of *a.* wrought
Matt. 10. 2. names of the twelve
Luke 11. 49. I will send proph. and *a.*
1 Cor. 4. 9. God hath sent forth us *a.*
15. 9. I am the least of the *a.*
2 Cor. 11. 13. such are false *a.*
Rev. 2. 2. say they are *a.* and
18. 20. holy *a.* and prophets, Eph. 3. 5.
21. 14. names of twelve *a.* of the
Acts 1. 25. part of this *apostleship*
Rom. 1. 5. received grace and *a.*
1 Cor. 9. 2. seal of my *a.* are ye
Gal. 2. 8. to *a.* of circumcision
R. V. Acts 5. 34. men

APPAREL, Isa. 63. 1. Zeph. 1. 8.
1 Tim. 2. 9. 1 Pet. 3. 3. Jas. 2. 2.
R. V. Isa. 3. 22——; Jas. 2. 2. clothing

APPEAR, Gen. 1. 9. Heb. 11. 3.
Ex. 23. 15. none shall *a.* before me empty, 34. 20. Deut. 16. 16.
2 Chron. 1. 7. did God *a.* to Solomon
Ps. 42. 2. when shall I *a.* before God
90. 16. let work *a.* to servants
Isa. 1. 12. when ye *a.* before me who
66. 5. shall *a.* to your joy, but they
Matt. 6. 16. may *a.* to men to fast
Luke 19. 11. kingdom of God immediately *a.*
Rom. 7. 13. sin that it might *a.* sin
2 Cor. 5. 10. we must all *a.* before the
Col. 3. 4. when Christ shall *a.* ye also *a.*
1 Tim. 4. 15. thy profiting *a.* to all
28. *a.* second time without sin to salvation
1 Pet. 5. 4. when the chief shepherd shall *a.*
1 John 3. 2. not yet *a.* what we shall
1 Sam. 16. 7. man looks—*appearance*
John 7. 24. judge not according to *a.*
1 Thes. 5. 22. abstain from all *a.* of
2 Tim. 1. 10. manifest by *a.* of Jesus
4. 1. judge quick and dead at his *a.*
8. all them that love his *a.*
Tit. 2. 13. look for glorious *a.* of
1 Pet. 1. 7. unto praise at *a.* of Jesus
Tit. 2. 11. grace hath *a.* to all men
Heb. 9. 26. he *a.* to put away sin
R. V. 1 Sam. 2. 27. reveal myself; S. of S. 4. 1; 6. 5. lie along the side; Acts 22. 30. come together; Rom. 7. 13. shewn to be; 2 Cor. 5. 10; 7. 12; Col. 3. 4; 1 Pet. 5. 4; 1 John 2. 28. manifested; 2 Cor. 10. 7. that are before your face; 1 Thes. 5. 22. every form; 1 Pet. 1. 7. revelation

APPETITE, Prov. 23. 2. Isa. 29. 8.

APPLE of eye, Deut. 32. 10. Ps. 17. 8. Prov. 7. 2. Lam. 2. 18. Zech. 2. 8.
Apple-trees, S. of S. 2. 3. & 8. 5.
Apples, Prov. 25. 11. S. of S. 2. 5. 7. 8.

APPOINT, Gen. 30. 28.
Isa. 61. 3. *a.* to them that mourn in Zion
26. 1. salvation will God *a.* for walls
Matt. 24. 51. *a.* him portion with the hypocrites
Luke 22. 29. I *a.* unto you a kingdom
Job 7. 1. is there not an *appointed* time
14. 14. all the days of my *a.* time
30. 23. to house *a.* for all living
Ps. 79. 11. preserve those *a.* to die
Jer. 5. 24. reserve *a.* weeks for harvest
Mic. 6. 9. hear rod and him who *a.* it
Hab. 2. 3. vision is for an *a.* time
Heb. 9. 27. *a.* to men once to die
1 Pet. 2. 8. whereunto they were *a.*
R. V. Num. 35. 6. give; 2 Sam. 15. 15. choose; Ezek. 21. 22. set; 1 Sam. 19. 20. as head; 2 Chr. 34. 22. commanded; Acts 1. 23. put forward

APPLY heart to wisdom, &c. Ps. 90. 12. Prov. 2. 2. & 22. 17. & 23. 12. Eccl. 7. 25. & 8. 9, 16. Hos. 7. 6.
R. V. Eccl. 7. 25. heart was set

APPREHENDED, take fast hold of, Phil. 3. 12, 13. Acts 12. 4. 2 Cor. 11. 32.
R. V. Acts 12. 4. taken; 2 Cor. 11. 32. take

APPROACH, come near to, marry
Lev. 18. 6. *a.* to any near of kin, 20. 16.
Ps. 65. 4. blessed whom thou causest to *a.*
Jer. 30. 21. engageth heart to *a.* to
1 Tim. 6. 16. light to which none can *a.*
Isa. 58. 2. delight in *approaching* to God
Heb. 10. 25. as ye see the day *a.*
R. V. Ezek. 42. 13; 43. 19. are near

APPROVE, like, commend
Ps. 49. 13. posterity *a.* their sayings
Phil. 1. 10. may *a.* things excellent
Acts 2. 22. man *approved* of God
Rom. 14. 18. *acceptable* to God, *a.* of
16. 10. Apelles *a.* in Christ
2 Tim. 2. 15. show thyself *a.* to God
Rom. 2. 18. *approvest* things excellent
Lam. 3. 36. to subvert Lord *approveth* not
2 Cor. 6. 4. in all things *approving* ourselves

APT to teach, 1 Tim. 3. 2. 2 Tim. 2. 24.

ARE, seven years, Gen. 41. 26, 27.
1 Cor. 1. 28. bring to nought things that *a.*
30. of him *a.* ye in Christ Jesus
8. 6. of whom *a.* all things
Heb. 2. 10. for and by whom *a.* all
Rev. 1. 19. write things that *a.*
20. *a.* angels; *a.* seven churches

ARGUE, Job 6. 25. & 23. 4.

ARIGHT, set not their hearts, Ps. 78. 8.
50. 23. ordereth conversation *a.*
Prov. 15. 2. useth knowledge *a.*
Jer. 8. 6. they spake not *a.*
R. V. Prov. 23. 31. smoothly

ARISE for our help, Ps. 44. 26.
1 Chron. 22. 16. *a.* be doing
Amos 7. 2. by whom shall Jacob *a.* 5.
Mic. 7. 8. when I fall I shall *a.*
Mal. 4. 2. Son of righteousness *a.*
Ps. 112. 4. to the upright *ariseth* light
Matt. 13. 21. persecution *a.* because

ARM of flesh with him, 2 Chron. 32. 8.
Job 40. 9. hast thou an *a.* like God
Ps. 44. 3. own *a.* did not save them
Isa. 33. 2. be thou their *a.* every
51. 5. mine *a.* shall judge; on my *a.*
9. put on strength, O *a.* of Lord
52. 10. Lord made bare his holy *a.*
53. 1. *a.* of Lord revealed, John 12. 38.
63. 12. led them by his glorious *a.*
1 Pet. 4. 1. *a.* yourselves with same
His arm, Ps. 98. 1. Isa. 40. 10, 11. & 59. 16. Jer. 17. 5. Ezek. 31. 17. Zech. 11. 17. Luke 1. 51.
Stretched-out arm, Ex. 6. 6. Deut. 4. 34. & 5. 15. & 7. 19. & 11. 2. & 26. 8. 2 Chron. 6. 32. Ps. 136. 12. Jer. 27. 5. & 32. 17, 21. Ezek. 20. 33, 34.
Gen. 49. 24. *arms* of his hands made strong
Deut. 33. 27. underneath everlast.
Luke 11. 21. strong man *armed* keep
R. V. Job 31. 22. shoulder

ARMIES of living God, 1 Sam. 17. 2.
Job 25. 3. any number of his *a.*
Ps. 44. 9. goest not forth with our, 60. 10. & 108. 11.
S. of S. 6. 13. company of two *a.*
Rev. 19. 14. *army* in heaven followed
R. V. Gen. 26. 26; 1 Chr. 27. 34. host; Rev. 9. 16. armies.

ARMOR of light, Rom. 13. 12.
2 Cor. 6. 7. by *a.* of righteousness
Eph. 6. 7. put on whole *a.* of God
R. V. 1 Sam. 17. 38, 39. apparel

ARRAY, in order of battle, 2 Sam. 10. 9. Job 6. 4. Jer. 50. 14.
Array, to clothe, Esth. 6. 9. Job 40. 10. Jer. 43. 12. Matt. 6. 29. 1 Tim. 2. 9. Rev. 7. 13. & 17. 4. & 19. 8.
R. V. 1 Tim. 2. 9. raiment

ARROGANCY, presumptuous self-conceit, 1 Sam. 2. 3. Prov. 8. 13. Isa. 13. 11.

ARROWS of the Almighty, Job 6. 4.
Ps. 91. 5. nor for *a.* that flieth by day
Deut. 32. 23. I will spend my *a.* upon
Ps. 38. 2. thine *a.* stick fast in me
45. 5. thine *a.* are sharp in heart
Lam. 3. 12. set me as a mark for *a.*
R. V. Lam. 3. 13. shafts

ARTIFICER, Tubal-Cain the first, Gen. 4. 22.
ASCEND into hill of Lord, Ps. 24. 3.
Ps. 139. 8. if I *a.* to heaven, Rom. 10. 6.
John 20. 17. I *a.* to my Father
Ps. 68. 18. hast *ascended* on high
Prov. 30. 4. who hath *a.* into heaven
John 3. 13. no man hath *a.* up to
Rev. 8. 4. smoke of incense *a.* before God
Gen. 28. 12. angels *ascending* and descending, John 1. 51. upon Son of man
ASCRIBE greatness to God, Deut. 32. 3.
Job. 36. 3. I will *a.* righteousness to
Ps. 68. 34. *a.* strength unto God
ASHAMED and blush to lift, Ezra 9. 6.
Gen. 2. 25. man and wife naked not *a.*
Ezek. 16. 61. remember ways and be *a.*
Mark 8. 38. shall be *a.* of me
Rom. 1. 16. I am not *a.* of gospel
5. 5. hope maketh not *a.* because
Not be ashamed, Ps. 25. 2. & 119. 6, 80.
Isa. 49. 23. Rom. 9. 33. 2 Tim. 2. 15.
R. V. Job 6. 20. confounded; Luke 13. 17; Rom. 9. 33; 10. 11; 2 Cor. 7. 14; 9. 4; 10. 8; Phil. 1. 20; Heb. 11. 16; 1 Pet. 3. 16. put to shame
ASHES, Gen. 18. 27. Job 2. 8. & 13. 12. & 30. 19. & 42. 6. Ps. 102. 9. Isa. 44. 20. & 61. 3. Jer. 6. 26. Ezek. 28. 18. Mal. 4. 3.
R. V. 1 Kings 20. 38, 41. his headband
ASK the way to Zion, Jer. 50. 5.
Matt. 7. 7. *a.* and it shall be given
20. 22. ye know not what ye *a.*
Luke 12. 48. of him they will *a.* more
John 14. 13, 14. whatsoever ye *a.* in my name, & 15. 16. & 16. 23.
16. 24. *a.* and ye shall receive—*asked*
Eph. 3. 20. above all we can *a.* or
Jas. 1. 5. wisdom let him *a.* of God
6. let him *a.* in faith, not wavering
4. 2, 3. *a.* not; *a.* receive not; *a.* amiss
Isa. 65. 1. sought of—*asked* not for me
Jer. 6. 16. *a.* for good old paths
Matt. 7. 8. every one that *asketh* receiveth
ASLEEP, 1 Cor. 15. 16. 1 Thes. 4. 13.
ASP, poisonous serpent, Deut. 32. 33. Job 20. 14, 16. Isa. 11. 8. Rom. 3. 13.
ASS knows master's crib, Isa. 1. 3.
Zech. 9. 9. riding upon an ass, Matt. 21. 5. John 12. 15.
ASSEMBLY of wicked, Ps. 22. 16.
89. 7. God feared in *a.* of his saints
Heb. 12. 23. general *a.* of first-born
Eccl. 12. 11. nails fastened by masters of *a.*
Isa. 4. 5. create on her *a.* a cloud
Heb. 10. 25. forsake not *assembling*
R. V. Lev. 8. 4; Num. 8. 9; 10. 2. 3; 16. 2; 2 Chr. 30. 23. congregation; Ps. 89. 7; 111. 1; Ezek. 13. 9. council; Jas. 2. 2. synagogue
ASSUAGE, Gen. 8. 1. Job 16. 5, 6.
ASSURANCE, firm persuasion
Isa. 32. 17. effect of righteousness *a.*
1 Thes. 1. 5. gospel came in much *a.*
Heb. 6. 11. to full *a.* of hope unto end
10. 22. in full *a.* of faith
1 John 3. 19. *assure* our hearts before
R. V. Heb. 6. 11; 22. 10. fulness
ASTRAY, Ps. 119. 176. Isa. 53. 6. Matt. 18. 12. Luke 15. 4. 1 Pet. 2. 25.
ATHIRST, sore, and called, Judg. 15. 18.
Rev. 21. 6. give to him *a.* of fountain
22. 17. him that is *a.* come take of
ATONEMENT, pacifying, satisfaction for sin, Lev. 16. 11. & 24.
2 Sam. 21. 3. wherewith shall I make *a.*
Rom. 5. 11. by whom we received *a.*
R. V. Rom. 5. 11. reconciliation
ATTAIN to wise counsels, Prov. 1. 5.
Ezek. 46. 7. according as hand shall *a.*
Phil. 3. 11, 12. *a.* to resurrection not already *attained*
R. V. Acts 27. 12. could reach
ATTEND to my cry, Ps. 55. 2. & 61. 1. & 66. 19. & 86. 6. & 142. 6.
Prov. 4. 1. *a.* to know understand.
20. *a.* to my words, 7. 24.
Acts 16. 14. she *attended* to—spoken
Attendance, 1 Kings 10. 5. 1 Tim. 4. 13. Heb. 7. 13. Rom. 13. 6.
Attentive, 1 Chron. 6. 40. & 7. 15. Neh. 1. 6. & 8. 3. Ps. 130. 2. Luke 19. 48.
R. V. Ps. 86. 6. hearken; Acts 16. 14. to give heed
AUTHOR of confusion, 1 Cor. 14. 33.
Heb. 5. 9. *a.* of eternal salvation
12. 2. Jesus *a.* and finisher of our
R. V. Rom. 16. 17. turn away from; 2 Tim. 2. 23. refuse; Tit. 3. 9. shun
AUTHORITY, power to govern
Matt. 7. 29. taught as one having *a.*
John 5. 27. given him *a.* to execute
1 Cor. 15. 24. down all *a.* and power
1 Tim. 2. 2. prayer for all in *a.*
1 Pet. 3. 22. angels and *a.* subject
Rev. 13. 2. dragon gave him *a.*
R. V. 1 Tim. 2. 2. high place; 2. 12. have dominion
AVAILETH, Esth. 5. 13. Gal. 5. 6. & 6. 15. Jas. 5. 16.
AVENGE not, nor grudge, Lev. 19. 18.
Lev. 26. 25. shall *a.* quarrel of covenant
Deut. 32. 43. he will *a.* blood of
Isa. 1. 24. I will *a.* me of mine enemies
Luke 18. 7. shall not God *a.* his
Luke 18. 8. he will *a.* them speed.
Rom. 12. 19. *a.* not yourselves
Rev. 6. 10. dost thou not *a.* our blood
Rev. 18. 20. God hath *a.* you on her
Avenger, Num. 35. 12. Ps. 8. 2. & 44. 16. 1 Thes. 4. 6.
2 Sam. 22. 48. God that *avengeth* me
Judg. 5. 2. praise Lord for *avenging* Israel.
R. V. Lev. 19. 18. take vengeance; 26. 25. execute; Rev. 18. 20. judged your judgment.
AVOUCHED, Deut. 26. 17, 18.
AVOID it, pass not by it, Prov. 4. 15.
Rom. 16. 17. cause divisions, *a.*
AWAKE for thee, Job 8. 6.
Ps. 35. 23. *a.* to my judgment
139. 18. when I *a.* I am still with
1 Cor. 15. 34. *a.* to righteousness
Eph. 5. 14. *a.* thou that sleepest
Ps. 78. 65. Lord *awaked* out of sleep
73. 20. when thou *awakest* thou
AWE, stand in *a.* sin not, Ps. 4. 4.
Ps. 33. 8. would stand in *a.* of him
119. 161. heart stands in *a.* of word
AXE, Deut. 19. 5. 1 Kings 6. 7. & 2 Kings 6. 5. Isa. 10. 15. Jer. 51. 20.
Axes, 2 Sam. 12. 31. Ps. 74. 3, 6. Jer. 46. 22.
R. V. Ps. 74. 6. hatchet.

B

BABBLER, Eccl. 10. 11. Acts 17. 18.
1 Tim. 6. 20. avoid vain *babblings*, 2 Tim. 2. 16. Prov. 23. 29.
R. V. Eccl. 10. 11. charmer.
BABE leaped in womb, Luke 1. 41.
Heb. 5. 13. unskil. in words is a *b.*
Ps. 8. 2. out of mouth of *babes*
Isa. 3. 4. *b.* shall rule over them
1 Cor. 3. 1. as unto *b.* in Christ
1 Pet. 2. 2. as new-born *b.* desire
BACK to go from Samuel, 1 Sam. 10. 9.
1 Kings 14. 9. cast me behind *b.*
Prov. 26. 3. rod for the fool's *b.*
Isa. 38. 17. cast my sins behind thy *b.*
50. 6. gave my *b.* to smiters
Jer. 2. 27. turned their *b.* 32. 33.
18. 17. I will shew them *b.* not face
Ex. 33. 23. shall see my *b.* parts
Ps. 19. 13. keep *b.* thy servant from
53. 6. when God bringeth *b.* captivity
Acts 20. 20. kept *b.* nothing profit.
Neh. 9. 26. cast law behind *backs*
Backbiters, haters of God, Rom. 1. 30.
Ps. 15. 3. *backbiteth* not with his
Prov. 25. 23. *backbiting* tongue
2 Cor. 12. 20. strifes, *backbitings*
Backslider in heart, Prov. 14. 14.
Jer. 2. 19. thy *backslidings* reprove thee
3. 6, 12. return thou *b.* Israel, 14. 7. & 31. 22. & 49. 4.
14. 7. *b.* are many, we have sinned
Hos. 11. 7. my people are bent to *b.*
14. 4. I will heal their *b.*
Isa. 1. 4. they are gone away *b.*
59. 14. judgment is turned away *b.*
John 18. 6. went *b.* and fell to the ground
BAG, sack, or pouch, Deut. 25. 13. Job 14. 17. Prov. 16. 11. Mic. 6. 11. Hag. 1. 6. Luke 12. 33. John 13. 29.
R. V. Luke 12. 33. purses
BALANCE, Job 31. 6. & 6. 2. Ps. 62. 9. Isa. 40. 12, 15. & 46. 6. Dan. 5. 27.
16. 11. just weight and *b.* are
Mic. 6. 11. count pure with wick. *b.*
BALD, 2 Kings 2. 23. Jer. 16. 6. & 48. 37. Ezek. 27. 31. Mic. 1. 16.
Baldness, Lev. 21. 5. Deut. 14. 1. Isa. 3. 24. & 15. 2. & 22. 12. Ezek. 7. 18.
BALM, Gen. 37. 25. & 43. 11.
Jer. 8. 22. is there no *b.* in Gilead
46. 11. & 51. 8. Ezek. 27. 17.
BANNER, Isa. 13. 2. Ps. 20. 5.
Ps. 60. 4. *b.* to them that fear thee
S. of S. 2. 4. his *b.* over me was love
6. 4. terrible as an army with *banners*
R. V. Isa. 13. 2. ensign
BAPTISM of water, Matt. 3. 7.
Baptism of John, Matt. 21. 25. Mark 11. 30. Luke 7. 29. & 12. 50. Acts 1. 22. & 10. 37. & 18. 25. & 19. 3, 4.
Baptism of repentance, Mark 1. 4. Acts 13. 24. & 19. 4.
Baptism of suffering, Matt. 20. 22, 23. Mark 10. 38, 39. Luke 12. 50.
Rom. 6. 4. buried with him by *baptism*, Col. 2. 12.
Eph. 4. 5. one faith, one *b.*
1 Pet. 3. 21. *b.* doth now save us
Heb. 6. 2. doctrine of *baptisms*
BAPTIZE with water, with the Holy Ghost, Matt. 3. 11. Mark 1. 8. Luke 3. 16. Acts 1. 5. John 1. 26, 28, 31, 33.
Mark 1. 4. John did *b.* in wilder.
5. were all *baptized* of him, 8.
Mark 16. 16. believeth and is *b.*
Luke 3. 7. came to be *b.* 12.
7. 29, 30. publicans *b.* lawyers not *b.*
John 4. 1. Jesus *b.* more disciples
2. though Jesus himself *b.* not
Acts 2. 38. repent and be *b.* every one
8. 13. Simon believed and was *b.*
10. 47. that these should not be *b.*
48. Peter command. them to be *b.*
18. 8. believed and were *b.*
Rom. 6. 3. as many as were *b.* were
1 Cor. 1. 13. were ye *b.* in name of
15. none—*b.* in own name
10. 2. were all *b.* unto Moses
Gal. 3. 27. as have been *b.* into Christ
Matt. 28. 19. *baptizing* in name
BARE you on eagles' wings, Ex. 19. 4.
Isa. 53. 12. he *b.* the sins of many

Matt. 8. 17. himself *b.* our sicknesses
1 Pet. 2. 24. *b.* our sins in his own
BARN, Matt. 13. 30. Prov. 3. 10. Matt. 6. 26. Luke 12. 18, 24.
R. V. Job 39. 12; 2 Kings 6. 27. threshing-floor
BARREL of meal, 1 Kings 17. 14.
BARREN, Gen. 11. 30. & 25. 21. & 29. 31. Judg. 13. 2. Luke 1. 7.
Ex. 23. 26. nothing shall be *b.*
1 Sam. 2. 5. *b.* hath borne seven
S. of S. 4. 2. none is *b.* among, 6. 6.
Luke 23. 29. blessed are *b.* wombs
2 Pet. 1. 8. neither *b.* nor unfruitful
R. V. 2 Kings 2. 19. miscarrieth; Job 39. 6. salt; S. of S. 4. 2; 6. 6. bereaved; 2 Pet. 1. 8. idle
BASE in my own sight, 2 Sam. 6. 22.
1 Cor. 1. 28. *b.* things of this world
2 Cor. 10. 1. who in presence am *b.*
Ezek. 29. 14, 15. *basest* of kingdoms
BASTARD not enter, Deut. 23. 2.
Zech. 9. 6. *b.* shall dwell in Ashdod
Heb. 12. 8. without chastisement are *bastards*
BATTLE not to strong, Eccl. 9. 11.
Jer. 8. 6. as horse rusheth into *b.*
Ps. 140. 7. covered head in day of *b.*
R. V. Num. 31. 14; Josh. 22. 33; 2 Sam. 21. 18, 19, 20; 1 Cor. 14. 8; Rev. 9. 7, 9; 28. 8. war
BEAM out of timber, Hab. 2. 11.
Matt. 7. 3. considered not *b.* in own eye
S. of S. 1. 1, 17. *b.* of our house are
BEAR, Gen. 49. 15. Deut. 1. 9, 31. Prov. 9. 12. & 30. 21. Lam. 3. 27.
Gen. 4. 13. punishment greater than I can *b.*
Num. 11. 14. not able to *b.* all this people
Prov. 18. 14. wounded spirit who can *b.*
Amos 7. 10. land not able to *b.* words
Luke 14. 27. whoso doth not *b.* his
18. 7. though he *b.* long with them
John 16. 12. ye cannot *b.* them now
Rom. 15. 1. strong *b.* the infirmities
1 Cor. 3. 2. hitherto not able to *b.* it
10. 13. that may be able to *b.* it
Gal. 6. 2. *b.* ye one another's burdens
5. every man *b.* his own
17. I *b.* in my body the marks
Heb. 9. 28. offered to *b.* sins of many
Rev. 2. 2. canst not *b.* which are evil
Bear fruit, Ezek. 17. 8. Hos. 9. 16. Joel 2. 22. Matt. 13. 23. Luke 13. 9. John 15. 2, 4, 8.
Ps. 106. 4. favor thou *bearest* to
Rom. 11. 18. *b.* not root but
13. 4. *beareth* not sword in vain
1 Cor. 13. 7. charity *b.* all things
Ps. 126. 6. *bearing* precious seed
Heb. 13. 13. *b.* his reproach
BEASTS, animals without reason, Gen. 1. 24, 25. & 3. 1.—for ministers, Rev. 4. 6, 7, 8, 9. & 5. 6, 14. & 6. 1, 3. & 7. 11. & 14. 3. & 15. 7. & 19. 4.—for antichrist, Dan. 7. 11. Rev. 11. 7. & 13. 1, 11. & 15. 2. & 16. 13. & 17. 8. & 19. 19. & 20. 10.
Prov. 9. 2. wisdom killed her *b.*
Dan. 7. 17. four *b.* are four kings
1 Cor. 15. 32. I fought with *b.* at Ephesus
R. V. Ex. 11. 5; Num. 20. 8; Isa. 63. 14. cattle; in Rev. generally, living creatures
BEAT, Prov. 23. 14. Isa. 3. 15. Luke 12. 47, 48. 1 Cor. 9. 26.
R. V. Judg. 8. 17; 2 Kings 13. 25. smite; Mat. 7. 27. smote.
BEAUTY, Ex. 28. 2.
1 Chron. 16. 29. in the *b.* of holiness
Ps. 27. 4. to behold *b.* of the Lord
39. 11. makest his *b.* to consume
45. 11. king greatly desire thy *b.*
Prov. 20. 29. *b.* of old men gray head
31. 30. favor deceitful *b.* is vain
Isa. 3. 24. be burning instead of *b.*
33. 17. see the king in his *b.* and
Isa. 61. 3. give them *b.* for ashes
Zech. 11. 7. two staves, one called *b.*
Beautify, Ps. 149. 4. Isa. 60. 13
Beautiful, Eccl. 3. 11. S. of S. 6. 4. & 7. 1.
Isa. 52. 1, 7. & 64. 11. Jer. 13. 20. Ezek. 16. 12, 13. Matt. 23. 27. Acts 3. 2. Rom. 10. 15.
R. V. 2 Sam. 1. 19. glory; Job 40. 10; Lam. 1. 6. majesty; Isa. 61. 3. garland
BED, set for him, 2 Kings 4. 10.
Ps. 41. 3. make all his *b.* in sickness
S. of S. 3. 1. by night on my *b.* I
Isa. 28. 20. the *b.* is shorter than
Heb. 13. 4. marriage *b.* undefiled
Rev. 2. 22. I will cast her into a *b.*
Isa. 57. 2. rest in their *beds*
Amos 6. 4. lie on *b.* of ivory
R. V. many places in O. T., couch
BEFORE, in sight, Gen. 20. 15. & 43. 14. Ex. 22. 9. 1 Kings 17. 1. & 18. 15. 2 Kings 3. 14.—(in time or place) Gen. 31. 2. Job 3. 24. Josh. 8. 10. Luke 22. 47.
2 Chron. 13. 14.—(in dignity) 2 Sam. 6. 21. John 1. 15, 27.
Phil. 3. 13. those things which are *b.*
Col. 1. 17. he is *b.* all things and
R. V. Rev. 13. 12; 19. 20. in his sight
BEG, Ps. 109. 10. & 37. 25. Prov. 20. 4. Luke 16. 3. & 23. 52. John 9. 8.
Beggar, 1 Sam. 2. 8. Luke 16. 20, 22.
Beggarly elements, Gal. 4. 9.
R. V. Matt. 27. 58; Luke 23. 52. asked for
BEGIN at my sanctuary, Ezek. 9. 6.
Ex. 12. 2. the *beginning* of months
Gen. 49. 3. *b.* of strength, Deut. 21. 17.
Ps. 111. 10. fear of Lord is the *b.* of wisdom, Prov. 1. 7. & 9. 10.
Heb. 7. 3. neither *b.* of days nor end
2 Pet. 2. 20. latter end is worse than *b.*
Rev. 1. 8. I am Alpha and Omega, *b.* and the ending, 21. 6. & 22. 13.
3. 14. saith the *b.* of creation of
R. V. 1 Chr. 17. 9; Acts 26. 5; 2 Pet. 2. 20. first
BEGOTTEN drops of dew, Job 38. 28.
Ps. 2. 7. this day have I *b.* thee, Acts 13. 33. Heb. 1. 5, 6.
John 1. 14. only *b.* of the Father, 18.
3. 16. sent his only *b.* Son, 18.
1 Pet. 1. 3. *b.* us again to a lively
1 John 4. 9. sent his only *b.* Son
Rev. 1. 5. first *b.* of the dead
BEGUILE, Col. 2. 4, 18. Gen. 3. 13. 2 Cor. 11. 3. 2 Pet. 2. 14.
R. V. Col. 2. 4. delude; 2. 18. rob; 2 Pet. 2. 14. enticing
BEGUN to fall, Esth. 6. 13.
Gal. 3. 3. having *b.* in the spirit
Phil. 1. 6. hath *b.* a good work in
BEHAVE myself wisely, Ps. 101. 2.
Ps. 131. 2. I *b.* myself as a child
1 Tim. 3. 2. bishop of good *behavior*
Tit. 2. 3. in *b.* as becometh holiness
R. V. 1 Tim. 3. 2. orderly; Tit. 2. 3. reverent in demeanor.
BEHELD not iniquity in Jacob, Num. 23. 21.
Luke 10. 18. I *b.* Satan fall
John 1. 14. we *b.* his glory
Rev. 11. 12. their enemies *b.* them
BEHIND, Lev. 25. 51. Judg. 20. 40.
Ex. 10. 26. not an hoof left *b.*
Ps. 139. 5. beset me *b.* and before
Isa. 38. 17. cast all my sins *b.* thy
1 Cor. 1. 7. ye come *b.* in no gift
Col. 1. 24. fill up that is *b.* of afflict.
R. V. Col. 1. 24. lacking
BEHOLD with thine eyes, Deut. 3. 27.
Job 19. 27. my eyes shall *b.* and not
Ps. 11. 4. his eyes *b.* his eyelids try
7. countenance *b.* upright
17. 15. I will *b.* thy face in right.
27. 4. desired to *b.* beauty of Lord
37. 37. *b.* the upright man
113. 6. humbles himself to *b.*
Hab. 1. 13. of purer eyes than to *b.*
Matt. 18. 10. their angels *b.* face of
John 17. 24. they may *b.* my glory
19. 5. *b.* the man, 14. *b.* your king
26. *b.* thy son, 27. *b.* thy mother
1 Pet. 3. 2. *b.* your chaste conver.
Ps. 33. 13. Lord *beholdeth* all the
Jas. 1. 24. he *b.* himself and go.
Prov. 15. 3. *beholding* evil and good
Ps. 119. 37. turn eyes from *b.* vanity
Eccl. 5. 11. save *b.* of them with
Col. 2. 5. joying and *b.* your order
Jas. 1. 23. like man *b.* natural
BEING, Ps. 104. 33. & 146. 2. Acts 17. 28.
BELIAL, devil, furious and obstinate in wickedness, Deut. 13. 13. Judg. 19. 22. & 20. 13. 1 Sam. 1. 16. & 2. 12. & 10. 27. & 25. 17, 25. & 30. 22. 2 Sam. 16. 7. & 20. 1. & 23. 6. 1 Kings 21. 10, 13. 2 Chron. 13. 7. 2 Cor. 6. 15.
BELIEVE, credit as testimony, Ex. 4. 1. Num. 14. 11. & 20. 12.
Deut. 1. 32. ye did not *b.* the Lord
2 Chron. 20. 20. *b.* Lord, *b.* prophets
Isa. 7. 9. will not *b.* surely not
Matt. 9. 28. *b.* ye that I am able
Mark 1. 15. repent and *b.* the gos.
24. Lord I *b.* help my unbelief
11. 24. *b.* that ye receive them
Luke 8. 13. for a while *b.* and
24. 25. slow of heart to *b.* all
John 1. 12. even to them that *b.*
6. 29. ye *b.* on him whom he sent
69. we *b.* and are sure thou art
7. 39. they that *b.* him should
8. 24. if ye *b.* not I am he ye shall
11. 42. may *b.* thou hast sent me
13. 19. ye may *b.* that I am he
14. 1. ye *b.* in God, *b.* also in me
17. 20. pray for them who shall *b.*
20. 31. written that ye might *b.*
Acts 8. 37. I *b.* Jesus Christ is the
13. 39. all that *b.* are justified
16. 31. *b.* on the Lord Jesus and thou shalt be saved
Rom. 3. 22. on all them that *b.*
10. 9. shalt *b.* in thine heart
14. how shall they *b.* on him
2 Cor. 4. 13. we *b.* and therefore
Phil. 1. 29. not only to *b.* but suffer
1 Tim. 4. 10. especially those that *b.*
Heb. 10. 39. *b.* to saving of the soul
11. 6. cometh to God must *b.* that he is
Jas. 2. 19. devils also *b.* and
1 Pet. 2. 7. to you who *b.* he is prec.
1 John 3. 23. his command that we *b.* on Jesus Christ
Believe not, Isa. 7. 9. John 4. 48. & 8. 24. & 10. 26. & 12. 39. & 16. 9, 20, 25. Rom. 3. 3. 2 Cor. 4. 4. 2 Tim. 2. 13. 1 John 4. 1.
Gen. 15. 6. *believed* in Lord and he counted, Rom. 4. 3. Gal. 3. 6. Jas. 2. 23.
Ps. 27. 13. fainted unless I had *b.*
119. 66. I *b.* thy commandments
Isa. 53. 1. who hath *b.* our report, John 12. 38. Rom. 10. 16.
Dan. 6. 23. because he *b.* in his God
Jonah 3. 5. people of Nineveh *b.*
Matt. 8. 13. as thou hast *b.* so be it
21. 32. publicans and harlots *b.*
John 4. 53. himself *b.* and his house
17. 8. have *b.* thou didst send me
20. 29. blessed—not seen and yet *b.*
Acts 4. 32. that *b.* were of one heart
8. 13. Simon *b.* and was baptized
11. 21. great number *b.* and turned
48. as many as were ordained to eternal life *b.*
Rom. 4. 18. against hope *b.* in hope
Eph. 1. 13. after ye *b.* ye were
1 Tim. 3. 16. God was *b.* on in the
2 Tim. 1. 12. know whom I have *b.*
Believed not, Ps. 78. 22, 32. & 106. 24. Luke 24. 41. Acts 9. 26. Rom. 10. 14. 2 Thes. 2. 12. Heb. 3. 18. Jude 5.
Believers, Acts 5. 14. 1 Tim. 4. 12.
Believest, Luke 1. 20. John 1. 50. & 11. 26. & 14. 10. Jas. 2. 19.
Acts 8. 37. if thou *b.* with all thy
26. 27. *b.* thou prophets — thou *b.*
Believeth, Job 15. 22. & 39. 24.

Prov. 14. 15. simple *b.* every word
Isa. 28. 16. that *b.* — not make haste
Mark 9. 23. all things possible to—*b.*
16. 16. he that *b.* shall be saved, he that *b.* not shall be damned
John 3. 15, 16. *b.* in him should not
18. he that *b.* is not condemned
5. 24. *b.* on him that sent me
6. 35. *b.* on me shall never thirst
40. seeth the Son and *b.* may
11. 25. *b.* in me though he were d.
26. he that *b.* in me shall never d.
12. 44. *b.* on me, *b.* not on me, but
46. *b.* on me shall not abide in
Acts 10. 43. *b.* in him — receive remission
Rom. 1. 16. power of God—to every one that *b.*
3. 26. justifier of him that *b.* in
4. 5. worketh not, but *b.* on him
9. 33. *b.* on him — not ashamed, 10. 11.
10. for with the heart man *b.* unto righteousness
1 Cor. 7. 12. wife that *b.* not
13. husband that *b.* not
13. 7. charity *b.* all things
14. 24. come in one that *b.* not
2 Cor. 6. 15. he that *b.* with infidel
1 Pet. 2. 6. *b.* on him shall not be confounded
1 John 5. 1. whoso *b.* that Jesus is
5. overcom. world, but he that *b.*
10. he that *b.* on Son of God hath
—*b.* not God hath made him a liar because he *b.* not record that
Matt. 21. 22. ask in prayer, *believing*
John 20. 27. be not faithless, but *b.*
31. that *b.* ye might have life
Acts 16. 34. *b.* in God with all his
Rom. 15. 13. all joy and peace in b.
1 Pet. 1. 8. yet *b.* ye rejoice with joy
2 Thes. 2. 13. *belief* of the truth
R. V. Acts 19. 9; Heb. 3. 18. disobedient

BELLOWS are burnt, Jer. 6. 29.

BELLY, on *b.* shalt go, Gen. 3. 14.
Num. 5. 21. *b.* to swell and thigh
25. 8. thrust them through the *b.*
Job 3. 11. when I came out of *b.*
15. 2. fill his *b.* with east wind
35. their *b.* prepareth deceit
20. 15. God cast them out of his *b.*
20. not feel quietness in his *b.*
Ps. 17. 14. whose *b.* thou fillest with
22. 10. art my God from mother's *b.*
Prov. 20. 27. search inw. parts of *b.*
Isa. 46. 3. borne by me from the *b.*
Jonah 1. 17. in the *b.* of the fish, Matt. 12. 40.
2. 1. prayed to God out of fish's b.
2. out of the *b.* of hell cried I
Luke 15. 16. fill his *b.* with husks
John 7. 38. out of his belly shall
Rom. 16. 18. serve their own *b.*
Phil. 3. 19. whose God is their *b.*
Rev. 10. 9. make thy *b.* bitter
Tit. 1. 12. Cretians slow *bellies*
R. V. Job 20. 20. within him; 31. 9. body; S. of S. 5. 14. body; Jer. 51. 34. maw; Tit. 1. 12. gluttons

BELONG, Lev. 27. 24. Luke 23. 7.
Gen. 40. 8. interpretations *b.* to
Deut. 29. 29. secret things *b.* to Lord, things revealed *b.* to us and to our children
Ps. 47. 9. shields of earth *b.* to God
68. 20. to God *b.* issues from death
Dan. 9. 9. to the Lord *b.* mercies
Mark 9. 41. because ye *b.* in Christ
Luke 19. 42. things that *b.* to thy
Deut. 32. 35. to me *b.* vengeance
Ps. 94. 1. Heb. 10. 30. Rom. 12. 19.
Ezra 19. 4. this matter *belongeth* to
Ps. 3. 8. salvation *b.* to the Lord
62. 11. power *b.* to God, 12. *b.* mercy
Dan. 9. 7. righteousness *b.* to thee
Heb. 5. 14. strong meat *b.* to them

BELOVED — other hated, Deut. 21. 15.
Deut. 33. 12. *b.* of Lord shall dwell
Neh. 13. 26. Solomon *b.* of his God
Ps. 60. 5. thy *b.* may be delivered
127. 2. Lord giveth his *b.* sleep
S. of S. 1. 14. *my beloved*, 2. 3, 9, 16, 17. & 4. 16. & 5. 2, 6, 10, 16. & 6. 2, 3. & 7. 10, 13. Isa. 5. 1.
S. of S. 5. 9. thy *b.* more than another *b.*
Dan. 10. 11, 19. O man, greatly *b.* 9. 23.
Matt. 3. 17. my *b.* Son, 17. 5.
Rom. 9. 25. *b.* which was not *b.*
11. 28. *b.* for the Father's sake
16. 8. Amplias *b.* in the Lord
Eph. 1. 6. accepted in the *b.*
2 Pet. 3. 15. *b.* brother Paul
Rev. 20. 9. compassed *b.* city
R. V. Luke 9. 35. my chosen; Phile. 2. sister

BEMOAN, Jer. 15. 5. & 16. 5. & 22. 10. & 31. 18. & 48. 18.

BEND bow, Ps. 11. 2. & 64. 3. & 58. 7. & 7. 12. & 37. 1. Lam. 2. 4. & 3. 12. Isa. 5. 28.
Jer. 9. 3. *b.* their tongues like a bow
Isa. 60. 14. afflicted thee shall come *bending* unto thee
Hos. 11. 7. people *bent* to backslid.
Zech. 9. 13. I have *b.* Judah for me
R. V. Ps. 58. 7. aimeth

BENEATH, Prov. 15. 24. John 8. 23.

BENEFACTORS, Luke 22. 25.

BENEFITS, loaded us with, Ps. 68. 19.
Ps. 103. 2. forget not all his *b.*
116. 12. render to the Lord for all his *b.*
R. V. Phile. 14. goodness

BENEVOLENCE, due, 1 Cor. 7. 3.
R. V. 1 Cor. 7. 3. her due

BEREAVE soul of good, Eccl. 4. 8.
Jer. 15. 7. *b.* them of children, 18. 21.
Gen. 42. 36. & 43. 14. Ezek. 5. 17. & 36. 12, 13, 14. Lam. 1. 20. Hos. 9. 12. & 13. 8.
R. V. Jer. 18. 21. childless

BESEECH God to be gracious, Mal. 1. 9.
2 Cor. 5. 20. as though God did b.
R. V. In O. T. mostly changed to pray; Phil. 4. 2; 1 Thes. 4. 10; Heb. 13. 22. exhort

BESET me behind and before, Ps. 139. 5.
Hos. 7. 2. own doings have *b.* them
Heb. 12. 1. sin which doth easily *b.* us

BESIDE waters, Ps. 23. 2. Isa. 32. 20.
S. of S. 1. 8. feed kids *b.* shepherd's
Isa. 56. 8. others *b.* I have gathered
R. V. Judg. 20. 36. against; Mat. 25. 20 —; Acts 26. 24. mad; 2 Pet. 1. 5. for this very cause

BESIDE SELF, Mark. 3. 21. Acts 26. 24. 2 Cor. 5. 13.

BESOM of destruction, Isa. 14. 23.

BESOUGHT the Lord, Deut. 3. 23.
2 Sam. 12. 16. 1 Kings 13. 6. 2 Kings 13. 4. 2 Chron. 33. 12. Ezra 8. 23. 2 Cor. 12. 8.

BEST estate is vanity, Ps. 39. 5.
Mic. 7. 4. *b.* of them is as a brier
Luke 15. 22. bring forth *b.* robe
1 Cor. 12. 31. covet earnestly *b.* gifts
R. V. 1 Cor. 12. 31. greater

BESTEAD, hardly, Isa. 8. 21.

BESTOW a blessing, Ex. 32. 29.
Luke 12. 17. room to *b.* my fruits
13. 3. *b.* all my goods to feed the
John 4. 38. *bestowed* no labor
1 Cor. 15. 10. his grace *b.* on me
2 Cor. 1. 11. gift *b.* on us by means
8. 1. grace of God *b.* on churches
Gal. 4. 11. lest *b.* labor in vain
1 John 3. 1. love the Father hath *b.* on us
R. V. 2 Cor. 8. 1. which hath been given in; John 4. 38. ye have not labored

BETIMES, 2 Chron. 36. 15. Job 8. 5. & 24. 5. Prov. 13. 24. Gen. 26. 31.
R. V. 2 Chron. 36. 15. early; Job 8. 5; 24. 5. diligently

BETRAY, Matt. 24. 10. & 26. 21. Mark 13. 12. & 14. 18.
R. V. In N. T. mostly, delivered up

BETROTH, Deut. 28. 30. Hos. 2. 19, 20.

BETTER than ten sons, 1 Sam. 1. 8.
Judg. 8. 2. gleanings *b.* than vintage
1 Kings 19. 4. I am not *b.* than
Prov. 15. 16. *b.* is little with the fear
17. *b.* is a dinner of herbs with love
16. 8. *b.* is a little with righteous.
16. how much *b.* to get wisdom
27. 10. *b.* is a neighbor near that
Eccl. 4. 9. two are *b.* than one
13. *b.* is a poor and wise child than
7. 1. *b.* is a good name than precious
2. *b.* to go to the house of mourning
3. *b.* is sorrow than laughter
5. *b.* to hear rebuke of the wise
9. 16. wisdom is *b.* than strength
18. wisdom is *b.* than weapons of
S. of S. 4. 10. how much *b.* is thy love than wine
Matt. 6. 26. are ye not much *b.* than
1 Cor. 9. 15. were *b.* for me to die
Phil. 1. 23. with Christ is far *b.*
2. 3. esteem others *b.* than them.
Heb. 1. 4. made so much *b.* than the angels.
6. 9. persuaded *b.* things of you
22. Jesus made surety of a *b.* testament
10. 34. a *b.* enduring substance
35. obtain a *b.* resurrection
40. provided some *b.* things
12. 24. blood speaketh *b.* than Abel
2 Pet. 2. 21. *b.* not to have known
R. V. Mat. 12. 12. of more value; Mark 9. 43; Luke 5. 39; 1 Cor. 9. 15. good

BETWEEN thy seed and her, Gen. 3. 15.
1 Kings 3. 9. discern *b.* good and
18. 21. how long halt ye *b.* two
Ezek. 22. 26. no difference *b.* holy and profane, 44. 23. & 34. 17. Lev. 10. 10.
Phil. 1. 23. in a strait *b.* two having
1 Tim. 2. 5. one mediator *b.* God

BEWARE of men, Matt. 10. 17.
Matt. 7. 15. *b.* of false prophets
16. 6. *b.* of leaven of Pharisees, 11. Mark 8. 15.
Luke 12. 15. *b.* of covetousness
Col. 2. 8. *b.* lest any man spoil you
R. V. Ex. 23. 21; Col. 2. 8. take heed; Luke 12. 15. keep yourselves from

BEYOND or defraud, 1 Thes. 4. 6.
R. V. 1 Thes. 4. 6. transgress

BIBBER, Prov. 23. 20. Matt. 11. 19.

BID, Matt. 22. 9. & 23. 3. Luke 14. 10, 24. 2 John 10, 11.

BIDE, not in unbelief, Rom. 11. 23.

BILL, Deut. 24. 1, 3. Isa. 50. 1. Jer. 3. 8. Mark 10. 4. Luke 16. 6, 7.
R. V. Luke 16. 6. bond

BILLOWS, Ps. 42. 7. Jonah 2. 3.

BIND sweet influences, Job 38. 31.
Job 31. 36. I would *b.* it as a crown
Ps. 105. 22. to *b.* his princes at
118. 27. *b.* the sacrifice with cords
Prov. 3. 3. *b.* them about thy neck
Isa. 8. 16. *b.* up testimony, seal law
Matt. 12. 29. first *b.* strong man and
13. 30. *b.* them in bundles to burn
16. 19. thou shalt *b.* on earth, 18. 18.
22. 13. *b.* him hand and foot, and
Bindeth up, Job 5. 18. Ps. 147. 3.

BIRD hasteth to snare, Prov. 7. 23.
Ps. 124. 7. escaped as a *b.* out of the
Eccl. 10. 20. *b.* of air tell the matter
Isa. 46. 11. ravenous *b.* from the east
Jer. 12. 9. heritage as a speckled *b.*
Birds, Gen. 15. 10. & 40. 17. Lev. 14. 4. 2 Sam. 21. 10. Ps. 104. 17. Eccl. 9. 12. S. of S. 2. 12. Isa. 31. 5. Jer. 5. 27. & 12. 4, 9. Matt. 8. 20.

BIRTH, 2 Kings 19. 3. Eccl. 7. 1. Isa. 66. 9. Ezek. 16. 3. Gal. 4. 19.
Birthday, Gen. 40. 20. Matt. 14. 6.
Birthright, Gen. 25. 31, 32, 33. & 27. 36. & 43. 33. 1 Chron. 5. 1. Heb. 12. 16.

BISHOP, 1 Tim. 3. 1, 2. Tit. 1. 7.
1 Pet. 2. 25. return to *b.* of souls
Phil. 1. 1. with *bishops* and deacons

BITE, Num. 21. 6, 8, 9. Eccl. 10. 8, 11. Jer. 8. 17. Amos 9. 3. Hab. 2. 7.

Mic. 3. 5. prophets *b.* with their
Gal. 5. 15. if ye *b.* and devour one another
Prov. 23. 32. at the last it *b.* like a
BITTER made their lives, Ex. 1. 14.
Ex. 12. 8. with *b.* herbs eat it, Num. 9. 11.
Deut. 32. 24. devoured with *b.* destruction
32. their grapes of gall, clusters are *b.*
2 Kings 14. 26. affliction was very *b.*
Job 3. 20. why is life given to the *b.* in soul
Ps. 64. 3. their arrows even *b.* words
Prov. 27. 7. every *b.* thing is sweet
Isa. 5. 20. woe to them put *b.* for
Jer. 2. 19. evil thing and *b.* that
Col. 3. 19. wives be not *b.* against
Rev. 10. 9. it shall make thy belly *b.*
Judg. 5. 23. curse *bitterly* inhabit.
Ruth 1. 20. Almighty dealt *b.* with
Isa. 22. 4. I will weep *b.*, 33. 7.
Hos. 12. 14. provoked him most *b.*
Matt. 26. 75. wept *b.*, Luke 22. 62.
Bitterness of soul, 1 Sam. 1. 10.
1 Sam. 15. 32. *b.* of death is past
2 Sam. 2. 26. it will be *b.* in end
Prov. 14. 10. heart knows its own *b.*
Zech. 12. 10. in *b.* for first-born
Acts 8. 23. in gall of *b.* and bond of
Rom. 3. 14. mouth full of cursing and *b.*
Heb. 12. 15. root of *b.* springing up
R. V. Job 23. 2. rebellious
BITTERN, Isa. 14. 23. & 34. 11.
BLACK, 1 Kings 18. 45. Matt. 5. 36.
S. of S. 1. 5. I am *b.* but comely, 6.
Blackness of darkness, Heb. 12. 18
Jude 13.
R. V. S. of S. 1. 6. swarthy
BLAME, Gen. 43. 9. & 44. 32. 2 Cor. 8. 20. Eph. 1. 4.
Blamed, 2 Cor. 6. 3. Gal. 2. 11.
Blameless, Gen. 44. 10. Josh. 2. 17. Judg. 15. 3. Matt. 12. 5. Phil. 3. 6. 1 Tim. 5. 7.
Luke 1. 6. in all the ordinances of the Lord *b.*
1 Cor. 1. 8. be *b.* in the day of our
1 Thes. 5. 23. be preserved *b.*
1 Tim. 3. 2. bishop must be *b.*
Tit. 1. 6, 7, 10. office of deacon found *b.*
2 Pet. 3. 14. without spot and *b.*
R. V. Eph. 1. 4. blemish; Matt. 12. 5. guiltless; 1 Tim. 3. 2; 5. 7. without reproach
BLASPHEME, revile God, &c.
Ps. 74. 10. enemy *b.* thy name
Mark 3. 29. *b.* against Holy Ghost
Acts 26. 11. compelled them to *b.*
1 Tim. 1. 20. may learn not to *b.*
Lev. 24. 11. *blasphemed* the name of the Lord
2 Kings 19. 6. servants *b.* me, Isa. 37. 6.
Isa. 52. 5. my name continually is *b.*
Rom. 2. 24. the name of God is *b.*
Tit. 2. 5. word of God be not *b.*
Rev. 16. 9, 11, 21. *b.* the God of
Lev. 24. 16. *blasphemeth* put to death
Matt. 9. 3. said this man *b.*
Luke 12. 10. to him that *b.* against the Holy Ghost
Blasphemer, 1 Tim. 1. 13. & 2 Tim. 3. 2.
Blasphemy, 2 Kings 19. 3. Isa 37. 3. Matt. 12. 31. Mark 7. 22. Col. 3. 8. Rev. 2. 9.
R. V. 2 Tim. 3. 2. railers; 2 Kings 19. 3; Isa. 37. 3. contumely; Mark 7. 22; Col. 3. 8. railing
BLAST, Ex. 15. 8. 2 Sam. 22. 16. 2 Kings 19. 7. Job 4. 9. Isa. 25. 4.
Blasting, Deut. 28. 22. 1 Kings 8. 37.
BLEMISH, without, Ex. 12. 5. & 29. 1. Lev. 1. 3, 10. & 4. 23.
Dan. 1. 4. children and no *b.*
Eph. 5. 27. church holy, and without *b.*
1 Pet. 1. 19. as a lamb without *b.*
BLESS them that *b.* thee, Gen. 12. 3.
Gen. 22. 17. in blessing I will *b.* thee
Gen. 32. 26. not let thee go except thou *b.* me
Ex. 23. 25. *b.* thy bread and water
Num. 6. 24. Lord *b.* and keep thee
Ps. 5. 12. wilt *b.* the righteous
29. 11. will *b.* his people with peace
67. 1. be merciful to us and *b.* us
115. 13. he will *b.* them that fear
Matt. 5. 44. *b.* them that curse you
Rom. 12. 14. *b.* them that persecute
Acts 3. 26. sent him to *b.* you in turning many
1 Cor. 4. 12. being reviled we *b.*
Bless the Lord, Deut. 8. 10. Judg. 5. 9. Ps. 16. 7. & 34. 1. & 103. 1, 21, 22. & 104. 1, 35. & 26. 12.
Bless thee, Ps. 63. 4. & 145. 2, 10.
Gen. 1. 22. God *blessed* them and
2. 3. God *b.* the seventh day
Ex. 20. 11. the Lord *b.* the sabbath
Ps. 33. 12, 13. *b.* whose God is the
Prov. 10. 7. memory of the just is *b.*
Matt. 13. 16. *b.* are eyes, they see, Luke 10. 23.
24. 46. *b.* is that servant when his
43. Lord cometh, Luke 12. 37, 38.
Mark 10. 16. took them in his arms and *b.* them
Luke 1. 28, 42. *b.* art thou among
48. all generations shall call me *b.*
Acts 20. 35. more *b.* to give than to
Rom. 1. 25. Creator *b.* for ever, 9. 5.
2 Cor. 11. 31. Eph. 1. 3. 1 Pet. 1. 3.
1 Tim. 1. 11. glorious gospel of *b.*
Ps. 119. 1 *b.* are the undefiled in
84. 4. *b. are they* that dwell in thy
106. 3. *b.* — that keep judgment
Prov. 8. 32. *b.* — that keep my ways
Isa. 30. 18. *b.* — that wait for him
Matt. 5. 3—11. *b.*—the poor in spirit — mourn — meek — hunger and thirst — merciful — pure in heart — peacemakers, persecuted — when men revile you, Luke 6. 21, 22.
Luke 11. 28. *b.* — that hear the word and do it
John 20. 29. *b.* — that have not seen, and yet have believed
Rom. 4. 7. *b.* — whose iniquities are forgiven
Rev. 19. 9. *b.* — called to the marriage supper
22. 14. *b.* — that do his command.
Num. 24. 9. *b.* is *he* that blesseth
Ps. 32. 1. *b.* — whose transgression is forgiven
41. 1. *b.* — that considereth the
Dan. 12. 12. *b.* — that waiteth and cometh
Matt. 11. 6. *b.* — who shall not be off
21. 9. *b.* — cometh in the name of the Lord, 23. 39. Mark 11. 19. Luke 13. 35.
Rev. 1. 3. *b.* — that readeth this
16. 15. *b.* — that watcheth and keep.
20. 6. *b.* — that hath part in the first resurrection
22. 7. *b.* — that keepeth the sayings of this book
Ps. 1. 1. *b. is the man* that walketh not in the counsel of the ungodly
34. 8. *b.* — that trusteth in him, 84. 12.
65. 4. *b.* — whom thou choosest
84. 5. *b.* — whose strength is in thee
112. 1. *b.* — that feareth the Lord
Prov. 8. 34. *b.* — that heareth me
Isa. 56. 2. *b.* — that doeth this, and
Ps. 49. 18. he *blesseth* his soul
Blessedness, Rom. 4. 6, 9. Gal. 4. 15.
Gen. 12. 2. thou shalt be a *blessing*
27. 36. he hath taken away my *b.*
28. 4. give thee *b.* of Abraham
Deut. 11. 26. set before you a *b.* and a curse, 30. 19. Jas. 3. 9, 10.
23. 5. turned curse into *b.*, Neh. 13. 2.
Neh. 9. 5. exalted above all *b.*
Job 29. 13. *b.* of him ready to perish
Ps. 3. 8. thy *b.* is upon thy people
129. 8. the *b.* of Lord be upon you
Isa. 65. 8. destroy it not for a *b.* is
Joel 2. 14. leaveth a *b.* behind him
1 Cor. 10. 16. the cup of *b.* which
Gal. 3. 14. *b.* of Abraham might
Blessings, Gen. 49. 25, 26. Josh. 8. 34. Ps. 21. 3. Prov. 10. 6. & 28. 20.
BLIND, Ex. 4. 11. Lev. 21. 18.
Job 29. 15. I was eyes to the *b.*
Ps. 146. 8. openeth the eyes of the *b.*
Isa. 42. 7. to open the *b.* eyes, 18.
19. who is *b.* but my servant?
43. 8. bring the *b.* people that have
56. 10. his watchmen are *b.*
Matt. 11. 5. the *b.* receive sight, Luke 7. 21.
23. 16. woe to you, *b.* guides, 24.
Luke 4. 18. recovery of sight to *b.*
Rev. 3. 17. thou art *b.* and naked
John 12. 40. *blinded* their eyes
Rom. 11. 7. the rest were *b.*
2 Cor. 3. 14. their minds were *b.*
4. 4. the God of this world hath *b.* the minds
1 John 2. 11. darkness hath *b.* his
R. V. Rom. 11. 7; 2 Cor. 3. 14. hardened
BLOOD of grapes, Gen. 49. 11.
Job. 16. 18. cover not thou my *b.*
Ps. 9. 12. maketh inquisition for *b.*
72. 14. precious their *b.* in his
Isa. 26. 21. the earth shall disclose her *b.*
Ezek. 3. 18. his *b.* will I require
9. 9. the land is full of *b.*
16. 6. polluted in thine own *b.*
Hos. 4. 2. they break out, and *b.*
Mic. 3. 10. they build up Zion with *b.*
Matt. 26. 28. *b.* of New Testament
Mark 14. 24. Luke 22. 20. 1 Cor. 11. 25. & 27. 8. field of *b.*, Acts 1. 19.
25. his *b.* be on us and on our child.
Luke 13. 1. whose *b.* Pilate had
22. 44. as it were great drops of *b.*
John 1. 13. born not of *b.* nor of flesh
6. 54, 56. whoso drink. my *b.* hath
55. my *b.* is drink indeed
19. 34. out of his side came *b.* and
Acts 17. 26. made of one *b.* all
18. 6. your *b.* be upon your own
Rom. 3. 25. through faith in his *b.*
5. 9. being justified by his *b.*
1 Cor. 11. 27. guilty of body and *b.* of Christ
Col. 1. 20. made peace through the *b.* of the cross
Heb. 9. 20. this is the *b.* of the test.
22. without shedding of *b.* no
10. 19. into the holiest by the *b.* of
12. 4. ye have not yet resisted unto *b.*
24. *b.* of sprinkling that speaketh
1 Pet. 1. 2. sprinkling of the *b.* of
19. with precious *b.* of Christ
1 John 1. 7. his *b.* cleanseth from
5. 6. came by water and *b.*
Rev. 1. 5. washed us in his own *b.*
6. 10. dost thou not avenge our *b.*
7. 14. made white in the *b.* of the
8. 7. hail and fire mingled with *b.*
12. 11. overcame by the *b.* of the
16. 6. shed *b.* — given them *b.* to
17. 6. drunken with the *b.* of saints
Blood-guiltiness, Ps. 51. 14.
Bloody, Ex. 4. 25, 26. Ps. 5. 6. & 55. 23.
R. V. Ps. 5. 6; 55. 23; 59. 2; 139. 19. bloodthirsty; Acts 28. 8. dysentery
BLOSSOM, man's rod shall, Num. 17. 5.
Isa. 5. 24. their *b.* shall go up as dust
27. 6. Israel shall *b.* and bud
35. 1. the desert shall *b.* as the
Hab. 3. 17. the fig-tree shall not *b.*
Ezek. 7. 10. rod hath *blossomed* pride
R. V. Num. 17. 5. *bud.*
BLOT, Job 31. 7. Prov. 9. 7.
Ex. 32. 32, 33. *b.* me out of thy book, Num. 5. 23. Ps. 69. 28. Rev. 3. 5.
Blot out their *name* or remem. Deut. 9. 14. & 25. 19. & 29. 20. 2 Kings 14. 27. Ps. 109. 13.
Blot out sin, transgression, ini-

quity, Neh. 4. 5. Ps. 51. 1, 9. & 109. 14.
Isa. 43. 25. & 44. 22. Jer. 18. 23. Acts 3. 19.
Col. 2. 14. *blotting* out the handwriting
R. V. Job. 31. 7. spot.
BLOW on my garden, S. of S. 4. 16.
Hag. 1. 9. I did *b.* upon it
John 3. 8. wind *bloweth* where it
BLUSH to lift up my face, Ezra 9. 6.
Jer. 6. 15. neither could they *b.* 8. 12.
BOAST, Ps. 10. 3. & 34. 2. & 49. 6. & 52. 1.
Prov. 20. 14. & 25. 14. Jas. 3. 5.
Ps. 44. 8. in God we *b.* all the day
Prov. 27. 1. *b.* not of to-morrow
Boasting, Acts 5. 36. Rom. 3. 27.
Jas. 4. 16. now ye rejoice in your *b.*
Rom. 1. 30. proud *boasters*, 2 Tim. 3. 2.
R. V. Rom. 11. 18; 2 Cor. 9. 2; 10. 8. glory.
BODY of heaven, Ex. 24. 10.
Job 19. 26. though worms destroy this *b.*
Matt. 6. 22. *b.* full of light, Luke 11. 34.
10. 28. them that kill the *b.*, Luke 12. 4.
Matt. 26. 26. this is my *b.*, 1 Cor. 11. 24.
Rom. 6. 6. the *b.* of sin be destroyed
7. 4. dead to the law by the *b.* of
24. deliver me from the *b.* of this
8. 10. *b.* is dead because of sin
13. do mortify deeds of the *b.*
23. the redemption of our *b.*
1 Cor. 6. 13. *b.* is not for fornication, for the Lord; and the Lord for the *b.*
18. every sin a man doeth is without the *b.*
19. your *b.* is the temple of the Holy Ghost
7. 4. wife hath not power of her own *b.*
9. 27. I keep under my *b.* and
10. 16. communion of *b.* of Christ
11. 27. guilty of *b.* and blood of the
29. not discerning the Lord's *b.*
12. 14. the *b.* is not one member
27. ye are the *b.* of Christ
15. 35. with what *b.* do they come?
44. sown a natural *b.* raised a spiritual *b.*
Eph. 3. 6. fellow heirs of the same *b.*
5. 23. he is the Saviour of the *b.*
Phil. 3. 21. who shall change our vile *b.*
Col. 1. 18. he is the head of the *b.* the church
2. 11. putting off the *b.* of sins of
17. shadow — but the *b.* is of Christ
23. neglecting of the *b.*
1 Thes. 5. 23. spirit, soul, and *b.* be
Jas. 3. 6. able to bridle the whole *b.*
Jude 9. disputed about the *b.* of
John 2. 21. his own *b.*, 1 Cor. 6. 18. 1 Pet. 2. 24.
1 Cor. 5. 3. in the *b.*, 2 Cor. 5. 6, 10. & 12. 2. Phil. 1. 20. Heb. 13. 3.
Deut. 28. 11, 18, 53. fruit of the *b.*, 30. 9. Ps. 132. 11. Mic. 6. 7.
Rom. 8. 11. quicken your mortal *bodies*
12. 1. present your *b.* a living sacri.
1 Cor. 6. 15. your *b.* are members of
Eph. 5. 28. husbands love your wives as your own *b.*
Luke 3. 22. Holy Ghost descended in a *bodily* shape
2 Cor. 10. 10. his *b.* presence is
Col. 2. 9. dwelleth the fulness of the godhead *b.*
1 Tim. 4. 8. *b.* exercise profiteth
R. V. Isa. 51. 23. back; Matt. 14. 12; 15. 45. corpse
BOLD as a lion, Prov. 28. 1.
2 Cor. 10. 1. being absent am *b.*
11. 21. if any is *b.* I am *b.* also
Phil. 1. 14. are much more *b.* to
Mark 15. 43. went *boldly* unto Pilate
Heb. 4. 16. come *b.* to the throne of
2 Cor. 7. 4. great is my *boldness* of
Heb. 10. 19. *b.* to enter into the
1 John 4. 17. *b.* in the day of judg.
R. V. 2 Cor. 10. 1. good courage; 7. 26. openly; Eph. 6. 19 ——; Heb. 13. 6. with good courage; Eccl. 8. 1. hardness
BOND of the covenant, Ezek. 20. 37.
Acts 8. 23. in gall and *b.* of iniquity
1 Cor. 12. 13. *bond and free*, Gal. 3. 28. Eph. 6. 8. Col. 3. 11. Rev. 6. 15. & 13. 16. & 19. 18.
Ps. 116. 16. has loosed my *bonds*
Job. 12. 18. he looseth *b.* of kings
Acts 20. 23. *b.* and afflictions abide
23. 29. worthy of death or of *b.*
26. 29. such as I am except these *b.*
Eph. 6. 20. I am an ambassador in *b.*
Phil. 1. 16. to add affliction to my *b.*
2 Tim. 2. 9. suffer trouble even unto *b.*
Phile. 10. whom I have begotten in my *b.*
Heb. 10. 34. compassion in my *b.*
13. 3. remember them that are in *b.*
Ex. 13. 3. house of *bondage*, 20. 2.
1. 14. lives bitter with hard *b.*
2. 23. sighed by reason of the *b.*
Rom. 8. 15. received again the spirit of *b.*
1 Cor. 7. 15. brother or sister is not in *b.*
Gal. 4. 24. Sinai which gendereth to *b.*
5. 1. entangled with the yoke of *b.*
Bondwoman, Gen. 21. 10. Gal. 4. 23, 30.
BONDMAID, laws concerning, Lev. 19. 20. & 25. 44.
BONDMAN, laws concerning, Lev. 25. 39. Deut. 15. 12.
R. V. Ex. 1. 14; Isa. 14. 3. serve; Deut. 7. 8; Jer. 34. 13. bondage; 1 Kings 9. 22 'ondservants; Gal. 4. 23, 30, 31. handmaid
BONE of my bone and flesh of my, Gen. 2. 23. & 29. 14. Judg. 9. 2. 2 Sam. 5. 1. & 19. 13. 1 Chron. 11. 11.
Ex. 12. 46. not break a *b.* of it
John 19. 36. *b.* of him shall not be
Ps. 51. 8. *b.* thou hast broken may
Eccl. 11. 5. how the *b.* grow in the
Matt. 23. 27. full of dead men's *b.*
His bones, Ps. 34. 20. Eph. 5. 30. Job 20. 11. Ezek. 32. 27. Prov. 12. 4.
Ps. 6. 2. *my bones* are vexed
22. 14. all — are out of joint
31. 10. — are consumed
38. 3. there is no rest —
102. 3. — are burnt as an hearth
5 — cleave to my skin
BONNETS, of the priests, directions for making, Ex. 28. 40. & 29. 9. & 39. 28. Ezek. 44. 18. *See* MITRE.
BOOK, Gen. 5. 1. Esth. 6. 1.
Ex. 32. 32. blot me out of thy *b.*
Job 19. 23. O that they were printed in a *b.*
31. 35. mine adversary had written a *b.*
Ps. 40. 7. in the volume of the *b.*, Heb. 10. 7.
Book of life, Phil. 4. 3. Rev. 3. 5. & 13. 8. & 17. 8. & 20. 12, 15. & 21. 27. & 22. 19.
Books, Eccl. 12. 12. Dan. 7. 10. & 9. 2. John 21. 25. 2 Tim. 4. 13. Rev. 20. 12.
R. V. 1 Chr. 29. 29; 2 Chron. 9. 29; 12. 15; 20. 34. history; Jer. 32. 12.
BOOTHS, Lev. 23. 42, 43. Neh. 8. 14.
BORDER of his garment, Mark 6. 56.
BORING of the ear, Ex. 21. 6.
BORN to trouble, man is, Job 5. 7.
Job 14. 1. *b.* of a woman, 15. 14. & 25. 4. Matt. 11. 11. Luke 7. 28.
Ps. 58. 3. the wicked go astray as soon as they are *b.*
Ps. 87. 5. this and that man was *b.* in her
Prov. 17. 17. a brother is *b.* for
Eccl. 3. 2. a time to be *b.* and a time to die
Isa. 9. 6. unto us a child is *b.* a son
66. 8. shall a nation be *b.* at once
Jer. 15. 10. *borne* me a man of strife
Matt. 11. 11. among them that are *b.* of women
John 3. 4. can a man be *b.* when
5. *b.* of water and of the Spirit
Rom. 9. 11. children being not yet *b.*
1 Cor. 15. 8. one *b.* out of due time
Gal. 4. 23. *b.* after the flesh, 29.
1 Pet. 2. 2. as new *b.* babes desire sincere milk of
John 3. 3, 5, 7. *b.* again
John 1. 13. *born of God*, 1 John 3. 9. & 4. 7. & 5. 1, 4, 18.
BORROW, Deut. 15. 6. & 28. 12.
Ex. 22. 14. *b.* aught of his neighbor, 3. 22. & 11. 2. & 12. 35.
Matt. 5. 42. would *b.* of thee turn
Ps. 37. 21. the wicked *borroweth* and payeth not
Prov. 22. 7. *borrower* is servant to
Isa. 24. 2. as with the lender so with *b.*
R. V. Ex. 3. 22; 11. 2; 12. 35. ask
BOSOM, Gen. 16. 5. Ex. 4. 6.
Num. 11. 12. carry them in *b.* as a
Deut. 13. 6. wife of thy *b.*, 28. 54, 56.
Ps. 35. 13. prayer returned into my own *b.*
Prov. 5. 20. why embrace the *b.* of a
6. 27. take fire in his *b.* and not be
17. 23. gift out of *b.* to pervert, 21. 14.
19. 24. hideth his hands in his *b.* 26. 15.
Isa. 40. 11. carry them in his *b.*
65. 6, 7. recompense into their *b.*
Ps. 79. 12. Jer. 32. 18.
Mic. 7. 5. her that lieth in thy *b.*
Luke 6. 38. shall men give into your *b.*
16. 22. carried into Abraham's *b.*, 23.
John 1. 18. who is in the *b.* of the Father, 13. 23. leaning on Jesus' *b.*
R. V. Prov. 19. 24; 26. 15. dish
BOTH, Gen. 2. 25. & 3. 7. & 19. 36.
Zech. 6. 13. counsel of peace between *b.*
Eph. 2. 14. our peace made *b.* one
18. we *b.* have access by one spirit
BOTTLE, Gen. 21. 14, 15, 19.
Ps. 56. 8. put my tears into thy *b.*
Jer. 13. 12. every *b.* filled with wine
Job 38. 37. who can stay *bottles* of
Matt. 9. 17. new wine into old *b.*
Mark 2. 22. new wine into new *b.* Matt. 9. 17.
R. V. generally, skins or wine skins
BOTTOMLESS pit, Rev. 9. 1. & 11. 7. & 17. 8.
Satan bound there, Rev. 20. 1, 2.
BOUGHT, Gen. 17. 12, 13. & 33. 19.
Deut. 32. 6. he thy father that *b.*
Matt. 13. 46. sold all and *b.* it
1 Cor. 6. 20. *b.* with a price, 7. 23.
2 Pet. 2. 1. denying the Lord that *b.* them
BOUND Isaac, Gen. 22. 9.
Job 36. 8. if they be *b.* in fetters
Ps. 107. 10. being *b.* in affliction
Prov. 22. 15. foolishness *b.* in heart
Matt. 16. 19. whatsoever ye bind on earth shall be *b.* in heaven, 18 18.
Acts 20. 22. I go *b.* in the spirit
21. 13. ready not to be *b.* only, but
Rom. 7. 2. wife is *b.* to her husband, 1 Cor. 7. 39.
1 Cor. 7. 27. art thou *b.* to a wife, seek
2 Tim. 2. 9. the word of God is not *b.*
Heb. 13. 3. in bonds as *b.* with them
Isa. 1. 6. closed nor *bound up*
Ezek. 30. 21. not — to be healed
34. 4. neither have ye *b.* the broken
Hos. 13. 12. iniquity of Ephraim is

BOUNTY, 1 Kings 10. 13. 2 Cor. 9. 5.
Prov. 22. 9. *bountiful* eye be blessed
Ps. 13. 6. dealt *bountifully* with me, 116. 7. & 119. 17. & 142. 7.
2 Cor. 9. 6. he that sows *b.* shall reap *b.*
BOW in the clouds, Gen. 9. 13, 14, 16.
Gen. 49. 24. his *b.* abode in strength
Josh. 24. 12. not with sword nor *b.*
2 Sam. 1. 18. teach children use of *b.*
Ps. 7. 12. he hath bent his *b.*
44. 6. I will not trust in my *b.*
78. 57. turned aside like a deceit. *b.*
Jer. 9. 3. bend tongue like a *b.* for
Lam. 2. 4. bent his *b.* like an enemy
Lam. 3. 12. bent his *b.* and set me
Hos. 1. 5. break the *b.* of Israel
17. I will not save them by *b.*
7. 16. turned like a deceitful *b.*
1 Sam. 2. 4. Ps. 37. 15. *bows*, & 64. 3. & 78. 9. Jer. 51. 56.
Bow down thine ear, 2 Kings 19. 16. Ps. 31. 2. & 86. 1. Prov. 22. 17.
Job 31. 10. let others — upon her
Ps. 95. 6. let us — and worship
Gen. 23. 12. Abraham *bowed down* himself before the people, 27. 29.
Judg. 7. 5, 6. — on their knees to
Ps. 38. 6. I am—greatly, I go mourning all the day long
Isa. 2. 11. haughtiness of men —, 17.
BOWELS did yearn, Gen. 43. 30. 1 Kings 3. 26. 2 Chron. 21. 15, 18.
Ps. 71. 6. took me out of my mother's *b.*
Isa. 63. 15. where is the sounding of thy *b.*
Jer. 4. 19. my *b.* my *b.* I am pained
31. 20. my *b.* are troubled for him, Lam. 1. 20. & 2. 11. S. of S. 5. 4.
Acts 1. 18. all his *b.* gushed out
2 Cor. 6. 12. straitened in your *b.*
Phil. 1. 8. I long after you in the *b.* of Christ
2. 1. if any comfort, if any *b.* and
Col. 3. 12. put on *b.* of mercies
1 John 3. 17. shutteth up *b.* of
R. V. Ps. 109. 18. inward parts; 2 Cor. 6. 12. affections; Phil. 1. 8; 2. 1. tender mercies; Col. 3. 12; Phile. 7. 20. heart
BOWL, Num. 7. 85. Eccl. 12. 6. Zech. 4. 2, 3. & 9. 15. & 14. 20.
R. V. Ex. 25. 31, 33, 34; 37. 17, 19, 20; 1 Kings 7. 50; 2 Kings 12. 13. cups; 2 Kings 25. 15; 1 Chr. 28. 17; Jer. 52. 18. basons
BOYS, Gen. 25. 27. Zech. 8. 5.
BRAKE the tables, Ex. 32. 19. & 34. 1. Deut. 9. 17. & 10. 2.
Judg. 16. 12. Samson *b.* the new
1 Sam. 4. 18. Eli *b.* his neck and
1 Kings 19. 11. wind *b.* in pieces the
2 Kings 11. 18. *b.* Baal's image, 10. 27.
18. 4. *b.* the images and brazen ser.
23. 14. *b.* in pieces the images, 2 Chron. 31. 1.
Job 29. 17. *b.* the jaws of the wick.
Ps. 76. 3. *b.* the arrows of the bow
105. 16. *b.* the whole staff of bread
Jer. 31. 32. my covenant they *b.*, Ezek. 17. 16.
Dan. 2. 1. his sleep *b.* from him
6. 24. *b.* all their bones to pieces
Matt. 14. 19. blessed, and *b.* and gave, 15. 36. & 26. 26. Mark 6. 41. & 8. 6. & 14. 22. Luke 9. 16. & 22. 19. & 24. 30. 1 Cor. 11. 24.
Mark 14. 3. *b.* box and poured the
Brake down images—altars of Baal, 2 Kings 10. 27. & 11. 18. 2 Chron. 14. 3. & 23. 17. & 34. 4. — wall of Jerusalem, 2 Kings 14. 13. & 25. 10. 2 Chron. 25. 23. & 36. 19. Jer. 39. 8. & 52. 14. — houses of Sodomites — high places — altars — altar of Bethel, 2 Kings 23. 7, 8, 12, 15.
BRAMBLE, Judg. 9. 14. Luke 6. 44.
R. V. Isa. 34. 13. thistles

BRANCH, with clusters of grapes, Num. 13. 23. Isa. 17. 9. & 18. 5.
Job 15. 32. his *b.* shall not be green
Ps. 80. 15. *b.* thou madest strong
Prov. 11. 28. the right. flourish as a *b.*
Isa. 4. 2. *b.* of the Lord be beautiful
9. 14. cut off *b.* and root, 19. 15.
14. 19. cast out like an abomi. *b.*
25. 5. *b.* of terrible ones be brought
Jer. 23. 5. unto David a righteous *b.*
Ezek. 8. 17. they put *b.* to their nose
Zech. 3. 8. bring forth my servant *b.*
6. 12. behold man whose name is *b*
Mal. 4. 1. leave neither root nor *b.*
Matt. 24. 32. when his *b.* is yet ten.
John 15. 2. every *b.* in me that bear
4. *b.* cannot bear fruit of itself
Lev. 23. 40. take *branches* of palm-trees, Neh. 8. 15. John 12. 13.
Job 15. 30. flame shall dry up his *b.*
Ps. 80. 11. sent her *b.* unto the river
104. 12. fowls sing among the *b.*
Isa. 16. 8. her *b.* are stretched out
Jer. 11. 16. the *b.* of it are broken, Ezek. 17. 6, 7. & 19. 10, 14.
Dan. 4. 14. hewn down tree, cut off *b.*
Hos. 14. 6. his *b.* shall spread as
Zech. 4. 12. what be these two olive *b.*
John 15. 5. I am the vine, ye are the *b.*
Rom. 11. 6. if root be holy, so are *b.*
17. if some of the *b.* be broken off
21. God spared not natural *b.*, 24.
BRAND, Judg. 15. 5. Zech. 3. 2.
BRASS, Gen. 4. 22. Dan. 5. 4.
Num. 21. 9. made serpent of *b.*
Deut. 8. 9. out of whose hills mayest dig *b.*
28. 23. heaven over thy head shall *b.*
Job 6. 12. is my strength of *b.*—flesh
41. 27. he esteemeth *b.* as rotten
Isa. 48. 4. thy neck iron, and brow *b.*
60. 17. for wood I will bring *b.*
Dan. 2. 32. belly and thighs of *b.*
Zech. 6. 1. were mountains of *b.*
1 Cor. 13. 1. become as sounding *b.*
Rev. 1. 15. feet like fine *b.*, 2. 18.
Brazen, Num. 16. 39. 2 Kings 18. 4. & 25. 13. 2 Chron. 6. 13. Jer. 1. 18. & 15. 20. & 52. 20. Mark 7. 4.
BRAWLER, 1 Tim. 3. 3. Tit. 3. 2.
Prov. 21. 9. & 25. 24. *brawling* woman
R. V. 1 Tim. 3. 3. contentious
BRAY, Job 6. 5. Prov. 27. 22.
BREACH, be upon thee, Gen. 38. 29.
Num. 14. 34. know my *b.* of promise
Judg. 21. 15. Lord made *b.* in tribes
2 Sam. 6. 8. Lord made *b.* on Uzza, 1 Chron. 13. 11. & 15. 13.
Job 16. 14. break. me with *b.* upon *b.*
Ps. 106. 23. Moses stood in the *b.*
Isa. 30. 13. this iniq. shall be as *b.*
Lam. 2. 13. thy *b.* is great like sea
Ps. 60. 2. heal *breaches* thereof
R. V. Num. 14. 34. alienation; Judg. 5. 17. creeks; Isa. 30. 26. hurt
BREAD shall be fat, Gen. 49. 20.
Ex. 16. 4. I will rain *b.* from heaven
Lev. 21. 6. *b.* of their God they offer
Num. 14. 9. they are *b.* for us
21. 5. soul loatheth this light *b.*
Deut. 8. 3. not live by *b.* only, Matt. 4. 4.
Ruth 1. 6. visited his people giving *b.*
1 Sam. 2. 5. hired themselves for *b.*
1 Kings 18. 4. fed them with *b.* and
Neh. 5. 14. not eaten *b.* of gover., 18
9. 15. gavest them *b.* from heaven
Ps. 37. 25. nor his seed begging *b.*
78. 20. can he give *b.* also
80. 5. feedest them with *b.* of tears
102. 9. I have eaten ashes like *b.*
132. 15. satisfy her poor with *b.*
Prov. 9. 17. *b.* eaten in secret
31. 27. she eateth not *b.* of idleness

Eccl. 9. 11. nor yet *b.* to the wise
11. 1. cast thy *b.* upon the waters
Isa. 3. 1. whole stay of *b.*, 7.
30. 20. Lord give you *b.* of adversi.
55. 2. spend money for that is not *b.*
10. give seed to sower, *b.* to eater
Lam. 4. 4. the young children ask *b.*
Ezek. 18. 7. hath given *b.* to hun.
Hos. 2. 5. give me my *b.* and water
Amos 4. 6. want of *b.* in all your
Mal. 1. 7. ye offer polluted *b.* on
Matt. 4. 3. these stones be made *b.*
4. not live by *b.* alone, Luke 4. 4.
6. 11. this day our daily *b.*, Luke 11. 11.
7. 9. son ask *b.* will he give a stone
15. 26. meet to take the children's *b.*
26. 26. took *b.* and blessed it
Mark 8. 4. satisfy these men with *b.*
Luke 7. 33. neither eating *b.* nor
15. 17. servants have *b.* enough
24. 35. known in breaking of *b.*
John 6. 32. Moses gave you not that *b.*
33. the *b.* of God is he that cometh
34. evermore give us this *b.*
35. I am *b.* of life, 48. true *b.* 32.
41. I am the *b.* which came down
50. this is the *b.* that cometh down
13. 18. he that eateth *b.* with me
Acts 2. 42. breaking *b.* and in pray.
20. 7. came together to break *b.*
27. 35. he took *b.* and gave thanks
1 Cor. 10. 16. *b.* we break is it not
11. 23. night he was betrayed took *b.*
26. as often as ye eat this *b.*, 27.
Deut. 16. 3. *bread of affliction*, 1 Kings 22. 27. 2 Chron. 18. 26. Isa. 30. 20.
Gen. 3. 19. *shall eat bread*, 28. 20. Ps. 14. 4. & 127. 2. Prov. 25. 21. Eccl. 9. 7. Mark 7. 5. Luke 14. 15. 1 Cor. 11. 26. 2 Thes. 3. 12.
1 Sam. 2. 36. *piece of bread*, Prov. 6. 26. & 28. 21. Jer. 37. 21. Ezek. 13. 19.
Lev. 26. 26. *break staff of bread*, Ps. 105. 16. Ezek. 4. 16. & 5. 16. & 14. 13.
Gen. 19. 3. *unleavened bread*, Ex. 12. 8, 15. & 18. 20. & 13. 6, 7. Mark 14. 12. Luke 22. 7. Acts 12. 3. & 20. 6. 1 Cor. 5. 8.
BREAK, Gen. 19. 9. Ex. 34. 13.
Judg. 7. 19. *b.* the pitchers that were
9. 53. and all to *b.* his skull
Ezra 9. 14. should we again *b.* thy
Ps. 2. 3. let us *b.* their bands asunder
9. shalt *b.* them with a rod of iron
58. 6. *b.* their teeth in their mouth
89. 31. if they *b.* my statutes
141. 5. oil which shall not *b.* head
S. of S. 2. 17. till the day *b.* and the shadows, 4. 6.
Isa. 42. 3. bruised reed not *b.*, Matt. 12. 20.
58. 6. that ye *b.* every yoke
Jer. 14. 21. *b.* not covenant with us
15. 12. shall iron *b.* northern iron
Ezek. 4. 16. *b.* the staff of bread, 5. 16. & 14. 13. Ps. 105. 16.
17. 15. shall he *b.* covenant and be
Hos. 1. 5. *b.* the bow of Israel, 2. 18.
Zech. 11. 10. might *b.* my covenant
14. might *b.* the brotherhood
Matt. 5. 19. *b.* one of these least
Acts 21. 13. mean ye to *b.* my heart
1 Cor. 10. 16. bread which we *b.*
Ex. 23. 24. *break down*, Deut. 7. 5. Ps. 74. 6. Eccl. 3. 3. Jer. 31. 28. & 45. 4. Hos. 10. 2.
Ex. 19. 22, 24. *break forth*, Isa. 55. 8. Jer. 1. 14. Gal. 4. 27.
Isa. 14. 7. *break forth into singing*, 44. 23. & 49. 13. & 54. 1. & 55. 12. & 52. 9.
Dan. 4. 27. *break off thy sins by right.*
Ex. 22. 6. *break out*, Isa. 35. 6. Hos. 4. 2. Amos 5. 6.
Job 19. 2. *break in pieces*, 34. 24. Ps. 72. 4. & 94. 5. Isa. 45. 2. Jer. 51. 20, 21, 22. Dan. 2. 40, 44. & 7. 23.
Ex. 19. 21, 24. *break through*, and Matt. 6. 19, 20. where thieves — and
Jer. 4. 3. *break up* your fallow ground, Hos. 10. 10.

Ps. 74. 13, 14. *breakest* heads of dra.
Gen. 32. 26. let me go, for the day *breaketh*
Job 9. 17. he *b.* me with a tempest
16. 14. he *b.* me with breach
Ps. 29. 5. voice of the Lord *b.* the
119. 20. my soul *b.* for the longing
Prov. 25. 15. a soft tongue *b.* the
Eccl. 10. 8. whoso *b.* a hedge, a serpent shalt bite them
Jer. 19. 11. as one *b.* a potter's vessel
23. 29. like a hammer that *b.* rocks
Hos. 13. 13. a place of *breaking* forth of children, 1 Chron. 14. 11.
Luke 24. 35. known of them in *b.*
Acts 2. 42. *b.* of bread, 46.
Rom. 2. 23. through *b.* the law dishonorest thou
R. V. Gen. 27. 40. shake; Ex. 34. 13; Deut. 7. 5; 12. 3. dash in pieces; Job 13. 25. harass; 39. 15. trample; S. of S. 2. 17; 4. 5. be cool; Isa. 54. 3. spread; Ezek. 23. 34. gnaw; Matt. 9. 17. burst; Rom. 2. 25. transgressors; Job 41. 25. consternation; Rom. 2. 23. thy transgression of

BREASTS, Gen. 49. 25. Job 3. 12.
Job 21. 24. his *b.* are full of milk
Ps. 22. 9. I was upon my mother's *b.*
Prov. 5. 19. let her *b.* satisfy thee at
S. of S. 1. 13. shall lie all night between my *b.*
4. 5. thy *b.* are like two roes, 7. 3.
7. 7. thy *b.* to clusters of grapes, 8.
8. 1. sucked the *b.* of my mother
10. I am a wall and my *b.* like
Isa. 28. 9. weaned and drawn from *b.*
60. 16. suck the *b.* of kings, 49. 23.
Ezek. 16. 7. thy *b.* are fashioned
8. bruised the *b.* of her virginity
Hos. 2. 2. adulteries from between her *b.*
Joel 2. 16. gather those that suck *b.*
Luke 23. 48. smote *b.* and returned
Rev. 15. 6. their *b.* girded with
Ex. 28. 4. *breastplate*, Rev. 9. 9, 17.
Isa. 59. 17. put on righteousness as *b.*
Eph. 6. 14. *b.* of righteousness
1 Thes. 5. 8. *b.* of faith and love

BREATH of life, Gen. 2. 7. & 6. 17. & 7. 15, 22. Isa. 2. 22. Hab. 2. 19.
Job 12. 10. in whose hands is *b.* of all
19. 17. my *b.* is strange to my wife
Ps. 33. 6. made by *b.* of his mouth
104. 29. thou takest away their *b.*
150. 6. all that hath *b.* praise Lord
Eccl. 3. 19. they have all one *b.*
Isa. 2. 22. whose *b.* is in his nostrils
11. 4. with *b.* of his lips shall slay
Lam. 4. 20. the *b.* of our nostrils
Dan. 5. 23. in whose hand thy *b.* is
Acts 17. 25. giveth life and *b.* and all
Ps. 27. 12. *breathe* out cruelty
Ezek. 37. 9. come *b.* upon these slain
John 20. 22. he *breathed* on them
Acts 9. 1. *breathing* out slaughter
R. V. Job 4. 9. blast; 17. 1. spirit

BRETHREN, we be, Gen. 13. 8.
Gen. 49. 29. him that was separate from his *b.*, Deut. 33. 16.
Deut. 17. 20. be not lifted up above *b.*
33. 9. neither did he acknowledge his *b.*
24. let him be acceptable to his *b.*
1 Chron. 4. 9. more honorable than his *b.*
Job 6. 15. my *b.* have dealt deceit.
19. 13. put my *b.* far from me
Ps. 22. 22. declare thy name unto my *b.*
69. 8. I am become a stranger to my *b.*
Hos. 13. 15. fruitful among his *b.*
Matt. 23. 8. all ye are *b.*, Acts 7. 26.
12. 48. who are my *b.*
25. 40. the least of these my *b.*
28. 10. go tell my *b.* that they go
Mark 10. 29. left house of *b.*, Luke 18. 29.
John 7. 5. neither did his *b.* believe
20. 17. go to my *b.* and say, I ascend
Acts 11. 29. send relief to the *b.*
Rom. 8. 29. firstborn among many *b.*
9. 3. accursed from Christ for my *b.*
1 Cor. 6. 5. to judge between his *b.*
15. 6. seen of above 500 *b.* at once.
Gal. 2. 4. false *b.* unawares brought
1 Tim. 4. 6. put *b.* in remembrance
Heb. 2. 11. not ashamed to call them *b.*
1 Pet. 1. 22. unfeigned love of the *b.*
1 John 3. 14. because we love the *b.*
16. to lay down our lives for the *b.*
3 John 10. neither doth he receive *b.*
Gen. 27. 29. *thy brethren*, 48. 22. & 49. 8. Deut. 15. 7. & 18. 15. 1 Sam. 17. 18. Matt. 12. 47. Mark 3. 32. Luke 8. 20. & 14. 12. & 22. 32.
Jer. 12. 6. —have dealt treacherous.
Rev. 19. 10. I am of —, 22. 9.
1 Kings 12. 24. *your brethren*, 2 Chron. 30. 7, 9. & 35. 6.
Neh. 4. 14. fight for — your sons and
Isa. 66. 5. — that hated you
Acts 3. 22. raise up of — prophet like unto me, 7. 37. Deut. 18. 15.
Matt. 5. 47. if you salute — only
R. V. Acts 20, 32; Rom. 15. 15; 1 Cor. 11. 2 —; 1 John 2. 7. beloved

BRIBES, 1 Sam. 8. 3. Amos 5. 12.
1 Sam. 12. 3. have I received any *b.*
Ps. 26. 10. right hand full of *b.*
Isa. 33. 15. hands from holding *b.*
Job 15. 34. tabernacles of *bribery*
R. V. 1 Sam. 12. 3. ransom

BRICK, Gen. 11. 3. Ex. 1. 14. & 5. 7, 8, 14, 16, 19. Isa. 65. 3. & 9. 10.
2 Sam. 12. 31. *brick-kiln*, Jer. 43. 9. Nah. 3. 14.

BRIDE, doth clothe with an orna., Isa. 49. 18.
Isa. 61. 10. as a *b.* adorneth herself
Jer. 2. 32. can a *b.* forget her attire
Joel 2. 16. *b.* go out of her closet
John 3. 29. that hath *b.* is bridegr.
Rev. 21. 2. as a *b.* adorned for her
9. I will shew thee *b.* Lamb's wife
22. 17. spirit and *b.* say, come
Matt. 9. 15. *bride-chamber*, Mark 2. 19. Luke 5. 34.

BRIDEGROOM, Joel 2. 16. John 2. 9.
Ps. 19. 5. as a *b.* coming out of
Isa. 61. 10. as a *b.* decketh himself
62. 5. as a *b.* rejoiceth over the
Jer. 7. 34. cease the voice of *b.* and bride, 16. 9. & 25. 10. & 33. 11. Rev. 18. 23.
Matt. 9. 15. as long as the *b.* is — them, Mark 2. 19, 20. Luke 5. 34.
Matt. 25. 1. went forth to meet *b.* 6.

BRIDLE for the ass, Prov. 26. 3.
Ps. 32. 9. mouth held with *b.*
Isa. 37. 29. put my *b.* in thy lips, 30. 28. 2 Kings 19. 28. Rev. 14. 20.
Jas. 3. 2. able to *b.* the whole body
1. 26. *bridleth* not his tongue

BRIERS, Judg. 8. 7, 16. Isa. 7. 23, 24, 25. & 32. 13. Heb. 6. 8. Mic. 7. 4.
Isa. 5. 6. come up *b.* and thorns
9. 18. wickedness, shall devour *b.*, 10. 17.
27. 4. set *b.* against me in battle
Ezek. 2. 6. though *b.* and thorns be
28. 24. no more a pricking *b.* unto
R. V. Heb. 6. 8. thistles

BRIGHTNESS, 2 Sam. 22. 13. Ezek. 1. 4, 27, 28. & 8. 2. & 28. 7, 17.
Job 31. 26. beheld moon walking in *b.*
Ezek. 10. 4. full of the *b.* of Lord's
Dan. 12. 3. wise shall shine as the *b.* of the firmament
Amos 5. 20. very dark and no *b.* in it.
Hab. 3. 4. his *b.* was as the light
Acts 26. 13. a light above *b.* of sun
2 Thes. 2. 8. Lord destroy with *b.*
Heb. 1. 3. being the *b.* of his glory
R. V. Heb. 1. 3. effulgence

BRIMSTONE, Gen. 19. 24. Deut. 29. 23. Job 18. 15. Ps. 11. 6. Isa. 30. 33. & 34. 9. Ezek. 38. 22. Luke 17. 29. Rev. 14. 10. & 19. 20. & 21. 8.

BRING a flood, Gen. 6. 17.
Josh. 23. 15. *b.* upon you all the evil
1 Kings 8. 32. to *b.* his way upon
Job 14. 4. who can *b.* a clean thing
Ps. 60. 9. who *b.* me into strong, 72. 10. Isa. 60. 9. & 66. 20.
72. 3. mountains *b.* peace to people
Eccl. 11. 9. God will *b.* thee into judgment, 12. 14. Job 14. 4. & 30. 23.
S. of S. 8. 2. *b.* thee to my mother's
Isa. 1. 13. *b.* no more vain oblations
43. 5. I will *b.* thy seed from east
46. 13. I *b.* near my righteousness
66. 9. shall I *b.* to the birth and
Hos. 2. 14. allure and *b.* her into
Zeph. 3. 5. every morning *b.* his
Luke 2. 10. I *b.* you good tidings
John 14. 26. *b.* all things to remem.
Acts 5. 28. intend to *b.* this man's blood
1 Cor. 1. 28. *b.* to nought things
1 Thes. 4. 14. God will *b.* with him
1 Pet. 3. 18. that he might *b.* us to
Gen. 1. 11, 20, 24. *bring forth*, 3. 16. Matt. 1. 21. Job 39. 1. Ex. 3. 10.
2 Kings 19. 3. there is not strength to —
Job 15. 35. conceive mischief and — vanity
Ps. 37. 6. he shall — thy righteous.
92. 14. still — fruit in old age
Prov. 27. 1. what a day may —
Isa. 41. 21. — your strong reasons
42. 1. — judgment to the Gentiles, 4.
66. 8. made to — in one day
Zeph. 2. 2. before the decree —
Mark 4. 20. — fruit some thirty fold
Luke 3. 8. — fruits worthy of repentance
8. 15. — fruit with patience
John 15. 2. that it may — more fruit
Ps. 1. 3. *bringeth forth* fruit in its
Hos. 10. 1. — fruit to himself
Matt. 3. 10. *b.* not forth good fruit, 7. 19. & 12. 35. Luke 6. 43.
John 12. 24. if it die it — much fruit
Jas. 1. 15. — sin — death

BROAD, Num. 16. 38, 39. Nah. 2. 4. Matt. 23. 5.
Job 36. 16. out of strait into *b.* place
Isa. 33. 21. Lord a place of *b.* rivers
Matt. 7. 13. *b.* is way to destruction
R. V. Num. 16. 38. beaten

BROIDERED work, Ezek. 16. 10.

BROKEN my covenant. Gen. 17. 14. Ps. 55. 20. Isa. 24. 5. & 33. 8. & 36. 6. Jer. 11. 10. & 33. 21.
Ps. 34. 18. night to them of *b.* heart
44. 19. sore *b.* us in place of drag.
17. *b.* spirit, *b.* and contrite heart
147. 3. healeth the *b.* in heart
Isa. 61. 1. to bind up the *b.* hearted
Jer. 2. 13. hewed out *b.* cisterns
Dan. 2. 42. strong and partly *b.*
Hos. 5. 11. Ephraim is *b.* in judgment
Matt. 21. 44. shall fall on stone, shall be *b.*
John 10. 35. Scripture cannot be *b.*

BROOK, Num. 15. 23. Deut. 2. 13.
Ps. 110. 7. drink of the *b.* in the way
Job 20. 17. the *b.* of honey and
Isa. 19. 6. *b.* of defence shall be
R. V. Num. 21. 14, 15. valleys

BROTHER, born for adversity, Prov. 17. 17.
Prov. 18. 19. a *b.* offended is harder
24. is a friend that sticketh closer than a *b.*
27. 10. neighbor near, than *b.* far
Jer. 9. 4. trust not in any *b.* for every *b.*
Matt. 10. 21. *b.* shall deliver up *b.* to death, Mark 13. 12. Mic. 7. 2.
1 Cor. 5. 11. *b.* be a fornicator
6. 6. but *b.* goeth to law with *b.*
7. 15. *b.* or sister is not in bondage
2 Thes. 3. 15. admonish him as a *b.*
Jas. 1. 9. let *b.* of low degree
Ps. 35. 14. *my brother*, S. of S. 8. 1. Matt. 12. 50. & 18. 21. 1 Cor. 8. 13.
Ps. 50. 20. *thy brother*, Matt. 5. 23, 24. & 18. 15. Rom. 14. 10, 15.
Gen. 45. 4. *your brother*, Rev. 1. 9.
Zech. 11. 14. *brotherhood*, 1 Pet. 2. 17.

Amos 1. 9. remember not *brotherly* covenant
Rom. 12. 10. kindly affectioned with *b.*
Heb. 13. 1. let *b.* love continue
2 Pet. 1. 7. to godliness *b.* kindness
R. V. Luke 6. 16; Acts 1. 13. son
BROUGHT me hitherto, 2 Sam. 7. 18.
Neh. 4. 15. God *b.* their counsel to
Ps. 45. 14. be *b.* unto the king in
79. 8. we are *b.* very low
107. 39. *b.* low through oppression
116. 6. I was *b.* low and he helped
Isa. 1. 2. nourished and *b.* up child.
Matt. 10. 18. *b.* before governors, Mark 13. 9. Luke 12. 12.
1 Cor. 6. 12. not be *b.* under power
Gal. 2. 4. false brethren, unawares *b.* in
1 Tim. 6. 7. *b.* nothing into this world
Ps. 107. 12. *brought down*, Matt. 11. 23.
Deut. 33. 14. *brought forth*, Ps. 18. 19.
BRUISE thy head—his heel, Gen. 3. 15.
Isa. 53. 10. it pleased Lord to *b.* him
Isa. 42. 3. *bruised* reed not break, Matt. 12. 20.
53. 5. he was *b.* for our iniquities
Ezek. 23. 3, 21. *b.* breasts, *b.* teats
R. V. Jer. 30. 12; Nah. 3. 19. hurt; Dan. 2. 40. crush; Isa. 28. 28. ground
BRUIT, report, Jer. 10. 22. Nah. 3. 19.
BRUTISH man knows not, Ps. 92. 6.
Ps. 94. 8. understand, ye *b.* among
Jer. 10. 14. man is *b.* in his knowledge, 51. 17.
BUCKLER to all that trust, Ps. 18. 30.
Ps. 18. 2. my *b.* and horn of my
91. 4. his truth shall be thy *b.*
Prov. 2. 7. a *b.* to them that walk
R. V. 2 Sam. 22. 31; Ps. 18. 2; Prov. 2. 7. shield; 1 Chron. 12. 8. spear
BUDDING of Aaron's rod, Num. 17.
BUFFETED, 2 Cor. 12. 7. Matt. 26. 67. 1 Cor. 4. 11. 1 Pet. 2. 20.
BUILD walls of Jerusalem, Ps. 51. 18.
Ps. 102. 16. Lord shall *b.* up Zion
Eccl. 3. 3. a time to *b.* up
Mic. 3. 10. *b.* up Zion with blood
Acts 20. 32. able to *b.* you up
Job 22. 23. if thou return shalt be *built* up
Ps. 89. 2. mercy shall be *b.* up for
Matt. 7. 24. *b.* his house on a rock
Eph. 2. 20. ye are *b.* on foundation
Col. 2. 7. rooted and *b.* up in him
Heb. 3. 4. he that *b.* all things is
1 Pet. 2. 5. *b.* up a spiritual house
Heb. 11. 10. *builder* and maker is
Ps. 118. 22. stone which the *b.* refused, Matt. 21. 42. Mark 12. 10. Luke 20. 17. Acts 4. 11. 1 Pet. 2. 7.
1 Cor. 3. 10. *master builder*
Josh. 6. 26. cursed that *buildeth*
Jer. 22. 13. woe to him that *b.* house
Amos 9. 6. *b.* his stories in heaven
Hab. 2. 12. *b.* a town with blood
1 Cor. 3. 10. another *b.* thereon
9. ye are God's *building*
2 Cor. 5. 1. we have a *b.* of God
Heb. 9. 11. tabernacle not of this *b.*
Jude 20. *b.* up yourselves in faith
BULLS compassed me, Ps. 22. 12.
Ps. 50. 13. will I eat the flesh of *b.*
Heb. 9. 13. if blood of *b.* and goats
Ps. 69. 31. than *bullock* with horns
Jer. 31. 18. as a *b.* unaccustomed to
Ps. 51. 19. offer *b.* on thy altar
Isa. 1. 11. delight not in blood of *b.*
R. V. Isa. 51. 20. antelope; Lev. 4. 10; 9. 18; Deut. 17. 1. ox; Jer. 31. 18. calf; Jer. 50. 11. strong horses

BULRUSHES, Ex. 2. 3. Isa. 18. 2. & 58. 5.
R. V. Isa. 58. 5. rush; 18. 2. papyrus
BULWARKS, Ps. 48. 13. Isa. 26. 1.
R. V. 2 Chr. 26. 15. battlements
BUNDLE, Gen. 42. 35. Acts 28. 3.
1 Sam. 25. 29. bound in the *b.* of
S. of S. 1. 13. *b.* of myrrh is my
Matt. 13. 30. bind tares in *bundles* to burn
BURDEN, 2 Kings 5. 17. & 8. 9.
Ex. 18. 22. shall bear the *b.* with thee, Num. 11. 17.
23. 5. ass lying under his *b.*
Deut. 1. 12. how can I bear your *b.*
2 Sam. 15. 33. thou shalt be a *b.*
2 Kings 5. 17. two mules *b.* of earth
2 Chron. 35. 3. not be *b.* on should.
Neh. 13. 19. shall be no *b.* brought in on Sabbath day, Jer. 17. 21. & 22. 24, 27.
Job 7. 20. I am a *b.* to myself
Ps. 38. 4. a *b.* too heavy for me
55. 22. cast thy *b.* upon the Lord
Eccl. 12. 5. grasshopper shall be a *b.*
Isa. 9. 4. broken the yoke of his b.
10. 27. *b.* taken from thy shoulder
Zeph. 3. 18. reproach of it was a *b.*
Zech. 12. 3. all that *b.* themselves
Matt. 11. 30. my yoke is easy, my *b.*
20. 12. borne the *b.* and heat of day
Acts 15. 28. no greater *b.* than nec.
2 Cor. 12. 16. I did not *b.* you
Gal. 6. 5. every man bear his own *b.*
Rev. 2. 24. put on you no other *b.*
Isa. 13. 1. *b.* threatening of heavy judgments, 14. 28. & 15. 1. & 17. 1. & 19. 1. & 21. 1, 11. & 22. 1. & 23. 1. Ezek. 12. 10. Nah. 1. 1. Hab. 1. 1. Zech. 9. 1. & 12. 1.
Mal. 1. 1. *b.* of the word
2 Cor. 5. 4. we groan being *burdened*
Gen. 49. 14. *burdens*, Ex. 1. 11. & 2. 11. & 5. 4.
Isa. 58. 6. to undo the heavy *b.*
Lam. 2. 14. seen for thee false *b.*
Matt. 23. 4. bind heavy *b.*, Luke 11. 46.
Gal. 6. 2. bear one another's *b.*
Zech. 12. 3. *burdensome*, 2 Cor. 11. 9. & 12. 13, 14. 1 Thes. 2. 6.
R. V. Gen. 49. 14. sheepfolds; Amos 5. 11. exactions; 2 Cor. 8. 13. distressed
BURN upon altar, Ex. 29. 13, 18, 25. Lev. 1. 9, 15. & 2. 2. & 3. 5, 11, 16. & 5. 12. & 6. 15. & 9. 17.
Gen. 44. 18. let not thine anger *b.*
Deut. 32. 22. shall *b.* to lowest hell
Isa. 27. 4. go through them and *b.*
Mal. 4. 1. day cometh shall *b.* as an
Luke 3. 17. chaff he will *b.* with unquenchable fire
Luke 24. 32. did not our heart *b.*
1 Cor. 7. 9. it is better to marry than *b.*
Rev. 17. 6. eat her flesh and *b.* her
Ex. 3. 2. the bush *burned* with fire
Deut. 9. 15. and mount *b.* with fire
Ps. 39. 3. while I was musing fire *b.*
1 Cor. 3. 15. if any man's work shall be *b.*
13. 3. though I give my body to *b.*
Heb. 6. 8. whose end is to be *b.*
Ps. 46. 9. *burneth* the chariot in fire
97. 3. *b.* up his enemies round
Isa. 9. 18. wickedness *b.* as the fire
Rev. 21. 8. lake which *b.* with fire
Gen. 15. 17. *burning* lamp that passed between those pieces
Jer. 20. 9. his word was as *b.* fire
Hab. 3. 5. *b.* coals went forth at his
Luke 12. 35. loins girded and your lights *b.*
John 5. 35. a *b.* and a shining light
Ex. 21. 25. *b.* for *b.* wound for wou.
Deut. 28. 22. smite thee with extreme *b.*
Isa. 3. 24. *b.* instead of beauty
4. 4. by the spirit of judgment and *b.*
Amos 4. 11. firebrand plucked out of the *b.*
Isa. 33. 14. dwell with everlasting *b.*

Gen. 8. 20. *burnt-offerings*, Deut. 12. 6. 1 Sam. 15. 22. Ps. 50. 8. Isa. 1. 11. & 56. 7. Jer. 6. 20. & 7. 21, 22.
Hos. 6. 6. knowledge of God more than—
Mark 12. 33. more than all whole—
Heb. 10. 6. in—for sin and sacrifices
Ps. 74. 8. *burnt* up all synagogues
Isa. 64. 11. our beautiful house is—
Matt. 22. 7. destroyed and—their city
2 Pet. 3. 10. works that are therein be—
BURST thy bands, Jer. 2. 20.
Prov. 3. 10. presses *b.* out with new
Mark 2. 22. new wine doth *b.* the bottles, Luke 5. 37. Job 32. 19.
Acts 1. 18. *b.* asunder in the midst
R. V. Prov. 3. 10. overflow; Isa. 30. 14. pieces
BURY my dead out of my sight, Gen. 23. 4.
Gen. 49. 29. *b.* me with my fathers
Ps. 79. 3. there was none to *b.* them
Matt. 8. 21. first to go and *b.* my
Rom. 6. 4. *buried* with him by baptism into death, Col. 2. 12.
1 Cor. 15. 4. he was *b.* and rose again
Gen. 23. 4. a possession of a *burying*
47. 30. *b.* me in the *b.* place
Mark 14. 8. anoint my body to the *b.*
John 12. 7. against the day of my *b.*
2 Chron. 26. 23. *burial*, Acts 8. 2.
Eccl. 6. 3. that he have no *b.*
Isa. 14. 20. not joined with them in *b.*
Jer. 22. 19. buried with *b.* of an ass
Matt. 26. 12. she did it for my *b.*
BUSH is not burnt, Ex. 3. 2, 3, 4. Acts 7. 30. Mark 12. 26.
Deut. 33. 16. good will of him that dwelt in *b.*
R. V. Isa. 7. 10. pastures
BUSHEL, Matt. 5. 15. Luke 11. 33.
BUSHY and black, S. of S. 5. 11.
BUSINESS, Gen. 39. 11. Rom. 16. 2.
Ps. 107. 23. do *b.* in great waters
Prov. 22. 29. seest a man diligent in *b.*
Luke 2. 49. must be about Father's *b.*
Acts 6. 3. we may appoint over this *b.*
Rom. 12. 11. not slothful in *b.*
1 Thes. 4. 11. study to do your own *b.*
BUSY-BODIES censured, Prov. 20. 3. & 26. 17. 1 Thes. 4. 11. 2 Thes. 3. 11. 1 Tim. 5. 13. 1 Pet. 4. 15.
BUTTER and milk, Gen. 18. 8. Deut. 32. 14. Judg. 5. 25. 2 Sam. 17. 29. Prov. 30. 33.
Job 20. 17. brooks of honey and *b.*
Ps. 55. 21. words were smoother than *b.*
Isa. 7. 15. *b.* and honey shall he eat, 22.
BUY the truth, Prov. 23. 23.
Isa. 55. 1. *b.* and eat, yea, *b.* wine
1 Cor. 7. 30. they that *b.* as possessed
Jas. 4. 13. *b.* and sell, and get gain
Rev. 3. 18. I counsel thee *b.* gold
Prov. 20. 14. it is nought saith *buyer*
Isa. 24. 2. as with *b.* so with seller
Ezek. 7. 12. let no *b.* rejoice
Prov. 31. 16. considereth a field and *buyeth* it
Matt. 13. 44. selleth all and *b.* field
Rev. 18. 11. no man *b.* her merchan.
BY and by, Matt. 13. 21. Mark 6. 25. Luke 17. 7. & 21. 9.
By-word among all nations, Deut. 28. 37.
1 Kings 9. 7. Israel shall be a—
2 Chron. 7. 20. make this house a—
Job 17. 6. made a—of the people
30. 9. I am their song and their—
Ps. 44. 14. makest us a—among the heathen

C

CAGE, Jer. 5. 27. Rev. 18. 2.
R. V. Rev. 18. 2. hold
CAIN and Abel, Gen. 4. 1-17. Heb. 11. 4. & 12. 24. Jude 11.

CAKE of bread tumbled into host, Judg. 7. 13.
1 Kings 17. 12. I have not a *c*. but
Hos. 7. 8. Ephraim is a *c*. not turned
Cakes, Gen. 18. 6. Judg. 6. 19.
Jer. 7. 18. make *c*. to queen of
44. 19. made *c*. to worship her
R. V. 1 Chr. 23. 29. wafers
CALAMITY at hand, Deut. 32. 35.
Job 6. 2. my *c*. laid in the balance
Ps. 18. 18. prevented me in the day of my *c*.
Prov. 1. 26. I will laugh at your *c*.
6. 15. his *c*. shall come suddenly
Jer. 18. 17. the face in day of their *c*.
46. 21. day of thy *c*. is come, 48. 16. & 49. 8, 32. Ezek. 35. 5. Obad. 13.
Ps. 57. 1. till these *calamities* be overpast
Prov. 17. 5. that is glad at *c*. shall
24. 22. their *c*. shall rise suddenly
R. V. Ps. 141. 5. wickedness
CALDRON, 1 Sam. 2. 14. Job 41. 20. Ezek. 11. 3, 7, 11. Mic. 3. 3. Jer. 52. 18.
R. V. Job 41. 20. burning rushes; Jer. 52. 18, 19. pots
CALEB and Joshua, Num. 13. 30. & 14. 6, 24, 38. & 26. 65. & 32. 12.
CALF, Gen. 18. 7. Job 21. 10. Ps. 29. 6. Isa. 27. 10. Rev. 4. 7.
Ex. 32. 4. made a molten *c*., 20. Deut. 9. 16. Neh. 9. 18. Ps. 106. 19.
Isa. 11. 6. *c*. and young lion lie
Hos. 8. 5. thy *c*. O Samaria, hath
8. 6. the *c*. of Samaria shall be
Luke 15. 23. bring hither the fatted *c*.
27. thou hast killed the fatted *c*. 30.
CALL them what he would, Gen. 2. 19.
Gen. 24. 57. we will *c*. the damsel
30. 13. daughters will *c*. me bless.
Deut. 4. 7. all that we *c*. upon him
1 Sam. 3. 6. here am I, for thou didst *c*. me
1 Kings 8. 52. in all they *c*. to thee
17. 18. to *c*. my sin to remembrance
1 Chron. 16. 8. *c*. upon his name
13. 22. *c*. thou and I will answer
27. 10. will he always *c*. upon God
Ps. 4. 1. hear me when I *c*. O God
49. 11. *c*. lands after their names
72. 17. all nations shall *c*. him
80. 18. we will *c*. on thy name
86. 5. plenteous in mercy to all that *c*.
145. 18. nigh to all them that *c*. upon
Prov. 31. 28. children rise and *c*. her
Isa. 5. 20. woe to them that *c*. evil
55. 6. *c*. upon him while he is near
65. 24. before they *c*. I will answer
Jer. 25. 29. I will *c*. for a sword upon all
Joel 2. 32. remnant whom the Lord shall *c*.
Jonah 1. 6. sleeper arise, *c*. upon
Zech. 13. 9. they shall *c*. upon my
Mal. 3. 12. all nations shall *c*. you
Matt. 9. 13. I came not to *c*. right. but sinners, Mark 2. 17.
22. 3. to *c*. them that were bidden
Luke 1. 48. all generations shall *c*.
6. 46. why *c*. ye me Lord, Lord?
John 4. 16. *c*. thy husband and
13. 13. ye *c*. me master and Lord
Acts 2. 39. as many as Lord shall *c*.
10. 15. God hath cleansed *c*. not
Rom. 9. 25. I will *c*. them my people
10. 12. rich in mercy to all that *c*. on
2 Cor. 1. 23. I *c*. God for a record
Heb. 2. 11. not ashamed to *c*. them
Jas. 5. 14. *c*. for the elders of the
1 Pet. 1. 17. if ye *c*. on the Father
Call on the name of the Lord, Gen. 4. 26. & 12. 8. & 13. 4. & 21. 33. & 26. 25. 1 Kings 18. 24. 2 Kings 5. 11. Ps. 116. 4, 13, 17. Joel 2. 32. Zeph. 3. 9. Acts 2. 21. Rom. 10. 13. 1 Cor. 1. 2.
I will call unto, or, *on the Lord*, 1 Sam. 12. 17. 2 Sam. 22. 4. Ps. 18. 3. & 55. 16. & 86. 7.
Call upon me, Ps. 50. 15. & 91. 15. Prov. 1. 28. Jer. 29. 12.
Gen. 21. 17. angel of God *called* to Hagar
22. 11. the angel of the Lord *c*. to Abraham out of heaven, 15.
Ex. 3. 4. God *c*. unto him out of the
19. 3. Lord *c*. unto him out of the
Judg. 15. 18. was athirst, and *c*. on
2 Kings 8. 1. Lord hath *c*. for a
1 Chron. 4. 10. Jabesh *c*. on God of
21. 26. David *c*. on the Lord and he
Ps. 17. 6. I have *c*. upon thee, 31. 17.
18. 6. in my distress I *c*. upon Lord
79. 6. not *c*. on thy name, Jer. 10. 25.
88. 9. I have *c*. daily upon thee
118. 5. I *c*. upon the Lord in my dis.
Prov. 1. 24. I have *c*. and ye refused
S. of S. 5. 6. I *c*. him, he gave me
Isa. 41. 2. who *c*. him to his foot
42. 6. I the Lord *c*. thee in right.
43. 1. I have *c*. thee by thy name
22. thou hast not *c*. upon me
48. 1. *c*. by the name of Israel, 44. 5.
49. 1. Lord *c*. me from the womb
50. 2. when I *c*. was none to answer
51. 2. I *c*. him alone, and blessed
61. 3. be *c*. trees of righteousness
62. 4. thou shalt be *c*. Hephzibah
Lam. 1. 19. I *c*. for my lovers they
3. 55. I *c*. upon thy name, O Lord
Hos. 11. 1. I *c*. my son out of Egypt
Amos 7. 4. Lord *c*. to contend by
Hag. 1. 11. I *c*. for a drought on
Matt. 20. 16. many be *c*. but few chosen, 22. 14.
Mark 14. 72. Peter *c*. to mind word of the Lord
Luke 15. 19. not worthy to be *c*. thy
John 1. 48. before that Philip *c*. thee
10. 35. if he *c*. them gods to whom
15. 15. I have *c*. you friends
Acts 9. 41. when he had *c*. saints
21. destroy them that *c*. on this
10. 23, 24. *c*. in — *c*. together his kinsmen
Acts 11. 26. disciples were *c*. Christians
13. 2. for work whereto I *c*. them
19. 40. we are in danger to be *c*. in question, 23. 6. & 24. 21.
20. 1. Paul *c*. to him the disciples
Rom. 1. 1. *c*. to be an apos. 1 Cor. 1. 1.
6. *c*. of Jesus Christ, 7. *c*. to be
2. 17. thou that art *c*. a Jew
8. 28. *c*. according to his purpose
30. predestinate, them he also *c*.
9. 24. whom he hath *c*. Jews also
1 Cor. 1. 9. faithful by whom ye were *c*.
26. not many wise, — noble are *c*.
5. 11. if any man *c*. a brother be
7. 18. *c*. being circumcised
21, 22. *c*. servant
24. every man wherein he is *c*.
15. 9. I am not meet to be *c*. an
Gal. 1. 6. *c*. you into the grace of
15. God who *c*. me by his grace
Eph. 2. 11. who are *c*. uncircum.
4. are *c*. in one hope of your calling
Col. 3. 15. to which ye are *c*. in one
1 Thes. 2. 12. *c*. you unto his king.
4. 7. God hath not *c*. us to unclean
2 Thes. 2. 4. above all that is *c*. God
1 Tim. 6. 12. whereunto thou art *c*.
2 Tim. 1. 9. *c*. us with a holy calling
Heb. 3. 13. exhort while it is *c*. to.
5. 4. *c*. of God, as was Aaron
10. *c*. of God a high priest
9. 15. that they who are *c*. may
11. 16. not ashamed to be *c*. their
24. refusing to be *c*. the son of Pharaoh's daughter
Jas. 2. 7. name by which ye are *c*.
1 Pet. 1. 15. as he that *c*. you is holy
21. hereunto were ye *c*.
2 Pet. 1. 3. *c*. us to glory and virtue
1 John 3. 1. we should be *c*. sons of
Jude 1. preserved in Christ Jesus and *c*.
Rev. 17. 14. with him *c*. and chosen
19. 9. are *c*. unto marriage supper
2 Chron. 7. 14. *called by my name*, Isa. 43. 7. & 65. 1. Jer. 7. 10, 11, 14, 30. & 25. 29. & 32. 34. & 34. 15. Amos 9. 12.
1 Kings 8. 43. *called by thy name*, 2 Chron. 6. 33. Isa. 4. 1. & 43. 1. & 45. 4. & 63. 19. Jer. 14. 9. & 15. 16. Dan. 9. 18, 19.
2 Kings 8. 43. to all that the stranger *calleth* for, 2 Chron. 6. 33.
Job 12. 4. who *c*. on God and he ans.
Ps. 42. 7. deep *c*. unto deep at noise
Isa. 59. 4. none *c*. for justice nor for
Hos. 7. 7. none among them that *c*.
Amos 5. 8. that *c*. for waters of sea
Luke 15. 6. *c*. together his friends, 9.
John 10. 3. he *c*. his own sheep by
Rom. 4. 17. *c*. those things which be
Gal. 5. 8. persuasion not of him that *c*.
1 Thes. 5. 24. faithful is he that *c*.
Rom. 11. 29. gifts and *calling* of God
1 Cor. 1. 26. ye see your *c*. brethren
7. 20. let every man abide in same *c*.
Eph. 1. 18. what is the hope of his *c*.
4. 4. called in one hope of your *c*.
Phil. 3. 14. prize of high *c*. of God
2 Thes. 1. 11. count you worthy of this *c*.
2 Tim. 1. 9. called with a holy *c*.
Heb. 3. 1. partakers of heavenly *c*.
2 Pet. 1. 10. make your *c*. and elect.
Isa. 41. 4. *c*. the generation from the beginning
Matt. 11. 16. sitting and *c*. their
Mark 11. 21. Peter *c*. to remembrance
Acts 7. 59. stoned Stephen *c*. upon
22. 16. *c*. upon the name of Lord
1 Pet. 3. 6. obeyed Abraham, *c*. him
CALM, Ps. 107. 29. Jonah 1. 11, 12. Matt. 8. 26. Mark 4. 39. Luke 8. 24.
CALVE (cow), Job 21. 10. (hinds) 39. 1. Ps. 29. 9. Jer. 14. 5.
1 Kings 12. 28. made two *calves* of
Hos. 14. 2. we will render *c*. of our
Mic. 6. 6. come with *c*. of a year old
Heb. 9. 12. blood of goats and *c*., 19.
CAME, Ps. 18. 6. & 88. 17. Matt. 1. 18. & 9. 14. John 1. 7, 11. & 8. 14, 42. & 18. 37. Rom. 5. 18. & 9. 5. 1 Tim. 1. 15. 1 John 5. 6.
Came down, 2 Kings 1. 10, 12, 14. 2 Chron. 7. 1, 3. Lam. 1. 9. John 3. 13. & 6. 38, 41, 51, 58. Rev. 20. 9.
Came forth, Num. 11. 20. Judg. 14. 14. Eccl. 5. 15. Zech. 10. 4.
John 16. 28. I — from the Father
CAMEL, Gen. 24. 19. Lev. 11. 4. Matt. 3. 4. raiment of *c*.'s hair, Mark 1. 6.
19. 24. easier for a *c*. to go through
23. 24. strain at a gnat, and swallow *c*.
CAMP, Ex. 32. 17. & 36. 6.
Ex. 14. 19. angel went before the *c*.
16. 13. quails came and covered *c*.
Num. 11. 26. they prophesied in *c*.
31. let the quails fall by the *c*.
Deut. 23. 14. Lord walketh in midst of *c*. therefore shall thy *c*. be holy
Judg. 13. 25. began to move him in *c*.
2 Kings 19. 35, smote in the *c*. of the Assyrians
Heb. 13. 13. go unto him without *c*.
Rev. 20. 9. compassed *c*. of saints
CAN we find such a one, Gen. 41. 38.
Deut. 1. 12. how *c*. I myself alone
32. 38. neither is there any *c*. deliver
2 Sam. 7. 20. what *c*. David say more
2 Chron. 1. 10. who *c*. judge this
Esth. 8. 6. how *c*. I endure to see the destruction of my people
Job 8. 11. *c*. the rush grow without
25. 4. how *c*. man be justified with
Ps. 40. 5. more than *c*. be number.
Ps. 49. 7. none *c*. redeem his brother
89. 6. who *c*. be likened unto Lord
Eccl. 4. 11. how *c*. one be warm
Isa. 49. 15. *c*. a woman forget her
Jer. 2. 32. *c*. a maid forget her orna.
Ezek. 22. 14. *c*. thy heart endure
37. 3. *c*. these dry bones live
Amos 3. 3. *c*. two walk together
Matt. 12. 34. how *c*. ye speak good
19. 25. who then *c*. be saved

Mark 2. 7. who *c.* forgive sins but
19. *c.* children of bride-chamber
10. 38. *c.* ye drink of the cup that I
John 3. 4. how *c.* man be born again
9. how *c.* these things be, Luke 1. 34.
5. 19. Son *c.* do nothing of him., 30.
6. 44. no man *c.* come to me except
9. 4. night, when no man *c.* work
15. 4. no more *c.* ye except ye abide
1 Cor. 12. 3. no man *c.* say that Jesus
2 Cor. 13. 8. *c.* do nothing against
1 Tim. 6. 7. we *c.* carry nothing out
Heb. 10. 11. *c.* never take away sins
Jas. 2. 14. *c.* faith save him
Rev. 3. 8. open door and no man *c.*
Gen. 32. 12. which *cannot* be numbered for multitude, 1 Kings 3. 8. Hos. 1. 10.
Num. 23. 20. he hath blessed; and I *c.* reverse it
Josh. 24. 19. ye *c.* serve the Lord
1 Sam. 12. 21. vain things which *c.*
1 Kings 8. 27. heaven of heavens *c.* contain thee, 2 Chron. 6. 18.
Ezra 9. 15. we *c.* stand before thee
Job 9. 3. he *c.* answer for one of a
23. 8, 9. I *c.* perceive him — *c.* behold
28. 15. it *c.* be gotten for gold
36. 18. a great ransom *c.* deliver
Ps. 40. 5. they *c.* be reckoned up in
77. I am so troubled that I *c.* speak
93. 1. world establish. that it *c.* be
139. 6. too high, I *c.* attain unto it
Isa. 38. 18. the grave *c.* praise thee
44. 18. they *c.* see; they *c.* under.
20. he *c.* deliver his soul
50. 2. hand shortened that it *c.* redeem
56. 11. shepherds that *c.* understand
Jer. 4. 19. I *c.* hold my peace
6. 10. are uncircumcised, they *c.*
7. 8. ye trust in lying words that *c.*
14. 9. as a mighty man *c.* save
18. 6. *c.* I do with you as this potter
29. 17. like the vile figs that *c.* be
33. 22. the host of heaven *c.* be
Lam. 3. 7. hath hedged me, that I *c.* get
Matt. 6. 24. ye *c.* serve God and mammon, Luke 16. 13.
7. 18. a good tree *c.* bring forth evil
27. 42. himself he *c.* save, Mark 15. 31.
Luke 14. 26. *c.* be my disciple, 27. 33.
16. 26. would pass from hence to you *c.*
John 3. 3. *c.* see the kingdom of
5. he *c.* enter into the kingdom of
8. 43. because ye *c.* hear my word
10. 35. the Scripture *c.* be broken
14. 17. whom the world *c.* receive
15. 4. branch *c.* bear fruit of itself
Acts 4. 20. we *c.* but speak the things
5. 39. if it be of God ye *c.* overthrow
27. 31. except these abide in the ship, ye *c.* be saved
Rom. 8. 8. that are in flesh *c.* please God
26. groanings which *c.* be uttered
Cor. 7. 9. if they *c.* contain, let
10. 21. ye *c.* drink cup of the Lord
15. 50. flesh and blood *c.* inherit the kingdom of God
2 Cor. 12. 2. in body or out, I *c.* tell
Gal. 5. 17. ye *c.* do the things that
2 Tim. 2. 13. he *c.* deny himself
Tit. 1. 2. God who *c.* lie hath
2. 8. sound speech *c.* be condemned
Heb. 4. 15. high priest which *c.* be
9. 5. we *c.* now speak particularly
12. 27. those things which *c.* be
28. kingdom that *c.* be moved
Jas. 1. 13. God *c.* be tempted with
1 John 3. 9. he *c.* sin because born
Ex. 33. 20. *canst* not see my face
Deut. 28. 27. *c.* not be healed
Job 11. 7. *c.* thou by searching find
22. darkness that thou *c.* not see
Matt. 8. 2. if thou wilt, thou *c.*
Mark 9. 22. if *c.* do any thing have

John 3. 8. *c.* not tell whence it
13. 36. thou *c.* not follow me now
CANDLE shall be put out, Job 18. 6. & 21. 17. Prov. 24. 20.
Job 29. 3. when his *c.* shined on
Ps. 18. 28. the Lord will light my *c.*
Prov. 20. 27. spirit of man is *c.* of
31. 18. her *c.* goeth not out by
Matt. 5. 15. do men light a *c.* and — it, Mark 4. 21. Luke 8. 16. & 11. 33.
Luke 11. 36. shining of *c.* doth give
15. 8. light a *c.* and sweep house
Rev. 18. 23. light of *c.* shine no more at all, Jer. 25. 10.
Rev. 22. 5. they need no *c.* neither
Zeph. 1. 22. search Jerusalem with *candles*
Ex. 25. 31. *candlestick*, & 37. 17, 20. Lev. 24. 4. Num. 8. 2. 2 Kings 4. 10. Dan. 5. 5.
Zech. 4. 2. behold a *c.* all of gold
Matt. 5. 15. but on a *c.* and it giveth light to all, Mark 4. 21. Luke 11. 33.
Rev. 1. 20. seven *c.* are the seven
2. 5. I will remove thy *c.* out of his
R. V. Matt. 5. 15; Mark 4. 21; Luke 8. 16. stand
CANKER, 2 Tim. 2. 17. Jas. 5. 3.
CAPTAIN, Num. 2. 3. & 14. 4.
Josh. 5. 14, 15. *c.* of the Lord's host
2 Chron. 13. 12. God himself is our *c.*
Heb. 2. 10. *c.* of their salva. perfect
R. V. 1 Sam. 9. 16; 10. 1; 13. 4. prince; Jer. 51. 23, 28, 57; Dan. 3. 2, 3, 27; 6. 7. governors
CAPTIVE, Gen. 14. 14. & 34. 29.
Judg. 5. 12. lead thy captivity *c.*
Isa. 49. 24. shall the lawful *c.* be
Jer. 22. 12. die whither they led him *c.*
Amos 7. 11. Israel shall be led away *c.*
2 Tim. 2. 26. taken *c.* by him at his
Deut. 30. 3. I will turn thy *captivity*
Job 42. 10. the Lord turned the *c.*
Ps. 14. 7. Lord bringeth back the *c.*
68. 18. lead *c.* captive, Eph. 4. 8.
85. 1. brought back the *c.* of Jacob
126. 1. turned again the *c.* of Zion
Jer. 15. 2. such as are for *c.* to *c.*
29. 14. I will turn away your *c.*
30. 3. bring again *c.* of my people
Hos. 6. 11. when I returned *c.* of
Zeph. 2. 7. Lord shall turn away their *c.*
Rom. 7. 23. bringing me into *c.* of
2 Cor. 10. 5. bringing into *c.* every
Rev. 13. 10. lead into *c.* shall go into *c.*
R. V. Isa. 20. 4; 45. 13; 49. 21. exile
CARCASS, Matt. 24. 28. Luke 17. 37.
R. V. Lev. 11. 26; Judg. 14. 8. body
CARE, Luke 10. 40. 1 Cor. 7. 21.
Matt. 13. 22. *c.* of this world choke, Mark 4. 19. Luke 8. 14.
1 Cor. 9. 9. doth God take *c.* for
12. 25. have the same *c.* one for
2 Cor. 11. 28. *c.* of all the churches
1 Tim. 3. 5. how shall he take *c.* of
1 Pet. 5. 7. casting all your *c.* on
Ps. 142. 4. no man *cared* for my
John 12. 6. not that he *c.* for the
Acts 18. 17. Gallio *c.* for none of these things
Matt. 22. 16. *carest*, Mark 4. 38.
Deut. 11. 12. land thy God *careth*
John 10. 13. hireling *c.* not for
1 Cor. 7. 32, 33, 34. unmarried *c.* for things of Lord, married *c.* for things of the world
1 Pet. 5. 7. for he *c.* for you
2 Kings 4. 13. been *careful* for us
Jer. 17. 8. not be *c.* in the year of
Dan. 3. 16. not *c.* to answer thee
Luke 10. 41. art *c.* and troubled about many things
Phil. 4. 6. be *c.* for nothing; but
10. were *c.* but ye lacked opportunity
Tit. 3. 8. be *c.* to maintain good

Ezek. 12. 18, 19. *carefulness*, 1 Cor. 7. 32. 2 Cor. 7. 11.
Isa. 32. 9. *careless* daughters, 10. 11.
R. V. Ezek. 4. 16. carefulness; 1 Pet. 5. 7. anxiety; Phil. 4. 10. did take thought; Deut. 15. 5; Phil. 2. 28; Heb. 12. 17. diligently; Mic. 1. 12. anxiously; 1 Cor. 7. 32. be free from cares; 2 Cor. 7. 11. earnest care; Judg. 18. 7. in security; Ezek. 39. 6. securely
CARNAL, sold under sin, Rom. 7. 14.
Rom. 8. 7. *c.* mind is enmity against God
15. 27. minister to them in *c.*
1 Cor. 3. 1. not speak but as to *c.*
3. ye are yet *c.* — are ye not *c.*
9. 11. if we reap your *c.* things
2 Cor. 10. 4. our weapons are not *c.*
Heb. 7. 16. law of a *c.* commandment
Rom. 8. 6. to be *c.* minded is death
R. V. 1 Cor. 3. 4. men; 2 Cor. 10. 4. of the flesh; Rom. 8. 6, 7. mind of the flesh
CARPENTER, 2 Sam. 5. 11. Isa. 41. 7. Jer. 24. 1. Zech. 1. 20.
Matt. 13. 55. *carpenter's son*, Mark 6. 3.
R. V. Jer. 24. 1; 29. 2. craftsmen; Zech. 1. 20. smiths
CARRY us not up hence, Ex. 33. 15.
Num. 11. 12. *c.* them in thy bosom
Eccl. 10. 20. bird of air shall *c.*
Isa. 40. 11. *c.* lambs in his bosom
Luke 10. 4. *c.* neither purse nor scrip
1 Tim. 6. 7. can *c.* nothing out
Luke 16. 22. *carried* by angels into Abraham's bosom
Eph. 4. 14. *c.* about with every
Heb. 13. 9. *c.* about with divers
Rev. 17. 3. *c.* me away in spirit, 21. 10.
CART is pressed full, Amos 2. 13.
Isa. 5. 18. as it were with a *c.* rope
CASE, Ex. 5. 19. Ps. 144. 15.
R. V. Deut. 22. 1; 24. 13. surely
CAST law behind their backs, Neh. 9. 26.
Ps. 22. 10. *c.* upon thee from the
55. 22. *c.* thy burden on the Lord
Prov. 1. 14. *c.* in thy lot among us
Eccl. 11. 1. *c.* thy bread upon
Isa. 2. 20. a man shall *c.* his idols
Ezek. 23. 35. *c.* me behind thy back
Dan. 3. 20. *c.* them into the fiery
6. 24. *c.* them into the den of lions
Jonah 2. 4. I am *c.* out of thy sight
Mic. 7. 19. *c.* all their sins into the
Mal. 3. 11. vine shall not *c.* her fruit
Matt. 3. 10. hewn down and *c.* into the fire, 7. 19. Luke 3. 9.
5. 25. thou be *c.* into prison
7. 6. neither *c.* pearls before swine
15. 26. children's bread, and *c.* it to
22. 13. *c.* him into outer darkness
29, 30. *c.* it from — *c.* into hell, 18. 8, 9.
Mark 11. 23. be thou *c.* into the sea
12. 44. she *c.* in all, Luke 21. 4.
Luke 1. 29. she *c.* in her mind what
58. lest the officer *c.* thee into prison
John 8. 7. let him first *c.* a stone at
Acts 16. 23. they *c.* them into prison
Rev. 2. 10. devil shall *c.* some of you into prison
20. 3. *c.* him into the bottomless
Lev. 26. 44. I will not *cast away*
2 Sam. 1. 21. shield is vilely —
Job 8. 20. God will not — perfect man
Ps. 2. 3. let us — their cords from us
51. 11. *c.* me not away from thy
Isa. 41. 9. I will not *c.* thee away
Ezek. 18. 31. — all your transgress.
Rom. 11. 1. hath God — his people, 2.
Heb. 10. 35. *c.* not away your confid.
1 Cor. 9. 27. myself be a —
2 Chron. 25. 8. God hath power to *cast down*

Job 22. 29. when men are — then
Ps. 37. 24. though he fall he shall not be —
42. 5. why art thou —, 11. & 43. 5.
Ps. 102. 10. lifted me up and — again
2 Cor. 4. 9. — but not destroyed
Ps. 44. 9. thou hast *cast off* and put
23. *c.* us not off for ever
71. 9. *c.* me not off in time of old
94. 14. Lord will not — his people
Jer. 31. 37. I will—all seed of Israel
Lam. 3. 31. Lord will not—for ever
Hos. 8. 3. Israel hath—thing is good
Rom. 13. 12. let us — the works of
1 Tim. 5. 12. they — their first love
Gen. 21. 10. *cast out* this bond woman and her son, Gal. 4. 30.
Ex. 34. 24. I will — the nations
Lev. 18. 24. which I — before thee
Deut. 7. 1. — many nations before
Ps. 78. 55. he—heathen before them
Prov. 22. 10.—the scorner,and contention
Isa. 14. 9. thou art — of thy grave
26. 19. the earth shall — the dead
66. 5. *c.* you out for my name's sake
Jer. 7. 15. I will *c.* out of my sight
15. 1. *c.* them out of my sight
Matt. 7. 5. *c.* beam out of thine eye
8. 12. children of kingdom shall be —
12. 24. doth not— devils but by Beelzebub
21. 12. — them that sold and
Mark 9. 28. why could not we *c.* out
16. 9. he had — seven devils
17. in my name shall they—devils
Luke 6. 22. — your name as evil
John 6. 37. that cometh will in no wise —
Rev. 12. 9. the dragon was —
Ps. 73. 18. thou *castedst* them down
Job 15. 4. thou *castest* off fear
Ps. 50. 17. *c.* my words behind thee
Job 21. 10. cow *casteth* not her calf
Ps. 147. 6. *c.* the wicked to ground
Jer. 6. 7. so she *c.* out her wicked.
Matt. 9. 34. he *c.* out devils through Beelzebub, Mark 3. 22. Luke 11. 15.
1 John 4. 18. perfect love *c.* out fear
3 John 10. *c.* them out of the
Job 6. 21. ye see my *casting* down
Rom. 11. 15. if *c.* away of them
2 Cor. 10. 5. *c.* down imaginations
1 Pet. 5. 7. *c.* all your care on him
CASTOR and Pollux, Acts 28. 11.
CATCH every man his wife, Judg. 21. 21.
Ps. 10. 9. he lieth in wait to *c.* poor
Jer. 5. 26. they set a trap, they *c.* men
Mark 12. 13. they *c.* him in his
Luke 5. 10. henceforth thou shalt *c.* men
R. V. Matt. 13. 19; John 10. 12. snatcheth
CATTLE on a thousand hills are mine, Ps. 50. 10.
104. 14. he causeth grass to grow for *c.*
Ezek. 34. 17. I judge between *c.* and *c.*
John 4. 12. drank thereof and his *c.*
R. V. Gen. 30. 40-43. flock
CAUGHT him and kissed him, Prov. 7. 13.
John 21. 3. that night they *c.* noth.
Acts 8. 39. Spirit of the Lord *c.* away Philip
2 Cor. 12. 4. he was *c.* up into para.
16. being crafty I *c.* you with guile
1 Thes. 4. 17. *c.* up together with
Rev. 12. 5. her child was *c.* up to
CAUL, Isa. 3. 18. Hos. 13. 8.
CAUSE come before judges, Ex. 22. 9.
Ex. 23. 2. not speak in a *c.* to
6. nor wrest judgment of poor in *c.*
Deut. 1. 17. *c.* that is too hard for
1 Kings 8. 45. maintained their *c.*, 49.
Job 5. 8. to God would I commit my *c.*

Ps. 9. 4. maintain my right and my *c.*
Prov. 18. 17. that is first in his own *c.*
Eccl. 7. 10. what is *c.* that former
Isa. 51. 22. pleadeth *c.* of his people
Jer. 5. 28. judge not *c.* of fatherless, 22. 16.
11. 20. to thee I revealed my *c.*, 20. 12.
Lam. 3. 36. to subvert a man in his *c.*
Matt. 19. 3. put away his wife for every *c.*
2 Cor. 4. 16. for which *c.* we faint
5. 13. if we be sober it is for your *c.*
Ex. 9. 16. *for this cause*, Matt. 19. 5. Ex. 5. 31. John 12. 27. & 18. 37. Rom. 1. 13. & 13. 6. 1 Cor. 11. 30.
1 Tim. 1. 16. — I obtained mercy
Ps. 119. 161. *without cause*, Prov. 23. 29. Matt. 5. 22. John 15. 25.
Job 6. 24. *c.* me to understand
Ps. 10. 17. wilt *c.* thine ear to hear
67. 1. *c.* his face to shine, 80. 3, 7, 19.
143. 8. *c.* me to know the way
Isa. 3. 12. lead thee, *c.* thee to err, 9. 16.
58. 14. I will *c.* thee to ride on
66. 9. and not *c.* to bring forth
Jer. 3. 12. not *c.* my anger to fall
7. 3. *c.* you to dwell in his place, 7.
15. 4. *c.* them to be removed
11. *c.* the enemy to treat thee
44. *c.* their captivity to return, 33. 7. & 34. 22. & 42. 12.
32. 37. *c.* them to dwell safely
Lam. 3. 32. though he *c.* grief, yet
Ezek. 36. 27. *c.* you to walk in my statutes
Dan. 9. 17. *c.* thy face to shine on sanctuary
Rom. 16. 17. mark them which *c.* division
Prov. 7. 21. fair speech *caused* him
Prov. 10. 5. a son *causeth*, 17. 2. & 19. 26.
Matt. 5. 32. *c.* her to commit adultery
2 Cor. 2. 14. always *c.* us to triumph
Prov. 26. 2. curse *causeless* shall not
R. V. 2 Chron. 19. 10. controversy; Prov. 31. 9. judgment; John 18. 37. to this end; Matt. 5. 32; Rev. 13. 12. maketh; 2 Cor. 9. 11. worketh
CAVE, and a stone lay on it, John 11. 41.
Gen. 19. 30. Lot dwelt in a *c.* he and
23. 19. buried Sarah his wife in *c.*
25. 9. buried him in the *c.*
49. 29. bury me with my fathers in *c.*
Josh. 10. 16. hid themselves in a *c.*
1 Kings 18. 4. hid them by 50 in a *c.*
Isa. 2. 19. go into *caves* for fear of
Ezek. 33. 27. that be in the *c.* shall die
Heb. 11. 38. wandered in *c.* of the
R. V. Job 30. 6; Heb. 11. 38. holes
CEASE not day nor night, Gen. 8. 22.
Deut. 15. 11. poor shall never *c.* out of
Neh. 6. 3. why should the work *c.*
Job 3. 17. there the wicked *c.*
Ps. 37. 8. *c.* from anger and wrath
46. 9. he maketh wars to *c.* unto
Prov. 19. 27. *c.* to hear instruction
23. 4. *c.* from thine own wisdom
Isa. 1. 16. *c.* to do evil, learn to do
1. 22. *c.* ye from man whose breath
Acts 13. 10. wilt thou not *c.* to per.
1 Cor. 13. 8. there be tongues, they *c.*
Eph. 1. 16. *c.* not to give thanks for
Col. 1. 9. *c.* not to pray for you
2 Pet. 2. 14. that cannot *c.* from sin
Ps. 12. 1. the godly man *ceaseth*
Prov. 26. 20. no talebearer, strife *c.*
1 Thes. 5. 17. pray without *ceasing*, 2. 13. 1 Sam. 12. 23. Acts 12. 5. Rom. 1. 9. 2 Tim. 1. 3.
R. V. Rom. 1. 9; 2 Tim. 1. 3. unceasingly; Acts 12. 5. earnestly
CEDAR, Lev. 14. 4. Jer. 22. 14, 15.
2 Sam. 7. 2. I dwell in a house of *c.*

2 Kings 14. 9. thistle sent to *c.* in
Ps. 29. 5. voice of Lord breaketh *c.*
92. 12. grow like a *c.* in Lebanon
S. of S. 1. 17. the beams of our house are *c.*
Isa. 9. 10. we will change them into *c.*
Ezek. 17. 22. of the high *c.*
23. goodly *c.*
Amos 2. 9. like the height of the *c.*
CELEBRATE, death cannot, Isa. 38. 18.
R. V. Lev. 23. 32. keep
CELESTIAL, 1 Cor. 15. 40.
CHAFF, wicked as, Job 21. 18. Ps. 1. 4. & 35. 5. Isa. 5. 24. & 17. 13. & 29. 5. & 41. 15. Dan. 2. 35. Hos. 13. 3. Luke 3. 17.
Isa. 33. 11. ye shall conceive *c.* ye
Jer. 23. 28. what is the *c.* to the
Zeph. 2. 2. before the day pass as the *c.*
Matt. 3. 12. burn up *c.* in unquench.
R. V. Isa. 5. 24. dry grass; Jer. 23. 28. straw
CHAIN, Gen. 41. 42. Dan. 5. 7. Ezek. 19. 4, 9. Mark 5, 3. 4.
Ps. 73. 6. pride compasseth them as a *c.*
S. of S. 4. 9. with one *c.* of thy neck
Acts 28. 20. I am bound with this *c.*
2 Tim. 1. 16. was not ashamed of my *c.*
Ps. 149. 8. bind their kings with *chains*
Prov. 1. 9. shall be a *c.* about neck
2 Pet. 2. 4. delivered into *c.* of dark.
Jude 6. reserved in everlasting *c.*
R. V. Num. 31. 50. ankle chains; S. of S. 1. 10. strings; Isa. 3. 19. pendants; Jer. 39. 7; 52. 11. fetters Ezek. 19. 4. hooks; Jude 6. bonds
CHALDEANS, Job. 1. 17. Isa. 43 14. & 48. 20. Jer. 38. 2. & 39. 8. & 40 9. & 50. 35. Ezek. 23. 14. Dan. 1. 4 & 9. 1.
CHAMBER, Ps. 19. 5. Joel 2. 16.
Job 9. 9. maketh the *chambers* of the
Ps. 104. 3. beams of *c.* in the waters
Prov. 7. 27. going down to the *c.* of
S. of S. 1. 4. king brought me into his *c.*
Isa. 26. 20. enter into *c.* and shut thy
Matt. 24. 26. he is in the secret *c.*
Rom. 13. 13. not in *chambering* and wantonness
R. V. 1 Kings 6. 6. story; Ezek. 40. 7. lodge
CHANCE, happens, 1 Sam. 6. 9. Eccl. 9. 11. 2 Sam. 1. 6. Luke 10. 31.
CHANGE of raiment, Judg. 14. 12, 13. Zech. 3. 4. Isa. 3. 22.
Job 14. 14. patiently wait till my *c.* come
Heb. 7. 12. made of necessity a *c.* of law
Job 17. 12. they *c.* the night into
Ps. 102. 26. as a vesture shalt thou *c.*
Jer. 13. 23. can Ethiopian *c.* his skin
Mal. 3. 6. I am the Lord, I *c.* not
Phil. 3. 21. who shall *c.* our vile
1 Sam. 21. 13. *changed* his behavior
Ps. 102. 26. and they shall be *c.*
Jer. 2. 11. hath a nation *c.* their gods
Rom. 1. 23. *c.* the glory of God
1 Cor. 15. 51. shall all be *c.*, 52.
2 Cor. 3. 18. *c.* into the same image
Job 10. 17. *changes* and war are against
Ps. 55. 19. they have no *c.* therefore
15. 4. sweareth and *changeth* not
Dan. 2. 21. he *c.* the times and seas.
Mark 11. 15. *money changers*, Matt. 21. 12. John 2. 14, 15.
R. V. Job 30. 18. disfigured
CHANT to sound of viol, Amos 6. 5.
CHAPEL, the king's, Amos 7. 13.
CHARGE, Gen. 26. 5. & 28. 6.
Ps. 91. 11. give his angels *c.* over
Acts 7. 60. lay not this sin to their *c.*
Rom. 8. 33. any thing to the *c.* of
S. of S. 2. 7. I *c.* you, O daughters of Jerusalem, 3. 5. & 5. 8. & 8. 4.

1 Tim. 6. 17. *c.* them that are rich
Job 1. 22. nor *charged* God foolishly
1 Thes. 2. 11. *c.* every one as a father
2 Cor. 11. 9. *chargeable*, 1 Thes. 2. 9. 2 Thes. 3. 8.
R. V. 1 Thes. 2. 9; 2 Thes. 3. 8. burden
CHARIOT, Gen. 41. 43. & 46. 29.
Ex. 14. 25. took off their *c.* wheels
2 Kings 2. 11. appeared a *c.* of fire
S. of S. 3. 9. Solomon made himself *c.*
Mic. 1. 13. bind the *c.* to swift beasts
Acts 8. 29. join thyself to this *c.*
Ps. 20. 7. some trust in *chariots*
68. 17. *c.* of God are 20,000
S. of S. 6. 12. made me like the *c.*
Hab. 3. 8. ride upon thy *c.* of salva.
R. V. S. of S. 3. 9. palanquin; Isa. 21. 7, 9. troop; 2 Sam. 8. 4 —
CHARITY edifieth, 1 Cor. 8. 1.
13. 1. if I have not *c.* I am nothing, 2. 3.
4. *c.* suffereth long, 8. *c.* never fail.
13. now abideth faith, hope, *c.*
Col. 3. 14. above all things put on *c.*
1 Thes. 3. 6. tidings of your faith and *c.*
1 Tim. 1. 5. end of the commandment is *c.*
2. 15. if they continue in faith and *c.*
2 Tim. 2. 22. follow righteousness, faith, *c.*
2 Tim. 3. 10. know my doctrine, faith, *c.*
Tit. 2. 2. sound in faith, in *c.*, in patience
3 John 6. borne witness of thy *c.*
1 Pet. 4. 8. have fervent *c.* among yourselves
5. 14. greet one another with a kiss of *c.*
2 Pet. 1. 7. add to brotherly kindness, *c.*
Jude 12. spots in your feasts of *c.*
Rom. 14. 15. walketh not *charitably*
CHARMED, Jer. 8. 17.
Deut. 18. 11. *charmers*, Ps. 58. 5. Isa. 19. 3.
CHASTE virgin, 2 Cor. 11. 2.
Tit. 2. 5. to be discreet, *c.*, good
1 Pet. 3. 2. your *c.* conversa., with
R. V. 2 Cor. 11. 2. pure
CHASTEN with rod of men, 2 Sam. 7. 14.
Ps. 6. 1. neither *c.* me in thy, 38. 1.
Prov. 19. 18. *c.* thy son while there is
Dan. 10. 12. to *c.* thyself before thy
Rev. 3. 19. as many as I love, I *c.*
Ps. 69. 10. *chastened* my soul with
1 Cor. 11. 32. we are *c.* of the Lord
Heb. 12. 10. for a few days *c.* us
Ps. 94. 12. blessed is the man whom thou *chastenest*
Deut. 8. 5. as a man *c.* his son
Prov. 13. 24. loveth him *chasteneth* him betimes
Heb. 12. 6. whom Lord loveth he *c.*
Job 5. 17. despise not thou *chastening* of the Lord, Prov. 3. 11. Heb. 12. 5.
Isa. 26. 16. when thy *c.* was upon
11. no *c.* for present is joyous
R. V. Dan. 10. 12. humble
CHASTISE you seven times, Lev. 26. 28.
Deut. 22. 18. elders shall *c.* him
1 Kings 12. 11. I will *c.* with scorpions, 14.
Hos. 7. 12. *c.* them as their congre.
Luke 23. 16. *c.* and release him, 22.
1 Chron. 10. 11, 14. father *chastised* with whips
Ps. 94. 10. *c.* the heathen
Deut. 11. 2. not seen *chastisement* of the
Isa. 53. 5. *c.* of our peace was upon
Jer. 30. 14. with the *c.* of a cruel one
Heb. 12. 8. if ye be without *c.* then
R. V. Heb. 12. 8. chastening
CHATTER like a crane, Isa. 38. 14.
CHEEK, 1 Kings 22. 24. Job 16. 10. Isa. 50. 6. Lam. 3. 30. Mic. 5. 1. Matt. 5. 39. Luke 6. 29. Deut. 18. 3.

S. of S. 1. 10. thy *cheeks* are comely
5. 13. his *c.* are as a bed of spices
R. V. Joel 1. 6. jaw
CHEER *be of good*, Matt. 9. 2. & 14. 27. Mark 6. 50. John 16. 33. Acts 23. 11. & 27. 22, 25.
Prov. 15. 13. *cheerful*, Zech. 9. 17.
2 Cor. 9. 6. *cheerfulness*, Rom. 12. 8.
Acts 24. 10. *cheerfully* answer for my.
R. V. Zech. 9. 17. flourish
CHERISH, Eph. 5. 29. 1 Thes. 2. 7.
CHERUBIMS, between, 1 Sam. 4. 4. 2 Sam. 6. 2. 2 Kings 19. 15. 1 Chron. 13. 6. Ps. 80. 1. & 99. 1. Isa. 37. 16.
R. V. cherubim
CHICKENS, hen gathereth, Matt. 23. 37.
CHIDE, not always, Ps. 103. 9.
R. V. Ex. 17. 2. strive, strove.
CHIEF, Ezra 9. 2. Neh. 11. 3.
Matt. 20. 27. that will be *c.* among
Luke 22. 26. that is *c.* as he that ser.
Eph. 2. 20. Jesus Christ himself being *c.*
1 Tim. 1. 15. sinners, — of whom I am *c.*
S. of S. 5. 10. *chiefest* among 10,000
Rom. 3. 2. *chiefly*, Phil. 4. 22. 2 Pet. 2. 10.
R. V. In O. T. frequently, prince, head, captain; Matt. 20. 27. first; Luke 11. 15. prince; 14. 1. rulers; Acts 18. 8-17 —; Luke 19. 47; Acts 25. 2. principal men; Mark 10. 44. first; Rom. 3. 2. first of all; Phil. 4. 22. especially
CHILD, Gen. 37. 30. 1 Cor. 13. 11.
Ex. 2. 2. saw he was a goodly *c.*
2 Sam. 12. 16. David besought God for the *c.*
Ps. 131. 2. quieted myself as a *c.* weaned
Prov. 29. 15. *c.* left to himself bring.
Eccl. 4. 8. hath neither *c.* nor brother
Isa. 3. 5. *c.* behave himself proudly
9. 6. unto us a *c.* is born
11. 6. a little *c.* shall lead them
Jer. 1. 6. cannot speak for I am a *c.*
31. 20. dear son is he a pleasant *c.*
Hos. 11. 1. when Israel was a *c.* I loved
Matt. 18. 2. Jesus called a little *c.*
Mark 9. 36. took a *c.* and set him in
10. 15. receive kingdom of God as little *c.*
2. 43. *c.* Jesus tarried behind in Jerusalem
Acts 4. 27. against thy holy *c.* Jesus
13. 10. thou *c.* of the devil, thou
1 Cor. 13. 11. when I was a *c.*
Gal. 4. 1. as long as a *c.* differs noth.
2 Tim. 3. 15. from a *c.* hast known
Rev. 12. 4. to devour her *c.* as soon
5. her *c.* was caught up to God
1 Tim. 2. 15. to be saved in *childbearing*
Eccl. 11. 10. *childhood* and youth are
1 Cor. 13. 11. put away *childish* things
Gen. 15. 2. *childless*, Jer. 22. 30.
25. 22. *children* struggled together
30. 1. give me *c.* or else I die
Ps. 17. 14. they are full of *c.* and
Prov. 17. 6. the glory of *c.* are their fathers
S. of S. 1. 6. mother's *c.* were angry
Isa. 1. 2. I brought up *c.* and they
3. 12. *c.* are their oppressors
30. 9. lying *c.* — *c.* that will not hear
Mal. 4. 6. turn hearts of fathers to *c.*
Matt. 3. 9. of these stones to raise up *c.*
15. 26. not meet to take *c.*'s bread
16. 8. *c.* of this world wiser than *c.*
Acts 3. 25. ye are *c.* of the prophets
Rom. 8. 17. if *c.* then heirs, heirs of
1 Cor. 7. 14. else were your *c.* unclean
14. 20. be not *c.* in understanding
Eph. 2. 3. are by nature *c.* of wrath

Eph. 5. 6. cometh the wrath of God upon the *c.* of disobedience. Col. 3. 6.
6. 1. *c.* obey your parents, Col. 3. 20.
Heb. 12. 5. speaketh unto you as *c.*
1 Pet. 1. 14. as obedient *c.* not fashioning
Rev. 2. 23. kill her *c.* with death
Ex. 34. 7. *children's children*, Jer. 2. 9. Ps. 103. 17. & 128. 6. Prov. 13. 22.
Prov. 17. 6. — are crown of old men
Matt. 5. 9. *children of God*, Luke 20. 36. John 11. 52. Rom. 8. 21. & 9. 8, 26. Gal. 3. 26. 1 John 3. 10. & 5. 2.
Ps. 89. 30. *his children*, 103. 13.
Luke 16. 8. *children of light*, John 12. 36. Eph. 5. 8. 1 Thes. 5. 5.
Matt. 18. 3. *little children*, 19. 14. Mark 10. 14. Luke 18. 16. John 13. 33. Gal. 4. 19. 1 John 2. 1, 12, 13. & 4. 4.
Rom. 9. 8. *children of promise*, Gal. 4. 28.
Ps. 128. 3, 6. *thy children*, 147. 13. Isa. 54. 13. Matt. 23. 37. Luke 13. 34. 2 John 4.
Ps. 115. 14. *your children*, Matt. 7. 11. Luke 11. 13. Acts 2. 39.
Job 19. 18. *young children*, Lam. 4. 4. Nah. 3. 10. Mark 10. 13.
CHOKE, Matt. 13. 7, 22. Mark 4. 7, 19. & 5. 13. Luke 8. 14, 33.
CHOOSE life, Deut. 30. 19.
Josh. 24. 15. *c.* you whom ye will
2 Sam. 24. 12. *c.* thee one of them
Ps. 25. 12. teach in the way that he shall *c.*
47. 4. *c.* our inheritance for us
Prov. 1. 29. did not *c.* the fear of
Isa. 7. 15. *c.* good and refuse evil, 16.
Phil. 1. 22. what I shall *c.* I wot not
Ps. 65. 4. man whom thou *choosest*
Heb. 11. 25. *choosing* rather to suf.
Josh. 24. 22. ye have *chosen* the Lord
1 Chron. 16. 13. children of Jacob his *c.*
Ps. 33. 12. *c.* for his own inheritance
105. 6. children of Jacob his *c.*, 43.
Prov. 16. 16. rather to be *c.* than
22. 1. a good name is rather to be *c.* than
Isa. 66. 3. have *c.* their own ways
Jer. 8. 3. death shall be *c.* rather
Matt. 20. 16. many are called, but few *c.*, 22. 14.
Mark 13. 20. elect's sake whom he hath *c.*
Luke 10. 42. Mary hath *c.* that good
John 15. 16. ye have not *c.* me
Acts 9. 15. he is a *c.* vessel to me
22. 14. God hath *c.* thee that thou
1 Cor. 1. 27. God hath *c.* the foolish
Eph. 1. 4. hath *c.* us in him before
2 Thes. 2. 13. from beginning *c.* you
1 Pet. 2. 4. *c.* of God and precious
9. ye are a *c.* generation
Rev. 17. 14. are called, and *c.* and
Isa. 41. 9. *I have chosen*, 43. 10. & 58. 6. Matt. 12. 18.
Ps. 119. 30. — the way of truth
173. — thy precepts
Isa. 44. 1, 2. Israel — Jeshurun whom
48. 10. — thee in the furnace of affli
John 13. 18. I know whom —
15. 16, 19. — you out of the world
R. V. Acts 22. 14; 2 Cor. 8. 19. appointed
CHRIST should be born, Matt. 2. 4.
16. 16. thou art *C.* son of the living
23. 8. one is your master even *C.*, 10.
Mark 9. 41. because ye belong to *C.*
Luke 24. 26. ought not *C.* to have suffered
46. it behooved *C.* to suffer and
John 4. 25. Messias which is call.
13. 34. that *C.* abideth for ever

Acts 8. 5. preached *C.* to them
Rom. 5. 6. *C.* died for the ungodly
8. while yet sinners *C.* died for us
10. if *C.* be in you the body is dead
10. 4. *C.* is the end of the law for
15. 3. *C.* pleased not himself
1 Cor. 1. 24. *C.* the power of God
3. 23. ye are *C.*'s and *C.* is God's
Gal. 2. 20. crucified with *C. C.* liveth
3. 13. *C.* hath redeemed us from
5. 24. that are *C*'s have crucified
Eph. 2. 12. ye were without *C.* being alienated
4. 20. ye have not so learned *C.*
5. 14. *C.* shall give thee light
23. as *C.* is the head of the church
6. 5. in singleness of heart as unto *C.*
Phil. 1. 21. to me to live is *C.*
23. I desire to dep., and be with
3. 8. that I may win *C.*
4. 13. can do all things through *C.*
Col. 1. 27. *C.* in you hope of glory
3. 4. when *C.* who is our life shall
Rom. 8. 1. to them in *Christ Jesus*
2. law of the spirit of life in—
1 Cor. 1. 30. of him are ye in—
2. 2. save—and him crucified
2 Cor. 13. 5. how that—is in you
Gal. 3. 28. ye are all one in—, 26.
Eph. 1. 1. saints and to faithful in—
2. 10. created in—unto works, 1. 1.
Phil. 2. 11. confess that—is Lord
3. 3. rejoice in—and have no confidence
12. for which I am apprehended of—
Col. 2. 6. received—the Lord, 3. 24.
1 Tim. 1. 15. that—that came into
1 Tim. 2. 5. one mediator, the man—
Heb. 13. 8. —the same yesterday
Rom. 12. 5. one body *in Christ*
16. 3, 7. were—before me, 10.
1 Cor. 15. 18. fallen asleep—are perished
19. in this life only have hope—
2 Cor. 5. 17. if any man be—he is a
19. God was—reconciling world
Gal. 1. 22. churches which were—
Phil. 1. 13. my bonds—are manifest
2. 1. if there be any consolation—
Col. 1. 2. saints and faithful breth.
1 Thes. 4. 16. the dead—shall rise
John 1. 25. *that Christ*, 6. 69.
Matt. 16. 20. *the Christ*, 26. 63. Mark 8. 29. & 14. 61. Luke 3. 15. & 9. 20. & 22. 67. John 1. 20, 41. & 3. 28. & 4. 29, 42. & 7. 41. & 10. 24. & 11. 27. & 20. 31. 1 John 2. 22. & 5. 1.
Rom. 6. 8. if we be dead *with Christ*
8. 17. heirs of God and joint heirs—
Gal. 2. 20. I am crucified—
Eph. 2. 5. quickened us together—
Col. 2. 20. if ye be dead—from the
Rev. 20. 4. reigned—1000 years
Acts 26. 28. persuadest me to be a *Christian*
1 Pet. 4. 15. suffer as a *C.* let him not be
Acts 11. 26. first called *Christians* at Antioch

CHURCH, Acts 14. 27. & 15. 3. 1 Cor. 4. 17. & 14. 4, 23. 3 John 9.
Matt. 16. 18. on this rock will I build my *c.*
18. 17. tell it to the *c.* neglect to hear the *c.*
Acts 2. 47. Lord added to *c.* daily
8. 1. great persecution against *c.*
11. 26. assembled themselves with *c.*
14. 23. ordained elders in every *c.*
1 Cor. 14. 4, 5. that *c.* may receive edifying
Eph. 1. 22. head over all things to *c.*
3. 10. known by *c.* the wisdom of
Eph. 5. 25. as Christ loved the *c.* and gave
32. concerning Christ and the *c.*
4. 15. no *c.* communic. with me
Col. 1. 18. head of the body, the *c.*
1 Tim. 5. 16. let not *c.* be charged
Heb. 12. 23. assembly and *c.* of first-born
3 John 6. witness of charity before *c.*
Acts 7. 38. *in the church*, 13. 1. 1 Cor. 6. 4. & 11. 18. & 12. 28. & 14. 19, 28, 35. Eph. 3. 21. Col. 4. 16.
Acts 20. 28. *the church of God*, 1 Cor. 1. 2. & 10. 32. & 15. 9. 2 Cor. 1. 1. Gal. 1. 13. 1 Tim. 3. 5.
9. 31. then had *churches* rest
15. 41. confirming the *c.*
16. 5. so were the *c.* established in
Rom. 16. 16. *c.* of Christ salute you
1 Cor. 7. 17. and so ordain I in all *c.*
14. 33. as in all *c.* of saints
34. women keep silence in the *c.*
1 Thes. 2. 14. became followers of *c.*
2 Thes. 1. 4. glory in you in the *c.*
Rev. 1. 4. seven *c.* in Asia, 11.
20. angels of the seven *c.* and
2. 7. hear what the Spirit saith to the *c.*, 11. 17, 29. & 3. 6, 13, 22.
2. 23. and all the *c.* shall know I
22. 16. testify these things in the *c.*

CHURL, Isa. 32. 5, 7. *Churlish*, 1 Sam. 25. 3.

CIRCUIT, 1 Sam. 7. 16. Job 22. 14. Ps. 19. 6. Eccl. 1. 6.

CIRCUMCISE the flesh, Gen. 17. 11.
Deut. 10. 16. *c.* the foreskin of your
Josh. 5. 2. *c.* again Israel
4. Joshua did *c.*
Jer. 4. 4. *c.* yourselves to the Lord
Gen. 17. 10. every male shall be *circumcised*, 14. 23, 26. Phil. 3. 5.
21. 4. Abraham *c.* his son Isaac
Josh. 5. 3. *c.* the children of Israel
Acts 15. 1. except ye be *c.* ye cannot be
Acts 16. 3. *c.* him because of the
Gal. 2. 3. neither was compelled to be *c.*
John 7. 22. Moses gave unto you *circumcision*
Acts 7. 8. God gave him the covenant of *c.*
Rom. 2. 25. *c.* profiteth if thou
29. *c.* is that of the heart in the
3. 1. what profit is there of *c.*
30. which shall justify *c.* by faith
4. 9. comes this blessedness on the *c.* only
11. he received the sign of *c.*
15. 8. Christ was minister of the *c.*
1 Cor. 7. 19. *c.* is nothing but keep.
Gal. 2. 7. gospel of the *c.* was unto
Phil. 3. 3. we are the *c.* which
Col. 2. 11. circumcised with *c.*
Tit. 1. 10. especially they of the *c.*

CIRCUMSPECT, Ex. 23. 13.
Eph. 5. 15. that ye walk *circumspectly*
R. V. take ye heed

CISTERN, Prov. 5. 15. Eccl. 12. 6.
Jer. 2. 13. hewed them out *cisterns*

CITY, Cain builded a, Gen. 4. 17.
Ps. 107. 4. found no *c.* to dwell in
7. might go to *c.* of habitation
127. 1. except the Lord keep the *c.*
S. of S. 3. 2. I will go out about the *c.* in
Isa. 1. 21. the faithful *c.* is become
33. 20. the *c.* of our solemnities
Jer. 3. 14. take one of a *c.* two of a
Amos 3. 6. shall there be evil in a *c.*
Zeph. 2. 15. this is the rejoicing *c.*
Zech. 8. 3. shall be called *c.* of truth
Matt. 5. 14. a *c.* set on a hill
Luke 10. 8. into whatsoever *c.* ye
19. 41. he beheld *c.* and wept over
Heb. 11. 10. he looked for a *c.*
12. 22. to the *c.* of the living God
Rev. 3. 12. name of the *c.* of my
Neh. 11. 1, 18, *holy city*, Isa. 48. 2.
Isa. 52. 1. Dan. 9. 24. Matt. 4. 5. & 27. 53. Rev. 11. 2. & 21. 2. & 22. 19.
Num. 35. 6. *cities of refuge*, Josh. 21. 13, 21, 27, 32, 38.
Amos 4. 8. two or three *cities* wandered unto one city
Luke 19. 17. have thou authority over ten *c.*
Acts 26. 11. persecuted unto strange *c.*
Rev. 16. 19. the *c.* of the nations
Luke 15. 15. *citizen*, & 19. 14.
Eph. 2. 19. fellow *citizens* with saints

CLAMOR, Eph. 4. 31. Prov. 9. 13.

CLAY, Job 27. 16. & 38. 14.
4. 19. them that dwell in houses of *c.*
10. 9. thou hast made me as the *c.*
Isa. 64. 8. we are the *c.* thou our potter, 45. 9. Jer. 18. 6.
Ps. 40. 2. brought me out of miry *c.*
Dan. 2. 33. part of iron, part of *c.*
Hab. 2. 6. that ladeth himself with thick *c.*

CLEAN beasts, Gen. 7. 2. & 8. 20.
Lev. 10. 10. between unclean and *c.*, 11. 47. Ezek. 22. 26. & 44. 23.
Job 14. 4. who bring *c.* thing out
15. 14. what is man that he should be *c.*
Ps. 19. 9. the fear of the Lord is *c.* enduring for ever
Prov. 16. 2. ways of man are *c.* in
Isa. 1. 16. wash ye, make you *c.* put
Jer. 13. 27. wilt thou not be made *c.*
Ezek. 36. 25. sprinkle *c.* water, ye shall be *c.*
Matt. 8. 3. I will, be thou *c.*, Luke 5. 13.
23. 25. make *c.* outside of, Luke 11. 39.
Luke 11. 41. all things are *c.* to you
John 13. 11. ye are *c.* but not all
Rev. 19. 8. fine linen, *c.* and white
Job 17. 9. *clean hands*, Ps. 24. 4.
Ps. 51. 10. *clean heart*, 73. 1.
18. 24. according to the *cleanness*
Amos 4. 6. given you *c.* of teeth in all cities
Ps. 19. 12. *cleanse* me from secret
119. 9. shall a young man *c.* his way
Jer. 33. 8. I will *c.* them fr. all sin
Ezek. 36. 25. from your idols will I *c.* you
Matt. 10. 8. heal sick, *c.* the lepers
2 Cor. 7. 1. let us *c.* ourselves from
Eph. 5. 26. *c.* it with the washing of
Jas. 4. 8. *c.* your hands, ye sinners
1 John 1. 9. *c.* us from all unright.
2 Chron. 30. 19. though not *cleansed* according
Ps. 73. 13. I have *c.* my heart in vain
Ezek. 36. 33. *c.* you from all iniqui.
Matt. 11. 5. the lepers are *c.*
Luke 17. 17. were there not ten *c.*, 9.
Acts 10. 15. what God hath *c.*, 11. 9.
1 John 1. 7. blood of Jesus Christ *c.*
R. V. Matt. 23. 25; Luke 11. 39. cleanse; Neh. 13. 22. purify; Ps. 19. 12. clear

CLEAR the guilty, Ex. 34. 7.
Ps. 51. 4. be *c.* when thou judgest
Zech. 14. 6. light shall not be *c.* nor
R. V. Zech. 14. 6. with brightness; 2 Cor. 7. 11; Rev. 21. 18. pure; 22. 1. bright; Job 33. 3. sincerely

CLEAVE to his wife, Gen. 2. 24. Matt. 19. 5. Mark 10. 7. Eph. 5. 31.
Deut. 4. 4. ye did *c.* to the Lord, 10. 20. & 11. 22. & 13. 4. & 30. 20. Josh. 22. 5. & 23. 8.
Ps. 22. 15. tongue *cleaveth* to my
119. 25. my soul *c.* unto the dust
137. 6. my tongue *c.* to the roof
Rom. 12. 9. *c.* to that which is good

CLIMB, Jer. 4. 29. Joel 2. 7, 9.
Amos 9. 2. though they *c.* up to
John 10. 1. *climbeth* some other way

CLOAK, Matt. 5. 40. Luke 6. 29.
Isa. 59. 17. clad with zeal as with *c.*
John 15. 22. have no *c.* for their sin
1 Thes. 2. 5. nor used *c.* of covetous.
1 Pet. 2. 16. liberty for *c.* of malic

I'm not afraid to
Trust him for he's
on my side

CLOSET, Joel 2. 16. Matt. 6. 6.
R. V. Luke 12. 3. inner chamber
CLOTHE, Matt. 6. 30. Luke 12. 28.
Job 10. 11. *clothed* me with skin and
Ps. 35. 26. be *c.* with shame, 132. 18.
109. 18. he *c.* himself with cursing
132.16.*c.* her priests with salvation
Ezek. 16. 10. I *c.* thee with broid.
Zeph. 1. 8. *c.* with strange apparel
Matt. 11. 8. *c.* in soft raiment
25. 36. naked, and ye *c.* me
43. *c.* me not
2 Cor. 5. 2. desiring to be *c.* upon
1 Pet. 5. 5. be *c.* with humility
Rev. 3. 5. be *c.* with white raiment
11. 3. prophecy *c.* in sackcloth and
12. 1. a woman *c.* with the sun
19. 14. *c.* in fine linen, clean and white
Job 22. 6. *clothing*, 24. 27. Mark 12. 38. Acts 10. 30. Jas. 2. 3.
Ps. 45. 13. her *c.* is of wrought gold
Isa. 59. 17. garment of vengeance for *c.*
Matt. 7. 15. come in sheep's *c.*
11. 8. that wear soft *c.* are in
CLOUD, Gen. 9. 13. Isa. 18. 4.
Isa. 44. 22. blotted out as a *c.* and
1 Cor. 10. 1. our fathers were under *c.*
2. baptized unto Moses in the *c.*
Heb. 12. 1. so great a *c.* of witness.
Rev. 11. 12. ascended to heaven in *c.*
Hos. 6. 4. *morning cloud*, 13. 3.
Judg. 5. 4. *clouds* dropped water
2 Sam. 23. 4. as a morning without *c.*
Ps. 36. 5. faithfulness reacheth to *c.*
57. 10. thy truth unto the *c.*, 108. 4.
104. 3. who maketh *c.* his chariot
Matt. 24. 30. coming in the *c.* of heaven, 26. 64. Mark 13. 26. & 14. 62.
1 Thes. 4. 17. caught up in *c.* to meet
2 Pet. 2. 17. *c.* carried with a temp.
Jude 12. *c.* without water, carried
Rev. 1. 7. he cometh with *c.*
R. V. In Job and Ps. mostly skies
CLOVEN tongues, Acts 2. 3.
R. V. Acts 2. 3. parting asunder
COAL, 2 Sam. 14. 7. Isa. 47. 14. & 6. 6. Lam. 4. 8. Ps. 18. 8, 12. & 120. 4. & 140. 10.
Prov. 6. 28. can one go on hot *coals*
25. 22. heap *c.* of fire on head, Rom. 12. 20.
26. 21. as *c.* are to burning
S. of S. 8. 6. *c.* thereof are *c.* of fire
R. V. Prov. 26. 21. embers; S. of S. 8. 6. flashes; Hab. 3. 5. bolts
COAT, Gen. 3. 21. & 37. 3. Ex. 28. 4.
S. of S. 5. 3. put off my *c.* how put
Matt. 5. 40. if any man take away thy *c.*
R. V. 1 Sam. 2. 19. robe; Dan. 3. 21, 27. hosen
COLD, Gen. 8. 22. Job 24. 7. & 37. 9.
Matt. 24. 12. the love of many wax *c.*
Rev. 3. 15. neither *c.* nor hot, 16.
R. V. Prov. 20. 4. winter
COLLECTION, 1 Cor. 16. 1.
R. V. 2 Chron. 24. 6, 9. tax.
COME not into my secret, Gen. 49. 6.
Ex. 20. 24. I will *c.* and bless thee
1 Sam. 17. 45. I *c.* to thee in name
1 Chron. 29. 14. all things *c.* of thee, 12.
Job 22. 21. good shall *c.* unto thee
Ps. 22. 31. they shall *c.* and shall
40. 7. lo I *c.*, Heb. 10. 9.
Eccl. 9. 2. all things *c.* alike to all
S. of S. 4. 16. awake north wind, *c.* thou south
Isa. 26. 20. *c.* my people enter into
35. 4. God will *c.* and save you
Ezek. 33. 31. *c.* to thee as the people cometh
Mic. 6. 6. wherewith shall I *c.* before the Lord
Mal. 3. 1. Lord shall suddenly *c.* to
4. 6. lest I *c.* and smite the earth
Matt. 8. 11. many shall *c.* from the east and west, Luke 7. 19, 20.
11. 28. *c.* unto me all ye that labor
16. 24. if any man will *c.* after me
Luke 7. 8. I say *c.* and he cometh
Luke 14. 20. I have married a wife, I cannot *c.*
John 1. 39. *c.* and see, 46. & 4. 29.
Rev. 6. 1, 3, 5, 7. & 17. 1. & 21. 9.
John 5. 40. ye will not *c.* to me to
6. 44. no man can *c.* to me, except
7. 37. if any man thirst, let him *c.*
Acts 16. 9. *c.* over, and help us
1 Cor. 11. 26. show the Lord's death till he *c.*
2 Cor. 6. 17. *c.* out from among them
7. 25. save them that *c.* to God by
10. 37. he that shall *c.* will *c.*
Rev. 18. 4. *c.* out of her, my people
22. 7. I *c.* quickly, 12. 20.
17. Spirit and the bride say, *c.* athirst *c.*
20. amen, even so *c.* Lord Jesus
Ps. 118. 26. that *cometh* in the name
Eccl. 11. 8. all that *c.* is vanity
Matt. 3. 11. he that *c.* after me, is mightier
Luke 6. 47. whosoever *c.* to me and
John 3. 31. he that *c.* from above, is above all
6. 37. *c.* to me, I will in no wise cast
45. hath learned of Father, *c.* unto me
14. 6. no man *c.* to Father, but
Heb. 11. 6. that *c.* to God must
Jas. 1. 17. gift *c.* down from Father
Heb. 10. 1. make the *comers* perfect
Ps. 19. 5. as a bridegroom *coming*
121. 8. Lord shall preserve thy *c.* in
Mal. 3. 2. who may abide the day of his *c.*
4. 5. before the *c.* of the great day
Matt. 24. 3. what shall be sign of thy *c.*
27. so shall the *c.* of Son of man
48. my Lord delayeth his *c.*, Luke 12. 45.
John 1. 27. *c.* after me is preferred before
1 Cor. 1. 7. waiting for the *c.* of our
1 Cor. 15. 23. that are Christ's at his *c.*
1 Pet. 2. 4. to whom *c.* as to a living
2 Pet. 1. 16. the power and *c.* of
3. 12. hasting unto *c.* of day of God
1 Thes. 4. 15. *coming of the Lord*, 2 Thes. 2. 1. Jas. 5. 7, 8.
COMELY, 1 Sam. 16. 18. Job 41. 12.
Ps. 33. 1. praise is *c.* for the upright, 147. 1.
Prov. 30. 29. yea, four are *c.* in go.
S. of S. 1. 5. I am black but *c.*
10. thy cheeks are *c.* with rows
2. 14. thy countenance is *c.*
6. 4. thou art *c.* as Jerusalem
1 Cor. 7. 35. for that which is *c.*
Isa. 53. 2. no form nor *comeliness*
Ezek. 16. 14. perfect through my *c.*
R. V. Prov. 30. 29. stately; 1 Cor. 7. 35; 11. 13. seemly; Ezek. 16. 14. majesty
COMFORT in my affliction, Ps. 119. 50.
Matt. 9. 22. be of good *c.*, Mark 10. 49. Luke 8. 48. 2 Cor. 13. 11.
Acts 9. 31. walking in *c.* of the
Rom. 15. 4. patience and *c.* of the
1 Cor. 14. 3. to exhortation and *c.*
2 Cor. 7. 4. I am filled with *c.*
Col. 4. 11. have been a *c.* to me
Job 7. 13. my bed shall *c.* me
Ps. 23. 4. thy rod and staff they *c.*
119. 82. when wilt thou *c.* me
S. of S. 2. 5. *c.* me with apples, for
Isa. 40. 1. *c.* ye, *c.* ye my people
51. 3. Lord shall *c.* Zion, Zech. 1. 17.
61. 2. to *c.* all that mourn
Jer. 31. 13. I will *c.* and make them
Lam. 1. 2. none to *c.* her, 21.
2 Cor. 1. 4. be able to *c.* them — by *c.*
Eph. 6. 22. might *c.* your hearts
1 Thes. 4. 18. *c.* one another with
5. 14. *c.* the feeble minded, support
2 Thes. 2. 17. *c.* your heart and
Isa. 40. 2. *comfortably*, Hos. 2. 14.
2 Sam. 19. 7. 2 Chron. 30. 22. & 32. 6.
Gen. 24. 67. *comforted*, 37. 35.
Ps. 77. 2. my soul refused to be *c.*
119. 52. I have *c.* myself
Isa. 49. 13. God hath *c.* his people
Matt. 5. 4. that mourn, they shall be *c.*
Luke 16. 25. now is he *c.* and thou
Rom. 1. 12. I may be *c.* together
1 Cor. 14. 31. learn and all may be *c.*
2 Cor. 1. 4. wherewith we ourselves are *c.*
Col. 2. 2. that their hearts might be *c.*
1 Thes. 3. 7. were *c.* over you in all
John 14. 16, 26. *comforter*, 15. 26. & 16. 7.
Job 16. 2. *comforter*, Ps. 69. 20.
Isa. 51. 12. I am he that *comforteth*
2 Cor. 1. 4. *c.* us in all our tribula.
John 14. 18. *comfortless*
Ps. 94. 19. *comforts*, Isa. 57. 18.
R. V. Mal. 9. 22; Mark 10. 49. cheer; 1 Cor. 14. 3; Phil. 2. 1. consolation; 1 Thes. 2. 11. encouraging; 5. 11. exhort one another
COMMAND, Ex. 8. 27. & 18. 23.
Gen. 18. 19. he will *c.* his children
Lev. 25. 21. I will *c.* my blessing
Deut. 28. 8. Lord shall *c.* the bless.
Ps. 42. 8. Lord will *c.* his loving kindness
44. 4. *c.* deliverance for Jacob
Isa. 45. 11. work of my hands, *c.* ye
Matt. 4. 3. *c.* that these stones be
John 15. 14. if ye do whatsoever I *c.*
1 Cor. 7. 10. unto the unmarried I *c.*
2 Thes. 3. 4. do things which we *c.*
1 Tim. 4. 11. these things *c.* and
Ps. 68. 28. God hath *commanded* thy strength
111. 9. he hath *c.* his covenant
133. 3. *c.* blessing, even life for
Matt. 28. 20. whatsoever I have *c.* you
Heb. 12. 20. could not endure that was *c.*
Lam. 3. 37. when Lord *commandeth*
Acts 17. 30. now *c.* all men every.
Gen. 49. 33. end of *commanding* his
1 Tim. 4. 3. *c.* to abstain from meats
Num. 23. 20. receive *commandment* to bless
Ps. 119. 96. thy *c.* is exceed. broad
Prov. 6. 23. the *c.* is a lamp
Hos. 5. 11. willingly walked after *c.*
Matt. 22. 38. is the first and great *c.*
John 10. 18. this *c.* I received of
12. 49. the Father gave me a *c.*
50. his *c.* is life everlasting
13. 34. a new *c.* give I unto you
15. 12. this is my *c.* that ye love
Rom. 7. 8. sin taking occasion by *c.*
1 Tim. 1. 5. end of the *c.* is charity
Heb. 7. 16. law of a carnal *c.*
2 Pet. 2. 21. turn from the holy *c.*
1 John 2. 7. an old *c.* which ye had
Ex. 34. 28. wrote ten *commandments*, Deut. 4. 13. & 10. 4.
Ps. 111. 7. all his *c.* are sure
112. 1. delight greatly in his *c.*
119. 6. I have respect unto all thy *c.*
10. let me not wander from thy *c.*
19. hide not thy *c.* from me
21. which do not err from thy *c.*
35. make me to go in path of thy *c.*
47. I will delight myself in thy *c.*
48. thy *c.* which I have loved
66. I have believed thy *c.*
86. all thy *c.* are faithful
98. thy *c.* hath made me wiser
127. I love thy *c.*
131. longed for *c.*
143. thy *c.* are my delights
151. all thy *c.* are truth
166. I have done thy *c.*
172. all thy *c.* are righteousness
176. I do not forget thy *c.*
Matt. 15. 9. for doctrines *c.* of men
Matt. 22. 40. on these two *c.* hang all
Mark 10. 19. knowest the *c.*, Luke 18. 20.
Luke 1. 6. walking in all the *c.* of
Col. 2. 22. after the *c.* of men
1 John 3. 24. keepeth his *c.* dwelleth
2 John 6. love that walk after his *c.*
Num. 15. 40. *do all, — these, — my*

— *his c.*, Deut. 6. 25. & 15. 5. & 28. 1, 15. & 19. 9. & 27. 10. & 30. 8. 1 Chron. 28. 7. Neh. 10. 29. Ps. 103. 18, 20. & 111. 10. Rev. 22. 14.
R. V. very frequently, especially in N. T., charged or enjoined. Frequently, word, decree, precept, charge, statute.

COMMEND, Gen. 12. 15. Rom. 16. 1. 2 Cor. 3. 1. & 5. 12. & 10. 12.
Luke 23. 46. into thy hands I *c.*
Acts 20. 32. I *c.* you to God and to
14. 13. *commended* them to Lord
Luke 16. 8. Lord *c.* unjust steward
Rom. 5. 8. God *commendeth* his love
1 Cor. 8. 8. meat *c.* us not to God
2 Cor. 4. 2. *commending* ourselves to every man's conscience
6. 4. *c.* ourselves as ministers of
2 Cor. 3. 1. epistles of *commendation*
Ezra 8. 36. *commission*, Acts 26. 12.

COMMIT adultery, thou shalt not, Ex. 20. 14. Deut. 5. 18. Matt. 5. 27. & 19. 18. Rom. 13. 9. Lev. 5. 17. Luke 18. 20.
Gen. 39. 8, 22. *c.* or to *give in charge*
Job 5. 8. to God would I *c.* my cause
Ps. 31. 5. into thy hands I *c.* my
37. 5. *c.* thy way unto the Lord
Prov. 16. 3. *c.* thy works unto Lord
Luke 12. 48. *c.* things worthy of
John 2. 24. did not *c.* himself to
Rom. 1. 32. *c.* such things worthy
1 Tim. 1. 18. this charge I *c.* unto
Jer. 2. 13. *committed* two evils
Luke 12. 48. men have *c.* much
1 Tim. 1. 11. gospel *c.* to my trust, 1 Cor. 9. 17. 2 Cor. 5. 19. Tit. 1. 3. Gal. 2. 7.
6. 20. keep that which is *c.* to thee
2 Tim. 1. 12. which I have *c.* to him
1 Pet. 2. 23. *c.* himself to him that judgeth righteously
Jude 15. which they have ungodly *c.*
Ps. 10. 14. poor *committeth* himself
John 8. 34. who *c.* sin is the servant
1 John 3. 8. who *c.* sin is of the devil

COMMON, Num. 16. 29. 1 Sam. 21. 4, 5. Eccl. 6. 1. Ezek. 23. 42.
Acts 2. 44. had all things *c.*, 4. 32.
1 Cor. 10. 13. temptation *c.* to man
Tit. 1. 4. son after the *c.* faith
Jude 3. write of the *c.* salvation
Eph. 2. 12. *commonwealth* of Israel
Matt. 28. 15. *commonly*, 1 Cor. 5. 1.
R. V. Eccl. 6. 1. heavy upon; Jer. 31. 5. enjoy the fruits thereof; Acts 5. 18. public; 1 Cor. 10. 13. can bear; Matt. 28. 15. was spread abroad; 1 Cor. 5. 1. actually

COMMUNE with your own heart, Ps. 4. 4. & 77. 6. Eccl. 1. 16.
R. V. Gen. 42. 24; 43. 19; Judg. 9. 1; 1 Sam. 25. 39. spake; Zech. 1. 14. talked

COMMUNICATE to him that teacheth in all good things, Gal. 6. 6.
Phil. 4. 14. *c.* with my affliction
1 Tim. 6. 18. distribute, willing to *c.*
Heb. 13. 16. to *c.* forget not
Gal. 2. 2. *communicated* to them the
Phil. 4. 15. no church *c.* with me in
2 Kings 9. 11. *communication*
Matt. 5. 37. let your *c.* be yea, nay
Eph. 4. 29. let no corrupt *c.* proceed
Luke 24. 17. what manner of *c.* are
1 Cor. 15. 33. evil *c.* corrupt good
10. 16. *communion* of the blood of Christ — *c.* of the body of Christ
2 Cor. 6. 14. what *c.* hath light
13. 14. *c.* of the Holy Ghost be with
R. V. Gal. 2. 2. laid before them; Phil. 4. 14, 15. had fellowship; 2 Kings 9. 11. talk; Matt. 5. 37; Eph. 4. 29. speech; Col. 3. 8. speaking; Phile. 6. fellowship

COMPACT, Ps. 122. 3. Eph. 4. 16.

COMPANY, Gen. 32. 8, 21.
Ps. 55. 14. to the house of God in *c.*
Prov. 29. 3. keepeth *c.* with harlots
S. of S. 6. 13. as the *c.* of two armies
Acts 4. 23. went to their own *c.*
Rom. 15. 24. first filled with your *c.*
1 Cor. 5. 11. not to keep *c.* with
2 Thes. 3. 14. have no *c.* with him
Heb. 12. 22. innumerable *c.* of angels
Ps. 119. 63. I am a *companion* of all
Mal. 2. 14. thy *c.* and wife of cove.
Phil. 2. 25. Epaphroditus my *c.* in
Rev. 1. 9. your *c.* in tribulation
Ps. 45. 14. *companions* that follow
122. 8. for my *c.* sakes — peace be
S. of S. 1. 7. aside by flocks of thy *c.*
Isa. 1. 23. princes *c.* of thieves
Heb. 10. 33. became *c.* of them
R. V. Num. 14. 7; 16. 16; 22. 4. congregation; Luke 5. 29; 23. 27. multitude; Acts 17. 5. crowd; Heb. 12. 22. hosts; Job 41. 6. bands of fishermen; 1 Chron. 27. 33. friend; Phil. 2. 25. fellow-worker; Rev. 1. 9. partaker with you

COMPARE, Isa. 40. 18. & 46. 5.
Ps. 89. 6. who in heaven can be *c.* to
Prov. 3. 15. not to be *c.* to wisdom, 8. 11.
S. of S. 1. 9. I have *c.* my love to company
Rom. 8. 18. not worthy to be *c.*
1 Cor. 2. 13. *c.* spiritual things with
Judg. 8. 2. *comparison*, Hag. 2. 3. Mark 4. 30.
R. V. Mark 4. 30. set it forth

COMPASS, Ex. 27. 5. & 38. 4. 2 Sam. 5. 23. 2 Kings 3. 9. Prov. 8. 27.
Ps. 5. 12. with favor *c.* him about
Isa. 50. 11. *c.* yourselves with sparks
Jer. 31. 22. a woman shall *c.* a man
Hab. 1. 4. wicked doth *c.* about the
Matt. 23. 15. ye *c.* sea and land to
Ps. 16. 4. sorrow *compassed* me, 116. 3.
Jonah 2. 3. floods *c.* me about, 5.
Heb. 12. 1. we are *c.* about with a
Ps. 73. 6. pride *compasseth* them
Hos. 11. 12. Ephraim *c.* me about
R. V. Prov. 8. 27. circle; Isa. 44. 13. compasses; 2 Kings 3. 9; Acts 28. 13. made circuit. Frequently in O. T., turned about

COMPASSION, 1 Kings 8. 50. 2 Chron. 30. 9. 1 John 3. 17.
Matt. 9. 36. *moved with compassion*, 14. 14. & 18. 27.
Ps. 78. 38. *full of compassion*, 86. 15. & 111. 4. & 112. 4. & 145. 8.
Deut. 13. 17. *have compassion*, 33. 3. 2 Kings 13. 23. 2 Chron. 36. 15. Jer. 12. 15. Lam. 3. 32. Mic. 7. 19. Rom. 9. 15. Heb. 5. 2. & 10. 34. Jude 22.
Lam. 3. 22. his *compassions* fail not
R. V. Matt. 18. 33; Mark 5. 19; Jude 22. mercy; Heb. 5. 2. bear gently with

COMPEL them to come in, Luke 14. 23.
Esth. 1. 8. drinking, none did *c.*
2 Chron. 21. 11. *compelled* Judah
Acts 26. 11. I *c.* them to blaspheme
2 Cor. 12. 11. I am a fool, ye *c.* me
Gal. 2. 3. not *c.* to be circumcised
14. why *compellest* Gentiles to live
R. V. 1 Sam. 28. 23; Luke 14. 23. constrain

COMPLAIN, Num. 11. 11. Job 7. 11.
Lam. 3. 39. why doth a living man *c.*
Num. 11. 1. *complainers*, Jude 16.
Ps. 144. 14. *complaining* in streets
Job 21. 4. *complaint*, 23. 2. Ps. 142. 2.
R. V. Acts 25. 7. bringing charges

COMPLETE in him, Col. 2. 10.
4. 12. stand *c.* in all the will of God
R. V. Col. 2. 10. made full; 4. 12. fully assured

COMPREHEND, Job 37. 5. Eph. 3. 18. Isa. 40. 12. John 1. 4. Rom. 13. 9.
R. V. John 1. 5; Eph. 3. 18. apprehend; Rom. 3. 9. summed up

CONCEAL his blood, Gen. 37. 26.
Job 27. 11. with Almighty I will not *c.*
Job 41. 12. I will not *c.* parts nor proportion
Prov. 25. 2. glory of God to *c.* a thing
Ps. 40. 10. I have not *concealed* thy loving kindness
Prov. 12. 23. prudent man *concealeth* knowledge
R. V. Job 6. 10. denied; 4. 12. keep silence concerning

CONCEIT, own, Prov. 18. 11. & 26. 5, 12, 16. & 28. 11. Rom. 11. 25. & 12. 16.
R. V. Prov. 18. 11. imagination

CONCEIVE, Judg. 13. 3. Luke 1. 31.
Job 15. 35. they *c.* mischief, Isa. 59. 4.
Ps. 51. 6. in sin did my mother *c.*
Isa. 7. 14. a virgin shall *c.* a son
Num. 11. 12. have I *conceived* all this people
Ps. 7. 14. hath *c.* mischief — falsehood
Jer. 49. 30. *c.* a purpose against you
Acts 5. 4. why hast thou *c.* in thy heart

CONCISION, Phil. 3. 2.

CONCLUDED them all in unbelief, Rom. 11. 32.
Gal. 3. 22. Scripture *c.* all under sin
Eccl. 12. 13. *conclusion* of matter
R. V. Rom. 11. 32. shut up; Acts 21. 25. given judgment

CONCUPISCENCE, sinful lust. Rom. 7. 8. Col. 3. 5. 1 Thes. 4. 5.
R. V. Rom. 7. 8. coveting; Col. 3. 5. desire; 1 Thes. 4. 5. lust

CONDEMN wicked, Deut. 25. 1.
Job 9. 20. my own mouth shall *c.*
Ps. 37. 33. nor *c.* him when he is judged
94. 21. they *c.* innocent blood
Isa. 50. 9. Lord will help me who *c.* me
Luke 6. 37. *c.* not and ye shall not be *c.*
John 3. 17. God sent not his Son into the world to *c.* the world
1 John 3. 20. heart *c.* us, 21.
Matt. 12. 37. by words—*condemned*
John 3. 18. who believe is not *c.*
Rom. 8. 3. for sin *c.* sin in the flesh
1 Cor. 11. 32. not be *c.* with world
Tit. 2. 8. speech that cannot be *c.*
Prov. 17. 15. *condemneth* the just
Rom. 8. 34. who is he that c.
Luke 23. 40. same *condemnation*
John 3. 19. this is the *c.* that light
Rom. 8. 1. no *c.* to them in Christ
1 Tim. 3. 6. fall into *c.* of the devil
Jas. 3. 1. receive the greater *c.*
5. 12. swear not, lest ye fall into *c.*
R. V. Ps. 109. 31; John 3. 17. judge; John 3. 19; 5. 24; 1 Cor. 11. 34; Jas. 5. 12. judgment

CONDESCEND, Rom. 12. 16. to low

CONFESS, Lev. 5. 5. & 16. 21.
Lev. 26. 40. if they *c.* their iniquit.
Ps. 32. 5. I will *c.* my transgres.
Matt. 10. 32. shall *c.* me before men
Luke 12. 8. him will I *c.* before my
Rom. 10. 9. *c.* with thy mouth
Jas. 5. 16. *c.* your faults one to
1 John 1. 9. if we *c.* our sins, he is faithful
4. 15. *c.* Jesus is Son of God, 2. 3. 2 John 7.
Heb. 11. 13. *confessed*, Ezra 10. 1.
Prov. 28. 13. *confesseth* and forsak.
Josh. 7. 19. *confession*, 2 Chron. 30. 22. Ezra 10. 11. Dan. 9. 4.
1 Tim. 6. 13. witnessed a good *c.*

CONFIDENCE, Job 4. 6. & 31. 24.
Ps. 65. 5. *c.* of all the ends of the earth
118. 8. than to put *c.* in man
Prov. 3. 26. Lord shall be thy *c.*
Mic. 7. 5. put not *c.* in a guide,
Phil. 3. 3. have no *c.* in the flesh
Heb. 3. 6. if we hold fast the *c.*, 14.
10. 35. cast not away your *c.*
1 John 2. 28. appear we may have *c.*
Ps. 27. 2. *confident*, Prov. 14. 16.

R. V. Judg. 9. 26. trust; Acts 28. 31; Heb. 3. 6; 10. 35; 1 John 2. 28; 3. 21. boldness; 2 Cor. 5. 6, 8. of good courage
CONFIRM feeble knees, Isa. 35. 3.
Dan. 9. 27. shall *c*. the covenant
Rom. 15. 8. to *c*. the promises
1 Cor. 1. 8. shall *c*. you to the end
Isa. 44. 26. *confirmeth* word of his servant
Acts 14. 22. *confirming* souls of the
R. V. 2 Kings 14. 5; 1 Chron. 14. 2. established; Dan. 9. 27. made firm; Heb. 6. 17. interposed with
CONFLICT, Phil. 1. 30. Col. 2. 1.
CONFORMED to the image, Rom. 8. 29.
Rom. 12. 2. be not *c*. to this world
R. V. Rom. 12. 2. fashioned according
CONFOUND language, Gen. 11. 7.
Jer. 1. 17. lest I *c*. thee before them
1 Cor. 1. 27. foolish things to *c*. wise
Ps. 97. 7. *confounded* that serve
Jer. 17. 18. let not me be *c*.
Ezek. 16. 52. *c*. and bear shame, 54.
1 Pet. 2. 6. believeth shall not be *c*.
Ezra 9. 7. *confusion* of face, Dan. 9. 7, 8.
Ps. 44. 15. my *c*. is continually
1 Cor. 14. 33. God is not author of *c*.
R. V. Jer. 1. 17. dismay; 1 Cor. 1. 27. that he might put to shame; Ps. 66. 6. brought to dishonor; 83. 17; Ezek. 16. 54; Mic. 7. 16. ashamed; Jer. 10. 14; 46. 24; 50. 2. put to shame
CONGREGATION, Lev. 4. 21.
Job 15. 34. *c*. of hypocrites desolate
Ps. 1. 5. sinners in *c*. of righteous
26. 5. hated *c*. of evil doers
74. 19. forget not *c*. of thy poor
89. 5. faithfulness in *c*. of saints
Prov. 21. 16. remain in *c*. of dead
Hos. 7. 12. chastise as *c*. hath heard
Joel 2. 16. sanctify the *c*.
R. V. in O. T. generally, assembly, meeting; Acts 13. 43. synagogue
CONIES, Ps. 104. 18. Prov. 30. 26.
CONQUER, Rev. 6. 2.
Rom. 8. 37. more than *conquerors*
CONSCIENCE, John 8. 9. Acts 23. 1.
Acts 24. 16. a *c*. void of offence
Rom. 2. 15. *c*. bearing witness, 9. 1.
2 Cor. 1. 12. estimony of our *c*.
1 Tim. 3. 9. mystery of faith in
Tit. 1. 15. mind and *c*. is defiled
Heb. 9. 14. purge *c*. from dead
10. 2. worshippers no more *c*. of
Acts 23. 1. *good conscience*, 1 Tim. 1. 5. Heb. 13. 18. 1 Pet. 3. 21.
R. V. John 8. 9 ——
CONSENT, with one, Ps. 83. 5. Zeph. 3. 9. Luke 14. 18. 1 Cor. 7. 5.
Prov. 1. 10. entice thee, *c*. thou not
Rom. 7. 16. I *c*. to law that it is
Ps. 50. 18. *consentedst* to thief
Acts 8. 1. *consenting*, 22. 20.
R. V. 1 Sam. 11. 7. as one man; Dan. 1. 14. hearkened unto
CONSIDER, Lev. 13. 13. Judg. 18. 14.
Deut. 4. 39. *c*. it in thy heart
32. 29. O that—*c*. their latter end
Ps. 8. 3. when I *c*. the heavens
Eccl. 5. 1. *c*. not that they do evil
7. 13. *c*. the work of God
Isa. 1. 3. my people doth not *c*.
5. 12. neither *c*. operation of hands
Hag. 1. 5, 7. Lord *c*. your ways, 2. 15, 18.
2 Tim. 2. 7. *c*. what I say and Lord
Heb. 3. 1. *c*. apostle and high priest
10. 24. *c*. one another to provoke
12. 3. *c*. him that endured such
Job 1. 8. hast thou *considered* my
Ps. 31. 7. hast *c*. my trouble
Mark 6. 52. *c*. not miracle of loaves
Rom. 4. 19. *c*. not his own body
Matt. 7. 3. *considerest* not the beam
Ps. 41. 1. blessed *considereth* poor
Prov. 31. 16. she *c*. a field and buy.
Isa. 44. 19. none *c*. in his heart

Heb. 13. 7. *considering* end of conversation
R. V. Jer. 23. 20; 32. 24. understand; Lam. 1. 11; 2. 20; 5. 1. behold; Mark 6. 52. understood
CONSIST. Col. 1. 17. Luke 12. 15.
CONSOLATION, Acts 4. 36. & 15. 31.
Luke 2. 25. waited for *c*. of Israel
Rom. 15. 5. God of *c*. grant you be
2 Cor. 1. 5. so our *c*. aboundeth by
Phil. 2. 1. if any *c*. in Christ
2 Thes. 2. 16. given us everlasting *c*.
Heb. 6. 18. might have strong *c*.
Job 15. 11. *consolations*
R. V. Acts 4. 36. exhortation; Rom. 15. 5; 2 Cor. 1. 5; 7. 7; 2 Thes. 2. 16; Phile. 7. comfort; Heb. 6. 18. encouragement
CONSPIRACY against Christ, Matt. 26. 3; Mark 3. 6; 14. 1; Luke 22. 2; John 11. 55; 13. 18.
against Paul, Acts 23. 12.
CONSTANCY of Ruth, Ruth 1. 14.
Rom. 16. 3. of Priscilla and Aquila
CONSTRAIN, Gal. 6. 12. Acts 16. 15.
2 Cor. 5. 14. for the love of Christ *constraineth* us because we
1 Pet. 5. 2. not by *constraint*
R. V. Gal. 6. 12. compel
CONSUME, Deut. 5. 25. & 7. 16.
Ex. 33. 3. lest I *c*. thee in the way
Ps. 37. 20. they shall *c*. into smoke
78. 33. days did he *c*. in vanity
Ezek. 4. 17. *c*. away for iniquity
2 Thes. 2. 8. Lord shall *c*. with spirit
Jas. 4. 3. *c*. it upon your lusts
Ex. 3. 2. bush was not *consumed*
Ps. 90. 7. we are *c*. by thy anger
Prov. 5. 11. thy flesh and body are *c*.
Isa. 64. 7. *c*. us because of our
Lam. 3. 22. of Lord's mercy we are not *c*.
Gal. 5. 15. be not *c*. one of another
Deut. 4. 24. Lord is *consuming* fire
Lev. 26. 16. *consumption*, Deut. 28. 22. Isa. 10. 22, 23. & 28. 22.
R. V. Frequently in O. T. devour; 2 Thes. 2. 8. Jesus shall slay
CONTAIN, Ezek. 23. 32. & 45. 11.
1 Kings 8. 27. heaven of heavens cannot *c*. thee, 2 Chron. 2. 6. & 6. 18.
John 21. 25. world not *c*. the books
1 Cor. 7. 9. if they cannot *c*. let
R. V. 1 Cor. 7. 9. have not continency
CONTEMN, God, — wicked, Ps. 10. 13.
Ezek. 21. 13. if sword *c*. the rod, 10.
Ps. 15. 4. a vile person is *contemned*
Job 12. 21. pours *contempt* on prin.
Ps. 123. 3. filled with *c*., 4.
Dan. 12. 2. some to everlasting *c*.
Mal. 1. 7. the table of the Lord is *contemptible*
2. 9. made you *c*. before all people
2 Cor. 10. 10. his speech is *c*.
R. V. Ps. 15. 4. despised
CONTEND, Deut. 2. 9. Job 9. 3.
Isa. 49. 25. I will *c*. with them that *c*.
Jer. 12. 5. how canst *c*. with horses
Amos 7. 4. Lord calleth to *c*. by fire
Jude 3. *c*. earnestly for the faith
Job 10. 2. cause why thou *contendest*
40. 2. that *contendeth* with the mighty instruct
Hab. 1. 3. *contention*, Acts 15. 39. 1. 16. 1 Thes. 2. 2.
Prov. 13. 10. by pride cometh *c*.
Jer. 15. 10. borne me a man of *c*.
Prov. 18. 18, 19. *contentions*, 19. 13. & 23. 29. & 27. 15. 1 Cor. 1. 11. Tit. 3. 9.
21. 19. *contentious*, 26. 21. & 27. 15. Rom. 2. 8. 1 Cor. 11. 16.
R. V. Prov. 29. 9. hath controversy
CONTENT, Gen. 37. 27. Luke 3. 14.
Phil. 4. 11. state therewith to be *c*.
1 Tim. 6. 8. raiment let us be *c*.
Heb. 13. 5. be *c*. with such things
3 John 10. with malicious words not *c*.

1 Tim. 6. 6. godliness with *contentment*
CONTINUAL, Ex. 29. 42. Num. 4. 7. Prov. 15. 15. Isa. 14. 6. Rom. 9. 2.
Gen. 6. 5. only evil *continually*
Ps. 34. 1. his praise *c*. in my
71. 3. I may *c*. resort
73. 23. yet I am *c*. with thee
119. 44. keep thy law *c*. for ever
Prov. 6. 21. bind them *c*. upon thy
Isa. 58. 11. Lord shall guide thee *c*.
Hos. 12. 6. wait on thy God *c*.
Acts 6. 4. give ourselves *c*. to prayer
Heb. 13. 15. sacrifice of praise to God *c*.
Deut. 28. 59. *continuance*, Ps. 139. 16. Isa. 64. 5. Rom. 2. 7.
R. V. Rom. 9. 2. unceasing; 1 Chron. 16. 11. evermore; Ps. 44. 15. all day long; 58. 7. apace; 109. 10——; Ps. 139. 16. day by day; Isa. 64. 5. them have we been of long time; Rom. 2. 7. patience
CONTINUE, Ex. 21. 21. Lev. 12. 4.
1 Sam. 12. 14. *c*. following the Lord
1 Kings 2. 4. Lord may *c*. his word
Ps. 36. 10. *c*. thy loving-kindness
John 8. 31. if ye *c*. in my word
15. 9. *c*. ye in my love, 10.
Acts 13. 43. to *c*. in grace of God
14. 22. to *c*. in the faith
Rom. 6. 1. shall we c. in sin that
11. 22. if thou *c*. in his goodness
Col. 1. 23. if ye *c*. in faith and not
4. 2. *c*. in prayer and watch
1 Tim. 2. 15. if they *c*. in faith
4. 16. doctrine *c*. in them
2 Tim. 3. 14. *c*. in things learned
Heb. 13. 1. let brotherly love *c*.
Rev. 13. 5. to *c*. forty-two months
Gen. 40. 4. *continued*, Neh. 5. 16.
Luke 6. 12. *c*. all night in prayer
22. 28. *c*. with me in temptations
Acts 1. 14. *c*. with one accord in
Heb. 8. 9. *c*. not in my covenant
1 John 2. 19. would have *c*. with us
Job 14. 2. shadow and *continueth* not
Gal. 3. 10. that *c*. not in all things
1 Tim. 5. 5. *c*. in supplication
Jas. 1. 25. looketh into the law and *c*.
Jer. 30. 23. *continuing*, Rom. 12. 12. Acts 2. 46. Heb. 13. 14.
R. V. John 2. 12; 8. 31; 15. 9. abide, abode; Acts 15. 35. tarried; 18. 11. dwelt; 20. 7. prolonged; in O. T. frequent changes to, abide
CONTRADICT-ING-ION, Acts 13. 45. Heb. 7. 7. & 12. 3.
R. V. Heb. 7. 7. any dispute; 12. 3. gainsaying
CONTRARY, Esth. 9. 1. Matt. 14. 24.
Lev. 26. 21. walk *c*. to, 23. 27, 28, 40, 41.
Acts 18. 13. *c*. to the law, 23. 3.
26. 9. many things *c*. to the name
Rom. 11. 24. grafted *c*. to nature
1 Thes. 2. 15. are *c*. to all men
1 Tim. 1. 10. is *c*. to sound doctrine
CONTRIBUTION, Rom. 15. 26.
CONTRITE heart, or spirit, Ps. 34. 18. & 51. 17. Isa. 57. 15, 16. & 66. 2.
CONTROVERSY, Deut. 17. 8. & 21. 5. & 25. 1. 2 Chron. 19. 8. Ezek. 44. 24.
Jer. 25. 31. Lord hath a *c*., Isa. 34. 8. Hos. 4. 1. & 12. 2. Mic. 6. 2.
1 Tim. 3. 16. without *c*. great is the
R. V. 2 Sam. 15. 2. suit
CONVENIENT, Jer. 40. 4, 5. Acts 24. 25.
Prov. 30. 8. feed with food *c*. for me
Rom. 1. 28. to do things — not *c*.
Phile. 8. to enjoin thee which is *c*.
R. V. Prov. 30. 8. that is needful; Rom. 1. 28. fitting; Eph. 5. 4; Phile. 8. befitting; 1 Cor. 16. 12. opportunity
CONVERSATION, Gal. 1. 13. Eph. 2. 3. & 4. 22. Heb. 13. 7. 1 Tim. 4. 12.

Ps. 37. 14. such as be of upright *c.*
50. 23. orders his *c.* aright, I will
2 Cor. 1. 12. in sincerity had our *c.*
Phil. 1. 27. let *c.* be as becometh
Heb. 13. 5. let *c.* be without covetousness
Jas. 3. 13. show out of good *c.* works
1 Pet. 1. 15. holy in all manner of *c.*
2 Pet. 2. 7. vexed with filthy *c.* of the
3. 11. in all holy *c.* and godliness
R. V. Ps. 37. 14. in the way; Gal. 1. 13; Phil. 1. 27; 1 Tim. 4. 12; 1 Pet. 3. 16. manner of life; 1 Pet. 2. 12; 3. 1. behavior; Heb. 13. 7; 2 Pet. 2. 7. life; 2 Pet. 3. 11. living
CONVERSION of Gentiles, Acts 15. 3.
CONVERT, and be healed, Isa. 6. 10.
Jas. 5. 19. err, and one *c.* him, 20.
Ps. 51. 13. sinners—*converted* to thee
Isa. 60. 5. abundance of the sea, *c.* to thee
Matt. 13. 15. should be *c.* and I heal
Luke 22. 32. when thou art *c.* strengthen
Acts 3. 19. repent and be *c.*
Ps. 19. 7. *converting* the soul
R. V. Ps. 19. 7. restoring; Isa. 60. 5. turned; Matt. 13. 15; 18. 3; Mark 4. 12; Luke 22. 32; John 12. 40; Acts 3. 19; 28. 27. turn, or turn again
CONVINCE, Tit. 1. 9. Jude 15.
Job 32. 12. *convinced*, Acts 18. 28. 1 Cor. 14. 24. Jas. 2. 9.
John 8. 46. who *convinceth* me of sin
R. V. 1 Cor. 14. 24. reproved by; Acts 18. 28. comforted; John 8. 46; Tit. 1. 9; Jas. 2. 9; Jude 15. convict
COPY of the law to be written by the king, Deut. 17. 18.
CORD, Josh. 2. 15. Mic. 2. 5.
Job 30. 11. he hath loosed my *c.*
Eccl. 4. 12. a threefold *c.* is not brok.
Isa. 54. 2. lengthen thy *c.* and strengthen
Job 36. 8. holden *in cords* of affliction
Ps. 2. 3. cast away their *c.* from us
Prov. 5. 22. holden with *c.* of his sins
Isa. 5. 18. draw iniquity with *c.* of vanity
Hos. 11. 4. drew them with *c.* of
R. V. Judg. 15. 13. ropes; Mic. 2. 5. the line
CORN, Gen. 41. 57. & 42. 2, 19.
Josh. 5. 11. eat of the old *c.* of the land, 12.
Job 5. 26. as a shock of *c.* cometh in
Ps. 65. 13. valleys covered with *c.*
72. 16. handful of *c.* in the earth
Prov. 11. 26. withholdeth *c.* people curse
Isa 62. 8. I will no more give *c.* to
Ezek. 36. 29. call for *c.* and increase
Hos. 2. 9. take away my *c.* in
10. 11. loveth to tread out the *c.*
14. 7. shall revive as *c.* and grow as
Zech. 9. 17. *c.* make young men cheer.
Matt. 12. 1. to pluck the ears of *c.*
John 12. 24. except *c.* of wheat fall
R. V. Matt. 12. 1. cornfield; John 12. 24. grain
CORNER, Prov. 7. 8, 12. Lev. 21. 5.
Prov. 21. 9. better dwell in *c.*, 25. 24.
Isa. 30. 20. teachers removed into *c.*
Zech. 10. 4. out of him came forth *c.*
Matt. 21. 42. become head of *c.*
Ps. 118. 22. *corner stone*, Isa. 28. 16. 1 Pet. 2. 6. Eph. 2. 20. Matt. 21. 42.
R. V. Ex. 25. 12; 37. 3; 1 Kings 7. 30. feet; Ex. 30. 4; 37. 27. ribs; Ex. 36. 25; 2 Kings 11. 11. side; Zech. 10. 4. corner stone
CORRECT thy son and he, Prov. 29. 17.
Ps. 39. 11. with rebuke dost *c.* man
Jer. 2. 19. own wicked. shall *c.* thee
Job 5. 17. happy is man whom God *c.*
Prov. 3. 12. whom Lord loveth he *c.*
Job 37. 13. whether for *correction*
Prov. 3. 11. but be not weary of his *c.*
23. 13. withhold not *c.* from child
Jer. 2. 30. they received not *c.*, 5. 3. & 7. 28. Zeph. 3. 2.
Hab. 1. 12. established them for *c.*
2 Tim. 3. 16. Scripture profitable for *c.*
R. V. Prov. 3. 12. reproveth; Heb. 12. 9. to chasten; Prov. 3. 11. reproof; Jer. 7. 28. instruction
CORRUPT, Job 17. 1. Ps. 38. 5.
Gen. 6. 11, 12. earth *c.* before God.
Ps. 14. 1. they are *c.*, 53. 1. & 73. 8.
Mal. 1. 14. sacrificeth to the Lord a *c.*
Matt. 7. 17, 18. a *c.* tree brings—
Eph. 4. 22. old man which is *c.*
29. let no *c.* communication
1 Tim. 6. 5. of *c.* minds, 2 Tim. 3. 8.
Matt. 6. 19. rust doth *c.*, 20.
1 Cor. 15. 33. evil communications *c.*
Gen. 6. 12. all flesh had *corrupted* his
Deut. 9. 12. thy people *c.* themsel.
Hos. 9. 9. have deeply *c.* themselves
2 Cor. 7. 2. we have *c.* no man
1 Cor. 9. 25. *corruptible*, 15. 53. 1 Pet. 1. 18, 23.
Job 17. 14. *corruption*, Ps. 16. 10. & 49. 9. Isa. 38. 17. Dan. 10. 8. John 2. 6. Acts 2. 27, 31. & 13. 34, 37. Rom. 8. 21. 1 Cor. 15. 42, 50. Gal. 6. 8. 2 Pet. 1. 4. & 2. 12, 19.
R. V. Job. 17. 4. consumed; Ps. 73. 8. scoff; Dan. 11. 32. pervert; Mal. 1. 14. blemished; Matt. 6. 19. consume; Jude 10. destroyed; Jonah 2. 6. pit; 2 Pet. 2. 12. destroying
COST, 2 Sam. 19. 42. & 24. 24. 1 Chron. 21. 24. Luke 14. 28.
R. V. John 12. 3. precious
COUNSEL, Num. 27. 21. & 31. 16.
Job 5. 13. *c.* of froward carried headlong
12. 13. he hath *c.* and understanding
21. 16. *c.* of the wicked far, 22. 18.
38. 2. who is this that darkeneth *c.* by words without knowledge, 42. 3.
Ps. 1. 1. walks not in *c.* of ungodly
33. 10. 11. *c.* of Lord stands for ever, Prov. 1 . 21. Isa. 46. 10, 11.
55. 14. we took sweet *c.* together
Prov. 1. 25. set at nought all my *c.*
8. 14. *c.* is mine and sound wisdom
11. 14. where no *c.* is people fall
20. 18. purpose established by *c.*
24. 6. by wise *c.* make war
27. 9. sweetness—by hearty *c.*
Isa. 11. 2. spirit of *c.* and might
28. 29. Lord wonderful in *c.* and
Jer. 32. 19. God great in *c.* mighty
Zech. 6. 13. *c.* of peace between them
Luke 7. 30. rejected *c.* of God against
Acts 2. 23. by determinate *c.*, 4. 28.
20. 27. to declare all the *c.* of God
Eph. 1. 11. after *c.* of his own will
Ezra 4. 5. *counsellors*, 7. 14. Job 3. 14. & 12. 17. Dan. 3. 24.
Ps. 119. 24. thy testimonies are my *c.*
Prov. 11. 14. in the multitude of *c.* is safety, 24. 26. & 15. 22.
12. 20. to *c.* of peace is joy
Isa. 9. 6. Wonderful, *C.*, the mighty
19. 11. wise *c.* of Pharaoh—brutish
R. V. Num. 27. 21; Judg. 20. 23——; Prov. 11. 14; 24. 6. guidance; Isa. 19. 17. purpose; Acts 5. 33. were minded
COUNT, Ex. 12. 4. Lev. 23. 15.
Num. 23. 10. who can *c.* the dust of
Job 31. 4. doth not he *c.* all my steps
Ps. 139. 18. if I *c.* them—more than
22. hate thee, I *c.* them my ene.
Acts 20. 24. neither *c.* I my life dear
Phil. 3. 7, 8, 9. I *c.* all things loss—dung
13. I *c.* not myself to have apprehended
Jas. 1. 2. *c.* it all joy when ye fall
5. 11. we *c.* them happy who endure
Gen. 15. 6. *counted* to him for righteousness, Ps. 106. 31. Rom. 4. 3.
Isa. 40. 17. *c.* to him less than nothing
Hos. 8. 12. of law *c.* as a strange thing
Luke 21. 36. *c.* worthy to escape
Acts 5. 41. that *c.* worthy to suffer
2 Thes. 1. 5. *c.* worthy of kingdom
1 Tim. 1. 12. he *c.* me faithful
5. 17. *c.* worthy of double honor
Heb. 3. 3. *c.* worthy of more glory
R. V. Mark 11. 32. verily held; Rom. 2. 26; 4. 3, 5; 9. 8. reckoned
COUNTENANCE, Gen. 4. 5. & 31. 2.
Num. 6. 26. lift up his *c.* on thee
1 Sam. 1. 18. her *c.* was no more sad
16. 7. look not on his *c.* nor height
Neh. 2. 2. why is thy *c.* sad
Job 29. 24. light of thy *c.* they cast
Ps. 4. 6. lift up light of thy *c.*, 80. 3, 7.
90. 8. settest secret sins in light of *c.*
S. of S. 2. 14. let me see thy *c.* comely
Matt. 6. 16. as hypocrites of a sad *c.*
Acts 2. 28. full of joy with thy *c.*
R. V. Ex. 23. 3. favor; Ps. 11. 7; 2 Cor. 3. 7. face; Ps. 21. 6. presence; S. of S. 5. 15. aspect; Matt. 28. 3. appearance
COUNTRY, far, Matt. 21. 33. & 25. 14. Mark 12. 1. Luke 15. 13. & 19. 12. & 20. 9. Prov. 25. 25.
Heb. 11. 14. declare they seek a *c.*
16. they desire a better *c.*—heavenly
2 Cor. 11. 26. *countrymen*, 1 Thes. 2. 14.
R. V. Matt. 9. 31; Acts 7. 3. land, Matt. 14. 35; Luke 3. 3; 4. 37. region; in O. T. mostly land, region, inheritance
COURAGE, Josh. 2. 11. Acts 28. 15.
Num. 13. 20. be of good *c.*, Deut. 31. 6. & 7. 23. Josh. 1. 6, 7, 9, 18. & 10. 25. & 23. 6. 2 Sam. 10. 12. & 13. 28. 1 Chron. 22. 13. & 28. 20. Ezra 10. 4. Ps. 27. 14. & 31. 24. Isa. 41. 6.
COURSE, Acts 13. 25. & 16. 11.
Acts 20. 24. finish my *c.* with joy
2 Thes. 3. 1. may have free *c.* and
2 Tim. 4. 7. I have finished my *c.*
R. V. Acts 21. 7. voyage; 1 Cor. 17. 27. in turn; 2 Thes. 3. 1. run; Jas. 3. 6. wheel
COURT, Ex. 27. 9. Isa. 34. 13.
Amos 7. 13. Bethel is king's *c.*
Ps. 65. 4. may dwell in thy *c.*
84. 10. day in thy *courts* better
92. 13. flourish in *c.* of our God
Isa. 1. 12. who required to tread my *c.*
62. 9. drink it in *c.* of my holiness
Luke 7. 25. delicate are in king's *c.*
Rev. 11. 2. *c.* without temple leave
1 Pet. 3. 8. be pitiful, *courteous*
Acts 27. 3. *courteously*, 28. 7.
R. V. 2 Kings 20. 4. part of the city; Amos 7. 13. royal house; 1 Pet. 3. 8. humble minded; Acts 27. 3. treated kindly
COVENANT, Gen. 17. 2. & 26. 28.
Gen. 9. 12. token of the *c.*, 13. 17.
17. 4. my *c.* is with thee, 7. 19.
11. a token of the *c.* betwixt
13. my *c.* shall be in the flesh
14. he hath broken my *c.*
Ex. 2. 24. God remembered his *c.*
31. 16. sabbath for a perpetual *c.*
34. 28. wrote words of *c.*
Lev. 26. 15. ye brake my *c.*
Judg. 2. 1. never brake *c.* with you
1 Chron. 16. 15. always mindful of his *c.*, Ps. 105. 8. & 111. 5.
Neh. 9. 38. we may make a sure *c.*
Job 31. 1. I made a *c.* with mine
Ps. 25. 14. Lord will show them *c.*
44. 17. not dealt falsely in thy *c.*
55. 20. broken his *c.*, Isa. 33. 8.
74. 20. have respect to the *c.*
78. 37. not steadfast in his *c.*, 10.

Ps. 78. 28. my *c*. shall stand fast, 34.
132. 12. children will keep my *c*.
Prov. 2. 17. forgetteth *c*. of her God
Isa. 28. 18. your *c*. with death
42. 6. given thee for *c*. of people
56. 4. take hold of my *c*., 6.
Jer. 14. 21. break not *c*. with us
Ezek. 20. 37. bring into bond of *c*.
Dan. 9. 27. confirm *c*. with many
Hos. 6. 7. have transgressed the *c*.
10. 4. swearing falsely in making *c*.
Mal. 2. 14. the wife of thy *c*.
3. 1. messenger of the *c*.
Acts 3. 25. the children of the *c*.
Rom. 1. 31. *c*. breakers
Heb. 8. 6. he is the mediator of a better *c*., 7. 9.
Gen. 9. 16. *everlasting covenant*, 17. 7, 13, 19. Lev. 24. 8. 2 Sam. 23. 5. 1 Chron. 16. 17. Ps. 105. 10. Isa. 24. 5. & 55. 3. & 61. 8. Jer. 32. 40. Ezek. 16. 60. & 37. 26. Heb. 13. 20.
Gen. 17. 9, 10. *keep*, *keepest*, *keepeth*, *covenant*, Ex. 19. 5. Deut. 7. 9, 12. & 29. 9. & 33. 9. 1 Kings 8. 23. & 11. 11. 2 Chron. 6. 14. Neh. 1. 5. & 9. 32. Ps. 25. 10. & 103. 18. & 132. 12. Dan. 9. 4.
Gen. 15. 18. Lord *made covenant*, Ex. 34. 27. Deut. 5. 2, 3. 2 Kings 23. 3. Job 31. 1.
Jer. 31. 31. *new covenant*, Heb. 8. 8, 13. & 12. 24.
Gen. 9. 15. *remember covenant*, Ex. 6. 5. Lev. 26. 42, 45. Ps. 105. 8. & 106. 45. Ezek. 16. 60. Amos 1. 9. Luke 1. 72.
Lev. 2. 13. *covenant of* salt, Num. 18. 19. 2 Chron. 13. 5.
Deut. 17. 2. *transgressed the covenant*, Josh. 7. 11, 15. & 23. 16. Judg. 2. 20. 2 Kings 18. 12. Jer. 34. 18. Hos. 6. 7. & 8. 1.
Rom. 9. 4. *covenants*, Gal. 4. 24.
Eph. 2. 12. *c*. of promise
R. V. Matt. 26. 15. weighed unto

COVER, Ex. 10. 5. & 40. 3.
Ex. 21. 33. dig a pit and not *c*. it
33. 22. I will *c*. thee with my hand
Deut. 33. 12. Lord shall *c*. him all
1 Sam. 24. 3. *c*. his feet, Judg. 3. 24.
Neh. 4. 5. *c*. not their iniquity
Job 16. 18. *c*. thou not my blood
Ps. 91. 4. *c*. thee with his feathers
Isa. 58. 7. naked that thou *c*. him
11. 9. as waters *c*. sea, Hab. 2. 14.
Hos. 10. 8. say to mountains, *c*. us, Luke 23. 30. Rev. 6. 16.
1 Cor. 11. 7. man ought not *c*. head
1 Pet. 4. 8. charity shall *c*. a multi.
Job 31. 33. if I *covered* my trans.
Ps. 32. 1. whose sin is *c*., Rom. 4. 7.
85. 2. hast *c*. all their sin
Lam. 3. 44. *c*. thyself with a cloud
Matt. 10. 26. nothing *c*. that shall not
Ps. 104. 2. *coverest* thyself with
73. 6. violence *covereth* them as a
Prov. 10. 12. love *c*. all sins
Isa. 28. 20. *covering*, 1 Cor. 11. 15.
Isa. 4. 6. *covert*, 16. 4. & 32. 2. Ps. 61. 4. Jer. 25. 38.
R. V. Ex. 40. 21. screened; 1 Kings 6. 35; Prov. 26. 23. overlaid; 1 Cor. 11. 6. veiled; Ex. 35. 12; 39. 34; 40. 21. screen; Prov. 7. 16; 31. 22. carpets; Isa. 30. 22. overlaying; S. of S. 3. 10. seat

COVET, Ex. 20. 17. Mic. 2. 2.
1 Cor. 12. 31. *c*. earnestly best gifts
Acts 20. 33. *coveted*, 1 Tim. 6. 10.
Prov. 21. 26. *coveteth*, Hab. 2. 9.
Ps. 10. 3. wicked blesseth *covetous*
Luke 16. 14. Pharisees who were *c*.
1 Cor. 5. 10. or with the *c*., 11.
6. 10. nor *c*. shall inherit kingdom
Eph. 5. 5. nor *c*. who is an idolater
1 Tim. 3. 3. bishop must not be *c*.
2 Pet. 2. 14. exercised with *c*. pract.
Ex. 18. 21. hating *covetousness*
Ps. 119. 36. to testimonies and not to *c*.
Ezek. 33. 31. heart goeth after their *c*.
Luke 12. 15. beware of *c*. for man's
Col. 3. 5. *c*. which is idolatry
Heb. 13. 5. conversation without *c*.
R. V. Hab. 2. 9. getteth; 1 Cor. 12. 31. desire; 14. 39. desire earnestly; 1 Tim. 6. 10. reaching; Luke 16. 14; 1 Tim. 3. 3; 2 Tim. 3. 2. lovers of money; Ex. 18. 21. unjust gain; Ezek. 33. 31; Hab. 2. 9. gain; Mark 7. 22. covetings; 2 Cor. 9. 5. extortions; Heb. 13. 5. free from love of money

CRAFT, Dan. 8. 25. Mark 14. 1. Acts 18. 3. & 19. 25, 27. Rev. 18. 22.
Job 5. 12. disappointeth devices of the *crafty*
15. 5. uttereth iniquity, choosest tongue of *c*.
Ps. 83. 3. taken *c*. counsel against
2 Cor. 12. 16. being *c*. I caught you with guile
Job 5. 13. *craftiness*, 1 Cor. 3. 19. Luke 20. 23. 2 Cor. 4. 2. Eph. 4. 14.
R. V. Mark 14. 1. with subtilty; Acts 18. 3; 19. 27. trade; 19. 25. business

CREATE, Gen. 1. 1, 21, 27. & 2. 3.
Ps. 51. 10. *c*. in me a clean heart
Isa. 4. 5. *c*. upon every dwelling-place
45. 7. I form light and *c*. darkness
57. 19. I *c*. the fruit of the lips, peace
65. 17. I *c*. new heavens and new earth
18. rejoice in what I *c*. I *c*. Jerusalem
Ps. 104. 30. spirit they are *created*
Isa. 43. 7. I have *c*. him for my
Jer. 31. 22. *c*. a new thing in earth
Mal. 2. 10. hath not one God *c*. us
Eph. 2. 10. *c*. in Christ Jesus unto good
3. 9. *c*. all things by Jesus Christ
Col. 1. 16. all things were *c*. by him
3. 10. image of him that *c*. him
1 Tim. 4. 3. which God *c*. to be received
Rev. 4. 11. hast *c*. all—are and were *c*.
10. 6. *c*. heaven and things therein
Amos 4. 13. *createth* the wind
Mark 10. 6. *creation*, 13. 19. Rom. 1. 20. & 8. 22. Rev. 3. 14.
Rom. 1. 25. creature — *Creator*
Eccl. 12. 1. remember thy *C*. in days
Isa. 40. 28. *C*. of ends of earth
43. 15. Lord the *C*. of Israel, your king
1 Pet. 4. 19. as to a faithful *C*.
Gen. 1. 20. *creature*, Lev. 11. 46.
Mark 16. 15. preach the gospel to every *c*.
2 Cor. 5. 17. man in Christ is a new *c*.
Gal. 6. 15. availeth but a new *c*.
Col. 1. 15. first-born of every *c*.
1 Tim. 4. 4. every *c*. of God is good
Heb. 4. 13. nor any *c*. not manifest
Isa. 13. 21. *creatures*, Jas. 1. 18.
Ezek. 1. 5, 19. *living creatures*, 3. 13. Rev. 4. 6, 9. & 5. 6, 11, 14.
R. V. Mark 16. 15. whole creation; Col. 1. 15. all creation

CREDITOR, parable of the, Luke 7. 41; of two creditors, Matt. 18. 23.

CREEP, Lev. 11. 31. Ps. 104. 20.
2 Tim. 3. 6. who *c*. into houses
Jude 4. *crept* in unawares
R. V. Gen. 8. 19; Lev. 11. 44. moveth

CRIB, Prov. 14. 4. Isa. 1. 3.

CRIME, Job 31. 11. Ezek. 7. 23.

CRIMSON, as wool, Isa. 1. 18. Jer. 4. 30. 2 Chron. 2. 7. & 3. 14.
R. V. Jer. 4. 30. scarlet

CRIPPLE healed at Lystra, Acts 14. 8.

CROOKED generation, Deut. 32. 5.
Ps. 125. 5. aside to their *c*. ways
Prov. 2. 15. whose ways are *c*. and
Eccl. 1. 15. that which is *c*. cannot
Isa. 40. 4. *c*. shall be made straight
Phil. 2. 15. in midst of *c*. generation
R. V. Job 26. 13. swift; Isa. 45. 2. rugged

CROSS, John 19. 17-31. Luke 23. 26.
Matt. 10. 38. takes not up his *c*. and follows, 16. 24. Luke 9. 23. & 14. 27.
1 Cor. 1. 17. lest the *c*. of Christ be made
18. preaching of *c*. is to them fool.
Gal. 5. 11. then is offence of the *c*. ceased
6. 12. suffer persecution for *c*. of Christ
14. glory save in *c*. of Lord Jesus
Phil. 2. 8. obedient to death of *c*.
3. 18. they are enemies of the *c*.
Col. 2. 14. took—nailing it to his *c*.
Heb. 12. 2. for joy — endured the *c*.

CROWN, Lev. 8. 9. Esth. 1. 11.
Job 31. 36. bind it as *c*. to me
Ps. 89. 39. hast profaned his *c*.
Prov. 12. 4. virtuous woman is a *c*.
14. 24. *c*. of wise is their riches
16. 31. hoary head is a *c*. of glory
17. 6. children's children are *c*. of
S. of S. 3. 11. behold king Solomon with *c*.
Isa. 28. 5. Lord of hosts for *c*. of glory
62. 3. thou shalt be a *c*. of glory
1 Cor. 9. 25. to obtain corruptible c.
Phil. 4. 1. my joy and *c*., 1 Thes. 2. 19.
2 Tim. 4. 8. laid up—a *c*. of righte.
Jas. 1. 12. receive a *c*. of life
1 Pet. 5. 4. receive a *c*. of glory
Rev. 2. 10. give thee a *c*. of life
Ps. 8. 5. *crowned* with glory and honor
Prov. 14. 18. prudent are *c*. with knowledge
Ps. 65. 11. *crownest* the year with
103. 4. *crowneth* with loving-kind.
Zech. 6. 11, 14. *crowns*, Rev. 4. 4, 10. & 9. 7. & 12. 3. & 13. 1. & 19. 12.
R. V. Rev. 12. 3; 13. 1; 19. 12. diadems

CRUCIFY, Matt. 20. 19. & 23. 34. Luke 23. 21. John 19. 6, 15.
Acts 2. 23. *crucified* and slain, 4. 10.
Rom. 6. 6. our old man is *c*. with him
1 Cor. 1. 13. was Paul *c*.
23. Christ *c*.
2. 2. save Jesus Christ and him *c*.
Gal. 2. 20. I am *c*. with Christ nevertheless
3. 1. Christ is set forth *c*. among
6. 14. world is *c*. to me and I to
Rev. 11. 8. where also our Lord was *c*.

CRUEL, Prov. 5. 9. & 11. 17. & 27. 4.
Gen. 49. 7. cursed wrath for it was *c*.
Job 30. 21. thou art become *c*. to me
Prov. 12. 10. tender mercies of the wicked are *c*.
S. of S. 8. 6. jealousy is *c*. as grave
Isa. 13. 9. day of Lord cometh *c*. with
Jer. 6. 23. *c*. and have no mercy, 50. 42.
Heb. 11. 36. had trial of *c*. mockings

CRUELTY condemned, Ex. 23. 5. Ps. 27. 12. Prov. 11. 17. & 12. 10. Ezek. 18. 18.
of Simeon and Levi, Gen. 34. 25. & 49. 5.
of Pharaoh, Ex. 1. 8.
of Adoni-bezek, Judg. 1. 7.
of Herod, Matt. 2. 16. (Judg. 9. 5. 2 Kings 3. 27. & 10. & 15. 16.)
R. V. Heb. 11. 36 ——; Gen. 49. 5; Judg. 9. 24; Ps. 74. 20. violence; Ezek. 34. 4. rigor

CRUMBS, Matt. 15. 27. Luke 16. 21.

CRY, Ex. 5. 8. & 3. 7, 9.
Gen. 18. 21. to the *c*. that is come
Ex. 2. 23. their *c*. came up to God
22. 23. I will surely hear their *c*.
2 Sam. 22. 7. my *c*. did enter into
Job 34. 28. he hears *c*. of afflicted
Ps. 9. 12. he forgets not the *c*. of
34. 17. his ears are open to their *c*.

Ps. 145. 19. he will hear their *c*.
Jer. 7. 16. neither lift up *c*. nor prayer for them, 11. 11, 14.
Matt. 25. 6. at midnight a *c*. made
Ps. 34. 15. righteous *c*. and Lord
Isa. 40. 6. voice said *c*. — what *c*.
42. 2. not *c*. nor lift up voice
58. 1. *c*. aloud, spare not
Ezek. 9. 4. that *c*. for all the abom.
Joel 1. 19. to thee will I *c*.
Jonah 3. 8. *c*. mightily to God
Matt. 12. 19. shall not strive nor *c*.
Luke 18. 7. *c*. day and night to him
Luke 19. 40. stones would *c*. out
Rom. 8. 15. spirit *c*. Abba, Father
Ps. 22. 5. *cried* and were delivered
34. 6. this poor man *c*. and Lord
Lam. 2. 18. their heart *c*. to Lord
Prov. 2. 3. thou *criest* after know.
Gen. 4. 10. brother's blood *crieth*
Prov. 1. 20. wisdom *c*. without
Mic. 6. 9. Lord's voice *c*. to the city
Prov. 19. 18. *crying*, Zech. 4. 7. Matt. 3. 3. Heb. 5. 7. Rev. 21. 4.
R. V. Rev. 14. 18. great voice
CUBIT unto his stature, Matt. 6. 27.
CUMBER, Luke 10. 40. & 13. 7.
CUP, Gen. 40. 11. & 44. 2.
Ps. 11. 6. portion of their *c*.
23. 5. my *c*. runneth over
73. 10. waters of a full *c*. are wrung out
116. 13. take *c*. of salvation
Isa. 51. 17. *c*. of trembling, 22. Zech. 12. 2.
Jer. 16. 7. nor give *c*. of consola.
25. 15. wine *c*. of fury, 17. 28. Lam. 4. 21. Ezek. 23. 31, 32.
Hab. 2. 16. *c*. Lord's right hand, Ps. 75. 8.
Matt. 10. 42. *c*. of cold water only
20. 22. able to drink of the *c*.
26. 39. let this *c*. pass from me
John 18. 11. the *c*. which my Father hath given
1 Cor. 10. 16. *c*. of blessing which we
21. drink *c*. of the Lord and *c*. of devils
11. 25. this *c*. is new testament
26. drink this *c*., 27. 28. Luke 22. 20.
Rev. 16. 19. *c*. of his wrath, 14. 10.
CURIOUS, Ex. 35. 32. Acts 19. 19.
Ps. 139. 15. *curiously* wrought
CURSE them, Num. 5. 18, 19, 22, 24, 27.
Gen. 27. 12. bring a *c*. upon me
13. on me be thy *c*. my son
Deut. 11. 26. blessing and *c*., 30. 1.
23. 5. turned *c*. into blessing, Neh. 13. 2.
Prov. 3. 33. *c*. of the Lord in house of
26. 2. *c*. causeless shall not come
Mal. 2. 2. send a *c*. upon you
3. 9. ye are cursed with a *c*.
Isa. 65. 15. *for*, or, *to be a c*., Jer. 24. 9. & 25. 18. & 29. 18. & 42. 18. & 44. 8, 12. & 26. 6. & 49. 13.
Gen. 8. 21. I will not again *c*. the ground
12. 3. *c*. him that curseth thee
Ex. 22. 28. nor *c*. ruler of people
Lev. 19. 14. shall not *c*. the deaf
Num. 22. 6. come, *c*. me this people, 17.
Deut. 23. 4. hired Balaam to *c*., Josh. 24. 9. Neh. 13. 2.
Judg. 5. 23. *c*. ye Meroz, *c*. bitterly
Job 1. 11. he will *c*. thee to face, 2.5.
2. 9. *c*. God and die
Ps. 109. 28. let them *c*. but bless
Prov. 11. 26. people shall *c*. him, 24. 24.
Eccl. 10. 20. *c*. not king in chamber
Jer. 15. 10. every one doth *c*. me
Mal. 2. 2. I will *c*. your blessings
Matt. 5. 44. bless them that *c*. you
Rom. 12. 14. bless and *c*. not
Gen. 49. 7. *cursed* be their anger
Job 3. 1. opened Job his mouth, and *c*. his day, 8.
5. 3. I *c*. his habitation, 24. 18.

Ps. 119. 21. proud are *c*., 37. 22.
Jer. 11. 3. *c*. be man that obeys not
17. 5. *c*. be man that trusteth in
Deut. 30. 19. *cursing*, Rom. 3. 14. Heb. 6. 8. Ps. 10. 7. & 59. 12. & 109. 17.
R. V. Josh. 6. 18. accursed; Jer. 29. 18. execration; Deut. 7. 26; 13. 17. devoted; Job 1. 5. renounced; John 7. 49. accursed; Prov. 29. 24. adjuration
CURTAINS of the tabernacle described, Ex. 26. 36.
CUSTOM, Gen. 31. 35. Rom. 13. 7. Luke 4. 16. 1 Cor. 11. 16. Jer. 10. 3.
R. V. Gen. 31. 35. manner; Ex. 3. 4. ordinance; Matt. 9. 9; Mark 2. 14; Luke 5. 27. place of toll; Matt. 17. 25. receive toll
CUT, Lev. 1. 6, 12. & 22. 24.
Zech. 11. 10. *cut asunder*, Matt. 24. 51. Luke 12. 46. Jer. 48. 2. & 50. 23. Ps. 129. 4.
Luke 13. 7, 9. *cut down*, Job 22. 16, 20.
Job 4. 7. *cut off*, 8. 14. Ps. 37. 9, 28. & 76. 12. & 90. 10. & 101. 5. Prov. 2. 22. Matt. 5. 30. & 18. 8. Rom. 11. 22. 2 Cor. 11. 12. Gal. 5. 12.
Acts 5. 33. *cut to heart*, 7. 54.
R. V. Isa. 38. 10. noontide
CUTTING the flesh forbidden, Lev. 19. 28; Deut. 14. 1; practised by prophets of Baal, 1 Kings 18. 28.
CYMBAL, Ezra 3. 10. Ps. 150. 5.
1 Cor. 13. 1. I am become a tinkling *c*.

D

DAINTY, Job 33. 20. Prov. 23. 6.
Gen. 49. 20. yield royal *dainties*
Ps. 141. 4. not eat of their *d*.
Prov. 23. 3. not desirous of his *d*.
DAMNED who believe not, Mark 16. 16. 2 Thes. 2. 12.
Rom. 14. 23. doubteth, is *d*. if he eat
2 Pet. 2. 1. *damnable* heresies
Matt. 23. 14. greater *damnation*
33. how can ye escape *d*. of hell
Mark 3. 29. in danger of eternal *d*.
John 5. 29. come forth to resurrection of *d*.
1 Cor. 11. 29. eateth and drinketh *d*.
R. V. Mark 16. 16; Rom. 14. 23. condemned; 2 Thes. 2. 12. judged; Matt. 23. 14—; 22. 33; John 5. 29; Rom. 13. 2. judgment; Mark 3. 29. sin; 12. 40; Luke 20. 47; Rom. 3. 8; 1 Tim. 5. 12. condemnation
DANCE turned to mourning, Lam. 5. 15. Ps. 30. 11. Luke 15. 25.
DANCING, as a mark of rejoicing, Ex. 15. 20. & 32. 19. Judg. 11. 34. 1 Sam. 21. 11. 2 Sam. 6. 14. Eccl. 3. 4. of Herodias's daughter pleases Herod, Matt. 14. 6; Mark 6. 22.
DANDLED on knees, Isa. 66. 12.
DANGER of the judgment, Matt. 5. 22.
Matt. 5. 21, 22. *d*. of the council—hell fire
Mark 3. 39. in *d*. of damnation
Acts 19. 27. craft in *d*.
40. we in *d*.
R. V. Mark 3. 29. guilty
DARE, 1 Cor. 6. 1. 2 Cor. 10. 12.
Rom. 5. 7. some would *d*. to die
R. V. 2 Cor. 16. 12. not bold to
DARK, Gen. 15. 17. Job 18. 6. & 24. 16.
Lev. 13. 6. if plague be *d*., 21. 26.
Num. 12. 8. speak not in *d*. speech.
2 Sam. 22. 12. *d*. waters, Ps. 18. 11.
Ps. 49. 4. *d*. sayings, 78. 2.
Dan. 8. 23. understanding *d*. sent.
2 Pet. 1. 19. light shineth in *d*.
1 Cor. 13. 12. through a glass *darkly*
Ex. 10. 15. *darkened*, Eccl. 12. 2, 3.
Ps. 69. 23. let eyes be *d*., Rom. 11. 10.

Zech. 11. 17. his right eye utterly *d*.
Rom. 1. 21. foolish heart was *d*.
Gen. 1. 2, 5, 18. *darkness*, 15. 12.
2 Sam. 22. 29. Lord will lighten my *d*.
1 Kings 8. 12. Lord dwell in thick *d*.
Job 34. 22. no *d*. where workers
Ps. 104. 20. makest *d*. and it is night
Isa. 5. 20. put *d*. for light, and light for *d*.
45. 7. I form light and create *d*.
Matt. 6. 23. whole body full of *d*.
8. 12. outer *d*., 22. 13. & 25. 30.
John 1. 5. *d*. comprehended it not
3. 19. men loved *d*. rather than lig.
Acts 26. 18. turn them from *d*. to
Rom. 13. 12. cast off works of *d*.
2 Cor. 4. 6. light to shine out of *d*.
6. 14. communion hath light with *d*.
Eph. 5. 8. were sometimes *d*. but
Col. 1. 13. delivered us from power of *d*.
1 Pet. 2. 9. called you out of *d*.
2 Pet. 2. 4. reserved in chains of *d*.
1 John 1. 5. in him is no *d*. at all
Jude 13. blackness of *d*. for ever
Deut. 28. 29. *in darkness*, 1 Sam. 2. 9. Ps. 107. 10. & 112. 4. Isa. 9. 2. & 50. 10. Matt. 4. 16. & 10. 27. John 1. 5. 1 Thes. 5. 4.
R. V. Zech. 14. 6. with gloom; Luke 23. 45. failing
DARLING, Ps. 22. 20. & 35. 17.
DARTS, fiery, of devil, Eph. 6. 16.
R. V. Job 41. 29. clubs; 2 Chron. 32. 5. weapons; Prov. 7. 23. arrow; Heb. 12. 20 —
DASH, 2 Kings 8. 12. Ex. 15. 6. Isa. 13. 16, 18. Hos. 10. 14. & 13. 16. Ps. 137. 9. Jer. 13. 14.
Ps. 2. 9. *d*. them in pieces like a potter's vessel
19. 12. lest thou *d*. thy foot against a stone
DAVID, for Christ, Ps. 89. 3. Jer. 30. 9. Ezek. 34. 23, 24. & 37. 24, 25. Hos. 3. 5. Isa. 55. 3.
DAY, Gen. 1. 5. & 32. 26.
Ps. 19. 2. *d*. unto *d*. uttereth speech
84. 10. a *d*. in thy courts is better
118. 24. this is the *d*. which the Lord
Prov. 27. 1. what *d*. may bring forth
Amos 6. 3. put far away evil *d*.
Zech. 4. 10. despised the *d*. of small
Matt. 6. 34. sufficient to *d*. is the
25. 13. know neither the *d*. nor
John 8. 56. rejoiced to see my *d*.
1 Cor. 3. 13. the *d*. shall declare it
Phil. 1. 6. till *d*. of Jesus Christ
1 Thes. 5. 5. children of the *d*.
Matt. 10. 15. *day of judgment*, 11. 22, 24. & 12. 36. Mark 6. 11. 2 Pet. 2. 9. & 3. 7. 1 John 4. 17.
Isa. 2. 12. *day of the Lord*, 13. 6, 9. & 34. 8. Jer. 46. 10. Lam. 2. 22. Ezek. 30. 3. Joel 1. 15. & 2. 1, 31. & 3. 14. Amos 5. 18. Obad. 15. Zeph. 1. 8, 18. & 2. 2, 3. Zech. 1. 7. & 14. 1. Mal. 4. 5. 1 Cor. 5. 5. Rev. 1. 10. 2 Cor. 1. 14. 1 Thes. 5. 2. 2 Pet. 3. 10.
Ps. 20. 1. Lord hear thee in the *day of trouble*
50. 15. call on me in —, 91. 15.
59. 16. my defence and refuge in—
77. 2. in — I sought the Lord
Isa. 37. 3. it is a — and rebuke
Ezek. 7. 7. time is come, — is near
Hab. 3. 16. I might rest in —
Zeph. 1. 15. a — and distress, desolation
Job 8. 9. *days* on earth as a shadow
14. 1. of few *d*. and full of trouble
Ps. 90. 12. teach us to number our *d*.
Prov. 3. 16. length of *d*. is in her right
Eccl. 7. 10. former *d*. better than
11. 8. remember *d*. of darkness, many
12. 1. while evil *d*. come not
Jer. 2. 32. forgotten me *d*. without
Matt. 24. 22. except those *d*. be shortened

Gal. 4. 10. observe *d.* months, and
Eph. 5. 16. because the *d.* are evil
1 Pet. 3. 10. would see good *d.*
Gen. 49. 1. *last days*, Isa. 2. 2. Mic. 4. 1. Acts 2. 17. 2 Tim. 3. 1. Heb. 1. 2. Jas. 5. 3. 2 Pet. 3. 3.
Num. 24. 14. *latter days*, Deut. 31. 29. Jer. 23. 20. & 30. 24. Dan. 10. 14. Hos. 3. 5.
Job 10. 20. *my days*, 17. 1, 11.
7. 6. — are swifter than a shuttle
16. I loathe it, — are vanity
9. 25. — are swifter than a post
Ps. 39. 4. know measure of —
5. made — as a handbreadth
Isa. 39. 8. peace and truth in —
Jer. 20. 18. — are consumed with
Ps. 61. 8. *daily* perform my vows
Prov. 8. 34. watching *d.* at my gates
Isa. 58. 2. seek me *d.* and delight in
Acts 2. 47. added to church *d.*
Heb. 3. 13. exhort one another *d.*
Job 9. 33. *day's-man*, or umpire
38. 12. *day-spring*, Luke 1. 78.
2 Pet. 1. 19. *day-star* arise in your hearts
R. V. Matt. 27. 62; John 1. 29; Acts 14. 20; 21. 8; 25. 6. on the morrow

DEACON, Phil. 1. 1. 1 Tim. 3. 8, 10, 12, 13.

DEAD, Gen. 20. 3. & 23. 3.
Num. 16. 48. stood between *d.* and
1 Sam. 24. 14. after a *d.* dog after
Ps. 88. 10. shall *d.* praise, 115. 17.
Eccl. 9. 5. the *d.* know not any thing
10. 1. *d.* flies cause the ointment
Matt. 8. 22. let the *d.* bury their *d.*
22. 32. not God of *d.* but of living
Luke 8. 52. the maid is not *d.* but
John 5. 25. *d.* shall hear the voice
11. 25. though he were *d.* yet
Rom. 6. 8. *d.* with Christ
11. *d.* to sin
Gal. 2. 19. I through law am *d.* to law
Eph. 2. 1. who were *d.* in trespasses
Col. 2. 13. being *d.* in your sins
1 Thes. 4. 16. *d.* in Christ shall rise
2 Tim. 2. 11. *d.* with him, we shall
Heb. 11. 4. being *d.* yet speaketh
Rev. 14. 13. blessed are *d.* — in Lord
Ps. 17. 9. *deadly*, Jas. 3. 8. Rev. 13. 3.
R. V. Rev. 13. 3, 12. death stroke

DEAF, Ex. 4. 11. Ps. 38. 13. Isa. 29. 18. & 35. 5. Mic. 7. 16.
Lev. 19. 14. shalt not curse the *d.*
Isa. 42. 18. hear, ye *d.* and look, ye blind
19. who is *d.* as my messenger
43. 8. *d.* people that have ears
Matt. 11. 5. *d.* hear, dead are raised

DEAL, a measure, Ex. 29. 40. Lev. 14. 10.

DEATH, Gen. 21. 16. Ex. 10. 17.
Num. 23. 10. let me die the *d.* of the
Deut. 30. 15. set before you life and *d.*
Ps. 6. 5. in *d.* no remembrance of
33. 19. deliver soul from *d.*, 116. 8.
73. 4. have no bands in their *d.*
89. 48. liveth and shall not see *d.*
116. 15. precious — is *d.* of saints
Prov. 2. 18. her house inclines to *d.*
8. 36. they that hate me, love *d.*
18. 21. *d.* and life in power of tong.
Eccl. 7. 26. more bitter than *d.* the
8. 8. hath no power in day of *d.*
Isa. 25. 8. swallow up *d.* in victory
28. 15. made covenant with *d.*
Jer. 8. 3. *d.* chosen rather than life
21. 8. way of life, way of *d.*
Hos. 13. 14. O *d.* I will be thy plagues
Matt. 16. 28. not taste of *d.*, Luke 9. 27.
26. 38. sorrowful even unto *d.*
John 5. 24. passed from *d.* to life, 1 John 3. 14.
John 8. 51. shall never see *d.*
12. 33. what *d.* he should die, 21. 19.
Acts 2. 24. loosed the pains of *d.*
Rom. 5. 12. sin entered, and *d.* by
6. 3. baptized into his *d.*
Rom. 6. 4. buried by baptism into *d.*
5. 9. *d.* hath no more dominion
21. end of these things is *d.*
23. the wages of sin is *d.* but gift of God
8. 2. free from law of sin and *d.*
6. to be carnally minded is *d.*
38. *d.* nor life shall separate from
1 Cor. 3. 22. or life, or *d.* or things present
11. 26. ye show Lord's *d.* till he come
15. 21. by man came *d.* by man
54. *d.* is swallowed up in victory
55. O *d.* where is thy sting
56. sting of *d.* is sin, and strength
2 Cor. 1. 9. had the sentence of *d.*
10. deliver from so great a *d.*
2. 16. we are savour of *d.* unto *d.*
4. 11. delivered to *d.* for Jesus'
12. *d.* worketh in us, but life in you
Phil. 2. 8. obedient to *d.* the *d.* of
Heb. 2. 9. tasted *d.* for every man
15. through fear of *d.* are subject
11. 5. should not see *d.*, Luke 2. 26.
Jas. 1. 15. sin finished brings *d.*
5. 20. save a soul from *d.* and hide
1 Pet. 3. 18. put to *d.* in the flesh
1 John 5. 16. there is a sin unto *d.*
17. there is a sin unto *d.* I do not
Rev. 1. 18. I have the keys of hell and *d.*
2. 10. be faithful unto *d.* and I will
20. 6. second *d.* hath no power
21. 4. there shall be no more *d.*
R. V. Mark 14. 1; Luke 18. 33. kill him

DEBATE, Prov. 25. 9. Isa. 27. 8. & 58. 4. Rom. 1. 29. 2 Cor. 12. 20.
R. V. Isa. 58. 4. contention; Rom. 1. 29. strife; 2 Cor. 12. 20. should be strife; Isa. 27. 8. dost contend

DEBT, Rom. 4. 4. Matt. 6. 12, 18, 27. Ezek. 18. 7, 11. *debtor*, Gal. 5. 3. Rom. 1. 14. & 8. 12. & 15. 27. Luke 7. 41. Matt. 6. 12.
R. V. Matt. 18. 30. which was due

DECEASE, Luke 9. 31. 2 Pet. 1. 15.

DECEIT, Jer. 5. 27. & 9. 6, 8.
Ps. 72. 14. redeem their souls from *d.*
101. 7. worketh *d.* shall not dwell
Prov. 20. 17. bread of *d.* is sweet
Isa. 53. 9. any *d.* in his mouth
Jer. 8. 5. they hold fast *d.* and refuse
Col. 2. 8. spoil you through vain *d.*
Ps. 35. 20. *deceitful*, 109. 2. Prov. 11. 18. & 14. 25. & 23. 3. & 27. 6.
Ps. 5. 6. abhor bloody and *d.* man
78. 57. turn like a *d.* bow, Hos. 7. 16.
120. 2. from a *d.* tongue, 52. 4. Mic. 6. 12. Zeph. 3. 13.
Prov. 31. 30. favor is *d.* and beauty vain
Jer. 17. 9. heart is *d.* above all things
Eph. 4. 22. according to *d.* lusts
Matt. 13. 22. *deceitfulness* of riches
Ps. 24. 4. *deceitfully*, Jer. 48. 10. Job 13. 7. 2 Cor. 4. 2.
R. V. Ps. 55. 11; 72. 14. oppression; Prov. 20. 17. falsehood; 1 Thes. 2. 3. error; Prov. 27. 6. profuse; 29. 13. oppressor; Eph. 4. 22. deceit; Gen. 34. 13. with guile

DECEIVE, 2 Kings 4. 28. & 18. 29.
Prov. 24. 28. *d.* not with thy lips
Matt. 24. 4. take heed that no man *d.* you
24. if possible *d.* the very elect
1 Cor. 3. 18. let no man *d.* himself
2 Thes. 2. 10. *deceivableness*
Deut. 11. 16. heart be not *deceived*
Job 12. 16. the *d.* and the deceiver are
Isa. 44. 20. a *d.* heart hath turned
Jer. 20. 7. O Lord, thou hast *d.* me
Ezek. 14. 9. I the Lord have *d.*
Obad. 3. thy pride hath *d.* thee
Rom. 7. 11. *d.* me, and by it slew me
1 Tim. 2. 14. Adam was not *d.* but
2 Tim. 3. 13. *deceiving* and being *d.*
Gal. 27. 12. *deceiver*, Mal. 1. 14. 2 John 7. 2 Cor. 6. 8. Tit. 1. 10.
Prov. 26. 19. *deceiveth*, Rev. 12. 9.
Jas. 1. 26. *d.* his own heart, 22.
R. V. Matt. 24. 4, 5, 11, 24; Mark 13. 5, 6; 1 John 3. 7. lead astray; Rom. 16. 18; 2 Thes. 2. 3. beguile; Lev. 6. 2. oppressed; Job 31. 9. enticed; Prov. 20. 1. erreth; Luke 21. 8; John 7. 47. led astray; Rom. 7. 11. 1 Tim. 2. 14. beguiled; Jas. 1. 22. deluding

DECENTLY, 1 Cor. 14. 40.

DECLARE, Gen. 41. 24. Isa. 42. 9.
Ps. 22. 2. I will *d.* thy name unto
38. 18. I will *d.* my iniquity and
145. 4. shall *d.* thy mighty acts
Isa. 3. 9. they *d.* their sin as Sodom
53. 8. who shall *d.* his generation
Mic. 3. 8. to *d.* to Jacob his transgression
Acts 17. 23. worship, him *d.* I unto
20. 17. not shunned to *d.* all counsel
Rom. 3. 25. to *d.* his righteousness
Heb. 11. 14. say such things *d.* plain.
1 John 1. 3. seen and heard *d.* we
Rom. 1. 4. *declared* — Son of God with
2 Cor. 3. 3. manifestly *d.* to be the epistle
Amos 4. 13. *d.* to man what his thought
1 Cor. 2. 1. I *d.* to you test. of God
R. V. Ps. 2. 7; 73. 28; 75. 1; 78. 6. tell of; Eccl. 9. 1. explore; Isa. 43. 26. set forth thy cause; Matt. 13. 36. explain; Rom. 3. 25. shew; John 17. 26; Col. 4. 7. make known; 1 John 1. 5. announce; Acts 15. 4, 14. rehearsed; Rom. 9. 17. published

DECLINE, Ps. 119. 51, 157.

DECREE, Ezra 5. 13, 17. & 6. 1, 12.
Ps. 2. 7. I will declare the *d.*
Prov. 8. 15. princes *d.* justice
Isa. 10. 1. that *d.* unrighteous decr.
Zeph. 2. 2. before *d.* bring forth
Isa. 10. 22. *decreed*, 1 Cor. 7. 37.
R. V. Dan. 2. 9. law; 6. 7, 8, 9, 12, 13, 15. interdict; Esth. 9. 32. commandment

DEDICATE, Deut. 20. 5. 2 Sam. 8. 11. 1 Chron. 26. 20, 26, 27. Ezek. 44. 29.
Num. 7. 84. *dedication*, Ezra 6. 16, 17. Neh. 12. 17. John 10. 22.
R. V. 2 Kings 12. 4. hallowed; Ezek. 44. 29. devoted

DEED, Gen. 44. 15. Judg. 19. 30.
Rom. 15. 18. obedient in word and *d.*
Col. 3. 17. whatsoever ye do in word or *d.*
Neh. 13. 14. wipe not out my good *deeds*
Ps. 28. 4. give them according to their *d.*, Jer. 25. 14. Rom. 2. 6. 2 Cor. 5. 10.
John 3. 19. because their *d.* were evil
Rom. 3. 20. by *d.* of law no flesh
Jude 15. of all their ungodly *d.*
R. V. In N. T. mostly, works

DEEP, Gen. 1. 2. Job. 38. 30.
Ps. 36. 6. thy judg. are a great *d.*
42. 7. *d.* calleth unto *d.* at the noise
1 Cor. 2. 10. yea, *d.* things of God
2 Cor. 11. 25. I have been in the *d.*
Isa. 31. 6. *deeply* revolted
Hos. 9. 9. *d.* corrupted themselves
Mark 8. 17. sighed *d.* in spirit
R. V. Isa. 63. 13; Jonah 2. 3. depth; Luke 8. 31; Rom. 2. 7. abyss; Ps. 135. 6. deeps; Ezek. 32. 14; 34. 18. clear

DEFAME, 1 Cor. 4. 13. Jer. 20. 10.

DEFENCE, 2 Chron. 11. 5. Isa. 19. 6.
Num. 14. 9. their *d.* is departed
Job 22. 25. Almighty shall be thy *d.*
Ps. 7. 10. my *d.* is of God who save.
Eccl. 7. 12. wisdom is a *d.* money is a *d.*
Isa. 4. 5. on all the glory shall be *d.*
33. 16. place of *d.* the munitions
R. V. Job 22. 25. treasure; Ps. 7. 10; 89. 18. shield; 59. 9, 16; 62. 2, 6;

94. 22. high tower; Isa. 4. 5. canopy; 19. 6. Egypt; Nah. 2. 5. mantelet
DEFER, Eccl. 5. 4. Isa. 48. 9. Dan. 9. 19. Prov. 13. 12. & 19. 11.
R. V. Prov. 19. 11. maketh him slow
DEFILE, Lev. 11. 44. & 15. 31.
S. of S. 5. 3. how shall I *d.* them
Dan. 1. 8. would not *d.* himself
Matt. 15. 18. they *d.* the man, 20.
1 Cor. 3. 17. if any *d.* temple of God
Mark 7. 2. eat bread with *defiled* hands
Isa. 24. 5. earth is *d.* under inhabit.
Tit. 1. 15. are *d.* and unbelieving
Heb. 12. 15. thereby many be *d.*
Rev. 3. 4. have not *d.* their gar.
14. 4. are not *d.* with women
21. 27. any thing that *defileth*
R. V. Ex. 31. 14; Ezek. 7. 24; 28. 18. profaned; Num. 35. 33; Isa. 24. 5; Jer. 3. 9; 16. 18. polluted; Gen. 34. 2. humbled; Deut. 22. 9. forfeited; Lev. 13. 14; 15. 32; Num. 5. 2; Ezek. 4. 13; Rev. 21. 27. unclean
DEFRAUD, Lev. 19. 13. Mark 10. 19. 1 Cor. 6. 7, 8. & 7. 5. 1 Thes. 4. 6. 1 Sam. 12. 3, 4. 2 Cor. 7. 2.
R. V. Lev. 19. 13. oppress; 2 Cor. 7. 2. took advantage of; 1 Thes. 4. 6. wrong
DELAY, Ex. 22. 29. & 32. 1.
Ps. 119. 60. I *delayed* not to keep
Matt. 24. 48. my lord *delayeth* his coming
R. V. Matt. 24. 48. tarrieth
DELICATE, Deut. 28. 56. Isa. 47. 1. Jer. 6. 2. Mic. 1. 16. Jer. 51. 34.
1 Sam. 15. 32. *delicately*, Prov. 29. 21.
Lam. 4. 5. Luke 7. 25.
R. V. Mic. 1. 16. of . . delight
DELIGHT, Gen. 34. 19. Num. 14. 8.
Deut. 10. 15. Lord had *d.* in fathers
1 Sam. 15. 22. hath the Lord as great *d.* in burnt offerings
Job 22. 26. have thy *d.* in Almighty
27. 10. will he *d.* himself in Almighty
Ps. 1. 2. his *d.* is in the law of God
16. 3. saints in whom is all my *d.*
37. 4. *d.* thyself in Lord, he will give
40. 8. I *d.* to do thy will, O my God
94. 19. thy comforts *d.* my soul
119. 24. thy testimonies are my *d.*, 174.
Prov. 11. 20. upright are his *d.*, 12. 22.
15. 8. prayer of upright is his *d.*
S. of S. 2. 3. under shadow with great *d.*
Isa. 55. 2. let your soul *d.* itself in fatness
58. 2. *d.* to know — take *d.* in approaching
13. call the sabbath a *d.* holy of
Rom. 7. 22. I *d.* in the law of God
Ps. 112. 1. *delighteth* greatly in his commandments
Prov. 3. 12. son in whom he *d.*
Isa. 42. 1. elect in whom my soul *d.*
Mic. 7. 18. because he *d.* in mercy
Ps. 119. 92. thy law hath been my *delights*, 143. Eccl. 2. 8.
Prov. 8. 31. my *d.* with sons of men
S. of S. 7. 6. how pleasant, O love, for *d.*
Mal. 3. 12. for ye shall be a *delightsome* land
R. V. Prov. 19. 10. delicate living
DELIVER, Ex. 3. 8. & 5. 18.
Job 5. 19. *d.* thee in six troubles and
10. 7. none can *d.* out of thy hand
Ps. 33. 19. to *d.* their souls from death
50. 15. I will *d.* thee, and thou, 91. 15.
56. 13. wilt thou not *d.* my feet
74. 19. *d.* not the soul of thy turtle
91. 3. *d.* thee from snare of fowler
Eccl. 8. 8. shall wickedness *d.* those
Ezek. 14. 14. should *d.* but their own
Dan. 3. 17. our God is able to *d.* us
Hos. 11. 8. how shall I *d.* thee, Israel
Rom. 7. 24. who shall *d.* from body
1 Cor. 5. 5. to *d.* such a one to Satan
2 Tim. 4. 18. the Lord shall *d.* me
Heb. 2. 15. *d.* them who thro. fear
2 Pet. 2. 9. Lord knows how to *d.*
2 Kings 5. 1. *deliverance*, 13. 17. 2 Chron. 12. 7. Esth. 4. 14. Ps. 32. 7. & 44. 4. Isa. 26. 18. Joel 2. 32. Obad. 17. Luke 4. 18. Heb. 11. 35.
Gen. 45. 7. *great deliverance*, Judg. 15. 18. 1 Chron. 11. 14. Ps. 18. 50.
Ezra 9. 13. given us such *d.* as this
Heb. 11. 35. not accepting *d.*
Prov. 11. 8. righteous is *delivered* out of trouble, and the wicked cometh, 9. 21.
28. 26. walketh wisely shall be *d.*
Isa. 38. 17. in love to soul, *d.* it
49. 24, 25. lawful captive — prey be *d.*
Jer. 7. 10. *d.* to do all abominations
Ezek. 3. 19. hast *d.* thy soul, 21. & 33. 9.
Dan. 12. 1. thy people shall be *d.*
Mic. 4. 10. Babylon, there shalt thou be *d.*
Matt. 11. 27. all things are *d.* to me
Acts 2. 23. *d.* by determinate coun.
Rom. 4. 25. who was *d.* for our offences
7. 6. we are *d.* from the law that
8. 32. God *d.* him up for us all
2 Cor. 1. 10. who *d.* us from so great
4. 11. *d.* unto death for Jesus' sake
1 Thes. 1. 10. which *d.* us from the
1 Tim. 1. 20. whom I have *d.* to
2 Pet. 2. 7. *d.* just Lot vexed with
Jude 3. faith once *d.* to the saints
R. V. Lev. 6. 4; 2 Sam. 10. 10; 1 Chron. 19. 11. committed; Deut. 5. 22. gave; Judg. 2. 16, 18; 3. 9, 31; 8. 22; 10. 12; 12. 2, 3. saved; 2 Kings 18. 30; 19. 10; Isa. 36. 15. given; 1 Chron. 11. 14. defended; Ps. 55. 18; 78. 42. redeemed; 81. 6. freed; Ezek. 6. 21; Mark 9. 31; 15. 1, 10. delivered up; Mic. 4. 10. rescued; 2 Kings 5. 1; 13. 17; 1 Chron. 11. 14. victory; Joel 2. 32; Obad. 17. those that escape; Luke 4. 18. release; Judg. 3. 9, 15. savior
DELUSION, 2 Thes. 2. 11. Isa. 66. 4.
R. V. 2 Thes. 2. 11. working of error
DEMONSTRATION, 1 Cor. 2. 4.
DEN, Judg. 6. 2. Job 37. 8. Heb. 11. 38. Rev. 6. 15. Ps. 104. 22.
Ps. 10. 9. *den of lions*, S. of S. 4. 8. Dan. 6. 7, 24. Amos 3. 4. Nah. 2. 12.
Jer. 7. 11. *den of robbers* — of thieves, Matt. 21. 13. Mark 11. 17.
Jer. 9. 11. *den of dragons*, 10. 22.
R. V. Jer. 9. 11; 10. 22. dwelling place; Job 37. 8. coverts; Rev. 6. 15. caves
DENY, 1 Kings 2. 16. Job 8. 18.
Prov. 30. 9. lest I be full and *d.* thee
Matt. 10. 33. shall *d.* me before men
26. 34. before the cock crow thou shalt *d.*
35. I will not *d.* thee, Mark 14. 31.
2 Tim. 2. 12. if we *d.* him he will *d.*
Tit. 1. 16. in works they *d.* him
1 Tim. 5. 8. hath *denied* the faith
Rev. 2. 13. hast not *d.* my faith
2 Tim. 3. 5. godliness *denying* the power
Tit. 2. 12. *d.* ungodliness and
2 Pet. 2. 1. *d.* Lord that bought th.
DEPART from, Job 21. 14. & 22. 17.
28. 28. to *d.* from evil, is understanding
Ps. 34. 14. *d.* from evil, 37. 27. Prov. 3. 7. & 13. 19. & 16. 6, 17.
Hos. 9. 12. woe to me when I *d.* from
Matt. 7. 23. *d.* from me, ye that work
Luke 2. 29. lettest thy servant *d.* in
5. 8. *d.* from me — a sinful man, O Lord
1 Tim. 4. 1. some shall *d.* from faith
2 Tim. 2. 19. name of Christ *d.* fr.
Ps. 18. 21. wickedly *departed* from
Prov. 14. 16. feareth and *departeth* from evil
Isa. 59. 15. *d.* from evil makes him.
Acts 20. 29. after my *departing*, wolves
2 Tim. 4. 6. *departure*, Ezek. 26. 18.
R. V. very largely, go, went away, withdrew
DEPTH, Job 28. 14. & 38. 16. Prov. 8. 27. Matt. 18. 6. Mark 4. 5.
Rom. 8. 39. nor *d.* separate us
11. 33. O the *d.* of riches of wisdom
Eph. 3. 18. *d.* of the love of Christ
Ex. 15. 5, 8. *depths*, Ps. 68. 22. & 71. 20. & 130. 1. Prov. 3. 20. & 9. 18.
Mic. 7. 19. cast sins into *d.* of sea
Rev. 2. 24. known *d.* of Satan
R. V. Ex. 15. 5, 8; Ps. 33. 7. deeps; Job 28. 14; 38. 16; Prov. 8. 27. deep; Mark 4. 5. deepness
DERISION, Job 30. 1. Ps. 2. 4. & 44. 13. & 59. 8. & 119. 51. Jer. 20. 7, 8.
R. V. Jer. 20. 7. laughing stock
DESCEND, Ex. 19. 18. & 33. 9.
Ps. 49. 17. glory shall not *d.* after
Isa. 5. 14. rejoiceth shall *d.* into it
Gen. 28. 12. angels of God ascending and *descending*, John 1. 51.
Matt. 3. 16. Spirit of God *d.* like dove, Mark 1. 10. John 1. 32, 33.
Rev. 21. 10. city *d.* out of heaven
R. V. Num. 34. 11; 1 Sam. 26. 10. go down; Mark 15. 32; Ps. 133. 3; Acts 24. 1; Jas. 3. 15; Rev. 21. 10. come or came down; Josh. 17. 9; 18. 13, 16, 17. went down; Heb. 7. 3, 6. genealogy
DESERT, Ex. 3. 1. & 19. 2. Num. 20. 1. Isa. 21. 1. & 35. 1. & 40. 3. & 43. 19. & 51. 3. Jer. 25. 24. & 50. 12. Ezek. 47. 8. Matt. 24. 26.
R. V. Ps. 102. 6. waste places; Ezek. 47. 8. Arabah; Ex. 3. 1; 5. 3; 19. 2; 23. 31; Num. 21. 1; 27. 14; 33. 16; 2 Chron. 26. 10; Isa. 21. 1; Jer. 25. 24; Matt. 24. 26; John 6. 31. wilderness
DESIRE, Deut. 18. 6. & 21. 11.
Gen. 3. 16. thy *d.* shall be to thy husband
4. 7. to thee shall be his *d.* and thou
Ex. 34. 24. nor any man *d.* thy land
Deut. 18. 6. with all the *d.* of his heart
2 Sam. 23. 5. this is all my *d.* though
2 Chron. 15. 15. with their whole *d.*
Job 14. 15. wilt have a *d.* to work
21. 14. we *d.* not knowledge of thy
Ps. 38. 9. all my *d.* is before thee
73. 25. none that I *d.* besides thee
145. 16. fulfil the *d.* of them that
Prov. 10. 24. *d.* of righteous shall
11. 23. *d.* of righteous is only good
21. 25. *d.* of slothful killeth him
Eccl. 12. 5. *d.* shall fail, because
Isa. 26. 8. *d.* of our soul is to thy
Ezek. 24. 16. take the *d.* of thy eyes
Hag. 2. 7. the *d.* of all nations shall
Luke 22. 15. with *d.* I have desired
Jas. 4. 2. *d.* to have and cannot
Rev. 9. 6. *d.* to die, and death shall flee
Ps. 19. 10. more to be *desired* are they
Isa. 26. 9. with my soul have I *d.* thee
Jer. 17. 16. nor have I *d.* woeful day
Ps. 37. 4. give the *desires* of heart
Eph. 2. 3. fulfilling *d.* of the flesh
Ps. 51. 6. thou *desirest* truth in
16. thou *d.* not sacrifice, else
Job 7. 2. servant earnestly *desireth*
12. what man *d.* life and
68. 16. hill which God *d.* to dwell
Prov. 12. 12. wicked *d.* not of evil
13. 4. soul of sluggard *d.* and hath
21. 10. soul of wicked *d.* evil
R. V. Job. 31. 35. signature; 2 Cor. 7. 7; Rom. 15. 23. longing; Ps. 78. 29. lusteth after; Job 20. 20. delighteth; Ps. 27. 4; Matt. 16. 1; Mark 15. 6; John 12. 21; Acts 3. 14; 7. 46; 9. 2; 13. 21, 28; 18. 20; 1 John 5. 15. asked; Hos. 6. 6; Mic. 7. 1. desire; Luke 9. 9; Acts 3. 7.

sought; 2 Cor. 8. 6; 12. 18. exhorted
DESOLATE, 2 Sam. 13. 20. Job 15. 28. & 16. 7. Ps. 25. 16. Isa. 49. 21. & 54. 1. Matt. 23. 38. Rev. 17. 16.
Isa. 49. 6. *desolations*, 61. 4. Jer. 25. 9, 12. Ezek. 35. 9. Dan. 9. 2, 18, 26.
R. V. Jer. 49. 13, 17. astonishment; Prov. 1. 27. storm; Lam. 3. 47. devastation; Job 30. 14; Ezra 9. 9; Ps. 74. 31. ruins
DESPAIR, 2 Cor. 4. 8. & 1. 8. Eccl. 2. 20.
1 Sam. 27. 1. *d. i. e.* to be past hope
Job 6. 20. *desperate*, Isa. 17. 11.
Jer. 17. 9. *desperately* wicked
DESPISE my statutes, Lev. 26. 15.
1 Sam. 2. 30. that *d.* me shall be lightly
Job 5. 17. *d.* not chastening of
Ps. 102. 17. will not *d.* their prayer
Prov. 23. 22. *d.* not mother when
Matt. 6. 24. hold to one and *d.* other
Rom. 14. 3. *d.* him that eateth not
Gen. 16. 4. mistress was *despised* in
2 Sam. 6. 16. she *d.* him in her
Prov. 12. 9. is *d.* and hath a serv.
S. of S. 8. 1. kiss thee I should not be *d.*
Isa. 53. 3. he is *d.* and rejected, Ps. 22. 6.
Zech. 4. 10. who *d.* the day of small
Luke 18. 9. righteous and *d.* others
Heb. 10. 28. that *d.* Moses' law died
Acts 13. 41. *despisers*, 2 Tim. 3. 3.
Rom. 2. 4. *despisest* thou riches of goodness
Job 36. 5. God *despiseth* not any
Prov. 11. 12. void of wisdom *d.* neighbor
13. 13. *d.* the word shall be destroyed
14. 21. that *d.* his neighbor sinneth
15. 32. refuseth instruction *d.* his
Isa. 33. 15. *d.* gain of oppression
49. 7. whom man *d.* nation abho.
Luke 10. 16. *d.* you, *d.* me, *d.* him
1 Thes. 4. 8. *d.* not man but God
Heb. 12. 2. *despising* the shame
10. 29. done *despite* to the Spirit of grace
R. V. Lev. 26. 15. reject; 26. 43; Num. 11. 20; 14. 31; Ps. 53. 5; Ezek. 20. 13, 16, 24; Amos 2. 4. rejected; Luke 18. 9; Heb. 10. 28. set at nought; Jas. 2. 6; 1 Cor. 4. 10. dishonor; Acts 19. 27. made of no account; Prov. 19. 16. careless of; Luke 10. 16; 1 Thes. 4. 8. rejecteth; 2 Tim. 3. 3. no lovers of
DESTROY, Gen. 18. 23. & 19. 13.
Ps. 101. 8. I will *d.* all wicked of the
Prov. 1. 32. the prosper. of fools *d.*
Matt. 5. 17. not come to *d.* but to fulfil
10. 28. able to *d.* both soul and body
John 2. 19. *d.* this temple, and I will raise
Rom. 14. 15. *d.* not him with thy
20. for meat *d.* not work of God
1 Cor. 3. 17. if defile temple, him God will *d.*
6. 13. God shall *d.* both it and them
Jas. 4. 12. able to save and to *d.*
1 John 3. 8. might *d.* works of devil
Hos. 4. 6. my people are *destroyed*
13. 9. Israel, thou hast *d.* thyself
2 Cor. 4. 9. cast down but not *d.*
Job 15. 21. *destroyer*, Ps. 17. 4. Prov. 28. 24. Jer. 4. 7. 1 Cor. 10. 10.
Esth. 4. 14. *shall be destroyed*, Ps. 37. 38. & 92. 7. Prov. 13. 13, 20. & 29. 1. Isa. 10. 27. Dan. 2. 44. Hos. 10. 8. Acts 3. 23. 1 Cor. 15. 26.
Deut. 7. 23. *destruction*, 32. 24.
Job 5. 22. at *d.* and famine shall laugh
18. 12. *d.* is ready at his side
Ps. 90. 3. thou turnest man to *d.*
91. 6. *d.* that wasteth at noonday
Prov. 10. 29. *d.* shall be to workers of iniquity, 21. 15. Job. 21. 30. & 31. 3.
15. 11. hell and *d.* are before the Lord
16. 18. pride goeth before *d.*
18. 12. before *d.* the heart of man
Jer. 4. 20. *d.* upon *d.* is cried, for land is spoiled
Hos. 13. 14. O grave, I will be thy *d.*
Matt. 7. 13. way that leads to *d.*
1 Cor. 5. 5. for the *d.* of the flesh
2 Cor. 10. 8. not for your *d.*, 13. 10.
1 Thes. 5. 3. peace and safety; then sudden *d.* cometh upon them
2 Thes. 1. 9. punished with everlasting *d.*
2 Pet. 2. 1. bring on themselves swift *d.*
3. 16. wrest Scriptures to their *d.*
R. V. Gen. 18. 23, 24; 1 Chron. 21. 12. consume; Ex. 23. 27; Deut. 7. 23; Ps. 144. 6. discomfit; Ex. 34. 13; Num. 24. 17; Deut. 7. 5; Ps. 28. 5. break down; Deut. 7. 24; 9. 3; 28. 51; Josh. 7. 7. perish; 2 Sam. 22. 41; Ps. 18. 40; 54. 5; 69. 4; 101. 5; 1 Kings 15. 13. cut off, or down; Ps. 5. 10. hold guilty; Prov. 15. 25. root up; Acts 9. 21; Gal. 1. 23. made havoc; Rom. 14. 20. overthrow; 1 Cor. 6. 13; Heb. 2. 14; 2 Thes. 2. 8. bring to nought; Rom. 6. 6. done away; 1 Cor. 15. 26. abolished; 1 Cor. 10. 9, 10; 2 Pet. 2. 12. perish; Acts 19. 27. despised; Jer. 50. 11. that plunder; Job 15. 21. spoiler; Ps. 17. 4. violent
DETERMINED, 2 Chron. 25. 16. Job 14. 5. Isa. 10. 23. & 28. 22. Dan. 9. 24. Acts 2. 23. & 4. 28. & 17. 26.
R. V. 2 Chron. 2. 1; Isa. 19. 17; Acts 20. 3. purposed; Dan. 9. 24. decreed; Acts 15. 37. was minded; 19. 39. settled in the regular; 15. 2. the brethren appointed
DETESTABLE, Deut. 7. 26. Jer. 16. 18. Ezek. 5. 11. & 7. 20. & 11. 18. & 37. 23. 1 Cor. 2. 2.
DEVICE, Eccl. 9. 10. Job 5. 12. Ps. 33. 10. Prov. 1. 31. & 12. 2. & 14. 17. & 19. 21. Jer. 18. 11, 12, 18. 2 Cor. 2. 11.
R. V. Ps. 33. 10. thoughts; Lam. 3. 62. imagination
DEVIL, Matt. 4. 5. & 8. 11. & 9. 32.
Matt. 4. 1. to be tempted of the *d.*
11. 18. they say he hath a *d.*
13. 39. enemy that sowed is the *d.*
25. 41. fire prepared for the *d.* and
John 6. 70. twelve, and one of you is a *d.*
7. 20. thou hast a *d.*, 8. 48.
8. 44. of your father the *d.*, 49.
13. 2. *d.* having now put it into, 27.
Acts 13. 10. thou child of the *d.*
Eph. 4. 27. neither give place to *d.*
2 Tim. 2. 26. recover out of the snare of the *d.*
Jas. 4. 7. resist *d.* and he will
1 Pet. 5. 8. your adversary the *d.* goeth
1 John 3. 8. to destroy works of *d.*
10. children of God and children of the *d.*
Jude 9. Michael contending with *d.*
Rev. 2. 10. the *d.* shall cast some
Lev. 17. 7. offer sacrifice to *devils*
Deut. 32. 17. they sacrifice to *d.*
Ps. 106. 37. sacrificed their sons to *d.*
Matt. 4. 24. possessed with *d.*, 8. 16, 28, 33. Luke 4. 41. & 8. 36.
10. 8. raise the dead, cast out *d.*
Mark 16. 9. cast out seven *d.*, Luke 8. 2.
Luke 10. 17. even *d.* are subject to
1 Cor. 10. 20. have fellowship with *d.* sacrifice to *d.*
21. cup of *d.* table of *d.*
Jas. 2. 19. *d.* believe and tremble
R. V. Lev. 17. 7; 2 Chron. 11. 15. he-goats, Deut. 32. 17; Ps. 106. 37. demons
DEVISE not evil against, Prov. 3. 29.
14. 22. do they not err that *d.* evil
16. 30. shutteth eyes to *d.* froward
Jer. 18. 18. come let us *d.* devices
Mic. 2. 1. woe to them that *d.* iniquity
DEVOTED, Lev. 27. 21, 28. Num. 18. 14.
Ps. 119. 38. servant who is *d.* to thy
Acts 17. 23. I beheld your *devotions*
DEVOUR, Gen. 49. 27. Isa. 26. 11.
Matt. 23. 14. ye *d.* widows' houses
Gal. 5. 15. if ye bite and *d.* one another
Heb. 10. 27. which shall *d.* the ad.
1 Pet. 5. 8. seeking whom he may *d.*
Isa. 1. 20. ye shall be *devoured*
Jer. 3. 24. shame hath *d.* the labor
Hos. 7. 7. *d.* judges
9. *d.* strength
Mal. 3. 11. I will rebuke *devourer*
Ex. 24. 17. *devouring fire*, Isa. 29. 6. & 30. 27, 30. & 33. 14.
Ps. 52. 4. lovest all *devouring* words
R. V. Ps. 80. 13. feed on; Isa. 42. 14. pant together; Prov. 19. 28; Hab. 1. 13. swalloweth up; Prov. 20. 25. rashly to say; Matt. 23. 14 ——
DEVOUT, Luke 2. 25. Acts 2. 5. & 10. 27. & 17. 4, 17. & 22. 12.
DEW, Gen. 27. 28. Deut. 32. 2.
Ps. 110. 3. hast the *d.* of thy youth
Isa. 26. 19. thy *d.* is as the *d.* of
Hos. 6. 4. goodness is as the early *d.*
Mic. 5. 7. Jacob — as *d.* from Lord
R. V. Ps. 133. 3 ——
DIADEM, Job 29. 14. Isa. 28. 5. & 62. 3. Ezek. 21. 26.
R. V. Ezek. 21. 26. mitre
DIE, Gen. 5. 5. & 6. 17.
Gen. 2. 17. thou shalt surely *d.*, 3. 4. & 20. 7. 1 Sam. 14. 44. & 22. 16. 1 Kings 2. 37, 42. Jer. 26. 8. Ezek. 3. 18. & 33. 8, 14.
Job 14. 14. if a man *d.* shall he live
Ps. 82. 7. ye shall *d.* like men
Prov. 23. 13. with rod he shall not *d.*
Eccl. 3. 2. there is a time to *d.*
Isa. 22. 13. to-morrow we shall *d.*
Ezek. 3. 19. *d.* in his iniquity, 33. 8.
18. 4. soul that sinneth shall *d.*
31. why will ye *d.* O house of
Jonah 4. 3. better for me to *d.* than
Matt. 26. 35. though I should *d.*
Luke 20. 36. neither can *d.* any more
John 8. 21. ye shall *d.* in your sins, 24.
11. 50. expedient that one *d.* for
Rom. 14. 8. we *d.* we *d.* unto Lord
1 Cor. 9. 15. better for me to *d.* than
15. 22. as in Adam all *d.* so in Christ
Phil. 1. 21. to live is Christ, to *d.* is gain
Heb. 9. 27. it is appointed for men to *d.*
Rev. 3. 2. that are ready to *d.*
14. 13. blessed are the dead who *d.*
Rom. 5. 6. Christ *died* for ungodly
8. while yet sinners, Christ *d.* for us
6. 9. being raised he *d.* no more
14. 9. to this end Christ *d.* and rose
1 Cor. 15. 3. Christ *d.* for our sins
2 Cor. 5. 15. he *d.* for all, that they
1 Thes. 5. 10. who *d.* for us that whether
Heb. 11. 13. these all *d.* in faith, not
Rom. 14. 7. no man *dieth* to himself
2 Cor. 4. 10. *dying*, 6. 9. Heb. 11. 21.
DIFFER, who makes, 1 Cor. 4. 7.
Phil. 1. 10. that *d.*, Rom. 2. 18.
Lev. 10. 10. *difference*, Ezra 22. 26. & 44. 23.
Acts 15. 9. no *d.*, Rom. 3. 22. & 10. 12.
R. V. Lev. 20. 25. separate; Acts 15. 9; Rom. 3. 22; 10. 12. distinction; Ezek. 22. 26. discern; 1 Cor. 12. 5. diversities; Jude 22. who are in doubt
DILIGENCE, 2 Tim. 4. 9, 21.
Prov. 4. 23. keep thy heart with all *d.*
Luke 12. 58. art in way give *d.* that

2 Pet. 1. 5. giving all *d.* add to faith
10. give *d.* to make calling and election
Jude 3. I gave all *d.* to write unto
Deut. 19. 18. *diligent*, Josh. 22. 5.
Prov. 10. 4. hand of *d.* maketh rich
12. 24. hand of *d.* shall bear rule
21. 5. thoughts of the *d.* tend to
22. 29. man *d.* in his business
2 Pet. 3. 14. be *d.* to be found of him
Ex. 15. 26. will *diligently* hearken to voice of, Deut. 11. 13. & 28. 1. Jer. 17. 24. Zech. 6. 15.
Deut. 4. 9. keep thy soul *d.*
6. 7. teach them *d.* unto thy children
17. *d.* keep the commandments, 11. 22.
24. 8. that thou observe *d.* and
Ps. 119. 4. to keep thy precepts *d.*
Heb. 11. 6. rewarder of them that *d.* seek
R. V. Cor. 8. 7. earnestness; 2 Cor. 8. 22. earnest; Tit. 3. 12; 2 Pet. 3. 14. give diligence
DIMINISH, Deut. 4. 2. Prov. 13. 11.
Rom. 11. 12. *diminishing* of them the riches of
R. V. Isa. 21. 17. few; Rom. 11. 12. their loss
DIMNESS of anguish, Isa. 8. 22. & 9. 1.
DIRECT, Eccl. 10. 10. Isa. 45. 13.
Ps. 5. 3. will I *d.* my prayer to thee
Prov. 3. 6. he shall *d.* thy paths
Isa. 61. 8. I will *d.* their work in truth
Jer. 10. 23. that walks to *d.* his steps
2 Thes. 3. 5. Lord *d.* your hearts
Isa. 40. 13. who *directed* the Spirit
Ps. 119. 5. ways were *d.* to keep
Prov. 16. 9. a man's heart deviseth, Lord *directeth* his steps
R. V. Gen. 46. 28. shew; Ps. 5. 3; Prov. 21. 29. order; Ps. 119. 5. established; Isa. 45. 13. make straight; 61. 8. give them; Num. 19. 4. toward front of
DISCERN, Eccl. 8. 5. 2 Sam. 14. 17. & 19. 35. 1 Kings 3. 9, 11. 1 Cor. 2. 14.
Mal. 3. 18. *d.* between righteous and
Heb. 5. 14. to *d.* both good and
4. 12. *discerner* of thoughts
1 Cor. 11. 29. not *discerning* Lord's body
12. 10. to another *d.* of spirits
R. V. Luke 12. 56. know how to interpret; 1 Cor. 2. 14. judge
DISCHARGE, in war, Eccl. 8. 8.
R. V. 1 Kings 5. 9. broken up
DISCIPLE, John 9. 28. & 19. 38.
Matt. 10. 24. the *d.* is not above
42. in the name of a *d.*
Luke 14. 26. ye cannot be my *d.*
John 8. 31. then are ye my *d.* ind.
Acts 21. 16. an old *d.* with whom
R. V. Matt. 26. 20; 28. 9; Mark 2. 18; Luke 9. 11; John 6. 11 ——; Acts 1. 15. brethren
DISCORD, soweth, Prov. 6. 14, 19.
DISCRETION, Ps. 112. 5. Prov. 1. 4. & 2. 11. & 3. 21. & 11. 22. & 19. 11. Isa. 28. 26. Jer. 10. 12.
R. V. Ps. 112. 5. in judgment; Isa. 28. 26. aright
DISEASE, Ps. 38. 7. & 41. 8. Eccl. 6. 2. Matt. 4. 23. & 9. 35. & 10. 1. Ex. 15. 26. Deut. 28. 60. 2 Chron. 21. 19.
Ps. 103. 3. who healeth all thy *d.*
Ezek. 34. 4. *diseased*, have ye not, 21.
R. V. 2 Kings 1. 2; 8. 8, 9; Matt. 9. 35. sickness; John 5. 4 ——; Matt. 14. 35; Mark 1. 32; John 6. 2. sick
DISFIGURE bodies, Matt. 6. 16.
DISGRACE not, Jer. 14. 21.
DISGUISES resorted to, 1 Sam. 28. 8. 1 Kings 14. 2. & 20. 38. & 22. 30. 2 Chron. 18. 29. & 35. 22.
disfiguring of face for the dead forbidden, Lev. 19. 28. Deut. 14. 1.

DISHONOR, Ps. 35. 26. Prov. 6. 33. Mic. 7. 6. son *d.* his father
Ps. 71. 13. cloth. with shame and *d.*
Rom. 1. 24. to *d.* their own bodies
1 Cor. 15. 43. it is sown in *d.* it is raised
DISOBEDIENCE, 2 Cor. 10. 6. Eph. 2. 2. & 5. 6. Col. 3. 6.
Rom. 5. 19. by one man's *d.* many
DISOBEDIENT, 1 Kings 13. 26. Neh. 9. 26.
Luke 1. 17. *d.* to wisdom of the just
Rom. 1. 30. *d.* to parents, 2 Tim. 3. 2.
Tit. 1. 16. abominable and *d.*
3. 3. *d.* deceived, serving divers lusts
1 Pet. 2. 7, 8. stumble being *d.*
R. V. 1 Pet. 2. 7. such as disbelieve
DISORDERLY, 2 Thes. 3. 6, 7, 11.
DISPENSATION, 1 Cor. 9. 17. Eph. 1. 10. & 3. 2. Col. 1. 25.
DISPERSED, Ps. 112. 9. Prov. 5. 16. Isa. 11. 12. Zeph. 3. 10. John 7. 35.
R. V. John 7. 35. Dispersion; Acts 5. 37; 2 Cor. 9. 9. scattered
DISPLEASED, Gen. 38. 10. 2 Sam. 11. 27. 1 Chron. 21. 7. Zech. 1. 2, 15. Isa. 59. 15. Mark 10. 14. 1 Kings 1. 6. Ps. 60. 1.
Deut. 9. 19. *hot* or *sore displeasure*, Ps. 2. 5. & 6. 1. & 38. 1.
R. V. Gen. 31. 35; Ps. 60. 1. angry; Gen. 38. 10. evil in sight of; Num. 11. 1. speak evil in ears of; Matt. 21. 15; Mark 10. 14, 41. moved with indignation; Judg. 15. 3. mischief
DISPOSING is of the Lord, Prov. 16. 33.
Acts 7. 53. *disposition* of angels
R. V. As if ordained by
DISPUTE, Job 23. 7. Mark 9. 33. Acts 6. 9. & 9. 29. & 17. 17. & 19. 8, 9.
Rom. 14. 1. doubtful *disputations*
Phil. 2. 14. *disputings*, 1 Tim. 6. 5.
R. V. Job 23. 7. reason; Mark 9. 33. were ye reasoning; Acts 17. 17. reasoned; Acts 15. 2. questioning; Acts 19. 8, 9. reasoning; 1 Tim. 6. 5. wranglings
DISQUIETED, Ps. 39. 6. & 42. 5, 11.
R. V. Prov. 30. 21. doth tremble
DISSEMBLE, Josh. 7. 11. Jer. 42. 20. Gal. 2. 13. Ps. 26. 4. Prov. 26. 24.
Rom. 12. 9. *dissimulation*, Gal. 2. 13.
R. V. Jer. 42. 20. dealt deceitfully; Rom. 12. 9. hypocrisy
DISSENSION, Acts 15. 2. & 23. 7, 10.
DISSOLVED, Ps. 75. 3. Isa. 24. 19. 2 Cor. 5. 1. 2 Pet. 3. 11. Job 30. 22.
R. V. Isa. 14. 31. melted away
DISTINCTLY, read law, Neh. 8. 8.
DISTRACTED, suffer terrors, Ps. 88. 15.
1 Cor. 7. 35. *distraction* without
DISTRESS, Gen. 42. 21. Deut. 2. 9, 19. Neh. 9. 37. Luke 21. 23, 25.
Gen. 35. 3. answered in day of my *d.*
2 Sam. 22. 7. in my *d.* I called on
1 Kings 1. 29. redeemed my soul out of all *d.*
2 Chron. 28. 22. in his *d.* trespassed
Ps. 4. 1. enlarged my heart in *d.*
Isa. 25. 4. strength to needy in *d.*
Zeph. 1. 15. that day is a day of *d.*, 17.
Rom. 8. 35. shall *d.* separate from Christ
1 Sam. 28. 15. *distressed*, 30. 6. 2 Sam. 1. 26.
2 Cor. 6. 4. in *distresses*, 12. 10.
Ps. 25. 17. *out of my distresses*, 107. 6, 13, 19, 28. Ezek. 30. 16. 2 Cor. 6. 4.
R. V. Ezek. 30. 16. adversaries; 1 Kings 1. 20. adversity; Neh. 2. 17. evil case; Rom. 8. 35. anguish; Deut. 2. 9, 19. vex; 2 Cor. 4. 8. straitened
DISTRIBUTE, Luke 18. 22. 1 Tim. 6. 18. 1 Cor. 7. 17. Job 21. 17. Rom. 12. 13.

Acts 4. 35. *distribution*, 2 Cor. 9. 13.
R. V. 1 Chron. 24. 3. divided; Rom. 12. 13. communicating; 2 Cor. 10. 13. apportioned
DITCH, Job 9. 31. Ps. 7. 15. Prov. 23. 27. Isa. 22. 11. Matt. 15. 14. Luke 6. 39.
R. V. 2 Kings 3. 16. trenches; Isa. 22. 11. reservoir; Matt. 15. 14; Luke 6. 39. pit
DIVERSITIES, 1 Cor. 12. 4, 6, 28.
R. V. 1 Cor. 12. 28. divers kinds
DIVIDE, Gen. 1. 6, 14. Job 27. 17.
1 Kings 3. 25. *d.* living child, 26.
Ps. 55. 9. destroy—*d.* their tongues
Isa. 53. 12. I will *d.* him a portion
Luke 12. 13. to *d.* inheritance with
2 Sam. 1. 23. in death not *divided*
Dan. 2. 41. kingdom shall be *d.*
Matt. 12. 25. kingdom, house *d.* against itself shall not stand, 26. Luke 11. 17.
12. 11. *dividing* to every man sever.
2 Tim. 2. 15. rightly *d.* the word of
Heb. 4. 12. to *d.* asunder of joints
Judg. 5. 15, 16. *divisions*, Luke 12. 51. Rom. 16. 17. 1 Cor. 1. 10. & 3. 3.
R. V. Lev. 11. 4, 7; Deut. 14. 7, 8. part; Num. 33. 54. inherit; Josh. 19. 45. distributing; 23. 4; Neh. 9. 22. allot; Matt. 25. 32. separateth; Acts 13. 19. gave them their land for an inheritance; 2 Tim. 2. 13. handling aright; Dan. 7. 25. half a; Judg. 5. 15, 16. watercourses; 1 Cor. 3. 3 ——
DIVINE sentence, Prov. 16. 10.
Heb. 9. 1. ordinance of *d.* service
2 Pet. 1. 3. his *d.* power hath given
Mic. 3. 11. prophets *d.* for money
Num. 22. 7. *divination*, 23. 23. Deut. 18. 10. Acts 16. 16.
Deut. 18. 14. *diviners*, Isa. 44. 25. Mic. 3. 6, 7. Zech. 10. 2. Jer. 29. 8.
DIVORCE, Jer. 3. 8. Lev. 21. 14. & 22. 13. Num. 30. 9. Matt. 5. 32.
Deut. 24. 1, 3. *divorcement*, Isa. 50. 1. Matt. 5. 31. & 19. 7. Mark 10. 4.
R. V. divorcement; Matt. 5. 32. put away
DO, Gen. 16. 6. & 18. 25. & 31. 16.
Matt. 7. 12. men should *d.* to you, *d.*
John 15. 5. without me ye can *d.*
Rom. 7. 15. what I would that *d.* I not
Phil. 4. 13. I can *d.* all things throu.
Heb. 4. 13. with whom we have to *d.*
Rev. 19. 10. see thou *d.* it not, 22. 9.
Rom. 2. 13. the *doers* of it shall
Jas. 1. 22. be ye *d.* of word and not
1 Chron. 22. 16. *doing*, Ps. 64. 9. & 66. 5. & 118. 23. Prov. 20. 11. Isa. 1. 16. Jer. 7. 3, 5. & 18. 11. & 26. 13. & 32. 19. Zech. 1. 4. Ezek. 36. 31. Zeph. 3. 11. Mic. 2. 7.
Rom. 2. 7. *well-doing*, Gal. 6. 9. 2 Thes. 3. 13. 1 Pet. 2. 15. & 3. 17. & 4. 19.
R. V. 2 Kings 22. 5. workmen; Ps. 101. 8. workers of iniquity; 2 Tim. 2. 9. malefactor
DOCTOR, Acts 5. 34. Luke 2. 46. & 5. 17.
Deut. 32. 2. *doctrine* shall drop as rain
Jer. 10. 8. the stock is a *d.* of vanities
Matt. 7. 28. astonished at his *d.*, 22. 33. Mark 1. 22. & 11. 18. Luke 4. 32.
Matt. 16. 12. beware of the *d.* of
Mark 1. 27. what new *d.* is this
John 7. 17. shall know of the *d.*
Acts 2. 42. apostles' *d.* and fellowship
Rom. 6. 17. form of *d.* which was
16. 17. contrary to *d.* ye have learn.
Eph. 4. 14. with every wind of *d.*
1 Tim. 5. 17. labor in word and *d.*
2 Tim. 3. 16. profitable for *d.*
Tit. 2. 7. in *d.* showing uncorrupt
10. may adorn the *d.* of God
Heb. 6. 1. principles of *d.* of Christ
Matt. 15. 9. teaching for *d.* the
Col. 2. 22. after *doctrines* of men

Heb. 13. 9. carr. about by strange *d.*
R. V. in N. T. generally, teaching
DOG, Ex. 11. 7. Deut. 23. 18.
1 Sam. 17. 43. am I a *d.*, 2 Kings 8. 13.
Prov. 26. 11. *d.* return to his vomit, 2 Pet. 2. 22.
Eccl. 9. 4. living *d.* better than
Isa. 56. 10. all dumb *dogs*
11. greedy *d.*
Matt. 7. 6. cast not that which is holy to *d.*
15. 27. *d.* eat of crumbs, Mark 7. 28.
Rev. 22. 15. without are *d.* and sorcerers
DOMINION, Gen. 27. 40. & 37. 8.
Num. 24. 19. he that shall have *d.*
Job 25. 2. *d.* and fear are with him
Ps. 8. 6. have *d.* over the works of
19. 13. not have *d.* over me, 119. 133.
49. 14. upright have *d.* over them
145. 13. thy *d.* endureth through
Isa. 26. 13. other lords had *d.* over
Dan. 4. 3. his *d.* is from generation
34.—an everlasting *d.*, 7. 14.
7. 27. all *d.* shall serve and obey
Rom. 6. 9. death has no more *d.*
14. sin shall not have *d.* over you
Col. 1. 16. thrones or *d.* or principalities
Jude 8. despise *d.* and speak evil
25. to God *d.*, 1 Pet. 4. 11. & 5. 11.
R. V. Judg. 14. 4. rule; 2 Chron. 21. 8. hand; Neh. 9. 37. power; 2 Cor. 1. 24. lordship; Matt. 20. 25. lord it
DOOR, Judg. 11. 31. & 16. 3.
Gen. 4. 7. sin lieth at the *d.*
Ps. 84. 10. *d.* keeper in the house
141. 3. keep *d.* of my lips
Prov. 26. 14. as *d.* turns on hinges
Hos. 2. 15. valley of Achor, *d.* of
John 10. 1. entereth not by the *d.* is
7. I am the *d.* of sheep
9. I am *d.*
Acts 14. 27. opened *d.* of faith
1 Cor. 16. 9. great *d.* and effectual
2 Cor. 2. 12. a *d.* was opened to me
Jas. 5. 9. judge stands before *d.*
Rev. 3. 8. I set before thee an open *d.*
20. I stand at *d.* and knock, if any
Ps. 24. 7. lift up ye everlasting *doors*
Mal. 1. 10. shut ye the *d.* for nought
Matt. 24. 33. near, even at the *d.*
R. V. Amos 9. 11. chapters; Ezek. 41. 2, 3. entrance; 41. 16. thresholds; 1 Kings 14. 17. house
DOTING, 1 Tim. 6. 4. Ezek. 23. 5, 20.
DOUBLE, Ex. 22. 4. Deut. 21. 17.
2 Kings 2. 9. *d.* portion of thy spirit
1 Chron. 12. 33. not of a *d.* heart
Job 11. 6. secrets are *d.* to that
Ps. 12. 2. with a *d.* heart do they speak
Isa. 40. 2. *d.* for all her sins, Jer. 16. 18.
Jer. 17. 18. destroy with *d.* destruct.
1 Tim. 3. 8. deacons not *d.* tongued
Jas. 1. 8. *d.* minded man, 4. 8.
Rev. 18. 6. *d.* to her, fill to her *d.*
R. V. Job 11. 6. manifold
DOUBT, Deut. 28. 66. Gal. 4. 20.
Matt. 14. 31. of little faith, why dost *d.*
21. 21. have faith and *d.* not
Mark 11. 23. and shall not *d.* in
Rom. 14. 23. he that *doubteth* is dam.
1 Tim. 2. 8. without wrath or *doubting*
Luke 12. 29. be not of *doubtful* mind
Rom. 14. 1. not to *d.* disputations
R. V. Luke 11. 20. then; 1 Cor. 9. 10. yea; Gal. 4. 20. perplexed; John 10. 24. hold us in suspense; Acts 5. 24; 10. 17; 25. 20. much perplexed; 1 Tim. 2. 8. disputing
DOUGH, Ex. 12. 34. Num. 15. 20. Neh. 10. 37. Ezek. 44. 30.
DOVE, Ps. 55. 6. & 68. 13. & 74. 19.
S. of S. 1. 15. & 2. 14. & 5. 2. & 6. 9.
Matt. 3. 16. Luke 3. 22. John 1. 32.
Isa. 38. 14. mourn as *d.*, 59. 11.
60. 8. fly as *d.* to their windows
Hos. 7. 11. Ephr. is like a silly *d.*
Matt. 10. 16. wise as serpents, and harmless as *d.*

DOWN sitting, Ps. 139. 2.
Isa. 37. 31. *downward*, Eccl. 3. 21.
DRAGON, Ps. 91. 13. Isa. 27. 1. & 51. 9. Jer. 51. 34. Ezek. 29. 3. Rev. 12. 3-17. & 13. 2, 4, 11. & 16. 13. & 20. 2.
Deut. 32. 33. *dragons*, Job 30. 29. Ps. 44. 19. & 74. 13. & 148. 7. Isa. 13. 22. & 34. 13. & 43. 20. Jer. 9. 11. & 14. 6. Mic. 1. 8. Mal. 1. 3.
R. V. Job 30. 29; Ps. 44. 19; Isa. 13. 22; 34. 13; 35. 7; 43. 20; Jer. 9. 11; 10. 22; 14. 6; 49. 33; 51. 37; Mic. 1. 8; Mal. 1. 3. jackals
DRAUGHTS of fishes, miraculous, Luke 5. 4, 5, 6. John 21. 6, 11.
DRAW, Gen. 24. 44. 2 Sam. 17. 13.
Job 21. 33. every man shall *d.*
Ps. 28. 3. *d.* me not away with
S. of S. 1. 4. *d.* me, we will run after
Isa. 5. 18. woe unto that *d.* iniquity
Jer. 31. 3. with loving kindness I *d.*
John 6. 44. except Father—*d.* him
12. 32. I will *d.* all men to me
Heb. 10. 38. if any man *d.* back, 39.
Ps. 73. 28. good for me to *d.* near to
Eccl. 12. 1. years *d.* nigh when say
Isa. 29. 13. *d.* near me with their
Heb. 7. 19. by which we *d.* nigh to
Jas. 4. 8. *d.* nigh to God, and he will *d.*
Ps. 18. 16. *drew* me out of many waters
Hos. 11. 4. I *d.* with cords of love
R. V. Mark 6. 53. moved; Luke 15. 1; Acts 27. 27. were drawing; Acts 19. 33. brought; Acts 14. 19; 17. 6; 21. 30. dragged
DREAD, Ex. 15. 16. Job 13. 11, 21.
Deut. 1. 29. *d.* not, nor be afraid
1 Chron. 22. 13. be strong *d.* not
Isa. 8. 13. let him be your fear and *d.*
Dan. 9. 4. great and *dreadful* God
Gen. 28. 17. how *d.* is this place
Mal. 1. 14. my name is *d.* among
4. 5. great and *d.* day of the Lord
R. V. Dan. 7. 7, 19; Mal. 1. 14; 4. 5. terrible
DREAM, Gen. 37. 5. & 40. 5. & 41. 7.
Gen. 20. 3. God came to Abimelech in a *d.*
31. 11. angel spake to Jacob in a *d.*
Num. 12. 6. speak to him in a *d.*
1 Kings 3. 5. the Lord appeared to Solomon in a *d.*
Ps. 73. 20. as *d.* when one awaketh
Eccl. 5. 3. *d.* comes through multitude
Isa. 29. 7. that fight—be as a *d.*
Dan. 2. 3. I *d.* a *d.*
4. 5. saw a *d.*
Matt. 1. 20. angel appeared in a *d.*
2. 12. Joseph warned of God in a *d.*
27. 19. suffered many things in a *d.*
Acts 2. 17. old men shall *d. dreams*, Joel 2. 28.
Job 7. 14. scarest me with *d.*
DRINK, Ex. 15. 24. & 32. 20.
Job 21. 20. *d.* of wrath of Almighty
Ps. 36. 8. *d.* of the river of thy pleasure
60. 3. *d.* wine of astonishment
80. 5. givest them tears to *d.*
Prov. 4. 17. *d.* the wine of violence
5. 15. *d.* waters out of own cistern
31. 4. it is not for kings to *d.* wine
7. *d.* and forget his poverty
S. of S. 5. 1. *d.* yea *d.* abundantly, O
Isa. 22. 13. let us eat and *d.*, 1 Cor. 15. 32.
43. 20. to give *d.* to my people
Hos. 4. 18. their *d.* is sour, committed
Amos 4. 1. say to masters, bring, and let us *d.*
Matt. 10. 42. give to *d.* to one of these little ones
20. 22. able to *d.* of cup, 23.
26. 27. *d.* ye all of it, this is my blood
29. I will not henceforth *d.* of fruit
John 6. 55. my blood is *d.* indeed
18. 11. cup Father given, shall I not *d.* it

Rom. 14. 17. king. of God is not *d.*
1 Cor. 10. 4. drink same spiritual *d.*
11. 25. as often as ye *d.* it in rem.
12. 13. all made to *d.* into one spirit
Lev. 10. 9. not *d.* wine nor *strong drink*, Judg. 13. 4, 7, 14. 1 Sam. 1. 15.
Prov. 31. 6. give—to those ready to perish
Isa. 5. 11. follow—
22. mingle—
28. 7. prophet erred through—
Mic. 2. 11. prophecy to them of—
Job 15. 16. *drinketh* iniquity like
John 6. 54. *d.* my blood hath eter.
56. that *d.* my blood dwells in me
1 Cor. 11. 29. eateth and *d.* unworth.
Heb. 6. 7. earth which *d.* in rain
Eph. 5. 18. be not *drunk* with wine
Rev. 17. 2. *d.* with wine of fornication
Deut. 21. 20. glutton and *drunkard*
Prov. 23. 21. *d.* shall come to poverty
Isa. 24. 20. earth shall reel like a *d.*
1 Cor. 5. 11. with railer and *d.* not eat
Ps. 69. 12. *drunkards*, Isa. 28. 1, 3. Joel 1. 5. Nah. 1. 10. 1 Cor. 6. 10.
Job 12. 25. stagger like a *drunken* man, Ps. 107. 27. Jer. 23. 9. Isa. 19. 14.
Isa. 29. 9. *d.* not with wine, 51. 21.
Acts 2. 15. these are not *d.* as ye suppose
1 Cor. 11. 21. one hungry another is *d.*
1 Thes. 5. 7. they that be *d.* are *d.*
Deut. 29. 19. *drunkenness*, Eccl. 10. 17. Jer. 13. 13. Ezek. 23. 33. Luke 21. 34. Rom. 13. 13. Gal. 5. 21.
DROP, Deut. 33. 28. Judg. 5. 4.
Deut. 32. 2. doctrine shall *d.* as rain
Ps. 65. 11. thy paths *d.* fatness, 12.
Prov. 5. 3. *d.* as honey-comb, S. of S. 4. 11.
Isa. 40. 15. all nations are as a *d.* of
S. of S. 5. 5. my hands *dropped* myrrh
2. locks with *drops* of the night
Luke 22. 44. sweat as it were great *d.*
DROSS, Ps. 119. 119. Isa. 1. 25. Ezek. 22. 18.
DROUGHT, Deut. 28. 24. 1 Kings 17. Hag. 1. 11.
DROWN, S. of S. 8. 7. 1 Tim. 6. 9.
R. V. Ex. 15. 4. sunk; Amos 8. 8; 9. 5. sink again; Heb. 11. 29. swallowed up
DROWSINESS clothe, Prov. 23. 21.
DRY, Judg. 6. 37, 39. Job 13. 25.
Prov. 17. 1. Isa. 44. 3. & 56. 3. Jer. 4. 11. Ezek. 17. 24. & 37. 2, 4. Hos. 9. 14.
R. V. Lev. 2. 14; Isa. 5. 13. parched; Joel 1. 12; Mark 11. 20. withered
DUE, Lev. 10. 13. Deut. 18. 3.
1 Chron. 15. 13. sought him not after *d.*
1 Chron. 16. 29. give Lord glory *d.* to his name, Ps. 29. 2. & 96. 8.
Prov. 3. 27. withhold not—whom it is *d.*
Matt. 18. 34. should pay all that was *d.*
Luke 23. 41. we received *d.* reward
Ps. 104. 27. meat in *due season*, 145. 15. Matt. 24. 45. Luke 12. 42.
Prov. 15. 23. a word spoken in—
Eccl. 10. 17. princes eat in—for strength
Gal. 6. 9. in—we shall reap, if we
Deut. 32. 35. foot shall slide in *due time*
Rom. 5. 6. in—Christ died for the
1 Cor. 15. 8. as one born out of—
1 Tim. 2. 6. to be testified in—
Tit. 1. 3. hath in—manifested
R. V. 1 Tim. 2. 6. its own; Tit. 1. 3. his own
DULL of hearing, Matt. 13. 15.
DUMB, Hab. 2. 18. Mark 9. 17.
Ex. 4. 11. who maketh *d.* or deaf
Ps. 38. 13. I was as a *d.* man

Ps. 39. 2. I was *d.* with silence, 9.
Prov. 31. 8. open thy mouth for *d.*
Isa. 35. 6. tongue of *d.* to sing
53. 7. sheep before shearers is *d.*
R. V. Luke 1. 20. silent
DUMBNESS of Zacharias, Luke 1. 20.
DUNG of solemn feasts, Mal. 2. 3.
Phil. 3. 8. I count them but *d.* to
DURABLE riches and righteousness, Prov. 8. 18.
Isa. 23. 18. merchandise for *d.* clothing
DUST thou art, and to *d.*, Gen. 3. 19.
18. 27. who am but *d.* and ashes
Job 30. 19. I am become like *d.*
Ps. 22. 15. brought me into *d.* of
30. 9. shall the *d.* praise thee
103. 14. remembereth that we are *d.*
119. 25. soul cleaveth to the *d.*
Eccl. 12. 7. then shall *d.* retu. to *d.*
Matt. 10. 14. shake off *d.* of your feet, Luke 10. 11. Acts 13. 51.
R. V. Lev. 14. 41. mortar
DUTY of marriage, Ex. 21. 10.
2 Chron. 8. 14. as the *d.* of every day
Eccl. 12. 13. this is whole *d.* of man
Luke 17. 10. which was our *d.* to do
R. V. Rom. 15. 27. owe it to them
DWARFS not to minister, Lev. 21. 20.
DWELL in thy holy hill, Ps. 15. 1.
Ps. 23. 6. I will *d.* in the house of
84. 10. than to *d.* in the tents of wickedness
120. 5. that I *d.* in tents of Kedar
133. 1. good for brethren to *d.* together
Isa. 33. 14. who shall *d.* with devouring fire—*d.* with everlasting burnings
16. he shall *d.* on high his place
Rom. 8. 9. Spirit of God *d.* in you, 11
2 Cor. 6. 16. I will *d.* in them, Ezek. 43. 7.
Col. 1. 19. in him shall all fulness *d.*
1 John 4. 13. that we *d.* in him
Rev. 21. 3. he will *d.* with them
John 6. 56. *dwelleth* in me, and I in
14. 10. Father that *d.* in me
17. he *d.* with and shall be in you
Acts 7. 48. *d.* not in temples, 17. 24.
Rom. 7. 17. sin that *d.* in me, 20.
18. in my flesh *d.* no good thing
8. 11. by his Spirit that *d.* in you
1 Cor. 3. 16. Spirit of God *d.* in you
Col. 2. 9. in him *d.* all fulness of
2 Tim. 1. 14. Holy Ghost who *d.* in
Jas. 4. 5. the Spirit which *d.* in
2 Pet. 3. 13. wherein *d.* righteous.
1 John 3. 17. how *d.* the love of God
4. 12. God *d.* in us, and his love is
16. *d.* in love, *d.* in God, and God
2 John 2. truth's sake which *d.* in
1 Tim. 6. 16. *dwelling* in light
Heb. 11. 9. *d.* in tabernacles with
2 Pet. 2. 8. righteous man *d.* among
Ps. 87. 2. more than all *d.* of Jacob
94. 17. almost *dwelt* in silence
John 1. 14. Word made flesh
Acts 13. 17. *d.* as strangers in it
2 Tim. 1. 5. faith *d.* first in grandmother
R. V. frequently in O. T., sit, sojourn

E

EAGLE stirreth up her nest, Deut. 32. 11.
Job 9. 26. as *e.* hasteth to the prey
Prov. 23. 5. fly away as *e.* towards
Jer. 49. 16. make nest as high as *e.*
Ezek. 17. 3. great *e.* with great wings
Mic. 1. 16. enlarge thy bald. as *e.*
Rev. 12. 14. to woman given wings of a great *e.*
Ex. 19. 4. bare you on *e.* wings
2 Sam. 1. 23. swifter than *eagles*
Ps. 103. 5. youth renewed like *e.*
Prov. 30. 17. young *e.* shall eat it
Isa. 40. 31. mount up with wings as *e.*
Jer. 4. 13. horses swifter than *e.*
Matt. 24. 28. there *e.* be gathered
R. V. Lev. 11. 18; Deut. 14. 17. vulture
EAR, Num. 14. 28. Ex. 9. 31.
Ex. 21. 6. bore his *e.*, Deut. 15. 17.
2 Kings 19. 16. bow down *e.*, Ps. 31. 2.
Neh. 1. 6. let thy *e.* be attentive, 11.
Job 12. 11. *e.* try words, 34. 3.
36. 10. openeth *e.* to discipline
Ps. 10. 17. cause thine *e.* to hear
Ps. 94. 9. planted the *e.* shall he not
Prov. 18. 15. *e.* of wise seek know.
20. 12. hearing *e.* and seeing eye
Eccl. 1. 8. nor *e.* filled with hearing
Isa. 50. 4. awaketh my *e.* to hear
59. 1. neither is *e.* heavy
Jer. 6. 10. their *e.* is uncircumcised
Matt. 10. 27. what ye hear in the *e.*
1 Cor. 2. 9. eye seen nor *e.* heard
Rev. 2. 7. he that hath an *e.* let him hear, 11. 17, 29. & 3. 6, 13, 22. & 13. 9. Matt. 11. 15. & 13. 9, 43.
Ex. 15. 26. *give ear*, Deut. 32. 1. Judg. 5. 3. Ps. 5. 1. & 17. 1. & 39. 12. & 49. 1. & 54. 2. & 78. 1. & 80. 1. & 84. 8. & 141. 1. Isa. 1. 2, 10. & 8. 9. & 28. 23. & 32. 9. & 42. 23. Jer. 13. 15. Hos. 5. 1. Joel 1. 2. Ps. 55. 1. & 86. 6.
Ps. 17. 6. *incline ear*, 45. 10. & 71. 2. & 88. 2. & 102. 2. & 116. 2. Isa. 37. 17. Dan. 9. 18.
49. 4. — to a parable
78. 1. — to words of my mouth
Prov. 2. 2. — to wisdom
4. 20. — to my sayings
Isa. 55. 3. — and come unto me
Jer. 11. 8. *nor inclined their ear*, 17. 23. & 25. 4. & 35. 15.
Deut. 29. 4. Lord not given *ears* to
1 Sam. 3. 11. both *e.* shall tingle, 2 Kings 21. 12. Jer. 19. 3.
2 Sam. 22. 7. cry did enter in. his *e.*
Job 33. 16. open the *e.* of men
Ps. 34. 15. his *e.* are open to their cry
40. 6. my *e.* hast thou opened
44. 1. we have heard with our *e.*
Isa. 6. 10. make their *e.* heavy, lest
35. 5. *e.* of deaf shall be unstopped
Matt. 13. 15. their *e.* dull of hearing
Luke 9. 44. these sayings sink down into your *e.*
2 Tim. 4. 4. turn away their *e.* from
2 Chron. 6. 40. *thine ears* be open to
Ps. 10. 17. cause — to hear
130. 2. let — be attentive
Prov. 23. 12. apply — to words of knowledge
Isa. 30. 21. — shall hear a word
Ezek. 3. 10. hear with —, 40. 4. & 44. 5.
Gen. 45. 6. *earing*, Ex. 34. 21.
1 Sam. 8. 12. *ear his ground*, Isa. 30. 24.
Ex. 9. 31. *in the ear*, Mark 4. 28.
Job 42. 11. gave *ear-ring* of gold
Prov. 25. 12. as an *e.* of gold so is
R. V. Gen. 24. 22, 47; 35. 4; Ex. 32. 2, 3; Job 42. 11. ring, rings; Isa. 3. 20. amulets
EARLY, Gen. 19. 2. John 18. 28. & 20. 1.
Ps. 46. 5. God shall help her, and that right *e.*
57. 8. will awake right *e.*, 108. 2.
63. 1. my God, *e.* will I seek thee
90. 14. satisfy us *e.* with mercy
Prov. 1. 28. seek me *e.* and not find
8. 17. that seek me *e.* shall find me
Isa. 26. 9. with my spir. I seek thee *e.*
Jer. 7. 13. rising up *e.*, 25. & 11. 7. & 25. 3, 4. & 26. 5. & 29. 19. & 32. 33. & 35. 14, 15. & 44. 4. 2 Chron. 36. 15.
Hos. 5. 15. in affliction will seek me *e.*
Jas. 5. 7. receive *e.* and latter rain
R. V. Judg. 7. 3; Ps. 57. 8. right early; 9. 14. in the morning; 101. 8. morning by morning; Ps. 1. 28; 8. 17. diligently; Hos. 5. 15. earnestly; Mark 16. 2. early in the morning; Acts 5. 21. about daybreak
EARNEST of Spirit given, 2 Cor. 1. 22. & 5. 5.
Eph. 1. 14. *e.* of your inheritance
Rom. 8. 19. *e.* expectation of the
2 Cor. 7. 7. told us of your *e.* desire
Heb. 2. 1. give the more *e.* heed
Job 7. 2. servant *earnestly* desireth the shadow
Jer. 11. 7. I *e.* protested to your fathers
31. 20. I do *e.* remember him still
Mic. 7. 3. do evil with both hands *e.*
Luke 22. 44. in an agony, prayed more *e.*
1 Cor. 12. 31. covet *e.* the best gifts
2 Cor. 5. 2. in this we groan *e.*
Jas. 5. 17. prayed *e.* it might not
Jude 3. *e.* contend for the faith
R. V. Mic. 7. 3. diligently; Luke 22. 56; Acts 23. 1. stedfastly; Acts 3. 12. fasten your eyes; Jas. 5. 17. fervently
EARNETH wages, Hag. 1. 6.
EARTH was corrupt, Gen. 6. 11, 12.
Gen. 6. 13. *e.* is filled with violence
11. 1. whole *e.* of one language
41. 47. *e.* brought forth by handfuls
Ex. 9. 29. *e.* is the Lord's, Deut. 10. 14. Ps. 24. 1. 1 Cor. 10. 26, 27, 28.
Num. 16. 32. *e.* opened her mouth, 26. 10. Deut. 11. 6. Ps. 106. 17.
Deut. 28. 23. *e.* under thee be iron
32. 1. O *e.* hear the words of my mouth
Judg. 5. 4. *e.* trembleth and heaven
1 Sam. 2. 8. pillars of *e.* are Lord's
2 Sam. 22. 8. *e.* shook and trembled
1 Chron. 16. 31. let *e.* rejoice, Ps. 96. 11.
Job 9. 6. shakes *e.* out of her place
24. *e.* is given into hand of wicked
11. 9. longer than *e.* broader than
16. 18. O *e.* cover not my blood
26. 7. hangeth *e.* upon nothing
28. 5. out of *e.* cometh bread and
38. 4. I laid the foundations of *e.*
Ps. 33. 5. *e.* is full of the goodness of
65. 9. visitest *e.* and waterest it
67. 6. *e.* shall yield her increase, 85. 12.
72. 19. let the whole *e.* be filled
75. 3. *e.* and inhabitants dissolved, Isa. 24. 19.
78. 69. like *e.* established for ever
97. 4. *e.* saw and trembled
104. 24. *e.* is full of thy riches, 13.
114. 7. tremble, O *e.* at presence of
115. 16. *e.* given to children of men
119. 64. *e.* is full of thy mercy
139. 15. in lowest parts of the *e.*
Prov. 25. 3. *e.* for depth is unsearchable
Isa. 6. 3. whole *e.* is full of his glory
11. 9. *e.* full of the knowledge of
24. 1. Lord maketh the *e.* empty
4. *e.* mourneth and fadeth, 33. 9.
5. *e.* is defiled under inhabitants
19. *e.* utterly broken down and
20. *e.* shall reel and stagger like a
26. 19. *e.* shall cast out her dead
Jer. 22. 29. O *e. e. e.* hear the word
Ezek. 34. 27. the *e.* shall yield her
43. 2. the whole *e.* shined with his
Hos. 2. 22. *e.* shall hear the corn
Hab. 3. 3. *e.* was full of his praise
Matt. 13. 5. stony ground had not much *e.*
John 3. 31. that is of *e.* earthly
Heb. 6. 7. *e.* which drinketh in rain
Rev. 12. 16. *e.* opened and swallowed
Ps. 67. 2. way known *upon earth*
73. 25. none — I desire besides thee
Eccl. 5. 2. God is in heaven and thou —
7. 20. there is not a just man —

Luke 5. 24. the Son of man hath power—
Col. 3. 5. mortify your members—
Lev. 6. 28. *earthen*, Jer. 19. 1. & 32. 14. Lam. 4. 2. 2 Cor. 4. 7.
John 3. 12, 31. *earthly*, 2 Cor. 5. 1. Phil. 3. 19. Jas. 3. 15.
1 Cor. 15. 47, 48, 49. *earthy*
1 Kings 19. 11, 12. *earthquake*, Isa. 29. 6. Amos 1. 1. Zech. 14. 5. Matt. 24. 7, 27, 54. & 28. 2. Acts 16. 26.
Rev. 6. 12. a great *e.*, 8. 5. & 11. 19. & 16. 18.
R. V. very frequently in O. T., land; John 3. 31. of the earth

EASE, Job 12. 5. & 16. 12. & 21. 23. Ps. 25. 13. & 123. 4. Deut. 28. 65. Isa. 32. 9, 11. Jer. 46. 27. & 48. 11. Ezek. 23. 42. Amos 6. 1. Zech. 1. 15.
Isa. 1. 24. I will *e.* me of mine adversaries
Luke 12. 19. take thine *e.* be merry
Matt. 11. 30. my yoke is *easy*, and burden light
Prov. 14. 6. knowledge is *e.* to him
1 Cor. 14. 9. words *e.* to be underst.
Jas. 3. 17. gentle, *e.* to be entreated
Matt. 9. 5. *easier*, 19. 24. Luke 16. 17.
1 Cor. 13. 5. charity is not *easily* provoked
Heb. 12. 1. sin—doth so *e.* beset us
R. V. Deut. 23. 13. sitteth down; 2 Chron. 10. 4, 9. make

EAST, Gen. 28. 14. & 29. 1. Matt. 2. 1, 2. Ps. 75. 6. & 103. 12.
Isa. 43. 5. bring thy seed from *e.*
Matt. 8. 11. many shall come from *e.*
Rev. 16. 12. way of kings of the *e.* may
Gen. 41. 6. *east wind*, Ex. 14. 21. Job 27. 21. Ps. 48. 7. Isa. 27. 8. Hos. 12. 1. & 13. 15. Hab. 1. 9.
R. V. Jer. 19. 2. Harsith; Rev. 7. 2; 16. 12. sunrising; Gen. 2. 14. in front; Num. 3. 38. toward the sunrising

EAT, Gen. 3. 5, 6, 12, 13. & 18. 8. & 19. 3.
Gen. 2. 16, 17. of every tree freely *e.*
3. 14. dust shalt thou *e.* all the
17. in sorrow thou shalt *e.* of it
Neh. 8. 10. *e.* the fat, drink the sweet
Ps. 22. 26. the meek shall *e.* and
53. 4. eat up my people as bread, 14. 4.
78. 25. man did *e.* angels' food
29. they did *e.* and were filled
Prov. 1. 31. *e.* fruit of their own way
S. of S. 5. 1. *e.* O friends; drink, yea
Isa. 1. 19. if obedient ye shall *e.*
3. 10. shall *e.* fruit of doings
55. 1. buy and *e.* yea, come buy
2. *e.* that which is good, and let
65. 13. my servants shall *e.* but ye
Dan. 4. 33. did *e.* grass as an ox
Hos. 4. 10. shall *e.* and not have enough, Hag. 1. 6. Mic. 6. 14.
Mic. 3. 3. *e.* flesh of my people
Matt. 6. 25. what shall we *e.* and
26. 26. take *e.* this is my body, Mark 14. 22. 1 Cor. 11. 24, 26, 28.
Luke 10. 8. *e.* such things as are set
15. 23. let us *e.* and be merry
17. 27. they did *e.* they drank, 28.
John 6. 26. because ye did *e.* of
53. except ye *e.* flesh of Son of man
Acts 2. 46. did *e.*—with gladness
1 Cor. 5. 11. with such, no, not to *e.*
31. whether ye *e.* or drink, do all
2 Thes. 3. 10. if not work neither *e.*
2 Tim. 2. 17. *e.* as doth a canker
Jas. 5. 3. *e.* your flesh as fire
Rev. 17. 16. shall *e.* her flesh, and
Ps. 69. 9. the zeal of thy house hath *eaten* me up, John 2. 17. Ps. 119. 139.
Prov. 9. 17. bread *e.* in secret is
S. of S. 5. 1. *e.* my honeycomb with
Hos. 10. 13. having *e.* fruit of lies
Luke 13. 26. *e.* and drunk in thy
Acts 12. 23. Herod was *e.* of worms
Judg. 14. 14. out of *eater* came meat
Isa. 55. 10. give bread to *e.* and seed
Nah. 3. 12. fall into mouth of *e.*
Eccl. 4. 5. *eateth* his own flesh
Matt. 9. 11. why *e.* your master with publicans and sinners, Luke 15. 2.
John 6. 54. whoso *e.* my flesh
57. he that *e.* me shall live by me
58. he that *e.* this bread shall live
Rom. 14. 6. he that *e. e.* to the Lord
20. evil for that man who *e.* with offence
1 Cor. 11. 29. *e.* and drinketh unworthily, *e.* and drinketh damnation, 27.
Matt. 11. 18. John came neither *eating* nor drinking, Luke 7. 33.
19. Son of man came *e.*
24. 38. were *e.* and drinking, Luke 17. 27.
Matt. 26. 26. as they were *e.* Jesus
1 Cor. 8. 4. concerning *e.* of those

EDIFY, or build up, Rom. 14. 19. 1 Thes. 5. 11. 1 Cor. 8. 1. & 10. 23. & 14. 17. Acts 9. 31.
Rom. 15. 2. please neighbor to *edification*
1 Cor. 14. 3. speak unto men to *e.*
1 Cor. 14. 12. excel to *edifying* of church
26. let all things be done to *e.*, 5. 17.
2 Cor. 12. 19. we do all for your *e.*
Eph. 4. 29. but what is good to the use of *e.*
1 Tim. 1. 4. minister questions rather than *e.*
R. V. 1 Thes. 5. 11. build each . . up; Eph. 4. 12; 4. 16. building up; 1 Tim. 1. 4. a dispensation of God; Rom. 15. 2. unto edifying; 2 Cor. 10. 8; 13. 10. building up

EFFECT, 2 Chron. 34. 22. Ezek. 12. 23.
Isa. 32. 17. *e.* of righteousness quietness
Matt. 15. 6. commandment of God *of none effect*
Mark 7. 13. making work of God—
Rom. 3. 3. make faith of God—
9. 6. not as though word hath—
1 Cor. 1. 17. lest cross of Christ—
Gal. 5. 4. Christ is become—to you
1 Cor. 16. 9. door and *effectual* is opened
2 Cor. 1. 6. which is *e.* in enduring
Eph. 3. 7. *e.* working of his power
Phile. 6. faith may become *e.*
Jas. 5. 16. *e.* fervent prayer of the righteous
Gal. 2. 8. *effectually*, 1 Thes. 2. 13.
R. V. Num. 30. 8; Matt. 15. 6; Mark 7. 13; 1 Cor. 1. 17. void; Rom. 9. 6. come to nought; Gal. 5. 4. severed from Christ; Jer. 48. 30. have wrought nothing; 2 Cor. 1. 6. worketh patient; Eph. 3. 7. according to; 4. 16. working in due measure; Jas. 5. 16. supplication; Gal. 2. 8. for; 1 Thes. 2. 13——

EFFEMINATE, 1 Cor. 6. 9.

EGG, Deut. 22. 6. Job 6. 6. & 39. 14. Isa. 10. 14. & 59. 5. Jer. 17. 11. Luke 11. 12.

ELDER, Gen. 10. 21. 2 John 1. 3 John 1.
Gen. 25. 23. *e.* shall serve younger, Rom. 9. 12.
1 Tim. 5. 1. rebuke not an *e.* but
2. entreat *e.* women as mothers
1 Pet. 5. 1. *elders*, I who am an *e.*
5. younger submit yourselves to *e.*
Deut. 32. 7. ask *e.* they will tell thee
Ezra 10. 8. according to counsel of *e.*
Joel 2. 16. assemble *e.*, Ps. 107. 32.
Acts 14. 23. ordain *e.* in every
15. 23. *e.* and brethren send greeting, 6.
1 Tim. 5. 17. *e.* rule well, counted worthy
Tit. 1. 5. ordain *e.* in every church
Heb. 11. 2. *e.* obtained good report
Rev. 4. 4. four and twenty *e.* sitting, 10. & 5. 6, 8, 11, 14. & 11. 16. & 19. 4. & 7. 11, 13. & 14. 3.
R. V. Joel 1. 14; 2. 16. old men; Matt. 26. 59——

ELECT, *chosen, choice one*
Isa. 42. 1. *e.* in whom my soul delighteth
45. 4. for Israel my *e.* I have called
65. 9. my *e.* shall inherit it
22. my *e.* shall long enjoy work
Matt. 24. 22. for *e.* sake the days are shortened
24. if possible deceive very *e.*
31. gather together his *e.* from the
Luke 18. 7. God avenge his own *e.*
Rom. 8. 33. to charge of God's *e.*
1 Tim. 5. 21. charge thee before the *e.* angels
2 Tim. 2. 10. endure all things for *e.*
Tit. 1. 1. according to the faith of God's *e.*
1 Pet. 1. 2. *e.* according to the fore.
2. 6. corner stone, *e.* precious
2 John 1. *e.* lady
13. *e.* sister
1 Pet. 5. 13. church *elected* with you
Rom. 9. 11. purpose of God according to *election*
11. 5. remnant according to the *e.* of grace
7. *e.* hath obtained it, and rest blinded
28. touching the *e.* they are beloved
1 Thes. 1. 4. knowing your *e.* of God
2 Pet. 1. 10. make calling and *e.* sure
R. V. Isa. 42. 1; 45. 4; 65. 9, 22. my chosen

ELEMENTS, Gal. 4. 3, 9. 2 Pet. 3. 10, 12.
R. V. Gal. 4. 3, 9. rudiments

ELOQUENT, Ex. 4. 10. Isa. 3. 3. Acts 18. 24.
R. V. Isa. 3. 3. skilful; Acts 18. 24. learned

EMBALMING, of Jacob, Gen. 50. 2. of Joseph, Gen. 50. 26. of Christ, John 19. 39.

EMPTY, Gen. 31. 42. & 37. 24. & 41. 27.
Ex. 23. 15. none shall appear before me *e.*, 34. 20. Deut. 16. 16.
Deut. 15. 13. not let him go away *e.*
Judg. 7. 16. with *e.* pitchers and lamps
2 Sam. 1. 22. sword of Saul returned not *e.*
Hos. 10. 1. Israel is an *e.* vine
Luke 1. 53. rich hath he sent *e.* away
Isa. 34. 11. stones of *emptiness*
R. V. Hos. 10. 1. luxuriant

EMULATION, Rom. 11. 14. Gal. 5. 20.

END of all flesh is come, Gen. 6. 13.
Deut. 32. 20. see what their *e.* shall
Ps. 37. 37. *e.* of that man is peace
39. 4. make me to know my *e.*
Prov. 5. 4. her *e.* is bitter as worm.
14. 12. *e.* thereof are ways of death
Eccl. 4. 8. no *e.* of all his labor
7. 2. that is the *e.* of all men
Isa. 9. 7. of his government shall be no *e.*
Jer. 5. 31. what will ye do in the *e.* thereof
29. 11. to give an expected *e.*
Lam. 4. 18. our *e.* is come. our *e.* is near, Ezek. 7. 2, 6. Amos 8. 2.
Ezek. 21. 25. when iniquity shall have an *e.*
Dan. 12. 8. what shall be the *e.* of these
13. go thy way till the *e.* be
Hab. 2. 3. at the *e.* it shall speak
Matt. 13. 39. harvest is *e.* of world
24. 6. but *e.* is not yet, Luke 21. 9.
Rom. 6. 21. *e.* of those things is death
10. 4. Christ is *e.* of law for righteousness
Rom. 14. 9. to this *e.* Christ both
1 Tim. 1. 5. *e.* of commandment is
Heb. 6. 8. whose *e.* is to be burned
16. oath—make an *e.* of all strife
13. 7. considering *e.* of their
Jas. 5. 11. seen the *e.* of the Lord
1 Pet. 1. 9. receiving the *e.* of your
4. 7. *e.* of all things is at hand
Rev. 21. 6. beginning and *e.*, 22. 13. & 1. 8. 1 Sam. 3. 12.

Jer. 4. 27. *make a full end*, 5. 10, 18. & 30. 11. Ezek. 11. 13.
Num. 23. 10. *last end*, Jer. 12. 4. Lam. 1. 9. & 4. 18. Dan. 8. 19. & 9. 24.
Deut. 8. 16. *latter end*, 32. 29. Job 42. 12. Prov. 19. 20. 2 Pet. 2. 20.
Ps. 119. 33. *unto the end*, Dan. 6. 26. Matt. 24. 13. & 28. 20. John 13. 1. 1 Cor. 1. 8. Heb. 3. 6, 14. & 6. 11. Rev. 2. 26.
1 Tim. 1. 4. *endless*, Heb. 7. 16.
Ps. 22. 27. all the *ends* of the world
65. 5. confidence of all *e.* of earth
67. 7. all *e.* of earth shall fear him
Prov. 17. 24. eyes of fool in *e.* of
Isa. 45. 22. be ye saved, all *e.* of the
52. 10. all *e.* of the earth shall see
Zech. 9. 10. his dominion to *e.* of
Acts 13. 47. for salvation to the *e.*
1 Cor. 10. 11. on whom *e.* of world
R. V. Josh. 15. 8; 18. 15; Isa. 13. 5; Acts 13. 47. uttermost part; Dan. 12. 8; Heb. 13. 7. issue; Luke 22. 37. hath fulfilment; Matt. 28. 1. now late on; 1 Pet. 1. 13. perfectly on; 2 Pet. 2. 20. last state . . become; Gen. 2. 2; Deut. 31. 30; 1 Kings 7. 51. finished; Ezek. 4. 8. accomplished; Luke 4. 2, 13; Acts 21. 27. completed; John 13. 2 ——

ENDOWED, Gen. 30. 20. 2 Chron. 2. 12, 13. Luke 24. 49. Jas. 3. 13.

ENDURE, Job 8. 15. & 31. 23.
Gen. 33. 14. as children are able to *e.*
Ps. 30. 5. weeping may *e.* for a night
132. 26. they perish, but thou shalt *e.*
Prov. 27. 24. doth crown *e.* to
Ezek. 22. 14. can thy heart *e.* or
Mark 4. 17. no root, and *e.* but for a
13. 13. that shall *e.* unto end shall
2 Tim. 2. 3. *e.* hardness as a soldier
10. *e.* all things for elect's sakes
4. 5. watch thou, *e.* afflictions, do
Heb. 12. 7. if ye *e.* chastening
Jas. 5. 11. we count happy who *e.*
Ps. 81. 15. should have *endured* for ever
Rom. 9. 22. *e.* with much long suffering
2 Tim. 3. 11. what persecutions I *e.*
Heb. 6. 15. had patiently *e.* he obtained
10. 32. ye *e.* a great fight of afflic.
12. 2. *e.* cross
3. *e.* contradiction
Ps. 30. 5. his anger *endureth* but a
52. 1. the goodness of God *e.* continually
100. 5. his truth *e.* to all generations
Matt. 10. 22. that *e.* to end, shall be saved, 24. 13. Mark 13. 13.
John 6. 27. meat which *e.* unto life
1 Cor. 13. 7. charity *e.* all things
Jas. 1. 12. blessed that *e.* temptation
Ps. 9. 7. *endure for ever*, the Lord, 102. 12, 26. & 104. 31. his name, Ps. 72. 17. his seed, 89. 29, 36.
1 Chron. 16. 34, 41. *endureth for ever*, his mercy, 2 Chron. 5. 13. & 7. 3, 6. & 20. 21. Ezra 3. 11. Ps. 106. 1. & 107. 1. & 118. 1, 2 3, 4, 29. & 136. 1-26. & 138. 8. Jer. 33. 11.
Ps. 111. 3. his righteousness —, 112. 39.
10. his praise —
117. 2. truth of the Lord —
119. 160. every one of thy judgments —
135. 13. thy name —
1 Pet. 1. 25. word of Lord —
Ps. 19. 9. fear of Lord *enduring* for ever
Heb. 10. 34. in heaven *e.* substance
R. V. Gen. 33. 14. according to the pace; Job 31. 23. do nothing; Ps. 9. 7. sitteth; 30. 5. tarry; John 6. 27; 1 Pet. 1. 25. abideth; Heb. 10. 34. abiding

ENEMY, Ex. 15. 6, 9. Ps. 7. 5.
Ex. 23. 22. I will be an *e.* unto thine enemies
Deut. 32. 27. I feared wrath of the *e.*
1 Sam. 24. 19. find his *e.* will he let
Job 33. 10. counteth me for his *e.*
Ps. 7. 5. let *e.* persecute my soul
8. 2. mightest still the *e.* and
Prov. 27. 6. kisses of *e.* are deceitful
Isa. 63. 10. he turned to be their *e.*
1 Cor. 15. 26. the last *e.* destroyed
Gal. 4. 16. am I become your *e.*
2 Thes. 3. 15. count him not as *e.*
Jas. 4. 4. friend of world, *e.* of God
1 Kings 21. 20. *mine enemy*, Ps. 7. 4. Mic. 7. 8, 10. Job 16. 9. Lam. 2. 22.
Ex. 23. 4. *thy enemy*, Prov. 25. 21. Rom. 12. 20. Matt. 5. 43.
Mic. 7. 6. man's *enemies* are men of
Rom. 5. 10. if when *e.* we were reconciled
1 Cor. 15. 25. put all *e.* under his feet
Phil. 3. 18. *e.* to the cross of Christ
Col. 1. 21. *e.* in your minds by wicked
Gen. 22. 17. *his enemies*, Ps. 68. 1, 21. & 112. 8. & 132. 18. Prov. 16. 7. Isa. 59. 18. & 66. 6. Heb. 10. 13.
Deut. 32. 41. *my enemies*, Ps. 18. 17, 48. & 23. 5. & 119. 98. & 139. 22. & 143. 12. Isa. 1. 24. Luke 19. 27.
Deut. 32. 31. *our enemies*, Luke 1. 71, 74.
Ex. 23. 22. *thy enemies*, Num. 10. 35. Deut. 28. 48, 53, 55, 57. & 33. 29. Judg. 5. 31. Ps. 21. 8. & 92. 9. & 110. 1. Matt. 22. 44. Heb. 1. 13.
Gen. 3. 15. I will put *enmity* between
Rom. 8. 7. carnal mind is *e.* against God
Eph. 2. 15. abolished *e.*
16. slain *e.*
R. V. Very frequently in O. T., especially in Ps., adversary

ENGAGETH his heart, Jer. 30. 21.

ENJOIN, Philc. 8. Esth. 9. 31. Job 36. 23. Heb. 9. 20.
R. V. Heb. 9. 20. commanded to you ward

ENJOY, Num. 36. 8. Deut. 28. 41.
Lev. 26. 34. land *e.* her sabbaths, 43.
Acts 24. 2. we *e.* great quietness
1 Tim. 6. 17. giveth richly all things to *e.*
Heb. 11. 25. *e.* pleasures of sin for
R. V. Num. 36. 8; Josh. 1. 15. possess

ENLARGE, Ex. 34. 24. Mic. 1. 16.
Gen. 9. 27. God shall *e.* Japheth
Deut. 33. 20. blessed be he that *enlargeth* Gad
2 Sam. 22. 37. *enlarged* steps, Ps. 18. 36.
Ps. 4. 1. *e.* me when in distress
25. 17. troubles of my heart are *e.*
119. 32. when thou shalt *e.* my
Isa. 5. 14. hell hath *e.* herself
54. 2. *e.* the place of thy tent
Hab. 2. 5. *e.* his desires as hell
2 Cor. 6. 11. our heart is *e.*, 13.
Esth. 4. 14. *enlargement*
R. V. Ps. 4. 1. set me at large; 2 Cor. 10. 15. magnified in

ENLIGHTEN darkness, Ps. 18. 28.
Eph. 1. 18. understanding being *enlightened*
Ps. 19. 8. commandment is pure, *enlightening* the eyes
Heb. 6. 4. impossible for those once *e.*
R. V. Ps. 18. 28. lighten

ENMITY between God and man, Rom. 8. 7. Jas. 4. 4; how abolished, Eph. 2. 15. Col. 1. 20.

ENOUGH, I have, Gen. 33. 9, 11.
Gen. 45. 28. it is *e.* Joseph is alive
Ex. 36. 5. bring more than *e.*
1 Kings 19. 4. it is *e.* take away
Prov. 30. 15, 16. say not, it is *e.*
Hos. 4. 10. eat, and not *e.*, Hag. 1. 6.
Matt. 10. 25. it is *e.* for disciple
Mark 14. 41. it is *e.* the hour is
Luke 15. 17. bread *e.* and to spare
R. V. Ex. 2. 19——

ENQUIRE after iniquity, Job 10. 6.
Ps. 27. 4. to *e.* in his temple
78. 34. returned and *e.* early after God
Eccl. 7. 10. thou dost not *e.* wisely
Isa. 21. 12. if ye will *e.* *e.* ye
Ezek. 36. 37. this I will be *enquired* of by the house of Israel
Zeph. 1. 6. have not *e.* for him
Matt. 2. 7. Herod *e.* of them diligently
Judg. 20. 27. *enquired of the Lord*, 1 Sam. 23. 2, 4. & 30. 8. 2 Sam. 2. 1. & 5. 19, 23. & 21. 1. Jer. 21. 2.
Prov. 20. 25. after vows make *enquiry*
R. V. Almost always changed to inquire; Matt. 27. 7, 16. learned; 1 Pet. 1. 10. sought

ENRICHED, 1 Cor. 1. 5. 2 Cor. 9. 11.
Ps. 65. 9. thou greatly *e.* it with

ENSAMPLE, 1 Cor. 10. 11. Phil. 3. 17. 1 Thes. 1. 7. 2 Thes. 3. 9. 1 Pet. 5. 3. 2 Pet. 2. 6.
R. V. 1 Cor. 10. 11. by way of example; 2 Pet. 2. 6. example

ENSIGN, Isa. 5. 26. Zech. 9. 16.
Isa. 11. 10. stand for *e.* to people, 12.
Ps. 74. 4. set up their *e.* for signs
R. V. Zech. 9. 16. on high

ENTER, Gen. 12. 11. Num. 4. 23. Judg. 18. 9. Dan. 11. 17, 40, 41.
Job 22. 4. will he *e.* into judg.
Ps. 100. 4. *e.* into his gates with
Isa. 2. 10. *e.* into rock and hide
26. 2. open, righteous nation may *e.*
20. *e.* into thy chambers, and shut
57. 2. he shall *e.* into peace
Matt. 5. 20. in no case *e.* into the
6. 6. when thou prayest, *e.* closet
7. 13. *e.* at strait gate, Luke 13. 24.
21. shall *e.* into kingdom of heaven
18. 8. better to *e.* into life, halt
19. 23. rich man hardly *e.* into
24. than for rich man to *e.* into the kingdom of heaven, Mark 10. 25. Luke 18. 25.
25. 21. *e.* thou into joy of Lord
Mark 14. 38. watch and pray, lest ye *e.* into temptation, Luke 22. 46.
Luke 13. 24. seek to *e.* but not able
24. 26. suffered and *e.* into his glory
John 3. 4. can he *e.* the second time
5. he cannot *e.* into the kingdom
Acts 14. 22. through much tribulation *e.* kingdom of God.
Heb. 4. 3. believed, do *e.* into rest
Rev. 15. 8. no man able to *e.* into temple
21. 27. *e.* into it, any thing defileth
Rev. 22. 14. *e.* through gates into
Ps. 143. 2. *enter not into* judgment
Prov. 4. 14. *e.* not into path of
23. 10. *e.* not into the fields of the
Matt. 26. 41. that ye *e.* not into temptation
Ps. 119. 130. *entrance*, 2 Pet. 1. 11.
Luke 11. 52. ye *entered* not yoursel.
John 4. 38. ye *e.* into their labors
10. 1. that *e.* not by door, but
Rom. 5. 12. sin *e.* into the world
Heb. 4. 6. *e.* not in because of unbelief
10. that is *e.* into his rest, he ceased
Matt. 23. 13. *entering*, Luke 11. 52. Mark 4. 19. & 7. 15. 1 Thes. 1. 9. Heb. 4. 1.
R. V. Mark 5. 40; 7. 18. goeth. The same change is frequent in O. T. Ex. 35. 15. door; 2 Chron. 18. 9; 23. 13. entrance; Mark 7. 15. going; Acts 27. 2. embarking; Num. 34. 8; 1 Chron. 4. 39; 1 Thes. 2. 1. entering; 2 Chron. 12. 10. door; Ps. 119. 130. opening

ENTERTAIN strangers, Heb. 13. 2.
R. V. Show love unto
ENTICE, Ex. 20. 16. Deut. 13. 6.
2 Chron. 18. 19, 20, 21. Prov. 1. 10.
Job 31. 27. *enticed,* Jas. 1. 14.
1 Cor. 2. 4. *enticing words,* Col. 2. 4.
R. V. 1 Cor. 2. 4. persuasive; Col. 2. 4. persuasiveness of
ENVY slayeth silly one, Job 5. 2.
Prov. 3. 31. *e.* not the oppressor
14. 30. *e.* is the rottenness of bones
23. 17. let not thy heart *e.* sinners
Eccl. 9. 6. their *e.* is perished
Isa. 11. 13. *e.* of Ephraim shall depart, not *e.* Judah
Ezek. 35. 11. do according to thine *e.*
Matt. 27. 18. for *e.* they delivered
Acts 7. 9. moved with *e.*, 17. 5.
13. 45. Jews filled with *e.* spake
Rom. 1. 29. full of *e.* murder
Phil. 1. 15. preach Christ of *e.*
1 Tim. 6. 4. whereof cometh *e.*
Jas. 4. 5. spirit in us lusteth to *e.*
1 Pet. 2. 1. laying aside all *e.*
Gen. 26. 14. Philistines *envied* him
30. 1. Rachel *e.* her sister
Ps. 106. 16. they *e.* Moses in camp
Eccl. 4. 4. man is *e.* of his neigh.
Num. 11. 29. *enviest* thou for my sake
1 Cor. 13. 4. charity *envieth* not
Rom. 13. 13. not in strife and *envying*
1 Cor. 3. 3. there is among you *e.*
2 Cor. 12. 20. debates, *e.* wraths
Gal. 5. 26. *e.* one another
Jas. 3. 14. ye have bitter *e.* and
Gal. 5. 21. *envyings,* murders
Ps. 37. 1. *envious,* 73. 3. Prov. 24. 1, 19.
R. V. Isa. 26. 11. see thy zeal for the people; Job 5. 2; Prov. 27. 4; Acts 7. 9; 13. 45; 17. 5. jealousy; Rom. 13. 13; 1 Cor. 3. 3; 2 Cor. 12. 20; Jas. 3. 14, 16. jealousy
EPHOD, Ex. 39. 2. Judg. 8. 27. & 17. 5. 1 Sam. 2. 18. & 21. 9. & 23. 9. & 30. 7. 2 Sam. 6. 14. Hos. 3. 4.
EPISTLE, Acts 15. 30. & 23. 33. Rom. 16. 22. 1 Cor. 5. 9. 2 Cor. 7. 8. Col. 4. 16. 1 Thes. 5. 27. 2 Thes. 2. 15. & 3. 14, 17. 2 Pet. 3. 1.
2 Cor. 3. 2. *e.* written in our hearts
3. ye are declared the *e.* of Christ
1. *epistles,* 2 Pet. 3. 16.
R. V. Acts 23. 33. letter
EQUAL, Job 28. 17, 19. Ps. 17. 2. & 55. 13. Prov. 26. 7. Lam. 2. 13.
Isa. 40. 25. to whom shall I be *e.*
46. 5. to whom will ye make me *e.*
Ezek. 18. 25. way of Lord is not *e.*
29. & 33. 17, 20. their way is not *e.*
Matt. 20. 12. made them *e.* to us
Luke 20. 36. *e.* to the angels
John 5. 18. making himself *e.* with
Rev. 21. 16. length, breadth, and height *e.*
Gal. 1. 14. *equals,* Ps. 55. 13.
2 Cor. 8. 14. *equality*
Ps. 99. 4. dost establish *equity*
Prov. 1. 3. receive instruction of *e.*
17. 26. to strike princes for *e.*
Eccl. 2. 21. whose labor is in *e.*
Isa. 11. 4. reprove with *e.* for
59. 14. truth is fallen, and *e.* can.
Mic. 3. 9. that pervert all *e.*
Mal. 2. 6. walked with me in *e.*
R. V. Ps. 17. 2. equity; Prov. 26. 7. hang loose; Gal. 1. 14. of mine own age
ERR, 2 Chron. 33. 9. Isa. 19. 14.
Ps. 95. 10. *e.* in heart, Heb. 3. 10.
119. 21. do *e.* from thy command.
Prov. 14. 22. do they not *e.* that devise ill
Isa. 3. 12. lead — cause to *e.*, 9. 16.
63. 17. why made us to *e.* from thy
Jer. 23. 13. prophet caused to *e.* by lies, 32.
Amos 2. 4. lies caused them to *e.*
Mic. 3. 5. prophets make my people to *e.*
Matt. 22. 29. ye *e.* not knowing the
Jas. 1. 16. do not *e.* my brethren
5. 19. if any of you *e.* from truth
Num. 15. 22. if ye have *erred*
1 Sam. 26. 21. I have *e.* exceedingly
Job 6. 24. understand wherein I have *e.*
19. 4. be it that I have *e.*, my error
Ps. 119. 110. yet I *e.* not from
Isa. 28. 7. have *e.* through wine
29. 24. they that *e.* in spirit
1 Tim. 6. 10. have *e.* from the faith
21. *e.* concerning faith, 2 Tim. 2. 18.
Prov. 10. 17. *erreth,* Ezek. 45. 20.
2 Sam. 6. 7. *error,* Job 19. 4. Eccl. 5. 6. & 10. 5. Dan. 6. 4.
Isa. 32. 6. will utter *e.* against Lord
Jer. 10. 15. vanity work of *e.*, 51. 18.
Dan. 6. 4. neither was there any *e.* or fault found
Matt. 27. 64. last *e.* be worse than the first
Rom. 1. 27. recompense of their *e.*
Jas. 5. 20. sinner from *e.* of his
2 Pet. 2. 18. them who live in *e.*
1 John 4. 6. know we the spirit of *e.*
Jude 11. after the *e.* of Balaam
Ps. 19. 12. who can under. his *errors*
Heb. 9. 7. for the *e.* of the people
R. V. 1 Tim. 6. 10. been led astray; Jas. 1. 16. be not deceived; Jer. 10. 15; 51. 18. delusion
ERRAND, Judg. 3. 19. 2 Kings 9. 5.
ESCAPE, Gen. 19. 17, 22. & 32. 8.
Ezra 9. 8. leave a remnant to *e.*
Esth. 4. 13. think not that thou shalt *e.*
Job 11. 20. but the wicked shall not *e.*
Ps. 56. 7. shall they *e.* by iniquity
71. 2. deliver me and cause me to *e.*
141. 10. let wicked fall whilst I *e.*
Prov. 19. 5. he that speaks lies shall not *e.*
Eccl. 7. 26. pleaseth God, shall *e.* her
Isa. 20. 6. we flee — how shall we *e.*
Jer. 11. 11. evil — not be able to *e.*
Ezek. 17. 15. shall *e.* that doeth
Matt. 23. 33. how can ye *e.* damna.
Luke 21. 36. accounted worthy to *e.*
Rom. 2. 3. *e.* the judgment of God
1 Cor. 10. 13. with temptation make a way to *e.*
1 Thes. 5. 3. destruction they shall not *e.*
Heb. 2. 3. how shall we *e.* if neglect
12. 25. much more shall not we *e.*
Ezra 9. 15. we remain yet *escaped*
Job 1. 15, 16, 17, 19. I only am *e.* to
Ps. 124. 7. soul is *e.* we are *e.*
Isa. 45. 20. ye are *e.* of the nations
John 10. 39. he *e.* out of their hands
Heb. 12. 25. if they *e.* not who refused
2 Pet. 1. 4. *e.* corruption of the world
2. 18. those that were clean *e.*
20. have *e.* pollutions of the world
ESCHEW evil, Job 1. 8. & 2. 3. 1 Pet. 3. 11.
R. V. 1 Pet. 3. 11. turn away from
ESPECIALLY, Deut. 4. 10. Ps. 31. 11.
Gal. 6. 10. good *e.* to household of
1 Tim. 4. 10. *e.* of those that believe
5. 17. *e.* those that labor in word
R. V. Ps. 31. 11. exceedingly
ESPOUSALS, S. of S. 3. 11. Jer. 2. 2.
2 Cor. 11. 2. *espoused* to Christ
R. V. 2 Sam. 3. 14; Matt. 1. 18; Luke 1. 27. betrothed
ESPY, Josh. 14. 7. Ezek. 20. 6.
R. V. Josh. 14. 7. spy
ESTABLISH, Num. 30. 13. 1 Kings 15. 4. Deut. 28. 9. Job 36. 7.
Gen. 6. 18. *e.* my covenant, 9. 9. & 17. 7, 9, 21. Lev. 26. 9. Deut. 8. 18.
1 Sam. 1. 23. the Lord *e.* his word
2 Sam. 7. 12. I will *e.* his kingdom, 13.
25. *e.* the word for ever, and do as
2 Chron. 9. 8. God loved Israel to *e.*
7. 18. *e.* throne of kingdom
Ps. 7. 9. but *e.* the just, 48. 8.
89. 2. faithfulness shalt *e.* in heav.
4. thy seed will I *e.* for ever
99. 4. dost *e.* equity, executest
119. 38. *e.* thy word to servant
Prov. 15. 25. he will *e.* border of
Isa. 9. 7. to *e.* with judgment and
49. 8. give thee for a covenant to *e.*
62. 7. no rest till he *e.* Jerusalem
Ezek. 16. 60. I will *e.* an everlast.
Rom. 3. 31. yea, we *e.* the law
10. 3. going about to *e.* their own
1 Thes. 3. 13. may *e.* your hearts
2 Thes. 2. 17. *e.* you in every good
3. 3. Lord shall *e.* and keep you
Jas. 5. 8. patient; *e.* your hearts
1 Pet. 5. 10. God of all grace *e.* you
Gen. 41. 32. thing is *established*
Ex. 6. 4. have *e.* my covenant with
15. 17. which thy hands have *e.*
Ps. 40. 2. on rock he *e.* my goings
78. 5. he *e.* a testimony in Jacob
93. 2. thy throne is *e.* of old
112. 8. his heart is *e.* trusting
119. 90. hast *e.* the earth, and it
148. 6. hath *e.* them for ever
Prov. 3. 19. Lord hath *e.* the heav.
4. 26. let all thy ways be *e.*
12. 3. man shall not be *e.* by wickedness
16. 12. throne is *e.* by righteous.
30. 4. *e.* all the ends of the earth
Isa. 7. 9. if believe not — not be *e.*
16. 5. in mercy shall throne be *e.*
Jer. 10. 12. *e.* world by wisdom, 51. 15.
Hab. 1. 12. *e.* them for correction
Matt. 18. 16. two or three witness. *e.*
2 Cor. 13. 1. word may be *e.*
Acts 16. 5. so were the churches *e.*
Rom. 1. 11. to the end you may be *e.*
Col. 2. 7. built up — *e.* in the faith
Heb. 8. 6. *e.* upon better promises
2 Pet. 1. 12. *e.* in the present truth
Lev. 25. 30. *shall be established,* Deut. 19. 15. Ps. 89. 21. 2 Cor. 13. 1.
2 Chron. 20. 20. believe in God so ye —
Job 22. 28. shall decree a thing and it —
Ps. 102. 28. their seed—before thee
Prov. 12. 19. lip of truth —
25. 5. his throne — in righteousness, 29. 14.
Isa. 2. 2. Lord's house —, Mic. 4. 1.
54. 14. in righteousness thou —
Jer. 30. 20. their congregation —
Prov. 29. 4. king by judgment *establisheth* the land
Hab. 2. 12. woe to him that *e.* city by
2 Cor. 1. 21. who *e.* us with you is God
R. V. 2 Sam. 7. 25. confirm; Isa. 49. 8. raise up; Lev. 25. 30; 2 Sam. 7. 16. made sure; Prov. 8. 28. made firm; Zech. 5. 11. prepared; Heb. 8. 6. hath been enacted; Acts 16. 5. strengthened
ESTATE, Gen. 43. 7. Esth. 1. 7, 19.
Ps. 39. 5. man at best *e.* is vanity
Prov. 27. 23. know *e.* of thy flocks
Matt. 12. 45. last *e.* of that man is worse than the first, Luke 11. 26.
Luke 1. 48. regarded low *e.* of
Rom. 12. 16. condescend to men of low *e.*
Phil. 4. 11. in whatsoever *e.* I am — content
Jude 6. angels kept not first *e.*
R. V. Dan. 11. 7, 20, 21, 38. place; Mark 6. 21. chief men; Rom. 12. 16. things lowly; Jude 6. own principality
ESTEEM, Job 36. 19. Isa. 29. 16, 17.
Ps. 119. 128. I *e.* all thy precepts
Phil. 2. 3. *e.* each other better than
1 Thes. 5. 13. *e.* them very highly in
Deut. 32. 15. lightly *esteemed* the
1 Sam. 2. 30. despise me, lightly *e.*
Job 23. 12. I have *e.* words of his
Isa. 53. 3. despised — we *e.* him not
4. did *e.* him stricken, smitten of
Luke 16. 15. is highly *e.* among men
Rom. 14. 5. *esteemeth* one day above

another, another e. every day alike
Rom. 14. 14. to him that e. it to be unclean
Heb. 11. 26. *esteeming* the reproach
R. V. Job 23. 12. treasured up; 41. 27; Isa. 27. 17. counted; Luke 16. 15. exalted; Rom. 14. 14. accounteth; Heb. 11. 26. accounting
ESTRANGED, Job 19. 13. Jer. 19. 4.
Ps. 58. 3. wicked are e. from womb
78. 30. not e. from their lusts
Ezek. 14. 5. they are all e. from me
ETERNAL God thy refuge, Deut. 33. 27.
Isa. 60. 15. make thee an e. excell.
Mark 3. 29. in danger of e. damna.
Rom. 1. 20. even his e. power and
2 Cor. 4. 17. exceeding e. weight of
18. things not seen which are e.
5. 1. have house e. in the heavens
Eph. 3. 11. according to e. purpose
1 Tim. 1. 17. unto the King e. be honor
2 Tim. 2. 10. salvation with e. glory
Heb. 5. 9. author of e. salvation
6. 2. baptisms, and of e. judgment
9. 12. obtained e. redemp. for us
1 Pet. 5. 10. called us to e. glory
Jude 7. vengeance of e. fire
Matt. 19. 16. that I may have *eternal life*, Mark 10. 17. Luke 10. 25.
25. 46. the righteous shall go into—
Mark 10. 30. in world to come—
John 3. 15. not perish but have—
4. 36. gathereth fruit unto—
5. 39. in Scriptures ye think ye have—
6. 54. hath—and I will raise him
68. thou hast the words of—
10. 28. I give unto them—
12. 25. shall keep it unto—
17. 2. should give—to as many
3. this is—to know only true God
Acts 13. 48. ordained to—believed
Rom. 2. 7. who seek for glory and—
5. 21. grace might reign to—
6. 23. the gift of God is—through
1 Tim. 6. 12. lay hold on—, 19.
Tit. 1. 2. in hope of—which God
3. 7. heirs according to hope of—
2. 25. promise promised us, even—
3. 15. no murderer hath—
5. 13. may know that ye have—
Jude 21. for mercy unto—
R. V. Rom. 1. 20. everlasting
ETERNITY, that inhabits, Isa. 57. 15.
EUNUCH, 2 Kings 9. 32. & 20. 18.
Isa. 56. 3. let no e. say, I am a dry
Matt. 19. 12. some e. born made e.
Acts 8. 27. e. had come to Jerusa.
R. V. Jer. 52. 35. officer
EVEN balances, Job 31. 6.
Ps. 26. 12. foot stands in e. place
Luke 19. 44. lay thee e. with ground
EVEN or **EVENING**, Gen. 1. 5, 8, 31. & 19. 1. Ex. 12. 6, 18.
1 Kings 18. 29. at e. sacrifice, Ezra 9. 4, 5. Ps. 141. 2. Dan. 9. 21.
Hab. 1. 8. e. wolves, Zeph. 3. 3.
Zech. 14. 7. at e. time shall be light
R. V. Mark 11. 19. every evening
EVENT, Eccl. 2. 14. & 9. 2, 3.
EVER, a long time, constantly, eternally, Josh. 4. 7. & 14. 9.
Deut. 19. 9. to walk e. in his way
Ps. 5. 11. let them e. shout for joy
25. 15. my eyes e. toward the Lord
51. 3. my sin is e. before me
Luke 15. 31. son thou art e. with
John 8. 35. in house son abideth e.
1 Thes. 4. 17. we shall be e. with
5. 15. e. follow that which is good
2 Tim. 3. 7. e. learning, and never
Heb. 7. 24. this man continueth e.
25. he e. liveth to make interces.
Jude 25. to God be glory now and e.
Gen. 3. 22. eat and live *for ever*
Deut. 32. 40. I lift up hand and live—
Josh. 4. 24. fear Lord your God—
1 Kings 10. 9. Lord loved Israel—
1 Kings 11. 39. afflict the seed of David but not—
Ps. 9. 7. Lord shall endure—
12. 7. thou wilt preserve them—
22. 26. your heart shall live—
23. 6. I will dwell in the house of the Lord—
30. 12. I will give thanks to thee—
37. 18. their inheritance shall be—
28. saints are preserved—
29. in land righteous shall dwell—
49. 9. that he should still live—
52. 9. I will praise thee—
61. 4. I will abide in tabernacle—
74. 19. forget not congregation of poor—
81. 15. their time should endure—
92. 7. that they shall be destroyed—
102. 12. but thou, O Lord, shalt endure—
103. 9. the Lord will not keep his anger—
105. 8. remember his covenant—
112. 6. righteous shall not be moved—
119. 111. testimonies as heritage—
132. 14. this is my rest—I have
146. 6. who keepeth truth—
Prov. 27. 24. riches are not—crown
Eccl. 1. 4. the earth abideth—
Isa. 26. 4. trust in Lord—for in Lord
32. 17. quietness and assurance—
40. 8. word of Lord shall stand—
59. 21. my words shall not depart—
Jer. 3. 5. will he reserve anger—, 12.
17. 4. kindled fire shall burn—
Lam. 3. 31. Lord will not cast off—
Mic. 7. 18. retaineth not his anger—
Zech. 1. 5. prophets, do they live—
John 6. 51. eateth shall live—, 58.
Rom. 1. 25. Creator who is blessed—
9. 5. over all God blessed—
2 Cor. 9. 9. his righteousness remaineth—
Heb. 13. 8. Jesus Christ, the same yesterday, and—
1 John 2. 17. doeth will of God, abideth—
Ex. 15. 18. Lord reigns *for ever and*
1 Chron. 16. 36. blessed be God—, 29. 10. Neh. 9. 5. Dan. 2. 20.
Ps. 10. 16. the Lord is king—
45. 6. thy throne, O God, is—, Heb. 1. 8.
52. 8. I will trust in God—
111. 8. command. stand fast—
119. 44. I will keep thy law—
145. 1. I will bless thy name—, 2. 21.
Dan. 12. 3. they shine as stars—
Mic. 4. 5. walk in name of God—
Gal. 1. 5. to whom be glory—, Phil. 4. 20. 1 Tim. 1. 17. 2 Tim. 4. 18. Heb. 13. 21. 1 Pet. 4. 11. & 5. 11. Rev. 1. 6. & 5. 13. & 7. 12. Rom. 11. 36. & 16. 27.
Rev. 4. 9. who liveth—, 10. & 10. 6. & 15. 7. Dan. 4. 34. & 12. 7.
22. 5. they shall reign—
EVERLASTING hills, Gen. 49. 26.
Gen. 17. 8. Canaan, an e. possession, 48. 4.
21. 33. called on name of e. God
Ex. 40. 15. e. priesthood, Num. 25. 13.
Lev. 16. 34. this should be an e. statute
Deut. 33. 27. underneath are e. arms
Ps. 24. 7. be lifted up ye e. doors
41. 13. blessed be God from e. to e.
90. 2. thou art from e. to e., 106. 48.
100. 5. his mercy is e.
103. 17. mercy of Lord from e. to e.
119. 142. thy righteousness is e.
139. 24. lead me in the way e.
145. 13. e. kingdom, Dan. 4. 3.
Prov. 10. 25. the righteous is an e.
Isa. 9. 6. mighty God the e. Father
26. 4. in Lord Jehovah is e. strength
33. 14. who dwell with e. burnings
35. 10. shall come to Zion with songs of e. joy, 51. 11. & 61. 7.
40. 28. e. God, Creator, fainteth
54. 8. with e. kindness will I gather
Isa. 56. 5. an e. name, 63. 12, 16.
60. 19. Lord shall be an e. light, 20.
Jer. 10. 10. true living God, e. King
20. 11. e. confusion never forgotten
23. 40. I will bring e. reproach
31. 3. I loved thee with an e. love
Dan. 4. 34. e. dominion, 7. 14.
9. 24. to bring in e. righteousness
Mic. 5. 2. goings forth of old from e.
Hab. 1. 12. art thou not from e. my God
3. 6. e. mountains scattered; his ways e.
Matt. 18. 8. cast into e. fire, 25. 41.
2 Thes. 1. 9. punished with e. destruction
2. 16. God hath given us e. conso.
Luke 16. 9. receive into e. habita.
1 Tim. 6. 16. to whom be power e.
2 Pet. 1. 11. e. kingdom of our
Jude 6. reserved in e. chains of darkness
Rev. 14. 6. having the e. Gospel to
Dan. 12. 2. awake to *everlasting life*
Matt. 19. 29. shall inherit—
Luke 18. 30. in world to come—
John 3. 16. not perish but have—, 36.
4. 14. well springing up to—
5. 24. heareth my word hath—
6. 27. meat which endureth to—
47. that believeth on me hath—
Acts 13. 46. yourselves unworthy of—
Rom. 6. 22. ye have the end—
Gal. 6. 8. soweth to the Spirit, of the Spirit reap—
1 Tim. 1. 16. believe on him to—
R. V. 1 Chron. 16. 36; Ps. 100. 5; 119. 44. for ever; Hab. 3. 6; Matt. 18. 8; 19. 29; 25. 41, 46; Luke 16. 9; 18. 30; John 3. 16, 36; 5. 24; 6. 27, 40, 47; 12. 50; Acts 13. 46; Rom. 6. 22; 16. 26; Gal. 6. 8; 2 Thes. 1. 9; 2. 16; 1 Tim. 1. 16; 6. 16; Heb. 3. 20; 2 Pet. 1. 11. eternal
EVERMORE, Ps. 16. 11. & 105. 4. & 133. 3. John 6. 34. 2 Cor. 11. 31. 1 Thes. 5. 16. Rev. 1. 18.
R. V. 1 Thes. 5. 16. always
EVERY imagination evil, Gen. 6. 5.
Ps. 32. 6. for this e. one godly pray
119. 101. refrained feet from e. evil
104. I hate e. false way, 128.
Prov. 2. 9. understand e. good path
15. 3. eyes of Lord are in e. place
30. 5. e. word of God is pure
Eccl. 3. 1. a time to e. purpose
Isa. 45. 23. e. knee bow, and e. tongue, Rom. 14. 11. Phil. 2. 11.
1 Tim. 4. 4. e. creature of God is good
Tit. 3. 1. ready to e. good work
Heb. 12. 1. lay aside e. weight and
1 John 4. 1. believe not e. spirit
EVIDENCE, Jer. 32. 10. Heb. 11. 1.
Job 6. 28. *evidently*, Acts 10. 3. Gal. 3. 1, 11. Phil. 1. 28. Heb. 7. 14, 15.
R. V. Jer. 32. 10, 11, 12, 14, 16, 44. deed
EVIL, Gen. 2. 9, 17. & 3. 5, 22.
Deut. 29. 21. I will separate him to e.
30. 15. set before thee death and e.
Josh. 24. 15. if it seem e. to you
Job 2. 10. we receive good and not e.
5. 19. in trouble no e. touch thee
30. 26. looked for good e. came
Ps. 23. 4. I will fear no e. for thou
34. 21. e. shall slay the wicked
52. 3. lovest e. more than good
91. 10. no e. shall befall thee
97. 10. ye that love Lord, hate e.
Prov. 5. 14. I was almost in all e.
12. 21. no e. shall happen to just
31. 12. will do him good and not e.
Eccl. 2. 21. vanity and a great e.
5. 13. sore e. riches kept to hurt
9. 3. heart of men is full of e.
Isa. 5. 20. call e. good, and good e.
45. 7. I make peace and create e.
59. 7. feet run to e. and make haste
Jer. 17. 17. art my hope in day of e.
18. 11. I frame e. against you
44. 11. set my face against you for e.
27. I will watch over them for e.

Lam. 3. 38. proceedeth not *e.* and good
Ezek. 7. 5. an *e.* an only *e.* is come
Dan. 9. 12. on us a great *e.*, 13. 14.
Amos 3. 6. shall there be *e.* in a city
5. 14. seek good and not *e.* that live
15. hate *e.* love good, Mic. 3. 2.
Hab. 1. 13. of purer eyes than to behold *e.*
Matt. 5. 11. all manner of *e.* against
6. 34. sufficient to day is *e.* thereof
Rom. 2. 9. upon every soul that doeth *e.*
7. 19. *e.* I would not that I do
12. 17. recompense no man *e.* for *e.*
16. 19. simple concerning *e.*
1 Cor. 13. 5. charity thinketh no *e.*
1 Thes. 5. 15. let no man render *e.* for *e.*, 1 Pet. 3. 9.
22. abstain from all appearance of *e.*
1 Tim. 6. 10. love of money is the root of all *e.*
Tit. 3. 2. to speak *e.* of no man
Heb. 5. 14. discern both good and *e.*
Gen. 6. 5. thoughts only *e.*, 8. 21.
47. 9. few and *e.* have been the days
Prov. 14. 19. *e.* bow before the good
15. 15. all days of afflicted are *e.*
Isa. 1. 4. a seed of *e.* doers, 14. 20.
Matt. 5. 45. sun to rise on *e.* and good
7. 11. if ye being *e.* know, Luke 11. 13.
12. 34. how can ye being *e.* speak good
Luke 6. 35. kind to the unthankful and *e.*
Eph. 5. 16. because the days are *e.*
3 John 11. follow not that which is *e.*
Jude 10. speak *e.* of those things
R. V. Judg. 9. 5. wickedness; 2 Sam. 13. 16. great wrong; 1 Chron. 2. 3; 21. 17. wickedly; Ps. 40. 17. hurt; Prov. 16. 27. mischief; Jer. 24. 3, 8; 29. 17. bad; Matt. 5. 37; 6. 13; John 17. 15; 2 Thes. 3. 3. evil one; Jas. 3. 16. vile; Jas. 4. 11; 1 Pet. 3. 16 ——; Eph. 4. 31. railing

EXACT, Deut. 15. 2, 3. Ps. 89. 22. Isa. 58. 3. Luke 3. 13.
Job 39. 7. *exactor*, Isa. 60. 17.

EXALT, Dan. 11. 14, 36. Obad. 4.
Ex. 15. 2. my father's God, I will *e.*
1 Sam. 2. 10. *e.* the horn of his anointed
Ps. 34. 3. let us *e.* his name together
37. 34. *e.* thee to inherit the land
99. 5. *e.* the Lord our God for he
118. 28. my God I will *e.* thee, Isa. 25. 1.
Ezek. 21. 26. *e.* him that is low
1 Pet. 5. 6. may *e.* you in due time
Num. 24. 7. his kingdom be *exalted*
2 Sam. 22. 47. *e.* be the God of my
Neh. 9. 5. *e.* above all blessing and
Job 5. 11. *e.* to safety, 36. 7.
Ps. 89. 16. in righteousness shall be *e.*, 17.
Prov. 11. 11. by blessing of upright city is *e.*
Isa. 2. 2. Lord's house *e.* above hills
11. Lord alone shall be *e.*, 17. & 5. 16. & 30. 18. & 33. 5, 10.
40. 4. every valley shall be *e.* and
52. 13. my servant shall be *e.*
Hos. 13. 1. Eph. was *e.* in Israel, 6.
Matt. 11. 23. Capernaum which art *e.* to heaven, Luke 10. 15.
23. 12. humbleth himself shall be *e.*, Luke 14. 11. & 18. 14.
Luke 1. 52. *e.* them of low degree
Acts 2. 33. by right hand of God *e.*
5. 31. him hath God *e.* with his
2 Cor. 12. 7. I be *e.* above measure
Phil. 2. 9. God hath highly *e.* him
Jas. 1. 9. low rejoice that he is *e.*
Prov. 14. 34. righteous. *exalteth* a
Luke 14. 11. *e.* himself be abased, 18. 14.
2 Cor. 10. 5. casting down that *e.* itself
2 Thes. 2. 4. *e.* himself above all—
R. V. Job 36. 22. doeth loftily; Ps. 148. 14; Ezek. 31. 10. hath lifted up; Prov. 17. 19. raiseth high; Jas. 1. 9. his high estate

EXAMINE, Ezra 10. 16. Luke 23. 14. Acts 4. 9. & 12. 19. & 22. 24, 29. & 28. 18. 1 Cor. 9. 3.
Ps. 26. 2. *e.* me, O Lord, prove and
1 Cor. 11. 28. let a man *e.* himself
2 Cor. 13. 5. *e.* yourselves, prove
R. V. 1 Cor. 11. 28. prove; 2 Cor. 13. 5. try your own selves

EXAMPLE, 1 Thes. 1. 7. Jas. 5. 10.
Matt. 1. 19. not make her a public *e.*
John 13. 15. I have given you an *e.*
Phil. 3. 17. ye have us for an *e.*
2 Thes. 3. 9. make ourselves an *e.*
Heb. 4. 11. fall after the same *e.* of unbelief
8. 5. *e.* shadow of heavenly things
1 Pet. 2. 21. Christ leaving us an *e.*
5. 3. not lords but *e.* to the flock
2 Pet. 2. 6. making them an *e.*
Jude 7. Sodom—set forth for an *e.*
R. V. 1 Tim. 4. 12. example to those that believe; Heb. 8. 5. that which is a copy

EXCEED, Deut. 25. 3. 1 Kings 10. 7.
Matt. 5. 20. except your righteousness *e.* the righteous. of scribes
Gen. 17. 6. *exceeding* fruitful
15. 1. I am thy shield and *e.* great reward
Num. 14. 7. land is *e.* good
1 Sam. 2. 3. why talk so *e.* proudly
1 Kings 4. 29. wisdom *e.* much
1 Chron. 22. 5. house *e.* magnifical
Ps. 43. 4. I will go to God, my *e.* joy
Matt. 5. 12. rejoice and be *e.* glad
26. 38. my soul is *e.* sorrowful, to
Rom. 7. 13. sin might become *e.* sinful
2 Cor. 4. 17. work a far more *e.* weight
7. 4. I am *e.* joyful in all tribulation
Eph. 1. 19. *e.* greatness of his power
1 Tim. 1. 14. grace was *e.* abundant
1 Pet. 4. 13. rejoice, glad with *e.* joy
2 Pet. 1. 4. *e.* great and precious promise
Jude 24. present you with *e.* joy
Gen. 13. 13. sinners before the Lord *exceedingly*, 1 Sam. 26. 21. 2 Sam. 13. 15.
Ps. 68. 3. let righteous. rejoice *e.*
1 Thes. 3. 10. praying *e.* that
R. V. Job 36. 9. behave themselves proudly; 2 Chron. 14. 14 ——; 2 Cor. 7. 4. overflow with joy; 1 Tim. 1. 14. abounded exceedingly; Gen. 16. 10. greatly; Ps. 68. 3. with gladness; 2 Chron. 28. 6. waxed exceeding strong

EXCEL, Gen. 49. 4. 1 Kings 4. 30.
Prov. 31. 29. thou *excellest* them all
Eccl. 2. 13. wisdom *e.* folly, as far
1 Cor. 14. 12. seek that ye may *e.*
2 Cor. 3. 10. by reason of the glory that *e.*
Gen. 49. 3. *excellency* of dignity, and *e.*
Ex. 15. 7. in greatness of thy *e.*
Deut. 33. 26. rideth in his *e.* on sky
Job 13. 11. his *e.* make you afraid
Ps. 47. 4. *e.* of Jacob, whom he loved
Isa. 35. 2. see glory and *e.* of our God
Amos 6. 8. I abhor the *e.* of Jacob
8. 7. the Lord hath sworn by the *e.* of Jacob
1 Cor. 2. 1. not with *e.* of speech
2 Cor. 4. 7. *e.* of power may be of God
Phil. 3. 8. count all loss for the *e.* of Christ
Esth. 1. 4. *excellent* majesty, Job 37. 23.
Ps. 8. 1. how *e.* is thy name in the earth, 9.
16. 3. saints, *e.* in whom all my delight
Ps. 36. 7. how *e.* is thy lovingkind.
Prov. 12. 26. righteous is more *e.*
Isa. 12. 5. the Lord hath done *e.* things
28. 29. wonderful in counsel, *e.* in
Dan. 5. 12. an *e.* spirit in Daniel, 6. 3.
Rom. 2. 18. approvest things more *e.*
1 Cor. 12. 31. shew you a more *e.* way
Phil. 1. 10. approve things that are *e.*
Heb. 1. 4. obtained a more *e.* name
8. 6. obtained a more *e.* ministry
11. 4. offered a more *e.* sacrifice
2 Pet. 1. 17. came a voice from *e.*
R. V. 1 Chron. 15. 21. lead; Ps. 103. 20. ye mighty; 1 Cor. 14. 12. abound unto; Gen. 37. 4. majesty; Isa. 13. 19; Ezek. 24. 21. pride; Ps. 36. 7. precious; 141. 5. as upon the head; 148. 13. exalted; Prov. 17. 27. cool; 12. 26. guide to

EXCESS, Matt. 23. 25. Eph. 5. 18. 1 Pet. 4. 3, 4.
R. V. Eph. 5. 18. riot; 1 Pet. 4. 3. wine bibbings

EXCHANGE, Matt. 16. 26. Mark 8. 37.
Matt. 25. 27. *exchangers*

EXCLUDE, Rom. 3. 27. Gal. 4. 17.

EXCUSE, Luke 14. 18, 19. Rom. 1. 20. & 2. 15. 2 Cor. 12. 19.
R. V. 2 Cor. 12. 19. are excusing

EXECRATION, Jer. 42. 18. & 44. 12.

EXECUTE, Num. 5. 30. & 8. 11.
Ps. 149. 7. *e.* vengeance, Mic. 5. 15.
Rom. 13. 4. revenger to *e.* wrath
Ex. 12. 12. *execute judgment*, Deut. 10. 18. Ps. 119. 84. Isa. 16. 3. Jer. 7. 5. & 21. 12. & 22. 3. & 23. 5. Mic. 7. 9. Zech. 7. 9. & 8. 16. John 5. 27. Jude 15.
R. V. Num. 8. 11. be to do; Jer. 5. 1. doeth; Isa. 46. 11. of; Rom. 13. 4. for

EXERCISE, Ps. 131. 1. Matt. 20. 25. Acts 24. 16. 1 Tim. 4. 7, 8. Heb. 5. 14. & 12. 11. 2 Pet. 2. 14.
Jer. 9. 24. Lord *e.* lovingkindness
R. V. Matt. 20. 25; Mark 10. 42. lord it; Luke 22. 25. have

EXHORT, Acts 2. 40. & 11. 23. & 15. 32. & 27. 22. 2 Cor. 9. 5. 1 Thes. 2. 11. & 4. 1. & 5. 14. 1 Tim. 2. 1. 2 Tim. 4. 2. Tit. 1. 9. & 2. 6, 9, 15. 1 Pet. 5. 1, 12. Jude 3.
2 Thes. 3. 12. we command and *e.* by
Heb. 3. 13. *e.* one another daily
10. 25. *exhorting* one another; and
Luke 3. 18. *exhortation*, Acts 13. 15. & 20. 2. Rom. 12. 8. 1 Cor. 14. 3. 2 Cor. 8. 17. 1 Thes. 2. 3. 1 Tim. 4. 13. Heb. 12. 5. & 13. 22.
R. V. 2 Cor. 9. 5. entreat

EXPECTATION, Luke 3. 15. Acts 12. 11.
Ps. 9. 18. *e.* of the poor shall not perish
62. 5. for my *e.* is from him
Prov. 10. 28. *e.* of the wicked shall
11. 7. dieth, his *e.* shall perish
23. *e.* of the wicked is wrath
23. 18. *e.* shall not be cut off, 24. 14.
Isa. 20. 5. be ashamed of their *e.*, 6.
Rom. 8. 19. *e.* of creature waiteth
Phil. 1. 20. according to my earnest *e.*
Jer. 29. 11. give you an *expected* end
R. V. Prov. 23. 18; 24. 14. thy hope; Hope in your latter

EXPEDIENT for us that one man die for the people, John 11. 50. & 18. 14.
John 16. 7. *e.* for you that I go away
1 Cor. 6. 12. all things not *e.*, 10. 23.
2 Cor. 8. 10. this is *e.* for you
12. 1. it is not *e.* for me to glory

EXPERIENCE, Gen. 30. 27. Eccl. 1. 16. Rom. 5. 4.
2 Cor. 9. 13. by the *experiment* of
R. V. Gen. 30. 27. divined; Rom.

5. 4. probation: seeing that the proving of you by
EXPERT in war, 1 Chron. 12. 33, 35, 36. S. of S. 3. 8. Jer. 50. 9.
Acts 26. 3. know thee to be *e*. in all
EXPOUNDED, riddle, Judg. 14. 19. Mark 4. 34. Luke 24. 27. Acts 11. 4. & 18. 26. & 28. 23.
R. V. Judg. 14. 14. declare; Luke 24. 27. interpreted
EXPRESS, Heb. 1. 3. 1 Tim. 4. 1.
R. V. 1 Sam. 20. 21 —
EXTEND mercy, Ezra 7. 28. & 9. 9. Ps. 109. 12.
Ps. 16. 2. my goodness *e*. not to thee
Isa. 66. 12. I will *e*. peace to her like a river
EXTINCT, Job 17. 1. Isa. 43. 17.
EXTOL, Ps. 30. 1. & 66. 17. & 68. 4. & 145. 1. Isa. 52. 13. Dan. 4. 37.
R. V. Ps. 68. 4. cast up a highway for; Isa. 52. 13. lifted up
EXTORTION, Ezek. 22. 12. Matt. 23. 25. Ps. 109. 11. *extortioner*, Isa. 16. 4. Luke 18. 11. 1 Cor. 5. 10, 11. & 6. 10.
R. V. Ezek. 22. 12. oppression
EXTREME, Deut. 28. 22. Job 35. 15.
R. V. neither doth he greatly regard arrogance
EYE for *e*. Ex. 21. 24. Lev. 24. 20. Matt. 5. 38.
Deut. 32. 10. as the apple of his *e*., Ps. 17. 8.
Job 24. 15. no *e*. shall see me
Ps. 33. 18. *e*. of the Lord on them that
Prov. 20. 12. the seeing *e*. Lord hath
Eccl. 1. 8. the *e*. not satisfied with
Isa. 64. 4. neither hath the *e*. seen
Matt. 6. 22. light of the body is the *e*., Luke 11. 34.
18. 9. if thine *e*. offend thee, 5. 29.
Rev. 1. 7. every *e*. shall see him
Prov. 23. 6. *evil eye*, 28. 22. Matt. 6. 23. & 20. 15. Mark 7. 22. Luke 11. 34.
Job 16. 16. *eyelids*, 41. 18. Ps. 11. 4. & 132. 4. Prov. 4. 25. & 6. 4, 25. & 30. 13. Jer. 9. 18.
Rev. 3. 18. *eyesalve*
Eph. 6. 6. *eyeservice*, Col. 3. 22.
2 Sam. 22. 25. *eyesight*, Ps. 18. 24.
Luke 1. 2. *eye-witnesses*, 2 Pet. 1. 16.
Gen. 3. 5. your *eyes* shall be opened
Job 10. 4. hast thou *e*. of flesh
29. 15. I was *e*. to the blind
Ps. 15. 4. in whose *e*. a vile person
145. 15. *e*. of all things wait on thee
Eccl. 2. 14. wise man's *e*. are in his
11. 7. pleasant for *e*. to behold sun
Isa. 3. 16. walk with wanton *e*.
5. 15. the *e*. of the lofty shall be
29. 18. *e*. of the blind shall see out of obscurity
32. 3. *e*. of them that see shall
35. 5. *e*. of blind shall be opened
42. 7. to open blind *e*. and give
Jer. 5. 21. have *e*. and see not
Dan. 7. 20. horn that had *e*.
Hab. 1. 13. of purer *e*. than to beh.
Matt. 13. 16. blessed are your *e*. for
18. 9. having two *e*. to be cast into
Mark 8. 18. having *e*. see ye not
Luke 4. 20. *e*. were fastened on him
10. 23. blessed are the *e*. which see
John 9. 6. anointed *e*. of blind man
Eph. 1. 18. *e*. of your understand.
Heb. 4. 13. all things are opened unto *e*. of him
2 Pet. 2. 14. *e*. full of adultery
1 John 2. 16. lust of the *e*. and pride
Rev. 1. 14. his *e*. as a flame of fire
3. 18. anoint thine *e*.
4. 6. four beasts full of *e*., 8.
Deut. 13. 18. right in the *eyes of the Lord*, 1 Kings 15. 5, 11. & 22. 43.
Gen. 6. 8. Noah found grace in the —
1 Sam. 26. 24. life set by in —
2 Sam. 15. 25. find favor in —
2 Chron. 16. 9. — run to and fro
Ps. 34. 15. — are on righteous
Prov. 5. 21. ways of man are before —
15. 3. — are in every place behold.
Isa. 49. 5. I shall be glorious in —
Amos 9. 8. — are upon sinful king.
Zech. 4. 10. — which run to and fro
Ps. 25. 15. *my eyes* are ever towards
119. 123. — fail for thy salvation
141. 8. — are unto thee, O God
Isa. 1. 15. I will hide — from you
38. 14. — fail with looking upward
Jer. 9. 1. O that — were a fountain of
13. 17. — shall weep sore, because
14. 17. — run down with tears
Amos 9. 4. I will set — on them for evil
Luke 2. 30. — have seen thy salvation
Ps. 123. 2. so *our eyes* wait on the Lord
Matt. 20. 33. that — may be opened
1 John 1. 1. that we have seen with —
Deut. 12. 8. right *in his own eyes*, Judg. 17. 6. & 21. 25.
Job 32. 1. righteous —
Neh. 6. 16. cast down *in their own eyes*
Ps. 139. 16. *thine eyes* did see my
Prov. 23. 5. set — on that which is
S. of S. 6. 5. turn away — from me
Isa. 30. 20. — shall see thy teachers
Jer. 5. 3. are not — upon the truth
Ezek. 24. 16. take away desire —, 25.
R. V. 1 Kings 16. 25; 2 Chron. 21. 6; 29. 6; Jer. 52. 2. sight; Ruth 2. 10. thy sight

F

FABLES, 1 Tim. 1. 4. & 4. 7. 2 Tim. 4. 4. Tit. 1. 14. 2 Pet. 1. 16.
FACE, Gen. 3. 19. & 16. 8.
Lev. 19. 32. honor the *f*. of old man
Num. 6. 25. Lord make his *f*.
2 Chron. 6. 42. turn not away *f*., Ps. 132. 10.
Ps. 17. 15. I will behold thy *f*.
31. 16. make thy *f*. shine, 119. 135.
67. 1. cause his *f*. to shine on, 80. 3, 7, 19.
84. 9. behold *f*. of thine anointed, 132. 10.
Ezek. 1. 10. *f*. of a man, a lion. Rev. 4. 7.
Dan. 9. 17. cause thy *f*. to shine on
Hos. 5. 5. testify to his *f*., 7. 10.
Matt. 11. 10. my messenger before thy *f*., Mark 1. 2. Luke 7. 27. & 9. 52.
Acts 2. 25. set the Lord always before my *f*.
1 Cor. 13. 12. but then see *f*. to *f*.
2 Cor. 3. 18. with open *f*. beholding
Jas. 1. 23. his natural *f*. in a glass
R. V. Gen. 24. 47. nose; 46. 28. way; 1 Sam. 26. 20; Joel 2. 6. presence; 1 Kings 13. 6. favor; 20. 38, 41; 2 Kings 9. 30; Jer. 4. 30. eyes; Ezek. 38. 19. nostrils; 40. 15. forefront; Joel 2. 20. forepart; Deut. 14. 2; 2 Sam. 14. 7; Jer. 25. 33; Luke 22. 64 —
FADE, we all, as a leaf, Isa. 64. 6.
Jas. 1. 11. rich man *f*. away in
1 Pet. 1. 4. inheritance that *fadeth*
5. 4. receive a crown of glory that *f*.
R. V. Ezek. 47. 12. wither
FAIL, Deut. 28. 32. Job. 11. 20.
Deut. 31. 6. Lord will not *f*. nor, 8. Josh. 1. 5. 1 Chron. 28. 20.
Ps. 12. 1. faithful *f*. from among
69. 3. my eyes *f*. while I wait for my God
Lam. 3. 22. his compassions *f*. not
Luke 16. 9. when ye *f*. they may
22. 32. prayed that thy faith *f*. not
Heb. 12. 15. lest any *f*. of the grace
S. of S. 5. 6. soul *failed* when he spake
Ps. 31. 10. my strength *faileth*, 38. 10. & 71. 9.
Ps. 40. 12. my heart *f*. me, 73. 26.
143. 7. hear me, my spirit *f*.
Luke 12. 33. lay up treasure that *f*. not
1 Cor. 13. 8. charity never *f*.
Deut. 28. 65. for *failing* of eyes
Luke 21. 26. men's hearts *f*. them
R. V. Judg. 11. 30. indeed; Gen. 47. 15. was all spent; Josh. 3. 16. wholly; Ez. 4. 22. be slack; Ps. 40. 26; 59. 15. is lacking; Isa. 19. 3. make void; 34. 16. be missing; Jer. 48. 33. cease; Luke 16. 17. fall; 1 Cor. 13. 8. be done away; Heb. 12. 15. that falleth short; Luke 21. 26. fainting
FAINT, Deut. 25. 18. Judg. 8. 4, 5.
Isa. 1. 5. head sick, whole heart is *f*.
40. 30. youths shall *f*. and be weary
Luke 18. 1. to pray always and not *f*.
2 Cor. 4. 1. received mercy we *f*. not
Heb. 12. 5. nor *f*. when rebuked of
Ps. 27. 13. I had *fainted* unless I
Rev. 2. 3. hast labored and not *f*.
Ps. 84. 2. soul *fainteth* for courts of the Lord
119. 81. my soul *f*. for thy salvation
R. V. Isa. 13. 7. feeble; Deut. 20. 8; Ezek. 21. 15. melt; Josh. 2. 9, 24. melt away; Isa. 13. 7. feeble; Jer. 45. 3; Rev. 2. 3. weary; Matt. 9. 36. distressed; Isa. 7. 4. faint; Jer. 49. 23. melted away
FAIR, Gen. 6. 2. & 24. 16.
Prov. 7. 21. *f*. speech, Rom. 16. 18.
S. of S. 1. 15. behold thou art *f*., 4. 1, 7. & 2. 10. & 6. 10. & 7. 6. Gen. 12. 11.
4. 10. how *f*. is thy love, better
Jer. 12. 6. they speak *f*. words
Acts 7. 20. Moses was exceeding *f*.
Ps. 45. 2. thou art *fairer* than the
Dan. 1. 15. their countenance appeared *f*.
R. V. Ezek. 27. 12-17. wares; Job 37. 22. golden
FAITH, Acts 3. 16. & 13. 8.
Deut. 32. 20. children in whom is no *f*.
Matt. 6. 30. O ye of little *f*., 8. 26. & 16. 8. & 14. 31. Luke 12. 28.
8. 10. not found so great *f*. no
17. 20. had *f*. as a grain of mustard
21. 21. have *f*. and doubt not
Mark 4. 40. how is it that ye have no *f*.
11. 22. Jesus saith have *f*. in God
Luke 7. 9. so great *f*. no not in Israel
17. 5. Lord increase our *f*.
Acts 3. 16. the *f*. which is by him
6. 5. Stephen, a man full of *f*.
Acts 6. 7. company of priests obedient to *f*.
14. 9. he had *f*. to be healed
27. God opened door of *f*. to
16. 5. churches established in the *f*.
20. 21. *f*. towards our Lord Jesus
Rom. 1. 5. for obedience to the *f*.
3. 3. make *f*. of God without effect
27. but by the law of *f*.
4. 5. his *f*. is counted for righteousness
12. in the steps of that *f*. of Abraham, 16.
13. through the righteousness of *f*., 9. 30. & 10. 6.
14. if of law be heirs, *f*. is made
16. of *f*. that by grace promise sure
10. 17. *f*. cometh by hearing, and
12. 3. God dealt the measure of *f*
6. according to the propor. of *f*
14. 23. eateth not of *f*. is not of *f*. is
1 Cor. 12. 9. to another *f*. by the same spirit
13. 2. though I have all *f*. to
13. now abideth *f*. hope, charity
2 Cor. 4. 13. we have the same spirit of *f*.
Gal. 1. 23. preach the *f*. which once
3. 7. they which are of *f*., 9.
12. the law is not of *f*. but the man
23. before *f*. came, we were under
5. 6. but *f*. which worketh by love
22. fruit of the Spirit is *f*.
Eph. 4. 5. one Lord, one *f*. one

Eph. 4. 13. until we come in the unity of *f.*
6. 16. above all take shield of *f.*
23. love with *f.* from God the
Phil. 1. 25. I shall abide for your joy of *f.*
27. striving together for *f.* of gosp.
1 Thes. 1. 3. remem. your work of *f.*
5. 8. putting on breastplate of *f.*
2 Thes. 1. 11. fulfil work of *f.* with power
3. 2. for all men have not *f.*
1 Tim. 1. 5. charity out of *f.* unfeign.
14. exceeding abundantly with *f.*
19. holding *f.* and a good conscience; concerning *f.* have made shipwreck
4. 6. nourished up in the words of *f.*
5. 8. hath denied the *f.*
12. cast off their first *f.*
6. 10. erred from the *f.*
21. concerning the *f.*
12. fight the good fight of *f.*
2 Tim. 1. 5. unfeigned *f.* that is in
2. 18. overthrow *f.* of some
22. follow righteous. *f.* charity
3. 10. fully known my doctrine, life, *f.*
4. 7. fought a good fight, I have kept the *f.*
Tit. 1. 1. according to *f.* of God's elect
4. my son after the common *f.*
Heb. 4. 2. word did not profit, not being mixed with *f.*
10. 22. draw near in full assur. of *f.*
23. hold fast the profess. of our *f.*
11. 6. without *f.* it is impossible to
12. 2. Jesus the author and finisher of our *f.*
13. 7. whose *f.* follow, considering
Jas. 2. 1. have not *f.* of our Lord
14. say that he hath *f.* can *f.* save
17. *f.* if it hath not works, is dead, 26.
18. thou hast *f.* and I works; show *f.*—*f.* by my works
22. *f.* wrought with works
5. 15. prayer of *f.* shall save
2 Pet. 1. 1. like precious *f.* with us
1 John 5. 4. overcometh world, even our *f.*
Jude 3. contend earnestly for the *f.*
20. build up yourselves on holy *f.*
Rev. 2. 13. hast not denied my *f.*
19. I know thy works and *f.*
13. 10. here is the *f.* of the saints
14. 12. which keep the *f.* of Jesus
Hab. 2. 4. just shall live *by faith*, Rom. 1. 17. Gal. 3. 11. Heb. 10. 38.
Acts 15. 9. purifying their hearts—
26. 18. sanctified—that is in me
Rom. 1. 12. comforted by mutual *f.*
3. 22. righteousness which is—of Christ
28. conclude a man is justified—
5. 1. being justified—we have peace
2. have access—, Eph. 3. 12.
9. 32. sought it not—but works
2 Cor. 1. 24. of your joy for—ye stand
5. 7. we walk—and not by sight
Gal. 2. 16. not justified, but—, 3. 24.
20. I live—of the Son of God
3. 22. promise—might be given
26. ye are all children of God—in Christ Jesus.
5. 5. wait for hope of righteousness—
Eph. 3. 17. Christ may dwell in your hearts—
Phil. 3. 9. righteousness through *f.*
Heb. 11. 4.—Abel, 5.—Enoch, etc.
7 heir of righteousness which is—
Jas. 2. 24. justified by works, not—
Rom. 4. 19. not weak *in faith*
20. strong—giving glory to God
1 Cor. 16. 13. stand fast—quit you
2 Cor. 8. 7. ye abound—in utter.
Col. 1. 23. if ye continue—
2. 7. built up in him, established—

1 Tim. 1. 2. Timothy, my own son—
4. godly edifying which is—
2. 15. if they continue—and charity
3. 13. purchase great boldness—
4. 12. be an example—in purity
2 Tim. 1. 13. of sound words—and
Tit. 1. 13. they may be sound—2. 2.
Heb. 11. 13. all these died—not having
Jas. 1. 6. let him ask—nothing
1 Pet. 5. 9. whom resist, steadfast—
Matt. 9. 2. Jesus, seeing *their faith*, Mark 2. 5. Luke 5. 20.
Acts 3. 16. *through faith* in his Son
Rom. 3. 25. propitiation—in his blood
31. do we make void the law—, 30.
Eph. 2. 8. by grace ye are saved—
Col. 2. 12.—of the operation of God
2 Tim. 3. 15. salvation—which is
Heb. 6. 12.—and patience inherit
11. 3.—we understand the worlds
11.—Sarah received strength to
28.—Moses kept the passover
33.—subdued kingdoms
11. 39. obtained a good report—, 2.
1 Pet. 1. 5. kept by power of God—
Matt. 9. 22. *thy faith* hath made thee whole, Luke 8. 48. & 17. 19.
15. 28. O woman, great is—be
Luke 7. 50.—hath saved thee, 18. 42.
22. 32. I have prayed that—fail not
Jas. 2. 18. show me—without thy
Luke 8. 25. where is *your faith*
Matt. 9. 29. according to—be it to
Rom. 1. 8.—is spoken of through
1 Cor. 2. 5. that—not stand in wisdom
15. 14.—is also vain, 17.
2 Cor. 1. 24. not dominion over—
Eph. 1. 15. after I heard of—, Col. 1. 4.
Phil. 2. 17. offered upon service of—
Col. 2. 5. beholding steadfast. of—
1 Thes. 1. 8.—to God-ward is spread
3. 2. establish you, comfort you, concerning—
5. I sent to know—lest the tempter
7. comforted in affliction by—
10. perfect what is lacking in—
2 Thes. 1. 3.—groweth exceedingly
Jas. 1. 3. trying of—worketh patience
1 Pet. 1. 7. trial of—being precious
9. receiving end of—salvation
21. that—and hope might be in God
2 Pet. 1. 5. add to—virtue, knowledge
R. V. Acts 6. 8. grace; Rom. 3. 3; Gal. 5. 22. faithfulness

FAITHFUL, 1 Sam. 2. 35. & 22. 14. 2 Sam. 20. 19. Neh. 13. 13. Dan. 6. 4. 1 Tim. 6. 2. 1 Pet. 5. 12.
Num. 12. 7. *f.* in all my house
Heb. 3. 2, 5. Moses *f.* in all as a ser.
Deut. 7. 9. *f.* God which keepeth
Neh. 7. 2. a *f.* man, and feared
Ps. 12. 1. the *f.* fail from among men
31. 23. Lord preserveth the *f.*
101. 6. my eyes be upon *f.* in land
119. 86. thy commandments are *f.*
138. thy testimonies are very *f.*
Prov. 11. 13. is of a *f.* spirit, concealeth
13. 17. a *f.* ambassador is health
14. 5. a *f.* witness will not lie
20. 6. a *f.* man who can find
27. 6. *f.* are wounds of a friend
28. 20. *f.* man shall abound with
Isa. 1. 21. how *f.* city became a har.
26. city of righteousness, *f.* city
8. 2. I took *f.* witness to record
49. 7. Lord is *f.* and Holy One of
Jer. 42. 5. the Lord be a true and *f.*
Hos. 11. 12. Judah is *f.* with saints

Matt. 25. 21. well done, *f.* servant, 24. 45.
23. hast been *f.* in a few, Luke 19. 17.
Luke 12. 42. who is that *f.* steward
16. 10. *f.* in least is *f.* also in much
Acts 16. 15. judge me *f.* to the Lord
1 Cor. 1. 9. God is *f.* by whom ye
4. 2. required in stewards, a man *f.*
17. Timothy who is *f.* in the Lord
7. 25. obtained mercy of the Lord to be *f.*
10. 13. God is *f.* and will not suffer
Eph. 1. 1. the saints and *f.* in Christ Jesus, Col. 1. 2.
6. 21. *f.* minis., Col. 1. 7. & 4. 7, 9.
1 Thes. 5. 24. *f.* is he that calleth
2 Thes. 3. 3. the Lord is *f.* and shall
1 Tim. 1. 12. he counted me *f.*
15. this is a *f.* saying and worthy, 4. 9. 2 Tim. 2. 11. Tit. 3. 8.
3. 11. wives grave, sober, *f.* in all
2 Tim. 2. 2. heard of me, commit to *f.* men
13. he abideth *f.* cannot deny himself
Tit. 1. 6. blame. having *f.* children
9. holding fast the *f.* word as
Heb. 2. 17. might be a *f.* high priest
10. 23. *f.* is he that promised, 11. 11.
1 Pet. 4. 19. as unto a *f.* Creator
1 John 1. 9. he is *f.* to forgive all
Rev. 1. 5. *f.* and true witness, 3. 14
2. 10. be *f.* to death
13. *f.* martyr
Rev. 21. 5. words are true and *f.*, 22. 6.
1 Sam. 26. 23. render to every man his *faithfulness*
Ps. 5. 9. no *f.* in their mouth
40. 10. declared thy *f.*, 89. 1.
89. 1. make known thy *f.* to all
2. thy *f* shalt establish in heavens
5. praise thy *f.* in the great congregation
8. who like thy *f.* round about thee
24. my *f.* shall be with him
33. I will not suffer my *f.* to fail
119. 75. in *f.* thou hast afflicted me
90. thy *f.* is to all generations
143. 1. in thy *f.* answer me, and
Isa. 11. 5. *f.* is the girdle of his reins
25. 1. thy counsels of old are *f.*
Lam. 3. 23. mercies new, great thy *f.*
Hos. 2. 20. I will betroth thee to me in *f.*
Matt. 17. 17. O *faithless* and perverse generation, Mark 9. 19. Luke 9. 41.
John 20. 27. be not *f.* but believing
R. V. 1 Tim. 6. 2. believing; Tit. 1. 6. that believe who are

FALL, Num. 11. 31. & 14. 29, 32.
Gen. 45. 24. see that ye *f.* not out
2 Sam. 24. 14. let us *f.* into the
Ps. 37. 24. though he *f.* he shall not
45. 5. whereby they *f.* under thee
82. 7. *f.* like one of the princes
141. 10. let the wicked *f.* into their
145. 14. Lord upholdeth all that *f.*
Prov. 11. 5. wicked *f.* by his own
24. 16. wicked shall *f.* into mischief
26. 27. digs a pit shall *f.* into it, Eccl. 10. 8.
28. 14. hardeneth his heart shall *f.*
Eccl. 4. 10. if they *f.* one will lift
Isa. 8. 15. many shall stumble and *f.*
Dan. 11. 35. some shall *f.* to try them
Hos. 10. 8. mountains and hills *f.* on us, Luke 23. 30. Rev. 6. 16.
Mic. 7. 8. rejoice not when I *f.*
Matt. 7. 27. great was the *f.* of it
10. 29. sparrow not *f.* on ground

Matt. 15. 14. blind both *f.* into the ditch
21. 44. upon whomsoever it *f.*, Luke 20. 18.
Luke 2. 34. set for the *f.* and rising
Rom. 11. 11. stumbled that they should *f.* through their *f.* salvation is come to the Gentiles
1 Cor. 10. 12. stands, take heed lest he *f.*
1 Tim. 3. 6. *f.* into condemnation
6. 9. rich *f.* into temptation
Heb. 4. 11. *f.* after the same exam.
10. 31. fearful thing to *f.* into the hands of God
2 Pet. 1. 10. if these ye shall never *f.*
3. 17. lest ye *f.* from your steadfastness
Luke 8. 13. in time of temptation *fall away*
Heb. 6. 6. impossible if they—to renew them
Gal. 5. 4. ye are *fallen* from grace
Ps. 16. 6. *f.* to me in pleasant places
Hos. 14. 1. hast *f.* by thine iniquity
Prov. 24. 16. just *falleth* seven times
Rom. 14. 4. to his own master he *f.*
Ps. 56. 13. thou hast delivered my feet from *falling*, 116. 8.
2 Thes. 2. 3. there come a *f.* away
Jude 24. able to keep you from *f.*
R. V. Lev. 26. 37; Ps. 64. 8; Isa. 31. 3; Jer. 6. 21; 46. 16; Ezek. 36. 15; Hos. 4. 5; 5. 5; 2 Pet. 1. 10. stumble; Acts 27. 17. cast; 27. 34. perish; Isa. 34. 4. fading; Acts 27. 41. lighting upon; Jude 24. stumbling

FALLOW, Jer. 4. 3. Hos. 10. 12.
R. V. Deut. 14. 5; 1 Kings 4. 23. roebuck

FALSE, Jer. 14. 14. & 37. 14.
Ex. 23. 1. not raise a *f.* report
7. keep thee far from a *f.* matter
Ps. 119. 104. hate every *f.* way, 128.
Prov. 11. 1. *f.* balance is abomina.
Zech. 8. 17. love no *f.* oath
Matt. 24. 24. *f.* Christs, *f.* prophets
2 Cor. 11. 13, 26. *f.* apostles, *f.* brethren, Gal. 2. 4.
2 Tim. 3. 3. *f.* accusers, Tit. 2. 3.
2 Pet. 2. 1. *f.* prophets, *f.* teachers
Ps. 119. 118. their deceit is *falsehood*
144. 8. whose right hand—of *f.*
Isa. 59. 13. from heart words of *f.*
Lev. 6. 3. sweareth *falsely*, 19. 12.
Ps. 44. 17. neither dealt *f.* in coven.
Zech. 5. 4. thief and that swears *f.*
Matt. 5. 11. evil against you *f.* for
Luke 3. 14. neither accuse any *f.*
1 Pet. 3. 16. *f.* accuse your good
Acts 13. 6. *false prophet*, Rev. 16. 13. & 19. 20. & 20. 10.
Matt. 7. 15. *false prophets*, 24. 11, 24. Luke 6. 26. 2 Pet. 2. 1. 1 John 4. 1.
Ex. 20. 16. *false witness*, Deut. 5. 20. & 19. 16. Prov. 6. 19. & 12. 17. & 14. 5. & 19. 5, 9. & 21. 28. & 25. 18. Matt. 15. 19. & 19. 18. Rom. 13. 9. 1 Cor. 15. 15.
R. V. Ps. 35. 11. unrighteous; 120. 3. deceitful; Prov. 17. 4. wicked; Jer. 14. 14; 23. 32. lying; Lam. 2. 14. vanity; Matt. 26. 60——; Luke 19. 8. wrongfully; Rom. 13. 9. covet; Tit. 2. 3. slanderers; Luke 3. 14. wrongfully; 1 Pet. 3. 16——

FAMILIAR, Job. 19. 14. Ps. 41. 9. Lev. 19. 31. & 20. 6, 27. Isa. 8. 19.
R. V. Jer. 20. 10. familiar friends

FAMILY, Gen. 10. 5. Lev. 20. 5.
Zech. 12. 12. mourn every *f.* apart
Eph. 3. 15. whole *f.* in heaven and
Ps. 68. 6. setteth solitary in *families*
107. 41. maketh him *f.* like a flock
Amos 3. 2. known of all the *f.* of
R. V. 2 Chron. 35. 5. fathers' houses

FAMINE, Gen. 12. 10. & 41. 27.
Job 5. 20. in *f.* he shall redeem thee
Ps. 33. 19. keep them alive in *f.*
Ps. 37. 19. in the days of *f.* shall be
Ezek. 5. 16. evil arrows of *f.*, 6. 11.
Amos 8. 11. not a *f.* of bread, but
R. V. Job 5. 22. dearth

FAMISH, Gen. 41. 55. Prov. 10. 3. Isa. 5. 13. Zeph. 2. 11.

FAN, Isa. 41. 16. Jer. 4. 11. & 51. 2. Matt. 3. 12. Luke 3. 17.

FAR, Ex. 8. 28. Neh. 4. 19.
Ex. 23. 7. keep *f.* from false matter
Ps. 73. 27. *f.* from thee shall perish
Amos 6. 3. put *f.* away the evil day
Mark 12. 34. not *f.* from the kingd.
Phil. 1. 23. with Christ, which is *f.*
Eph. 2. 13. sometimes *f.* off, now
R. V. Job 30. 10. aloof; Judg. 9. 17; Ps. 27. 9; Isa. 19. 6; 26. 15; Ezek. 7. 20; Mark 13. 34——; Matt. 21. 33; 25. 14; Mark 12. 1. another; 2 Cor. 4. 17. more and more

FARTHING, Matt. 5. 26. & 10. 29.

FASHION, 1 Cor. 7. 31. Phil. 2. 8.
Job 10. 8. thy hands have *fashioned* me, Ps. 119. 73.
Ps. 139. 16. in continuance were *f.*
Ezek. 16. 7. thy breasts are *f.*
Phil. 3. 21. be *f.* like his glorious
Ps. 33. 15. he *fashions* their hearts
Isa. 45. 9. the clay say to him that *fashioneth* it
1 Pet. 1. 14. not *fashioning* yourselves
R. V. Acts 7. 44. figure; Phil. 3. 21. conformed to

FAST, 2 Sam. 12. 21. Esth. 4. 16.
Isa. 58. 4. ye *f.* for strife; not *f.* as
Jer. 14. 12. when they *f.* I will not
Zech. 7. 5. did ye at all *f.* unto me
Matt. 6. 16. when ye *f.* be not as
18. appear not to men to *f.*
9. 14. why do we *f.* and thy disc.
Luke 18. 12. I *f.* twice a week
1 Kings 21. 9. proclaim a *fast*, 12. 2 Chron. 20. 3. Ezra 8. 21. Isa. 58. 3, 5, 6. Jer. 36. 9. Joel 1. 14. & 2. 15. Jonah 3. 5. Zech. 8. 19. Acts 27. 9.
Judg. 20. 26. *fasted* that day
1 Sam. 7. 6. *f.* on that day
31. 13. *f.* seven days, 1 Chron. 10. 12.
2 Sam. 1. 12. they wept and *f.* till even
1 Kings 21. 27. Ahab *f.* and lay in
Ezra 8. 23. we *f.* and besought the Lord
Isa. 58. 3. why have we *f.* and thou
Zech. 7. 5. when ye *f.* in filth and
Matt. 4. 2. when he had *f.* forty days
Acts 13. 2. ministered and *f.*
3. *f.* and prayed
Neh. 9. 1. assembled with *fasting*
Esth. 4. 3. were *f.* and weeping, 9. 31.
Ps. 35. 13. humbled soul with *f.*, 69. 10.
109. 24. my knees weak through *f.*
Jer. 36. 6. read the roll on *f.* day
Dan. 6. 18. king passed the night *f.*
9. 3. to seek by prayer with *f.*
Joel 2. 12. turn ye to me with *f.*
Matt. 15. 32. not send them away *f.*
Luke 2. 37. with *f.* and prayers
Acts 10. 30. was *f.* till this hour
14. 23. ordained elders, prayed with *f.*
1 Cor. 7. 5. give yourselves to *f.*
2 Cor. 6. 5. in *f.* often, 11. 27.

FASTENED, Job 38. 6. Eccl. 12. 11. Isa. 22. 25. Luke 4. 20.
R. V. Ex. 28. 14. shalt put; 28. 25. put on; 40. 18. laid; Judg. 4. 21. pierced through; 1 Kings 6. 6. have hold; Matt. 17. 21; Mark 9. 29——

FAT is the Lord's, Lev. 3. 16. & 4. 8.
Prov. 11. 25. liberal shall be made *f.*
13. 4. soul of the diligent shall be made *f.*
15. 30. good report maketh bones *f.*
Isa. 25. 6. *f.* things full of marrow
11. 6. *fatling*, Matt. 22. 4.
Gen. 27. 28. God give thee of *fatness* of the earth
Job 36. 16. table should be full of *f.*
Ps. 36. 8. satisfied with *f.* of house
63. 5. shall be satisfied as with *f.*
Isa. 55. 2. let your soul delight . in *f.*
Jer. 31. 14. satiate the soul with *f.*
Rom. 11. 17. root and *f.* of olive-tree
R. V. Ps. 92. 14. full of sap; Isa. 58. 11. strong; Jer. 50. 11. wanton as an; Deut. 32. 15. become sleek

FATHER, Gen. 2. 24. & 4. 20, 21.
Gen. 17. 4. be a *f.* of many nations
Job 29. 16. I was a *f.* to the poor
Ps. 68. 5. a *f.* of fatherless is God
103. 13. as a *f.* pitieth his children
Isa. 9. 6. the everlasting *F.* prince
Jer. 31. 9. I am a *F.* to Israel and
Mal. 1. 6. if I be a *F.* where is my honor
2. 10. have we not all one *F.*
John 5. 19. what he seeth the *F.* do.
20. *F.* loveth the Son, 3. 35.
22. *F.* judgeth no man but
26. *F.* hath life in himself
8. 18. *F.* beareth witness of me
44. *f.* devil is a liar and *f.* of it
16. 32. I am not alone *F.* is with
Acts 1. 4. promise of the *F.*
Rom. 4. 11. be the *f.* of all them
12. *f.* of circumcision
16. *f.* of us all
17. made thee a *f.* of many nations
1 Cor. 8. 6. the *F.* of whom are all
1 Cor. 1. 3. God and *F.* of our Lord Jesus Christ, *F.* of mer. and God of all com., Eph. 1. 3. 1 Pet. 1. 3.
6. 18. I will be a *F.* to you and
1 Tim. 5. 1. entreat him as a *f.*
Heb. 1. 5. I will be to him a *F.* and
12. 9. subjection to the *F.* of spirits
Jas. 1. 17. gift from *F.* of lights
John 5. 17. *my Father* worketh and I work
10. 30. I and my *F.* are one
14. 28. my *F.* is greater than I
Ezek. 16. 45. *your father* an Amorite
Matt. 5. 16. glorify your *F.* in heaven, 6. 1, 8, 9, 32. & 7. 11. & 45. 48.
John 8. 41. ye do deeds of your *f.*
44. ye are of your *f.* the devil
20. 17. I ascend to my *F.* and your
Ex. 15. 2. my *f.*'s God I will exalt
Neh. 9. 9, 16. *our fathers* dealt proudly
Ps. 22. 4. our *f.* trusted in thee
44. 1. our *f.* have told us, 78. 3.
Lam. 5. 7. our *f.* have sinned
Acts 15. 10. our *f.* not able to bear
Ex. 22. 22. not afflict *fatherless*
Deut. 10. 18. execute judgment of *f.*
Ps. 10. 14. thou helper of the *f.*
82. 3. defend the poor and *f.*
146. 9. Lord relieveth the *f.* and widow
Isa. 1. 17. judge *f.* plead for widow
Jas. 1. 27. visit *f.* in affliction

FAULT, Gen. 41. 9. Ex. 5. 16.
Ps. 19. 12. cleanse thou me from secret *f.*
Matt. 18. 15. if trespass, tell him his *f.*
Luke 23. 4. I find no *f.* in him, 14. John 18. 38. & 19. 4, 6.
1 Cor. 6. 7. utterly a *f.* among you
Jas. 5. 16. confess your *f.* one to
1 Pet. 2. 20. buffeted for your *f.*
Jude 24. able to present you *faultless*
R. V. Deut. 25. 2. wickedness; Mark 7. 2——; John 18. 38; 19. 4, 6. crime; 1 Cor. 6. 7. defect; Gal. 6. 1. any trespass; Jas. 5. 16. sins; Rev. 14. 5. blemish; Jude 24. blemish in

FAVOR, Gen. 39. 21. Deut. 33. 23.
1 Sam. 2. 26. Samuel in *f.* with
Job 10. 12. granted me life and *f.*
Ps. 5. 12. with *f.* wilt thou compass
106. 4. remember me with *f.* that
Prov. 31. 30. *f.* is deceitful and
Luke 2. 52. in *f.* with God and man
Ps. 41. 11. know thou *favorest* me
R. V. Ps. 112. 5. that dealeth graciously; Prov. 14. 9. good will; S. of S. 8. 10. peace; Ps. 102. 13, 14. have pity; 41. 11. delighted in

FEAR, Gen. 9. 2. Ex. 15. 16.
Ps. 53. 5. in *f.* where no *f.* was
119. 38. servant devoted to thy *f.*
120. flesh trembleth for *f.* of thee
Prov. 1. 26. mock when your *f.* cometh
Isa. 8. 12. *f.* not their *f.* nor be afraid
13. let him be your *f.*, Gen. 31. 42.
Jer. 32. 40. put my *f.* in their hearts
Mal. 1. 6. if master where is my *f.*
Rom. 13. 7. render *f.* to whom *f.*
2 Tim. 1. 7. spirit of *f.* but of power
Heb. 2. 15. who through *f.* of death
12. 28. with reverence and godly *f.*
1 Pet. 1. 17. time of sojourning here in *f.*
1 John 4. 18. no *f.* in love
Gen. 20. 11. *fear of God* not in this place
2 Sam. 23. 3. ruling in —
Neh. 5. 15. so did not I because of —
Ps. 36. 1. no — before his eyes, Rom. 3. 18.
2 Cor. 7. 1. perfecting holiness in —
Job 28. 28. *fear of the Lord*, that is wisdom
Ps. 19. 9. — is clean, enduring for ever
34. 11. children I will teach you —
Prov. 1. 29. they did not choose —
8. 13. — is to hate evil
10. 27. — prolongeth days
14. 26. in — is strong confidence
27. — is a fountain of life
15. 33. — is instruction of wisdom
22. 4. by — are riches, honor, life
23. 17. be thou in — all day long
Isa. 33. 6. — is his treasure
Acts 9. 31. walking in — and comfort
Ps. 2. 11. *with fear*, Phil. 2. 12.
Heb. 11. 7. Jude 23. save —
Deut. 4. 10. learn *to fear* me
5. 29. such a heart that would *f.* me
28. 58. mayest *f.* this glorious name
2 Kings 17. 39. Lord your God ye shall *f.*
1 Chron. 16. 30. *f.* before him all
2 Chron. 6. 31. that they may *f.* thee, 33.
Neh. 1. 11. servants, desire to *f.* thy name
Ps. 23. 4. I will *f.* no evil, for thou
31. 19. goodness laid up for those that *f.*
61. 5. heritage of those that *f.*
86. 11. incline my heart to *f.* thy name
Jer. 10. 7. who would not *f.* thee
32. 39. heart that may *f.* me for ever
Mal. 4. 2. to you that *f.* my name
Luke 12. 5. *f.* him who can cast, Matt. 10. 28.
Rom. 8. 15. not spirit of bondage again to *f.*
11. 20. be not high-minded but *f.*
Heb. 4. 1. *f.* lest a promise being left
12. 21. Moses said, I exceedingly *f.* and
Rev. 2. 10. *f.* none of these things
Gen. 42. 18. this do and live, for I *fear God*
Ex. 18. 21. such as — men of truth
Ps. 66. 16. come hear all ye that —
Eccl. 5. 7. dreams, vanities, *f.* thou God
8. 12. shall go well with them that —
12. 13. — and keep his commandments
Job 37. 24. therefore men do *fear him*
Ps. 25. 14. secret of Lord with them that —
33. 18. eye of Lord upon them that —
34. 9. there is no want to them that —
85. 9. his salvation is nigh to them that —
Ps. 103. 13. as father pities, so Lord them that —
111. 5. giveth meat to them that —
145. 19. fulfil the desire of them that —
Matt. 10. 28. — who is able to destroy
Luke 1. 50. his mercy on them that —
Deut. 6. 2. mightest *fear the Lord*
13. thou shalt — thy God, 10. 20.
24. — our God for our good always
10. 12. — thy God walk in his ways
14. 23. learn to — thy God, always, 17. 19. & 31. 12, 13.
Josh. 4. 24. that ye might — your
24. 14. therefore — serve in sincer.
1 Sam. 12. 14. if ye will — and serve
24. only — and serve him in truth
1 Kings 18. 12. thy servant did —, 2 Kings 4. 1.
2 Kings 17. 28. how they should —
Ps. 15. 4. he honoreth them that —
22. 23. ye that — trust in him, 115. 11.
33. 8. let all the earth —
115. 13. he will bless them that —
135. 20. ye that — bless the Lord
Prov. 3. 7. — and depart from evil
24. 21. my son — and meddle not
Jer. 5. 24. let us now — that giveth rain
26. 19. did not he — and besought
Hos. 3. 5. and shall — and his goodness
Jonah 1. 9. I — the God of heaven
Gen. 15. 1. *fear not*, I am thy shield
Num. 14. 9. Lord is with us — them
Deut. 1. 21. — neither be discour.
Ps. 56. 4. I will not *f.* what flesh can do, 118. 6. Heb. 13. 6.
Isa. 41. 10. — for I am with thee, I will help thee, 13. & 43. 5.
43. 1. — for I have redeemed thee
Jer. 5. 22. *f.* ye not me, saith the Lord
30. 10. — O my servant Jacob
Matt. 10. 28. — them that kill the body
Luke 12. 32 — little flock; for it is
Ex. 1. 17. midwives *feared* God, 21.
14. 31. people *f.* Lord and believed
1 Sam. 12. 18. all people greatly *f.* the Lord
1 Kings 18. 3. Obadiah *f.* the Lord
Neh. 7. 2. Hanani *f.* God above
Job 1. 1. one that *f.* God and
Ps. 76. 7. thou art to be *f.* who
89. 7. God is greatly to be *f.* in
96. 4. Lord is to be *f.* above all
Mal. 3. 16. they that *f.* the Lord
Acts 10. 2. one that *f.* the Lord
Heb. 5. 7. was heard in that he *f.*
Gen. 22. 12. that thou *fearest* God
Job 1. 8. that *feareth* God, 2. 3.
Ps. 25. 12. what man is he that *f.*
128. 1. every one that *f.* the Lord
Prov. 28. 14. happy is the man that *f.* alway
Isa. 50. 10. who among you *f.* Lord
Acts 10. 22. one that *f.* God and of
35. he that *f.* God and works righ.
13. 26. whosoever among you *f.* God
Ex. 15. 11. *fearful* in praises
Matt. 8. 26. why are ye *f.*, Mark 4. 40.
Heb. 10. 27. certain *f.* looking for
31. *f.* thing to fall into hands of
Rev. 21. 8. *f.* and unbelieving shall
Ps. 55. 5. *fearfulness* and trembling
Isa. 33. 14. *f.* hath surprised hypocrites
Ps. 139. 14. I am *fearfully* and
R. V. very often in O. T., terror; Luke 21. 11. terrors; Isa. 21. 4. horror hath; 33. 14. trembling

FEAST, Gen. 19. 3. & 21. 8.
Prov. 15. 15. merry heart has a continual *f.*
Eccl. 10. 9. a *f.* is made for laughter
Isa. 25. 6. Lord make to all people a *f.* of
1 Cor. 5. 8. let us keep *f.* but not
R. V. Lam. 1. 4; 2. 6, 7; Hos. 2. 11. assembly; Matt. 26. 17; Luke 23. 17; Acts 18. 21 ——

FEEBLE, Gen. 30. 42. Job 4. 4.
Ps. 105. 37. not one *f.* person among
Isa. 35. 3. confirm the *f.* knees
Zech. 12. 8. he that is *f.* shall be
1 Thes. 5. 14. comfort the *f.* minded
Heb. 12. 12. lift up the *f.* knees
R. V. 1 Sam. 2. 5. languisheth; Ps. 38. 8. faint; Isa. 16. 14. of no account; 1 Thes. 5. 14. fainthearted; Heb. 12. 12. palsied

FEED, *fed*, Gen. 25. 30. & 30. 36.
Ps. 28. 9. *f.* them and lift them up
37. 3. verily thou shalt be *f.*
49. 14. death shall *f.* on them
Prov. 10. 21. lips of righteous *f.*
Isa. 58. 14. *f.* thee with heritage of
Jer. 3. 15. pastors *f.* you with knowledge
Acts 20. 28. to *f.* the church of God
1 Cor. 13. 3. give all my goods to *f.*
3. 2. I have *f.* you with milk, and
Rev. 7. 17. Lamb in the throne *f.*
1 Kings 22. 27. *f.* him with bread
Prov. 30. 8. *f.* me with food convenient
S. of S. 1. 8. *f.* thy kids beside shepherds' tents
Mic. 7. 14. *f.* thy people with thy rod
John 21. 15. *f.* my lambs, *f.* my sheep, 16. 17.
Rom. 12. 20. if enemy hunger, *f.*
1 Pet. 5. 2. *f.* flock of God among
Isa. 44. 20. he *feedeth* on ashes
S. of S. 2. 16. he *f.* among lilies, 6. 3.
Hos. 12. 1. Ephraim *f.* on wind —
Matt. 6. 26. heavenly Father *f.* them, Luke 12. 24.
1 Cor. 9. 7. who *f.* a flock and eateth not
R. V. Gen. 46. 32. keepers of; John 21. 16; 1 Pet. 5. 2. tend; 2 Sam. 19. 33. sustain; Ps. 49. 14; Rev. 7. 17. be their shepherd; Rev. 12. 6. may nourish

FEEL, *feeling*, Gen. 27. 12. Acts 17. 27. Eph. 4. 19. Heb. 4. 15.
R. V. Job 20. 20. knew no; Eccl. 8. 5. know

FEET, Gen. 18. 4. & 19. 2. & 49. 10.
1 Sam. 2. 9. keep *f.* of his saints
Neh. 9. 21. their *f.* swelled not
Job 12. 5. is ready to slip with his *f.*
29. 15. eyes to the blind, and *f.*
Ps. 73. 2. my *f.* were almost gone
116. 8. delivered my *f.* from falling
119. 105. thy word is a lamp to my *f.*
Prov. 4. 26. ponder the path of thy *f.*
Isa. 59. 7. their *f.* run to evil, and
Luke 1. 79. guide our *f.* into way of
Eph. 6. 15. *f.* shod with the prep.
Heb. 12. 13. straight paths for your *f.*
Rev. 11. 11. they stood upon their *f.*
R. V. Isa. 3. 18; Matt. 18. 29 ——

FEIGNED, 1 Sam. 21. 13. Ps. 17. 1.
2 Pet. 2. 3. *feignedly*, Jer. 3. 10.

FELLOW, Gen. 19. 9. Ex. 2. 13.
Zech. 13. 7. man that is my *f.*
Acts 24. 5. a pestilent *f.*, 22. 22.
Rom. 16. 7. my *f.* prisoner, Col. 4. 10.
2 Cor. 8. 23. my *f.* helper, 3 John 8.
Eph. 2. 19. *f.* citizens
3. 6. *f.* heirs
Col. 1. 7. *f.* servant, 4. 7. Rev. 6. 11. & 19. 10. & 22. 9.
Phil. 4. 3. *f.* laborers, 1 Thes. 3. 2.
Ps. 45. 7. oil of gladness above *f.*, Heb. 1. 9.
94. 20. have *fellowship* with thee
Acts 2. 42. continued steadfastly in apostles' doctrine and *f.*
1 Cor. 1. 9. God by whom call. to *f.*
10. 20. should have *f.* with devils
2 Cor. 6. 14. what *f.* hath righteous.
8. 4. *f.* of ministering to saints

Gal. 2. 9. gave us right hand of *f.*
Eph. 5. 11. no *f.* with unfruitful
Phil. 1. 5. for your *f.* in the gospel
2. 1. if there be any *f.* of the Spi.
1 John 1. 3. *f.* with us, our *f.* with
R. V. Judg. 11. 37; Ezek. 37. 19; Dan. 2. 13. companions; 1 Sam. 29. 4; Matt. 12. 24; 26. 61; Luke 22. 59; 23. 2; John 9. 29; Acts 18. 13. man; Lev. 6. 2. bargain; 1 Cor. 10. 20. communion; Eph. 3. 9. dispensation

FERVENT in spirit, Acts 18. 25.
Rom. 12. 11. *f.* in spirit serving
2 Cor. 7. 7. your *f.* mind toward me
Jas. 5. 16. *f.* prayer of righteous
2 Pet. 3. 10. melt with *f.* heat, 12.
Col. 4. 12. Epaphras always laboring *fervently* for you in prayers
1 Pet. 1. 22. love one another *f.*
R. V. 2 Cor. 7. 7. zeal for; Jas. 5. 16. much in its workings; Col. 4. 12. striving

FEVER threatened for disobedience, Deut. 28. 22.
healed: Peter's wife's mother, Matt. 8. 14; nobleman's son, John 4. 52.

FEW, Gen. 29. 20. Ps. 105. 12.
Matt. 7. 14. way to life, *f.* find it
20. 16. many called, but *f.* chosen, 22. 14.
25. 21. been faithful in a *f.* things
Rev. 2. 14. I have a *f.* things

FIDELITY, all good, Tit. 2. 10.

FIERCENESS of anger, Deut. 13. 17. Josh. 7. 26. 2 Kings 23. 26. Job 4. 10. & 10. 16. & 39. 24. & 41. 10. Ps. 85. 3. Jer. 25. 38. Hos. 11. 9.

FIERY law, Deut. 33. 2.
Num. 21. 6. *f.* serpents, 8. Deut. 8. 15.
Ps. 21. 9. make them as a *f.* oven
Eph. 6. 16. quench *f.* darts of devil
Heb. 10. 27. *f.* indignation devour
1 Pet. 4. 12. not strange the *f.* trial
R. V. Heb. 10. 27. fierceness of fire

FIGHT, 1 Sam. 17. 20. Ex. 14. 14.
Acts 5. 39. found to *f.* against God
1 Cor. 9. 26. so *f.* I not as one that
2 Tim. 4. 7. I have fought a good *f.*
Heb. 10. 32. a great *f.* of afflictions
R. V. Heb. 10. 32. conflict of suffering

FIGS, Gen. 3. 7. Isa. 34. 4. & 38. 21.
Jer. 24. 2. very good *f.* naughty *f.*, 29. 17.
Matt. 7. 16. do men gather *f.* of thistles
Jas. 3. 12. can *f.* tree bear olive
Judg. 9. 10. *fig-tree*, 1 Kings 4. 25. Mic. 4. 4. Isa. 36. 16. Hos. 9. 10. Nah. 3. 12. Hab. 3. 17. Zech. 3. 10. Matt. 21. 19. & 24. 32. Luke 13. 6, 7. John 1. 48, 50. Rev. 6. 13.
R. V. Isa. 34. 4. fading leaf

FIGURE, Rom. 5. 14. 1 Cor. 4. 6. Heb. 9. 9, 24. & 11. 19. 1 Pet. 3. 21.
R. V. Heb. 9. 24. like in pattern to; 1 Pet. 3. 21. after a true likeness

FILL, Job 8. 21. & 23. 4.
Ps. 81. 10. open mouth wide, I will *f.* it
Jer. 23. 24. I *f.* heaven and earth
Rom. 15. 13. God *f.* you with all
Eph. 4. 10. ascended, might *f.* all
Col. 1. 24. I *f.* up that which is be.
Ps. 72. 19. earth *filled* with his glory
Luke 1. 53. hath *f.* hungry with
Acts 9. 17. *f.* with the Holy Ghost, 2. 4. & 4. 8, 31. & 13. 9, 52. Luke 1. 15.
Rom. 15. 14. *f.* with all knowledge
2 Cor. 7. 4. I am *f.* with comfort
Eph. 3. 19. might be *f.* with all
5. 18. not with wine but *f.* with
Phil. 1. 11. *f.* with the fruits of
Col. 1. 9. *f.* with knowledge of his
2 Tim. 1. 4. mindful of tears *f.* with
Eph. 1. 23. fulness of him that *filleth* all in all
R. V. Job 38. 39; Ezek. 32. 4. satisfy; Ps. 104. 28; Prov. 18. 20; 30. 16. satisfied, Matt. 5. 6; Mark 2. 21. should fill, Rev. 15. 1. finished; 18. 6. mingle unto; Rom. 15. 24. in some measure I shall have been satisfied

FILTH, Isa. 4. 4. 1 Cor. 4. 13.
Job 15. 16. more *filthy* is man
Ps. 14. 3. altogether become *f.*, 53. 3.
Isa. 64. 6. all our righteousness as *f.*
Col. 3. 8. put off *f.* communication
1 Tim. 3. 3. greedy of *f.* lucre, 8. Tit. 1. 7, 11. 1 Pet. 5. 2.
2 Pet. 2. 7. vexed with *f.* conver.
Jude 8. *f.* dreamers defile the flesh
Rev. 22. 11. that is *f.* let him be *f.*
Jas. 1. 21. lay apart all *filthiness*
Ezek. 36. 25. from all your *f.* I
2 Cor. 7. 1. cleanse ourselves from all *f.*
R. V. Ezra 9. 11. through the uncleanness; 2 Cor. 7. 1. defilement of; Rev. 17. 4. even the unclean things; Job 15. 16. corrupt; Isa. 64. 6. polluted; Zeph. 3. 11. rebellious; Col. 3. 8. shameful; 1 Tim. 3. 3. money; 2 Pet. 2. 7. lascivious; Jude 8 ——

FINALLY, 2 Cor. 13. 11. Eph. 6. 10. Phil. 3. 1. & 4. 8. 2 Thes. 3. 1. 1 Pet. 3. 8.

FIND, Gen. 19. 11. & 38. 22.
Num. 32. 23. your sin shall *f.* you
Job 11. 7. who by searching can *f.*
Prov. 1. 28. shall seek me and not *f.*
S. of S. 5. 6. I sought but could not *f.*
Jer. 6. 16. ye shall *f.* rest to your
29. 13. shall seek me and *f.* me
Matt. 7. 7. seek and ye shall *f.*
10. 39. *f.* life; loseth life shall *f.* it, 16. 25.
11. 29. ye shall *f.* rest to your souls
John 7. 34. seek me, and shall not *f.*
Rom. 7. 18. how to do good, I *f.* not
2 Tim. 1. 18. may *f.* mercy in that
Heb. 4. 16. may *f.* grace to help
Rev. 9. 6. seek death and shall not *f.*
Prov. 8. 35. whoso *findeth* me *f.* life
18. 22. whoso *f.* a wife, *f.* a good
Eccl. 9. 10. whatsoever thy hand *f.* to do
Matt. 7. 8. that seeketh *f.*, Luke 11. 10.
Isa. 58. 13. not *finding* thine own pl.
Rom. 11. 33. his ways past *f.* out

FINE, Job 28. 1. Isa. 3. 23. Lev. 2. 1. Ps. 81. 16. Prov. 25. 4.
R. V. Isa. 19. 9. combed; Lam. 4. 1; Dan. 10. 5. pure; Mark 15. 46. linen cloth; Rev. 1. 15; 2. 18. burnished.

FINGER of God, Ex. 8. 19. & 31. 18. Deut. 9. 10. Luke 11. 20.
1 Kings 12. 10. my little *f.* shall
Ps. 8. 3. heaven is work of thy *f.*
144. 1. he teacheth my *f.* to fight
Prov. 6. 13. he teacheth with his *f.*
Luke 11. 46. touch not with one of your *f.*
John 20. 27. reach hither thy *f.*

FINISH transgression, Dan. 9. 24.
John 17. 4. I have *f.* work
19. 30. it is *f.*
Acts 20. 24. *f.* my course with joy
2 Cor. 8. 6. would also *f.* in you
2 Tim. 4. 7. I have *f.* my course
Jas. 1. 15. sin when it is *f.* bringeth
Heb. 12. 2. author and *finisher* of
R. V. Luke 14. 28; 2 Cor. 8. 6. complete; John 3. 34, 5. 36; 17. 4. accomplish; Acts 20. 24. may accomplish, Jas. 1. 15. full-grown

FIRE, Ex. 3. 2. & 9. 23, 24. & 40. 38.
Gen. 19. 24. the Lord rained *f.*
Ps. 11. 6. rain *f.* and brimstone
39. 3. while musing the *f.* burned
Prov. 6. 27. can a man take *f.*
25. 22. heap coals of *f.* on his head, Rom. 12. 20.
S. of S. 8. 6. as coals of *f.* hath vehement
Isa. 9. 18. wickedness burneth as a *f.*
10. 17. light of Israel for a *f.* for a flame
31. 9. Lord of hosts whose *f.* is in Zion
43. 2. walkest through *f.* shall not
Jer. 23. 29. is not my word like *f.*, 20. 9.
Amos 5. 6. lest Lord break out like *f.*
7. 4. Lord God called to contend by *f.*
Zech. 2. 5. I will be a wall of *f.*
3. 2. brand plucked out of *f.*, Amos 4. 11.
Mal. 3. 2. he shall be as a refiner's *f.*
Matt. 3. 10. cut down and cast into the *f.*, 7. 19.
12. burn with unquenchable *f.*, Mark 9. 43, 44, 46, 48. Luke 3. 17.
Luke 9. 54. command *f.* to come
12. 49. I am come to send *f.* on the
1 Cor. 3. 13. revealed by *f.* —*f.* try, 15.
Heb. 12. 29. our God is consuming *f.*
Jude 23. pulling them out of the *f.*
Matt. 5. 22. *hell-fire*, 18. 9. Mark 9. 47.
Lev. 10. 1. *strange fire*, Num. 3. 4. & 26. 61.
R. V. Matt. 5. 22; 18. 9. the hell of fire; Mark 9. 44, 46, 47 ——

FIRST, Matt. 10. 2. Esth. 1. 14.
Isa. 41. 4. the Lord the *f.* and the last, 44. 6. & 48. 12. Rev. 1. 11, 17. & 2. 8. & 22. 13.
Matt. 6. 33. seek *f.* the kingdom of
7. 5. *f.* cast out the beam, Luke 6. 42.
19. 30. many that be *f.* shall be last, 20. 16. Mark 10. 31.
22. 38. this is the *f.* and great
Acts 26. 23. *f.* that should rise
Rom. 11. 35. who hath *f.* given to
1 Cor. 15. 45. *f.* man Adam
47. *f.* man of the earth
2 Cor. 8. 5. *f.* gave their own selves
12. accepted, if there be *f.* willing
1 Pet. 4. 17. if judgment *f.* begin
1 John 4. 19. because he *f.* loved us
Rev. 2. 4. left thy *f.* love
5. do *f.* works
20. 5. this is the *f.* resurrection, 6.
Matt. 1. 25. *first-born*, Luke 2. 7.
Rom. 8. 29. *f.* among many breth.
Col. 1. 15. *f.* of every creature
18. *f.* from the dead
Rom. 11. 16. if *first fruit* be holy
Prov. 3. 9. honor the Lord with *f.*
Rom. 8. 23. having *first fruits*
1 Cor. 15. 20. Christ *f.* of them
Jas. 1. 18. we a kind of *f.* creatures
Rev. 14. 4. redeemed are *f.* to God

FISH, Ezek. 29. 4, 5. & 47. 9, 10.
Jer. 16. 16. *fishers*, Ezek. 47. 10. Matt. 4. 18, 19. John 21. 7. Isa. 19. 8.
R. V. Isa. 19. 10. hire; Job 41. 1; John 21. 7 ——

FLAME, Ex. 3. 2. Judg. 13. 20.
Ps. 104. 4. maketh ministers a *f.*
106. 18. *f.* burnt up wicked, Num. 16. 35.
Isa. 10. 17. the Holy One of Israel for a *f.*
2 Thes. 1. 8. in *flaming* fire taking
R. V. Judg. 20. 38, 40. cloud; Dan. 7. 11. with fire; Isa. 13. 8. faces of flame: Nah. 2. 3. flash in the steel

FLATTER, Ps. 78. 36. Prov. 2. 16. & 20. 19. Job 32. 21, 22. 1 Thes. 2. 5.
R. V. Prov. 20. 19. openeth wide

FLEE, Isa. 10. 3. & 20. 6. Heb. 6. 18.
Prov. 28. 1. wicked *f.* when no
Matt. 3. 7. who warned you to *f.*
1 Cor. 6. 18. *f.* fornication
10. 14. *f.* from idolatry
1 Tim. 6. 11. man of God *f.* these
2 Tim. 2. 22. *f.* youthful lusts
Jas. 4. 7. resist the devil, he will *f.* from you
R. V. Job 30. 10. stand; 30. 3. gnaw the dry ground; Ps. 64. 8. wag the head; Jer. 48. 9. fly; Hos. 7. 13. wandered, Acts 16. 27. escaped

FLEECE, Gideon's, Judg. 6. 37.
FLESH, Gen. 2. 21. 1 Cor. 15. 39.
Gen. 2. 24. they shall be one *f.*, Matt. 19. 5. 1 Cor. 6. 16. Eph. 5. 31.
John 10. 11. clothed me with skin and *f.*
Ps. 56. 4. what *f.* can do to me
78. 39. remember that they were but *f.*
Jer. 17. 5. cursed that maketh *f.* his arm
Matt. 26. 41. spirit is willing, but *f.* weak
John 1. 14. the Word was made *f.*
6. 53. eat the *f.* of the Son of man, 52, 55, 56.
63. *f.* profiteth nothing, words are
Rom. 7. 25. serve with *f.* law of sin
8. 12. debtors not to the *f.*
9. 3. kinsmen according to the *f.*
5. of whom concerning *f.* Christ
13. 14. make not provision for *f.*
1 Cor. 1. 29. that no *f.* should glory
2 Cor. 1. 17. purpose according to *f.*
10. 2. walked according to the *f.*
Gal. 5. 17. *f.* lusts against the Spirit
24. Christ's have crucified *f.* with
Eph. 6. 5. masters according to *f.*
Heb. 12. 9. we had fathers of our *f.*
Jude 7. going after strange *f.*
23. hating garment spotted by *f.*
John 8. 15. ye judge *after the flesh*
Rom. 8. 1. walk not — but after
5. they that are — mind things of *f.*
13. if ye live — ye shall die, 12.
1 Cor. 1. 26. not many wise men —
10. 18. Israel —, Rom. 9. 8. Gal. 6. 13.
2 Cor. 5. 16. know no man — know Christ
10. 3. walk in *f.* not war —
2 Pet. 2. 10. walk — in lust of
Ps. 65. 2. to thee shall *all flesh* come
Isa. 40. 6. — is grass, 1 Pet. 1. 24.
49. 26. — shall know that I am thy
Jer. 32. 27. I am the Lord, the God of —
Joel 2. 28. I will pour my Spirit on —
Luke 3. 6. — shall see the salvation
John 17. 2. given him power over —
Rom. 7. 5. when we were *in the flesh*
8. 8. that are — cannot please God
1 Tim. 3. 16. mystery; God manifest —
1 Pet. 3. 18. he was put to death —, 4. 1.
Gen. 2. 23. *my flesh*, 29. 14. Job 19. 26.
Ps. 63. 1. & 119. 120. John 6. 51, 55, 56. Rom. 7. 18.
John 1. 13. born not of will *of the flesh*
3. 6. that which is born — is *f.*
Rom. 8. 5. after *f.* do mind things—
Gal. 5. 19. works — are manifest
6. 8. soweth to *f.* shall — reap cor.
Eph. 2. 3. lusts — desires —
1 Pet. 3. 21. not putting away filth—
1 John 2. 16. lust—of the eyes, pride
Matt. 16. 17. *flesh and blood* have
1 Cor. 15. 50. — cannot inherit the
Gal. 1. 16. I conferred not with —
Eph. 5. 30. members of his — and
6. 12. we wrestle not against — but
Heb. 2. 14. children are partakers of —
2 Cor. 1. 12. not with *fleshly* wisdom
1 Pet. 2. 11. abstain from *f.* lusts
R. V. Acts 2. 30; Rom. 8. 1; Eph. 5. 30 ——; 2 Cor. 3. 3. tables that are hearts of flesh
FLOCK, Gen. 32. 5. Ps. 77. 20. Isa. 40. 11. & 63. 11. Jer. 13. 17, 20.
Zech. 11. 4. feed *f.* of slaughter, 7.
Luke 12. 32. fear not, little *f.* for it
Acts 20. 28. take heed to all the *f.*, 29.
1 Pet. 5. 2. feed the *f.* of God
R. V. Ezek. 34. 3, 8, 10, 15, 19, 31. sheep
FLOURISH, Isa. 17. 11. & 66. 14.
Ps. 72. 7. shall the righteous *f.*, 16. & 92. 12, 13, 14. Prov. 11. 28. & 14. 11.
92. 7. when workers of iniquity *f.*
132. 18. on himself shall crown *f.*
R. V. Isa. 17. 11; Eccl. 12. 5. blossom; S. of S. 6. 11; 7. 12. budded; Phil. 4. 10. ye have revived
FOLLOW, Gen. 44. 4. Ex. 14. 4.
Ex. 23. 2. shall not *f.* a multitude
Deut. 16. 20. that is just shalt thou *f.*
Ps. 38. 20. I *f.* the thing that good is
Isa. 51. 1. my people that *f.*
Hos. 6. 3. know if we *f.* on to know
Rom. 14. 19. *f.* things that make for
1 Cor. 14. 1. *f.* after charity, desire
Phil. 3. 12. but I *f.* after that I may
1 Thes. 5. 15. ever *f.* that which is
1 Tim. 6. 11. *f.* after righteousness
2 Tim. 2. 22. *f.* righteousness, faith
Heb. 12. 14. *f.* peace with all men
13. 7. whose faith *f.* considering
1 Pet. 2. 21. example should *f.* his
3 John 11. *f.* not evil, but that whi.
Rev. 14. 13. their works do *f.* them
Ps. 23. 6. goodness and mercy shall *follow me*, Matt. 4. 19. & 9. 9. & 19. 21. Luke 5. 27. & 9. 59. John 1. 43. & 21. 19.
Matt. 16. 24. take up cross and —
Luke 18. 22. sell all that thou hast, and —
John 12. 26. if any man serve me, let him —
Num. 14. 24. hath *followed* me fully
32. 12. wholly *f.* the Lord, Deut. 1. 36. Josh. 14. 8, 9, 14.
Rom. 9. 30. *f.* not after righteousness
31. *f.* law of righteousness
Ps. 63. 8. soul *followeth* hard after
Matt. 10. 38. taketh not his cross and *f.* me
Mark 9. 38. he *f.* not us, Luke 9. 49.
R. V. Ex. 14. 17. go in after; Matt. 4. 19. come ye after; 27. 62. the day after; 2 Thes. 3. 7; Heb. 13. 7; 3 John 11. imitate; Phil. 3. 12. press on
FOLLY wrought in Israel, Gen. 34. 7. Deut. 22. 21. Josh. 7. 15. Judg. 20. 6.
Job 4. 18. angels he charged with *f.*
Ps. 49. 13. their way is their *f.*
85. 8. let them not turn again to *f.*
Prov. 26. 4, 5. answer a fool according to his *f.*
2 Tim. 3. 9. their *f.* shall be manifest
R. V. 2 Cor. 11. 1. foolishness
FOOD, Gen. 3. 6. Deut. 10. 18.
Job 23. 12. words more than necessary *f.*
Ps. 78. 25. men did eat angels' *f.*
136. 25. who giveth *f.* to all flesh
146. 7. who giveth *f.* to the hungry
Prov. 30. 8. feed me with *f.* conven.
Acts 14. 17. filling our hearts with *f.*
2 Cor. 9. 10. ministered bread for your *f.*
1 Tim. 6. 8. having *f.* and raiment
R. V. Gen. 42. 33. corn; Lev. 22. 7; 2 Sam. 9. 10. bread; Ps. 78. 25. bread of the mighty
FOOL said in his heart, Ps. 14. 1. & 53. 1.
Jer. 17. 11. at end of days shall be *f.*
Matt. 5. 22. whosoever shall say to brother, thou *f.*
Luke 12. 20. thou *f.* this night thy
1 Cor. 3. 18. let him become a *f.* that
2 Cor. 11. 16. think me a *f.*
Ps. 75. 4. *fools* deal not foolishly
94. 8. ye *f.* when will ye be wise
107. 17. *f.* because of their trans.
Prov. 1. 7. *f.* despise wisdom
22. *f.* hate knowledge
13. 20. companion of *f.* shall be
14. 8. folly of *f.* is deceitful
16. 22. instruction of *f.* is folly
Eccl. 5. 4. he hath no pleasure in *f.*
Matt. 23. 17. ye *f.* and blind, 19.
Rom. 1. 22. professing to be wise became *f.*
1 Cor. 4. 10. we are *f.* for Christ's sake
Eph. 5. 15. walk circumspectly, not as *f.*
Ps. 5. 5. *f.* shall not stand in thy sight
Ps. 73. 22. so *f.* was I and ignorant
Matt. 7. 26. on sand like to a *f.* man
25. 2. virgins, five were wise and five *f.*
Rom. 1. 21. their *f.* heart darkened
Gal. 3. 1. O *f.* Galatians, who bewitched
Eph. 5. 4. filthiness, nor *f.* talking
Tit. 3. 3. were sometimes *f.* disobe.
Gen. 31. 28. done *foolishly*, Num. 12. 11. 1 Sam. 13. 13. 2 Sam. 24. 10. 1 Chron. 21. 8. 2 Chron. 16. 9. Prov. 14. 17. 2 Cor. 11. 21.
Job 1. 22. Job sinned not, nor charged God *f.*
2 Sam. 15. 31. turn counsel into *foolishness*
Prov. 12. 23. heart of fools proclaimeth *f.*
14. 24. *f.* of fools is folly, 15. 2, 14.
22. 15. *f.* is bound in heart of child
27. 22. bray a fool, yet his *f.* will
1 Cor. 1. 18. preaching of the cross is to them that perish, *f.*
23. Christ crucified, to Greeks *f.*
25. *f.* of God is wiser than men
3. 19. wisdom of world is *f.* with God
R. V. 2 Cor. 11. 23. one beside himself; Prov. 11. 29; 12. 15; Luke 12. 20; 1 Cor. 15. 36; 2 Cor. 11. 16; 12. 6, 11. foolish; Ps. 75. 4. arrogant; Eph. 5. 15. unwise; Ps. 5. 5; 73. 3. arrogant; 73. 22. brutish; Prov. 9. 6. ye simple ones; Rom. 1. 21. senseless; 10. 19. void of understanding; Ps. 75. 4. arrogantly; Prov. 14. 24; 15. 2, 14. folly
FOOT shall not stumble, Prov. 3. 23.
Eccl. 5. 1. keep thy *f.* when thou
Isa. 58. 13. turn away *f.* from sabbath
Matt. 18. 8. if thy *f.* offend thee, cut
Heb. 10. 29. trodden under *f.* Son of God
R. V. Ex. 31. 9; 35. 16; 38. 8; 39. 39; 41. 11; Lev. 8. 11. base; Isa. 18. 7. down; Lam. 1. 15. set at nought
FORBEAR, Ex. 23. 5. 1 Cor. 9. 6.
Rom. 2. 4. goodness and *forbearance*, 3. 25.
R. V. Neh. 9. 30. bear with; Prov. 24. 11. hold not back; Ezek. 24. 17. sigh but not aloud
FORBID, Mark 10. 14. Luke 18. 16. & 6. 29. Acts 24. 23. & 28. 31.
1 Tim. 4. 3. *forbidding* to marry
1 Thes. 2. 16. *f.* us to speak to the Gentiles
R. V. Matt. 3. 14. would have hindered; Luke 6. 29. withhold not; Gal. 6. 14. far be it from me; 2 Pet. 2. 16. and stayed
FORCE, Matt. 11. 12. Heb. 9. 17.
Isa. 60. 5. *f.* of Gentiles shall come, 11.
Job 6. 25. how *forcible* right words
R. V. Deut. 20. 19. wielding; Isa. 60. 5, 11. wealth; Ezek. 35. 5. power; Dan. 11. 38. fortresses; Obad. 11. substance
FOREFATHERS, 2 Tim. 1. 3. Jer. 11. 10.
FOREHEAD, Ex. 28. 38. Lev. 13. 41.
Jer. 3. 3. thou hast a whore's *f.*
Ezek. 3. 8. thy *f.* strong against their *f.*
Rev. 7. 3. sealed in their *f.*, 9. 4.
13. 16. mark their *f.*, 14. 9. & 20. 4.
14. 1. Father's name written in *f.*, 22. 4.
R. V. Ezek. 16. 12. nose
FOREIGNERS, Ex. 12. 45. Deut. 15. 3. Obad. 11. Eph. 2. 19.
FOREKNOW, Rom. 8. 29. & 11. 2.
Acts 2. 23. *foreknowledge* of God, 1 Pet. 1. 2.
FOREORDAINED, 1 Pet. 1. 20.
FORERUNNER, Heb. 6. 20.
FORESEETH, Prov. 22. 3. & 27. 12.
R. V. Prov. 22. 3; 27. 12. seeth; Acts 2. 25. beheld

FOREWARN, Luke 12. 5.
R. V. Luke 12. 5. warn
FORGAT Lord, Judg. 3. 7. 1 Sam. 12. 9.
Ps. 78. 11. *f.* his works and wonders
106. 21. *f.* God their Saviour
Lam. 3. 17. I *f.* prosperity
Hos. 2. 13. *f.* me, saith the Lord
Deut. 9. 7. remember and *forget* not
Job 8. 13. paths of all that *f.* God
Ps. 45. 10. *f.* thy own people, and
103. 2. *f.* not all his benefits
119. 16. I will not *f.* thy words, 83, 93, 109, 141, 153, 176.
Prov. 3. 1. my son, *f.* not my law
Isa. 49. 15. can woman *f.* her sucking child
Jer. 2. 32. can a maid *f.* her orna.
Heb. 6. 10. God is not unrighteous to *f.* your
13. 16. to do good and to communicate *f.* not
Jas. 1. 25. be not a *f.* hearer
Ps. 44. 24. thou *forgettest* our afflict.
9. 12. he *f.* not the cry of humble
Prov. 2. 17. *f.* covenant of her God
Jas. 1. 24. *f.* what manner of man
Phil. 3. 13. *forgetting* those things
Ps. 10. 11. God hath *forgotten*
42. 9. why hast thou *f.* me
77. 9. hath God *f.* to be gracious
119. 61. I have not *f.* thy law
Isa. 17. 10. hast *f.* the God of thy
Jer. 2. 32. my people have *f.* me
3. 21. have *f.* their God, Deut. 32. 18.
50. 5. covenant that shall not be *f.*
Heb. 12. 5. *f.* the exhortation
FORGAVE their iniquity, Ps. 78. 38.
Matt. 18. 27. *f.* him the debt, 32.
Luke 7. 42. frankly *f.* them both
43. love most, to whom *f.* most
2 Cor. 2. 10. *f.* any thing, I *f.* it
Col. 3. 13. as Christ *f.* you, also do
Ps. 32. 5. *forgavest* the iniquity of
99. 8. thou wast a God that *f.* them
Ex. 32. 32. now *forgive* their sin
Ps. 86. 5. thou art good and ready to *f.*
Isa. 2. 9. therefore *f.* them not
Matt. 6. 12. *f.* us our debts as we
14. if ye *f.* men, 15. if you *f.* not
9. 6. Son of man hath power on earth to *f.*
Luke 6. 37. *f.* and ye shall be for.
17. 3. if he repent, *f.* him, 4.
23. 34. Father *f.* them, they know
1 John 1. 9. faithful to *f.* us
Ps. 32. 1. whose transgression is *forgiven*
85. 2. *f.* the iniquity of thy people
Isa. 33. 24. people shall be *f.* their
Matt. 9. 2. good cheer, thy sins be *f.*
12. 31. all manner of sin *f.* 32. not be *f.*
Luke 7. 47. to whom little is *f.* loveth
Rom. 4. 7. blessed whose iniquities are *f.*
Eph. 4. 32. as God hath *f.* you, Col. 3. 13.
Jas. 5. 15. if he have committed sins, they shall be *f.*
1 John 2. 12. your sins are *f.* you
Ps. 103. 3. who *forgiveth* all thy ini.
130. 4. is there *forgiveness* with thee
Dan. 9. 9. to the Lord belong mercy and *f.*
Acts 5. 31. to give repent. and *f.*
26. 18. may receive *f* of sins by faith
Eph. 1. 7. *f* of sins according to the riches
Col. 1. 14. redempt., even *f.* of sin
Ex. 34. 7. *forgiving* iniquity, transgression and sin, Num. 14. 18. Mic. 7. 18.
Eph. 4. 32. *f.* one another, Col. 3. 13.
R. V. Luke 6. 37. release; Mark 11. 26 —; Acts 5. 31. 13. 38; 26. 18. remission
FORM, Gen. 1. 2. 1 Sam. 28. 14.
Isa. 53. 2. hath no *f.* nor comeliness
Rom. 2. 20. hast the *f.* of knowl.
6. 17. obeyed from heart that *f.*
Phil. 2. 6. who being in *f.* of God
7. took upon him the *f.* of a ser.
2 Tim. 1. 13. hold *f.* of sound words
3. 5. having the *f.* of godliness
Isa. 45. 7. I *f.* the light and create
Deut. 32. 18. hast forgotten God that *formed* thee
Prov. 26. 10. God that *f.* all things
Isa. 27. 11. *f.* them will show no
43. 21. this people have I *f.* for myself
Rom. 9. 20. thing *f.* say to him
Gal. 4. 19. till Christ be *f.* in you
Ps. 94. 9. that *formeth* the eye
Zech. 12. 1. *f.* spirit of man within
Jer. 10. 16. he is the *former* of all things, 51. 19.
R. V. Gen. 1. 2; Jer. 4. 23. waste; Job 4. 16. appearance; Dan. 2. 31; 3. 25. aspect; 2 Tim. 1. 13. pattern; Deut. 32. 18. gave birth; Job 26. 5. tremble; 26. 13. pierced; Prov. 26. 10. wounded; Isa. 44. 10. fashioned; Zech. 14. 8. eastern; Mal. 3. 4. ancient; Job 30. 3. gloom of; Hos. 6. 3. rain that watereth; Rev. 21. 4. the first
FORNICATION, 2 Chron. 21. 11. Isa. 23. 17. Ezek. 16. 15, 26, 29.
Matt. 5. 32. put away wife for cause of *f.*
19. 9. except it be for *f.*
John 8. 41. we be not born of *f.*
Acts 15. 20. abstain from *f.*, 29. & 21. 25.
Rom. 1. 29. filled with all *f.* wickedness
1 Cor. 5. 1. there is *f.* among you
6. 13. body not for *f.*
18. flee *f.*
7. 2. to avoid *f.* every man have his wife
2 Cor. 12. 21. not repent. of their *f.*
Gal. 5. 19. works of flesh, adult. *f.*
Eph. 5. 3. but *f.* and all uncleanness
Col. 3. 5. mortify *f.* uncleanness
1 Thes. 4. 3. should abstain from *f.*
Jude 7. giving themselves to *f.*
Rev. 2. 14. taught to commit *f.*, 20.
21. I gave her space to repent of her *f.*
9. 21. neither repented of their *f.*
17. 4. abomination and filthiness of her *f.*
19. 2. did corrupt earth with her *f.*
Ezek. 16. 15. *fornications*, Matt. 15. 19.
1 Cor. 5. 9. *fornicators*, 10. 11. & 6. 9. Heb. 12. 16.
R. V. 2 Chron. 21. 11. go a whoring; Isa. 23. 17. play the harlot; Ezek. 16. 15, 29. whoredom, Rom. 1. 29 —
FORSAKE, Deut. 12. 19. & 31. 16.
Deut. 4. 31. Lord thy God will not *f.* thee, 31. 6, 8. 1 Chron. 28. 20. Heb. 13. 5.
Josh. 1. 5. I will not fail thee nor *f.* thee, Isa. 41. 17. & 42. 16.
1 Sam. 12. 22. Lord will not *f.* his people
1 Kings 6. 13. I will not *f.* my peo.
2 Chron. 15. 2. if ye *f.* him he will *f.*
Ps. 27. 10. father and mother *f.* me
94. 14. neither will he *f.* his inher.
Isa. 55. 7. let the wicked *f.* his way
Jer. 17. 13. they that *f.* thee shall
Jonah 2. 8. *f.* their own mercy
Ps. 71. 11. God hath *forsaken* him
22. 1. my God, why *f.* me, Matt. 27. 46.
37. 25. I have not seen the righteous *f.*
Isa. 49. 14. Lord hath *f.* my Lord
54. 7. small moment have I *f.* thee
Jer. 2. 13. *f.* me the fountain of liv.
Matt. 19. 27. we have *f.* all
29. *f.* houses or brethren or
2 Cor. 4. 9. persecuted but not *f.*
Prov. 2. 17. *forsaketh* the guide of
Prov 28. 13. confesseth and *f.* shall find
Heb. 10. 25. not *f.* the assembling
Deut. 32. 15. he *forsook* God which
Ps. 119. 87. I *f.* not thy precepts
2 Tim. 4. 16. all men *f.* me
R. V. Deut. 4. 31. fail; Judg. 9. 11. leave; 6. 13; 2 Kings 21. 14; Jer. 23. 33, 39. cast off; Job 20. 13. will not let it go; Jer. 15. 6. rejected; 18. 14. dried up; Amos 5. 2. cast down; Matt. 19. 27; 26. 56; Mark 14. 50; Luke 5. 11. left; Luke 14. 33. renounceth
FORSAKING God, danger of, Deut. 28. 20. Judg. 10. 13. 2 Chron. 15. 2. & 24. 20. Ezra 8. 22. & 9. 10. Isa. 1. 28. Jer. 1. 16. & 5. 19. & 17. 13. Ezek. 6. 9.
FORTRESS and rock, Lord is my, 2 Sam. 22. 2. Ps. 18. 2. & 31. 3. & 71. 3. & 91. 2. & 144. 2. Jer. 16. 19.
R. V. Jer. 10. 17. siege; 16. 19. stronghold; Mic. 7. 12. Egypt
FORTY DAYS, as the flood, Gen. 7. 17.
giving of the law, Ex. 24. 18.
spying Canaan, Num. 13. 25.
Goliath's defiance, 1 Sam. 17. 16.
Elijah's journey to Horeb, 1 Kings 19. 8.
Jonah's warning to Nineveh, Jonah 3. 4.
fasting of our Lord, Matt. 4. 2. Mark 1. 13. Luke 4. 2.
Christ's appearances during, Acts 1. 3.
FORTY STRIPES, Deut. 25. 3. save one; 2 Cor. 11. 24.
FORTY YEARS, manna sent, Ex. 16. 35. Num. 14. 33. Ps. 95. 10.
of peace, Judg. 3. 11. & 5. 31. & 8. 28.
FOUND, Gen. 26. 19. & 31. 37.
Eccl. 7. 27. this have I *f.* that, 29.
28. one man among a thousand have I *f.*
S. of S. 3. 1. I *f.* him not, 4. I *f.* him
Isa. 55. 6. seek the Lord while he may be *f.*
65. 1. I am *f.* of them that sought
Ezek. 22. 30. I sought a man but *f.*
Dan. 5. 27. weighed and *f.* wanting
Phil. 3. 9. *f.* in him, not having my
2 Pet. 3. 14. may be *f.* of him in
Matt. 7. 25. *founded* on a rock, Ps. 24. 2. Prov. 3. 19. Isa. 14. 32.
Ps. 11. 3. if the *foundations* be destroyed
Job 4. 19. whose *f.* is in the dust
Prov. 10. 25. righteous is an everlasting *f.*
Rom. 15. 20. lest I build upon another man's *f.*
1 Cor. 3. 10. laid *f.*
12. build on this *f.*
Eph. 2. 20. built on *f.* of the proph.
1 Tim. 6. 19. lay up a good *f.* for
2 Tim. 2. 19. the *f.* of God stands
Heb. 11. 10. a city which hath *f.*
Rev. 21. 14. the city hath twelve *f.*
Matt. 13. 35. *foundation of the world*, 25. 34. John 17. 24. Eph. 1. 4. 1 Pet. 1. 20. Rev. 13. 8. & 17. 8. Ps. 104. 5. Prov. 8. 29. Isa. 51. 13, 16.
R. V. Luke 6. 48. because it had been well builded; Isa. 16. 7. raisin cakes; Jer. 50. 15. bulwarks
FOUNTAIN, Gen. 7. 11. Deut. 8. 7.
Deut. 33. 28. *f.* of Jacob on a land
Ps. 36. 9. with thee is *f.* of life
Prov. 5. 18. let thy *f.* be blessed
13. 14. law of wise is a *f.* of life
14. 27. fear of Lord is a *f.* of life
Eccl. 12. 6. pitcher broken at the *f.*
S. of S. 4. 12. *f.* sealed
15. *f.* of gardens
Jer. 2. 13. Lord *f.* of liv. waters, 17. 13.
9. 1. my eyes were a *f.* of tears
Rev. 21. 6. give of *f.* of life freely, 22. 17
R. V. Num. 33. 9; Prov. 5. 16 springs; Jer. 6. 7. well

FOUR living creatures, vision of, Ezek. 1. 5. & 10. 10. Rev. 4. 6. & 5. 14. & 6. 6.
kingdoms, Nebuchadnezzar's vision of, Dan. 2. 36; Daniel's vision of, Dan. 7. 3, 16.
FOURFOLD compensation, Ex. 22. 1. 2 Sam. 12. 6. Luke 19. 8.
FOXES, Judg. 15. 4. Ps. 63. 10. S. of S. 2. 15. Lam. 5. 18. Ezek. 13. 4. Matt. 8. 20. Luke 13. 32.
FRAGMENTS, Matt. 14. 20. Mark 6. 43. & 8. 19, 20. John 6. 12, 13.
FRAIL I am, Ps. 39. 4.
FRAME, Ps. 50. 19. & 94. 20. & 103. 14. Isa. 29. 16. Jer. 18. 11. Eph. 2. 21. Heb. 11. 3.
R. V. Hos. 5. 4. their doings will not suffer them
FRAUD condemned, Lev. 19. 13. Mal. 3. 5. Mark 10. 19. 1 Cor. 6. 8. 1 Thes. 4. 6. *See* DECEIT.
FREE, Ex. 21. 2. Lev. 19. 20.
2 Chron. 29. 31. as many as were of a *f.* heart
Ps. 51. 12. uphold with thy *f.* Spirit
John 8. 32. truth shall make you *f.*
36. if Son make *f.* shall be *f.*
Rom. 5. 15. so also is *f.* gift
6. 7. *f.* from sin, 18.
20. *f.* from righteousness
7. 3. *f.* from law
8. 2. *f.* from the law of sin
1 Cor. 7. 22. the Lord's *f.* man
Gal. 3. 28. neither bond nor *f.*, Col. 3. 11.
5. 1. Christ hath made us *f.* not
1 Pet. 2. 16. as *f.* and not using lib.
Hos. 14. 4. I will love them *freely*
Matt. 10. 8. *f.* ye have received, *f.*
Rom. 3. 24. justified *f.* by his grace
8. 32. with him *f.* give us all
1 Cor. 2. 12. things *f.* given us of
Rev. 21. 6. of fount. of life *f.*, 22. 17.
R. V. Ex. 21. 11. for nothing; 36. 3. free will; 2 Chron. 29. 31; Amos 4. 5. willing; Ps. 88. 5. cast off; Acts 22. 28. am a Roman; Col. 3. 11. freeman; 2 Thes. 3. 1. run; Matt. 15. 6. Mark 7. 11 ——; Rom. 6. 7. justified
FREEWILL offerings, Lev. 22. 18. Num. 15. 3. Deut. 16. 10. Ezra 3. 5.
FREEWOMAN and bondwoman, illustration of, Gal. 4. 22.
FRET, Ps. 37. 1, 7, 8. Prov. 24. 19.
Prov. 19. 3. his heart *f.* against the
Ezek. 16. 43. hast *fretted* me in all
FRIEND, Jer. 6. 21. Hos. 3. 1.
Ex. 33. 11. as a man to his *f.*
Deut. 13. 6. *f.* which is as his own
2 Sam. 16. 17. is this kind. to thy *f.*
Job 6. 14. pity should be showed from his *f.*
Prov. 17. 17. *f.* loveth at all times
18. 24. a *f.* that sticketh closer than a brother
27. 10. own *f.* and father's *f.*
S. of S. 5. 16. my beloved and *f.*
Mic. 7. 5. trust ye not in a *f.* put
John 15. 13. lay down life for his *f.*
15. 14. ye are my *f.* if
15. called you *f.*
Jas. 4. 4. *f.* of the world is enemy of God, *friendship* of the world is enmity with God
Prov. 22. 24. make no *f.* with an
18. 24. hath *f.* must show himself *friendly*
R. V. 2 Sam. 19. 6. them that love thee; Prov. 6. 1; 17. 18. neighbor; Judg. 19. 3; Ruth 2. 13. kindly; Prov. 18. 24. doeth it to his own destruction
FROWARD, Job 5. 13. 1 Pet. 2. 18.
Deut. 32. 20. a very *f.* generation
Ps. 18. 26. will show thyself *f.*
Prov. 4. 24. *f.* mouth, 6. 12. & 8. 13. 10. 31. *f.* tongue, 11. 20. *f.* heart, 17. 20.
3. 32. the *f.* is abomination to the
Isa. 57. 17. went on *frowardly*
Prov. 6. 14. *frowardness* is in him
R. V. 2 Sam. 22. 27; Ps. 18. 26; Prov. 3. 32; 11. 20. perverse; 21. 8. him that is laden with guilt is exceeding crooked
FRUIT, Gen. 4. 3. Lev. 19. 24.
2 Kings 19. 30. bear *f.* upward, Isa. 37. 31.
Ps. 92. 14. shall bring forth *f.* in old
127. 3. *f.* of womb is his reward
Prov. 11. 30. *f.* of righteous is
S. of S. 2. 3. his *f.* was sweet
4. 13. with pleasant *f.*
6. 11. to see the *f.* of the valley
Isa. 3. 10. eat the *f.* of their doings
27. 9. all the *f.* to take away sin
57. 19. create *f.* of the lips, peace
Hos. 10. 1. empty vine brings *f.*
Mic. 6. 7. *f.* of my body for sin of
Matt. 7. 17. good tree brings forth good *f.*, 21. 19.
12. 33. *f.* good; tree known by his *f.*
26. 29. not drink of *f.* of vine till
Luke 1. 42. blessed is the *f.* of thy womb
John 4. 36. gathers *f.* to eternal life
15. 2. branch beareth not *f.* he tak.
Rom. 6. 21. what *f.* had
22. *f.* to holiness
Gal. 5. 22. *f.* of Spirit is love, joy
Eph. 5. 9. *f.* of Spirit is in all good.
Phil. 4. 17. desire *f.* that may abound
Heb. 12. 11. peaceable *f.* of righteousness
Jas. 3. 18. *f.* of righteousness is
Rev. 22. 2. yielded *f.* every month
Matt. 3. 8. bring forth *fruits* meet
7. 16. shall know them by their *f.*
2 Cor. 9. 10. increase the *f.* of right.
Phil. 1. 11. filled with the *f.* of righteousness
Jas. 3. 17. full of good *f.* without
R. V. Ex. 23. 10; Deut. 22. 9. increase; Lev. 25. 15. crops; Isa. 28. 4; S. of S. 6. 11. green plant; Mic. 7. 1. fig; Amos 7. 14. trees; Luke 12. 18. corn; Jude 12. autumn trees
FRUIT TREES saved in time of war, Deut. 20. 19.
FRUSTRATE, Isa. 44. 25. Gal. 2. 21.
R. V. Gal. 2. 21. make void
FUGITIVE servant, law of, Deut. 23. 15.
FULL, Gen. 15. 16. Ex. 16. 3, 8.
Deut. 34. 9. Joshua *f.* of the spirit
Ruth 1. 21. I went out *f.* and
1 Sam. 2. 5. that were *f.* have hired
Job 5. 26. come to grave in *f.* age
14. 1. of few days and *f.* of trouble
Ps. 17. 14. they are *f.* of children
Prov. 27. 7. *f.* soul loath the honey.
Luke 4. 1. Jesus being *f.* of the Holy Ghost
John 1. 14. of God *f.* of grace and
1 Cor. 4. 8. now ye are *f.* now ye
Col. 2. 2. riches of *f.* assurance
2 Tim. 4. 5. *f.* proof of thy ministry
10. 22. draw near in *f.* assurance
Gen. 29. 27. *fulfil*, Ex. 23. 26.
Matt. 3. 15. it becometh us to *f.* all righteousness
5. 17. not to destroy the law, but *f.*
Acts 13. 22. who shall *f.* all my will
Luke 21. 24. till times of Gentiles be *f.*
Gal. 5. 14. law is *f.* in one word
16. shall not *f.* lust of the flesh
6. 2. bear burden and so *f.* law
Eph. 2. 3. *f.* the desires of flesh and
Phil. 2. 2. *f.* ye my joy, that ye be
Col. 4. 17. ministry, in the Lord, that thou *f.* it
2 Thes. 1. 11. *f.* all the good pleas.
Jas. 2. 8. if ye *f.* the royal law
Rev. 17. 17. put in their hearts to *f.*
Job 20. 22. in *fulness* of sufficiency
Ps. 16. 11. in thy presence is *f.* of
John 1. 16. of his *f.* have we receiv.
Rom. 11. 25. till *f.* of the Gent.
15. 29. *f.* of blessing of the Gospel
Gal. 4. 4. when *f.* of time was come
3. 19. ye may be filled with the *f.* of God
Col. 1. 19. in him should all *f.* dwell
2. 9. in him dwells all the *f.* of
R. V. Lev. 2. 14; 2 Kings 4. 42. fresh; 1 Cor. 10. 28 ——
FURNACE, Deut. 4. 20. Jer. 11. 4. Ps. 12. 6. Isa. 31. 9. & 48. 10. Dan. 3. 6, 11. Matt. 13. 42, 50. Rev. 1. 15.
FURNISHED, Deut. 15. 14. Prov. 9. 2.
2 Tim. 3. 17. thoroughly *f.* to all
R. V. Ps. 78. 19. prepare; Isa. 65. 11. fill up; Matt. 22. 10. filled
FURY is not in me, Isa. 27. 4.
59. 18. repay *f.* to his adversaries
Jer. 6. 11. I am full of *f.* of the
10. 25. pour out thy *f.* on heathen
Prov. 22. 24. with *furious* man not
R. V. Job 20. 23. fierceness

G

GABRIEL, Dan. 8. 16. & 9. 21. Luke 1. 19, 26.
GAIN, Prov. 3. 14. Job 22. 3.
Isa. 33. 15. despiseth the *g.* of oppre.
Phil. 1. 21. to live is Christ, to die is *g.*
3. 7. what were *g.* to me I counted
1 Tim. 6. 5. supposing *g.* is godliness
Matt. 16. 26. if he should *g.* whole
1 Cor. 9. 19. servant to all, that I might *g.*
18. 15. thou hast *gained* thy bro.
Luke 19. 16. thy pound hath *g.* ten
Tit. 1. 9. convince *gainsayers*
Acts 10. 29. *gainsaying*, Rom. 10. 21. *g.* people
Jude 11. perished in the *g.* of Core
R. V. Prov. 28. 8; Dan. 11. 39. price; Acts 19. 24. little business; 2 Cor. 12. 17, 18. take advantage; Luke 19. 16, 18. made; Acts 27. 21. gotten . . . injury
GALL, Job 16. 13. & 20. 14, 25.
Deut. 29. 18. the root bears *g.*
32. 32. their grapes are grapes of *g.*
Ps. 69. 21. gave me *g.* for drink, Matt. 27. 34.
Jer. 8. 14. given us water of *g.*, 9. 15.
Lam. 3. 19. remembering the wormwood and *g.*, 5.
Acts 8. 23. thou art in the *g.* of bit.
GAP, to stand in, Ezek. 22. 30.
GARDEN, Gen. 2. 15. & 3. 23. & 13. 10.
S. of S. 4. 12. a *g.* enclosed is my sister
16. blow on my *g.*, 5. 1. & 6. 2, 11.
Jer. 31. 12. soul as a watered *g.*, Isa. 58. 11.
GARMENT, Josh. 7. 21. Ezra 9. 3.
Job 37. 17. how thy *garments* are warm
Ps. 22. 18. parted my *g.* among
Isa. 9. 5. battle with *g.* rolled in
61. 3. *g.* of praise for the spirit
Joel 2. 13. rend your hearts and not *g.*
Matt. 21. 8. spread their *g.* in way
Acts 9. 39. showing *g.* Dorcas made
Jas. 5. 2. your *g.* are moth-eaten
Rev. 3. 4. have not defiled their *g.*
16. 15. watcheth and keepeth his *g.*
R. V. Deut. 22. 11. mingled stuff; Judg. 14. 12, 13, 19; 1 Kings 10. 25; 2 Kings 5. 22, 23; Ps. 109. 19; Dan. 11. 9. raiment; Josh. 7. 21; Zech. 13. 4. mantle; Esth. 8. 15; Mark 16. 5. robe; 1 Sam. 18. 4; 2 Sam. 20. 8; Luke 24. 4. apparel; Mark 13. 16; Luke 22. 36. cloak; Ps. 69. 11. clothing; 104. 6. vesture; Matt. 27. 31 ——
GATE, Gen. 19. 1. & 34. 20, 24.
Gen. 22. 17. possess *g.* of his ene.
28. 17. this is the house of God, and the *g.* of heaven
Job 29. 7. I went to *g.* prepared
Ps. 118. 20. this *g.* of the Lord into

Matt. 7. 13. enter strait *g.*, Luke 13. 2.
Heb. 13. 12. suffered without the *g.*
Ps. 9. 13. up from *gates* of death
24. 7. lift up your heads, O *g.*, 9.
87. 2. Lord loveth *g.* of Zion
100. 4. enter his *g.* with thanks,
118. 19. open for me *g.* of right.
Isa. 38. 10. to go to *g.* of the grave
Matt. 16. 18. *g.* of hell shall not prevail
R. V. Esth. 5. 1. entrance, Ezek. 40. 6 —— ; Neh. 13. 19; Isa. 45. 1, 2; S. of S. 7. 13; Luke 13. 24; Acts 4. 2. door, doors
GATHER thee from all nations, Deut. 30. 3. Neh. 1. 9. Jer. 29. 14.
Ps. 26. 9. *g.* not my soul with sinners
Zeph. 3. 18. *g.* them that are sor.
Matt. 3. 12. *g.* his wheat into gar.
7. 16. do men *g.* grapes of thorns
Eph. 1. 10. to *g.* in one all things
Ex. 16. 18, 21. he that *gathered* much
Matt. 23. 37. *g.* thy children as hen *g.*
John 4. 36. *g.* fruit unto eternal
R. V. Gen. 49. 2; Ex. 35. 1, Lev. 8. 3; Num. 8. 9; 16. 3; 19. 42; 20. 2, 8; Deut. 4. 10; 31. 12, 18; Judg. 9. 6; 20. 1; 1 Chron. 13. 5, Ezek. 38. 13; Mic. 4. 11. assembled; Ex. 9. 19. hasten in; Job 11. 10. call unto judgment; Isa. 62. 9. garnered; Jer. 6. 1. flee for safety; 51. 11. hold firm; Joel 2. 6, Nah. 2. 10. waxed pale; Eph. 1. 10. sum up
GAVE, Gen. 14. 20. Ex. 11. 3.
Job 1. 21. Lord *g.* and Lord taketh
Ps. 81. 12. I *g.* them up unto
Eccl. 12. 7. spirit return to God that *g.* it
Isa. 42. 24. who *g.* Jacob for a spoil
John 1. 12. he *g.* power to become
3. 16. God *g.* his only begotten Son
1 Cor. 3. 6. God *g.* the increase, 7
2 Cor. 8. 5. first *g.* themselves to
Gal. 1. 4. who *g.* himself for our
2. 20. *g.* himself for me, Tit. 2. 14.
Eph. 4. 8. *g.* gifts unto men
11. *g.* some apostles
1 Tim. 2. 6. *g.* himself a ransom
Ps. 21. 4. asked life, thou *gavest* it
John 17. 4. work thou *g*
22. glory thou *g.* me
6. the men thou *g.* me, 12. & 18. 9.
which thou *g.* me, lost none
GENEALOGIES, 1 Tim. 1. 4. Tit. 3. 9.
GENERATION, Gen. 2. 4. & 6. 9.
Deut. 32. 5. they are a perverse and crooked *g.*
20. a very froward *g.* in whom
Ps. 14. 5. God is in the *g.* of the righteous
22. 30. accounted to Lord for a *g.*
24. 6. this is *g.* of them that seek
112. 2. *g.* of upright shall be
145. 4. one *g.* shall praise thy
Isa. 53. 8. who declare his *g.*, Acts 8. 33.
Matt. 3. 7. ye *g.* of vipers, 12. 34. & 23. 33.
Luke 16. 8. *g.* wiser than the child
Acts 13. 36. had served his *g* according
1 Pet. 2. 9. chosen *g.* to show praises
Ps. 33. 11. thoughts to all *generations*
45. 17. to be remembered in all *g.*
79. 13. show forth thy praise in all *g.*
89. 4. build thy throne to all *g.*
90. 1. our dwelling place in all *g.*
100. 5. his truth endureth to all *g.*
119. 90. thy faithfulness to all *g.*
Col. 1. 26. the mystery hid from ages and *g.*
R. V. Matt. 3. 7; 23. 33; 12. 34, Luke 3. 7. ye offspring; 1 Pet. 2. 9. an elect race
GENTILES, Gen. 10. 5. Jer. 4. 7.
Isa. 11. 10. to it shall the *g.* seek
Isa. 42. 6. a light of the *g.*, 49. 6. Luke 2. 32. Acts 13. 47.
60. 3. *g.* shall come to thy light
62. 2. *g.* shall see thy righteous.
Matt. 6. 32. after these things do the *g.* seek
John 7. 35. to the dispersed among the *g.*
Acts 13. 46. lo, we turn to the *g*
14. 27. opened door of faith unto *g.*
Rom. 2. 14. *g.* which have not law
3. 29. is he not also God of *g.* yea
15. 10. rejoice ye *g.* with his people
12. in his name shall the *g.* trust
Eph. 3. 6. *g.* be fellow heirs and
8. preach among *g.* unsearchable
1 Tim. 2. 7. a teacher of *g.*, 2 Tim. 1. 11.
3. 16. God manifest in flesh, preached to *g.*
GENTLE among you, 1 Thes. 2. 7.
Tit. 3. 2. be *g.* showing all meek.
Jas. 3. 17. wisdom from above is *g.*
1 Pet. 2. 18. not only to the *g.* but
Ps. 18. 35. thy *gentleness* made me
2 Cor. 10. 1. beseech by the *g.* of
Gal. 5. 22. fruit of the Spirit is love, joy, *g.*
Isa. 40. 11. *gently* lead those with
R. V. Gal. 5. 22. kindness
GIFT, 1 Cor. 1. 7. & 7. 7.
Ex. 23. 8. take no *g.* for a *g.* blindeth
Prov. 17. 8. *g* is a preci. stone, 23.
18. 16. a man's *g.* maketh room for
21. 14. a *g* in secret pacifieth anger
Eccl. 7. 7. a *g.* destroyeth the heart
Matt. 5. 24. leave there thy *g.* and
John 4. 10. if thou knewest *g.* of
Rom. 6. 23. *g.* of God is eternal
Eph. 2. 8. through faith it is the *g.* of
Phil. 4. 17. not because I desire a *g.*
1 Tim. 4. 14. neglect not the *g.* that
2 Tim. 1. 6. stir up *g.* of God
Heb. 6. 4. tasted of heavenly *g.*
Jas. 1. 17 every good and perfect *g.*
Ps. 68. 18. received *gifts* for men
Matt. 7. 11. give good *g.* to your children
Rom. 11. 29. for *g* and calling of God
Eph. 4. 8. led captivity and gave *g.*
R. V. 2 Sam. 8. 2, 6 1 Chron. 18. 2, 6. presents; Ezek. 22. 12. bribes; Luke 21. 5. offerings, 2 Cor. 8. 4. this grace
GIRD with strength, Ps. 18. 32.
Ps. 30. 11. *g.* me with gladness
Luke 12. 35. let your loins be *girded*, 1 Pet. 1. 13.
Eph. 6. 14. having your loins *g.* with
Isa. 11. 5. *girdle*, Matt. 3. 4. Rev. 1. 13. & 15. 6.
R. V. Job 12. 18. bindeth, Ex. 28. 8, 27, 28; 29 5; 39 5. 20, 21; Lev. 8. 7. band
GIRL, they have sold a *g.* for wine, Joel 3. 3.
Zech. 8. 5. streets full of *g*
GIVE, Gen. 12. 7. & 30. 31.
1 Kings 3. 5. ask what I shall *g.*
Ps. 2. 8. I shall *g.* thee the heathen
29. 11. Lord will *g.* strength to his
37. 4. *g.* the desires of thy heart
109. 4. I *g.* myself to prayer
104. 27. mayest *g.* them their meat
Jer. 17. 10. to *g.* every man accord.
Hos. 11. 8. how shall I *g.* thee up
Luke 6. 38. *g.* and it shall be given
John 10. 28. I *g.* to them eternal
Acts 3. 6. such as I have *g.* I unto
20. 35. more blessed to *g* than to receive
Eph. 4. 28. that he may have to *g.*
1 Tim. 4. 15. *g.* thyself wholly to
2 Sam. 22. 50. *give thanks*, 1 Chron. 16. 8, 34, 35, 41. Neh. 12. 24. Ps. 35. 18. & 79. 13. & 92. 1 & 105. 1. & 107. 1. & 118. 1. & 136. 1
Ps. 6. 5. in grave who shall—to thee
Ps. 30. 4. —at the remembrance of
119. 62. at midnight I will rise to—
Eph. 1. 16. cease not to—, 1 Thes. 1. 2. 2 Thes. 2. 13. Col. 1. 3.
1 Thes. 5. 18. in every thing —, Phil. 4. 6.
Matt. 13. 12. to him shall be *given*
11. it is *g.* to you to know the mys.
Luke 12. 48. to whom much is *g.*
John 6. 39. of all which he hath *g.*
65. can come to me except it be *g.*
19. 11. except it were *g.* thee from
Rom. 11. 35. hath first *g.* to him
2 Cor. 9. 7 God loves the cheerful *giver*
Ps. 37. 21. shows mercy and *giveth*
Prov. 28. 27. he that *g.* to poor shall
Isa. 40. 29. *g.* power to the faint
42. 5. *g.* breath to people on earth
1 Tim. 6. 17. *g.* us richly all things
Jas. 1. 5. *g.* to all men liberally
1 Pet. 4. 11. of the ability that God *g.*
GLAD, my heart is, Ps. 16. 9.
Ps. 31. 7. I will be *g.* and rejoice in
64. 10. righteous shall be *g.* in Lord
104. 34. I will be *g.* in the Lord
122. 1. I was *g.* when they said
Luke 1. 19. *glad tidings*, & 8. 1.
Mark 6. 20. heard him *gladly*, 12. 37.
Luke 8. 40. people *g.* received him
Acts 2. 41. that *g.* received his word
2 Cor. 12. 15. I will very *g.* spend
Ps. 4. 7. put *gladness* in my heart
30. 11. hast girded me with *g.*
51. 8. make me to hear joy and *g.*
97. 11. *g.* sown for the upright
100. 2. serve the Lord with *g.*
Isa. 35. 10. shall obtain joy and *g.*
51. 3. joy and *g.* shall be found
Acts 2. 46. eat their meat with *g.*
R. V. Ps. 48. 11; 104. 34; Acts 2. 26; 1 Cor. 16. 17; 2 Cor. 13. 9; 1 Pet. 4. 13; Rev. 19. 7. rejoice; Luke 1. 19; 8. 1; Acts 13. 32. good; Luke 8. 40; Acts 2. 41 —— ; Ps. 105. 43. singing; 2 Sam. 6. 12; Mark 4. 16; Acts 12. 14; Phil. 2. 29. joy
GLASS, we see through, 1 Cor. 13. 12.
2 Cor. 3. 18. beholding as in a *g.*
Rev. 4. 6. a sea of *g.*, 15. 2.
21. 18. the city was pure gold like clear *g.*
R. V. Job 37. 18. mirror; Isa. 3. 23. hand mirrors; Jas. 1. 23. mirror; Rev. 4. 6; 15. 2. glassy sea.
GLOOMINESS, Joel 2. 2. Zeph. 1. 15.
GLORY, Gen. 31. 1. Ps. 49. 16.
1 Sam. 4. 21. *g.* is departed from
1 Chron. 29. 11. thine the power and the *g.*, Matt. 6. 13.
Ps. 8. 5. crowned with *g.* and honor.
73. 24. afterward receive me to *g.*
145. 11. speak of the *g.* of thy king.
Prov. 3. 35. the wise shall inherit *g.*
16. 31. hoary head is a crown of *g.*
20. 29. *g.* of young men is their str.
25. 27. to search their own *g.* is not *g.*
Isa. 4. 5. upon all the *g.* shall be
24. 16. heard songs, even *g.* to the
28. 5. Lord shall be for a crown of *g.*
Jer. 2. 11. chang. their *g.*, Ps. 106. 20.
Ezek. 20. 6. the *g.* of all lands, 15.
Hos. 4. 7. change their *g.* into shame
Hag. 2. 7. I will fill this hou. with *g.*
9. *g.* of this latter house shall be
Zech. 2. 5. be the *g.* in the midst
Matt. 6. 2. may have *g.* of men
16. 27. come in *g.* of his Father
Luke 2. 14. *g.* to God in the highest
32. light of the Gentiles, *g.* of thy
John 1. 14. his *g.* the *g.* of the only
17. 5. *glorify* me with the *g.* I had
22. *g.* which thou gavest I have
Rom. 2. 7. seek for *g.* and honor
11. 36. to whom be *g.* for ever, 2 Tim. 4. 18. Heb. 13. 21.
16. 27. in God be *g.* through Christ
1 Cor. 11. 7. man is *g.* of God, woman is *g.* of man
15. 43. in dishonor, it is raised in *g.*
2 Cor. 3. 18. changed from *g.* to *g.*

2 Cor. 4. 17. an exceeding and eternal weight of *g.*
Eph. 1. 6. praise of *g.* of his grace
3. 21. to him be *g.* in the church
Phil. 3. 19. whose *g.* is in their shame
Col. 1. 27. Christ in you hope of *g.*
3. 4. appear with him in *g.*
1 Thes. 2. 12. hath called you to *g.*
1 Tim. 3. 16. received up into *g.*
1 Pet. 1. 8. joy unspeak., full of *g.*
4. 13. his *g.* be revealed
14. spirit of *g.*
5. 1. partaker of *g.* to be revealed
4. ye shall receive a crown of *g.*
10. called us to eternal *g.*
2 Pet. 1. 3. called us to *g.* and virtue
17. came a voice from the excellent *g.*
Rev. 4. 11. worthy to receive *g.*, 5. 12. Rom. 16. 27. 1 Tim. 1. 17. 1 Pet. 5. 11. Jude 25.
Josh. 7. 19. *give glory* to the God of Israel, 1 Sam. 6. 5. 1 Chron. 16. 29. Ps. 29. 2. & 96. 8. & 115. 1. Luke 17. 18. Rev. 14. 7.
Ps. 19. 1. *glory of God*, Prov. 25. 2. Acts 7. 55. Rom. 3. 23. & 5. 2. 1 Cor. 10. 31. & 11. 7. 2 Cor. 4. 6. Rev. 21. 11.
Ex. 16. 7. *glory of the Lord*, Num. 14. 21.
1 Kings 8. 11. Ps. 104. 31. & 138. 5. Isa. 35. 2. & 40. 5. & 60. 1. Ezek. 1. 28. & 3. 12, 23. & 43. 5. & 44. 4. Luke 2. 9. 2 Cor. 3. 18.
Ps. 29. 9. *his glory*, 49. 17. & 72. 19. & 113. 4. & 148. 13. Prov. 19. 11. Isa. 6. 3. Hab. 3. 3. Matt. 6. 29. & 19. 28. & 25. 31. John 2. 11. Rom. 9. 23. Eph. 1. 12. & 3. 16. Heb. 1. 3.
Job. 29. 20. *my glory*, Ps. 16. 9. & 30. 12. & 57. 8. & 108. 1. Isa. 42. 8. & 43. 7. & 48. 11. & 60. 7. & 66. 18. John 8. 50. & 17. 24.
Ex. 33. 18. *thy glory*, Ps. 8. 1. & 63. 2. Isa. 60. 19. & 63. 15. Jer. 14. 21.
1 Chron. 16. 10. *glory* ye in his holy
Ps. 64. 10. upright in heart shall *g.*
106. 5. I may *g.* with thy inherit.
Isa. 41. 16. shalt *g.* in Holy One of
45. 25. seed of Israel be justified, and *g.*
Jer. 9. 24. him that glorieth *g.* in this
Rom. 4. 2. hath *g.* but not bef. God
5. 3. we *g.* in tribulation
1 Cor. 1. 31. that glorieth *g.* in the
3. 21. let no man *g.* in men
2 Cor. 5. 12. to *g.* on our behalf—
11. 18. many *g.* after the flesh
12. 1. it is not exped. for me to *g.*
Gal. 6. 14. God forbid I should *g.*
Isa. 25. 5. strong people shall *glorify* thee
Matt. 5. 16. *g.* your Father in heav.
John 12. 23. Father *g.* thy name
17. 1. *g.* thy Son
21. 19. by what death he should *g.* God
1 Cor. 6. 20. *g.* God in your body
1 Pet. 2. 12. *g.* God in day of visita.
Rev. 15. 4. who shall not fear thee, and *g.* thy name
Lev. 10. 3. before all I will be *glorified*
Matt. 9. 8. they *g.* God, 15. 31.
John 7. 39. Jesus was not yet *g.*
15. 8. herein is my Father *g.*
Acts 3. 13. God of our fathers hath *g.* his
4. 21. all men *g.* God for that was
Rom. 1. 21. they *g.* him not as God
8. 30. whom he justified, them he *g.*
Gal. 1. 24. they *g.* God in me
2 Thes. 1. 10. shall come to be *g.* in
Heb. 5. 5. even Christ *g.* not him.
1 Pet. 4. 11. God in all things may be *g.*
14. on your part he is *g.*
1 Cor. 5. 6. *glorying*, 9. 15. 2 Cor. 7. 4. & 12. 11.
Ex. 15. 6. *glorious* in power
11. who is like thee, *g.* in holiness
Deut. 28. 58. fear this *g.* and fearful
1 Chron. 29. 13. praise thy *g.* name
Ps. 45. 13. king's daughter all *g.*
66. 2. make his praise *g.*
72. 19. blessed be his *g.* name
87. 3. *g.* things are spoken of
111. 3. his work is honorable and *g.*
145. 5. speak of *g.* honor of thy
12. make known his *g.* majesty
Isa. 4. 2. branch of Lord shall be *g.*
22. 23. be for a *g.* throne to his
30. 30. cause his *g.* voice to be heard
33. 21. *g.* Lord will be to us a place
49. 5. yet shall I be *g.* in eyes
60. 13. make the place of my feet *g.*
63. 1. who is this *g.* in his apparel
Jer. 17. 12. a *g.* high throne from
Rom. 8. 21. *g.* liberty of children
2 Cor. 3. 7. ministration was *g.*
4. 4. light of *g.* gospel should
Col. 1. 11. according to his *g.* power
Tit. 2. 13. looking for *g.* appearance
Ex. 15. 1. *gloriously*, Isa. 24. 23.
R. V. 1 Pet. 4. 14 ——; Ps. 111. 3. majesty; Isa. 49. 5. honorable; 1 Chron. 16. 27; Job 40. 10. honor; 1 Chron. 16. 35. triumph; Ps. 89. 44. brightness; Prov. 4. 9; Isa. 62. 3. beauty; Matt. 6. 13——; 2 Cor. 12. 11 —

GLUTTON, Deut. 21. 20. Prov. 23. 21.
Matt. 11. 19. *gluttonous*, Luke 7. 34.
R. V. Deut. 21. 20. riotous liver

GNASH, Job 16. 9. Ps. 35. 16. & 37. 12. & 112. 10. Lam. 2. 16. Mark 9. 18.
Matt. 8. 12. *gnashing of teeth*, 13. 42, 50. & 22. 13. & 24. 51. & 25. 30. Luke 13. 28.
R. V. Mark 9. 18. grindeth

GNAT, and swallow a camel, Matt. 23. 24.

GNAW, Zeph. 3. 3. Rev. 16. 10.
R. V. Zeph. 3. 3. leave nothing

GO, Judg. 6. 14. 1 Sam. 12. 21. Matt. 8. 9. Luke 10. 37. John 6. 68.
Job 10. 21. *I go*, Ps. 39. 13. & 139. 7. Matt. 21. 30. John 7. 33. & 8. 14, 21, 22. & 13. 33. & 16. 5.
Ex. 4. 23. *let my people go*, 5. 1.
Gen. 32. 26. *not let go*, Ex. 3. 19. Job 27. 6. S. of S. 3. 4.
Ex. 23. 23. *shall go*, 32. 34. & 33. 14. Acts 25. 12.
1 Sam. 12. 21. *should go*, Prov. 22. 6.
Judg. 11. 35. *go back*, Ps. 80. 18.
Num. 22. 18. *go beyond*, 1 Thes. 4. 6.
Gen. 45. 1. *go out*, Ps. 60. 10. Isa. 52. 11. & 55. 12. Jer. 51. 45. Ezek. 46. 9. Matt. 25. 6. John 10. 9. 1 Cor. 5. 10.
Deut. 4. 40. *go well* with thee, 5. 16. & 19. 13. Prov. 11. 10. & 30. 29.
Job 34. 21. seeth all his *goings*
Ps. 17. 5. hold up my *g.* in thy way
40. 2. set my feet and established my *g.*
68. 24. seen thy *g.* O God in
121. 8. Lord preserve thy *g.* out
Prov. 5. 21. he pondereth all his *g.*
Mic. 5. 2. whose *g.* are of old, from
The R. V. changes are frequent, but chiefly those relating to words before and after *go*

GOAT, Lev. 3. 12. & 16. 8, 21, 22.
Isa. 1. 11. I delight not in the blood of *goats*
Ezek. 34. 17. judge between rams and *g.*
Dan. 8. 5. he *g.*
8. rough *g.*, 21.
Matt. 25. 32, 33. set the *g.* on his
Heb. 9. 12. blood of *g.*, 13. 19. & 10. 4.

GOD, and *gods* for *men* representing God, Ex. 4. 16. & 7. 1. & 22. 28. Ps. 82. 1, 6. John 10. 34. for *idols* which are put in God's place, Deut. 32. 21. Judg. 6. 31. and 140 other places. for devil, god of this world, 2 Cor. 4. 4. and for the true God about 3120 times
Gen. 17. 1. I am Almighty *G.*, Job 36. 5. Isa. 9. 6. & 10. 21. Jer. 32. 18.
Gen. 17. 7. to be a *G.* to thee and thy seed, Ex. 6. 7, 21, 33. everlasting *G.* Ps. 90. 2. Isa. 40. 28. Rom. 16. 26.
Ex. 8. 10. none like Lord our *G.*, 1 Kings 8. 23. Ps. 35. 10. & 86. 8. & 89. 6.
18. 11. Lord is greater than all *gods*
Deut. 10. 17. *G.* of gods, Josh. 22. 22. Dan. 2. 47. Ps. 136 2.
Deut. 32. 39. there is no *g.* with me, 1 Kings 8. 23. 2 Kings 5. 15. 2 Chron. 6. 14. & 32. 15. Isa. 43. 10. & 44. 6, 8. & 45. 5, 14, 21, 22.
Job 33. 12. *G.* is greater than man, 36. 26.
Ps. 18. 31. who is *G.* save the Lord, 86. 10.
Mic. 7. 18. who is a *G.* like to thee
Matt. 6. 24. ye cannot serve *G.* and
19. 17. none good but one, that is *G.*
Mark 12. 27. not the *G.* of dead, but of the living
32. there is one *G.* and none other
John 17. 3. the only true *G.*, 1 John 5. 20.
Acts 7. 2. *G.* of glory appeared to
Rom. 8. 31. if *G.* be for us, who can
9. 5. over all *G.* blessed for ever
15. 5. *G.* of patience
13. *G.* of hope
2 Cor. 1. 3. *G.* of all comfort
1 Tim. 3. 16. *G.* manifest in flesh
1 Pet. 5. 10. *G.* of all grace, when
1 John 4. 12. no man seen *G.*, John 1. 18.
Deut. 10. 17. *great God*, 2 Sam. 7. 22. 2 Chron. 2. 5. Job 36. 26. Neh. 1. 5. Prov. 26. 10. Jer. 32. 18, 19. Dan. 9. 4. Tit. 2. 13. Rev. 19. 17.
Deut. 5. 26. *living God*, Josh. 3. 10. 1 Sam. 17. 26, 36. 2 Kings 19. 4, 16. and twenty-two other places
Ex. 34. 6. *God merciful*, Deut. 4. 31. 2 Chron. 30. 9. Neh. 9. 31. Ps. 116. 5. Jonah 4. 2.
Gen. 49. 24. *mighty God*, Deut. 7. 21. & 10. 17. Neh. 9. 32. Job 36. 5. Ps. 50. 1. & 132. 2, 5. Isa. 9. 6. & 10. 21. Jer. 32. 18. Hab. 1. 12.
2 Chron. 15. 3. *true God*, Jer. 10. 10. John 17. 3. 1 Thes. 1. 9. 1 John 5. 20.
Gen. 39. 9. do this wickedness and sin *against God*, Num. 21. 5. Ps. 78. 19. Hos. 13. 16. Acts 5. 39. & 23. 9. Rom. 8. 7. & 9. 20. Rev. 13. 6. Dan. 11. 36.
Ps. 42. 2. *before God*, 56. 13. & 61. 7. & 68. 3. Eccl. 2. 26. Luke 1. 6. Rom. 2. 13. & 3. 19. 1 Tim. 5. 21. Jas. 1. 27. Rev. 3. 2.
John 9. 16. *of God*, Acts 5. 39. Rom. 9. 16. 1 Cor. 1. 30. & 11. 12. 2 Cor. 3. 5. & 5. 18. Phil. 1. 28. 1 John 3. 10. & 4. 1, 3, 6. & 5. 19. 3 John 11.
Ex. 2. 23. *to God*, Ps. 43. 4. Eccl. 12. 7. Isa. 58. 2. Lam. 3. 41. John 13. 3. Heb. 7. 25. & 11. 6. & 12. 23. 1 Pet. 3. 18. & 4. 6. Rev. 5. 9. & 12. 5.
Gen. 5. 22. *with God*, 24. & 6. 9. & 32. 28. Ex. 19. 17. 1 Sam. 14. 45. 2 Sam. 23. 5. Job 9. 2. & 25. 4. Ps. 78. 8. Hos. 11. 12. John 5. 18. Phil. 2. 6.
Gen. 28. 21. *my God*, Ex. 15. 2. Ps. 22. 1. & 31. 14. & 91. 2. & 118. 28. Hos. 2. 23. Zech. 13. 9. John 20. 17. 28. and about 120 other places
Ex. 5. 8. *our God*, Deut. 31. 17. & 32. 3. Josh. 24. 18. 2 Sam. 22. 32. Ps. 67. 6. and 180 other places
Ex. 20. 2. *thy God*, 5, 7, 10, 12. Ps. 50. 7. & 81. 10. and about 340 other places
Ex. 6. 7. *your God*, Lev. 11. 44. & 19. 2, 3, 4. and 140 other places
Ex. 32. 11. *his God*, Lev. 4. 22. and about sixty other places
Gen. 17. 8. *their God*, Ex. 29. 45. Jer. 24. 7. & 31. 33. & 32. 38. Ezek. 11. 20. & 34. 24. & 37. 27. Zech. 8. 8. 2 Cor. 6. 16. Rev. 21. 3. and fifty other places

2 Chron. 36. 23. *God of heaven*, Ezra 5. 11. & 6. 10. & 7. 12, 23. Neh. 1. 4. & 2. 4. Ps. 136. 26. Dan. 2. 18, 19, 44. Jonah 1. 9. Rev. 11. 13. & 16. 11.
Ex. 24. 10. *God of Israel*, Num. 16. 9. Josh. 7. 19. & 13. 33. & 22. 16, 24. & 24. 23. Judg. 11. 23. Ruth 2. 12. Isa. 41. 17. Jer. 31. 1. Ezek. 8. 4. Matt. 15. 31.
Rom. 15. 33. *God of peace*, 16. 20. 2 Cor. 13. 11. 1 Thes. 5. 23. Heb. 13. 20.
Ps. 24. 5. *God of his salvation, of our salvation*, 65. 5. & 68. 19, 20. & 79. 9. & 85. 4. & 95. 1.
Acts 17. 29. *Godhead*, Rom. 1. 20. Col. 2. 9.
R. V. Rom. 1. 20. divinity

GODLY, Ps. 4. 3. & 12. 1. & 32. 6. Mal. 2. 15. 2 Pet. 2. 9. 3 John 6.
2 Cor. 1. 12. in *g.* sincerity, had our conversation
Tit. 2. 12. live soberly, righteously, and *g.*
1 Tim. 2. 2. quiet life in all *godliness*, 10. & 3. 16. & 6. 3, 5, 11. 2 Tim. 3. 5.
4. 8. *g.* is profitable to all things
6. 3. doctrine according to *g.*, Tit. 1. 1.
2 Tim. 3. 5. having a form of *g.* but
2 Pet. 1. 3. all that pertain to life and *g.*
6. add to patience *g.*
7. to *g.* brotherly kindness
R. V. 2 Cor. 1. 12. sincerity; 1 Tim. 1. 4. dispensation of God; Heb. 12. 28. awe; 3 John 6. worthily of God

GOLD, Gen. 2. 11. & 13. 2. Isa. 2. 7.
Job 23. 10. I shall come forth like *g.*
31. 24. if I made *g.* my hope or fine *g.*
Ps. 19. 10. more desired than *g.*
119. 127. love thy commandments above *g.* yea, fine *g.*, 72.
Prov. 8. 19. my fruit is better than *g.* or fine *g.*
Isa. 13. 12. man more precious than fine *g.*
Zech. 13. 9. I will try them as *g.* is
1 Tim. 2. 9. women adorn themselves in modest apparel, not with *g.*, 1 Pet. 3. 3.
1 Pet. 1. 7. trial of faith more precious than *g.*
Rev. 3. 18. buy of me *g.* tried in fire

GOLDEN CANDLESTICK, Ex. 25. 31.

GOOD, Deut. 6. 24. & 10. 13.
Gen. 1. 31. every thing he had made was very *g.*
2. 18. it is not *g.* for man to be alone
2 Kings 20. 19. *g.* is the word of the Lord, Isa. 39. 8.
Ps. 34. 8. taste and see that Lord is *g.*
73. 1. truly God is *g.* to Israel
106. 5. I may see *g.* of thy chosen
119. 68. thou art *g.* and doest *g.*
145. 9. Lord is *g.* to all, 136. 1.
Lam. 3. 25. Lord is *g.* to them that
Mic. 6. 8. he hath showed thee what is *g.*
Matt. 19. 17. why call me *g.* none
Rom. 3. 8. do evil that *g.* may come
1 Thes. 5. 15. follow that which is *g.*, 3 John 11.
Neh. 2. 18. hand for this *good work*
Matt. 26. 10. wrought a — on me
John 10. 33. for a — we stone thee not
2 Cor. 9. 8. abound to every —
Phil. 1. 6. begun a — will finish
Col. 1. 10. fruitful in every —
2 Thes. 2. 17. establish you in every —
1 Tim. 5. 10. followed every —
2 Tim. 2. 21. prepared to —, Tit. 3. 1.
Tit. 1. 16. to every — reprobate
Heb. 13. 21. perfect in every —
Matt. 5. 16. may see your *good works*
John 10. 32. many — have I showed you
Acts 9. 36. Dorcas was full of —
1 Tim. 2. 25. the — of some are manifest
Tit. 3. 8. be careful to maint. —, 14.
Heb. 10. 24. provoke to love and —
1 Pet. 2. 12. may by your — which
Ex. 33. 19. make my *goodness* pass
2 Chron. 6. 41. saints rejoice in *g.*
Neh. 9. 25. delight themselves in *g.*
35. not served thee in thy great *g.*
Ps. 16. 2. my *g.* extendeth not to
23. 6. *g.* and mercy shall follow
27. 13. believed to see *g.* of Lord
31. 19. how great is thy *g.*, Zech. 9. 17.
52. 1. the *g.* of God endureth
11. crownest the year with thy *g.*
Isa. 63. 7. great *g.* bestowed on Israel
Hos. 3. 5. fear the Lord and his *g.*
Rom. 2. 4. *g.* of God leadeth to repentance
11. 22. behold the *g.* and severity of God
Eph. 5. 9. fruit of Spirit in all *g.*, Gal. 5. 22.
R. V. changes are frequent, but nearly all based on words before or after the word *good*; 2 Sam. 7. 28; 1 Chron. 17. 26. good things; 2 Chron. 32. 32; 35. 26. good deeds; Ps. 33. 5; 144. 2. lovingkindness; Prov. 20. 6. kindness

GOSPEL, Mark 1. 1, 15. & 8. 35.
Matt. 4. 23. preaching *g.* of kingdo.
Mark 16. 15. preach the *g.* to
Acts 20. 24. *g.* of the grace of God
Rom. 1. 1. *g.* of God, 15. 16. 1 Tim. 1. 11.
1 Cor. 1. 17. but to preach the *g.*
4. 15. I have begotten you through the *g.*
2 Cor. 4. 3. if our *g.* be hid
4. glorious *g.*
11. 4. another *g.* which ye, Gal. 1. 6.
Gal. 1. 8. preach any other *g.*, 9.
Eph. 1. 13. *g.* of salvation
6. 15. *g.* of peace
Col. 1. 5. truth of *g.*, Gal. 2. 5.
23. hope of *g.*
Phil. 1. 5. fellowship in *g.*
1 Thes. 1. 5. our *g.* came in power
Heb. 4. 2. unto us was *g.* preached
1 Pet. 4. 6. *g.* was preached to dead
Rev. 14. 6. having everlasting *g.* to preach
R. V. Luke 4. 18; 7. 29; 1 Pet. 1. 25. good tidings; Rom. 10. 16. glad tidings; Rom. 10. 15——

GOVERNMENT, Isa. 9. 6, 7. & 22. 21. 1 Cor. 12. 28. 2 Pet. 2. 10
R. V. 2 Pet. 2. 10. dominion

GRACE, Ezra 9. 8. Esth. 2. 17.
Ps. 84. 11. Lord will give *g.* and glory
Prov. 3. 34. gives *g.* to the lowly
Zech. 4. 7. with shoutings, crying *g.* to it.
12. 10. spirit of *g.* and supplications
John 1. 14. of Father full of *g.* and
16. of fulness we receive *g.* for *g.*
17. *g.* and truth came by Jesus Christ
Acts 18. 27. helped them believe through *g.*
Rom. 3. 24. justified freely by his *g.*
5. 20. *g.* did much more abound
6. 14. not under law, but under *g.*
11. 5. according to the election of *g.*
2 Cor. 12. 9. my *g.* is sufficient for
Eph. 2. 5. by *g.* ye are saved, 8.
7. show exceed. riches of his *g.*, 1. 7.
4. 29. minister *g.* to hearers
Tit. 3. 7. justified by his *g.*
Heb. 4. 16. come boldly to the throne of *g.*
13. 9. heart be established with *g.*
1 Pet. 3. 7. heirs of the *g.* of life
5. 5. and giveth *g.* to the humble
2 Pet. 3. 18. grow in *g.* and in knowledge
Rom. 1. 7. *grace and peace* to you, 1 Cor. 1. 3. 2 Cor. 1. 2. Gal. 1. 3. Eph. 1. 2. Phil. 1. 2. Col. 1. 2. 1 Thes. 1. 1. 2 Thes. 1. 2. Phile. 3. 1 Pet. 1. 2. 2 Pet. 1. 2. Jude 2. Rev. 1. 4.
Luke 2. 40. *grace of God*, Acts 11. 23. & 13. 43. & 14. 3, 26. & 15. 40. & 20. 24, 32. Rom. 5. 15. 1 Cor. 1. 4. & 3. 10. & 15. 10. Eph. 3. 2, 7. Heb. 2. 9. & 12. 15.
2 Cor. 1. 12. by — we have had our conversation
6. 1. receive not — in vain
8. 1. of — bestowed on churches
9. 14. for the exceeding — in you
Gal. 2. 21. I do not frustrate —
Col. 1. 6. knew — in truth
1 Pet. 4. 10, stewards of manifold —
Jude 4. turning — into lascivious.
Acts 15. 11. *grace of our Lord Jesus Christ*, Rom. 16. 20, 24. 1 Cor. 16. 23. 2 Cor. 8. 9. & 13. 14. Gal. 6. 18. Phil. 4. 23. 1 Thes. 5. 28. 2 Thes. 3. 18. Phile. 25.
Rev. 22. 21. — be with you all
Gen. 43. 29. God be *gracious* to thee
Ex. 22. 27. I will hear for I am *g.*
33. 19. I will be *g.* to whom I will be *g.*
34. 6. Lord God merciful and *g.*
2 Chron. 30. 9. Neh. 9. 17, 31. Ps. 103. 8. & 116. 5. & 145. 8. Joel 2. 13.
Num. 6. 25. the Lord be *g.* to thee
Job 33. 24. then he is *g.* to him
Ps. 77. 9. hath God forgotten to be *g.*
86. 15. full of compassion and *g.*
Isa. 30. 18. the Lord wait that he may be *g.*
Amos 5. 15. may be, the Lord will be *g.*
Jonah 4. 2. knew that thou art a *g.* God
Mal. 1. 9. beseech God to be *g.*, Isa. 33. 2.
Gen. 33. 5. *graciously*, 11. Ps. 119. 29.
Hos. 14. 2. receive us *g.*
R. V. 2 Sam. 16. 4. favor; Rom. 11. 6; 16. 24——; Jer. 22. 23. to be pitied; Hos. 14. 2. accept . . . good

GRAFTED, Rom. 11. 17, 19, 23, 24

GRANT, Job 10. 12. Ps. 140. 8. Prov. 10. 24. Rom. 15. 5. Eph. 3. 16. 2 Tim. 1. 18. Rev. 3. 21.
R. V. 1 Chron. 21. 22; Rev. 3. 21. give; Matt. 20. 21. command; Rev. 19. 8. given unto

GRAPES, of gall, Deut. 32. 32.
S. of S. 2. 13. the tender *g.*, 15.
7. 7. clusters of *g.*
Isa. 5. 4. wild *g.*
Ezek. 18. 2. sour *g.*
Mic. 7. 1. soul desireth first ripe *g.*
R. V. Lev. 19. 10. fallen fruit; S. of S. 2. 13; 7. 12. in blossom

GRASS, Ps. 37. 2. & 90. 5. & 92. 7. & 102. 4, 11. Isa. 44. 4. & 51. 12.
Ps. 103. 15. man's days are like *g.*
Isa. 40. 6. all flesh is *g.*, 7. 8. 1 Pet. 1. 24. Jas. 1. 10, 11.
Matt. 6. 30. if God so clothe the *g.*
Rev. 8. 7. green *g.*
9. 4. not hurt *g.*
R. V. Isa. 15. 6. hay; Jer. 14. 6. herbage; Jer. 50. 11. treadeth out the corn

GRAVE, 1 Kings 2. 9. & 14. 13.
1 Sam. 2. 6. Lord brings down to *g.*
Job 5. 26. come to thy *g.* in full
14. 13. hide me in the *g.*, 17. 1, 13.
Ps. 6. 5. in *g.* who shall give thanks
Prov. 1. 12. swallow them up alive, as the *g.*
Isa. 38. 18. *g.* cannot praise thee
Hos. 13. 14. the power of the *g.* O *g.* I will be thy destruction
1 Cor. 15. 55. O *g.* where is thy vic.
Zech. 3. 9. I will *engrave* the graving

Job 19. 24. *graven* with an iron pen
Isa. 49. 16. I have *g.* thee upon
Jer. 17. 1. sin *g.* upon table of their
1 Tim. 3. 4, 8, 11. *grave*, Tit. 2. 2, 7.
R. V. Job 33. 22. pit; Matt. 27. 52; Luke 11. 44; John 5. 28; 11. 17, 31; Rev. 11. 9. tombs; 1 Cor. 15. 55. death; Isa. 14. 19. sepulchre; Job 30. 24. ruinous heap; Job 7. 9; 17. 13; Ps. 6. 5; 30. 3; 31. 17; 49. 14, 15; 88. 3; 89. 48; Prov. 1. 12; Hos. 13. 14. Sheol

GRAY, Ps. 71.18. Prov. 20.29. Hos. 7. 9.
R. V. Prov. 20. 29. hoary

GREAT, Gen. 12. 2. & 30. 8.
Deut. 29. 24. *g.* anger, 2 Chron. 34. 21.
1 Sam. 6. 9. *great evil*, Neh. 13. 27. Eccl. 2. 21. Jer. 44. 7. Dan. 9. 12.
Ps. 47. 2. *great king*, 48. 2. & 95. 3. Mal. 1. 14. Matt. 5. 35.
Job 32. 9. *great men*, Jer. 5. 5.
Ex. 32. 11. *great power*, Neh. 1. 10. Job 23. 6. Ps. 147. 5. Nah. 1. 3. Acts 4. 33. & 8. 10. Rev. 11. 17.
Ex. 32. 21. *so great*, Deut. 4. 7, 8. 1 Kings 3. 9. Ps. 77. 13. & 103. 11. Matt. 8. 10. & 15. 33. 2 Cor. 1. 10. Heb. 2. 3. & 12. 1. Rev. 16. 18. & 18. 17.
Job 5. 9. *great things*, 9. 10. & 37. 5. Jer. 45. 5. Hos. 8. 12. Luke 1. 49.
Gen. 6. 5. *great wickedness*, 39. 9. Job 22. 5. Joel 3. 13. 2 Chron. 28. 13.
Job 33. 12. God is *greater* than man
Matt. 12. 42. *g.* than Solomon is here
John 1. 50. see *g.* things than these
4. 12. art thou *g.* than, 8. 53.
14. 28. my Father is *g.* than I
1 Cor. 14. 5. *g.* is he that prophe.
1 John 4. 4. *g.* is he that is in you, 3. 20.
5. 9. witness of God is *g.*
1 Sam. 30. 6. David was *greatly* distressed
2 Sam. 24. 10. I have sinned *g.* in
1 Kings 8. 3. Obadiah feared the Lord *g.*
1 Chron. 16. 25. great is the Lord and *g.* to be praised, Ps. 48. 1. & 96. 4. & 145. 3.
2 Chron. 33. 12. humbled himself *g.* before God
Job 3. 25. thing I *g.* feared is come
Ps. 28. 7. my heart *g.* rejoiceth
47. 9. God is *g.* exalted
Dan. 9. 23. O man *g.* beloved, 10. 11, 19.
Mark 12. 27. ye do *g.* err
Ex. 15. 7. *greatness* of thy excellency
Num. 14. 19. pardon according to *g.*
Deut. 32. 3. ascribe ye *g.* to our God
1 Chron. 29. 11. thine is the *g.*
Neh. 13. 22. spare according to the *g.* of thy mercy
Ps. 66. 3. *g.* of thy power, 79. 11. Eph. 1. 19.
145. 3. his *g.* is unsearchable, 6.
Isa. 63. 1. travelling in the *g.* of his strength
The R. V. changes, which are frequent, mostly turn on antecedent and consequent words

GREEDY of gain, Prov. 1. 19. & 15. 27.
Isa. 56. 11. they are *g.* dogs, never
Eph. 4. 19. work uncleanness with *greediness*

GRIEF, Isa. 53. 3, 4, 10. Heb. 13. 17.
Gen. 6. 6. *grieved* him at his heart
Judg. 10. 16. his soul was *g.* for
Ps. 95. 10. forty years long was I *g.*
Isa. 54. 6. woman forsaken and *g.*
Jer. 5. 3. hast stricken them, they have not *g.*
Lam. 3. 33. nor *g.* children of men
Amos 6. 6. not *g.* for the affliction of Joseph
Mark 3. 5. being *g.* for hardness of heart
10. 22. went away *g.* for he had
Rom. 14. 15. if brother be *g.* at thy meat
Ps. 10. 5. his ways are always *grievous*
Matt. 23. 4. burdens *g.* to be borne
Acts 20. 29. shall *g.* wolves enter
Matt. 8. 6. *grievously* tormented, 15. 22.
R. V. 1 Sam. 1. 16. provocation; 2 Chron. 6. 29; Ps. 31. 10; 69. 29; Jer. 45. 3; 2 Cor. 2. 5. sorrow; Job 6, 2. vexation; Jer. 6. 7. sickness; Jonah 4. 6. evil case; 1 Sam. 15. 11. was wroth; 1 Chron. 4. 10. not to my sorrow; Prov. 26. 15. wearieth; Isa. 57. 10. faint; Mark 10. 22. sorrowful; Acts 4. 2; 16. 18. sore troubled; 2 Cor. 2. 4. made sorry; 2. 5. caused sorrow; Heb. 3. 10, 17. displeased; Gen. 12. 10. sore; Ps. 10. 5. firm; 31. 18. insolently; Isa. 15. 4. trembleth within; Jer. 23. 19. whirling; Phil. 3. 1. perilous; Isa. 9. 1. hath made it glorious; Jer. 23. 19. burst; Ezek. 14. 13. committing a trespass

GRIND the faces of the poor, Isa. 3. 15.
Matt. 21. 44. it will *g.* him to powder
Eccl. 12. 3. *grinders* cease because few, 4.
R. V. Lam. 5. 13. young men bare the mill; Matt. 21. 44; Luke 20. 18. scatter

GROAN earnestly, 2 Cor. 5. 2, 4.
John 11. 33. Jesus *groaned* in spirit
Rom. 8. 22. whole creation *groaneth*
Ps. 6. 6. weary with my *groaning*
Rom. 8. 26. *g.* that cannot be uttered

GROUNDED, or *correcting* staff, Isa. 30. 32.
Eph. 3. 17. rooted and *g.* in love
Col. 1. 23. if continue in the faith *g.*
R. V. Isa. 30. 32. appointed

GROW, Gen. 48. 16. 2 Sam. 23. 5.
Ps. 92. 12. *g.* like cedar in Lebanon
Hos. 14. 5. shall *g.* as a lily
7. *g.* as the vine
Mal. 4. 2. shall *g.* up as calves of
Eph. 2. 21. *g.* unto a holy temple
1 Pet. 2. 2. sincere milk that ye may *g.*
2 Pet. 3. 18. *g.* in grace and knowl.
R. V. Lev. 13. 39. hath broken out; Job 14. 19. overflowings; 18. 18. spring; 38. 38. runneth; Isa. 11. 1. bear fruit; Hos. 14. 5, 7. blossom; Mal. 4. 2. gambol; Matt. 21. 19. no fruit from

GRUDGE, Lev. 19. 18. Jas. 5. 9.
1 Pet. 4. 9. *grudging*, 2 Cor. 9. 7.
R. V. Ps. 59. 15. tarry all night; Jas. 5. 9; 1 Pet. 4. 9. murmur

GUIDE unto death, Ps. 48. 14.
Ps. 73. 24. shall *g.* me with thy counsel
Prov. 2. 17. forsaketh the *g.* of her youth
Isa. 58. 11. Lord shall *g.* thee con.
Jer. 3. 4. my Father thou art *g.* of
Luke 1. 79. *g.* our feet into way
John 16. 13. *g.* you into all truth
1 Tim. 5. 14. bear children, *g.* house
R. V. Ps. 55. 13. companion; Prov. 2. 17. friend; 6. 7. chief; Ps. 32. 8. counsel; 112. 5. shall maintain; 1 Tim. 5. 14. rule

GUILE, Ex. 21. 14. Ps. 55. 11. 2 Cor. 12. 16. 1 Thes. 2. 3.
Ps. 32. 2. in whose spirit is no *g.*
34. 13. keep thy lips from *g.*, 1 Pet. 3. 10.
John 1. 47. Israelite in whom there is no *g.*
22. neither was *g.* found in mouth
R. V. Rev. 14. 5. lie

GUILTY, Lev. 4. 13. & 22. 27.
Ex. 34. 7. by no means clear the *g.* Num. 14. 18. Gen. 42. 21.
Rom. 3. 19. all world *g.* before
1 Cor. 11. 27. *g.* of body and blood of Lord
Jas. 2. 10. offend in one point, is *g.* of all
Ex. 20. 7. not hold him *guiltless*
R. V. Num. 5. 31. free; Matt. 23. 18. debtor; 26. 66; Mark 14. 64. worthy; Rom. 3. 19. brought under judgment of

GULF, fixed, Luke 16. 26.

H

HABITABLE part, Prov. 8. 31.

HABITATION, 2 Chron. 6. 2. & 29. 6.
Deut. 26. 15. look down from thy holy *h.*, Ps. 68. 5. Jer. 25. 30. Zech. 2. 13.
Ps. 26. 8. have loved the *h.* of thy
74. 20. earth full of *h.* of cruelty
89. 14. are *h.* of thy throne, 97. 2.
91. 9. hast made Most High thy *h.*
Prov. 3. 33. he blesseth *h.* of the just
Isa. 33. 20. see Jerusalem a quiet *h.*
Jer. 31. 23. the Lord bless thee, O *h.* of justice
Luke 16. 9. receive you into everlasting *h.*
Jude 6. angels which left their own *h.*
Rev. 18. 2. Babylon is become *h.* of
R. V. Gen. 49. 5. their swords; Ex. 15. 2. praise him; Lev. 13. 46. dwelling; 1 Chron. 4. 41. Meunim (Mehunim); Job 5. 24; Jer. 25. 30, 37. fold; 41. 17. Geruth; Ps. 89. 14; 97. 2. foundation; Jer. 9. 10; 50. 19; Amos 1. 2. pasture; Luke 16. 9. eternal tabernacles

HAIL, Isa. 28. 2, 17. Rev. 8. 7. & 16. 21.

HAIR, Job 4. 15. S. of S. 4. 1.
Ps. 40. 12. more than the *h.* of my head, 69. 4.
Hos. 7. 9. gray *h.* are here and there
Matt. 5. 36. make one *h.* white or
10. 30. *h.* of your head are numbered, Luke 12. 7.
1 Cor. 11. 14. if man have long *h.*
1 Pet. 3. 3. not of plaiting the *h.*

HALT, between two, 1 Kings 18. 21.
Mic. 4. 6. will I assemble her that *halteth*
Jer. 20. 10. watched for thy *halting*
R. V. Luke 14. 21. lame

HAND, Gen. 3. 22. & 16. 12.
Deut. 33. 3. all his saints are in thy *h.*
Ezra 7. 9. the good *h.* of his God is upon him
8. 22. *h.* of our God is upon them
Job 12. 6. into whose *h.* God bring.
Prov. 10. 4. *h.* of diligent maketh
11. 21. though *h.* join in *h.*, 16. 5.
Isa. 1. 12. who required this at your *h.*
Matt. 22. 13. bind him *h.* and foot
John 13. 3. given all things into his *h.*
1 Pet. 5. 6. humble yourselves under the mighty *h.* of God
Num. 11. 23. *Lord's hand* waxed
2 Sam. 24. 14. let us fall into — not man
Job 2. 10. received good at — and not evil
12. 9. — hath wrought all this, Isa. 41. 20.
Isa. 40. 2. received of the — double
59. 1. — is not shortened that cannot
Ps. 16. 8. he is at my *right hand*, I shall not
11. at thy — are pleasures for ever.
18. 35. thy — hath holden me up

Ps. 73. 23. hast holden me by my —
137. 5. let my — forget her cunning
139. 10. thy h. lead and thy — hold
Prov. 3. 16. length of days is in her —
Eccl. 10. 2. wise man's heart is at his —
9. 1. wise and their works are in the h. of God
S. of S. 2. 6. his — doth embrace me, 8. 3.
Matt. 5. 30. if thy — offend thee, cut it off
6. 3. left h. know what thy — doeth
20. 21. one on the — and the other on the left
25. 33. sheep on his — goats on the left, 34. 41.
Mark 14. 62. sitting on — of power
16. 19. sat on — of God, Rom. 8. 34. Col. 3. 1. Heb. 1. 3. & 8. 1. & 10. 12. 1 Pet. 3. 22. Acts 2. 33. & 7. 55, 56.
Ps. 31. 5. into *thy hand* I commit
Prov. 30. 32. lay — upon thy mouth
Eccl. 9. 10. whatsoever — findeth to
Isa. 26. 11. when — is lifted up, they
Matt. 18. 8. if — or thy foot offend
Gen. 27. 22. *hands* are the h. of Esau
Ex. 17. 12. Moses' h. were heavy
Job 17. 9. hath clean h. shall be stronger
Ps. 24. 4. hath clean h. and a pure
76. 5. men of might found their h.
Prov. 31. 20. reacheth forth h. to the needy
31. give her of the fruit of her h.
Isa. 1. 15. spread forth your h. I will hide
Mic. 7. 3. do evil with both h. earn.
Matt. 18. 8. having two h. or feet
Luke 1. 74. delivered out of the h.
9. 44. delivered into h. of men
John 13. 9. but also my h. and head
2 Cor. 5. 1. house not made with h.
Eph. 4. 28. working with his h.
1 Tim. 2. 8. every where lifting up holy h.
Heb. 9. 11. tabernacle, not made with h.
10. 31. fearful thing to fall into the h. of the living God
Jas. 4. 8. cleanse your h. ye sinners
Col. 2. 14. *handwriting* of ordinances

HANDLE me and see, Luke 24. 39.
Col. 2. 21. touch not, taste not, h.
2 Cor. 4. 2. not h. the word of God

HANDMAID, Ps. 86. 16. & 116. 16. Prov. 30. 23. Luke 1. 38, 48.
R. V. 1 Sam. 1. 18; 25. 27; 2 Sam. 14. 15. servant

HANG, Ps. 137. 2. Josh. 8. 29.
Deut. 21. 33. h. is accursed of God, Gal. 3. 13.
Job 26. 7. he h. the earth on nothing
Matt. 18. 6. millstone h. about neck
22. 40. on these h. all the law and
Heb. 12. 12. hands which h. down

HAPPEN, Jer. 44. 23. Rom. 11. 25.
Prov. 12. 21. no evil shall h. to just, 1 Pet. 4. 12.
Eccl. 2. 14. one event h. to them all
8. 14. h. according to work of
1 Cor. 10. 11. these h. for ensamples
R. V. Rom. 11. 25. hath befallen

HAPPY am I, for the daughters, Gen. 30. 13.
Deut. 33. 29. h. art thou, O Israel
1 Kings 10. 8. h. are thy men, h. these
Job 5. 17. h. is the man whom God correcteth
Ps. 127. 5. h. is the man who hath his quiver full
137. 8. h. that rewards thee, 9.
144. 15. h. that people whose God is the Lord
Jer. 12. 1. why are they h. that deal treacherously
Prov. 3. 13. h. is the man that findeth wisdom, 18.
14. 21. he that hath mercy on poor, h. is
Prov. 16. 20. whoso trusteth in the Lord h. is he
29. 18. he that keepeth the law, h. is he
Mal. 3. 15. we call the proud h. that
John 13. 17. h. are ye, if ye do them
Rom. 14. 22. h. he that conde. not
Jas. 5. 11. count them h. which endure
1 Pet. 3. 14. suffer for righteousness' sake, h. are ye
1 Cor. 7. 40. *happier* if she so abide
R. V. Jer. 12. 1. at ease; John 13. 17; Jas. 5. 11; 1 Pet. 3. 14; 4. 14. blessed

HARD, Gen. 35. 16, 17. Ex. 1. 14. & 18. 26. 2 Sam. 13. 2. Ps. 88. 7.
Gen. 18. 14. is any thing too h. for the Lord
2 Sam. 3. 39. sons of Zeruiah be too h. for me
2 Kings 2. 10. thou askest a h. thing
Ps. 60. 3. hast showed thy people h. things
Prov. 13. 15. the way of transgressors is h.
Matt. 25. 24. that thou art a h. man
Mark 10. 24. how h. is it for them
John 6. 60. this is a h. saying; who
Acts 9. 5. h. for thee to kick, 26. 14.
Jude 15. of all their h. speeches
R. V. Job 41. 24. firm; Ps. 94. 4. arrogantly; Prov. 13. 15. rugged; Acts 9. 5 —

HARDEN, Ex. 4. 21. Deut. 15. 7. Josh. 11. 20. Job 6. 10. & 39. 16.
Heb. 3. 8. h. not your hearts as in the provocation, 15. & 4. 7. Ps. 95. 8.
Prov. 21. 29. h. his face
28. 14. h. his heart
29. 1. h. his neck shall be destroyed
Job 9. 4. hath *hardened* himself against
Isa. 63. 17. h. our heart from thy fear
Mark 6. 52. their heart was h., 3. 5.
Rom. 9. 18. whom he will, he *hardeneth*
Prov. 18. 19. a brother offended is *harder*
Jer. 5. 3. made faces h. than a rock
Ezek. 3. 9. h. than a flint thy fore.
Matt. 19. 8. because of *hardness* of your hearts
Mark 3. 5. grieved for the h. of their
2 Tim. 2. 3. endure h. as a good soldier
R. V. Job 6. 10. exult; Ex. 7. 14; 9. 7. stubborn; Jer. 7. 26; 19. 15. made stiff

HARLOT, Gen. 34. 31. Josh. 2. 1. Judg. 11. 1. Prov. 7. 10. Isa. 1. 21. & 23. 15.
Jer. 2. 20. play the h., 3. 1, 6, 8. Ezek. 16. 15, 16, 41. Hos. 2. 5. & 4. 15.
Matt. 21. 31. h. go into the kingdom
1 Cor. 6. 16. joined to h. is one body
Jas. 2. 25. was not Rahab the h. justified
Rev. 17. 5. mother of h. and abominations

HARM, Gen. 31. 52. Acts 28. 5.
1 Chron. 16. 22. do my prophets no h., Ps. 105. 15. Prov. 3. 30. Jer. 39. 12.
1 Pet. 3. 13. who is he that will h.
Matt. 10. 16. *harmless*, Phil. 2. 15.
Heb. 7. 26. holy, h. undefiled
R. V. Acts 27. 21. injury; 28. 6. nothing amiss; Heb. 7. 26. guileless

HARVEST, Gen. 8. 22. & 30. 14.
Ex. 34. 21. in h. thou shalt rest
Isa. 9. 3. joy before thee according to joy of h.
Jer. 5. 24. reserved appointed weeks of h.
8. 20. the h. is past, the summer
51. 33. time of h. shall come, Joel 3. 13.
Matt. 9. 37. h. plenteous
38. pray ye the Lord of the h.
Rev. 14. 15. h. of earth is ripe, Joel 3. 13.

HASTE, Ex. 12. 11, 33. Isa. 52. 12.
Ps. 31. 22. I said in my h., 116. 11.
Ps. 38. 22. make h. help me, 40. 13. & 70. 1, 5. & 71. 12. & 141. 1.
119. 60. I made h. and delayed not
S. of S. 8. 14. make h. my beloved
Isa. 28. 16. believ. shall not make h.
49. 17. thy children shall make h.
Ps. 16. 4. *hasten* after another god
Isa. 5. 19. let him h. his work that
60. 22. I the Lord will h. it in his time
Jer. 1. 12. I will h. my word to
Prov. 14. 29. *hasty* of spirit, Eccl. 7. 9.
20. 21. inheritance gotten *hastily*
R. V. Job 9. 26. swoopeth; 40. 23. trembleth; John 11. 31. quickly; Isa. 28. 4. first ripe; Dan. 2. 15. urgent

HATE, Gen. 24. 60. Deut. 21. 15.
Lev. 19. 17. shall not h. thy brother
Deut. 7. 10. repayeth them that h.
1 Kings 22. 8. I h. him for he doth not
Ps. 68. 1. let them that h. him flee
97. 10. ye that love Lord, h. evil
139. 21. do not I h. them that h.
Prov. 8. 13. fear of Lord is to h. evil
36. all they that h. me love death
Jer. 44. 4. abominable thing that I h.
Amos 5. 10. they h. him that rebuketh
15. h. the evil, and love the good
Mic. 3. 2. who h. the good and love
Luke 14. 26. and h. not his father
John 7. 7. world cannot h. you, but
15. 18. if the world h. you it hated
Rom. 7. 15. what I h. that do I
1 John 3. 13. marvel not if world h.
Rev. 2. 6. hatest the deeds, which I also h., 15.
17. 16. these shall h. the whore
Prov. 1. 29. for that they *hated* knowledge
5. 12. and say how have I h. instruction
Isa. 66. 5. your brother that h. you
Mal. 1. 3. I h. Esau, Rom. 9. 13.
Matt. 10. 22. shall be h. of all men, Mark 13. 13. Luke 21. 17.
Luke 19. 14. his citizens h. him
John 15. 24. h. me and my father, 18.
Eph. 5. 29. no man ever h. his own
Rom. 1. 30. backbiters, *haters* of God
2 Sam. 19. 6. *hatest* friends and lovest thine enemies
Ps. 5. 5. h. all workers of iniquity
Ex. 23. 5. ask of him that *hateth* thee
Prov. 13. 24. spareth rod, h. his son
John 12. 25. h. his life in this world
Ex. 18. 21. men of truth *hating* covetousness
Tit. 3. 3. *hateful* and h. one another
Jude 23. h. garment spotted by flesh
R. V. Gen. 49. 23; Ps. 55. 3. persecute; Matt. 5. 44 —

HAUGHTY, my heart is not, Ps. 131. 1.
Prov. 16. 18. h. spirit before fall, 18. 12.
21. 24. proud and h. scorner dealeth
Zeph. 3. 11. no more be h. because
Isa. 2. 11. *haughtiness*, 17. & 13. 11. & 16. 6.
R. V. Isa. 16. 6. arrogancy; Isa. 10. 33; 24. 4. lofty

HEAD, Gen. 2. 10. & 40. 13.
Gen. 3. 15. it shall bruise thy h.
49. 26. blessings on h. of him
Ezra 9. 6. iniquity increased over our h.
Prov. 16. 31. hoary h. is a crown of
20. 29. beauty of old men is gray h.
Eccl. 2. 14. wise men's eyes are in h.
Ps. 38. 4. iniquity gone over my h.
S. of S. 5. 2. my h. is filled with
Isa. 1. 5. whole h. is sick and heart
6. from sole of foot even unto h.
Jer. 9. 1. O that my h. were waters
Ezek. 9. 10. their way on h., 16. 4.
Dan. 2. 28. visions of thy h. on

Zech. 4. 7. bring forth *h.* stone thereof
Matt. 8. 20. not where to lay his *h.*
14. 8. give me *h.* of John Baptist
Rom. 12. 20. coals of fire on his *h.*, Prov. 25. 22.
1 Cor. 11. 3. *h.* of man is Christ, *h.* of woman is man, *h.* of Christ is God
Eph. 1. 22. gave him to be *h.* over
Col. 1. 18. he is *h.* of the body, 2. 19.
Rev. 19. 12. on his *h.* many crowns
Ps. 24. 7. lift up your *heads*, O ye gates, 9.
Isa. 35. 10. everlasting joy on their *h.*, 51. 11.
Luke 21. 28. lift up your *h.* for a
Rev. 13. 1. seven *h.* and ten horns
Job 5. 13. *headlong*, Luke 4. 29. Acts 1. 18.
2 Tim. 3. 4. *heady*, high-minded
HEAL her now, O God, Num. 12. 13.
Deut. 32. 39. I wound, I *h.* and I
2 Chron. 7. 14. I will *h.* their land
Ps. 6. 2. *h.* me, for my bones are
60. 2. *h.* breaches for land shaketh
Isa. 57. 18. I have seen his way and will *h.* him
Jer. 3. 22. I will *h.* your backsliding, Hos. 14. 4.
17. 14. *h.* me, and I shall be *h.*
Hos. 6. 1. hath torn and he will *h.*
Luke 4. 18. *h.* the broken-hearted
John 12. 40. convert, and I should *h.*
2 Chron. 30. 20. Lord *healed* the
Ps. 30. 2. I cried and thou hast *h.*
Isa. 6. 10. convert and be *h.*, Acts 28. 27.
53. 5. with his stripes we are *h.*, 1 Pet. 2. 24.
Jer. 6. 14. *h.* the hurt of the daughter of, 8. 11.
Hos. 7. 1. when I would have *h.* Israel
Matt. 4. 24. he *h.* them all, 12. 15. & 14. 14.
Heb. 12. 13. let it rather be *h.*
Jas. 5. 16. pray that ye may be *h.*
Rev. 13. 3. his deadly wound was *h.*
Ex. 15. 26. I am the Lord that *healeth* thee
Ps. 103. 3. who *h.* all thy diseases
147. 3. he *h.* the broken in heart
Isa. 30. 26. Lord *h.* stroke of their
Jer. 14. 19. looked for time of *healing*
30. 13. thou hast no *h.* medicine
Mal. 4. 2. with *h.* in his wings
Matt. 4. 23. *h.* all manner of sick.
1 Cor. 12. 9. to another the gifts of *h.*
Rev. 22. 2. leaves were for *h.* nations
Ps. 42. 11. *health* of my countenance, 43. 5.
Prov. 3. 8. shall be *h.* to thy navel
Jer. 8. 15. looked for a time of *h.*
30. 17. I will restore *h.* and heal
R. V. Mark 5. 23; Luke 8. 36; Acts 14. 9. made whole; 28. 9. cured: Nah. 3. 19. assuaging; 2 Sam. 20. 9. Is it well with thee
HEAP coals, Prov. 25. 22. Rom. 12. 20.
Deut. 32. 23. I will *h.* mischiefs
Job 36. 13. hypocrites in heart *h.*
2 Tim. 4. 3. *h.* to themselves teach.
Ps. 39. 6. he *heapeth* up riches, and
Jas. 5. 3. ye have *heaped* treasures
Judg. 15. 16. *heaps* upon *h.* with the
R. V. Isa. 17. 11. fleeth away; Jer. 31. 21. guide posts
HEAR, Gen. 21. 6. & 23. 6.
Deut. 30. 17. if heart turn away, so that thou wilt not *h.*
1 Kings 8. 30. *h.* thou in heaven thy dwelling place
2 Kings 19. 16. bow down thine ear, and *h.*
2 Chron. 6. 21. *h.* from thy dwelling
Job 5. 27. *h.* it and know it for
Ps. 4. 1. *h.* my prayer, 39. 12. & 54. 2. & 51. 8. & 84. 8. & 102. 1. & 143. 1. Dan. 9. 17, 19.
Ps. 4. 3. Lord will *h.*, 17. 6. & 145. 19. Zech. 10. 6.
51. 8. make me to *h.* joy and
59. 7. who, say they, doth *h.*, 10.
66. 16. come and *h.* all ye that
115. 6. they have ears, but *h.* not
Prov. 19. 27. cease to *h.* instruction
Eccl. 5. 1. be more ready to *h.* than
S. of S. 2. 14. let me *h.* thy voice, 8. 13.
Isa. 1. 2. *h.* O heavens, and give
6. 10. lest they *h.* with ears, Deut. 29. 4.
Matt. 10. 27. what ye *h.* in the ear
13. 17. to *h.* those things ye *h.*
17. 5. this is my beloved Son, *h.* ye
Mark 4. 24. take heed what ye *h.*
33. spake the word as they were able to *h.* it
Luke 8. 18. take heed how ye *h.*
16. 29. Moses and the prophets, let them *h.* them
John 5. 25. they that *h.* shall live
Acts 10. 33. to *h.* all things that
Jas. 1. 19. every man be swift to *h.*
Rev. 2. 7. let him *h.* what the Spirit saith to the churches, 3. 6, 13, 22. & 11. 17, 29.
3. 20. if any *h.* my voice, and open
Ex. 2. 24. God *heard* their groaning
Ps. 6. 9. Lord hath *h.* my supplica.
10. 17. hast *h.* desire of humble, 34. 6.
34. 4. I sought the Lord, and he *h.*
61. 5. thou hast *h.* my vows, 116. 1.
120. 1. I cried to Lord and he *h.*
Isa. 40. 28. hast thou not *h.* that God
64. 4. from beginning men have not *h.*
Jer. 8. 6. I hearkened and *h.* but
Jonah 2. 2. I cried to Lord and he *h.*
Mal. 3. 16. Lord hearkened and *h.*
Matt. 6. 7. be *h.* for much speaking
Luke 1. 13. thy prayer is *h.* and thy
John 3. 32. what he hath seen and *h.*
Rom. 10. 14. of whom they have not *h.*
1 Cor. 2. 9. eye hath not seen nor ear *h.*
Phil. 4. 9. what *h.* and seen in me
Heb. 4. 2. with faith in them that *h.*
Jas. 5. 11. ye have *h.* of patience of Job
Ex. 3. 7. *I have heard* their cry
6. 5. — the groaning, Acts 7. 34.
16. 12. — the murmurings, Num. 14. 27.
1 Kings 9. 3. — thy prayer and supplication, 2 Kings 19. 20. & 20. 5. & 22. 19.
Job 42. 5. — of thee by the hearing
Isa. 49. 8. in an acceptable time —
Ps. 65. 2. thou that *hearest* prayer
John 11. 42. I knew thou *h.* me
1 Sam. 3. 9. speak, Lord, thy servant *heareth*
Prov. 8. 34. blessed is man that *h.*
Matt. 7. 24. whoso *h.* these sayings
Luke 10. 16. he that *h.* you *h.* me
John 9. 31. God *h.* not sinners, but
Rev. 22. 17. let him that *h.* say come
Rom. 2. 13. not *hearers* but doers
Eph. 4. 29. minister grace to the *h.*
Jas. 1. 22. be doers of the word and not *h.*
Job 42. 5. of thee by *hearing* of ear
Prov. 20. 12. the *h.* ear, and seeing
28. 9. turneth away his ear from *h.*
Matt. 13. 14. *h.* they hear not, Acts 28. 27.
Rom. 10. 17. faith cometh by *h.* and *h.* by
Heb. 5. 11. seeing ye are dull of *h.*
2 Pet. 2. 8. in seeing and *h.* vexed his
R. V. The O. T. changes, which are numerous, are chiefly to *answer*
HEARKEN unto the voice of, Deut. 28. 15.
Deut. 28. 1. if thou *h.* diligently, 30. 10.
1 Sam. 15. 22. to *h.* better than the fat of rams
Ps. 103. 20. angels *h.* to voice of
Isa. 46. 12. *h.* unto me, ye stout
HEART, Ex. 28. 30. & 35. 5.
1 Sam. 1. 13. she spake in her *h.* only
16. 7. but Lord looketh on *h.*
24. 5. David's *h.* smote him after
1 Chron. 16. 10. let the *h.* of them rejoice that seek the Lord, Ps. 105. 3.
22. 19. set your *h.* to seek the Lord your God
2 Chron. 17. 6. his *h.* was lifted up
30. 19. prepareth his *h.* to seek God
Ps. 22. 26. your *h.* shall live for ever, 69. 32.
37. 31. law of his God is in his *h.*
51. 17. a broken and a contrite *h.*, Isa. 66. 2.
64. 6. inward thought, and *h.* is
Prov. 4. 23. keep thy *h.* with dili.
10. 20. *h.* of wicked is little worth
16. 9. a man's *h.* deviseth his way
27. 19. *h.* of man answereth to man
Eccl. 7. 4. *h.* of wise is in house
10. 2. wise man's *h.* is at his right hand, but a fool's *h.* is at his left
S. of S. 3. 11. in the day of gladness of his *h.*
Isa. 6. 10. make *h.* of this people fat
Jer. 11. 20. triest the reins and the *h.*, 17. 10.
12. 11. no man layeth it to *h.*, Isa. 42. 25.
17. 9. *h.* is deceitful above all
24. 7. I will give them a *h.* to know
32. 39. I will give them one *h.*, Ezra 11. 19.
Lam. 3. 41. lift up our *h.* with our
Ezek. 11. 19. take stony *h.* give *h.* of flesh
36. 26. new *h.* take stony *h.* give *h.*
Joel 2. 13. rend your *h.* not your
Mal. 4. 6. turn *h.* of fathers to
Matt. 6. 21. there will your *h.* be
12. 34. out of abundance of the *h.* the mouth speaketh
Luke 2. 19. pondered them in her *h.*, 51.
24. 25. O fools, and slow of *h.* to
32. did not our *h.* burn within us
John 14. 1. let not your *h.* be troubled, 27.
Acts 5. 33. were cut to the *h.*, 7. 54.
11. 23. with purpose of *h.* cleave to the Lord
13. 22. found man after mine own *h.*
Rom. 10. 10. with *h.* man believeth
1 Cor. 2. 9. nor entered into *h.* of man
2 Cor. 3. 3. in fleshly tables of the *h.*
1 Pet. 3. 4. in the hidden man of the *h.*
1 John 3. 20. if *h.* condemn us, God
Deut. 11. 13. serve him *with all heart*, Josh. 22. 5. 1 Sam. 12. 20.
13. 8. love Lord your God —, 30. 6. Matt. 22. 37. Mark 12. 30, 33. Luke 10. 27.
Deut. 26. 16. keep and do them —
30. 2. turn to the Lord — and soul, 10. 2 Kings 23. 25. Joel 2. 12.
1 Kings 2. 4. walk before me in truth —
8. 23, 48. return to thee —, 2 Chron. 6. 38.
2 Chron. 15. 12. seek the God of their fathers —
15. sworn —
Prov. 3. 5. trust in Lord — and be
Jer. 29. 13. search for me —
Zeph. 3. 14. sing, be glad, rejoice —
Acts 8. 37. if thou believest —
Ps. 86. 12. I will praise thee *with all my heart*
45. 1. *my heart* is inditing a
57. 7. — is fixed, O God, — is fixed
61. 2. what time — is overwhelmed
84. 2. my flesh and — crieth for

Ps. 109. 22. — is wounded within me
131. 1. Lord — is not haughty
S. of S. 5. 2. I sleep, but — waketh
Hos. 11. 8. — is turned within me
1 Kings 8. 61. *heart perfect* with the Lord, 11. 4. & 15. 3, 14. 2 Chron. 15. 17.
2 Kings 20. 3. and with —, 2 Chron. 19. 9.
1 Chron. 28. 9. serve him with —, 29. 9.
2 Chron. 16. 9. in behalf of them whose —
Ps. 101. 2. I will walk within my house with a —
24. 4. clean hands and *pure heart*
Matt. 5. 8. blessed are the pure in *h.*
1 Tim. 1. 5. charity out of a —
2 Tim. 2. 22. call on Lord out of —
1 Pet. 1. 22. love with — fervently
Ps. 9. 1. praise him *with my whole heart*
119. 2. seek him —
Jer. 3. 10. not turned with her whole *h.*
Col. 3. 23. do it *heartily* as to Lord
R. V. 2 Sam. 3. 21; Ezek. 25. 15; 27. 31; Lam. 3. 51. soul; Job 38. 36; Jer. 7. 31. mind

HEATH, Jer. 17. 16. & 48. 6.

HEATHEN, Lev. 25. 44. & 26. 45.
Ps. 2. 1. why do the *h.* rage
2. 8. give them the *h.* for
Matt. 18. 17. let him be as a *h.* man
Gal. 3. 8. justify the *h.* through faith

HEAVEN of *h.* cannot contain, 1 Kings 8. 27. 2 Chron. 2. 6. & 6. 18.
Ps. 103. 11. as *h.* is high above the
Prov. 25. 3. *h.* for height, and earth
Isa. 66. 1. *h.* is my throne, Acts 7. 49.
Jer. 31. 37. if *h.* above can be
Hag. 1. 10. *h.* over you is stayed
Matt. 5. 18. till *h.* and earth pass
Luke 15. 18. sinned against *h.*, 21.
John 1. 51. see *h.* open and angels
Ps. 73. 25. whom have I *in heaven*
Eccl. 5. 2. God is — and thou upon
Heb. 10. 34. have — a better sub.
1 Pet. 1. 4. inheritance reserved — for you
Ps. 8. 3. consider *the heavens*, the
19. 1. — declare the glory of God
89. 11. — are thine, and earth also
Isa. 65. 17. I create new *h.* and
Acts 3. 21. *h.* must receive him till
2 Cor. 5. 1. house eternal in the *h.*
Eph. 4. 10. ascend far above all *h.*
Matt. 6. 14. *heavenly* Father, 26. 32. & 15. 13. & 18. 35. Luke 11. 13.
John 3. 12. if I tell you of *h.* things
1 Cor. 15. 48. as is *h.* such are the *h.*
Eph. 1. 3. in *h.* places, 20. & 2. 6.
2 Tim. 4. 18. unto his *h.* kingdom
Heb. 3. 1. partak. of the *h.* calling
R.V. Mark 11. 26; Luke 11. 2; Heb. 10. 34; 1 John 5. 7; Rev. 16. 17 —

HEAVE OFFERING, Ex. 29. 27. Num. 15. 19. & 18. 8, 28, 29.

HEAVY, Num. 11. 14. Job 33. 7.
Ps. 38. 4. as a *h.* burden too *h.* for
Prov. 31. 6. wine to those of *h.* hearts
Isa. 6. 10. make their ears *h.* lest
58. 6. to undo the *h.* burden
Matt. 11. 28. labor and are *h.* laden
23. 4. bind *h.* burdens and griev.
Ps. 69. 20. I am full of *heaviness*
119. 28. my soul melteth for *h.*
Prov. 12. 25. *h.* in the heart
14. 13. the end of that mirth is *h.*
Rom. 9. 2. I have great *h.* and
1 Pet. 1. 6. in *h.* through
R. V. Ezra 9. 5. humiliation; Job 9. 27. sad countenance; Isa. 29. 2. mourning; 2 Cor. 2. 1. with sorrow; Phil. 2. 26. sore troubled; 1 Pet. 1. 6. have been put to grief; Prov. 31. 6. bitter; Isa. 30. 27. rising smoke; 46. 1. made a load; 58. 6. bands of the yoke; Matt. 26. 37; Mark 14. 33. troubled

HEDGE, Job 1. 10. Prov. 15. 19. Isa. 5. 5. Hos. 2. 6. Job 3. 23. Lam. 3. 7.
R. V. 1 Chron. 4. 23. Gederah; Ps. 80. 12; Eccl. 10. 8; Jer. 49. 3. fences; Lam. 3. 7. fenced; Matt. 21. 33. set a hedge about

HEED, 2 Sam. 20. 10. 2 Kings 10. 31.
Deut. 2. 4. take good *h.* to yoursel.
Josh. 22. 5. take diligent *h.* to do
Ps. 119. 9. by taking *h.* thereto
Eccl. 12. 9. he gave good *h.* sought
Jer. 18. 18. not give *h.* to any of his
R. V. Deut. 27. 9. silence; 2 Chron. 19. 6. consider; 33. 8. observe; Eccl. 12. 9. pondered; Matt. 18. 10. see; Luke 11. 35. look; Acts 8. 11. regard; 22. 26; Rom. 11. 21 —

HEEL, his, thou shalt bruise
Ps. 41. 9. lifted up his *h.* against
Hos. 12. 3. he took his brother by *h.*

HEIFER, Num. 19. 2. Jer. 46. 20. & 48. 34. Hos. 4. 16. & 10. 11. Heb. 9. 13.

HEIR, Gen. 15. 4. & 21. 10.
Prov. 30. 23. handmaid *h.* to her
Jer. 49. 1. hath Israel no sons, hath he no *h.*
Matt. 21. 38. this is the *h.* let us
Rom. 4. 13. Abraham should be *h.*
8. 17. if children, *h.* of God, joint *h.* with Christ
Gal. 3. 29. children *h.* according
4. 7. if a son, then an *h.* of God
Eph. 3. 6. Gentiles should be fellow *h.*
Heb. 1. 2. God hath appointed *h.* of
6. 17. might show to *h.* of promise
21. 7. became *h.* of righteousness
1 Pet. 3. 7. *h.* together of grace of
R. V. Jer. 49. 2; Mic. 1. 15. possess; Gal. 4. 30. inherit

HELD, Ps. 94. 18. S. of S. 3. 4.

HELL, Matt. 18. 9. Mark 9. 43, 45.
Deut. 32. 22. shall burn to lowest *h.*
2 Sam. 22. 6. the sorrows of *h.*
Job 11. 8. it is deeper than *h.*
26. 6. *h.* is naked before him and
Ps. 9. 17. wicked be turned into *h.*
16. 10. not leave my soul in *h.*
116. 3. pains of *h.* gat hold on me
139. 8. make my bed in *h.* thou art
Prov. 5. 5. her steps take hold of *h.*
7. 27. her house is the way to *h.*
9. 18. her guests are in depths of *h.*
15. 11. *h.* and destruction are
24. that he may depart from *h.*
23. 14. shalt deliver his soul from *h.*
27. 20. *h.* and destruction are
Isa. 5. 14. *h.* hath enlarged herself
14. 9. *h.* from beneath is moved to
28. 15. with *h.* are we at agree.
57. 9. debase thyself even to *h.*, Ezek. 31. 16, 17. & 32. 21, 27.
Amos 9. 2. though they dig into *h.*
Jonah 2. 2. out of belly of *h.* cried I
Hab. 2. 5. enlarged his desire as *h.*
Matt. 5. 22. be in danger of *h.* fire
29. body be cast into *h.*, 30. & 18. 9. Mark 9. 43, 45, 47.
10. 28. destroy both soul and body in *h.*
11. 23. brought down to *h.*, Luke 10. 15.
16. 18. the gates of *h.* shall not
23. 15. twofold more the child of *h.*
Luke 12. 5. power to cast into *h.*
16. 23. in *h.* he lifted up his eyes
Acts 2. 31. his soul not left in *h.*, 27.
Jas. 3. 6. tongue set on fire of *h.*
2 Pet. 2. 4. cast them down to *h.*
Rev. 1. 18. having keys of *h.* and
6. 8. death and *h.* followed with
20. 13. death and *h.* delivered up
14. death and *h.* were cast into
R. V. 2 Sam. 22. 6; Job 11. 8; 26. 6; Ps. 16. 10; 18. 5; 116. 3; 139. 8; Prov. 5. 5; 7. 27; 9. 18; 15. 11, 24; 23. 14; 27. 30. Sheol; Matt. 11. 23; 16. 18; Luke 10. 15; 16. 23; Acts 2. 27, 31; Rev. 1. 18; 6. 8; 20. 13, 14. Hades; Matt. 5. 22; 18. 9. hell of fire

HELMET, 1 Sam. 17. 5. 2 Chron. 26. 14.
Isa. 59. 17. a *h.* of salvation on head
Eph. 6. 17. take the *h.* of salvation
1 Thes. 5. 8. for a *h.* the hope of sal.

HELP meet for him, Gen. 2. 18.
Deut. 33. 29. Lord shield of thy *h.*
Judg. 5. 23. came not to the *h.* of
Ps. 27. 9. thou hast been my *h.*
33. 20. he is our *h.* and shield
40. 17. my *h.* and deliverer, 70. 5.
46. 1. God is a very present *h.* in trouble
60. 11. vain is *h.* of man, 108. 12.
71. 12. O my God, make haste for my *h.*
89. 19. laid *h.* upon one that is
115. 9. Lord is their *h.* and shield, 10. 11.
124. 8. our *h.* is in name of Lord
Hos. 13. 9. but in me is thy *h.*
Acts 26. 22. having obtained *h.* of God
1 Cor. 12. 28. *helps*, governments
2 Chron. 14. 11. nothing with thee to *h.*
Ps. 40. 13. make haste to *h.* me, 70. 1.
Isa. 41. 10. I will *h.* thee
63. 5. there was none to *h.*
Acts 16. 9. come unto Macedonia, and *h.* us
Heb. 4. 16. find grace to *h.* in time
1 Sam. 7. 12. hitherto hath the Lord *helped* us
Ps. 118. 13. I might fall; but Lord *h.* me
Isa. 49. 8. in day of salvation I *h.*
Zech. 1. 15. they *h.* forward afflicted
Acts 18. 27. *h.* them much who had
Rev. 12. 16. the earth *h.* the woman
Rom. 8. 26. Spirit *helpeth* our infirmities
Ps. 10. 14. thou art the *helper*
54. 4. God is my *h.*, Heb. 13. 6.
Job 9. 13. proud *helpers* do stoop
2 Cor. 1. 24. we are *h.* of your joy
3 John 8. fellow *h.* to the truth
R. V. 1 Sam. 11. 9. deliverance; 1 Chron. 18. 5. succor; 2 Chron. 20. 9. save; Job 8. 20. uphold; Ps. 116. 6. saved; Eccl. 4. 10. lift

HEM, Matt. 9. 20. & 14. 36.
R. V. Ex. 28. 33, 34; 39. 24, 25, 26. skirts; Matt. 9. 20; 14. 36. border

HEN, Matt. 23. 37. Luke 13. 34.

HERESY, Acts 24. 14. 1 Cor. 11. 19. Gal. 5. 20. 2 Pet. 2. 1.
Tit. 3. 10. a man that is a *heretic*
R. V. Acts 24. 14. a sect

HERITAGE appointed by God, Job 20. 29.
Ps. 16. 5. I have a goodly *h.*
61. 5. given me the *h.* of those
127. 3. lo, children are a *h.* of Lord
Isa. 54. 17. this is *h.* of servants
Jer. 3. 19. goodly *h.* of the host
Joel 2. 17. give not thy *h.* to rep.
1 Pet. 5. 3. not as lords over God's *h.*
R. V. 1 Pet. 5. 3. charge allotted

HEW tables of stone, Ex. 34. 1. Deut. 12. 3.
Jer. 2. 13. *hewed* them out cisterns
Hos. 6. 5. therefore have I *h.* them
Matt. 3. 10. *hewn* down, 7. 19.
R. V. 1 Kings 5. 18. fashion; 1 Sam. 11. 7. cut

HID themselves, Adam and wife, Gen. 3. 8.
Ps. 119. 11. word have I *h.* in heart
Zeph. 2. 3. it may be, ye shall be *h.*
Matt. 10. 26. nor *h.* that shall not be
11. 25. *h.* these things from wise
2 Cor. 4. 3. if Gospel be *h.* it is *h.*

Col. 2. 3. in whom are *h.* all treas.
3. 3. your life is *h.* with Christ
Ps. 83. 3. and consulted against thy *hidden* ones
1 Cor. 4. 5. bring to light *h.* things of
1 Pet. 3. 4. the *h.* man of heart
Rev. 2. 17. give to eat the *h.* manna
Gen. 18. 17. shall I *hide* from Abra.
Job 33. 17. may *h.* pride from man
Ps. 17. 8. *h.* me under the shadow
27. 5. in time of trouble he shall *h.*
30. 7. didst *h.* thy face and I
31. 20. shalt *h.* them in secret
Ps. 51. 9. *h.* thy face from my sin
143. 9. I flee to thee to *h.* me, 7.
Isa. 26. 20. *h.* thyself for a moment
Jas. 5. 20. *h.* a multitude of sins
Rev. 6. 16. *h.* us from the face of
Job 13. 24. why *hidest* thou thy face, Ps. 30. 7. & 44. 24. & 88. 14. & 143. 7.
Isa. 45. 15. thou art a God that *h.*
Job 34. 29. when he *hideth* his face
42. 3. who is he that *h.* counsel
Ps. 139. 12. darkness *h.* not from
Isa. 8. 17. I will wait on Lord that *h.*
Hab. 3. 4. *hiding* of his power
Ps. 32. 7. *h.* place, 119. 114.
R. V. Deut. 30. 11. too hard for; Job 15. 20; 20. 26; 24. 1; Prov. 2. 1. laid up; Prov. 19. 24; 26. 15. burieth; 27. 16. restraineth; Jer. 16. 17; Luke 9. 45. concealed; Luke 8. 17. secret; 2 Cor. 4. 3, 13. is veiled; Jas. 5. 20. cover

HID TREASURE, parable, Matt. 13. 44.

HIGH, Deut. 3. 5, 12. & 28. 43.
Deut. 26. 19. make thee *h.* above all
1 Kings 9. 8. house which is *h.*
1 Chron. 17. 17. man of *h.* degree
Job 11. 8. as *h.* as heaven, what
Ps. 49. 2. both low and *h.* rich and
89. 13. strong arm, and *h.* is right
97. 9. thou Lord art *h.* above all
103. 11. as heaven is *h.* above earth
131. 1. not in things too *h.* for me
Prov. 21. 4. a *h.* look and proud
Eccl. 12. 5. afraid of that which is *h.*
Isa. 57. 15. I dwell in the *h.* and
Ezek. 21. 26. abase him that is *h.*
Rom. 12. 16. mind not *h.* things
2 Cor. 10. 5. every *h.* thing that
Phil. 3. 14. for the prize of the *h.* calling of God
Num. 24. 16. *Most High*, Deut. 32. 8. 2 Sam. 22. 14. Ps. 7. 17. & 9. 2. & 21. 7. & 46. 4. & 50. 14. & 56. 2.
Ps. 47. 2. the Lord — is terrible
83. 18. Jehovah art — over all earth
92. 8. thou art — for evermore
Isa. 14. 14. I will ascend and be like the —
Acts 7. 48. — dwelleth not in temples
Job 5. 11. set up *on high* those that
Ps. 107. 41. setteth the poor — from
113. 5. like our God who dwelleth —
Isa. 26. 5. bring down those that dwell —
Luke 24. 49. be endued with power from —
Eccl. 5. 8. there be *higher* than they
Isa. 55. 9. heaven *h.* than earth
Heb. 7. 26. made *h.* than the heavens
Ps. 18. 13. *Highest* gave his voice
87. 5. *H.* himself shall establish
Eccl. 5. 8. he that is higher than *h.*
Luke 1. 35. power of the *H.* shall
2. 14. glory to God in the *h.*, 19. 38.
6. 35. children of the *H.*
14. 8. sit not down in the *h.* room
1. 28. thou that art *highly* favored
16. 15. which is *h.* esteemed
Rom. 12. 3. not think of himself more *h.*
1 Thes. 5. 13. esteem them very *h.*
2 Tim. 3. 4. heady, *high-minded*
Rom. 11. 20. be not — but fear
1 Tim. 6. 17. rich, that they be not—
Job 22. 12. *height*, Rom. 8. 39. Eph. 3. 18.
R. V. 2 Tim. 3. 4. puffed up

HILL, Ex. 24. 4. Ps. 68. 15, 16.
Ps. 2. 6. set my King on holy *h.* of Zion, 3. 4. & 15. 1. & 43. 3. & 68. 15. & 99. 9.
Gen. 7. 19. all high *h.* under heaven
Num. 23. 9. from the *h.* I behold
Ps. 65. 12. little *h.* rejoice on every
68. 16. why leap ye, high *h.*
98. 8. let *h.* be joyful together
Hos. 10. 8. to the *h.* fall on us, Luke 23. 30.
Hab. 3. 6. the perpetual *h.* did bow
R. V. Ex. 24. 4; 1 Kings 11. 7. mount; Gen. 7. 19; Num. 14. 44, 45; Deut. 1. 41, 43; Josh. 15. 9; 18. 13, 14; 24. 30; Judg. 2. 9; 16. 3; 1 Sam. 25. 20; 26. 13; 2 Sam. 21. 9; 1 Kings 22. 17; Ps. 18. 7; 68. 15, 16; 80. 10; 95. 4; 97. 5; 104. 10, 13, 18, 32; 121. 1; Luke 9. 37. mountain, or mountains; Deut. 1. 7; Josh. 9. 1; 11. 16; 17. 6. hill country; 1 Sam. 9. 11; 2 Sam. 16. 1. ascent; Acts 17. 22. the Areopagus

HIND, 2 Sam. 22. 34. Ps. 29. 9. Prov. 5. 19. S. of S. 2. 7. & 3. 5. Hab. 3. 19.

HIRE, Deut. 24. 15. Isa. 23. 18. Mic. 1. 7. & 3. 11. Luke 10. 7. Jas. 5. 4.
Job 7. 1. a *hireling*, John 10. 12, 13.
R. V. Gen. 31. 8. wages

HITHERTO Lord helped us, 1 Sam. 7. 12.
Job 38. 11. *h.* shalt thou come, but
John 16. 24. *h.* ye asked nothing
1 Cor. 3. 2. *h.* ye were not able to
R. V. 1 Sam. 7. 18; 1 Chron. 17. 16. thus far; 2 Sam. 15. 34. in time past; Isa. 18. 2, 7. onward; Dan. 7. 28. here; John 5. 17. even until now; 1 Cor. 3. 2. yet

HOLD, Gen. 21. 18. Ex. 9. 2. & 20. 7.
Judg. 9. 46. a *h.* of the house
Job 17. 9. righteous shall *h.* on way
Isa. 41. 13. God will *h.* thy right
62. 1. for Zion's sake will I not *h.*
Jer. 2. 13. cisterns that can *h.* no
Matt. 6. 24. *h.* to one and despise the
Rom. 1. 18. *h.* truth in unrighteous.
Phil. 2. 29. *h.* such in reputation
Heb. 3. 14. if we *h.* beginning of
1 Thes. 5. 21. prove all, *hold fast* that which is good
2 Tim. 1. 13. — form of sound words
Heb. 3. 6. if we — the confidence of hope
Heb. 4. 14. let us — our profession
Rev. 2. 25. what ye have — till I
3. 11. — that thou hast that no man
Ps. 77. 4. *holdest* my eyes waking
Rev. 2. 13. *h.* fast my name and
Job 2. 3. still he *holdeth* fast
Ps. 66. 9. which *h.* our soul in life
Prov. 17. 28. a fool, when he *h.*
Jer. 6. 11. I am weary with *holding*
Phil. 2. 16. *h.* forth the word of life
Col. 2. 19. not *h.* the head, from
1 Tim. 1. 19. *h.* faith and a good
3. 9. *h.* mystery of faith in
Tit. 1. 9. *h.* fast the faithful word
R. V. Jer. 51. 30. strongholds; Dan. 11. 39; Nah. 3. 12, 14. fortresses; Acts. 4. 3. ward
The R. V. changes are based on words before and after *hold*

HOLY ground, Ex. 3. 5.
Ex. 16. 23. *h.* sabbath, & 31. 14, 15.
19. 6. *h.* nation, 1 Pet. 2. 9.
29. 6. *h.* crown; 30. 25. *h.* ointment
Lev. 16. 33. *h.* sanctuary
27. 14. house to be *h.*; 30. *h.* tithes
Num. 5. 17. *h.* water; 31. 6. *h.* instruments
Lev. 11. 45. be ye *h.* for I am *h.*, 20. 7.
1 Sam. 2. 2. there is none *h.* as Lord
21. 5. vessels of young men are *h.*
Ps. 22. 3. thou art *h.* that inhabitest
99. 5. worship at his footstool, for he is *h.*
145. 17. Lord is *h.* in all his works
Prov. 20. 25. a snare to devour that which is *h.*
Isa. 6. 3. *h. h. h.* Lord God of hosts
Ezek. 22. 26. difference between *h.*
Matt. 7. 6. give not that which is *h.*
Luke 1. 35. *h.* thing which shall be
Acts 4. 27. thy *h.* child Jesus, 30.
Rom. 7. 12. law *h.* commandment *h.*
12. 1. sacrifice *h.* acceptable to God
1 Cor. 7. 14. children unclean, but now *h.*
Eph. 1. 4. be *h.* and without blame
2 Tim. 1. 9. called us with *h.* calling
3. 15. hast known the *h.* Scriptures
Tit. 1. 8. sober, just, *h.*, temperate
1 Pet. 1. 15. be ye *h.* in all manner
2. 5. a *h.* priesthood, 9. *h.* nation
2 Pet. 1. 21. *h.* men of God spake as
3. 11. *h.* in all conversation and
Rev. 3. 7. saith he that is *h.* and
4. 8. *h. h. h.* Lord God Almighty
15. 4. fear thee for thou only art *h.*
20. 6. blessed and *h.* is he that hath
22. 11. he that is *h.* let him be *h.*
Ex. 26. 33. *most holy place*, 34. & 29. 37. & 40. 10. 1 Kings 6. 16. & 7. 50. & 8. 6. Ezek. 44. 13. & 45. 3.
Lev. 6. 25. *most holy offering*, 7. 1, 6. & 10. 17. & 14. 13. Num. 18. 9, 10. Ezek. 48. 12.
21. 22. bread of his God most *h.*
27. 28. *most holy things*, Num. 4. 4, 19. 1 Chron. 6. 49. & 23. 13. 2 Chron. 31. 14.
Ezek. 43. 12. the whole limit shall be most *h.*
Jude 20. building up on your most *h.* faith
Ps. 42. 4. with multitude that kept *holy day*, Isa. 58. 13. Col. 2. 16. Ex. 25. 2.
Matt. 1. 18. with child of *Holy Ghost*
20. that is conceived in her is of —
3. 11. baptize you —, Mark 1. 8. John 1. 33. Acts 1. 5. & 11. 16.
12. 31. blasphemy against —, 32. Mark 3. 29.
Mark 12. 36. David said by —, Acts 1. 16.
13. 11. not ye that speak, but the —
Luke 1. 35. — shall come upon thee
2. 15 — was upon him
3. 22. — descended in bodily shape
12. 12. — shall teach you in that same
John 7. 39. for — was not yet given
14. 26. Comforter which is — whom
20. 22. receive ye the —
Acts 1. 2. though — had given
8. after that the — is come upon
2. 33. receive promise of the —
38. receive gift of —, 10. 45.
7. 51. ye do always resist the —
8. 15. receive —, 19.
18. — given
9. 31. walking in the fear of Lord and in the comfort of the —
10. 38. anointed Jesus with the —
44. — fell on all them, 11. 15.
47. received the —, 8. 17.
19. 2. be any —, 6.
13. 2. the — said, separate me Saul
4. they being sent forth by the —
15. 28. it seemed good to — and us
16. 6. forbidden of — to preach in
20. 23. save that — witnesseth
21. 11. thus saith — so shall the Jews
28. 25. well spake the — by Esaias
Rom. 5. 5. love of God shed abroad by —
14. 17. righteousness, peace, and joy in —
15. 13. abound in hope through power of —
16. offering of Gentiles sanctified by —
1 Cor. 2. 13. in words which the — teacheth
6. 19. temple of — which is in you
12. 3. can say Jesus is Lord but by the —
2 Cor. 6. 6. by — by love unfeigned
13. 14. communion of — be with you
1 Thes. 1. 5. in — much assurance
2 Tim. 1. 14. keep by — which dwell.
Tit. 3. 5. not by works, but by the renewing of —
Heb. 2. 4. miracles and gifts of —

Heb. 3. 7. wherefore, as — saith
6. 4. made partakers of —
9. 8.—this signifying that the way
10. 15. whereof — is a witness to
1 Pet. 1. 12. preach unto you—sent
2 Pet. 1. 21. holy men of God moved by —
1 John 5. 7. Father, Word, and — are
Jude 20. building up . . praying in —
Luke 1. 15. *filled with*, or *full of the Holy Ghost*, 41. 67. Acts 2. 4. & 4. 8. & 6. 3, 5. & 9. 17. & 11. 24. & 13. 9, 52.
Ps. 51. 11. take not thy *Holy Spirit* from me
Isa. 63. 10. rebell. and vexed his —
Luke 11. 13. give — to them that
Eph. 1. 13. ye were sealed with — of promise
4. 30. grieve not the — of God
Ps. 87. 1. *holy mountain*, Isa. 11. 9. & 56. 6. & 57. 13. & 65. 11, 25. & 66. 20. Dan. 9. 16. & 11. 45. Joel 2. 1. & 3. 17. Obad. 16. Zeph. 3. 11. Zech. 8. 3.
Lev. 20. 3. *holy name*, & 22. 2, 33. 1 Chron. 16. 10, 35. Ps. 33. 21. & 103. 1. & 111. 9. & 145. 21. Isa. 57. 15. Ezek. 36. 20, 21.
Deut. 33. 8. *Holy One*, Job 6. 10. Ps. 16. 10. & 89. 19. Isa. 10. 17. & 29. 23. & 40. 25. & 43. 15. & 49. 7. Hab. 1. 12. & 3. 3. Mark 1. 24. Acts 3. 14. & 4. 27, 30. 1 John 2. 20.
2 Kings 19. 22. *Holy One of Israel*, Ps. 71. 22. & 78. 41. & 89. 18. Isa. 1. 4. & 5. 19, 24. & 10. 20. & 12. 6. & 17. 7. & 29. 19. & 30. 11, 12. & 31. 1. & 41. 14. & 45. 11. & 47. 4. & 49. 7. & 55. 5. & 60. 9, 14. Jer. 50. 29. & 51. 5.
Deut. 7. 6. *holy people*, 14. 2, 21. & 26. 19. & 28. 9. Isa. 62. 12. Dan. 8. 24. & 12. 7.
Ex. 28. 29. *holy place*, Lev. 6. 16. & 10. 17. Eccl. 8. 10. and about thirty other texts
Ps. 5. 7. *holy temple*, 11. 4. & 65. 4. & 79. 1. & 138. 2. Jonah 2. 4. Mic. 1. 2. Hab. 2. 20. Eph. 2. 21.
Isa. 65. 5. I am *holier* than thou
Heb. 9. 3. the *holiest* of all, 8.
1 Thes. 2. 10. how *holily* and justly
Ex. 15. 11. glorious in *holiness*
28. 36. *h.* to Lord, 39. 30. Isa. 23. 18.
1 Chron. 16. 29. in beauty of *h.*, Ps. 29. 2. & 96. 9. & 110. 3. 2 Chron. 20. 21.
2 Chron. 31. 18. sanctified themselves in *h.*
Ps. 30. 4. at remembrance of his *h.*
47. 8. God sits on throne of his *h.*
48. 1. in mountain of his *h.*
89. 35. I have sworn by my *h.*
93. 5. *h.* becometh thy house
Isa. 23. 18. her hire shall be *h.* to
35. 8. it shall be called the way of *h.*
63. 15. habitation of thy *h.*
18. people of *h.*
Jer. 2. 3. Israel was *h.* to the Lord
Amos 4. 2. Lord hath sworn by his *h.*
Obad. 17. on mount Zion there shall be *h.*
Zech. 14. 20. on horse bells, *h.* to
Mal. 2. 11. Judah hath profaned *h.*
Luke 1. 75. in *h.* and righteousness
Acts 3. 12. as though by our own *h.*
Rom. 1. 4. Son of God according to the Spirit of *h.*
6. 19. yield members servants to righteousness unto *h.*
22. fruit unto *h* and end everlast.
2 Cor. 7. 1. perfecting *h.* in the fear
Eph. 4. 24. created in righteousness and true *h.*
1 Thes. 3. 13. unblameable in *h.*
4. 7. called not to uncleanness but to *h.*
1 Tim. 2. 15. in faith, love, *h.*
Tit. 2. 3. in behavi. as becometh *h.*
Heb. 12. 10. partakers of his *h.*
14. *h.* without which no man shall
R. V. Ex. 38. 24; Lev. 10. 17, 18; 14. 13; Ps. 68. 17; Ezek. 21. 2. sanctuary; Matt. 12. 31, 32; Mark 3. 29; Luke 2. 25, 26; John 1. 33; 7. 39; Acts 2. 4; 6. 5; 1 Cor. 2. 13. Holy Spirit

HOME, Gen. 39. 16. & 43. 16.
Ps. 68. 12. that tarried at *h.* divided
Eccl. 12. 5. man goeth to his long *h.*
2 Cor. 5. 6. while we are at *h.* in
Tit. 2. 5. obedient, keepers at *h.*
R. V. Gen. 43. 16; Josh. 2. 18; 1 Sam. 10. 26; Matt. 8. 6; Mark 5. 19. house; Luke 9. 61 ——; 1 Tim. 5. 4. family

HONEST and good heart, Luke 8. 15.
Acts 6. 3. men of *h.* report, full of
Rom. 12. 17. provide things *h.* in
2 Cor. 8. 21. providing for *h.* things
Phil. 4. 8. whatsoever things are *h.*
1 Pet. 2. 12. have your conversation *h.*
Rom. 13. 13. walk *honestly* as in day
1 Thes. 4. 12. walk *h.* towards them
Heb. 13. 18. in all things willing to live *h.*
1 Tim. 2. 2 in all godliness and *honesty*
R. V. Acts 6. 3. good; Rom. 12. 17; 1 Cor. 8. 21; 2 Cor. 13. 7; Phil. 4. 8. honorable; 1 Pet. 2. 12. behavior seemly

HONEY, Gen. 43. 11. Lev. 2. 11. Judg. 14. 8, 18. 1 Sam. 14. 26, 29.
Ps. 19. 10. sweeter than *h.* and
Prov. 25. 27. it is not good to eat much *h.*
S. of S. 4. 11. *h.* and milk are under
Isa. 7. 15. butter and *h.* shall he eat
Matt. 3. 4. his meat was locusts and wild *h.*
Rev. 10. 9. in mouth sweet as *h.*, 10.
1 Sam. 14. 27. dipt in *honeycomb*, Prov. 5. 3, 16, 24. & 24. 13. & 27. 7. S. of S. 4. 11. & 5. 1. Luke 24. 42.

HONOR, be not thou united
1 Chron. 29. 12. both riches and *h.*
Ps. 7. 5. lay mine *h.* in the dust
8. 5. crown. him with glory and *h.*
26. 8. place where thine *h.* dwell.
49. 12. man being in *h.* abideth not
20. man that is in *h.* and under.
Prov. 3. 16. in her left hand riches and *h.*
15. 33. before *h.* is humility
26. 1. *h.* is not seemly for a fool
29. 23. *h.* shall uphold the humble
Mal. 1. 6. if I be a father where is mine *h.*
Matt. 13. 57. prophet is not without *h.*
John 5. 41. I receive not *h.* from men
Rom. 2. 7. seek for glory and *h.* and immortality
12. 10. in *h.* preferring one another
13. 7. give *h.* to whom *h.* is due
2 Cor. 6. 8. by *h.* and dishonor
2 Tim. 2. 20. some to *h.* and some to
Heb. 5. 4. taketh this *h.* to himself
1 Pet. 1. 7. be found unto praise and *h.*
Ex. 20. 12. *h.* thy father and mother
1 Sam. 2. 30. that *h.* me I will *h.*
Prov. 3. 9. *h.* Lord with substance
Isa. 29. 13. with their lips do *h.* me
John 5. 23. should *h.* the Son as *h.*
12. 26. if any man serve me him will my Father *h.*
1 Pet. 2. 17. *h.* all men, love
Ps. 15. 4. he *honoreth* them that
Mal. 1. 6. a son *h.* his father
Matt. 15. 8. *h.* me with their lips
Heb. 13. 4. marriage is *honorable* in
R. V. Gen. 49. 6; Ps. 7. 5; 26. 8; 66. 2; Prov. 14. 28; 25. 2; Dan. 4. 30; John 5. 41, 44; 8. 54; 2 Cor. 6. 8. glory; Ps. 31. 25. dignity; Dan. 4. 36. majesty; Rev. 19. 1; 21. 24 ——; John 8. 54. glorify

HOOF, Ex. 10. 26. Lev. 11. 3-7.

HOOK, Ex. 26. 32. Ezek. 29. 4. & 38. 4.
Isa. 2. 4. *pruning hooks*, 18. 5. Mic. 4. 3.
R. V. Job 41. 1. fishhook; 2. rope

HOPE in Israel concerning this, Ezra 10. 2.
Job 8. 13. hypocrite's *h.* shall perish
27. 8. what is the *h.* of hypocrite
Ps. 78. 7. might set their *h.* in God
146. 5. whose *h.* is in Lord his God
Prov. 10. 28. *h.* of righteous shall
11. 7. the *h.* of unjust men perish.
14. 32. righteous hath *h.* in death
19. 18. chasten thy son while there is *h.*
Isa. 57. 10. saidst thou there is no *h.*, Jer. 2. 25. & 18. 12. Ezek. 37. 11.
Jer. 14. 8. O the *h.* of Israel, 17. 13. & 50. 7.
17. 7. blessed is the man that trusteth in the Lord, and whose *h.* the Lord is
Lam. 3. 29. if so be there may be *h.*
Hos. 2. 15 valley of Achor for door of *h.*
Joel 3. 16. Lord will be the *h.* of
Zech. 9. 12. turn to the strong hold ye prisoners of *h.*
Acts 24. 15. have *h.* towards God
Rom. 5. 4. experience *h.*
5. *h.* maketh not ashamed
8. 24. we are saved by *h.* but *h.* that is seen is not *h.*
15. 4. comfort of Scriptures, might have *h.*
1 Cor. 9. 10. husbandman partaker of his *h.*
13. 13. now abideth faith, *h.* and
15. 19. if in this life only, *h.*
Gal. 5. 5. wait for *h.* of righteous.
Eph. 2. 12. having no *h.* and with.
Col. 1. 23. not moved away from *h.*
1 Thes. 4. 13. sorrow not as others that have no *h.*
5. 8. for a helmet, the *h.* of salva.
1 Tim. 1. 1. Jesus Christ who is our *h.*
Tit. 2. 13. looking for that blessed *h.*
3. 7. according to the *h.* of eternal
Heb. 6. 11. to the full assurance of *h.*
19. which *h.* we have as an anchor
1 Pet. 1. 3. begotten us again to a lively *h.*
21. that your faith and *h.* might be
3. 15. asketh a reason of *h.* in you
1 John 3. 3. man that has his *h.* in
Ps. 16. 9. my flesh also shall rest *in hope*
Rom. 4. 18, against *h.* believed —
5. 2. rejoice — of glory of God, 12. 12.
Tit. 1. 2. — eternal life of which
Ps. 39. 7. *my hope* is in thee
71. 5. thou art —, Jer. 17. 17.
22. 9. didst make me *hope* when I
42. 5. *h.* thou in God, for, 11.
119. 49. thou hast caused me to *h.*
81. I *h.* in thy word, 114.
130. 7. let Israel *h.* in the Lord
147. 11. those that *h.* in his mercy
Lam. 3. 26. good that man should *h.*
Rom. 8. 25. if we *h.* for that we see
1 Pet. 1. 13. be sober and *h.* to end
Ps. 119. 43. I have *hoped* in thy
74. I have *h.* in thy word, 147.
166. I have *h.* in thy salvation
Heb. 11. 1. faith is the substance of things *h.* for
1 Cor. 13. 7. charity *hopeth* all
Luke 6. 35. lend, *hoping* for nothing
R. V. Job 8. 14. confidence; Ps. 16. 9. safety; Jer. 17. 17. refuge; Lam. 3. 18. expectation; Jer. 3. 23. look.

HORN of my salvation, Ps. 18. 2.
Ps. 75. 4. lift not up the *h.*, 5. 10.
92. 10. my *h.* shalt thou exalt as the *h.* of the unicorn
148. 14. he exalted the *h.* of his
Luke 1. 69. raised up *h.* of salva.
Mic. 4. 13. I will make thy *h.* iron
Dan. 8. 20. having two *horns*
Hab. 3. 4. *h.* coming out of his hand
Rev. 13. 1. beast having ten *h.*

Rev. 13. 11. had two *h.* like a lamb
5. 6. lamb having seven *h.*
R. V Ex. 21. 29 —— ; Hab. 3. 4. rays
HORRIBLE, Ps. 11. 6. & 40. 2. Jer.
5. 30. & 18. 13. & 23. 14. Hos. 6. 10.
Jer. 2. 12. Ezek. 32. 10.
R. V. Ps. 11. 6. burning
HORROR, Gen. 15. 12. Job 18. 20.
Ps. 55. 5. & 119. 53. Ezek. 7. 18.
R. V. Ps. 119. 53. hot indignation
HORSE and rider thrown, Ex.
15. 21.
Ps. 32. 9. be ye not as *h.* or mule
33. 17. *h.* is a vain thing for safety
Prov. 21. 31. *h.* is prepared for the
Eccl. 10. 7. I have seen serv. on *h.*
Jer. 8. 6. as *h.* rusheth into battle
12. 5. canst thou contend with *h.*
Hos. 14. 3. we will not ride upon *h.*
Zech. 1. 8. & 6. 2, 3, 6. *h.* red, white,
black, Rev. 6. 2, 4, 5, 8. & 9. 17.
Rev. 6. 2. and behold a white *h.*
HOSPITALITY, Rom. 12. 13.
1 Tim. 3. 2. Tit. 1. 8. 1 Pet. 4. 9.
HOST, Luke 10. 35. Rom. 16. 23.
Ps. 27. 3. & 33. 16. & 103. 21. & 108.
11. & 148. 2. Isa. 40. 26. Luke 2. 13.
Ps. 103. 21. Jer. 3. 19.
R. V. Ex. 16. 13; Deut. 2. 14, 15;
Josh. 1. 11; 3. 2; 18. 9; Judg. 7.
8, 10, 13, 15; 1 Sam. 11. 11; 14. 15,
19; 1 Chron. 9. 19. camp; 2 Kings
18. 17; 25. 1; 2 Chron. 14. 9; 24.
23; 26. 11. army
HOT, Ps. 38. 1. & 39. 3. Prov. 6. 28.
Hos. 7. 7. 1 Tim. 4. 2. Rev. 3. 15.
R. V. Judg. 2. 14; 3. 8; 6. 39; 10. 7.
kindled
HOUR, Dan. 3. 6, 15. & 4. 33.
Matt. 10. 19. shall be given you in
the same *h.*
24. 36. of that day and *h.* knoweth
25. 13. ye know neither day nor *h.*
Luke 12. 12. Holy Ghost shall teach
you that same *h.*
22. 53. this is your *h.* and power
of darkness
John 2. 4. my *h.* is not yet come
4. 23. the *h.* cometh and now is
12. 27. save me from this *h.*
Rev. 3. 3. not know what *h.* I come
10. will keep thee from the *h.* of
17. 12. power as kings one *h.* with
18. 10. in one *h.* is thy judgment
R. V. Matt. 24. 42. on what day;
1 Cor. 8. 7. until now
HOUSE, Ex. 20. 17. Lev. 14. 36.
Ex. 12. 30. not a *h.* where not one
Job 21. 28. where is the *h.* of prince
30. 23. *h.* appointed for all living
Prov. 3. 33. curse of the Lord is in
h.
12. 7. *h.* of righteous shall stand
19. 14. *h.* and riches are inherit.
Eccl. 7. 2. go to the *h.* of mourn.
12. 3. when keepers of *h.* treming
ble
S. of S. 2. 4. brought me to the
banqueting *h.*
Isa. 5. 8. woe to them that join *h.*
to *h.*
60. 7. I will glorify the *h.* of my
64. 11. our holy and beautiful *h.*
Matt. 10. 13. *h.* worthy
23. 38. *h.* left desolate, Luke
11. 17.
Luke 12. 3. proclaimed on *h.* tops
John 14. 2. in my father's *h.* are
Rom. 16. 5. church in their *h.*,
1 Cor. 16. 19. Col. 4. 15. Phile. 2.
2 Cor. 5. 1. earthly *h.* . . *h.* of God
not made with hands
2 Tim. 1. 16. give mercy to the *h.*
Heb. 3. 3. built *h.* hath more honor
than the *h.*
2 John 10. receive him not into *h.*
Ps. 105. 21. made him Lord of all
his house
112. 3. wealth and riches shall be
in —
Acts 10. 2. feared God with all —
16. 34. believed in God with all —
Heb. 3. 2. faithful in all —, 5. 6.
John 4. 53. his *whole house* believed
1 Tim. 5. 8. especially for those of
his own *h.*
Josh. 24. 15. as for me and *my
house*
2 Sam. 23. 5. though — be not so
Ps. 101. 2. will walk within — with
Isa. 56. 7. joyful in — of prayer,
Matt. 21. 13. Mark 11. 7. Luke 19.
46.
Matt. 12. 44. will return to —, Luke
11. 24.
Acts 16. 15. judged me faithful,
come into —
Deut. 6. 7. when sittest in *thy
house*
Ps. 26. 8. I loved habitation of —
Isa. 38. 1. set — in order, for thou
Acts 11. 14. thou and all — saved,
16. 31.
Gen. 28. 17. *house of God* or Lord,
Ps. 42. 4. & 55. 14. & 23. 6. & 27. 4.
Eccl. 5. 1. Isa. 2. 3. Mic. 4. 2.
1 Tim. 3. 15. 1 Pet. 4. 17. Ex. 23.
19. Josh. 6. 24. and about one hun-
dred other places
Job 4. 19. dwell in *houses* of clay
Ps. 49. 11. *h.* shall continue for
Matt. 11. 8. in soft linen sit in
kings' *h.*
19. 29. forsaken *h.* or lands
23. 14. devour widows' *h.*
Luke 16. 4. may receive me into *h.*
1 Cor. 11. 22. have ye not *h.* to eat
1 Tim. 3. 12. ruling their own *h.*
2 Tim. 3. 6. creep into *h.* and lead
Tit. 1. 11. subvert whole *h.* teach.
Acts 16. 15. baptized and her whole
household
Gal. 6. 10. *h.* of faith
Eph. 2. 19. *h.* of God
Matt. 13. 52. like *householder*, 20. 1.
R. V. Ex. 12. 3; 2 Kings 7. 11; 10.
5, 12; 15. 5; Isa. 36. 3; 1 Cor. 1. 11;
1 Tim. 5. 14. household; 2 Cor.
5. 2. habitation; Deut. 6. 22;
1 Sam. 25. 17; 2 Sam. 6. 11; 17. 23;
1 Kings 11. 20; 2 Tim. 4. 19. house
HOW long, Ps. 6. 3. & 13. 1. & 74. 9.
& 79. 5. & 80. 4. & 89. 46. Isa. 6. 11.
Jer. 4. 14. Dan. 8. 13. & 12. 6. Matt.
17. 17. Luke 9. 41. Rev. 6. 10.
Job 15. 16. *how much more*, Prov.
21. 27. Matt. 7. 11. Luke 12. 24, 28.
Heb. 9. 14.
Matt. 18. 21. & 23. 37. *how oft*, Luke
13. 34. Job 21. 17. Ps. 78. 40.
HOWL, Isa. 13. 6. & 14. 31. Jer. 4.
8. Joel 1. 5, 11, 13. Jas. 5. 1. Hos.
7. 14. Deut. 32. 10. Amos 8. 3.
HUMBLE person shall save, Job
22. 29.
Ps. 9. 12. forgett. not the cry of *h.*
10. 12. forget not the *h.*
17. desire of the *h.*
34. 2. *h.* shall hear of it, and be
69. 32. *h.* shall see this, and be
Prov. 16. 19. to be of an *h.* spirit
29. 23. honor shall uphold *h.* in
Isa. 57. 15. of contrite and *h.* spirit
Jas. 4. 6. giveth grace to the *h.*
Ex. 10. 3. thou refuse to *h.* thyself
Deut. 8. 2. to *h.* thee, and to prove
2 Chron. 7. 14. shall *h.* themselves
34. 27. because didst *h.* thyself
Prov. 6. 3. . . . thyself, and make
Jer. 13. 18. *h.* yourselves, sit down
Matt. 18. 4. whoso *h.* himself shall
2 Cor. 12. 21. my God will *h.* me
Jas. 4. 10. *h.* yourselves in sight
1 Pet. 5. 6. *h.* yourselves therefore
Lev. 26. 41. if uncircumcised
hearts be *humbled*
2 Kings 22. 19. hast *h.* thyself
2 Chron. 12. 6. princes and kings
h. themselves
33. 12, 23. *h.* not himself before
the Lord, 36. 12.
Ps. 35. 13. I *h.* my soul with fasting
113. 6. Lord who *h.* himself to
Isa. 2. 11. lofty looks shall be *h.*
10. 33. high and haughty shall be *h.*
Jer. 44. 10. are not *h.* unto this day
Lam. 3. 20. my soul is *h.* in me
Dan. 5. 22. hast not *h.* thy heart
Phil. 2. 8. *h.* himself and became
Deut. 21. 14. *humbled her*, 22. 24, 29.
Ezek. 22. 10, 11.
Col. 3. 12. put on *humbleness* of
Mic. 6. 8. walk *humbly* with thy
God
Prov. 22. 4. by *humility* are riches
Acts 20. 19. serv. Lord with all *h.*
Col. 2. 18. in a voluntary *h.*, 23.
1 Pet. 5. 5. be clothed with *h.*
R. V. Ps. 9. 12; 10. 12. poor; Ps.
10. 17; 34. 2; 69. 32; Prov. 16. 19;
29. 23. lowly; Ps. 35. 13. afflicted;
Isa. 2. 11; 10. 33. brought low;
Lam. 3. 20. brought down; 2 Sam.
16. 4. do; Acts 20. 19. lowliness
HUNGER, Ex. 16. 3. Deut. 28. 48.
Ps. 34. 10. young lions suffer *h.*
Prov. 19. 15. idle soul shall suffer *h*
Jer. 42. 14. no war nor have *h.* of
Lam. 4. 9. sword better than slain
with *h.*
Deut. 8. 3. suffered thee to *h.*
Isa. 49. 10. shall not *h.* nor thirst
Matt. 5. 6. blessed are they that *h.*
Luke 6. 21. blessed are ye that *h.*
John 6. 35. that cometh to me shall
never *h.*
Rom. 12. 20. if thine enemy *h.* feed
1 Cor. 4. 11. we both *h.* and thirst
11. 34. if any man *h.* let him eat
Ps. 107. 9. fill the *hungry* with
goodness
146. 7. God giveth food to the *h.*
Prov. 25. 21. if enemy be *h.* give
27. 7. to the *h.* every bitter thing
Isa. 58. 7. is it not to deal thy
bread to the *h.*
10. if thou draw out thy soul to *h.*
65. 13. shall eat; but ye shall be *h.*
Ezek. 18. 7. hath given his bread
to the *h.*, 16.
Luke 1. 53. filled the *h.* with good
Phil. 4. 12. how to be full and to
be *h.*
R. V. Jer. 38. 9; Ezek. 34. 29; Rev.
6. 8. famine
HUNT, 1 Sam. 26. 20. Job 38. 39.
Ps. 140. 11. evil doth *h.* the violent
Prov. 6. 26. adulteress will *h.* for
precious
Ezek. 13. 18. ye *h.* the souls of my
people
Job 10. 16. thou *huntest* me as
HURT, Gen. 4. 23. & 26. 29.
Josh. 24. 20. will turn and do you
h.
Ps. 15. 4. sweareth to his *h.* and
Eccl. 5. 13. riches kept for owners
to their *h.*
Jer. 6. 14. healed *h.* of the daugh.
Rev. 2. 11. shall not be *h.* of
6. 6. *h.* not the oil and wine
Ezra 4. 15. *hurtful*, Ps. 144. 10.
1 Tim. 6. 9. fall into foolish and *h.*
R. V. Josh. 24. 20. evil; Acts 27. 10.
injury; Acts 18. 10. harm
HUSBAND, Gen. 3. 6, 16. & 29. 32.
Ex. 4. 25. bloody *h.* art thou to me
Isa. 54. 5. thy Maker is thy *h.* Lord
Jer. 31. 32. though I was a *h.* to
Mark 10. 12. if a woman put away
her *h.*
John 4. 17. I have no *h.*
1 Cor. 7. 14. unbelieving *h.* is sanc.
34. careth how she may please *h.*
14. 35. let them ask *h.* at home
2 Cor. 11. 2. espoused you to one *h.*
Eph. 5. 22. wives submit to your *h.*
23. the *h.* is the head of wife, 24.
25. *h.* love your wives, as Christ
Eph. 5. 33. the wife see that she
reverence her *h.*
Col. 3. 18. wives submit to your *h.*
1 Pet. 3. 1. subject to their own *h.*
7. ye *h.* dwell with them, accord.
R. V. 1 Cor. 7. 14. brother
HUSBANDMAN, my Father is
John 15. 1.
1 Tim. 2. 6. *h.* that labors must be
Jas. 5. 7. *h.* waiteth for precious
1 Cor. 3. 9. ye are God's *husbandry*
HYMN, Matt. 26. 30. Eph. 5. 19
Col. 3. 16.

HYPOCRISY, Isa. 32. 6. Matt. 23. 28. Mark 12.15. Luke 12.1. 1 Tim. 4. 2. Jas. 3. 17. 1 Pet. 2. 1.
Matt. 7. 5. *hypocrite*, Luke 6. 42. & 13. 15.
Matt. 24. 51. appoint him portion with *h.*
Job 20. 5. joy of *h.* is but for a moment
27. 8. what is the hope of the *h.*
36. 13. *h.* in heart heap up wrath
Isa. 9. 17. every one is a *h.* and evil
33. 14. fearful. hath surprised *h.*
Matt. 6. 2. *hypocrites*, 6. 16. & 15. 7. & 16. 3. & 23. 13, 14, 15, 23.
Job 8. 13. the *h.* hope shall perish
15. 34. congregation of *h.* shall
R. V. Isa. 32. 6. profaneness; Job 8. 13; 13. 16; 17. 8; 20. 5; 27. 8; 34. 30; 36. 13; Prov. 11. 9; Isa. 33. 14. godless; Isa. 9. 17. profane; Matt. 16. 3; 23. 14; Luke 11. 44——

I

IDLE, they be, Ex. 5. 8, 17.
Prov. 19. 15. an *i.* soul shall suffer
Matt. 12. 36. every *i.* word give
20. 3. standing *i.*
6. why stand ye *i.*
Luke 24. 11. words seemed as *i.* tales
1 Tim. 5. 13. they learn to be *i.*
Prov. 31. 27. *idleness*, Eccl. 10. 18. Ezek. 16. 49.
R. V. Matt. 20. 6——; Ezek. 16. 49. ease

IDOL, 2 Chron. 15. 16. & 33. 7.
Isa. 66. 3. as if he blessed an *i.*
Zech. 11. 17. who to the *i.* shepherd
1 Cor. 8. 4. an *i.* is nothing in world
Ps. 96. 5. gods of nations are *idols*
Isa. 2. 8. land is full of *i.* they wor.
Jer. 50. 38. they are mad upon *i.*
Hos. 4. 17. Ephraim is joined to *i.*
Acts 15. 20. abstain from pollu. of *i.*
Rom. 2. 22. thou that abhorrest *i.*
1 Cor. 8. 1. touch. things offered to *i.*
2 Cor. 6. 16. temple of God with *i.*
1 John 5. 21. keep yourselves from *i.*
Rev. 2. 14. eat things sacrificed to *i.*
9. 20. worship devils and *i.* of gold
1 Cor. 5. 10, 11. *idolater*, 6. 9. & 10. 7. Eph. 5. 5. Rev. 21. 8. & 22. 15.
1 Sam. 15. 23. stubbornness as iniquity and *idolatry*
Acts 17. 16. city wholly given to *i.*
1 Cor. 10. 14. dearly beloved, flee *i.*
Gal. 5. 20. *i.* witchcraft, hatred
Col. 3. 5. covetousness, which is *i.*
1 Pet. 4. 3. walked in abominable *idolatries*
R. V. 1 Kings 15. 13; 2 Chron. 15. 16; Jer. 50. 2. image, and images; 2 Chron. 15. 18. abominations; Isa. 57. 5. among oaks; Jer. 22. 28. vessel; Zech. 10. 2. teraphim; 11. 17. worthless; 1 Cor. 12. 2——; 1 Sam. 15. 23. teraphim; Acts 17. 16. full of idols
2 Chron. 34. 7. hewed down all the *sun-images* throughout all the land of Israel

IGNORANCE, sin through, Lev. 4. 2, 13, 22, 27. Num. 15. 24, 25. Acts 3. 15.
Acts 17. 30. the times of this *i.*
Eph. 4. 18. alienated through *i.* in
Ps. 73. 22. so foolish was I and *ignorant*
Isa. 63. 16. though Abraham be *i.* of
Rom. 10. 3. being *i.* of God's righteousness
1 Cor. 14. 38. if any man be *i.* let
Heb. 5. 2. who can have compassion on *i.*
Acts 17. 23. *ignorantly*, 1 Tim. 1. 13.
R. V. Lev. 4. 2, 22, 27; 5. 18; Num. 15. 24, 26, 27, 28, 29. unwittingly; Lev. 4. 13. shall err; Num. 15. 25. was an error; Isa. 56. 10. without knowledge; 63. 16. knoweth not; Num. 15. 28. erreth; Deut. 19. 4. unawares

ILLUMINATED, Heb. 10. 32.

IMAGE, Lev. 26. 1. Dan. 2. 31.
Gen. 1. 26. let us make man in our own *i.*, 27. & 5. 1. & 9. 6. Col. 3. 10.
Gen. 5. 3. Adam begat a son after his *i.*
Ps. 73. 20. Lord, thou shalt despise their *i.*
Matt. 22. 20. whose *i.* is this, Luke 20. 24.
Rom. 8. 29. conformed to *i.* of Son
1 Cor. 15. 49. have borne the *i.* of the earthly we shall also bear *i.* of the heavenly
4. 4. Christ who is the *i.* of God
2 Cor. 3. 18. into same *i.* from glory
Heb. 1. 3. express *i.* of his person
Rev. 13. 14. make an *i.* to the beast
Ex. 23. 24. break down *images*, 34. 13.
R. V. Lev. 26. 1. figured stones; Ex. 23. 24; 34. 13; Lev. 26. 1; Deut. 7. 5; 16. 22; 1 Kings 14. 23; 2 Kings 17. 10; 18. 4; 23. 14; 2 Chron. 14. 3; 31. 1; Jer. 43. 13; Hos. 1. 2; Mic. 5. 13. pillar, and pillars; Job 4. 16. form; Rom. 11. 4——

IMAGINE, Ps. 2. 1. Nah. 1. 9. Zech. 7. 10. & 8. 17. Acts 4. 25.
Gen. 6. 5. every *imagination* of the thoughts was evil, 8. 21. Prov. 6. 18. Lam. 3. 60, 61. Rom. 1. 21. 2 Cor. 10. 5.
R. V. Lam. 3. 60, 61. devices; Rom. 1. 21. reasonings; Gen. 11. 6. purpose

IMMEDIATELY, Mark 4. 15. Acts 12. 23.

IMMORTAL, invisible, 1 Tim. 1. 17.
Rom. 2. 7. seek for *immortality*
1 Cor. 15. 53. this mortal must put on *i.*
1 Tim. 6. 16. who only hath *i.* in
2 Tim. 1. 10. brought *i.* to light
R. V. *incorruption*
Rom. 2. 7. seek for glory . . and *i.*

IMMUTABLE, Heb. 6. 17, 18.

IMPART, Luke 3. 11. Rom. 1. 11. 1 Thes. 2. 8.

IMPENITENT heart, Rom. 2. 5.

IMPERIOUS whorish woman, Ezek. 16. 30.

IMPLACABLE, unmerciful, Rom. 1. 31.
R. V. Rom. 1. 31——

IMPORTUNITY, Luke 11. 8.

IMPOSSIBLE, Matt. 17. 20. & 19. 26.
Luke 1. 37. with God nothing is *i.*
17. 1. it is *i.* but offences will come
Heb. 6. 4. it is *i.* for those once
18. in two things it is *i.* for God to
11. 6. without faith it is *i.* to please
R. V. Luke 1. 37. void of power; Heb. 6. 4. as touching

IMPUDENT, Prov. 7. 13. Ezek. 2. 4.
R. V. Ezek. 3. 7. of hard forehead

IMPUTE, 1 Sam. 22. 15. Lev. 7. 18. & 3. 7.
Ps. 32. 2. to whom Lord *i.* not iniq.
Rom. 4. 6. *i.* righteousness without
8. blessed to whom Lord will not *i.*
22. *i.* to him for righteousness
2 Cor. 5. 19. not *i.* their trespasses
Jas. 2. 23. *i.* to him for righteous.
R. V. Hab. 1. 11. even; Rom. 4. 6, 8, 11, 22, 23, 24. reckon; 2 Cor. 5. 19. reckoning; Jas. 2. 23. reckoned

IN Christ, Acts 24. 24. Rom. 12. 5. 1 Cor. 1. 2, 30. & 3. 1. & 15. 18, 22. 2 Cor. 1. 21. & 2. 14. & 3. 14. & 5. 17, 19. & 12. 2. Gal. 1. 22. Eph. 1. 1, 3, 10, 12, 20. & 2. 6, 10, 13. Phil. 1. 1, 13. & 2. 1, 5. & 3. 14. Col. 1. 2, 4.
1 Thes. 1. 1. *in God*, 4. 16. John 3. 21. Col. 3. 3.
Gen. 15. 16. *in the Lord*, Ps. 4. 5. & 31. 24. & 34. 2. & 35. 9. & 37. 4, 7. Isa. 45. 17, 24, 25. Jer. 3. 23. Zech. 12. 5. 1 Cor. 1. 31. & 4. 17. & 7. 22, 39. Eph. 2. 21. & 6. 10. Phil. 4. 2, 4. Col. 3. 18. & 4. 7, 17. 1 Thes. 5. 12. Phile. 16, 20. Rev. 14. 13.

INCEST condemned, Lev. 18. & 20. 17. Deut. 22. 30. & 27. 20. Ezek. 22. 11. Amos 2. 7. cases of, Gen. 19. 33. & 35. 22. & 38. 18. 2 Sam. 13. & 16. 21. Mark 6. 17. 1 Cor. 5. 1.

INCHANTMENT, Lev. 19. 26. Num. 23. 23. Eccl. 10. 11. Isa. 47. 9.

INCLINE heart, Josh. 24. 23. Judg. 9. 3. 1 Kings 8. 58. Ps. 119. 36, 112. & 141. 4.
Ps. 78. 1. *incline*, 40. 1. & 116. 2. Prov. 2. 2. & 5. 13. Jer. 7. 24, 26. & 11. 8. & 17. 23. & 25. 4. & 34. 14. & 35. 15. & 44. 5. Isa. 55. 3.
R. V. Ps. 71. 2. bow down

INCLOSED, Ps. 17. 10. & 22. 16. S. of S. 4. 12. & 8. 9. Lam. 3. 9.
R. V. S. of S. 4. 12. shut up; Lam. 3. 9. fenced up

INCONTINENT, 1 Cor. 7. 5. 2 Tim. 3. 3.

INCORRUPTIBLE God, Rom. 1. 23.
1 Cor. 9. 25. to obtain an *i.* crown
15. 52. dead shall be raised *i.*
1 Pet. 1. 4. begotten to inheritance *i.*
23. born not of corruptible seed, but of *i.*
1 Cor. 15. 42, 50, 53, 54. *incorruption*

INCREASE, Lev. 19. 25. & 25. 7.
Lev. 25. 36. take no usury nor *i.*, 37.
Deut. 16. 15. bless thee in all thine *i.*
Ps. 67. 6. earth yield her *i.*, 85. 12.
Prov. 3. 9. with first fruits of all *i.*
Isa. 9. 7. of the *i.* of his govern.
1 Cor. 3. 6. I planted; but God gave the *i.*, 7.
Col. 2. 19. increaseth with *i.* of God
Ps. 62. 10. if riches *i.* set not heart
Prov. 1. 5. wise man will *i.* learn.
Isa. 29. 19. meek shall *i.* their joy
Luke 17. 5. Lord, *i.* our faith
John 3. 30. he must *i.* but I decrease
1 Thes. 3. 12. Lord make you to *i.* in
2 Tim. 2. 16. will *i.* to more ungod.
Ezra 9. 6. iniquities are *increased*
Isa. 9. 3. multi. nation, not *i.* joy
Luke 2. 52. Jesus *i.* in wisdom and
Acts 6. 7. the word of God *i.* and the
Rev. 3. 17. am rich and *i.* with goods
Eccl. 1. 18. *increaseth* knowledge
Isa. 40. 29. have no might, he *i.*
Col. 2. 19. whole body *i.* with the
1 Chron. 11. 9. David went on *increasing*
Col. 1. 10. *i.* in knowledge of God
R. V. Gen. 47. 34. ingathering; Job 10. 16. exalteth; Prov. 28. 8. augmenteth; Ps. 7. 23. ascendeth; Isa. 52. 1. made many; Lam. 2. 5. Ezek. 16. 26; Hos. 4. 7; 10. 1; 12. 1. multiplied; Luke 2. 52. advanced; 2 Cor. 2. 15. groweth; Rev. 3. 17. have gotten

INCREDIBLE thing, Acts 26. 8.

INCURABLE wound, Job 34. 6. Jer. 15. 18.
Mic. 1. 9. *i.* bruise, Jer. 30. 12, 15.

INDEED, 1 Kings 8. 27. 1 Chron. 4. 10. Matt. 3. 11. Luke 4. 24. John 1. 47. & 4. 42. & 6. 55. & 8. 31, 36. 1 Tim. 5. 3, 5. 1 Pet. 2. 4.

INDIGNATION, Neh. 4. 1. Esth. 5. 9. Ps. 69. 24. & 78. 49. & 102. 10.
Isa. 10. 5. staff in their hand is my *i.*
26. 20. hide thee until *i.* be over.
Mic. 7. 9. I will bear the *i.* of Lord
Nah. 1. 6. who can stand before his *i.*
Matt. 20. 24. moved with *i.*
Rom. 2. 8. *i.* and wrath, tribulation
2 Cor. 7. 11. yea, what *i.* yea, what
Heb. 10. 27. fiery *i.* which shall
Rev. 14. 10. poured into cup of his *i.*
R. V. 2 Kings 3. 27; Esth. 5. 9. wrath; Acts 5. 17. jealousy; Heb. 10. 27. fierceness of fire; Rev. 14. 10. anger

INDITING a good matter, Ps. 45. 1.

INDUSTRY, Gen. 2. 15. & 3. 23. Prov. 6. 6. & 10. 4. & 12. 24. & 13. 4. & 21. 5. & 22. 29. & 27. 23. Eph. 4. 28. 1 Thes.

4. 11. 2 Thes. 3. 12. Tit. 3. 14; rewarded, Prov. 13. 11. & 31. 13.
INEXCUSABLE, O man, Rom. 2. 1.
INFALLIBLE proofs, many, Acts 1. 3.
INFANT, 1 Sam. 15. 3. Job 3. 16. Isa. 65. 20. Hos. 13. 16. Luke 18. 15.
R. V. Luke 18. 15. their babes
INFIDEL, 2 Cor. 6. 15. 1 Tim. 5. 8.
INFINITE iniquities, Job 22. 5.
Ps. 147. 5. his understanding is *i.*
Nah. 3. 9. her strength, and it was *i.*
R. V. Job 22. 5. end
INFIRMITY, this is my *i.*, Ps. 77. 10.
Prov. 18. 14. the spirit of a man will sustain his *i.*
Matt. 8. 17. himself took our *infirmities*
Rom. 8. 26. the Spirit also helpeth our *i.*
15. 1. strong ought to bear the *i.*
2 Cor. 12. 9. glory in my *i.*
10. pleasure in *i.*
1 Tim. 5. 23. drink wine for thine often *i.*
Heb. 4. 15. with the feeling of our *i.*
R. V. Lev. 12. 2. her sickness; Luke 7. 21; 2 Cor. 12. 5, 9, 10. weaknesses
INFLAME them, wine, Isa. 5. 11. & 57. 5.
INFLICTED punishment, 2 Cor. 2. 6.
INFLUENCES of Pleiades, Job 38. 31.
INGATHERING, feast of, Ex. 23. 16. & 34. 22.
INGRAFTED word, receive, Jas. 1. 21.
INGRATITUDE to God, Rom. 1. 21.
INHABIT, Prov. 10. 30. Isa. 65. 21, 22.
Ps. 22. 3. thou that *inhabitest* the praises of Israel
Isa. 57. 15. lofty One that *inhabiteth*
R. V. Prov. 10. 30; Jer. 48. 18. dwell in; Lev. 16. 22. solitary land; 1 Chron. 5. 9; Zech. 12. 6; 14. 10, 11. dwell
INHERIT, Gen. 15. 8. Ps. 82. 8.
1 Sam. 2. 8. to make them *i.* throne
Ps. 25. 13. his seed shall *i.* earth
27. 11. the meek shall *i.* the earth, Matt. 5. 5.
Ps. 37. 29. the righteous shall *i.* the land, Isa. 60. 21.
Prov. 3. 35. wise shall *i.* glory; but
Matt. 19. 29. hath forsaken, shall *i.* everlasting life
25. 34. *i.* king. prepared for you
Mark 10. 17. what shall I do that I may *i.* eternal life, Luke 10. 25. & 18. 18.
1 Cor. 6. 9. unrighteous not *i.* the kingdom of God, 10.
Gal. 5. 21. do such things not *i.* the kingdom of God
Heb. 6. 12. through faith *i.* prom.
1 Pet. 3. 9. that ye should *i.* bless.
Rev. 21. 7. overcometh shall *i.* all
Num. 18. 20. I the Lord am thy *inheritance,* Deut. 10. 9. & 18. 2. Ezek. 44. 28.
Deut. 4. 20. a people of *i.*, 9. 20, 29. & 32. 9. 1 Kings 8. 5. Ps. 28. 9. & 33. 12. & 68. 9. & 74. 2. & 78. 62, 71. & 79. 1. & 94. 14. & 106. 5, 40. Isa. 19. 25. Jer. 10. 16. & 51. 19.
Ps. 16. 5. Lord is portion of mine *i.*
Prov. 19. 14. riches are *i.* of fathers
Eccl. 7. 11. wisdom is good with an *i.*
Acts 20. 32. *i.* among the sanctified
Eph. 1. 11. among whom he obtained an *i.*
14. earnest of our *i.* and purchased
5. 5. hath an *i.* in the kingdom
Col. 1. 12. partakers of *i.* of saints
3. 24. shall receive the reward of *i.*
Heb. 9. 15. receive the promise of eternal *i.*
1 Pet. 1. 4. to an *i.* incorruptible

R. V. Isa. 54. 3; Jer. 8. 10; 49. 1. possess; Josh. 13. 15, 24, 32 ——; Job 31. 2; Eph. 1. 11. heritage; Ezek. 22. 16. be profaned
INIQUITY, Gen. 15. 16. & 19. 15.
Ex. 20. 5. visiting *i.* of the fathers
34. 7. forgiving *i.* transgression
Lev. 26. 41. accept the punishment of their *i.*, 43.
Num. 23. 21. hath not beheld *i.*
Deut. 32. 4. a God of truth, without *i.*
Job 4. 8. they that plough *i.* reap
11. 6. less than thine *i.* deserveth
15. 16. man drinketh in *i.* like
22. 23. put away *i.* far from thee
34. 32. if I have done *i.* I will do
Ps. 32. 5. mine *i.* have I not hid
39. 11. with rebukes correct man for *i.*
51. 5. behold I was shapen in *i.*
66. 18. if I regard *i.* in my heart
119. 3. they also do not *i.* they walk
Prov. 22. 8. that soweth *i.* shall
Eccl. 3. 16. place of righteousness *i.* was there
Isa. 1. 4. a people laden with *i.*
5. 18. woe to them that draw *i.*
27. 9. by this shall *i.* of Jacob
33. 24. people shall be forgiven their *i.*
53. 6. Lord laid on him the *i.* of us
57. 17. for *i.* of his covetousness
59. 3. defiled your fingers with *i.*
Jer. 2. 5. what *i.* have your
3. 13. only acknowledge thine *i.*
31. 30. every one shall die for *i.*
50. 20. *i.* of Israel be sought for
Ezek. 3. 18. he shall die in his *i.*
18. 30. so *i.* shall not be your ruin
Dan. 9. 24. makes reconcilia. for *i.*
Hos. 14. 2. take away all *i.* and
Mic. 7. 18. a God like thee, that pardoneth *i.*
Hab. 1. 13. Holy One canst not look on *i.*
Matt. 7. 23. depart from me ye that work *i.*
Acts 8. 23. in gall of bitterness and bond of *i.*
Rom. 6. 19. servants to uncleanness and to *i.* unto *i.*
1 Cor. 13. 6. charity rejoic. not in *i.*
2 Thes. 2. 7. mystery of *i.* already
2 Tim. 2. 19. that nameth Christ depart from *i.*
Tit. 2. 14. he might redeem us from all *i.*
Jas. 3. 6. tongue is a fire, a world of *i.*
Ps. 18. 23. *my iniquity,* 25. 11. & 32. 5. & 38. 18. & 51. 2.
Job 34. 22. *workers of iniquity,* Ps. 5. 5. & 6. 8. & 14. 4. & 92. 7. Prov. 10. 29. & 21. 15. Luke 13. 27.
Lev. 16. 21. confess over him all *iniquities*
26. 39. pine in their *i.* and *i.* of
Ezra 9. 6. our *i.* are increased
Neh. 9. 2. confessed the *i.* of
Job 13. 26. to possess *i.* of my youth
Ps. 38. 4. mine *i.* are gone over my
40. 12. mine *i.* have taken hold
51. 9. hide from my sins, blot out my *i.*
79. 8. remember not against us former *i.*
90. 8. thou hast set our *i.* before
103. 3. who forgiveth all thine *i.*
10. not rewarded us accord. to *i.*
130. 3. if thou, Lord, shouldest mark *i.*
8. he shall redeem Israel from all *i.*
Prov. 5. 22. his own *i.* shall take
Isa. 43. 24. hast wearied me with *i.*
53. 5. he was wounded, bruised for *i.*
Jer. 14. 7. though our *i.* testify
Dan. 4. 27. break off thy *i.* by show.
Mic. 7. 19. he will subdue our *i.*
Acts 3. 26. bless you in turning from *i.*
Rom. 4. 7. blessed are they whose *i.*

Rev. 18. 5. God hath remem. her *i.*
Isa. 53. 11. he shall bear *their iniquities*
Jer. 33. 8. I will cleanse them from all — and I will pardon all —
Ezek. 43. 10. may be ashamed of —
Heb. 8. 12. their sins, and — will I
Num. 14. 34. shall ye bear *your iniquities*
Isa. 50. 1. for — have ye sold
59. 2. — have separated between you and God
Jer. 5. 25. — turned away these things
Ezek. 24. 23. ye shall pine away for —
36. 31. loathe yourselves . . for —
33. I shall have cleansed you from all —
Amos 3. 2. I will punish you for all —
R. V. 1 Sam. 15. 23. idolatry; Job 6. 29, 30. injustice; Job 22. 23; 36. 23; Ps. 37. 1; 119. 13; Jer. 2. 5; Ezek. 28. 15, 18; Mal. 2. 6; 1 Cor. 13. 6; 2 Tim. 2. 19. unrighteousness; Ps. 94. 20; Eccl. 3. 16. wickedness; Dan. 9. 5. perversely; Hab. 1. 13. perverseness; 2 Thes. 2. 7. lawlessness; Heb. 8. 12 ——; 2 Pet. 2. 16. transgression
INJURED me, ye have not, Gal. 4. 12.
1 Tim. 1. 13. was a persecutor and *injurious*
INJUSTICE, Ex. 22. 21. & 23. 6. Lev. 19. 15. Deut. 16. 19. & 24. 17. Job 31. 13. Ps. 82. 2. Prov. 22. 16. & 29. 7. Jer. 22. 3. Luke 16. 10.
results of, Prov. 11. 7. & 28. 8. Mic. 6. 10. Amos 5. 11. & 8. 5. 1 Thes. 4. 6. 2 Pet. 2. 9.
INK, 2 John 12. 3 John 13.
INNER, 1 Kings 6. 27. Eph. 3. 16.
R. V. Eph. 3. 16. inward
INNOCENT, Ps. 19. 13. Prov. 28. 20.
Gen. 20. 5. in *innocency* of hands
Ps. 6. 6. wash my hands in *i.*, 73. 13.
Dan. 6. 22. before him *i.* was
Hos. 8. 5. how long ere they at. *i.*
R. V. Ps. 19. 3. clear; Prov. 6. 29; 28. 20. unpunished
INNUMERABLE, Job 21. 33. Ps. 40. 12. Luke 12. 1. Heb. 11. 12. & 12. 22.
INORDINATE, Ezek. 23. 11. Col. 3. 5.
R. V. *passion;* Col. 3. 5. uncleanness, *i.* affection
INQUISITION, Deut. 19. 18. Ps. 9. 12.
INSCRIPTION to unknown God, Acts 17. 23.
INSPIRATION, Job 32. 8. 2 Tim. 3. 16.
R. V. Job 32. 8. breath; 2 Tim. 3. 16. inspired
INSTANT, Isa. 29. 5. & 30. 13. Jer. 18. 7. Rom. 12. 12. 2 Tim. 4. 2. Acts 12. 5.
Luke 7. 4. besought him *instantly*
Acts 26. 7. *i.* serving God day and
R. V. Luke 2. 38. very hour; Rom. 12. 12. earnestly
INSTRUCT, Deut. 4. 36. & 32. 10.
Neh. 9. 20. thy good Spirit to *i.* them
Job 40. 2. contendeth with the Almighty *i.*
16. 7. my reins *i.* me in the night
32. 8. I will *i.* thee, and teach
S. of S. 8. 2. moth. who would *i.* me
Isa. 28. 26. his God doth *i.* him
Dan. 11. 33. that under. shall *i.*
1 Cor. 2. 16. Lord that he may *i.* him
Isa. 8. 11. Lord *instructed* me
Ps. 2. 10. be *i.* ye judges of earth
Matt. 13. 52. every scribe, *i.* unto
Phil. 4. 12. in all things I am *i.* both
2 Tim. 2. 25. in meekness *i.* those
Rom. 2. 20. an *instructor* of foolish
1 Cor. 4. 15. have ten thousand *i.*
Job 33. 16. sealeth their *instruction*
Ps. 50. 17. hatest *i.* and castest my

Prov. 4. 13. take fast hold of *i*. keep
5. 12. how have I hated *i*.
19. 27. cease to hear *i*. that causeth
23. 12. apply thy heart to *i*. and
2 Tim. 3. 16. profitable for *i*. in
R. V. Deut. 32. 10. cared for;-
2 Chron. 3. 3. laid; Job 40. 2. contend with Almighty; Matt. 13. 52. hath been made a disciple; 14. 8. put forward by; Phil. 4. 12. learned the secret; 2 Tim. 2. 25. correcting; Prov. 10. 17; 12. 1; 13. 18; 15. 5, 32; 16. 22; Zeph. 3. 7. correction

INSTRUMENTS of cruelty, Gen. 49. 5.
Ps. 7. 13. prepared for him *i*. of
Rom. 6. 13. neither yield members *i*. of unrighteousness; but *i*. of righteousness to God
Isa. 32. 7. the *i*. of the churl are
R. V. Gen. 49. 5; Isa. 54. 16. weapon; Ex. 25. 9; Num. 3. 8; 7. 1; 2 Sam. 24. 22. furniture; Num. 4. 12; 31. 6; 1 Chron. 9. 20; 28. 14; 2 Chron. 4. 16; 5. 1. vessels; Ps. 68. 25. minstrels; 87. 7. that dance; 33. 2; 144. 9 —

INTANGLE, Matt. 22. 15. Gal. 5. 1. 2 Tim. 2. 4. 2 Pet. 2. 20.

INTEGRITY of my heart, Gen. 20. 5.
Job 2. 3. still he holdeth fast his *i*.
27. 5. I will not remove mine *i*.
Ps. 7. 8. according to my *i*. that is
25. 21. let *i*. and uprightness
26. 1. I have walked in mine *i*.
Prov. 11. 3. *i*. of upright shall guide

INTERCESSION, Jer. 7. 16. & 27. 18.
Isa. 53. 12. made *i*. for transgress.
Rom. 8. 26. Spirit maketh *i*. for us, 27.
34. who also maketh *i*. for
11. 2. Elias maketh *i*. to God
1 Tim. 2. 1. prayers and *i*. be made
Heb. 7. 25. he ever liveth to make *i*.
Isa. 59. 16. wondered there was no *intercessor*
R. V. Rom. 11. 2. pleadeth with

INTERMEDDLE, Prov. 14. 10. & 18. 1.
R. V. Prov. 18. 1. rageth against

INTERPRETATION, Gen. 40. 5. & 41. 11. Judg. 7. 15. Dan. 2. 4, 7, 36. 1 Cor. 12. 10. & 14. 26. 2 Pet. 1. 20.
Job 33. 23. *interpreter* one among
R. V. 1 Pet. 1. 6. a figure

INTREAT, Gen. 12. 16. & 23. 8. Ex. 8. 8. & 9. 28. & 10. 17. Jer. 15. 11.
1 Sam. 2. 25. man sin, who shall *i*.
1 Cor. 4. 13. we suffer; being defamed we *i*.
1 Tim. 5. 1. but *i*. him as a father
Jas. 3. 17. gentle and easy to be *intreated*
Prov. 18. 23. the poor useth *intreaties*
2 Cor. 8. 4. praying us with much *i*.
R. V. Job 19. 17. my supplication; Phil. 4. 3. beseech; 1 Tim. 5. 1. exhort

INTRUDING into those things, Col. 2. 18.

INVENT, Amos 6. 5. Rom. 1. 30.
Ps. 99. 8. tookest vengeance of their *inventions*
106. 28. provoked him with their *i*.
Prov. 8. 12. find out knowledge of witty *i*.
Eccl. 7. 29. men have sought many *i*.
R. V. Ps. 99. 8; 106. 29, 39. doings; Prov. 8. 12. and discretion

INVISIBLE, Rom. 1. 20. Col. 1. 15, 16. 1 Tim. 1. 17. Heb. 11. 27.

INWARD friends abhorred me, Job 19. 19.
Ps. 5. 9. *inward part*, 51. 6. Prov. 20. 27. Jer. 31. 33. Luke 11. 39.
Rom. 7. 22. *inward man*, 2 Cor. 4. 16.
2 Cor. 7. 15. *inward affection* is
Ps. 62. 4. curse *inwardly*

Matt. 7. 15. *i*. wolves
Rom. 2. 29. he is a Jew that is one *i*.

IRON sharpeneth iron, Prov. 27. 17.
Eccl. 10. 10. if the *i*. be blunt, put
Isa. 48. 4. neck is an *i*. sinew, and
Jer. 15. 12. shall *i*. break northern *i*.
Dan. 2. 33. legs of *i*. his feet *i*. and
4. 23. even with a band of *i*. and
1 Tim. 4. 2. conscience seared with hot *i*.

ISSUES from death, Ps. 68. 20.
Prov. 4. 23. out of the heart are the *i*. of life
R. V. Lev. 12. 7. fountain; Matt. 22. 23. seed

ITCHING ears, 2 Tim. 4. 3.

IVORY, 1 Kings 10. 18. & 22. 39. Ps. 45. 8. S. of S. 5. 14. & 7. 4. Ezek. 27. 6. Amos 3. 15. & 6. 4. Rev. 18. 12.

J

JAW-BONE of an ass, Samson uses, Judg. 15. 15; water flows from, 15. 19.

JEALOUS God, I am a, Ex. 20. 5. & 34. 14. Deut. 5. 9. & 6. 15. Josh. 24. 19.
1 Kings 19. 10. I have been very *j*.
Ezek. 39. 25. be *j*. for my holy
Joel 2. 18. will Lord be *j*. for land
Nah. 1. 2. God is *j*. and the Lord
Zech. 1. 14. I am *j*. for Jerusalem
2 Cor. 11. 2. *j*. over you with godly *jealousy*
Deut. 29. 20. Lord's *j*. shall smoke
Ps. 79. 5. shall thy *j*. burn like fire
Prov. 6. 34. *j*. is the rage of a man
S. of S. 8. 6. *j*. is cruel as the grave
Rom. 10. 19. provoke you to *j*.
1 Cor. 10. 22. do we provoke Lord to *j*.

JEHOVAH, Ex. 6. 3. Ps. 83. 18. Isa. 12. 2. & 26. 4. Gen. 22. 14. Ex. 17. 15. Judg. 6. 24. it is about 2000 times translated Lord, in capitals

JERUSALEM, for the church, Isa. 24. 23. & 62. 1. & 66. 10, 13. Jer. 3. 17. Joel 2. 32. & 3. 16, 17. Zech. 12. 10. & 8. 22. Gal. 4. 25, 26. Heb. 12. 22. Rev. 3. 12. & 21. 2.

JESHURUN, i. e. Israel, Deut. 32. 15. & 33. 5, 26. Isa. 44. 2.

JESTING, evil, censured, Eph. 5. 4.

JESUS, or Joshua, Acts 7. 45. Heb. 4. 8.

JESUS the Saviour of men, Matt. 1. 21. & 2. 1. & 8. 29. & 14. 1. & 27. 37. 1 Cor. 12. 3. 2 Cor. 4. 5. Eph. 4. 21. Heb. 2. 9. & 12. 2. Rev. 22. 16. and in about 650 other places

JEWELS, I make up my, Mal. 3. 17.
R. V. 2 Chron. 32. 27. vessels; S. of S. 1. 10. hair; Ezek. 16. 12. ring

JEWS first, and also Greeks, Rom. 1. 16. & 2. 9, 10, 28. not a *J*. which is one outwardly, but is a *J*. which is one inwardly, 29.
Rom. 10. 12. no difference between *J*. and Greek
1 Cor. 9. 20. to *J*. I became as a *J*. to gain *J*.
Gal. 3. 28. neither *J*. nor Greek
Rev. 2. 9. say they are *J*. and are

JOIN, Ex. 1. 10. Ezra 9. 14.
Prov. 11. 21. though hand *j*. in
Isa. 5. 8. woe to them that *j*. house
Jer. 50. 5. let us *j*. ourselves to Lord
Acts 5. 13. of the rest durst no man *j*. himself
9. 26. assayed to *j*. himself to the
Hos. 4. 17. Ephraim is *joined* to idols
Num. 25. 3. Israel *j*. himself to Ba.
Eccl. 9. 4. *j*. to all living there is
Zech. 2. 11. many nat. shall be *j*.
Matt. 19. 6. what God hath *j*. let not
1 Cor. 1. 10. be perfectly *j*. together
6. 17. he that is *j*. to the Lord is
Eph. 5. 31. shall be *j*. to his wife
Col. 2. 19. all the body by *joints* and bands
Heb. 4. 12. dividing asunder of *j*.
R. V. Ex. 4. 12. repaired; Isa. 9. 11. stir up; Gen. 14. 8. set in array; Ezra 4. 12. repaired; Job 3. 6. rejoice; Ezek. 46. 22. inclosed; 1 Cor. 1. 10. perfected; Eph. 4. 16. framed; 5. 31. cleave to; Gen. 32. 25. strained

JOURNEY, Num. 9. 13. Rom. 1. 10.
R. V. Num. 33. 12; Deut. 10. 6. journeyed; Mark 13. 34. sojourning in another country; Rom. 1. 10 —

JOY, 1 Chron. 12. 40. 2 Chron. 20. 27.
Neh. 8. 10. *j*. of Lord is your strength
Esth. 8. 17. the Jews had *j*. and
Job 20. 5. *j*. of the hypocrite is
Ps. 16. 11. in thy presence is fulness of *j*.
30. 5. but *j*. cometh in the morn.
51. 8. make me hear *j*. and glad.
12. restore to me *j*. of thy salva.
126. 5. who sow in tears shall reap in *j*.
Eccl. 9. 7. eat thy bread with *j*.
Isa. 9. 3. hast not increased the *j*.
12. 3. with *j*. shall draw water out
35. 10. with songs and everlast. *j*.
61. 3. give them the oil of *j*. for
7. everlasting *j*. shall be to them
66. 5. shall appear to your *j*.
Zeph. 3. 17. the Lord will *j*. over
Matt. 2. 10. rejoiced with exceeding great *j*.
13. 20. hear the word and with *j*.
25. 21. enter into *j*. of thy Lord
Luke 1. 44. babe leaped in my womb for *j*.
15. 7. *j*. shall be in heaven over
24. 41. while they believe not for *j*.
John 15. 11. that your *j*. might be
16. 20. your sorrow be turn. into *j*.
22. your *j*. no man taketh from
Acts 20. 24. finish my course with *j*.
Rom. 14. 17. righteousness and peace and *j*. in the Holy Ghost
2 Cor. 1. 24. we are help. of your *j*.
Gal. 5. 22. fruit of the Spirit is love, *j*.
Phil. 4. 1. brethren, my *j*. and crown
1 Thes. 1. 6. receive word with *j*. of
Heb. 12. 12. who for the *j*. set be.
Jas. 1. 2. count it all *j*. when ye
1 Pet. 1. 8. rejoice with *j*. unspeak.
4. 13. rejoice, be glad with exceeding *j*.
1 John 1. 4. we write that your *j*.
Col. 2. 5. *joying* and beholding
Heb. 12. 11. no chastening is *joyous*
Ezra 6. 22. the Lord hath made them *joyful*
Ps. 35. 9. my soul shall be *j*. in Lord
63. 5. I will praise thee with *j*. lips
89. 15. blessed they that know *j*.
Eccl. 7. 14. in day of prosper. be *j*.
Isa. 56. 7. make them *j*. in my
61. 10. my soul shall be *j*. in God
2 Cor. 7. 4. exceeding *j*. in all our tribulations
Deut. 28. 47. servedst not the Lord with *joyfulness*
Col. 1. 11. patience and long suffering with *j*.
Eccl. 9. 9. live *joyfully* with the wife
R. V. Job 41. 22. terror danceth; Jer. 48. 27. the head; Acts 2. 28. gladness; Rom. 5. 11. rejoice; Ps. 96. 12; 149. 5. exult; 98. 8. sing for; Col. 1. 11. joy

JUDGE, Deut. 17. 9. & 25. 2.
Gen. 18. 25. shall not the *J*. of earth
Ex. 2. 14. who made thee a *j*.
Judg. 11. 27. Lord the *J*. be *j*. this

1 Sam. 2. 25. the *j.* shall *j.* him;
Isa. 33. 22. Lord is our *j.* and our
Ps. 68. 5. father of fatherless and *j.*
75. 7. God is the *j.* he putteth
Luke 12. 14. who made me a *j.* over
Acts 10. 42. to be the *J.* of quick
2 Tim. 4. 8. Lord the righteous *J.*
Heb. 12. 23. are come to God the *J.*
Jas. 5. 9. the *J.* standeth before
Gen. 16. 5. Lord *j.* between me and
Deut. 32. 36. the Lord shall *j.* his people, Ps. 135. 14. Heb. 10. 30.
Ps. 7. 8. Lord shall *j.* the people
9. 8. the Lord shall *j.* the world in righteous. 96. 13. & 98. 9. Acts 17. 31.
Mic. 3. 11. heads thereof *j.* for re.
Matt. 7. 1. *j.* not that ye be not jud.
John 5. 30. as I hear I *j.* and my
12. 47. I came not to *j.* the world
Acts 23. 3. sittest thou to *j.* me
Rom. 2. 16. when God shall *j.* the
3. 6. then how shall God *j.* the world
14. 10. why dost thou *j.* thy brother
1 Cor. 4. 3. I *j.* not mine own self
5. *j.* nothing before the time, until
11. 31. if we would *j.* ourselves, we
14. 29. let the prophets speak, and others *j.*
Col. 2. 16. let no man *j.* you in meat
2 Tim. 4. 1. who shall *j.* the quick
Jas. 4. 11. if ye *j.* the law
Ps. 51. 4. *judgest*, Rom. 14. 4. Jas. 4. 12.
7. 11. God *judgeth* the righteous
John 5. 22. the Father *j.* no man
1 Cor. 2. 15. he that is spiritual *j.*
Matt. 19. 28. *judging* twelve tribes
Deut. 1. 17. the *judgment* is God's
32. 4. all his ways are *j.* a God of
Ps. 1. 5. the ungodly shall not stand in the *j.*
9. 16. the Lord is known by the *j.*
101. 1. I will sing of mercy and *j.*
119. 66. teach me good *j.* for
143. 2. enter not into *j.* with thy
Prov. 21. 15. it is joy to just to do *j.*
29. 26. every man's *j.* cometh from
Eccl. 11. 9. God will bring into *j.*
Isa. 1. 27. Zion shall be redeemed with *j.*
28. 17. *j.* also will I lay to the line
30. 18. Lord is a God of *j.*
42. 1. shall bring forth *j.* to the
53. 8. was taken from prison and *j.*
61. 8. I the Lord love *j.* and hate
Jer. 5. 1. if there be any that executeth *j.*
8. 7. they know not the *j.* of Lord
Dan. 4. 37. all whose ways are *j.*
7. 22. *j.* was given to the saints
Hos. 12. 6. keep mercy and *j.* wait
Amos 5. 7. who turn *j.* to worm.
24. let. *j.* run down as waters, and
Matt. 5. 21. be in danger of the *j.*
12. 20. till he send forth *j.* unto victory
John 5. 22. Father committed all *j.*
27. given him author. to execute *j.*
9. 39. for *j.* I am come into the
16. 8. he will reprove the world of sin and *j.*
Acts 24. 25. he reasoned of *j.* to come
Rom. 5. 18. *j.* came on all men to
14. 10. must all stand before *j.* seat
Heb. 9. 27. all men once to die, but after this the *j.*
1 Pet. 4. 17. *j.* must begin at house
Jude 15. to execute *j.* upon all
Rev. 17. 1. show thee *j.* of great
Ps. 19. 9. *judgments* of Lord are
36. 6. thy *j.* are a great deep
119. 75. I know that thy *j.* are
108. O Lord, teach me thy *j.*
Isa. 26. 8. in the way of thy *j.* we
9. when thy *j.* are in the earth
Jer. 12. 1. let me talk with thee of *j.*
Rom. 11. 33. how unsearchable are his *j.*
R. V. 1 Sam. 2. 25. God; Job 9. 15. mine adversary; 1 Sam. 24. 15. give sentence; Jer. 5. 28. plead; Ezek. 28. 23. fall; 1 Cor. 6. 5. decide; 11. 31; 14. 29. discern; Heb. 11. 11. counted; Acts 24. 6; Jas. 4. 12 ——; Job 29. 14. justice; Ps. 76. 8; Acts 25. 15; 2 Pet. 2. 3. sentence; Judg. 5. 10. on rich carpets; Phil. 1. 9. discernment; Mark 6. 11 ——

JUST man was Noah, Gen. 6. 9.
Lev. 19. 36. *j.* balance, *j.* weights
Deut. 16. 20. that which is *j.* shalt
32. 4. a God of truth, *j.* and right
2 Sam. 23. 3. ruleth over men must be *j.*
Neh. 9. 33. *j.* in all that is brought
Job 4. 17. shall man be more *j.* than
9. 2. how should man be *j.* with
Prov. 4. 18. path of *j.* is as shining
10. 6. blessings are on head of *j.*
11. 1. but a *j.* weight is his delight
12. 21. no evil shall happen to *j.*
17. 26. to punish the *j.* is not good
20. 7. a *j.* man walketh in integrity
21. 15. it is joy to *j.* to do judgment
24. 16. *j.* man falleth seven times
Eccl. 7. 15. *j.* man that perisheth in
20. there is not a *j.* man on earth
Isa. 26. 7. way of the *j.* is upright.
45. 21. none beside me; a *j.* God
Ezek. 18. 9. he is *j.* he shall surely
Hab. 2. 4. *j.* shall live by his faith
Zeph. 3. 5. the *j.* Lord is in the
Zech. 9. 9. he is *j.* and having sal.
Matt. 1. 19. Joseph being a *j.* man
5. 45. sendeth rain on the *j.* and
Luke 15. 7. more than over ninety-nine *j.* persons
John 5. 30. my judgment is *j.*
Acts 7. 52. showed coming of *j.* one
24. 15. resurrection both of *j.* and
Rom. 2. 13. not the hearers of the law are *j.*
3. 26. he might be *j.* and justifier
7. 12. commandment holy, *j.* and
Phil. 4. 8. whatsoever things are true, *j.* pure
Col. 4. 1. give that which is *j.* and
Heb. 2. 2. received a *j.* recompense
12. 23. the spirits of *j.* men made
1 John 1. 9. he is faithful and *j.* to
Rev. 15. 3. *j.* and true are thy ways
Mic. 6. 8. to do *justly*, and love
Luke 23. 41. we indeed *j.* for we
1 Thes. 2. 10. how *j.* we behaved
Gen. 18. 19. to do *justice* and
Ps. 89. 14. *j.* and judgment are the
Prov. 8. 15. by me princes decree *j.*
Jer. 31. 23. O habitation of *j.*
Ezek. 45. 9. execute judg. and *j.*
R. V. For most part, righteous; Ps. 89. 14; Isa. 9. 7; 56. 1; 59. 9, 14. righteousness; 1 Thes. 2. 10. righteously

JUSTIFY not the wicked, Ex. 23. 7.
Deut. 25. 1. they shall *j.* righteous
Job 9. 20. if I *j.* myself, my mouth
27. 5. God forbid that I should *j.*
33. 32. speak, for I desire to *j.* thee
Isa. 5. 23. woe to them that *j.* the
Luke 10. 29. he, willing to *j.* himself
16. 15. ye are they which *j.* your.
Rom. 3. 30. God shall *j.* circumci.
Gal. 3. 8. God would *j.* heathen
Job 11. 2. should a man full of talk be *justified*
13. 18. I know I shall be *j.*
25. 4. can a man be *j.* with God
Ps. 51. 4. mightest be *j.* when thou
143. 2. in thy sight shall no man living be *j.*
Isa. 43. 9. that they may be *j.*, 26.
Jer. 3. 11. hath *j.* herself more
Ezek. 16. 51. *j.* thy sisters in all
Matt. 11. 19. wisdom is *j.* of child.
12. 37. by thy words thou shalt be *j.*
Luke 7. 29. *j.* God, being baptized
18. 14. went away *j.* rather than
Acts 13. 39. are *j.* from all things
Rom. 2. 13. doers of law shall be *j.*
3. 4. might be *j.* in thy sayings
20. there shall no flesh be *j.* in his
24. being *j.* freely by his grace
28. man is *j.* by faith without
4. 2. if Abraham were *j.* by works
5. 1. being *j.* by faith, we have
9. being *j.* by his blood, be saved
Rom. 8. 30. whom he *j.* them he also
1 Cor. 4. 4. yet am I not hereby *j.*
6. 11. ye are *j.* in name of the Lord
Gal. 2. 16. not *j.* by works of law
3. 11. no man is *j.* by the law
24. that we might be *j.* by faith
1 Tim. 3. 16. God manifest in flesh, *j.* in Spirit
Tit. 3. 7. that being *j.* by his grace
Jas. 2. 21. was not Abraham *j.* by
24. by works a man is *j.* not faith
25. was not Rahab *j.* by works
Prov. 17. 15. he that *justifieth* the wicked
Isa. 50. 8. he is near, that *j.* me
Rom. 4. 5. God that *j.* the ungodly
8. 33. it is God that *j.* who is he
3. 26. the *justifier* of him that
1 Kings 8. 32. condemning the wicked and *justifying* the righteous, 2 Chron. 6. 23.
Rom. 4. 25. raised for our *justification*
5. 16. gift is of many offences unto *j.*
18. free gift came on all men, to *j.*
R. V. Job 13. 18. am righteous; 25. 4. just; Job 9. 20; 13. 18. righteous

K

KEEP, Gen. 2. 15. & 33. 9.
Gen. 18. 19. they shall *k.* the way
28. 15. I am with thee and will *k.*
Ex. 23. 7. *k.* thee far from a false
20. I send an angel to *k.* thee in
Num. 6. 24. the Lord bless thee, and *k.* thee
Deut. 23. 9. *k.* thee from every
29. 9. *k.* words of this covenant
1 Sam. 2. 9. he will *k.* the feet of
1 Chron. 4. 10. thou wouldst *k.* me
Ps. 17. 8. *k.* me as the apple of the eye
25. 10. to such as *k.* his covenant
20. *k.* my soul
89. 28. my mercy will I *k.* for
91. 11. angels to *k.* thee in all
103. 9. not chide nor *k.* his anger
119. 2. *k.* his testimonies, 88, 129, 146; *k.* thy precepts, 4, 63, 69, 100; *k.* his statutes, 119. 33; *k.* his word and law, 17, 34, 57, 106, 136.
127. 1. except the Lord *k.* the city
140. 4. *k.* me, O Lord, from the
141. 3. *k.* the door of my lips
Eccl. 5. 1. *k.* thy foot when thou
Isa. 26. 3. Lord will *k.* him in per.
27. 3. I the Lord *k.* it; I will *k.* it
Jer. 3. 12. I will not *k.* anger for
Hos. 12. 6. *k.* mercy and judgment
Mic. 7. 5. *k.* the door of thy mouth
Mal. 2. 7. priest's lips *k.* knowledge
Luke 11. 28. hear the word of God and *k.* it
John 12. 25. he that hateth his life shall *k.* it
14. 23. if man love me, will *k.* my
17. 11. holy Father, *k.* through
15. thou shouldest *k.* them from
1 Cor. 5. 8. let us *k.* the feast, not
11. not to *k.* company with such
9. 27. I *k.* under my body, and
Phil. 4. 7. peace of God shall *k.*
1 Tim. 5. 22. *k.* thyself pure
6. 20. *k.* that is committed to thy
2 Tim. 1. 12. able to *k.* that which is
Jas. 1. 27. *k.* himself unspotted
Jude 21. *k.* yoursel. in love of God
24. who is able to *k.* you from
Rev. 1. 3. blessed are they that hear and *k.*
3. 10. I will *k.* thee from the hour
22. 9. thy brethren which *k.* say.
Lev. 26. 3. if ye *keep* my *commandments*
Deut. 6. 7. diligently—always
13. 4.—his—and obey his voice
Ps. 119. 60. I delayed not to—thy—
Prov. 4. 4.—my—and live, 7. 2.
Eccl. 12. 13. fear God and—his—

Matt. 19. 17. if ye will enter into life — the —
John 14. 15. if ye love me — my —
1 John 2. 3. we know him, if we — his —
5. 3. this is the love of God that we — his —
Rev. 14. 12. here are they that — the —
Judg. 3. 19. *keep silence*, Ps. 35. 22. & 50. 3, 21. & 83. 1. Eccl. 3. 7. Isa. 41. 1. & 62. 6. & 65. 6. Lam. 2. 10. Amos 5. 13. Hab. 2. 20. 1 Cor. 14. 28, 34.
1 Kings 8. 23. who *keepest* covenant and mer., 2 Chron. 6.14. Neh. 9. 32.
Deut. 7. 9. which *keepeth* covenant
Ps. 121. 3. he that *k.* thee will not
146. 6. which *k.* truth for ever
Prov. 13. 3. he that *k.* his mouth *k.*
29. 18. he that *k.* the law, happy
1 John 5. 18. that is of God *k.* him.
Rev. 16. 15. blessed is he that *k.*
22. 7. blessed is he that *k.* his
Ex. 34. 7. *keeping* mercy for thous.
Ps. 19. 11. in *k.* of them there is
Dan. 9. 4. *k.* the covenant and mercy
1 Pet. 4. 19. commit the *k.* of their
Ps. 121. 5. the Lord is thy *keeper*
Eccl. 12. 3. when *k.* of house shall
S. of S. 1. 6. made me *k.* of vine.
5. 7. *k.* took away my veil from me
Tit. 2. 5. chaste, *k.* at home, good
Deut. 32. 10. *k.* them as the apple
33. 9. they *kept* thy covenant
Josh. 14. 10. Lord hath *k.* me alive
2 Sam. 22. 22. *k.* ways of the Lord
23. *k.* myself from mine iniquity
Job 23. 11. his ways have I *k.* and
Ps. 17. 4. *k.* me from paths of the
30. 3. *k.* me alive, that I go not
S. of S. 1. 6. mine own vineyard have I not *k.*
Matt. 19. 20. these have I *k.* from
Luke 2. 19. Mary *k.* all these things
John 15. 20. if they have *k.* my say.
17. 6. they have *k.* thy word
12. all thou gavest me, I have *k.*
Rom. 16. 25. *k.* secret since the world
2 Tim. 4. 7. I have *k.* the faith
1 Pet. 1. 5. *k.* by the power of God
Rev. 3. 8. hast *k.* my word, and not
R. V. Deut. 5. 1, 12; 23. 23; 1 Chron. 28. 8; Ps. 105. 45; 119. 5, 8, 44, 57, 60, 63, 88. observe; Acts 12. 4; Phil. 4. 7; 2 Thes. 3. 3; 1 Tim. 6. 20; 2 Tim. 1. 12; 1 John 5. 21; Jude 24. guard; Matt. 28. 4. watchers; Acts 12. 6; 12. 19. guards; 16. 27. jailor; Tit. 2. 5. workers

KERCHIEFS, woe respecting, Ezek. 13. 18.

KEY of house of David, Isa. 22. 22. Rev. 3. 7.
Matt. 16. 19. *k.* of the kingdom of
Luke 11. 52. taken away the *k.* of
Rev. 1. 18. I have *k.* of hell
9. 1. *k.* of the bottomless pit

KICK, Deut. 32. 15. 1 Sam. 2. 29. Acts 9. 5. & 26. 14.

KID, Isa. 11. 6. Luke 15. 29.
S. of S. 1. 8. feed *k.* beside sheph.
R. V. In Gen. Lev. Num. and Ezek. mostly he-goat, or goat

KIDNEYS, for sacrifices, burnt, Ex. 29. 13. Lev. 3. 4.
— of wheat, fat of, Deut. 32. 14.

KILL, thou shalt not, Ex. 20. 13.
Deut. 32. 39. I *k.* and I make alive
2 Kings 5. 7. I am God to *k.* and
Eccl. 3. 3. time to *k.* and to heal
Matt. 10. 28. fear not them which *k.* the body, but are not able to *k.*
Mark 3. 4. lawful to save life, or *k.*
Acts 10. 13. rise, Peter, *k.* and eat
1 Kings 21. 19. hast thou *killed* and
Ps. 44. 22. we are *k.* all day long
Luke 12. 5. after he hath *k.* hath
Acts 3. 15. *k.* the Prince of Life
2 Cor. 6. 9. we are chast. and not *k.*
1 Thes. 2. 15. both *k.* the Lord
Rev. 13. 10. that *k.* with the sword
Matt. 23. 37. thou that *killest* the prophets, Luke 13. 34.
1 Sam. 2. 6. the Lord *killeth*, and
John 16. 2. who *k.* you will think
2 Cor. 3. 6. letter *k.* but spirit
R. V. Ex. 20. 13; Deut. 5. 17; Matt. 19. 18. do no murder; Num. 35. 27; 1 Sam. 19. 1; 2 Kings 11. 15; Acts 23. 15; Rev. 6. 4. slay; Mark 14. 12; Luke 22. 7. sacrificed

KIND, Gen. 1. 11. 2 Chron. 10. 7.
Luke 6. 35. he is *k.* to unthankful
1 Cor. 13. 4. charity suff. long . is *k.*
Eph. 4. 32. be *k.* to one another
1 Sam. 20. 14. show me the *kindness*
2 Sam. 9. 3. may show the *k.* of God
16. 17. is this thy *k.* to thy friend
Neh. 9. 17. a God slow to anger and of great *k.*
Ps. 117. 2. his merciful *k.* is great
Prov. 19. 22. the des. of man is his *k.*
31. 26. in her tongue is law of *k.*
Isa. 54. 8. with everlasting *k.* will
10. my *k.* shall not depart from
Jer. 2. 2. I remember thee, the *k.*
Joel 2. 13. God is of great *k.*
Col. 3. 12. put on bowels of mer., *k.*
2 Pet. 1. 7. to godliness, brother. *k.*
Ps. 25. 6. remember thy *loving kindness*
36. 7. how excellent is thy —
63. 3. thy — is better than life
103. 4. who crowneth thee with —
Isa. 63. 7. I will mention the — of
Jer. 9. 24. I am the Lord which exercise —
32. 18. thou showest — to thous.
Hos. 2. 19. I will betroth thee in —
R. V. Matt. 17. 21 ——

KINDLE, Prov. 26. 21. Isa. 10. 16.
Isa. 30. 33. breath of Lord doth *k.* it
Hos. 11. 8. my repentings are *kindled*
2 Sam. 22. 9. coals *k.* by it, Ps. 18. 8.
Ps. 2. 12. when his wrath is *k.* but a
Isa. 50. 11. walk in light of sparks ye have *k.*
Luke 12. 49. fire on earth, what if it be already *k.*
R. V. Prov. 26. 21. inflame; Jer. 33. 18. burn; Jas. 3. 5. much wood is kindled by how small a fire

KING, Gen. 14. 18. & 36. 31.
Job 18. 14. bring him to *k.* of ter.
34. 18. is it fit to say to a *k.* thou
Ps. 10. 16. Lord is *K.* for ever and
24. 7. the *K.* of glory shall come
33. 16. no *k.* saved by multitude
47. 7. God is *K.* of all the earth
74. 12. God is my *k.*, 5. 2. & 44. 4.
Prov. 30. 31. a *k.* against whom is
Eccl. 5. 9. *k.* himself is served by
8. 4. where word of *k.* is there
S. of S. 1. 4. the *k.* brought me into
12. while the *k.* sitteth at his table
7. 5. the *k.* is held in the galleries
Isa. 32. 1. a *k.* shall reign in
33. 22. the Lord is our lawgiver and our *k.*
43. 15. Creator of Israel, your *K.*
Jer. 10. 10. Lord is true God, and everlasting *K.*
23. 5. a *K.* shall reign and prosper
46. 18. saith the *K.* whose name
Hos. 3. 5. seek the Lord and David their *k.*
7. 5. in day of our *k.* the princes
13. 11. I gave them a *k.* in anger
Matt. 25. 34. then shall the *K.* say
Luke 23. 2. he himself is Christ, a *k.*
John 6. 15. come by force to make him *k.*
19. 14. behold your *k.*
15. no *k.* but Cæsar
1 Tim. 1. 17. to the *K.* eternal
6. 15. *K.* of kings, and Lord of lords, Rev. 16. 16. & 17. 14.
1 Pet. 2. 17. fear God, honor *k.*, 16.
Rev. 15. 3. just and true, thou *K.*
Ps. 76. 12. terrible to *kings* of the earth, 72. 11.
102. 15. *k.* of the earth see thy glory
144. 10. that giveth salva. to *k.*
149. 8. to bind their *k.* with fetters
Prov. 8. 15. by me *k.* reign, and
Hos. 8. 4. they set up *k.* but not by
Matt. 11. 8. soft clothing are in *k.* houses
Luke 22. 25. *k.* of Gentiles exercise
1 Cor. 4. 8. reigned as *k.* without us
1 Tim. 2. 2. give thanks for *k.* and
Rev. 1. 6. made us *k.* and priests
16. 12. that way of *k.* of the east
Ex. 19. 6. be a *kingdom* of priests
1 Sam. 10. 25. Samuel told man. of *k.*
1 Chron. 29. 11. thine is the *k.* O Lord, Matt. 6. 13.
Ps. 22. 28. for the *k.* is the Lord's
Dan. 2. 44. in last days shall God set up a *k.*
7. 27. whose *k.* is everlasting *k.*, 14.
Matt. 12. 25. every *k.* divided
38. good seed are the children of *k.*
25. 34. inherit *k.* prepared for you
Mark 11. 10. blessed be the *k.* of
Luke 12. 32. Father's pleasure to give you the *k.*
19. 12. to receive for himself a *k.*
John 18. 36. *k.* is not of this world
1 Cor. 15. 24. shall have delivered up the *k.*
Col. 1. 13. translated us into the *k.*
2 Tim. 4. 18. preserve me to his heavenly *k.*
Heb. 12. 28. we receiving a *k.* not to
Jas. 2. 5. rich in faith, heirs of *k.*
2 Pet. 1. 11. into everlasting *k.* of
Rev. 1. 9. in *k.* and patience of
11. 15. the *k.* of this world are *k.*
17. 17. to give their *k.* to the beast
Matt. 6. 33. *kingdom of God*, 12. 28. & 21. 43. Mark 1. 15. & 10. 14, 15. & 12. 34. & 15. 43. Luke 4. 43. & 6. 20. & 9. 62. & 10. 9, 11. & 13. 29. & 17. 20, 21. & 18. 16, 17, 29. & 21. 16.
John 3. 3. except born again, cannot see —, 5.
Rom. 14. 17. — is not meat and drink
1 Cor. 4. 20. — is not in word, but
6. 9. unright. shall not inherit —
15. 50. flesh and blood cannot inherit —
Eph. 5. 5. hath any inheritance in —
2 Thes. 1. 5. be counted worthy of —
Rev. 12. 10. now is come — and power
Matt. 3. 2. *kingdom of heaven*, 4. 17. & 10. 7. & 5. 3, 10. 19, 20. & 7. 21. & 8. 11. & 11. 11, 12. & 13. 11, 24, 31, 52. & 16. 19. & 18. 1, 3, 23. & 20. 1. & 22. 2. & 23. 13. & 25. 1, 14.

KISS the Son, lest he be angry, Ps. 2. 12.
S. of S. 1. 2. let him *k.* me with the *k.*
Rom. 16. 16. salute with a holy *k.*
1 Pet. 5. 14. greet with *k.* of charity
Ps. 85. 10. righteousness and peace have *kissed*
Luke 7. 38. *k.* his feet and anointed
Prov. 27. 6. *kisses* from an enemy

KNEELING in prayer, 2 Chron. 6. 13. Ezra 9. 5. Ps. 95. 6. Dan. 6. 10. Acts 7. 60. & 9. 40. & 21. 5. Eph. 3. 14.

KNEES, Gen. 30. 3. & 41. 43.
Job 4. 4. feeble *k.*, Isa. 35. 3. Heb. 12. 12.
Isa. 45. 23. to God every *k.* shall bow, Rom. 14. 11. Phil. 2. 10. Matt. 27. 29. Eph. 3. 14.
Nah. 2. 10. the *k.* smite together

KNIFE, Prov. 23. 2. & 30. 14.
R. V. Ezek. 5. 1, 2. sword

KNIT, 1 Sam. 18. 1. Col. 2. 2, 19.

KNEW, Gen. 3. 7. & 4. 1. & 42. 7.
Gen. 28. 16. God is in this place, I *k.* it not
Deut. 34. 10. whom Lord *k.* face to
Jer. 1. 5. before I formed thee, I *k.*
Matt. 7. 23. depart ye, I never *k.*
John 4. 10. if you *k.* the gift of God
Rom. 1. 21. when they *k.* God, they
2 Cor. 5. 21. made him to be sin who *k.* no sin
Deut. 8. 2. to *know* what was in thy
Josh. 22. 22. God knoweth, and Israel he shall *k.*
1 Sam. 3. 7. Samuel did not yet *k.*
1 Kings 8. 38. man shall *k.* plague

1 Chron. 28. 9. *k*. thou the God of
Job. 5. 27. *k*. thou it for thy good
13. 23. make me to *k*. my trans.
22. 13. how doth God *k*., Ps. 73. 11.
Ps. 4. 3. *k*. the Lord hath set apart
9. 10. that *k*. thy name will trust in
46. 10. be still, and *k*. that I am God
51. 6. God shall make me to *k*.
139. 23. *k*. my heart; and *k*. my
Eccl. 11. 9. *k*. that for all these
Isa. 58. 2. they seek and delight to *k*.
Jer. 17. 9. heart is dece. who can *k*.
22. 16. was not this to *k*. me
24. 7. I will give them a heart to *k*.
31. 34. saying, *k*. the Lord
Ezek. 2. 5. shall *k*. that a prophet hath, 33. 33.
Hos. 2. 20. in faithfulness thou shalt *k*. the Lord
Mic. 3. 1. is it not for you to *k*.
Matt. 6. 3. let not left hand *k*. what
7. 11. *k*. how to give good gifts
13. 11. given you to *k*. mystery
John 4. 42. we *k*. this is indeed
7. 17. he shall *k*. of the doctrine
10. 4. sheep follow him, for they *k*.
14. I *k*. my sheep and am known
13. 7. *k*. not now, but shalt *k*.
17. if ye *k*. these things, happy are
35. by this men *k*. ye are my
Acts 1. 7. it is not for you to *k*. the
Rom. 10. 19. did not Israel *k*. yes
1 Cor. 2. 14. neither can ye *k*. them
4. 19. I will *k*. not the speech
8. 2. *k*. any thing, *k*. nothing as he
Eph. 3. 19. to *k*. love of Christ
1 Thes. 5. 12. to *k*. them who labor
Tit. 1. 16. they profess that they *k*.
Ex. 4. 14. *I know*, Job 9. 2, 28.
Gen. 18. 19. — him that he will
22. 12. now — that thou fearest God
2 Kings 19. 27. — thy abode and thy
Job 19. 25. — that my Redeemer liveth
Ps. 41. 11. by this — that thou fav.
Jer. 10. 23. — that the way of man
Matt. 25. 12. — you not, Luke 13. 25.
John 13. 18. — whom I have chosen
Acts 26. 27. — that thou believest
Rom. 7. 18. — that in me
1 Cor. 4. 4. though — nothing by
13. 12. now — in part; but then
Phil. 4. 12. — how to be abased
2 Tim. 1. 12. — whom I have believed
1 John 2. 4. he that saith — him, is
Rev. 2. 2. — thy works, 9. 13, 19. & 3. 1, 3, 15.
Hos. 6. 3. *we know*, 8. 2. John 4. 22.
1 Cor. 2. 12. 1 John 2. 3, 5.
John 16. 30. *thou knowest* all things
21. 17. — all things — that I love thee
Ps. 1. 6. Lord *knoweth* the way of
94. 11. Lord *k*. thoughts of man
103. 14. he *k*. our frame, that we
139. 14. my soul *k*. right well
Eccl. 9. 1. no man *k*. either love or
Isa. 1. 3. ox *k*. his owner, and ass
Jer. 8. 7. stork *k*. appointed times
9. 24. understandeth and *k*. me to
Zeph. 3. 5. the unjust *k*. no shame
Matt. 6. 8. *k*. what things ye have
24. 36. of that day and hour *k*. no
1 Cor. 8. 2. *k*. any thing, he *k*. nothing yet
2 Tim. 2. 19. the Lord *k*. them that
Jas. 4. 17. that *k*. to do good doeth
2 Pet. 2. 9. Lord *k*. how to deliver
Rev. 2. 17. a name which no man *k*.
Ps. 9. 16. Lord is *known* by the
31. 7. hast *k*. my soul in adversity
67. 2. thy way may be *k*. on earth
Isa. 45. 4. thou hast not *k*. me, 5.
Amos 3. 2. you only have I *k*. of all
Matt. 10. 26. there is nothing hid that shall not be *k*., Luke 8. 17. & 12. 2.
Luke 19. 42. if thou hadst *k*. in this
Acts 15. 18. *k*. unto God are all his
Rom. 1. 19. that which may be *k*.
7. 7. I had not *k*. sin but by the
1 Cor. 8. 3. the same is *k*. of him
Gal. 4. 9. *k*. God, or rather are *k*. of
Rev. 2. 24. have not *k*. the depths of

Gen. 2. 17. *knowledge* of good and
1 Sam. 2. 3. the Lord is a God of *k*.
Ps. 19. 2. night unto night show. *k*.
73. 11. is there *k*. in the Most High
94. 10. he that teacheth men *k*.
139. 6. such *k*. is too wonderful
Prov. 8. 12. I find out *k*. of witty
14. 6. *k*. is easy to him that understandeth
19. 2. the soul be without *k*. is not
30. 3. I have not the *k*. of the holy
Eccl. 9. 10. there is no device nor *k*.
Isa. 28. 9. whom shall he teach *k*.
Jer. 3. 15. pastors shall feed you with *k*.
Dan. 12. 4. run to and fro, and *k*. be
Hos. 4. 6. are destroy. for lack of *k*.
Hab. 2. 14. earth filled with *k*. of the Lord, Isa. 11. 9.
Mal. 2. 7. priest's lips should keep *k*.
Rom. 2. 20. a teacher hast form of *k*.
3. 20. for by the law is *k*. of sin
10. 2. zeal for God not accord. to *k*.
1 Cor. 8. 1. all have *k*. *k*. puffeth up
Eph. 3. 19. the love of Christ which passeth *k*.
Phil. 3. 8. loss for excellency of the *k*.
Col. 2. 3. are hid treasures of wisdom and *k*.
3. 10. renewed in *k*. after image of
1 Pet. 3. 7. dwell with them according to *k*.
2 Pet. 1. 5. add to virtue *k*. and to *k*.
3. 18. grow in grace and in the *k*. of Jesus Christ
R. V. Many changes to, perceive, understand, learn, discern, etc., but none affecting general meaning. Prov. 2. 3. discernment; Eph. 3. 4. understanding

KNOCK, Matt. 7. 7. Rev. 3. 20.

L

LABOR, Gen. 31. 42. & 35. 16.
Ps. 90. 10. yet is their strength *l*.
104. 23. man goeth to his *l*. until eve
128. 2. thou shalt eat the *l*. of thine
Prov. 14. 23. in all *l*. there is profit
Eccl. 1. 8. all things are full of *l*.
4. 8. yet is there no end of all his *l*.
Isa. 55. 2. ye spend your *l*. for that
Hab. 3. 17. though *l*. of the olive
1 Cor. 15. 58. your *l*. is not in vain
1 Thes. 1. 3. work of faith, and *l*.
Heb. 6. 10. God will not forget your *l*. of
Rev. 14. 13. dead may rest from *l*.
Prov. 23. 4. *l*. not to be rich; cease
Matt. 11. 28. come all ye that *l*. and
John 6. 27. *l*. not for the meat
1 Thes. 5. 12. know them which *l*.
1 Tim. 5. 17. honor those who *l*.
Heb. 4. 11. let us *l*. to enter into
Isa. 49. 4. I have *labored* in vain
John 4. 38. other men *l*. and ye
1 Cor. 15. 10. I *l*. more abundantly
Phil. 2. 16. not run, nor *l*. in vain
Prov. 16. 26. he that *laboreth*, *l*.
Eccl. 5. 12. sleep of the *laboring* man is sweet
Col. 4. 12. Epaphras *l*. fervently
Luke 10. 7. the *laborer* is worthy
Matt. 9. 37. but *laborers* are few, Luke 10. 2.
1 Cor. 3. 9. we are *l*. toge. with God
R. V. Deut. 26. 7; Rev. 2. 2. toil; Eccl. 1. 8. weariness; Phil. 1. 22. work; Josh. 7. 3; 1 Cor. 4. 12. toil; Neh. 4. 21. wrought; Lam. 5. 5. are weary; 2 Cor. 5. 9. make it our aim; Col. 4. 12. striving; 1 Thes. 2. 9. working; Heb. 4. 11. give diligence; Rev. 2. 3 ——

LACK, Hos. 4. 6. Matt. 19. 20, 21.
2 Cor. 11. 9. 1 Thes. 3. 10. Jas. 1. 5.
R. V. 1 Thes. 4. 12. need

LADEN with iniquity, Isa. 1. 4.
Matt. 11. 28. labor and heavy *l*.
2 Tim. 3. 6. silly women, *l*. with

LADDER, Jacob's, Gen. 28. 12.

LADY of kingdoms, Isa. 47. 5.
Isa. 47. 7. I shall be a *l*. for ever
2 John 1. unto the elect *l*.
Esth. 1. 18. *ladies* of Persia
Judg. 5. 29. her wise *l*. answered
R. V. Esth. 1. 18. princesses

LAMB, Gen. 22. 7, 8. Ex. 12. 3.
2 Sam. 12. 3. man had nothing save one ewe *l*.
Isa. 11. 6. wolf shall dwell with *l*.
53. 7. he is brought as a *l*. to the
John 1. 29. behold the *L*. of God
1 Pet. 1. 19. as a *l*. without blem.
Rev. 5. 12. worthy is the *L*. that
6. 16. fall on us and hide us from the face of the *L*.
7. 14. robes made white in blood of the *L*., 12 11.
17. *L*. in the midst of the throne shall feed them
13. 8. *L*. slain from the foundation of the world
R. V. In Num., he-lamb

LAME, Lev. 21. 18. Mal. 1. 8, 13.
Job 29. 15. eyes to the blind and feet to the *l*.
Prov. 26. 7. legs of the *l*. are not
Isa. 35. 6. the *l*. man shall leap
Heb. 12. 13. lest the *l*. be turned

LAMP, Gen. 15. 17. Ex. 27. 20.
1 Kings 15. 4. Matt. 25. 1, 3, 4, 7, 8.
2 Sam. 22. 29. thou art my *l*. O Lord
Ps. 119. 105. thy word a *l*. to my
132. 17. I have ordained a *l*. for
Prov. 6. 23. the command. is a *l*.
13. 9. *l*. of wicked shall be put out
Isa. 62. 1. salvation as a *l*. that
Ex. 25. 37. *seven lamps*, 37. 23. Num. 8. 2. Zech. 4. 2. Rev. 4. 5.
R. V. Gen. 15. 17; Rev. 8. 10. torch; Judg. 7. 16, 20; Job 41. 19; Ezek. 1. 13. torches

LAND, Eccl. 10. 16, 17. Isa. 5. 30.
Deut. 19. 14. remove *landmark*, 27. 17. Job 24. 2. Prov. 22. 28. & 23. 10.
R. V. Many changes in O. T. to earth, ground, country, etc.

LANGUAGE, Gen. 11. 1. Neh. 13. 24.
Ps. 81. 5. Isa. 19. 18. Zeph. 3. 9.

LANGUISH, Isa. 24. 4. Ps. 41. 3.

LASCIVIOUSNESS, Mark 7. 22.
2 Cor. 12. 21. Gal. 5. 19. Eph. 4. 19.
1 Pet. 4. 3.
Jude 4. turning grace of God into *l*.

LAST end be like his, Num. 23. 10.
Lam. 1. 9. she remembered not her *l*. end
Luke 11. 26. *l*. state is worse than
1 Pet. 1. 5. *last time*, 20. 1 John 2. 18.
Jude 18. should be mockers in the —
R. V. Gen. 49. 1; Isa. 2. 2; Jer. 12. 4; Lam. 1. 9; Dan. 8. 19; Mic. 4. 1. latter; Matt. 21. 37; Luke 20. 32. afterward

LATTER day, Job 19. 25; *l*. end, Prov. 19. 20; *l*. house, Hag. 2. 9; *l*. time, 1 Tim. 4. 1. 2 Tim. 3. 1.

LAUGH, Gen. 17. 17. & 18. 12, 15.
2 Chron. 30. 10. but they *l*. them
Job 5. 22. at destruction and famine thou shalt *l*.
Ps. 2. 4. he that sitteth in the heavens shall *l*.
37. 13. the Lord shall *l*. at him
52. 6. righteous. shall see and *l*.
59. 8. thou, O Lord, shall *l*. at
Prov. 1. 26. I will *l*. at your calam.
Luke 6. 21. blessed that weep, for ye shall *l*.
Job 8. 21. he fill thy mouth with *laughing*
Ps. 126. 2. our mouth was filled with *laughter*
Prov. 14. 13. even in *l*. heart is sor.
Eccl. 7. 3. sorrow is better than *l*.
Jas. 4. 9. let your *l*. be turned

LAW, Gen. 47. 26. Prov. 28. 4.
Deut. 33. 2. from his right hand went a fiery *l*.

Neh. 8. 7. caused people to understand the *l.*
10. 28. separated from people to *l.*
Ps. 1. 2. his delight is in the *l.*
19. 7. *l.* of the Lord is perfect
37. 31. *l.* of his God is in his heart
119. 72. *l.* of thy mouth is better
Prov. 6. 23. *l.* is light
7. 2. keep my *l.* as apple of eye
28. 9. turns away from hearing *l.*
29. 18. keepeth the *l.* happy is he
Isa. 2. 2. shall go forth the *l.*
8. 16. seal the *l.* among my dis.
20. to the *l.* and the testimony
42. 21. magnify the *l.* and make
51. 7. peo. in whose heart is my *l.*
Jer. 18. 18. *l.* shall not perish from
31. 33. I will put my *l.* in inward
Ezek. 7. 26. *l.* shall perish from
Hos. 8. 12. writ. great things of my *l.*
Mal. 2. 7. people seek *l.* at his
Luke 16. 16. *l.* and prophets till
John 1. 17. *l.* was given by Moses
19. 7. we have a *l.* and by our *l.*
Acts 13. 39. not justified by the *l.*
Rom. 2. 12. sinned without *l.*
13. not hearers of *l.* but doers of *l.*
3. 20. by deeds of *l.* shall no flesh
27. boasting by what *l.* by *l.* of
31. do we make void the *l.*
5. 13. sin is not imput. where no *l.*
7. 7. had not known sin but by *l.*
8. for without the *l.* sin was dead
12. the *l.* is holy, just, and good
14. *l.* is spiritual, but I am carnal
22. I delight in the *l.* of God
23. *l.* in my members against *l.*
8. 2. *l.* of Spirit made free from *l.*
10. 4. Christ is end of the *l.* for
5. righteousness of *l.*, 9. 31, 32.
1 Cor. 6. 1. dare any of you go to *l.*
Gal. 2. 16. man not justified by works of the *l.*
3. 10. of works of the *l.* are under
12. the *l.* is not of faith, but the
13. Christ redeemed us from the curse of the *l.*
5. 23. love, faith, against such there is no *l.*
1 Tim. 1. 8. the *l.* is good if we use
9. that *l.* is not made for right.
Heb. 7. 19. *l.* made nothing perfect
Jas. 1. 25. whoso looketh into the perfect *l.*
1 John 3. 4. sin transgresseth the *l.* sin is transgression of *l.*
Neh. 9. 26. cast *thy law* behind their backs
Ps. 40. 8. — is within my heart
94. 12. whom thou teach. out of —
119. 70. I delight in —, 77. 92, 174.
18. wondrous things out of —
97. how I love —, 113. 163.
Ezek. 18. 5. do that which is *lawful* and right, 33. 14, 19.
1 Cor. 6. 12. all things are *l.* to
Isa. 33. 22. Lord is *lawgiver*
R. V. Gen. 47. 26; 1 Chron. 16. 17; Ps. 94. 20; 105. 10. statute; Acts 15. 24; 24. 6; Rom. 9. 32; 1 Cor. 7. 39; 9. 20 —; Acts 19. 39. regular; Gen. 49. 10. ruler's staff; Num. 21. 18; Ps. 60. 7; 108. 8. sceptre

LAY, Gen. 19. 33, 35. Job 29. 19.
Eccl. 7. 2. the living will *l.* it to
Isa. 28. 16. I *l.* in Zion a tried
Mal. 2. 2. I cursed, ye do not *l.*
Matt. 8. 20. hath not where to *l.*
Acts 7. 60. *l.* not this sin to their
15. 28. *l.* on you no greater bur.
Heb. 12. 1. *l.* aside every weight
Jas. 1. 21. *l.* apart all filthiness
John 10. 15. *lay down life*, 13. 37. & 15. 13.
1 Tim. 5. 22. *lay hands*, Heb. 6. 2.
6. 12. *lay hold* on eternal life
Heb. 6. 18. — on hope set before us
Matt. 6. 20. *lay up* for yourselves
Ps. 62. 9. to be *laid* in the balance
89. 19. I *l.* help on one that is
Isa. 53. 6. Lord *l.* on him iniquities
Matt. 3. 10. axe *l.* to root of trees
1 Cor. 3. 10. I have *l.* foundation
Heb. 6. 1. not *l.* again foundation
1 Sam. 21. 12. David *laid up* these
Ps. 31. 19. thy goodness — for them
Luke 1. 66. — in their hearts
Col. 1. 5. hope which is — for you
2 Tim. 4. 8. — for me a crown of
Job 21. 19. God *layeth* up his iniq.
24. 12. yet God *l.* not folly to them
Prov. 2. 7. *l.* up wisdom
26. 24. *l.* up deceit
Isa. 56. 2. blessed is the man that *l.* hold on
57. 1. no man *l.* to heart, 42. 25.
R. V. The frequent changes do not modify general meaning. *See* also the *v. i.* **Lie, lay, lain.**

LEAD, Ex. 15. 10. Job 19. 24. Zech. 5. 7, 8. Gen. 33. 14. Ex. 13. 21.
Ps. 5. 8. *lead me* in thy righteous.
25. 5. — in thy truth
27. 11. — in a plain path
61. 2. — to rock higher than I
24. — in the way everlasting
Isa. 11. 6. a little child shall *l.* them
40. 11. gently *l.* those with young
Matt. 15. 14. if blind *l.* the blind, Luke 6. 39.
1 Tim. 2. 2. may *l.* a quiet and
Rev. 7. 17. Lamb shall *l.* them to
Ps. 23. 2. *leadeth* me beside still
48. 17. God which *l.* thee by way
Matt. 7. 13. gate *l.* to destruction
John 10. 3. calleth sheep and *l.*
Rom. 2. 4. goodness of God *l.*
Gen. 24. 27. *Lord led*, 48. Ex. 13. 18. & 15. 13. Deut. 8. 2. & 29. 5. & 32. 10, 12. Neh. 9. 12. Ps. 77. 20. & 80. 1. & 78. 14, 53. & 106. 9. & 136. 16. & 107. 7.
Isa. 48. 2. & 63. 13, 14. Jer. 26. 17.
Rom. 8. 14. *led by Spirit*, Gal. 5. 18.
Isa. 55. 4. *leader* to people, 9. 16.
R. V. Ps. 25. 5; Matt. 15. 14; Luke 6. 39; Rev. 7. 17. guide

LEAF, Job 13. 25. Ezek. 47. 12. Rev. 22. 2.

LEAGUE with stones of field, Job 5. 23.
R. V. Josh. 9. 6, 7, 11, 15, 16; Judg. 2. 2; 2 Sam. 3. 21; 5. 3. covenant

LEAN not to own understanding, Prov. 3. 5.
Job 8. 15. he shall *l.* upon his
S. of S. 8. 5. that *l.* on her beloved
Mic. 3. 11. yet will they *l.* on Lord
John 13. 23. *l.* on Jesus' bosom
R. V. John 13. 23. reclining

LEANNESS, Job 16. 8. Ps. 106. 15. Isa. 10. 16. & 24. 16. my *l.* my *l.*
R. V. Isa. 24. 16. I pine away

LEAP, S. of S. 2. 8. Isa. 35. 6. Zeph. 1. 9.
Luke 1. 41. & 6. 23. rejoice and *l.* for

LEARN to fear me, Deut. 4. 10. & 5. 1. & 14. 23. & 31. 12, 13.
Ps. 119. 71. might *l.* thy statutes
Prov. 22. 25. lest thou *l.* his ways
Isa. 1. 17. *l.* to do well, seek
26. 10. yet will he not *l.* righteous.
Jer. 10. 2. *l.* not way of the heathen
Matt. 9. 13. *l.* what that means
11. 29. *l.* of me, for I am meek
1 Tim. 2. 11. let woman *l.* in silence
Tit. 3. 14. let ours *l.* to maintain
Rev. 14. 3. no man could *l.* that
Ps. 106. 35. *learned* their works
Isa. 50. 4. Lord God hath given me the tongue of the *l.*
John 6. 45. hath *l.* of Father cometh
Acts 7. 22. Moses was *l.* in all wis.
Eph. 4. 20. ye have not so *l.* Christ
Phil. 4. 11. I have *l.* in whatsoever
Heb. 5. 8. though a son, yet *l.* he
Prov. 1. 5. wise will incre. *learning*
Acts 26. 24. much *l.* doth make
Rom. 15. 4. was written for our *l.*
2 Tim. 3. 7. ever *l.* never come
R. V. Isa. 50. 4. are taught; Acts 7. 22. instructed

LEAST of thy mercies, Gen. 32. 10.
Jer. 31. 34. shall know me from *l.* to
Matt. 11. 11. *l.* in kingdom of God
Luke 16. 10. faithful in *l.* is faithful
1 Cor. 6. 4. judge who are *l.* esteemed
1 Cor. 15. 9. I am *l.* of all the apostles
Eph. 3. 8. less than the *l.* of all
R. V. 1 Sam. 21. 4. only; Matt. 13. 22. less than; 11. 11; Luke 7. 28. but little; Luke 16. 10. a very little; 1 Cor. 6. 4. of no account

LEAVE father and mother and cleave to his wife, Gen. 2. 24. Matt. 15. 9. Eph. 5. 31.
1 Kings 8. 57. let him not *l.* us, nor
Ps. 16. 10. not *l.* my soul in hell
27. 9. *l.* me not, neither forsake me
Matt. 5. 24. *l.* there thy gift before
23. 23. and not to *l.* other undone
John 14. 18. I will not *l.* you com.
27. peace I *l.* with you, my peace
Heb. 13. 5. I will never *l.* nor
Acts 14. 17. *left*, Rom. 9. 29. Heb. 4. 1. Jude 6. Rev. 2. 4.
R. V. Changes frequent, but usual meanings retained

LEAVEN, Ex. 12. 15. Lev. 2. 11.
Matt. 13. 33. the kingdom of heaven is like *l.*
16. 6. beware of *l.* of Pharisees
1 Cor. 5. 7. purge out the old *l.*
6. a little *l.* leaveneth lump

LEES, Isa. 25. 6. Jer. 48. 11. Zeph. 1. 12.

LEFT-HANDED slingers, Judg. 20. 16.

LEGS, Ps. 147. 10. Prov. 26. 7.
R. V. Isa. 47. 2. train

LEND, Ex. 22. 25. Deut. 23. 19, 20.
Jer. 15. 10. neither *l.* on usury
Luke 6. 35. do good and *l.* hoping
Ps. 37. 26. ever merci. and *lendeth*
Prov. 19. 17. giveth to the poor *l.*
22. 7. borrower is servant to *lender*
1 Sam. 1. 28. I have *lent* him to Lord
R. V. Lev. 25. 37. give; 1 Sam. 1. 28. granted

LEOPARD, S. of S. 4. 8. Isa. 11. 6. Jer. 5. 6. & 13. 23. Hos. 13. 7. Hab. 1. 8.

LEPROSY, in a house, Lev. 14. 33; of Miriam, Num. 12. 10; of Naaman and Gehazi, 2 Kings 5; of Uzziah, 2 Chron. 26. 19; symptoms of, Lev. 13; observances on healing, Lev. 14. & 22. 4. Deut. 24. 8; cured by Christ, Matt. 8. 3. Mark 1. 41. Luke 5. 12. & 17. 12.

LESS, Ezra 9. 13. Job 11. 6. Isa. 40. 17. Heb. 7. 9. Eph. 3. 8. Gen. 32. 10.

LETTER, Rom. 7. 2. 2 Cor. 3. 6.
R. V. 2 Cor. 7. 8; 2 Thes. 2. 2. epistle; Luke 23. 38; 2 Cor. 3. 1; Heb. 13. 22 —

LETTEST, Luke 2. 29. 2 Thes. 2. 7.

LEVIATHAN, Job 41. 1. Ps. 74. 14.

LIBERAL, Prov. 11. 25. Isa. 32. 5, 8. 2 Cor. 9. 13.
1 Cor. 16. 3. *liberality*, 2 Cor. 8. 2.
Jas. 1. 5. God giveth to all men *liberally*
R. V. 1 Cor. 16. 3. bounty

LIBERTINES, the, Acts 6. 9.

LIBERTY, Lev. 25. 10. Jer. 34. 8.
Ps. 119. 45. I will walk at *l.* for I
Isa. 61. 1. anoint. me to proclaim *l*
Luke 4. 18. sent me to set at *l.*
Rom. 8. 21. into glorious *l.* of the
2 Cor. 3. 17. where Spirit of Lord is there is *l.*
Gal. 5. 1. stand fast in *l.*
13. use not *l.* for an occasion to the
Jas. 1. 25. whoso looketh into the law of *l.*
2. 12. be judged by the law of *l.*
1 Pet. 2. 16. not using your *l.*
R. V. Acts 27. 3. leave; 1 Cor. 7. 39. free; Gal. 5. 13. freedom

LIE, Lev. 6. 3. & 19. 11. Job 11. 3.
Ps. 58. 3. wicked go astray speaking *l.*
62. 9. men of high degree are a *l.*
101. 7. that telleth a *l.* shall not
Hos. 11. 12. compasseth me about with *l.*
2 Thes. 2. 11. that they should believe a *l.*
1 Tim. 4. 2. speaking *l.* in hypocrisy
Rev. 22. 15. loveth and maketh a *l.*

Num. 23. 19. God is not a man,
that he should *l.*
Isa. 63. 8. children that will not *l.*
Hab. 2. 3. at the end it shall speak
and not *l.*
Col. 3. 9. *l.* not one to another
Tit. 1. 2. God that cannot *l.* hath
Heb. 6. 18. impossible for God to *l.*
Ps. 116. 11. I said, all men are *liars*
Tit. 1. 12. the Cretians are always *l.*
Rev. 2. 2. hast tried and found
them *l.*
21. 8. all *l.* shall have their part
John 8. 44. he is a *liar* and the
Rom. 3. 4. God be true, and every
man a *l.*
1 John 1. 10. we make him a *l.*
2. 4. keepeth not the command-
ments is a *l.*
Ps. 119. 29. remove from me the
way of *lying*
163. I abhor *l.* but love thy law
Prov. 12. 19. *l.* tongue but for a
Jer. 7. 4. trust not in *l.* words
Hos. 4. 2. by stealing and *l.* the,
Jonah 2. 8. observe *l.* vanities
R. V. Job 11. 3; Jer. 48. 30. boast-
ings; Ezek. 24. 12. toil; Ps. 101. 7;
Prov. 29. 12; Jer. 9. 3; Hos. 11. 12.
falsehood; Gen. 4. 7; 49. 25. couch-
eth
LIFE, Gen. 2. 7, 9. & 42. 15. & 44. 30.
Deut. 30. 15. set before you *l.* and
1 Sam. 25. 29. bound in bundle of *l.*
Ps. 16. 11. thou wilt show me the
path of *l.*
21. 4. asked *l.* of thee and thou
gavest
36. 9. with thee is the fountain of *l.*
63. 3. loving-kind. better than *l.*
66. 9. God holdeth our soul in *l.*
Prov. 8. 35. whoso findeth me findeth *l.*
15. 24. way of *l.* is above to wise
18. 21. death and *l.* are in power
Isa. 57. 10. hast found *l.* of thy
Matt. 6. 25. take no thought for *l.*
Luke 12. 15. man's *l.* consists not in
John 1. 4. in him was *l.* and the *l.*
3. 36. believ. on Son hath ever. *l.*
5. 40. not come, that ye might
have *l.*
6. 35. I am the bread of *l.*, 48. 40,
47, 54.
51. my flesh I give for *l.* of world
63. words I speak are spirit and *l.*
8. 12. followeth me shall have
light of *l.*
10. 10. I am come that they might
have *l.*
11. 25. I am the resurrection and *l.*
14. 6. I am the way, truth, and *l.*
Rom. 5. 17. reign in *l.* by Jesus
8. 2. law of Spirit of *l.* in Christ
Jesus
6. to be spiritually minded is *l.*
2 Cor. 2. 16. the savor of *l.* unto *l.*
3. 6. the letter killeth, but the
spirit giveth *l.*
4. 11. *l.* of Jesus might be mani.
Gal. 2. 20. the *l.* I now live in flesh
Eph. 4. 18. being alienated from *l.*
Col. 3. 3. your *l.* is hid with Christ
1 Tim. 2. 2. lead a peaceful *l.*
4. 8. having promise of the *l.* that
2 Tim. 1. 10. brought *l.* and immor.
2 Pet. 1. 3. that pertain to *l.* and
1 John 5. 12. he that hath the Son
hath *l.* he that hath not the Son
hath not *l.*
Job 2. 4. all that a man hath will
he give for *his life*
Prov. 13. 3. keepeth his mouth,
keepeth —
Matt. 20. 28. Son of man gave — a
ransom
Rom. 5. 10. much more saved by —
1 Kings 19. 4. to take away *my life*
Ps. 26. 9. gather not — with bloody
men
27. 1. the Lord is strength of
Jonah 2. 6. brought up — from cor.
John 10. 15. I lay down — for sheep
Acts 20. 24. neither count I — dear
Ps. 17. 14. *this life*, Luke 8. 14. & 21.
34. Acts 5. 20. 1 Cor. 15. 19. & 6. 3.
Deut. 30. 23. he is *thy life*, and
Ps. 103. 4. redeem — from destruc.
Jer. 39. 18.—shall be for a prey, 45. 5.
Prov. 10. 16. tends *to life*, 11. 19. &
19. 23. Matt. 7. 14. John 5. 24. Acts
11. 18. Rom. 7. 10. Heb. 11. 35.
1 John 3. 14.
LIFT *up* his countenance on thee,
Num. 6. 26.
1 Sam. 2. 7. Lord brings low—again
2 Kings 19. 4. — prayer for remnant
2 Chron. 17. 6. heart — in ways of
Ps. 4. 6. Lord—light of thy counte.
7. 6. Lord — thyself because
24. 7. -- ye gates, — ye doors, and
25. 1. to thee I — my soul, 86. 4.
75. 4. — not the horn, 5.
83. 2. — the head
102. 10. thou — me and castest me
121. 1. — mine eyes, 123. 1.
147. 6. Lord — the meek, but casts
Prov. 2. 3. — thy voice for under.
Eccl. 4. 10. one will — his fellow
Isa. 26. 11. Lord when thy hand
is —
33. 10. I will be exalted; now I —
myself
42. 2. he shall not cry, nor — voice
Jer. 7. 16. nor — a prayer for them
Lam. 3. 14. let us—our hearts with
Hab. 2. 4. his soul which is — is
Luke 21. 28. — your heads for day
of redemption
John 3. 14. so must the Son of man
be —, 12. 34.
8. 28. when ye have — Son of man
12. 32. if I be — I will draw all men
Heb. 12. 12. — hands which hang
Jas. 4. 10. the Lord shall *l.* you up
Ps. 3. 3. my glory and *lifter up* of
141. 2. *lifting* up of hands, 1 Tim.
2. 8.
R. V. Ps. 30. 1; Mark 1. 31; 9. 27;
Acts 3. 7; 9. 41. raised
LIGHT, Num. 21. 5. Deut. 27. 16.
Judg. 9. 4. 1 Kings 16. 31. Ezek. 8.
17. & 22. 7.
Isa. 49. 6. it is a *l.* thing to be my
Zeph. 3. 4. her prophets *l.* and
Matt. 11. 30. my yoke is easy and
my burden *l.*
2 Cor. 4. 17. *l.* affliction endureth
Ps. 62. 9. man is *lighter* than vanity
Jer. 3. 9. *lightness* of whoredoms
Gen. 1. 3. let there be *light*, 4, 5, 16.
& 44. 3.
Job 18. 5. *l.* of wicked men shall
33. 30. enlightened with *l.* of living
Ps. 4. 6. lift up *l.* of thy countenance
36. 9. in thy *l.* shall we see *l.*
43. 3. O send out thy *l.* and truth
90. 8. set secret sins in the *l.* of
97. 11. *l.* is sown for the righteous
104. 2. coverest thyself with *l.*
112. 4. to the upright ariseth *l.* in
119. 105. thy word is *l.* to my path
139. 12. darkness and *l.* are both
Prov. 4. 18. path of the just is as
the shining *l.*
6. 23. law is *l.* and reproofs are way
13. 9. *l.* of the righteous rejoiceth
15. 30. *l.* of the eyes rejoiceth the
Eccl. 11. 7. *l.* is sweet and a pleasant
Isa. 5. 20. darkness for *l.* and *l.* for
8. 20. because there is no *l.* in them
9. 2. walked in darkness, have
seen a great *l.*
30. 26. *l.* of moon as *l.* of sun
42. 6. keep thee, and give thee for
a *l.* of the Gentiles
50. 10. walketh in darkness and
hath no *l.*
11. walk ye in the *l.* of your fire
58. 8. shall thy *l.* break forth as
60. 1. arise, shine; for thy *l.* is
Zech. 14. 6. *l.* shall not be clear nor
7. evening time it shall be *l.*
Matt. 5. 14. ye are the *l.* of the world
16. let your *l.* so shine before men
6. 22. the *l.* of the body is the eye
Luke 2. 32. a *l.* to lighten Gentiles
John 1. 4. the life was the *l.* of men
John 1. 7. John came to bear witness of *l.*
9. true *l.* that lighteth every man
3. 19. men loved darkness rather
than *l.*
20. cometh not to the *l.*
21. cometh to the *l.*
5. 35. John burn. and a shining *l.*
8. 12. I am the *l.* of the world
12. 35, 36. walk while ye have the *l.*
Acts 13. 47. I have set thee for a *l.*
26. 18. turn them from dark. to *l.*
Rom. 13. 12. put on the armor of *l.*
1 Cor. 4. 5. bring to *l.* hidden
2 Cor. 4. 4. lest the *l.* of the Gospel
6. 14. what communion hath *l.* with
Eph. 5. 8. walk as children of *l.*
14. awake, and Christ shall give
thee *l.*
1 Thes. 5. 5. ye are the children of *l.*
1 Pet. 2. 9. called to his marvell. *l.*
1 John 1. 5. God is *l.* and in him is
Rev. 21. 23. the Lamb is the *l.*
thereof
Ps. 136. 7. *lights*, Ezek. 32. 8. Luke
12. 35. Phil. 2. 15. Jas. 1. 17.
2 Sam. 22. 29. *lighten*, Ezra 9. 8. Ps.
13. 3. & 35. 5. Rev. 21. 23.
Ex. 19. 16. *lightning*, Ps. 18. 14. Matt.
28. 3. & 24. 27. Luke 10. 18.
R. V. Jer. 23. 32. vain boasting;
2 Cor. 1. 17. fickleness; 2 Sam. 21.
17; 1 Kings 11. 36; 2 Kings 8. 19;
2 Chron. 21. 7; Matt. 6. 22; Luke
11. 34. lamp
LIKE men, quit you, 1 Cor. 16. 13.
Heb. 2. 17. to be made *l.* his breth.
1 John 3. 2. he appears we shall be *l.*
Phil. 2. 2. *like-minded*
20. no man —
Gen. 1. 26. after our *likeness*
5. 3. Adam begat a son in his own *l.*
Ps. 17. 15. I shall be sat. with thy *l.*
Rom. 6. 5. been planted in *l.* of his
8. 3. in *l.* of sinful flesh, Phil. 2. 7.
R. V. Rom. 1. 28. refused. Frequent changes to, as
LILY, S. of S. 2. 1, 2, 16. & 4. 5. & 5. 13.
& 6. 2, 3. & 7. 2. Hos. 14. 5. Matt. 6. 28.
LINE upon *l.* *l.* upon *l.* Isa. 28. 10, 13.
28. 17. judgment will I lay to the *l.*
34. 11. stretch on it *l.* of confusion
2 Cor. 10. 16. not boast in another
man's *l.*
Ps. 16. 6. *l.* are fallen in pleasant
R. V. Isa. 44. 13. pencil; 2 Cor. 10.
16. province
LINGER, Gen. 19. 16. 2 Pet. 2. 3.
LION, Gen. 49. 9. Judg. 14. 5, 18.
Job 4. 10, 11. & 10. 16. & 28. 8. Ps. 7. 2.
& 17. 12. & 10. 9. & 22. 13. Isa. 38. 13.
Prov. 22. 13. there is a *l.* without,
26. 13.
28. 1. righteous are bold as a *l.*
Eccl. 9. 4. living dog is better than
a dead *l.*
Isa. 11. 6. calf and young *l.*
35. 9. no *l.* shall be there, nor
Ezek. 1. 10. face as a *l.*, 10. 14.
Hos. 5. 14. be as a young *l.*
Mic. 5. 8. rem. of Jacob be as a *l.*
2 Tim. 4. 17. delivered out of mouth
of the *l.*
1 Pet. 5. 8. the devil as a roaring *l.*
Rev. 5. 5. *L.* of the tribe of Juda
R. V. Gen. 49. 9; Num. 23. 24; 24. 9;
Deut. 33. 20; Job 38. 39. lioness
LIPS, Ex. 6. 12, 30. Prov. 16. 10.
Ps. 12. 3. all flattering *l.*
17. 1. not feigned *l.*
31. 18. lying *l.*, 120. 2. Prov. 10. 18.
& 12. 22. & 17. 4, 7. Isa. 59. 3.
Ps. 63. 5. I will praise thee with
joyful *l.*
Prov. 10. 21. the *l.* of the righteous
26. 23. burning *l.* and wicked heart
S. of S. 7. 9. *l.* of those that are
asleep
Isa. 6. 5. man of unclean *l.* people
57. 19. create the fruit of the *l.*
Hos. 14. 2. render calves of our *l.*
Mal. 2. 7. priest's *l.* should keep
Ps. 51. 15. open thou *my lips*; and
63. 3. — shall praise thee, 71. 23.

Ps. 141. 3. keep the door of —
17. 4. *thy lips*, 34. 13. & 45. 2.
LITTLE, Ezra 9. 8. Neh. 9. 32.
Ps. 2. 12. when his wrath is kindled but a *l.*
8. 5. a *l.* lower than the angels
37. 16. a *l.* that a righteous man
Prov. 6. 10. a *l.* sleep, a *l.* slumber
10. 20. heart of wicked is *l.* worth
15. 16. better is *l.* with fear of the
Isa. 28. 10. here a *l.* and there a *l.*
54. 8. in a *l.* wrath I hid my face
Ezek. 11. 16. I will be as a *l.* sanc.
Zech. 1. 15. I was but a *l.* displeased
Matt. 6. 30. of *l.* faith, 8. 26. & 14. 31.
Luke 12. 32. fear not *l.* flock, it is
19. 17. thou hast been faithful in a very *l.*
1 Tim. 4. 8. bod. exercise profit. *l.*
Rev. 3. 8. hast *l.* strength, and kept
LIVE, Gen. 3. 22. & 17. 18.
Lev. 18. 5. if a man do, he shall *l.*, Neh. 9. 29. Ezek. 3. 21. & 18. 9. & 33. 13, 15, 16, 19. Rom. 10. 5. Gal. 3. 12.
Deut. 32. 40. *live for ever*, 1 Kings 1. 31. Neh. 2. 3. Ps. 22. 26. & 49. 9. Dan. 2. 4. & 3. 9. & 5. 10. & 6. 21. Zech. 1. 5. John 6. 51, 58. Rev. 4. 9. & 5. 14. & 10. 6. & 15. 7.
Job 14. 14. if a man die, shall he *l.*
Ps. 55. 23. bloody men not *l.* out
118. 17. I shall not die, but *l.* and
Isa. 38. 16. by these men *l.* and
55. 3. hear, and your soul shall *l.*
Ezek. 16. 6. said, when thou wast in thy blood, *L.*
18. 32. turn yourselves and *l.*
Hab. 2. 4. just shall *l.* by faith
Matt. 4. 4. man not *l.* by bread
John 14. 19. because I *l.* ye shall *l.*
Acts 17. 28. in him we *l.* and move
Rom. 8. 13. if *l.* after the flesh, ye
41. whether we *l.* we *l.* to Lord
2 Cor. 5. 15. who *l.* should not *l.* to
6. 9. as dying, and behold we *l.*
13. 11. be of one mind, *l.* in peace
Gal. 12. 20. I *l.* yet not I, but Christ
5. 25. if we *l.* in Spirit, walk in
Phil. 1. 21. to *l.* is Christ, 22.
2 Tim. 3. 12. all that will *l.* godly in
Tit. 2. 12. *l.* soberly, righteously
Heb. 13. 18. willing to *l.* honestly
1 Pet. 2. 24. should *l.* to righteous.
1 John 4. 9. that we might *l.*
Acts 23. 1. I *lived* in all good con.
Jas. 5. 5. ye have *l.* in pleasure
Rev. 18. 9. *l.* deliciously
20. 4. they *l.* and reigned with
Job 19. 25. I know that my Redeemer *liveth*
Rom. 6. 10. in that he *l.* he *l.* to God
14. 7. none *l.* to himself or dieth
1 Tim. 5. 6. *l.* in pleasure, dead
Heb. 7. 25. *l.* to make intercession
Rev. 1. 18. I am he that *l.* and was
3. 1. I know that thou *l.* and art
Acts 7. 38. received *lively* oracles
1 Pet. 1. 3. bego. again to a *l.* hope
2. 5. ye, as *l.* stones, are built up a
1 John 3. 16. *lives*, Rev. 12. 11.
Eccl. 7. 2. *living* will lay it to heart
Isa. 38. 19. the *l.* the *l.* shall praise
Jer. 2. 13. Lord fountain of *l.* waters
Matt. 22. 32. not the God of the dead, but of the *l.*
Mark 12. 44. cast in all her *l.*
John 4. 10. would have given thee *l.* water
7. 38. flow rivers of *l.* water
Rom. 12. 1. present your bodies a *l.* sacrifice
14. 9. Lord both of dead and *l.*
1 Cor. 15. 45. the first Adam was made a *l.* soul
Heb. 10. 20. by a new and *l.* way
1 Pet. 2. 4. coming as to a *l.* stone
Rev. 7. 17. lead them to *l.* fountains
R. V. 1 Cor. 9. 13. eat; Rev. 18. 7. waxed
LOAD, Ps. 68. 19. Isa. 46. 1.
LOATHE themselves for evil, Ezek. 6. 9. & 16. 5. & 20. 43. & 36. 31.
Jer. 14. 19. *loathed* Zion, Zech. 11. 8.
Num. 21. 5. soul *loatheth*, Prov. 27. 7.
Ps. 38. 7. *loathsome* disease
R. V. Job 7. 5. out afresh; Ps. 38. 7. burning
LOAVES, miraculous multiplication of, Matt. 14. 17. & 15. 32. Mark 6. 35. Luke 9. 12. John 6. 5.
LOFTY eyes, Ps. 131. 1. Prov. 30. 13.
Isa. 2. 11. *l.* looks humbled, 5. 15.
57. 15. *l.* One that inhabiteth
R. V. Isa. 2. 12. haughty; 57. 7. high
LOINS girt, Prov. 31. 17. Isa. 11. 5. Luke 12. 35. Eph. 6. 14. 1 Pet. 1. 13.
LONG, Ps. 91. 16. Eccl. 12. 5. Matt. 23. 14. Luke 18. 7. Jas. 5. 7.
Ex. 34. 6. Lord God, *long-suffering*, Num. 14. 18. Ps. 86. 15. Jer. 15. 15. Rom. 2. 4. & 9. 22. 1 Tim. 1. 16. 1 Pet. 3. 20. 2 Pet. 3. 9, 15.
Gal. 5. 22. fruit of Spirit is *l.*, Eph. 4. 2. Col. 1. 11. & 3. 12. 2 Tim. 3. 10. & 4. 2.
Ps. 63. 1. my flesh *longeth* for thee
84. 2. my soul *l.* for courts of
119. 40. *I have longed* after thy
131. — for thy commandments
174. — for thy salvation
20. my soul breaketh for *longing*
107. 9. he satisfieth the *l.* soul
R. V. Num. 9. 19; Deut. 28. 32; Ps. 94. 4; Matt. 23. 14; Mark 16. 5; Luke 1. 20 ——; Ex. 34. 6; Num. 14. 18; Ps. 86. 15. slow to anger
LOOK, Gen. 13. 14. Ex. 10. 10.
Ps. 5. 3. direct my prayer and I will *l.* up
Isa. 8. 17. wait upon the Lord, and *l.* for
45. 22. *l.* unto me and be saved
66. 2. to this man will I *l.* that is
Mic. 7. 7. I will *l.* unto the Lord
Luke 7. 19. do we *l.* for another
2 Cor. 4. 18. we *l.* at things not seen
Phil. 2. 4. *l.* not every one on own
3. 20. heaven, from whence we *l.*
Heb. 9. 28. to them that *l.* for him
1 Pet. 1. 12. angels desire to *l.* into
3. 14. seeing we *l.* for such things
Gen. 29. 32. the Lord *looked* on my affliction, Ex. 2. 25. & 3. 7. & 4. 31. Deut. 26. 7.
Ps. 34. 5. they *l.* to him and were
Isa. 5. 7. he *l.* for judgment, behold
22. 11. hath not *l.* to the maker
Jer. 8. 15. we *l.* for peace, but, 14. 19.
Obad. 13. not have *l.* on affliction
Hag. 1. 9. ye *l.* for much, and it
Luke 2. 38. *l.* for redemption in
22. 61. the Lord *l.* on Peter and
Heb. 11. 10. *l.* for a city whose
1 John 1. 1. which we have seen and *l.* on
1 Sam. 16. 7. man *looketh* on the outward appearance, but the Lord *l.* on the heart
S. of S. 2. 9. he *l.* forth at the win.
Matt. 5. 28. *l.* on a woman to lust
24. 50. come in a day he *l.* not for
Jas. 1. 25. *l.* into perfect law of
Ps. 18. 27. thou wilt bring down high *looks*
Isa. 38. 14. mine eyes fail with *looking* upward
Luke 9. 62. no man *l.* back is fit for
Tit. 2. 13. *l.* for that blessed hope
Heb. 10. 27. a fearful *l.* of judg.
12. 2. *l.* to Jesus, the author and
15. *l.* diligently, lest any fail
2 Pet. 3. 12. *l.* for and hasting
Jude 21. *l.* for the mercy of our
R. V. The changes are chiefly those brought about by subsequent words, and do not affect meanings
LOOSE, Deut. 25. 9. Josh. 5. 15
Ps. 146. 7. the Lord *l.* the prisoners
102. 20. to *l.* those appointed to
Isa. 58. 6. fast chosen to *l.* bands
Eccl. 12. 6. before the silver cord be *loosed*
Matt. 16. 19. *l.* on earth, *l.* in heav.
Acts 2. 24. having *l.* pains of death
1 Cor. 7. 27. bound to a wife, seek not to be *l.* art thou *l.* seek not a
R. V. Judg. 15. 14. dropped; Matt. 18. 27. released; Acts 13. 13; 16. 11; 27. 21. set sail; 27. 13. weighed anchor; Rom. 7. 2. discharged
LORD, ascribed to man, Gen. 18. 12. & 23. 11. Isa. 26. 13. 1 Cor. 8. 5. 1 Pet. 5. 3. and in about fourteen other places; and to God, Gen. 28. 16. Ex. 5. 2. 1 Cor. 12. 5. and in about three hundred other texts
Ex. 34. 6. the *L.* the *L.* God mer.
Deut. 4. 35. *L.* is God, 39. 1 Kings 18. 39.
6. 4. *L.* our God is one *L.*, 10.
17. *L.* of *l.*, Dan. 2. 47. 1 Tim. 6. 15. Rev. 17. 14. & 19. 16.
Neh. 9. 6. art *L.* alone, Isa. 37. 20.
Ps. 118. 27. God is the *L.*, 100. 3.
Zech. 14. 9. one *L.* and his name
Mark 2. 28. the Son of man is *L.* of
Acts 2. 36. made him *L.* and Christ
Rom. 10. 12. same *L.* over all
14. 9. *L.* of the dead and of the
1 Cor. 2. 8. *L.* of glory
15. 47. *L.* from heaven
8. 6. one God, one *L.* Jesus Christ
Eph. 4. 5. one *L.* one faith, one
Gen. 15. 6. and he believed *in the Lord*
1 Sam. 2. 1. heart rejoiceth —, Ps. 32. 11. & 33. 1. & 35. 9. & 97. 12. & 104. 34. Isa. 41. 16. & 61. 10. Joel 2. 13. Hab. 3. 18. Zech. 10. 7. Phil. 3. 1. & 4. 4.
1 Kings 18. 5. trust —, Ps. 4. 5. & 11. 1. & 31. 6. & 32. 10. & 37. 3. & 115. 9, 10, 11. & 118. 8. & 125. 1. Prov. 3. 5. & 16. 20. & 28. 25. & 29. 25. Isa. 26. 4. Zeph. 3. 2.
Ps. 31. 24. hope —, 130. 7. & 131. 3.
34. 2. soul make her boast —
37. 4. delight thyself —, 7. rest —
Isa. 45. 17. Israel shall be saved —
24. — have I righteousness and
42. 25. — shall all the seed of Israel
Rom. 16. 12. labor —, 1 Cor. 15. 58.
Eph. 6. 10. be strong — and power
1 Thes. 5. 12. over you —, Col. 4. 7, 17.
Rev. 14. 13. blessed are the dead which die —
LORD'S PRAYER, Matt. 6. 9.
LOSE, Eccl. 3. 6. Matt. 10. 39, 42. & 16. 26. John 6. 39. 2 John 8. Prov. 23. 8.
1 Cor. 3. 15. *loss*, Phil. 3. 7, 8.
Ps. 119. 176. astray like *lost* sheep
Ezek. 37. 11. our hope is *l.* we
Matt. 5. 13. if salt have *l.* its savor
10. 6. to the *l.* sheep of Israel
18. 11. save that was *l.*, Luke 19. 10.
Luke 15. 32. thy brother was *l.* and
John 18. 9. them thou gavest me, I have *l.* none
2 Cor. 4. 3. the Gospel be hid it is to them that are *l.*
R. V. Matt. 16. 26; Mark 8. 36. forfeit: John 17. 12. perished
LOT, Lev. 16. 8, 9, 10. Josh. 1. 6.
1 Sam. 14. 41. Saul said, give us a perfect *l.*, 42.
Ps. 16. 5. thou maintainest my *l.*
125. 3. rod of wicked not rest on *l.*
Prov. 16. 33. the *l.* is cast into lap
Acts 1. 26. the *l.* fell on Matthias
8. 21. hast neither *l.* nor part in
Ps. 22. 18. on my vesture they did cast *lots*
R. V. Matt. 27. 35 ——
LOVE, Gen. 27. 4. 2 Sam. 13. 15.
2 Sam. 1. 26. passing the *l.* of wo.
Eccl. 9. 1. no man knoweth either *l.*
S. of S. 2. 5. I am sick of *l.*, 5. 8.
7. 12. there I will give thee my *loves*
8. 6. *l.* is strong as death, jealous
Isa. 38. 17. thou hast in *l.* to my
Jer. 2. 2. remember the *l.* of
31. 3. loved thee with everlast. *l.*
Ezek. 16. 8. thy time was time of *l.*

Hos. 11. 4. draw them with bands of *l.*
Matt. 24. 12. the *l.* of many shall
John 15. 9. continue ye in my *l.*
13. greater *l.* hath no man than
Rom. 8. 35. who shall separate us from the *l.* of Christ, 39.
12. 9. let *l.* be without dissimula.
13. 10. *l.* is the fulfill. of the law
15. 30. for Christ's sake, and *l.*
2 Cor. 5. 14. *l.* of Christ constrain.
Gal. 5. 6. faith which worketh by *l.*
13. by *l.* serve one another
22. fruit of the Spirit is *l.* joy and
1 Thes. 1. 3. your labor of *l.*
5. 8. putting on breastplate of faith and *l.*
2 Thes. 2. 10. received not the *l.*
Heb. 13. 1. let brotherly *l.* continue
1 John 3. 1. what manner of *l.* the Father bestowed on us
4. 7. *l.* is of God
4. 9. manifest the *l.* of God
11. we ought to *l.* one another
18. perfect *l.* casteth out fear
21. who loveth God *l.* his brother
Rev. 2. 4. thou hast left thy first *l.*
Eph. 1. 4. without blame before God *in love*
4. 15. speaking truth —, 16.
5. 2. walk — as Christ hath loved
Col. 2. 2. knit together — and
1 Thes. 3. 12. abound —
5. 13. esteem —
Luke 11. 42. *love of God*, John 5. 42.
Rom. 5. 5. — is shed abroad in our
2 Cor. 3. 14. — be with you all
2 Thes. 3. 5. direct your hearts into —
1 John 2. 5. in him is — perfected
3. 16. perceive we —
17. dwelleth — in him
4. 9. in this was manifested — towards
5. 3. this is — keep his command.
Deut. 7. 7. his *love*, Zeph. 3. 17. Ps. 91. 14. Isa. 63. 9. John 15. 10. Rom. 5. 8.
Lev. 19. 18. thou shalt *l.* thy neighbor as thyself, 34. Matt. 19. 19. & 22. 39. Rom. 13. 8. Gal. 5. 14. Jas. 2. 8.
Deut. 6. 5. shalt *l.* the Lord thy God with all thy heart, Matt. 22. 37. Luke 10. 27.
Deut. 10. 12. to fear the Lord and to *l.*
Ps. 31. 23. O *l.* the Lord, all ye his
97. 10. ye that *l.* the Lord hate
145. 20. the Lord preserveth them that *l.* him
S. of S. 1. 4. the upright *l.* thee
Mic. 6. 8. to do justly, and *l.* mercy
Zech. 8. 19. *l.* the truth and peace
Matt. 5. 44. *l.* your enemies, bless
John 13. 34. *l.* one another, 15. 12, 17. Rom. 13. 8. 1 John 3. 11, 23. & 4. 7, 11, 12. 1 Pet. 1. 22.
14. 23. if a man *l.* me, my Father will *l.* him
1 Cor. 16. 22. if any man *l.* not Lord
Eph. 5. 25. *l.* your wives, Col. 3. 19.
2 Tim. 4. 8. to all them that *l.* his
1 Pet. 1. 8. whom having not seen, ye *l.*
2. 17. *l.* the brotherhood, 3. 8.
1 John 2. 15. *l.* not world nor
4. 19. we *l.* him because he first *loved* us
Ps. 116. 1. *I love* the Lord because, 18. 1.
119. 97. how — thy law, 113. 119, 127, 159, 163, 167. & 26. 8. Isa. 43. 1.
John 21. 15. *lovest* thou me — thee, 16. 17.
2 John 1. whom — in the truth
Rev. 3. 19. as many as — I rebuke
Deut. 7. 8. because the Lord *loved*
1 Sam. 18. 1. *l.* David as his own
2 Sam. 12. 24. called Solomon, and Lord *l.* him
1 Kings 3. 3. Solomon *l.* the Lord
10. 3. the Lord *l.* Israel

Hos. 11. 1. Israel was a child, then I *l.* him
Mark 10. 21. Jesus behold. him, *l.*
Luke 7. 47. sins are forgiven, she *l.*
2 Tim. 4. 10. having *l.* this present
Heb. 1. 9. hast *l.* righteousness
John 3. 16. God so *l.* the world
3. 19. men *l.* darkness rather
11. 36. behold how he *l.* him
12. 43. *l.* the praise of men more
13. 1. having *l.* his own, he *l.*
23. one of his disciples whom Jesus *l.*, 19. 26. & 20. 2. & 21. 7, 20.
14. 21. *l.* me, be *l.* of my Father
28. if ye *l.* me, ye would rejoice
15. 9. as my Father *l.* me, so have
16. 27. Father *loveth* you because
17. 23. I *l.* them as thou hast *l.* me
26. 1. wherewith thou hast *l.* them
Rom. 8. 37. conquerors through him that *l.* us
9. 13. Jacob I *l.* Esau I hated
Gal. 1. 20. Son of God, who *l.* me
Eph. 2. 4. great love where. he *l.* us
5. 2. as Christ *l.* us
25. as Christ *l.* church
2 Thes. 2. 16. God our Father *l.* us
2 Pet. 2.15. *l.* wages of unrighteous.
1 John 4. 10. not that we *l.* God but
Rev. 1. 5. that *l.* us and washed
12. 11. *l.* not their lives unto death
Ps. 11. 7. the righteous Lord *l.*
146. 8. the Lord *l.* the righteous
Prov. 3. 12. whom the Lord *l.* he
17. 17. a friend *l.* at all times
21. 17. he who *l.* pleasure, shall
S. of S. 1. 7. whom my soul *l.*, 3. 1, 4.
Matt. 10. 37. *l.* father or mother
John 3. 35. Father *l.* the Son, 15. 20.
16. 27. Father himself *l.* you
2 Cor. 9. 7. God *l.* a cheerful giver
3 John 9. *l.* to have preeminence
Rev. 22. 15. whoso *l.* and mak. a lie
2 Sam. 1. 23. *lovely*, S. of S. 5. 16. Ezek. 33. 32. Phile. 4. 8.
Ps. 88. 18. *lover*, Tit. 1. 8. Ps. 38. 11. Hos. 2. 5. 2 Tim. 3. 2, 4.
R. V. Tit. 1. 8. given to

LOW, Deut. 28. 43. Ezek. 17. 24.
1 Sam. 2. 7. Lord brings *l.* and lifts
Job 40. 12. look on every one that is proud and bring him *l.*
Ps. 49. 2. both high and *l.* rich and
136. 23. remem. us in our *l.* estate
Isa. 26. 5. lofty city he layeth it *l.*
32. 19. city shall be *l.* in a *l.* place
Luke 1. 48. he regard. the *l.* estate
52. he exalted them of *l.* degree, Job 5. 11. Ezek. 21. 26. Jas. 1. 9, 10.
Luke 3. 5. every mountain and hill be made *l.*
Rom. 12. 16. condescend to men of *l.* estate
Ps. 63. 9. *lower* parts of the earth, 139. 15. Isa. 44. 23. Eph. 4. 9.
138. 6. Lord hath respect to *lowly*
Prov. 3. 34. he giveth grace unto *l.*
11. 2. with the *l.* is wisdom
Matt. 11. 29. learn of me, for I am meek and *l.*
Eph. 4. 2. *lowliness*, Phil. 2. 3.
R. V. 2 Chron. 26. 10; 28. 18. lowland; Ps. 107. 39. bowed down; Ezek. 26. 20. nether

LUCRE, filthy, 1 Tim. 3. 3, 8. Tit. 1. 7. 1 Pet. 5. 2.

LUKEWARM, thou art, Rev. 3. 16.

LUMP, Isa. 38. 21. Rom. 9. 21. & 11. 16. 1 Cor. 5. 6, 7. Gal. 5. 9.
R. V. 2 Kings 20. 7; Isa. 38. 21. cake

LUST, Ex. 15. 9. Ps. 78. 18. Jas. 4. 2.
Ps. 81. 12. gave them up to their own hearts' *l.*
Matt. 5. 28. looketh on a woman to *l.*
Rom. 7. 7. not known *l.* except law
1 Cor. 10. 6. not *l.* after evil things
Gal. 5. 16. shall not fulfil *l.* of flesh
1 Thes. 4. 5. not in the *l.* of
Jas. 1. 15. when *l.* is conceived, it
1 John 2. 16. *l.* of the flesh, and *l.*
Mark 4. 19. *lusts* of other things
John 8. 44. *l.* of your father ye will
Rom. 6. 12. should obey it in the *l.*

Rom. 13. 14. for the flesh, to fulfil the *l.*
Gal. 5. 17. flesh *l.* against Spirit
24. crucified flesh with affec. and *l.*
Eph. 2. 3. *l.* of our flesh, and mind
1 Tim. 6. 9. foolish and hurtful *l.*
2 Tim. 2. 22. flee youthful *l.* follow
3. 6. laden with sins, led away with divers *l.*
Tit. 2. 12. denying ungodliness and worldly *l.*
3. 3. divers *l.* and pleasures
Jas. 4. 3. consume it on your *l.*
1 Pet. 2. 11. abstain from fleshly *l.*
2 Pet. 3. 3. walk after their own *l.*
R. V. Ps. 81. 12. stubbornness; Rom. 7. 7. coveting; Jas. 4. 1, 3. pleasures; Deut. 14. 26. desireth; Jas. 4. 5. long

M

MAD, Deut. 28. 34. 1 Sam. 21. 13.
Eccl. 2. 2. I said of laughter it is *m.*
Jer. 50. 38. they are *m.* upon idols
Hos. 9. 7. the prophet is a fool, the spiritual man is *m.*
John 10. 20. he hath a dev. and is *m.*
Acts 26. 11. exceedingly *m.* against
24. learning doth make thee *m.*
Deut. 28. 28. *madness*, Eccl. 1. 17. & 2. 12. & 9. 3. & 10. 13. Zech. 12. 4. Luke 6. 11. 2 Pet. 2. 16.
R. V. Eccl. 7. 7. foolish

MADE, Ex. 2. 14. 2 Sam. 13. 6.
Ps. 104. 24. thy works in wisdom hast thou *m.*
Prov. 16. 14. Lord *m.* all things
John 1. 3. all things were *m.* by him
Rom. 1. 3. Christ *m.* of the seed of David
1 Cor. 1. 30. Christ who of God is *m.*
9. 22. *m.* all things to all men
Gal. 4. 4. *m.* of a woman, *m.* under
Phil. 2. 7. *m.* in the likeness of men
R. V. The changes are mostly to such words as, created, wrought, become, manifested, etc.
See also MAKE.

MAGISTRATES, Ezra 7. 25; to be obeyed, Ex. 22. 8. Rom. 13. Tit. 3. 1. 1 Pet. 2. 14.

MAGNIFY, Josh. 3. 7. 1 Chron. 29. 25.
Job 7. 17. what is man that thou shouldst *m.* him
36. 24. remember to *m.* his work
Ps. 34. 3. *m.* the Lord with me
Isa. 42. 21. *m.* the law, and make
Luke 1. 46. my soul doth *m.* Lord
Acts 10. 46. spake with tongues and *m.* God
Gen. 19. 19. thou hast *magnified* thy
2 Sam. 7. 26. let thy name be *m.* for
Ps. 35. 27. let the Lord be *m.*
138. 2. hast *m.* thy word above
Acts 19. 17. the name of the Lord was *m.*
Phil. 1. 20. Christ shall be *m.* in
R. V. 2 Chron. 32. 23. exalted; Rom. 11. 13. glorify my ministry

MAID, Gen. 16. 2. Deut. 22. 14. Job 31. 1. Jer. 2. 32. Amos 2. 7. Zech. 9. 17.
R. V. Gen. 16. 2; 29. 24; 30. 7; Ex. 2. 5. handmaid; Matt. 9. 24. dam.

MAIMED healed by Christ, Matt. 15. 30.
animal, unfit for sacri. Lev. 22. 22.

MAINTAIN my cause, 1 Kings 8. 40, 45. Ps. 9. 4. & 140. 12. Job 13. 15.
Tit. 3. 8. care. to *m.* good works, 14.
Ps. 16. 5. thou *maintainest* my lot
R. V. 1 Chron. 26. 27. repair

MAJESTY, Dan. 4. 30, 36. & 5. 18, 19. Job 40. 10. Ps. 21. 5. & 45. 3, 4.
1 Chron. 29. 11. thine, O Lord, is *m.*
Job 37. 22. with God is terrible *m.*
Ps. 29. 4. voice of Lord is full of *m.*
93. 1. the Lord is clothed with *m.*
145. 5. glorious honor of thy *m.*
12. glorious *m.* of his kingdom

Isa. 2. 19. hide for fear of the glory of his *m.*
Heb. 1. 3. right hand of *M.* on high
8. 1. of the throne of the *M.*
2 Pet. 1. 16. eyewitnesses of his *m.*
Jude 25. to the only wise God be glory and *m.*
R. V. Dan. 4. 36; 5. 18, 19. greatness
MAKE, Gen. 1. 26. & 3. 6, 21. Deut. 32. 35. 1 Cor. 4. 15. 1 Sam. 20. 38.
Job 4. 17. shall man be purer than his *Maker*
32. 22. my *M.* would soon take me
35. 10. where is God my *M.*
36. 3. I will ascribe righ. to my *M.*
Ps. 95. 6. kneel before Lord our *M.*
Prov. 14.31. reproach. his *M.*, 17. 5.
22. 2. Lord is the *M.* of them all
Isa. 17. 7. that day shall man look to his *M.*
51. 13. forgettest the Lord thy *M.*
54. 5. thy *M.* is thy husband; the
Heb. 11. 10. whose builder and *m.*
MALE or female, Gen. 1. 27. Num. 5. 3. Mal. 1. 14. Matt. 19. 4. Gal. 3. 28.
MALEFACTORS, execution of, Deut. 21. 22.
crucified with Christ, Luke 23. 32.
MALICE, leaven of, 1 Cor. 5. 8.
1 Cor. 14. 20. in *m.* be children, in Eph. 4. 31. put away with all *m.*, Col. 3. 8. 1 Pet. 2. 1.
Tit. 3. 3. living in *m.* and envy
Rom. 1.29. filled with all *maliciousness;* full of envy, 1 Pet. 2. 1.
R. V. 1 Pet. 2. 1. wickedness
MAMMON, Matt. 6. 24. Luke 16. 9.
MAN, Gen. 1. 26, 27. 2 Kings 9. 11.
Job 4. 17. shall *m.* be more just
5. 7. *m.* is born to trouble, 14. 1.
7. 17. what is *m.* that thou
9. 2. how shall *m.* be just with God
14. 1. *m.* born of woman, is of
15. 14. what is *m.* that he should
6. *m.* is a worm
28. 28. unto *m.* he said, depart
Ps. 8. 4. what is *m.* that thou art
10. 18. *m.* of earth no more oppress
90. 3. thou turnest *m.* to destruc.
104. 23. *m.* goeth forth to his work
118. 6. not fear; what can *m.* do
144. 3. what is *m.* that thou takest
Prov. 20. 24. *m's* goings are of Lord
Eccl. 6. 10. it is known that it is *m.*
7. 29. God made *m.* upright, but
12. 5. *m.* goeth to his long home
Isa. 2. 22. cease ye from *m.* whose
Jer. 17. 5. cursed be the *m.* that
Zech. 13. 7. awake against the *m.* that is my fellow
Matt. 4. 4. *m.* shall not live by
26. 72. I know not the *m.*
John 7. 46. nev. *m.* spake like this *m.*
Rom. 6. 6. old *m.* crucified with
1 Cor. 2. 11. what *m.* knoweth the things of a *m.* save the spirit of *m.* in him
14. natural *m.* receiveth not things
11. 8. *m.* not of woman, but woman of *m.*
15. 47. first *m.* is earthy; second *m.*
2 Cor. 4. 16. though outward *m.* perish, yet inward *m.* is renewed
Eph. 4. 22. put off the old *m.* which
24. put on new *m.* renewed
1 Pet. 3. 4. be the hidden *m.* of heart
Ex. 15. 3. Lord is *a man* of war
Num. 23. 19. God is not — that he
Isa. 47. 3. I will not meet thee as —
53. 3. — of sorrows and acquainted
Jer. 15. 10. borne me — of strife
Matt. 8. 9. I am — under authority
16. 26. what shall — give in ex.
John 3. 3. except — be born again
Acts 10. 26. I myself also am —
2 Cor. 12. 2. I knew — in Christ, 3.
Phil. 2. 8. in fashion as — he hum.
1 Tim. 2. 5. one Meditator the *m.* Christ Jesus
Prov. 30. 2. *if any man,* Matt. 16. 24. John 6. 51. & 7. 17, 37. Rom. 8. 9. 2 Cor. 5.17. Gal. 1. 9. Rev. 22.19.

Ps. 39. 5. *every man,* Prov. 19. 6. Mic. 4. 4. & 7. 2. Gal. 6. 4, 5. Col. 1. 28. Heb. 2. 9.
Ps. 87. 4. *this man,* Isa. 66. 2. Mic. 5. 5. Luke 19. 14. John 7. 46. Jas. 1. 26.
Prov. 1. 5. *a wise man* will hear
9. 8. rebuke — and he will love thee
17. 10. reproof enters into — more
Eccl. 2. 14. — eyes are in his head
10. 2. — heart is at his right hand
Jer. 9. 23. let not — glory in wisdom
Jas. 3. 13. who is — among you
Deut. 33. 1. *man of God,* Judg. 13. 6, 8. 2 Kings 1. 9, 13. 1 Tim. 6. 11. 2 Tim. 3. 17.
R. V. Numerous changes in N. T. to one
MANDRAKES, Gen. 30. 14. S. of S. 7. 13.
MANIFEST, Eccl. 3. 18. 1 Cor. 15. 27.
Mark 4. 22. nothing hid which shall not be *m.*
John 14. 21. I will *m.* myself
2. 11. *m.* forth his glory to dis.
17. 6. I have *m.* thy name unto
1 Cor. 4. 5. make *m.* counsels
Gal. 5. 19. works of the flesh are *m.*
2 Thes. 1. 5. a *m.* token of right.
1 Tim. 3. 16. God was *m.* in the flesh
Heb. 4. 13. any creature not *m.* in
1 John 3. 5. he was *m.* to take
10. in this children of God are *m.*
4. 9. in this was *m.* the love of God
Luke 8. 17. *made manifest,* John 3. 21. 1 Cor. 3. 13. 2 Cor. 4. 10. & 5. 11. Eph. 5. 13.
Rom. 8. 19. *manifestation* of sons
1 Cor. 12. 7. *m.* of the Spirit is given
2 Cor. 4. 2. but by *m.* of the truth
R. V. 1 Cor. 15. 27; 1 Tim. 5. 25; 2 Tim. 3. 9. evident; Rom. 8. 19. revealing
MANIFOLD mercies, Neh. 9. 19, 27.
Ps. 104. 24. how *m.* are thy works
Amos 5. 12. I know your *m.* trans.
Luke 18. 30. *m.* more in this pre.
Eph. 3. 10. known *m.* wisdom of
1 Pet. 1. 6. in heaviness through *m.* temptations
MANNA, Ex. 16. 15. Num. 11. 6. Deut. 8. 3, 16. Josh. 5. 12. Neh. 9. 20. Ps. 78. 24. John 6. 31, 49, 58.
Rev. 2. 17. give to eat of hidden *m.*
R. V. Ex. 16. 15. what is it; John 6. 58 ——
MANNER, 1 Sam. 8. 9, 11. Isa. 5. 17. Jer. 22. 21. 1 Thes. 1. 5, 9. 1 John 3. 1.
2 Kings 17. 34. *manners,* Acts 13. 18. 1 Cor. 15. 33. Lev. 20. 23. Heb. 1. 1.
R. V. Numerous changes to custom, ordinance, form, etc.; and frequent omissions of the word
MANSIONS in my Father's house, John 14. 2.
MAN-STEALING, Ex. 21. 16. Deut. 24. 7.
MARK, set me as a, Job 7. 20. & 16. 12.
Lam. 3. 12. Gal. 6. 17. bear *marks*
Ezek. 9. 4. set a *m.* upon the foreheads, Rev. 13.16,17. & 14. 9. & 19. 20.
Phil. 3. 14. I press toward the *m.*
Ps. 37. 37. *m.* the perfect man
130. 3. if thou shouldest *m.* iniquity, Job 10. 14. Jer. 2. 22.
Rom. 16. 17. *m.* them which cause
Phil. 3. 17. *m.* them which walk
R. V. Gen. 4. 15. sign; Phil. 3. 14. goal; Rev. 15. 2 ——; Job 18. 2. consider; 22. 15. keep; 24. 16. shut themselves up
MARRIAGE, Gen. 38. 8. Deut. 25. 5.

Matt. 22. 2. king made a *m.* for son
25. 10. that were ready went into the *m.*
Heb. 13. 4. *m.* is honorable in all
Rev. 19. 7. the *m.* of the Lamb
Jer. 3. 14. I am *m.* to you, saith Lord
Luke 14. 20. I have *m.* a wife, and
17. 27. they drank, *m.* and
Isa. 62. 5. as a man *m.* a virgin
1 Cor. 7. 9. better to *m.* than to burn
1 Tim. 4. 3. forbidding to *m.* and
5. 14. that younger women *m.* and
R. V. Matt. 22. 2, 4, 9; 25. 10. marriage feast
MARROW, to bones, Prov. 3. 8. Job 21. 24.
Ps. 63. 5. soul is satis. as with *m.*
Isa. 25. 6. feast of fat things full of *m.*
Heb. 4. 12. dividing asunder joints and *m.*
MARTYR, Acts 22. 20. Rev. 2. 13. & 17. 6.
MARVEL not, Eccl. 5. 8. John 5. 28. Acts 3. 12. 1 John 3. 13.
Ps. 48. 5. they *marvelled,* Matt. 8. 27. & 9. 8, 33. & 21. 20. & 22. 22. Luke 1. 63. Acts 2. 7. & 4. 13.
Matt. 8. 10. Jesus *m.*, Mark 6. 6.
Job 5. 9. doeth *marvellous* things
10. 16. showed thyself *m.* against
Ps. 17. 7. show me thy *m.* kind.
98. 1. done *m.* things, Mic. 7. 15.
118. 23. it is *m.* in our eyes
1 Chron. 16. 12. remember his *m.* works, Ps. 105. 5. & 9. 1.
Ps. 139. 14. *m.* are thy works, Rev. 15. 3.
R. V. Ps. 48. 5. amazed; Matt. 9. 8. were afraid; Rev. 17. 7. wonder; Ps. 139. 14. wonderful; John 9. 30. the marvel
MASTER, Isa. 24. 2. Mal. 1. 6. & 2. 12.
Matt. 23. 10. one is your *M.*
Mark 10. 17. good *M.* what shall I
John 3. 10. art thou a *m.* in Israel
13. 13. ye call me *M.* and say well
14. if I your *M.* have washed
Rom. 14. 4. to his own *m.* he stands
Eccl. 12. 11. *masters* of assemblies
Matt. 6. 24. no man can serve two *m.*
23. 10. neither be ye called *m.*, Jas. 3. 1.
Col. 4. 1. *m.* give your servants
1 Cor. 3. 10. I as a *master builder*
R. V. 1 Sam. 24. 6; 26. 16; 29. 4, 10; 2 Sam. 2. 7; Amos 4. 1; Mark 13. 39; Rom. 14. 4; 2 Pet. 2. 1. lord; Matt. 26. 25, 49; Mark 9. 5; 11. 21; 14. 45; John 4. 31; 9. 2; 11. 8. Rabbi; Matt. 23. 8; John 3. 10; Jas. 3. 1. teacher
MATTER, Ex. 18. 22. & 23. 7. 1 Sam. 10. 16. Job 19. 28. & 32. 18. Ps. 45. 1. Dan. 7. 28. 2 Cor. 9. 5.
Acts 8. 21. part nor lot in this *m.*
Job 33. 13. account of any of his *matters*
Ps. 131. 1. exerc. myself in great *m.*
Matt. 23. 23. omitted the weight. *m.*
1 Pet. 4. 15. a busybody in other men's *m.*
R. V. Job 32. 18; Ps. 35. 20. words; 1 Sam. 16. 18. speech; Ps. 64. 5. purpose; Dan. 4. 17. sentence; Jas. 3. 5. much wood
MEAN, what, Ex. 12. 26. Deut. 6. 20, 24. Josh. 4. 6, 21. Ezek. 17. 12. Acts 17. 20. & 21. 13. Ezek. 37. 18. Jonah 1. 6.
Gen. 50. 20. ye thought ill; God *meant* good
Ps. 49. 7. *by any means,* Jer. 5. 31. 1 Cor. 9. 22. Phil. 3. 11. 1 Thes. 3. 15.
R. V. Acts 21. 13. do; 2 Cor. 8. 13. say not this; Acts 27. 2. which was about; Luke 15. 26. might be; Prov. 6. 26. on account; Luke 5

18 —— ; 8. 36; John 9. 21. how; Luke 10. 19; 2 Thes. 2. 3. in any wise; Judg. 5. 22; Rev. 13. 14. reason

MEASURE, Lev. 19. 35. Deut. 25. 15.
Job 11. 9. the *m.* is longer than
Ps. 39. 4. make me know the *m.*
Isa. 27. 8. in *m.* when it shooteth
Matt. 7. 2. with what *m.* ye mete
23. 32. fill up the *m.* of your
John 3. 34. giveth not Spirit by *m.*
Rom. 12. 3. gives to every man *m.*
2 Cor. 1. 8. were pressed out of *m.*
12. 7. I should be exalt. above *m.*
Eph. 4. 7. according to *m.* of the
13. to the *m.* of fulness of Christ
Rev. 11. 1. *m.* the temple of God
R. V. Mark 10. 26; 2 Cor. 1. 8. exceedingly; Mark 6. 51; Rev. 21. 15 —— ; 2 Cor. 10. 14; 12. 7. over much

MEAT, Job 6. 7. Ps. 42. 3. & 69. 21.
Ps. 104. 27. give *m.* in due season
111. 5. giveth *m.* to them that
Prov. 6. 8. provided *m.* in summer
Hos. 11. 4. I laid *m.* unto them
Hab. 1. 16. portion is fat and *m.*
3. 17. the fields shall yield no *m.*
Mal. 1. 12. that say his *m.* is con.
Matt. 6. 25. is not life more than *m.*
10. 10. workman worthy of his *m.*
John 4. 32. I have *m.* to eat ye
34. my *m.* is to do the will
6. 55. my flesh is *m.* indeed
Rom. 14. 15. destroy not him with thy *m.*
17. kingdom of God is not *m.* and drink
1 Cor. 6. 13. *m.* for belly, belly for
8. 8. *m.* commend. us not to God
10. 3. did all eat same spirit. *m.*
R. V. very frequent changes to food, meal, etc.

MEDDLE, 2 Kings 14. 10. Prov. 17. 14. & 20. 3, 19. & 24. 21. & 26. 17.
R. V. Deut. 2. 5, 19. contend; Prov. 17. 4; 20. 3. quarrelling; 26. 17. vexeth himself

MEDIATOR, is not *m.* of one, Gal. 3. 20.
Gal. 3. 19. ordained by angels in the hand of a *m.*
1 Tim. 2. 5. one *m.* between God
Heb. 8. 6. he is the *m.* of a better
9. 15. *m.* of New Testament
12. 24. *m.* of new covenant

MEDICINE, Prov. 17. 22. Jer. 30. 13. & 46. 11. Ezek. 47. 12.
R. V. Ezek. 47. 12. healing

MEDITATE, Isaac went to, Gen. 24. 63.
Josh. 1. 8. *m.* in thy law day and night, Ps. 1. 2. & 119. 15, 23, 48, 78, 148.
Ps. 63. 6. *m.* on thee in the night
77. 12. I will *m.* of thy works
Isa. 33. 18. thy heart shall *m.* terror
Luke 21. 14. not *m.* before what
1 Tim. 4. 15. *m.* upon these things
Ps. 5. 1. consider my *meditation*
19. 14. let the *m.* of my heart
49. 3. *m.* of my heart shall be
104. 34. my *m.* of him shall be sweet
119. 97. thy law is my *m.* all the day
99. thy testimonies are my *m.*
R. V. Isa. 33. 18. muse; 1 Tim. 4. 15. be diligent in

MEEK, Moses was very, Num. 12. 3.
Ps. 22. 26. the *m.* shall eat and be
25. 9. *m.* will he guide in judg.
37. 11. *m.* shall inherit the earth
76. 9. Lord rose to save all *m.* of
147. 6. the Lord lifteth up the *m.*
149. 4. he will beautify the *m.*
Isa. 11. 4. reprove for *m.* of the earth
29. 19. *m.* shall increase their joy
61. 1. preach good tidings to *m.*
Amos 2. 7. that turn aside way of *m.*
Zeph. 2. 3. seek the Lord all *m.*
Matt. 5. 5. blessed are *m.* for they
11. 29. I am *m.* and lowly in heart
21. 5. thy king cometh *m.* sitting
1 Pet. 3. 4. ornament of *m.* and
Zeph. 2. 3. seek righteousness, seek *meekness*
Ps. 45. 4. ride prosperously because of *m.*
1 Cor. 4. 21. come in the spirit of *m.*
2 Cor. 10. 1. I beseech you by the *m.* of Christ
Gal. 5. 23. faith, *m.* against such
6. 1. restore him in spirit of *m.*
Eph. 4. 2. walk with all lowliness and *m.*
Col. 3. 12. put on *m.* long-suffering
1 Tim. 6. 11. follow after faith, love, *m.*
2 Tim. 2. 25. in *m.* instructing those
Tit. 3. 2. showing all *m.* to all men
Jas. 1. 21. receive with *m.*
3. 13. show his works with *m.* of wisdom
1 Pet. 3. 15. of hope in you with *m.*

MEET, help, for him, Gen. 2. 18.
Job 34. 31. it is *m.* to be said to God
Matt. 3. 8. fruits *m.* for repent.
1 Cor. 15. 9. not *m.* to be called
Col. 1. 12. *m.* to be partakers of the
2 Tim. 2. 21. vessel *m.* for the master's use
Heb. 6. 7. *m.* for them by whom
Prov. 22. 2. rich and poor *m.*
Isa. 47. 3. I will not *m.* thee as a
64. 5. thou *m.* him that rejoiceth
Hos. 13. 8. I will *m.* them as a bear
Amos 4. 12. prepare to *m.* thy God
1 Thes. 4. 17. caught up to *m.* Lord
R. V. Deut. 3. 18. men of valor; Jer. 26. 14; 27. 5; Phil. 1. 7; 2 Pet. 1. 13. right; Judg. 5. 30. on; Ezek. 15. 4. profitable; Matt. 3. 8; Acts 26. 20. worthy of; Rom. 1. 27. due; Josh. 2. 16. light upon

MELODY in heart to the Lord, Eph. 5. 19.

MEMBER, body not one, 1 Cor. 12. 14.
Jas. 3. 5. tongue is a little *m.*
Ps. 139. 16. and in thy book all my *members*
Matt. 5. 29. one of thy *m.* perish
Rom. 6. 13. yield your *m.* as
7. 23. I see another law in my *m.*
12. 5. every one *m.* one of another
1 Cor. 6. 15. your bodies are *m.*
12. 12. the body is one, and hath many *m.*
Eph. 4. 25. we are *m.* one of anoth.
5. 30. *m.* of his body, his flesh
Col. 3. 5. mortify your *m.* on earth
R. V. 1 Cor. 12. 23. parts

MEMORY cut off, Ps. 109. 15.
Ps. 145. 7. utter the *m.* of thy
Prov. 10. 7. *m.* of the just is blessed
Eccl. 9. 5. *m.* of them is forgotten
Isa. 26. 14. made their *m.* to perish
1 Cor. 15. 2. if ye keep in *m.* what I
Ex. 3. 15. my *memorial* to all
13. 9. be for *m.* between thine eyes
17. 14. write this for a *m.* in book
Ps. 135. 13. thy *m.* through all
Hos. 12. 5. Lord of hosts; the Lord is his *m.*
Matt. 26. 13. be told for a *m.* of her
Acts 10. 4. come up for a *m.* before

MEN, Gen. 32. 28. & 42. 11.
Ps. 9. 20. know themselves to be but *m.*
17. 14. *m.* of thy hand; *m.* of
62. 9. *m.* of low degree are vanity
82. 7. ye shall die like *m.* and fall
Eccl. 12. 3. strong *m.* shall bow
Isa. 31. 3. Egyptians are *m.* not God
46. 8. remember this; show yourselves *m.*
Hos. 6. 7. they like *m.* transgress.
Rom. 1. 27. *m.* with *m.* working
Eph. 6. 6. *m.* pleasers, Col. 3. 22.
1 Thes. 2. 4.

MENSTRUOUS, Isa. 30. 22. Lam. 1. 17.
Ezek. 18. 6. neither come near a *m.* woman
R. V. Lam. 1. 17; Isa. 30. 22. unclean thing

MENTION, Ex. 23. 13. Job 28. 18.
Ps. 17. 16. I will make *m.* of thy
Isa. 26. 13. by thee only make *m.* of
62. 6. ye that make *m.* of the Lord
Rom. 1. 9. make *m.* of you in my prayers, Eph. 1. 16. 1 Thes. 1. 2. Phile. 4.
R. V. 2 Chron. 20. 34. inserted; Ezek. 18. 22, 24; 33. 16. remember.

MERCHANT, Hos. 12. 7. Matt. 13. 45.
Isa. 23. 18. *merchandise* be holiness, Matt. 22. 5. John 2. 16. 2 Pet. 2. 3.
R. V. Deut. 21. 14; 24. 7. deal with; Ezek. 27. 15. mart; 28. 16. traffic; Isa. 23. 11. concerning Canaan; 47. 15. that trafficked with thee; Ezek. 27. 20; Hos. 12. 7. trafficker; Ezek. 27. 13, 15, 17; 22. 23, 24. traffickers

MERCY, Gen. 19. 19. & 39. 21.
Ex. 34. 7. keep *m.* for thousands, Deut. 7. 9. 1 Kings 8. 23. Neh. 1. 5. & 9. 32. Dan. 9. 4.
Num. 14. 18. Lord is of great *m.*
Ps. 23. 6. goodness and *m.* shall
25. 10. all paths of the Lord are *m.*
33. 18. fear him and hope in his *m.*
52. 8. I trust in the *m.* of God for
57. 3. God shall send forth his *m.*
66. 20. not turned away his *m.*
86. 5. plenteous in *m.* to all, 103. 8.
101. 1. I will sing of *m.* and
103. 11. great is his *m.* to them
17. *m.* of the Lord is from ever.
106. 1. his *m.* endureth for ever, 107. 1. & 118. 1. & 136. 1-26. 1 Chron. 16. 34, 41. 2 Chron. 5. 13. & 7. 3, 6. & 20. 21. Ezra 3. 11. Jer. 33. 11.
Prov. 16. 6. by *m.* and truth, iniq.
20. 28. *m.* and truth preserve
Isa. 27. 11. he that made them will not have *m.*
Hos. 6. 6. I desired *m.* and not sacrifice
10. 12. reap in *m.*
12. 6. keep *m.*
14. 3. in thee fatherless findeth *m.*
Jonah 2. 8. they for. their own *m.*
Mic. 6. 8. what doth God require, but to love *m.*
20. *m.* to Abraham
Hab. 3. 2. in wrath remember *m.*
Luke 1. 50. his *m.* is on them that
78. through tender *m.* of our God
Rom. 9. 23. on vessels of *m.* pre.
15. *m.* on whom he will have *m.*
11. 31. through your *m.* they obtain *m.*
15. 9. may glorify God for his *m.*
2 Cor. 4. 1. as we have received *m.*
1 Tim. 1. 13. I obtained *m.* because I did it ignorantly
2. grace, *m.* and peace, Tit. 1. 4. 2 John 3. Jude 2.
2 Tim. 1. 18. grant may find *m.* in
Tit. 3. 5. according to his *m.* saved
Jas. 2. 13. shall have judgment without *m.* that showed no *m.* and *m.*
Heb. 4. 16. we may obtain *m.* and
Jas. 3. 17. full of *m.* and good
5. 11. Lord is pitiful and of tend. *m.*
Jude 21. looking for the *m.* of our
Gen. 32. 10. not worthy of the least of thy *mercies*
1 Chron. 21. 13. great are his *m.*
Ps. 69. 13. in multitude of thy *m.*
Isa. 55. 3. the sure *m.* of David
Lam. 3. 22. of Lord's *m.* we are
Dan. 9. 9. to the Lord belong *m.*
Rom. 12. 1. I beseech you by the *m.*
2 Cor. 1. 3. Father of *m.* and God of
Col. 3. 12. put on bowels of *m.*
Ps. 25. 6. *tender mercies*, 40. 11. & 51. 1. & 77. 9. & 79. 8. & 103. 4. & 119. 77, 156. & 145. 9.

Prov. 12. 10. —of wicked are cruel
Gen. 19. 19. *thy mercy*, Num. 14. 19.
Neh. 13. 22. Ps. 5. 7. & 6. 4. & 13. 5. & 25. 7. & 31. 7, 16. & 33. 22. & 36. 5. & 44. 26. & 85. 7. & 86. 13. & 90. 14. & 94. 18. & 108. 4. & 57. 10. & 119. 64. & 143. 12.
Ex. 34. 6. Lord God *merciful* and gracious, 2 Chron. 30. 9. Neh. 9. 17, 31. Ps. 103. 8. Joel 2. 13. Jonah 4. 2.
Ps. 18. 25. with *m.* show thyself *m.*
37. 26. he is ever *m.* and lendeth
117. 2. his *m.* kindness is great to
Prov. 11. 17. *m.* man doeth good
Isa. 57. 1. *m.* men are taken away
Jer. 3. 12. I am *m.* and will not
Matt. 5. 7. blessed are *m.* they
Luke 6. 36. be *m.* as your Father is *m.*
Heb. 2. 17. might be a *m.* high priest
8. 12. I will be *m.* to their
R. V. Ex. 34. 6; Neh. 9. 17; Ps. 103. 8; Joel 2. 13; Jonah 4. 2. full of compassion; Ps. 41. 4; 41. 10; 119. 132. have mercy; 37. 26. dealeth graciously; Gen. 39. 21; 2 Sam. 22. 51; 1 Kings 3. 6; 2 Chron. 1. 8; Ps. 5. 7; 18. 50; 21. 7; 25. 7, 10; 36. 5; 61. 7; 143. 12; Isa. 16. 5. kindness, or lovingkindness; Prov. 14. 21. pity; Isa. 9. 17; 14. 1; 27. 11; 49. 13; Jer. 13. 14; 30. 18; Heb. 10. 28. compassion

MERRY, be, Luke 12. 19. & 15. 23, 24, 29, 32.
Jas. 5. 13. is any *m.* let him sing
Prov. 15. 13. *merry-hearted*, 17. 22. Eccl. 9. 7. Isa. 24. 7.
R. V. Judg. 9. 27. festival; Prov. 15. 15; Jas. 5. 13. cheerful; 2 Chron. 7. 10. joyful; Eccl. 10. 19. glad in life

MESSAGE from God, Judg. 3. 20. Hag. 1. 13. 1 John 1. 5. & 3. 11.
Job 33. 23. if there be a *messenger*
Isa. 14. 32. what shall one answer the *m.*
42. 19. who is blind or deaf, as *m.*
44. 26. that performeth counsel of his *m.*
Mal. 2. 7. he is the *m.* of the Lord
3. 1. I send my *m.* even the *m.* of
R. V. Luke 19. 14. ambassage; Gen. 50. 16. message; 1 Sam. 4. 17. that brought tidings; Job 33. 23. angel; Isa. 57. 9. ambassador

MESSIAH, Dan. 9. 25, 26. John 1. 41. & 4. 25.

MICE, golden, 1 Sam. 6. 11.

MIDNIGHT, Egyptians smitten at, Ex. 12. 29.
prayer at, Ps. 119. 62. Acts 16. 25. & 20. 7.
bridegroom cometh at, Matt. 25. 6.
master of house cometh at, Mark 13. 35.

MIDST, Ps. 22. 14. & 46. 5. & 110. 2. Prov. 4. 21. Isa. 4. 4. & 41. 18. Ezek. 43. 7, 9. & 6. 10. Joel 2. 27. Zeph. 3. 5, 12, 15, 17. Phil. 2. 15. Rev. 1. 13. & 5. 6. & 7. 17. Lamb in *m.* of the throne

MIDWIVES of Egypt, Ex. 1. 16, 20.

MIGHT, Gen. 49. 3. Num. 14. 13.
Deut. 6. 5. love Lord with all thy *m.*
2 Kings 23. 25. turned to Lord with all his *m.*
2 Chron. 20. 12. no *m.* against
Ps. 76. 5. none of men of *m.* found
145. 6. men speak of the *m.* of thy
Eccl. 9. 10. findeth to do, do it with thy *m.*
Isa. 40. 29. that have no *m.* he
Zech. 4. 6. not by *m.* but by Spirit
Eph. 3. 16. his glory, to be strengthened with *m.*
6. 10. be strong in power of his *m.*
Col. 1. 11. strengthened with all *m.*
Deut. 7. 23. with *mighty* destruc.
10. 17. a great God, a *m.* and a
Ps. 24. 8. the Lord strong and *m.* the Lord *m.* in battle
Ps. 89. 10. I have laid help on one that is *m.*
Isa. 5. 22. *m.* to drink wine, men of
Jer. 32. 19. great in counsel, *m.* in work
1 Cor. 1. 20. not many *m.* are called
2 Cor. 10. 4. warfare not carnal but *m.*
Ps. 93. 4. Lord on high is *mightier*
Acts 18. 28. *mightily*, Col. 1. 29.
19. 20. so *m.* grew word of God
R. V. changes chiefly to great, strong, etc.

MILK, Gen. 18. 8. & 49. 12.
Job 10. 10. hast poured me out as *m.*
S. of S. 4. 11. honey and *m.* under
Isa. 55. 1. buy wine and *m.* without
Joel 3. 18. the hills shall flow with *m.*
Heb. 5. 12. become such as have need of *m.*
1 Pet. 2. 2. desire sincere *m.* of word

MILLSTONES, Ex. 11. 5. Matt. 24. 41. Rev. 18. 21.

MIND, Gen. 26. 35. Lev. 24. 12.
1 Chron. 28. 9. serve him with willing *m.*
Neh. 4. 6. people had a *m.* to work
Job 23. 13. he is of one *m.* who can
Isa. 26. 3. whose *m.* is stayed on thee
Luke 12. 29. be ye not of doubtful *m.*
Acts 17. 11. receive the word with readiness of *m.*
20. 19. serving the Lord with all humility of *m.*
Rom. 7. 25. with the *m.* I serve law
8. 7. carnal *m.* is enmity against
11. 34. who hath known the *m.* of
12. 16. be of same *m.* one
1 Cor. 1. 10. joined together in the same *m.*
2 Cor. 8. 12. be first a willing *m.* it is
13. 11. be of one *m.* live in peace, Phil. 1. 27. & 2. 2. & 4. 2. 1 Pet. 3. 8.
2 Tim. 1. 7. spirit of love and of a sound *m.*
Tit. 1. 15. their *m.* and conscience
Rom. 8. 5. of flesh, do *m.* things of
12. 16. *m.* not high things
Phil. 3. 16. *m.* same thing
19. *m.* earthly things
2 Cor. 3. 14. *minds* were blinded
Phil. 4. 7. God keep your hearts and *m.*
Heb. 10. 16. in their *m.* I will write
1 Pet. 3. 1. stir up your pure *m.* by
Rom. 8. 6. to be carnally *minded*
11. 20. be not high *m.* but fear
15. 5. God of patience grant you to be like *m.*
Tit. 2. 6. exhort young men to be sober *m.*
Jas. 1. 8. a double *m.* man, 4. 8.
Ps. 111. 5. ever *mindful* of his covenant, 1 Chron. 16. 15. Ps. 105. 8.
115. 12. Lord hath been *m.* of us
R. V. Acts 20. 13. intending

MINISTER, Josh. 1. 1. Luke 4. 20.
Matt. 20. 26. let him be your *m.*
Acts 26. 16. to make thee a *m.* and
Rom. 13. 4. he is *m.* of God to thee
15. 8. Christ was a *m.* of the
16. I be the *m.* of Jesus Christ to
Eph. 3. 7. was made a *m.* according
4. 29. may *m.* grace unto hearers
Rom. 15. 25. to *m.* unto the saints
15. 27. *m.* to them in carnal
1 Cor. 9. 13. they who *m.* about
2 Cor. 9. 10. *m.* seed to sower and
1 Pet. 4. 11. if any man *m.* let him
1 Tim. 4. 6. shall be a good *m.* of
Heb. 8. 2. *m.* of the sanctuary
Ps. 103. 21. *ministers* of his that do
104. 4. his *m.* a flaming fire
Isa. 61. 6. men call you the *m.* of
Luke 1. 2. from beginning, *m.* of
Rom. 13. 6. they are God's *m.*
1 Cor. 3. 5. *m.* by whom ye believed
4. 1. account of us as *m.* of Christ
2 Cor. 3. 6. made us able *m.* of
6. 4. approved ourselves as *m.* of
11. 23. are they *m.* of Christ, so
Matt. 4. 11. *ministered*, Luke 8. 3. Gal. 3. 5. Heb. 6. 10. 2 Pet. 1. 11.
Luke 1. 23. *ministration*, Acts 6. 1. 2 Cor. 3. 7, 8. & 9. 1, 13.
Heb. 1. 14. all *ministering* spirits
Rom. 15. 16. *m.* the gospel of God
Acts 6. 4. give ourselves to *ministry*
20. 24. I might finish the *m.* I have
2 Cor. 4. 1. seeing we have this *m.*
5. 18. given to us the *m.* of recon.
6. 3. that the *m.* be not blamed
Col. 4. 17. take heed to *m.* that thou
1 Tim. 1. 12. putting me into the *m.*
2 Tim. 4. 5. full proof of thy *m.*
Heb. 8. 6. obtained more excell. *m.*
R. V. Ezra 7. 24. servants; Luke 4. 24. attendant; 1 Chron. 28. 1. served; 2 Cor. 9. 10; Gal. 3. 5. supplieth; 1 Chron. 9. 28. vessels of service; Rom. 12. 7. ministry; Acts 12. 25; 2 Cor. 6. 3. ministration; Eph. 4. 12; 2 Tim. 4. 11. ministering; 1 Tim. 1. 12. his service

MIRACLE, Mark 6. 52. & 9. 39. Luke 23. 8. John 2. 11. & 6. 26. & 10. 41. & 11. 47. Acts 2. 22. & 4. 16. & 6. 8. & 19. 11. 1 Cor. 12. 10, 28, 29. Gal. 3. 5. Heb. 2. 4.
R. V. Heb. 2. 4. manifold powers. Elsewhere, for most part, changed to sign or signs

MIRTH, Prov. 14. 13. Eccl. 2. 2. & 7. 4. Isa. 24. 8, 11. Jer. 7. 34. & 16. 9. & 25. 10. Hos. 2. 11. Ezek. 21. 10.

MISCHIEF, Gen. 42. 4. & 44. 29.
Job 15. 35. they conceive *m.* bring
Ps. 10. 14. thou beholdest *m.* and
28. 3. *m.* is in their hearts, 10. 7.
36. 4. he deviseth *m.* upon his bed
94. 20. which frameth *m.* by a law
Prov. 10. 23. sport to a fool to do *m.*
11. 27. he that seeketh *m.* it shall
24. 16. wicked shall fall into *m.*
Acts 13. 10. full of all sub., and *m.*
R. V. Ex. 32. 12; Prov. 6. 14; 13. 17. evil; Ps. 52. 2; 119. 150; Prov. 10. 23. wickedness; 2 Kings 7. 9. punishment; Ps. 36. 4. iniquity; Prov. 24. 16. calamity; Acts 13. 10. villany

MISERY, Job 3. 20. Lam. 3. 19.
Judg. 10. 16. soul grieved for *m.*
Prov. 31. 7. drink and remember *m.*
Eccl. 8. 6. the *m.* of man is great
Rom. 3. 16. destruction and *m.*
Job 16. 2. *miserable* comforters are
1 Cor. 15. 19. are of all men most *m.*
Rev. 3. 17. knowest not thou art *m.*
R. V. 1 Cor. 15. 19. pitiable

MOCK when fear cometh
Prov. 14. 9. fools make a *m.* at sin
1 Kings 18. 27. Elijah *mocked* and
2 Chron. 36. 16. they *m.* the mes.
Prov. 17. 5. whoso *mocketh* the poor
30. 17. eye that *m.* at his father
20. 1. wine is a *mocker* and strong
Isa. 28. 22. be not *mockers*, lest
Jude 18. there should be *m.* in last
R. V. Job 13. 9. deceiveth; 12. 4. laughing stock; Isa. 28. 22. scorners; Jer. 15. 17. them that made merry

MODERATION known to all, Phil. 4. 5.

MODEST apparel, 1 Tim. 2. 9.

MOMENT, Ex. 33. 5. Isa. 27. 3.
Num. 16. 21. consume them in a *m.*
Job 7. 18. try him every *m.*
20. 5. joy of hypocrite is for a *m.*
Ps. 30. 5. his anger endureth but for a little *m.*
Isa. 26. 20. hide thee, as it were, for a little *m.*
54. 7. for a small *m.* have I for.
1 Cor. 15. 52. in a *m.* in the twink.
2 Cor. 4. 17. affliction is but for a *m.*

MONEY, Gen. 23. 9. & 31. 15.
Eccl. 7. 12. wisdom is def. and *m.*
10. 19. *m.* answereth all things
Isa. 55. 1. he that hath no *m.* come
2. wherefore spend *m.* for that

Mic. 3. 11. the prophets divine for *m.*
Acts 8. 20. thy *m.* perish with thee
1 Tim. 6. 10. love of *m.* is the root
R. V. Gen. 23. 9, 13; Ex. 21. 35. price of; Ex. 21. 30. ransom; Matt. 17. 24. half-shekel; 17. 27. shekel; Acts 7. 16. price in silver; 8. 20. silver

MORROW, Ex. 8. 23. & 16. 23.
Prov. 27. 1. boast not thy. of to *m.*
Isa. 22. 13. to *m.* we shall die
56. 12. to *m.* shall be as this day
Matt. 6. 34. take no thought for *m.*
Jas. 4. 14. know not what shall be on the *m.*

MORTAL man be just, Job 4. 17.
Rom. 6. 12. let not sin reign in *m.* body
8. 11. raised Christ, quicken *m.* body
1 Cor. 15. 53. this *m.* put on immor.
2 Cor. 5. 4. *mortality* be swallowed
Rom. 8. 13. *mortify* deeds of body
Col. 3. 5. *m.* your members on earth

MORTGAGES, Neh. 5. 3.

MOTE, Matt. 7. 3, 4, 5. Luke 6. 41.

MOTH, Job 4. 19. & 27. 18. Ps. 39. 11. Isa. 50. 9. & 51. 8. Hos. 5. 12. Matt. 6. 19, 20. Luke 12. 33.

MOTHER, Gen. 3. 20. & 21. 21. Judg. 5. 7. 2 Sam. 20. 19. 1 Kings 3. 27. Gal. 4. 26.
Job 17. 14. worm, thou art my *m.*
Ps. 27. 10. when father and *m.* for.
71. 6. took me out of my *m.'s* bowels
Matt. 12. 49. behold my *m.* and my
R. V. Luke 2. 43. his parents

MOUNT to be cast against Jerusalem, Jer. 6. 6.

MOURN, Neh. 8. 9. Job 5. 11.
Isa. 61. 2. to comfort all that *m.*
Matt. 5. 4. blessed are they that *m.*
Jas. 4. 9. be afflicted and *m.* and
Matt. 11. 17. we have *mourned*
1 Cor. 5. 2. are puffed up and have not rather *m.*
Eccl. 12. 5. *mourners* go about the
Isa. 57. 18. restore comfort to him and his *m.*
Ps. 30. 11. turned *mourning* into
Isa. 22. 12. Lord did call to weeping and *m.*
61. 3. to give the oil of joy for *m.*
Jer. 9. 17. call for the *m.* women
31. 13. I will turn their *m.* into joy
Joel 2. 12. turn to me with fasting and *m.*
Jas. 4. 9. let laughter be turned into *m.*
R. V. Gen. 50. 3; Num. 20. 29. wept; 2 Sam. 11. 26. made lamentation; Job 2. 11. bemoan; Gen. 50. 10; Isa. 19. 8. lament; Ps. 35. 14. bewaileth; 55. 2. am restless; 88. 9. wasteth away; Prov. 29. 2. sigh; Ezek. 24. 23. moan; Matt. 11. 17; Luke 7. 32. wailed; Job 3. 8. leviathan; Isa. 51. 11. sighing; Mic. 1. 11. wailing

MOUTH of babes and sucklings, Ps. 8. 2.
Ps. 37. 30. *m.* of righteous speaketh
Prov. 10. 14. *m.* of fools is near
10. 31. *m.* of the just bringeth
12. 6 *m.* of upright shall deliver
14. 3. in *m.* of fools is a rod of pride
15. 2. the *m.* of fools poureth out
18. 7. a fool's *m.* is his destruction
22. 14. *m.* of strange women is a
Lam. 3. 38. out of *m.* of the Most
Matt. 12. 34. out of abundance of the heart the *m.* speaketh
Luke 21. 15. will give you a *m.* and
Rom. 10. 10. with the *m.* confession
15. 6 with one mind and *m.* glorify
Prov. 13. 3. keepeth *his mouth*, keep.
Lam 3. 29. putteth — in dust if
Mal. 2. 7. they shall seek law at —
Ps. 17. 3. *my mouth* shall not transgress
39. 1. I will keep — with a bridle
49. 3. — shall speak of wisdom
Ps. 51. 15. — shall show forth thy
71. 15 — shall show forth thy
Eph. 6. 19. that I may open—boldly
Ps. 81. 10. open *thy mouth* wide
103. 5. who satisfieth — with good
Prov. 31. 8. open — for the dumb in
Eccl. 5. 6. suffer not—to cause flesh
R. V. Job 12. 11; 34. 3. palate; Ps. 32. 9. trappings; Isa. 19. 7. brink; Matt. 15. 8 ——

MOVE, Ex. 11. 7. Judg. 13. 25.
Acts 17. 28. in him we live and *m.*
20. 24. none of these things *m.* me
Ps. 15. 5. shall never be *moved*, 21. 7. & 26. 5. & 55. 22. & 62. 2, 6. & 66. 9. & 112. 6. & 121. 3. Prov. 12. 3.
Col. 1. 23. be not *m.* away from hope
1 Thes. 3. 3. no man be *m.* by these
Heb. 12. 28. a kingdom which cannot be *m.*
2 Pet. 1. 21. spake as *m.* by the Holy Ghost
Rom. 7. 5. *motions*
Prov. 5. 6. *moveable*
R. V. Gen. 9. 2. teemeth; 2 Kings 21. 8. wander; Ps. 23. 31. goeth down smoothly; Jer. 25. 16. reel to and fro; 46. 7, 8. toss themselves; 49. 21; 50. 46. trembleth; Ezek. 47. 9. swarmeth; Mic. 7. 17. trembling; Matt. 14. 14; Mark 6. 34. he had . . on; Matt. 21. 10; Mark 15. 11. stirred; Acts 20. 24 ——; Heb. 12. 28. shaken

MULTITUDE, Gen. 16. 10. & 28. 3. Ex. 12. 38. & 23. 2. Num. 11. 4.
Job 32. 7. *m.* of years should teach
Ps. 5. 7. *m.* of mercies
10. *m.* of transgressions
33. 16. no king saved by the *m.* of
51. 1. according unto the *m.* of thy
94. 19. in the *m.* of my thoughts
Prov. 10. 19. *m.* of words wanteth
11. 14. in the *m.* of counsellors
Eccl. 5. 3. *m.* of business, *m.* words
Jas. 5. 20. hide *m.* of sins, 1 Pet. 4. 8.
R. V. Gen. 28. 3; 48. 4; Luke 23. 1. company; Job. 39. 7; Jer. 3. 23; 10. 13; 51. 16. tumult; 46. 25. Amon; Ps. 42. 4. throng; Prov. 20. 15. abundance; Isa. 17. 12. ah, the uproar; Jer. 12. 6. aloud; Ezek. 31. 5; Matt. 12. 15. many; Mark 3. 9; Acts 21. 34. crowd; Luke 8. 37. all the people; Acts 23. 7. assembly; Job 33. 19; Acts 21. 22 ——

MURDER, Rom. 1. 29. Matt. 15. 19. Gal. 5. 21. Rev. 9. 21.
Job 24. 14. *murderer* rising with light
John 8. 44. devil was a *m.* from the
Hos. 9. 13. bring forth children to *m.*
1 Pet. 4. 15. none of you suffer as a *m.*
1 John 3. 15. who hateth his brother is a *m.* and no *m.* hath eternal life
R. V. Matt. 19. 18. not kill; Gal. 5. 21 ——; Num. 35. 16, 17, 18, 21. manslayer; Hos. 9. 13. slayer; Acts 21. 38. assassins

MURMUR, Deut. 1. 27. Ps. 106. 25. Jude 16. Ex. 16. 7. Phil. 2. 14.

MUSE, Ps. 39. 3. & 143. 5.
R. V. Luke 3. 15. reasoned

MUSIC, Lam. 3. 63. Amos 6. 5.
R. V. Lam. 3. 63. song

MUSTARD seed, Matt. 13. 31. & 17. 20.

MUZZLE, Deut. 25. 4. 1 Cor. 9. 9.

MYSTERY of the kingdom, Mark 4. 11.
Rom. 11. 25. not be ignorant of *m.*
16. 25. according to revelation of the *m.*
1 Cor. 2. 7. speak the wisdom of God in a *m.*
4. 1. stewards of the *m.* of God
13. 2. prophesy and understand *m.*
14. 2. in the Spirit he speaketh *m.*
15. 51. I show you a *m.* we shall
Eph. 1. 9. made known *m.* of his
3. 4. my knowledge in *m.*
5. 32. this is a great *m.* of Christ
Eph. 6. 19. make known *m.* of gospel
Col. 1. 2. *m.* which hath been hid
1. 27. glory of this *m.* among Gen.
2. 2. acknowledg. of *m.* of God
4. 3. open a door to speak *m.* of
2 Thes. 2. 7. *m.* of iniquity doth
1 Tim. 3. 9. holding *m.* of the faith
16. great is the *m.* of godliness
Rev. 1. 20. write the *m.* of seven
10. 7. *m.* of God should be finish.
17. 5. her name, *m.* Babylon the

N

NAIL, Judg. 4. 21. & 5. 26.
Ezra 9. 8. give us a *n.* in his
Eccl. 12. 11. *n.* fastened by the masters
Isa. 22. 23. fastened as a *n.* in a sure
Zech. 10. 4. out of him came the *n.*
R. V. Judg. 4. 21, 22. tent pin

NAKED, Gen. 2. 25. & 3. 7, 11.
Ex. 32. 25. when the people were *n.*
2 Chron. 28. 19. he made Judah *n.*
Job 1. 21. *n.* came I out of
Matt. 25. 26. I was *n.* and ye cloth.
1 Cor. 4. 11. we hunger and thirst and are *n.*
2 Cor. 5. 3. clothed may not be *n.*
Heb. 4. 13. all things are *n.* and
Rev. 3. 17. misera., poor, blind, *n.*
16. 15. keepeth his garments lest he walk *n.*
R. V. Ex. 32. 25. broken loose, let them loose for derision; 2 Chron. 28. 19. dealt wantonly; Hab. 3. 9. bare

NAME, Ex. 34. 14. Lev. 18. 21.
Ps. 20. 1. the *n.* of God of Jacob
109. 13. let their *n.* be blotted
Prov. 10. 7. *n.* of the wicked shall
22. 1. good *n.* is rather to be chos.
Eccl. 7. 1. a good *n.* is better than
Isa. 55. 13. shall be to the Lord for *n.*
56. 5. a *n.* better than of sons and
62. 2. thou shalt be call. by new *n.*
Jer. 13. 11. for a people, for a *n.* and
32. 20. made thee *n.* as at this day
33. 9. shall be to me a *n.* of joy, a
Mic. 4. 5. we will walk in the *n.* of
Matt. 10. 41. receive a prophet in *n.*
Luke 6. 22. cast out your *n.* as evil
Acts 4. 12. is none other *n.*
Rom. 2. 24. *n.* of God is blasphem.
Col. 3. 17. do all in the *n.* of Lord
2 Tim. 2. 19. that nameth *n.* of Ch.
Heb. 1. 4. obtained more excell. *n.*
1 Pet. 4. 14. if ye be reproached for the *n.* of Christ
1 John 3. 23. should believe on the *n.* of his Son
5. 13. that we believe on the *n.*
Rev. 2. 17. *n.* written, which no man
3. 1. I know thy works, that thou hast a *n.*
12. write on him *n.* of my God
14. 1. Father's *n.* on their fore.
Eph. 1. 21. every *n.* that is *named*, Phil. 2. 9.
Ps. 76. 1. *his name* is great in Israel
72. 17. — shall endure for ever
106. 8. he saved them for — sake
Prov. 30. 4. what is — and what
Isa. 9. 6.—shall be called Wonder.
Zech. 14. 9. shall be one Lord and — one
John 20. 31. might have life thro.—
Rev. 3. 5. I will confess — before
13. 17. the name of the beast, or the number of —, 15. 2.
Ex. 23. 21. *my name* is in him
3. 15. this is — for ever, and my
Judg. 13. 18. askest after —, Gen. 32. 29.
Isa. 48. 9. for — sake I will defer
Ezek. 20. 9. wrought for — sake
Mal. 1. 14. —is dreadful among the
2. 2. lay it to heart to give glory to—
Matt. 10. 22. hated of all for — sake
19. 29. forsaken houses for — sake

John 14. 13. ask in —, 15. 16. & 16. 23, 26.
16. 24. asked nothing in —
Acts 9. 15. he is a chosen vessel to bear —
Rev. 2. 3. for — hast labored, and
13. holdest fast —
3. 8. hast not denied my —
2 Chron. 14. 11. in *thy name* we go
Ps. 8. 1. how excellent is — in all
9. 10. that know — will put their
48. 10. according to — so is thy
75. 1.— is near, thy works declare
138. 2. magnified thy word above all —
S. of S. 1. 3.— is as ointment pour.
Isa. 26. 8. desire of our souls is to—
64. 7. none that calleth on —
Jer. 14. 7. do it for—sake, 21. Dan. 9. 6. Josh. 7. 9. Ps. 79. 9.
Mic. 6. 9. man of wisdom shall see —
John 17. 12. I kept them in —, 26.
Ex. 23. 13. make no mention of the *names* of other gods, Deut. 12. 3. Ps. 16. 4.
Ex. 28. 12. Aaron bear their *n*.
Ps. 49. 11. call lands after their *n*.
147. 4. stars he calleth by their *n*.
Luke 10. 20. *n*. written in heaven
Rev. 3. 4. hast a few *n*. in Sardis
R. V. Mark 9. 41; 11. 10; 1 John 5. 13 —— ; Luke 24. 18; Acts 7. 58; 28. 7. named; Matt. 9. 9; Mark 15. 7; Luke 19. 2. called; John 11. 1 —— ; John 11. 49; Acts 24. 1. one; 1 Cor. 5. 1. even

NARROW, 1 Kings 6. 4. Prov. 23. 27. Isa. 28. 20. & 49. 19. Matt. 7. 14.
R. V. 1 Kings 6. 4. fixed; Ezek. 40. 16; 41. 16, 26. closed; Matt. 7. 14. straitened

NATION, Gen. 15. 14. & 21. 13.
Gen. 20. 4. wilt thou slay a righteous *n*.
Num. 14. 12. make of thee a great *n*.
2 Sam. 7. 23. what *n*. is like thy
Ps. 33. 12. blessed is the *n*. whose
147. 20. not dealt so with any *n*.
Isa. 1. 4. ah sinful *n*. a people laden
2. 4. *n*. shall not lift up sword
49. 7. him whom the *n*. abhorreth
66. 8. shall a *n*. be born at once
Matt. 24. 7. *n*. shall rise against *n*.
Luke 7. 5. he loveth our *n*. and
Acts 10. 35. in every *n*. he that fear.
Rom. 10. 19. by a foolish *n*. I will
Phil. 2. 15. in midst of a crooked *n*.
1 Pet. 2. 9. ye are a holy *n*.
Rev. 5. 9. redeemed us out of every *n*.
Gen. 10. 32. *nations*, 17. 4, 6, 16.
Deut. 26. 19. high above all *n*., 28. 1.
Ps. 9. 20. *n*. may know themselves
113. 4. Lord is high above all *n*.
Isa. 2. 2. all *n*. shall flow unto it
40. 17. *n*. before him are as noth.
55. 5. *n*. that knew thee not shall
Jer. 4. 2. *n*. shall bless themselves
Zech. 2. 11. many *n*. be joined
Matt. 25. 32. before him be gathered all *n*.
Acts 14. 16. suffered all *n*. to walk
Rev. 21. 24. the *n*. of them that
R. V. Gen. 14. 1, 9; Josh. 12. 23. Goiim; Lev. 18. 26. homeborn; Ex. 2. 18; Deut. 2. 25; 4. 6, 19, 27; 14. 2; 28. 37; 30. 3; 1 Chron. 16. 24; 2 Chron. 7. 20; 13. 9; Neh. 1. 8; 19. 22; Ps. 96. 5; 106. 34; Ezek. 38. 8. peoples; Isa. 37. 18. countries; Mark 7. 26. race; Gal. 1. 14. countrymen; Phil. 2. 15. generation

NATURE, Rom. 2. 27. Jas. 3. 6.
Rom. 1. 26. that which is against *n*.
2. 14. do by *n*. things contained in
11. 24. olive wild by *n*. contr. to *n*.
1 Cor. 11. 14. doth not *n*. itself teach
Gal. 2. 16. are Jews by *n*. and
4. 8. served them which by *n*. are
Eph. 2. 3. were by *n*. the children
Heb. 2. 16. took not *n*. of angels
2 Pet. 1. 4. partakers of divine *n*.
Deut. 34. 7. *natural*, Rom. 1. 26, 27, 31. & 11. 21, 24. 1 Cor. 2. 14. & 15. 44, 46. 2 Tim. 3. 3. Jas. 1. 23. 2 Pet. 2. 12. Phil. 2. 20. Jude 10.
R. V. 2 Pet. 2. 12. creatures without reason

NAUGHT, it is, saith the buyer, Prov. 20. 14.
Jas. 1. 21. filthiness and superfluity of *naughtiness*
R. V. Prov. 11. 6. mischief; Jas. 1. 21. wickedness

NAVY of Solomon, 1 Kings 9. 26. 2 Chron. 8. 17.
of Jehoshaphat, 1 Kings 22. 48.

NEAR, nigh, Ps. 119. 151. & 148. 14. Isa. 55. 6. & 57. 19. Jer. 12. 2.
R. V. frequent changes to at, nigh, ——, etc.

NECESSARY, Job 23. 12. Acts 13. 46. & 15. 28. Tit. 3. 14. Heb. 9. 23.
Rom. 12. 13. *necessity*, Acts 20. 34. 1 Cor. 9. 16. 2 Cor. 6. 4. & 9. 7. & 12. 20. Phile. 14. Heb. 9. 16.
R. V. Acts 28. 10. we needed; Luke 23. 17 —— ; Heb. 8. 3. necessary; Phil. 4. 16. need

NECK, S. of S. 1. 10. Isa. 48. 4. Rom. 16. 4.
Acts 15. 10. put a yoke on *n*. of
2 Kings 17. 14. hardened their *necks*, Neh. 9. 16, 17, 29. Jer. 7. 26. & 19. 15.

NEED of all these things, Matt. 6. 32.
Matt. 9. 12. they that are whole *n*.
Luke 15. 7. the righteous *n*. no
Heb. 4. 16. find grace to help in time of *n*.
1 John 2. 27. *n*. not that any
Rev. 3. 17. rich, and have *n*. of
21. 23. no *n*. of sun
22. 5. *n*. no candle
Eph. 4. 28. give to him that *needeth*
2 Tim. 2. 15. *n*. not be ashamed of
Luke 10. 42. one thing is *needful*
Ps. 9. 18. *needy* not always be for.
72. 12. he shall deliver the *n*. and
82. 3. do justice to afflicted and *n*.
Isa. 14. 30. *n*. shall lie down in saf.
Jer. 22. 16. he judgeth cause of *n*.
R. V. Jude 3. was constrained

NEGLECT to hear, Matt. 18. 17.
1 Tim. 4. 14. *n*. not the gift that is
Heb. 2. 3. if we *n*. so great salva.
R. V. Matt. 18. 17. refuse; Col. 2. 23. severity of.

NEIGH, Jer. 5. 8. & 8. 16. & 13. 27.

NEIGHBOR, Ex. 3. 22. & 11. 2.
Ex. 20. 16. not bear false witness against thy *n*.
Lev. 19. 13. thou shalt not defr. *n*.
17. thou shalt rebuke thy *n*.
18. thou shalt love thy *n*. as thyself, Matt. 19. 19. & 22. 39. Rom. 13. 9. Gal. 5. 14. Jas. 2. 8. Matt. 7. 12. Heb. 13. 3.
Ps. 15. 3. nor doeth evil to his *n*.
Prov. 27. 10. better is a *n*. near
Jer. 22. 13. useth *n*.'s servant
31. 24. teach no more his *n*.
Luke 10. 29. who is my *n*., 36.
Rom. 13. 10. love worketh no ill to his *n*.
15. 2. let every one please his *n*.
R. V. 1 Kings 20. 35. fellow; Ps. 15. 3; Prov. 19. 4. friend; Heb. 8. 11. fellow-citizen

NEST, Job 20. 18. Ps. 84. 3. Prov. 27. 8. Isa. 10. 14. Hab. 2. 9. Matt. 8. 20.

NET, Job 18. 8. & 19. 6. Ps. 9. 15. & 25. 15. & 31. 4. & 35. 7, 8. & 57. 6. & 66. 11. Isa. 51. 20. Hab. 1. 15, 16. Matt. 13. 47. Ps. 141. 10. Eccl. 7. 20.

NEW, Lord make a *n*. thing, Num. 16. 30.
Judg. 5. 8. they chose *n*. gods, Deut. 32. 17.
Eccl. 1. 9. no *n*. thing under sun, 10.
Isa. 65. 17. *n*. heavens and a *n*. earth, 66. 22. 2 Pet. 3. 13. Rev. 21. 1.
Jer. 31. 22. created a *n*. thing in earth
Lam. 3. 23. his mercies are *n*.
Ezek. 11. 19. I will put a *n*. spirit
18. 31. make you a *n*. heart and *n*. spirit
36. 26. *n*. heart I will give, and a *n*. spirit
Matt. 9. 16. putteth *n*. cloth on old
17. neither put *n*. wine in old bot.
13. 52. bringeth forth things *n*.
Mark 1. 27. what *n*. doctrine is this, Acts 17. 19.
John 13. 34. a *n*. commandment I give unto you, 1 John 2. 7, 8.
Acts 17. 21. to tell or hear some *n*. thing
1 Cor. 5. 7. that ye may be a *n*.
2 Cor. 5. 17. if any man be in Christ, he is a *n*. creature
Gal. 6. 15. neither circumcision nor uncircumcision, but a *n*. creature
Eph. 4. 24. that ye put on *n*. man
1 Pet. 2. 2. as *n*. born babes desire
Rev. 2. 17. a *n*. name written
5. 9. sung a *n*. song, 14. 3.
Rom. 6. 4. should walk in *newness*
7. 6. we should serve in *n*. of spirit
R. V. Joel 1. 5; 3. 18. sweet; Matt. 9. 16; Mark 2. 21; Luke 5. 38. fresh; Matt. 9. 16; Mark 2. 21. undressed; Neh. 10. 39; Matt. 26. 28; Mark 2. 22; 14. 24 ——

NIGH, Lev. 25. 49. Num. 24. 17
Deut. 4. 7. who hath God so *n*.
Ps. 34. 18. Lord is *n*. them of brok.
85. 9. salvation is *n*. them that
145. 18. Lord is *n*. them that call
Matt. 15. 8. draweth *n*. with mouth
Eph. 2. 13. made *n*. by blood of
R. V. Gen. 47. 29; Ex. 24. 2; Lev. 21. 3; Luke 7. 12. near; Luke 21. 20; John 6. 4; Jas. 5. 8. at hand; Matt. 15. 8. honoreth

NIGHT, Gen. 1. 5, 14. & 26. 24.
Ex. 12. 42. this is that *n*. of Lord
Ps. 19. 2. *n*. unto *n*. showeth know.
30. 5. weeping may endure for a *n*.
Isa. 21. 11. what of the *n*.
Jer. 14. 8. as wayfaring man to tarry for a *n*.
Luke 6. 12. continued all *n*. in pray.
12. 20. this *n*. shall thy soul be
John 9. 4. *n*. cometh when no man
Rom. 13. 12. *n*. is far spent; day is
1 Thes. 5. 5. children not of *n*. nor
Rev. 21. 25. shall be no *n*. there
Ps. 134. 1. *by night*, S. of S. 3. 1. John 3. 2. & 7. 50. & 19. 39.
Job 35. 10. who giveth songs *in the night*
Ps. 16. 7. instruct me — seasons
42. 8. — his song shall be with me
77. 6. I call to remembrance my song —
119. 55. I have remem. thy name—
Isa. 26. 9. my soul desired thee —
59. 10. stumble at noon day as —
John 11. 10. if a man walk — he
1 Thes. 5. 7. sleep — and are drunk—
Ps. 63. 6. *night watches*, 119. 148.
R. V. Lev. 6. 20. evening; Isa. 21. 4; 59. 10. twi.; Judg. 19. 13; Matt. 27. 64; Mark 14. 27; 2 Pet. 3. 10 ——

NOBLE, Esth. 6. 9. Jer. 2. 21. Luke 19. 12. Acts 17. 11. Ex. 24. 11. Num. 21. 12.
1 Cor. 1. 26. not many *n*. are called
Col. 3. 5. *nobles* put not their necks
13. 17. I contended with the *n*. of
Ps. 149. 8. bind their *n*. with fetters
Prov. 8. 16. by me princes rule, and *n*.
Eccl. 13. 17. when thy king is the son of *n*.
R. V. Isa. 43. 14. as fugitives; Jer. 30. 21. prince; Nah. 3. 18. worthless; Acts 24. 3; 26. 25. excellent

NOISOME, Ps. 91. 3. Rev. 16. 2.

NOSE, Prov. 30. 33. Isa. 65. 5.
Isa. 2. 22. breath in *nostrils*, Lam. 4. 20.
R. V. S. of S. 7. 8. breath; Ezek. 39. 11. them that pass through; Job 4. 9. anger; 39. 20. snorting

NOTHING, Gen. 11. 6. Ex. 9. 4. &

12. 10. Num. 6. 4. & 16. 26. Josh. 11. 15.
2 Sam. 24. 24. offer that which costs me *n.*
1 Kings 8. 9. *n.* in ark save the two
Neh. 8. 10. send to them from whom *n.* is prepared
Job 6. 21. ye are *n.*
8. 9. of yesterday, and know *n.*
26. 7. hangeth earth on *n.*
34. 9. it profiteth *n.*
Ps. 17. 3. thou hast tried me and shalt find *n.*
39. 5. my age is as *n.* before thee
49. 17. when he dieth, shall carry *n.*
119. 165. *n.* shall offend them
Prov. 13. 4. the sluggard desireth and hath *n.*
7. that make. him. rich, yet hath *n.*
Isa. 40. 17. all nations before him are as *n.*
Jer. 10. 24. lest thou bring me to *n.*
Lam. 1. 12. is it *n.* to you, all ye
Hag. 2. 3. is it not in your eyes in comparison of it as *n.*
Luke 1. 37. with God *n.* shall be
John 8. 28. I do *n.* of myself
14. 30. prince of this world hath *n.* in me
15. 5. without me ye can do *n.*
1 Cor. 1. 19. bring to *n.* the under.
13. 2. I am *n.*
2 Cor. 12. 11. having *n.* yet possessing all, 2 Cor. 6. 10.
1 Tim. 6. 7. we brought *n.* into world

NOUGHT, Gen. 29. 15. Deut. 13. 17.
Isa. 41. 12. shall be as a thing of *n.*
49. 4. I have spent my strength for *n.*
52. 3. sold yourselves for *n.*
Amos 6. 13. rejoice in a thing of *n.*
Luke 23. 11. Herod and men set him at *n.*
Acts 19. 27. Diana in danger to be set at *n.*
Rom. 14. 10. why set at *n.* brother

NOVICE, not a, lest, 1 Tim. 3. 6.

NUMBER our days, teach us to, Ps. 90. 12.
Isa. 65. 12. I will *n.* you to the sword
Rev. 7. 9. multitude which no man could *n.*
Isa. 53. 12. was *numbered* with transgressors
Dan. 5. 26. God hath *n.* thy kingdom
Job 14. 16. thou *numberest* my steps
Ps. 71. 15. I know not the *numbers*
Rev. 13. 17. the *n.* of his name, 18.
R. V. Mark 10. 46; Acts 1. 15. multitude; 2 Sam. 24. 2. sum; Josh. 8. 10; 1 Kings 20. 15, 26, 27; 2 Kings 3. 6. mustered; 1 Tim. 5. 9. enrolled

NUMBERING of the people, by Moses, Num. 1. 26; by David, 2 Sam. 24. 1 Chron. 21, of the Levites, Num. 3. 14. & 4. 34.

NURSE, 1 Thes. 2. 7. Isa. 49. 23.

O

OATH, Gen. 24. 8. & 26. 3, 28.
1 Sam. 14. 26. people feared the *o.*
2 Sam. 21. 7. Lord's *o.* was between
2 Chron. 15. 15. Israel rejoiced at *o.*
Eccl. 8. 2. keep in regard of *o* of God
9. 2. that feareth and sweareth an *o.*
Ezek. 16. 59. despised the *o.*
Luke 1. 73. *o.* which he sware to
Heb. 6. 16. *o.* for confirmat. is end
Jas. 5. 12. swear not by heaven neither by any other *o.*

OBEY, Gen. 27. 8. Ex. 5. 2.
Deut. 11. 27. a blessing if ye *o.*
13. 4. walk after the Lord and *o.*
Josh. 24. 24. his voice will we *o.*
1 Sam. 12. 14. fear the Lord and *o.*
15. 22. to *o.* is better than sacrifice
Jer. 7. 23. *o.* my voice and I will
26. 13. amend your ways, and *o.*
Acts 5. 29. ought to *o.* God rather
Rom. 2. 8. contenti., and do not *o.*
6. 16. his servants ye are to whom ye *o.*
Eph. 6. 1. children *o.* your parents
Col. 3. 22. servants *o.* in all things
2 Thes. 1. 8. that *o.* not the Gospel
3. 14. if any man *o.* not your word
Tit. 3. 1. put them in mind to *o.*
Heb. 5. 9. salvation to all who *o.*
13. 17. *o.* them that have rule over
1 Pet. 3. 1. if any *o.* not the word
Rom. 6. 17. *obeyed* from heart that
1 Pet. 3. 6. Sarah *o.* Abraham
4. 17. the end of them that *o.* not
Isa. 50. 10. *obeyeth* voice, Jer. 11. 3.
1 Pet. 1. 22. purified in *obeying* truth
Rom. 1. 5. received grace for *obedience*
15. 19. by the *o.* of one many
6. 16. yield *o.* unto righteousness
16. 19. your *o.* is come abroad
26. made known for *o.* of faith
1 Cor. 14. 34. women to be under *o.*
2 Cor. 7. 15. remember the *o.* of you
10. 5. every thought to *o.* of Christ
Heb. 5. 8. learned he *o.* by things
1 Pet. 1. 2. sanctifi. of Spirit unto *o.*
Ex. 24. 7. will we do and be *obedient*
Num. 27. 20. children of Israel may be *o.*
Deut. 3. 30. turn and be *o.* to voice
8. 20. perish because not *o.* to Lord
2 Sam. 22. 45. strangers shall be *o.*
Isa. 1. 19. if ye be *o.* ye shall eat
42. 24. they were not *o.* to his law
Acts 6. 7. priests were *o.* to the faith
Rom. 15. 18. Gentiles *o.* by word
2 Cor. 2. 9. whether ye be *o.* in all
Eph. 6. 5. servants be *o.* to masters
Phil. 2. 8. he became *o.* unto death
Tit. 2. 5. discreet, *o.* to your hus.
1 Pet. 1. 14. as *o.* children, not
R. V. Ex. 5. 2; 23. 21, 22; Deut. 11. 27, 28; 28. 62; Josh. 24. 24; 1 Sam. 8. 19; 12. 14, 15; Job 36. 11, 12; Jer. 7. 23; Rom. 10. 16. hearken; Josh. 5. 6; 22. 2; Judg. 2. 2; 6. 10; 1 Sam. 28. 21; Jer. 17. 23, 28; 2 Chron. 11. 4. hearkened; Jer. 11. 3; 12. 17. hear; Gal. 3. 1——; 1 Cor. 14. 34. subjection; Deut. 8. 20; Dan. 4. 30. hearken; Num. 27. 20; 2 Sam. 22. 45. obey; Tit. 2. 5, 9. subjection; 1 Pet. 1. 22. obedience

OBSCURITY, Isa. 29. 18. & 58. 10.
R. V. 58. 10; 59. 9. darkness

OBSERVE, Ex. 12. 17. & 34. 11.
Ps. 107. 43. who is wise and will *o.*
119. 34. *o.* it with my whole heart
Prov. 23. 26. let thine eyes *o.* my
Jonah 2. 8. that *o.* lying vanities
Matt. 28. 20. teaching them to *o.*
Gal. 4. 10. ye *o.* days months and
Gen. 37. 11. his father *observed* the
Ex. 12. 42. a night to be much *o.*
Mark 6. 20. Herod fear. John and *o.*
10. 20. all these have I *o.* from my
Luke 17. 20. cometh not with *observation*
R. V. Lev. 19. 26; 2 Kings 21. 6; 2 Chron. 33. 6. practise; Deut. 16. 13; 2 Chron. 7. 17; Neh. 1. 5; Ps. 105. 45. keep; Prov. 23. 26. delight in; Hos. 14. 8; John 2. 8. regard; Gen. 37. 11; Mark 6. 20. kept; Ps. 107. 43. give heed; Hos. 13. 7. watch; Matt. 23. 3; Acts 21. 25——

OBSTINATE, Deut. 2. 30. Isa. 48. 4.

OBTAIN favor of Lord, Prov. 8. 35.
Isa. 35. 10. shall *o.* joy and gladness
Luke 20. 35. worthy to *o.* that world
1 Cor. 9. 24. so run, that ye may *o.*
Heb. 4. 16. may *o.* mercy and find
11. 35. might *o.* better resurrection
Hos. 2. 23. her that had not *obtained* mercy
Acts 26. 22. having *o.* help of God
Rom. 11. 7. the election hath *o.* it
Eph. 1. 11. in whom we have *o.* an
1 Tim. 1. 13. I *o.* mercy, because
Heb. 1. 4. *o.* a more excellent
6. 15. endured, he *o.* the promises
Heb. 9. 12. *o.* eternal redemption for us
R. V. Luke 20. 35; 1 Cor. 9. 24. attain; 1 Cor. 9. 25; Heb. 4. 16; Acts 1. 17. receive; Neh. 13. 6. asked

OCCASION, Gen. 43. 18. Judg. 14. 4.
2 Sam. 12. 14. given *o.* to enemies
Job 33. 10. he findeth *o.* against me
Jer. 2. 24. in her *o.* who can turn
Dan. 6. 4. could find none *o.*, 5.
Rom. 7. 8. sin taking *o.* by the
14. 13. *o.* to fall in brother's way
2 Cor. 11. 12. cut off *o.* from the
Gal. 5. 13. use not for *o.* to the flesh
1 Tim. 5. 14. give none *o.* to adver.
1 John 2. 10. none *o.* of stumbling

OCCUPY, Luke 19. 13. Heb. 13. 9.
R. V. Ex. 38. 24. used; Ezek. 27. 16, 19, 22. Luke 19. 13. trade, or traded; 1 Cor. 14. 16. filleth

ODOR, Phil. 4. 18. Rev. 5. 8.
R. V. Jer. 34. 5. make burning; Rev. 5. 8; 18. 13. incense

OFFENCE, 1 Sam. 25. 31. Isa. 8. 14.
Eccl. 10. 4. yield. pacifieth great *o.*
Hos. 5. 15. acknowledge their *o.*
Acts 24. 16. conscience void of *o.*
Rom. 4. 25. delivered for our *o.* and
Matt. 16. 23. thou art an *o.* unto me
18. 7. woe to the world because of *o.* for *o.* must come
Rom. 5. 15. not as *o.* so is free gift
16. the free gift is of many *o.*
17. by one man's *o.* death came
9. 33. rock of *o.*, 1 Pet. 2. 8. Isa. 8. 14.
14. 20. is evil for him that eateth with *o.*
16. 17. cause divisions and *o.*
1 Cor. 10. 32. give none *o.* neither
2 Cor. 6. 3. giving no *o.* in any
11. 7. committed an *o.* in abasing
Gal. 5. 11. then is the *o.* of the
Phil. 1. 10. without *o.* till day of Christ
R. V. Matt. 16. 23; Gal. 5. 11. stumbling block; Matt. 18. 7. occasion; Rom. 4. 25; 5. 15-18. trespass; Matt. 18. 7; Luke 17. 1; Rom. 16. 17; 2 Cor. 6. 3. occasion for stum.

OFFEND, I will not any more, Job 34. 31.
Ps. 73. 15. *o.* against generation
119. 165. nothing shall *o.* them
Jer. 2. 3. all that devour him shall *o.*
50. 7. we *o.* not because we have
Matt. 5. 29. if thy right eye *o.* thee
13. 41. gather out of his kingdom all that *o.*
17. 27. yet lest we should *o.* go
18. 6. whoso shall *o.* one of these
1 Cor. 8. 13. if meat make thy brother to *o.*
Jas. 2. 10. *o.* in one point is guilty
3. 2. in many things we *o.* all
Prov. 18. 19. brother *offended* is harder to be won
Matt. 11. 6. blessed who is not *o.*
26. 33. though all be *o.* I will
Mark 4. 17. immediate. they are *o.*
Rom. 14. 21. *o.* or is made weak
2 Cor. 11. 29. who is *o.* and I burn
Isa. 29. 21. make a man *offender* for
R. V. Gen. 20. 9; Jer. 37. 18; Acts 25. 8. sinned; Jer. 2. 3; Hab. 1. 11. guilty; Rom. 14. 21——. In most of the above references under the head of *Stumble*, the word stumble, stumbling or stumbleth has been introduced into R. V. text; Acts 21. 11. wrong doer

OFFER, Gen. 31. 54. Lev. 1. 3.
Matt. 5. 24. then come and *o.* thy gift
Heb. 13. 15. let us *o.* the sacrifice
Rev. 8. 3. *o.* it with prayers of
Mal. 1. 11. incense *offered* to my
Phil. 2. 17. *o.* upon sacrifice and service
2 Tim. 4. 6. I am now ready to be *o.*
Heb. 9. 14. *o.* himself without spot
28. Christ was once *o.* to bear

Heb. 11. 4. by faith Abel *o.* to God a
17. Abraham *o.* up Isaac
Ps. 50. 14. *o.* to God thanksgiving
23. whoso *offereth* praise glori.
Eph. 5. 2. *offering* a sacrifice to God
Heb. 10. 5. sacrifice and *o.* thou
14. by one *o.* hath perfected for
R. V. Frequent changes to sacrifice, present, bring or brought, especially in O. T. Frequent changes in Lev. and Num. to oblation
OFFSCOURING, Lam. 3. 45. 1 Cor. 4. 16.
OFFSPRING, Acts 17. 28. Rev. 22. 16.
R. V. Job 31. 8. produce
OFTEN reproved hardeneth, Prov. 29. 1.
Mal. 3. 16. spake *o.* one to another
Matt. 23. 37. how *o.* would I have
1 Cor. 11. 26. *o.* as ye eat this
Phil. 3. 18. of whom I have told you *o.*
Heb. 9. 25. needed not offer himself *o.*
OIL, Gen. 28. 18. Ex. 25. 6.
Ps. 45. 7. with *o.* of gladness
89. 20. with my holy *o.* I have
92. 10. be anointed with fresh *o.*
104. 15. *o.* to make his face shine
141. 5. *o.* which shall not break
Isa. 61. 3. *o.* of joy for mourning
Matt. 25. 3. took no *o.* in lamps
8. give us of your *o.* for our lamps
Luke 10. 34. pouring in wine and *o.*
OINTMENT, Ps. 133. 2. Prov. 27. 9, 16. Eccl. 7. 1. & 10. 1. S. of S. 1. 3. Isa. 1. 6. Amos 6. 6. Matt. 26. 7. Luke 7. 37.
R. V. Ex. 30. 25. perfume; 2 Kings 20. 13; Ps. 123. 2; Isa. 1. 6; 39. 2. oil
OLD, Gen. 5. 32. & 18. 12, 13.
Ps. 37. 25. been young, and now am *o.*
71. 18. when I am *o.* and gray.
Prov. 22. 6. when he is *o.* he will
Jer. 6. 16. ask for the *o.* paths and
Acts 21. 16. Mnason an *o.* disciple
1 Cor. 5. 7. purge out the *o.* leaven
2 Cor. 5. 17. *o.* things are passed
2 Pet. 1. 9. purged from his *o.* sins
Gen. 25. 8. *old age*, Judg. 8. 32. Job 30. 2. Ps. 71. 9. & 92. 14. Isa. 46. 4.
Rom. 6. 6. *old man*, Eph. 4. 22. Col. 3. 9.
Prov. 17. 6. of *old men*, 20. 29.
OLD PROPHET, the, 1 Kings 13. 11.
OMEGA, Alpha and, Rev. 1. 8, 11. & 21. 6. & 22. 13.
R. V. Rev. 1. 11 ——
ONE, Gen. 2. 24. Matt. 19. 5.
Jer. 3. 14. *o.* of a city, and two of
Zech. 14. 9. shall be *o.* Lord and
Matt. 19. 17. none good but *o.*
1 Cor. 8. 4. none other God but *o.*
10. 17. we being many are *o.* bread
Gal. 3. 20. mediator not of *o.* but
1 John 5. 7. these three are *o.*
Josh. 23. 14. not *one thing* hath failed
Ps. 27. 4. — have I desired of Lord
Mark 10. 21. — thou lackest, go sell
Luke 10. 42. but — is needful
Phil. 3. 13. this — I do, forgetting
OPEN thou my lips, Ps. 51. 15.
Ps. 81. 10. *o.* thy mouth wide
119. 18. *o.* thou mine eyes, that I
Prov. 31. 8. *o.* thy mouth for dumb
S. of S. 5. 2. *o.* to me, my sister, my
Isa. 22. 22. shall *o.* and none shall
42. 7. to *o.* blind eyes, Ps. 146. 8.
Ezek. 16. 63. never *o.* thy mouth
Matt. 25. 11. Lord *o.* to us
Acts 26. 18. to *o.* their eyes, and
Col. 4. 3. *o.* to us door of utterance
Rev. 5. 2. who is worthy to *o.*
Gen. 3. 7. eyes of them both were *opened*
Isa. 35. 5. eyes of the blind shall be *o.*
53. 7. he *o.* not his mouth
Matt. 7. 7. knock and it shall be *o.*
Luke 24. 45. then *o.* he their
Acts 14. 27. *o.* the door of faith
16. 14. Lydia whose heart Lord *o.*
1 Cor. 16. 9. a great door and effectual is *o.*
2 Cor. 2. 12. a door was *o.* to me of
Heb. 4. 13. naked and *o.* to eyes of
Ps. 104. 28. *openest* thy hand, 145. 16.
R. V. Gen. 38. 14. gate of Enaim; 2 Cor. 3. 18. unveiled; 1 Tim. 5. 24. evident; Job 38. 17; Jer. 20. 12. revealed; Mark 1. 10. rent asunder
OPERATION, Ps. 28. 5. Isa. 5. 12. Col. 3. 12. 1 Cor. 12. 6.
R. V. 1 Cor. 12. 6. workings; Col. 2. 12. in the working
OPINION, Job 33. 6. 10. 1 Kings 18. 21.
OPPORTUNITY, Matt. 26. 16. Gal. 6. 10. Phil. 4. 10. Heb. 11. 15.
OPPOSE, 2 Tim. 2. 25. 2 Thes. 2. 4.
R. V. Job 30. 21. persecutest
OPPRESS, Ex. 3. 9. Judg. 10. 12.
Ex. 22. 21. *o.* not a stranger, 23. 9.
Lev. 25. 14. *o.* not one another, 17.
Deut. 24. 14. shall not *o.* a hired
Ps. 10. 18. that man may no more *o.*
Prov. 22. 22. neither *o.* afflicted in
Zech. 7. 10. *o.* not the widow or
Mal. 3. 5. a witness against those that *o.*
Jas. 2. 6. do not rich men *o.* you
Ps. 9. 9. the Lord will be a refuge for the *oppressed*
10. 18. judge the fatherless and *o.*
Eccl. 4. 1. tears of such as were *o.*
Isa. 1. 17. relieve the *o.*, 58. 6.
38. 14. I am *o.* undertake for me
53. 7. he was *o.* and afflicted
Ezek. 18. 7. hath not *o.* any
Acts 10. 38. Jesus healed all *o.* of
Prov. 22. 16. *oppresseth*, 14. 31. & 28. 3.
Deut. 27. 7. Lord looked on our *oppression*
2 Kings 13. 4. the Lord saw the *o.*
Ps. 12. 5. for *o.* of poor and sighing
62. 10. trust not in *o.* and become
Eccl. 7. 7. *o.* maketh a wise man
Isa. 5. 7. looked for judgment but behold *o.*
33. 15. he that despiseth gain of *o.*
Ps. 72. 4. *oppressor*, 54. 3. & 119. 121.
Prov. 3. 31. & 28. 16. Eccl. 4. 1. Isa. 3. 12. & 14. 4. & 51. 13.
R. V. Lev. 25. 14, 17. wrong; Job 35. 9. cry out; Ezek. 18. 7, 12, 16. wronged; Ps. 12. 5. spoiling; Eccl. 7. 7. extortion; Ezek. 46. 18 ——; Job 3. 18. taskmaster; Ps. 54. 3. violent man; Zech. 10. 4. exactor
ORACLES of God, Acts 7. 38. Rom. 3. 2. Heb. 5. 12. 1 Pet. 4. 11.
ORDAIN, Isa. 26. 12. Tit. 1. 5.
Ps. 8. 2. hast *ordained* strength
132. 17. *o.* a lamp for mine anoint.
Isa. 30. 33. Tophet is *o.* of old, for
Jer. 1. 5. *o.* thee a prophet
Hab. 1. 12. thou hast *o.* them
Acts 13. 48. as were *o.* to eternal
14. 23. *o.* elders in every church
17. 31. judge by that man whom he hath *o.*
Rom. 7. 10. commandment which was *o.*
1 Cor. 9. 14. Lord *o.* that they
Gal. 3. 19. *o.* by angels in hand
Eph. 2. 10. God before *o.* we
1 Tim. 2. 7. *o.* a preacher and an
Heb. 5. 1. *o.* for men in things
Jude 4. *o.* to this condemnation
R. V. 1 Chron. 17. 9; Tit. 1. 5. appoint; Ps. 8. 2. established; 7. 13. maketh; Isa. 30. 33; Eph. 2. 10; Heb. 9. 6. prepared; 1 Cor. 2. 7. foreordained; 2 Chron. 11. 15; Ps. 81. 5; Jer. 1. 5; Dan. 2. 24; Mark 3. 14; John 15. 16; Acts 14. 23; 1 Tim. 2. 7; Heb. 5. 1; 8. 3. appointed
ORDER, Gen. 22. 9. Job 33. 5.
Job 23. 4. *o.* my cause before
Ps. 40. 5. be reckoned up in *o.*
50. 21. sins set them in *o.* before
119. 133. *o.* my steps in thy word
1 Cor. 14. 40. all things be done decently and in *o.*
Col. 2. 5. joying and beholding your *o.*
Tit. 1. 5. set in *o.* things wanting
2 Sam. 23. 5. everlasting covenant, *ordered* in all things
Ps. 37. 23. steps of a good man are *o.* by the Lord
50. 23. that *ordereth* his conversation aright
R. V. Ex. 40. 4; Luke 1. 1; Heb. 7. 21 ——; Ex. 26. 17. joined; 1 Chron. 15. 13; 23. 31; 2 Chron. 8. 14. ordinance; 1 Kings 20. 14. begin; Ps. 37. 23; Isa. 9. 7. establish
ORDINANCE of God, Isa. 58. 2. Rom. 13. 2.
1 Pet. 2. 13. submit to every *o.* of man
Neh. 10. 32. make *ordinances* for us
Isa. 58. 2. ask of me the *o.* of justice
Jer. 31. 35. *o.* of the moon and of
Ezek. 11. 20. keep mine *o.* and do them, Lev. 18. 4, 30. & 22. 9. 1 Cor. 11. 2.
Luke 1. 6. walking in all *o.* of Lord
Eph. 2. 15. law contained in *o.*
Col. 2. 14. handwriting of *o.* against
20. why are ye subject to *o.*
Heb. 9. 1. had *o.* of divine service
R. V. Lev. 18. 30; 22. 9; Mal. 3. 14. charge; Ex. 18. 20; Lev. 18. 3, 4, 30; 22. 9; Num. 9. 12, 14; 10. 8; 15. 15: 19. 2; 31. 21; Ps. 99. 7. statute, or statutes; Ezra 3. 10. order; Ezek. 45. 14. portion; 1 Cor. 11. 2. traditions
ORNAMENTS, Ex. 33. 5. Prov. 1. 9. & 25. 12. Isa. 49. 18. & 61. 10. Jer. 2. 32. Ezek. 16. 7, 11. 1 Pet. 3. 4.
R. V. Judg. 8. 21, 26. crescents; Prov. 1. 9; 4. 3. chaplet; Isa. 30. 22. plating; 61. 10. garland; 3. 20. ankle chains; 3. 18. anklets; 1 Pet. 3. 4. apparel
OSTENTATION condemned, Prov. 25. 14; 27. 2; Matt. 6. 1.
OUGHT ye to do, Matt. 23. 23. Jas. 3. 10.
OURS, Gen. 26. 20. Num. 32. 32.
Mark 12. 7. inheritance shall be *o.*, Luke 20. 14.
1 Cor. 1. 2. Christ our Lord both theirs and *o.*
Tit. 3. 14. let *o.* learn to maintain good works
OUTCASTS of Israel, Ps. 147. 2. Isa. 11. 12. & 16. 3. & 56. 8.
Isa. 16. 14. let mine *o.* dwell
OUTER, Ezek. 46. 21. & 47. 2. Matt. 8. 12. & 22. 13. & 25. 30.
OUTGOINGS, Josh. 17. 9. Ps. 65. 8.
R. V. In Josh. goings out
OUTRAGEOUS, Prov. 27. 4.
OUTSIDE, Ezek. 40. 5. Matt. 23. 25.
OUTSTRETCHED arm, Deut. 26. 8. Jer. 21. 5. & 27. 5.
OUTWARD, 1 Sam. 16. 7. Rom. 2. 28. 2 Cor. 4. 16. & 10. 7. 1 Pet. 3. 3.
Matt. 23. 28. *outwardly*, Rom. 2. 28.
OVEN, Ps. 21. 9. Hos. 7. 4. Mal. 4. 1.
R. V. Ps. 21. 9; Mal. 4. 1. furnace
OVERCHARGE, Luke 21. 31. 2 Cor. 2. 5.
OVERCOME, Gen. 49. 19. Num. 13. 30.
S. of S. 6. 5. thine eyes have *o.* me
John 16. 33. I have *o.* the world
Rom. 12. 21. be not *o.* of evil

1 John 2. 13. ye have *o.* the wick.
4. 4. ye are of God, and have *o.*
Rev. 17. 14. Lamb shall *o.* them
1 John 5. 4. born of God *overcometh*
Rev. 2. 7. to him that *o.* I will give
26. he that *o.* will I give power
3. 5. he that *o.* shall be clothed
12. him that *o.* will I make a pillar
21. him that *o.* will I grant to sit
21. 7. he that *o.* shall inherit all
R. V. Acts 19. 16. mastered
OVERMUCH, Eccl. 7. 16, 17. 2 Cor. 2. 7.
OVERPAST, Ps. 57. 1. Isa. 26. 20. Jer. 5. 28.
OVERSEER, Prov. 6. 7. Acts 20. 28.
R. V. Acts 20. 28. bishops
OVERSIGHT, Gen. 43. 12. 1 Pet. 5. 2.
R. V. Num. 4. 16. charge; Neh. 13. 4. who was appointed
OVERTAKE, Ex. 15. 9. Amos 9. 13. Hos. 2. 7. Gal. 6. 1. 1 Thes. 5. 4.
OVERTHROW, Deut. 12. 3. & 29. 23. Job 12. 19. Ps. 140. 4, 11. Prov. 13. 6. & 21. 12. Amos 4. 11. Acts 5. 39. 2 Tim. 2. 18.
R. V. Deut. 12. 3. break down; Ps. 140. 4. thrust aside; Prov. 18. 5. turn aside; 2 Sam. 17. 9. fallen; Job 19. 6. subverted
OVERTURN, Ezek. 21. 27. Job 9. 5. & 12. 15. & 28. 9. & 34. 25.
OVERWHELMED, Ps. 55. 5. & 61. 2. & 77. 3. & 124. 4. & 142. 3. & 143. 4.
R. V. Job 6. 27. cast lots upon
OVERWISE, neither make self, Eccl. 7. 16.
OWE, Rom. 13. 8. Matt. 18. 24, 28.
OWL, Job 30. 29. Ps. 102. 6. Isa. 13. 21. & 34. 11, 15. & 43. 20. Mic. 1. 8.
R. V. Lev. 11. 16; Deut. 14. 15; Job 30. 29; Isa. 13. 21; 34. 13; 43. 20; Jer. 50. 39; Mic. 1. 8. ostrich, or ostriches; Isa. 34. 14. night-monster; 34. 15. arrowsnake
OWN, Deut. 24. 16. Judg. 7. 2.
John 1. 11. his *o.* and his *o.* receiv.
1 Cor. 6. 19. ye are not your *o.*
10. 24. let no man seek his *o.*
Phil. 2. 4. look not on his *o.* things
21. all seek their *o.* not of Jesus
R. V. In very many instances, the word is omitted.
OX knoweth his owner, Isa. 1. 3. & 11. 7. Ps. 7. 22. & 14. 4. & 15. 17.
Ps. 144. 14, *oxen*, Isa. 22. 13. Matt. 22. 4. Luke 14. 19. John 2. 14. 1 Cor. 9. 9.
R. V. Gen. 34. 28; Ex. 9. 3. herds; Num. 23. 1. bullocks; Deut. 14. 5. antelope; 1 Sam. 14. 14. half furrow's length; Jer. 11. 19 —

P

PACIFY, Esth. 7. 10. Prov. 16. 14.
Ezek. 16. 63. when I am *pacified*
Prov. 21. 14. gift in secret *pacifieth* anger
Eccl. 10. 4. yield. *p.* great offences
R. V. Eccl. 10. 4. allayeth; Ezek. 16. 63. have forgiven
PAIN, Isa. 21. 3. & 26. 18. & 66. 7. Jer. 6. 24. Mic. 4. 10. Rev. 21. 4.
Ps. 116. 3. *pains* of hell gat hold
Acts 2. 24. loosed the *p.* of death
Ps. 55. 4. my heart is sore *pained*, Isa. 23. 5. Jer. 4. 19. Joel 2. 6.
Rev. 12. 2. travail. in birth and *p.*
Ps. 73. 16. *painful*, 2 Cor. 11. 27.
R. V. Nah. 2. 10. anguish; Acts 2. 24. pangs; Joel 2. 6. anguish
PAINTED, 2 Kings 9. 30. Jer. 4. 30. & 22. 14. Ezek. 23. 40.
PALACE, 1 Chron. 29. 19. Ps. 45. 8, 15. S. of S. 8. 9. Isa. 25. 2. Phil. 1. 13.
R. V 1 Kings 16. 18; 2 Kings 15. 25; Neh. 2. 8; 7. 2; Hos. 8. 14. castle; Ps. 78. 69. heights; 2 Chron. 9. 11. house; S. of S. 8. 9. turret; Amos 4. 3. Harmon; Matt. 26. 3, 29, 58; Mark 14. 54, 66; Luke 18. 21; John 18. 15. court; John 18. 28. judgment hall; Phil. 1. 13. prætorian guard; Ezek. 25. 14. encampments
PALM tree, Ps. 92. 12. S. of S. 7. 7.
PANT, Amos 2. 7. Ps. 38. 10. & 42. 1. & 119. 131. Isa. 21. 4.
R. V. Ps. 38. 10. throbbeth
PAPER REEDS of Egypt, Isa. 19. 7.
PARABLE, Ps. 49. 4. & 78. 2. Prov. 26. 7, 9. Ezek. 20. 49. Mic. 2. 4. Matt. 13. 3. Luke 5. 36. & 13. 6. & 21. 29.
PARADISE, Gen. 2. 15. Luke 23. 43. 2 Cor. 12. 4. Rev. 2. 7.
PARCHMENTS, 2 Tim. 4. 13.
PARDON our iniquity, Ex. 34. 9.
Ex. 23. 21. he will not *p.* your
Num. 14. 19. *p.* iniquity of people
1 Sam. 15. 25. *p.* my sin, 2 Kings 5. 18.
2 Kings 24. 4. which the Lord would not *p.*
2 Chron. 30. 18. the good Lord *p.*
Neh. 9. 17. a God ready to *p.*
Job 7. 21. why dost not *p.* my
Ps. 25. 11. for name's sake *p.*
Isa. 55. 7. our God, he will abundantly *p.*
Jer. 5. 7. how shall I *p.* thee for
33. 8. I will *p.* all their iniquities
Isa. 40. 2. cry that her iniquity is *pardoned*
Lam. 3. 42. we transgressed thou hast not *p.*
Mic. 7. 18. a God like thee that *p.*
PARENTS, Luke 2. 27. & 8. 56.
Matt. 10. 21. children rise up against their *p.*
Luke 18. 29. no man hath left house or *p.*
John 9. 2. who did sin, this man or his *p.*
Rom. 1. 30. disobedient to *p.*
2 Cor. 12. 14. children ought not to lay up for *p.* but *p.* for children
1 Tim. 5. 4. learn to requite their *p.*
PART, it shall be thy, Ex. 29. 26.
Num. 18. 20. I am thy *p.* and
Ps. 5. 9. their inward *p.* is very
51. 6. in hidden *p.* make me know
Luke 10. 42. hath chos. that good *p.*
John 13. 8. if I wash thee not, thou hast no *p.*
Acts 8. 21. neither *p.* nor lot in this
1 Cor. 13. 9. know in *p.* and proph.
10. that which is in *p.* shall be done
R. V. Frequent changes to portion; and many omissions of word. Also many changes due to preceding word
PARTAKER with adulterers, Ps. 50. 18.
Rom. 15. 27. *p.* of their spiritual
1 Cor. 9. 10. *p.* of this hope
13. *p.* with altar
10. 17. *p.* of one bread
21. *p.* of Lord's table
30. if I by grace be a *p.* why am
1 Pet. 5. 1. a *p.* of the glory reveal.
2 John 11. is *p.* of his evil deeds
Eph. 5. 7. be not *partakers* with
1 Tim. 5. 22. be not *p.* of other
Heb. 3. 14. *p.* of Christ
6. 4. *p.* of the Holy Ghost
12. 10. might be *p.* of his holiness
R. V. 1 Cor. 9. 14. have their portion; Heb. 2. 14. sharers in
PARTIAL, Mal. 2. 9. Jas. 2. 4.
1 Tim. 5. 21. *partiality*, Jas. 3. 17.
R. V. *divided in own mind;* Jas. 2. 4. Are ye not *p.* in yourselves; Jas. 3. 17. variance
PASS, Ex. 33. 19. Ezek. 20. 37. Zeph. 2. 2. Zech. 3. 4. 2 Pet. 3. 10.
Mark 14. 35. the hour might *p.* from
Luke 16. 17. easier for heaven and earth to *p.*
1 Pet. 1. 17. *p.* the time of sojourn.
John 5. 24. is *passed* from death to
Isa. 43. 2. when thou *passest* throu.
Mic. 7. 18. *passeth* by transgression
1 Cor. 7. 31. fashion of this world *p.*
Eph. 3. 19. love of Christ which *p.*
Phil. 4. 7. peace of God which *p.*
1 John 2. 17. world *p.* away and lusts
PASSION, Acts 1. 3. & 14. 15.
PASSOVER, Ex. 12. 11. Deut. 16. 2. Josh. 5. 11. 2 Chron. 30. 15. & 35. 1, 11. Heb. 11. 28.
1 Cor. 5. 7. Christ our *p.* is sacri.
PASTORS, Jer. 3. 15. & 17. 16. Eph. 4. 11.
Ps. 74. 1. sheep of thy *pasture*, 79. 13. & 95. 7. & 23. 2. & 100. 3. Isa. 30. 23. & 49. 9. Ezek. 34. 14, 18. John 10. 9.
R. V. Jer. 2. 8. rulers; 3. 15; 10. 21; 12. 10; 17. 16; 22. 22; 23. 1, 2. shepherds; Isa. 49. 9. all bare heights
PASTURE, spiritual, Ps. 23. 2. & 74. 1. & 79. 13. & 95. 7. & 100. Ezek. 34. 14. John 10. 9.
PATH, Num. 22. 24. Job 28. 7.
Ps. 16. 11. wilt show me *p.* of life
27. 11. lead me in a plain *p.*
119. 35. go in *p.* of thy
Prov. 4. 18. *p.* of the just is as
26. ponder the *p.* of thy feet
5. 6. lest thou ponder the *p.* of life
Isa. 26. 7. thou dost weigh *p.* of just
Ps. 17. 4. keep me from *paths* of
25. 4. show thy ways; teach me *p.*
10. all *p.* of the Lord are mercy
Prov. 3. 17. all her *p.* are peace
Isa. 59. 7. destruc. are in their *p.*
8. they have made them crook. *p.*
Jer. 6. 16. ask for old *p.* the good
Hos. 2. 6. shall not find her *p.*
Matt. 3. 3. make his *p.* straight
Heb. 12. 13. make straight *p.* for
R. V. Num. 22. 34. hollow way; Ps. 17. 4. ways; Jer. 18. 15. by paths
PATIENCE with me, Matt. 18. 26, 29.
Luke 8. 15. bring forth fruit with *p.*
21. 19. in your *p.* possess your souls
Rom. 5. 3. tribulation worketh *p.*
15. 4. that we through *p.* might have hope
2 Cor. 6. 4. as minist. of God, in *p.*
Col. 1. 11. strengthened unto all *p.*
1 Thes. 1. 3. *p.* of hope in our Lord
2 Thes. 1. 4. for your *p.* and faith
1 Tim. 6. 11. follow after *p.* meek.
2 Tim. 3. 10. my doctr., charity, *p.*
Tit. 2. 2. sound in faith, charity, *p.*
Heb. 6. 12. through *p.* inherit the
10. 36. have need of *p.* that after
12. 1. run with *p.* race set bef. us
Jas. 1. 3. trying of your faith worketh *p.*
4. let *p.* have her perfect work
5. 7. long *p.* for it till he receive
10. prophets for an example of *p.*
11. ye have heard of the *p.* of Job
2 Pet. 1. 6. to temperance *p.* to *p.*
Rev. 1. 9. brother in the *p.* of Jesus
2. 2. I know thy *p.*, 19.
Eccl. 7. 8. the *patient* in spirit
Rom. 2. 7. by *p.* continuance in
12. 12. *p.* in tribulation, instant in
1 Thes. 5. 14. be *p.* towards all men
2 Thes. 3. 5. *p.* waiting for Christ
1 Tim. 3. 3. not gree. of lucre but *p.*
2 Tim. 2. 24. gentle, apt to teach, *p.*
Jas. 5. 7. *p.* unto coming of Lord
8. be ye also *p.* establish your
Ps. 37. 7. wait *patiently* for the Lord
Heb. 6. 15. after he had *p.* endured
1 Pet. 2. 20. ye be buffeted for your faults take it *p.*
R. V. 1 Thes. 5. 14. long suffering; 1 Tim. 3. 3. gentle; 2 Tim. 2. 24. forbearing
PATRIARCH, Acts 2. 29. & 7. 8, Heb. 7. 4.
PATRIMONY, his, Deut. 18. 8.
PATTERN, 1 Tim. 1. 16. Tit. 2. 7. Ezek. 43. 10. Heb. 8. 5. & 9. 23.

R. V. 1 Tim. 1. 16; Tit. 2. 7. ensample; Heb. 9. 23. copies
PAVILION, Ps. 27. 5. & 31. 20. & 18. 11. 1 Kings 20. 12, 16. Jer. 43. 10.
PAY, Matt. 18. 28. Ps. 37. 21.
R. V. Num. 20. 19. give price; 2 Chron. 27. 5. render
PEACE, Lev. 26. 6. Num. 6. 26.
Job 22. 21. acquaint thyself with God, and be at *p.*
Ps. 34 14. seek *p.* and pursue it
37. 37. the end of that man is *p.*
85.10. righteousness and *p.* kissed
119. 165. great *p.* have they that
122. 6. pray for *p.* of Jerusalem
125. 5. *p.* shall be upon Israel
Prov. 16. 7. his enemies to be at *p.*
Isa. 9. 6. everl. Father, Prince of *p.*
26. 3. keep him in perfect *p.*
27.5. that he may make *p.* with me
45. 7. I make *p.* and create evil
48. 18. had thy *p.* been as a river
22. there is no *p.* to the wicked
57. 2. enter into *p.* shall rest in
19. *p. p.* to him that is far off
59. 8. way of *p.* they know not
63. 17. will make thy officers *p.*
66. 12. I will extend *p.* to her
Jer. 6. 14. saying, *p. p.* when there is no *p.*, 8. 11. Ezek. 13. 10. 2 Kings 9. 18, 22.
Jer. 8. 15. looked for *p.* but no
29. 7. seek *p.* of the city, for in
11. thoughts of *p.* and not of evil
Mic. 5. 5. this man shall be the *p.*
Zech. 8. 19. love the truth and *p.*
Matt. 10. 34. I came not to send *p.*
Mark 9. 50. have *p.* one with another
Luke 1. 79. guide our feet in the way of *p.*
2. 14. on earth *p.* good will towards
29. lettest thy servant depart in *p.*
John 14. 27. *p.* I leave; my *p.* I give
16. 33. in me ye might have *p.*
Rom. 5. 1. we have *p.* with God
8. 6. spiritual. minded is life and *p.*
15. 13. fill you with all *p.* and joy
1 Cor. 7. 15. God hath call. us to *p.*
2 Cor. 13. 11. live in *p.* and the God of *p.* shall
Gal. 5. 22. fruit of Spirit is love, *p.*
Eph. 2. 14. he is our *p.*
15. making *p.*
Phil. 4. 7. the *p.* of God, Col. 3. 15.
1 Thes. 5. 13. at *p.* among your.
Heb. 12. 14. follow *p.* with all men
Jas. 3. 18. sown in *p.* of them
1 Pet. 3. 11. let him seek *p.* and
2 Pet. 3. 14. found of him in *p.*
1 Tim. 2. 2. lead a *peaceable* life in
Heb. 12. 11. yielding *p.* fruit of
Jas. 3. 17. is first pure, then *p.*
Rom. 12. 18. live *peaceably* with all
Matt. 5. 9. blessed are the *peacemakers*
R. V. 1 Cor. 14. 30. silence; Rom. 10. 15 ——; Dan. 11. 21, 24. time of security; Rom. 12. 18. at peace
PEACE OFFERINGS, laws pertaining to, Ex. 20. 24. & 24. 5. Lev. 3. 6. & 7. 11. & 19. 5.
PEARL of great price, Matt. 13. 46.
Matt. 7. 6. cast not *pearls* before
1 Tim. 2. 9. gold, or *p.* or costly array
Rev. 21. 21. gates were twelve *p.*
R. V. Job 28. 18. crystal
PECULIAR treasure, Ex. 19. 5. Ps. 135. 4.
Eccl. 2. 8. *p.* treasure of provinces
Deut. 14. 2. *p.* people, 26. 18. Tit. 2. 14. 1 Pet. 2. 9.
PEN of iron, Job 19. 24. Jer. 17. 1.
Ps. 45. 1. tongue is as the *p.* of a ready writer
R. V. Tit. 2. 14; 1 Pet. 2. 9. own possession
PENURY, Prov. 14. 23. Luke 21. 4.
R. V. Luke 21. 4. want
PEOPLE, Gen. 27. 29. Ex. 6. 7.
Ps. 144. 15. happy is the *p.* whose
148. 14. Israel is a *p.* near unto him
Isa. 1. 4. sinful nation, a *p.* laden
10. 6. against the *p.* of my wrath
34. 5. upon the *p.* of my curse
Hos. 4. 9. like *p.* like priest
1 Pet. 2. 10. in time past were not *p.*
Ps. 73. 10. *his people* return hither
100. 3. we are — and sheep of his
Matt. 1. 21. Jesus shall save — from
Rom. 11. 2. God hath not cast away —
Ps. 50. 7. hear, O *my people*, and I will speak
81. 11. — would not hearken, 8. 13.
Isa. 19. 25. blessed be Egypt — and
63. 8. surely they are — that will
Jer. 30. 22. ye shall be — and I will be your God, 31. 33. & 24. 7. & 32. 38. Ezek. 11. 20. & 36. 38. & 37. 27. Zech. 2. 11. & 8. 8. & 13. 9. 2 Cor. 6. 16.
Hos. 1. 9. ye are not —
10. say to them which were not — thou art —
Heb. 11. 25. *p.* of God, 1 Pet. 2. 10.
R. V. Very frequent changes to peoples, multitude, multitudes, etc.
PERCEIVE, Deut. 29. 4. 1 John 3. 16.
R. V. Deut. 29. 4; Josh. 22. 31; 1 Sam. 12. 17; 1 John 3. 16. know; Judg. 6. 22; 1 Kings 22. 33; 2 Chron. 18. 32; Eccl. 3. 22; Luke 9. 27. saw; Neh. 6. 12; Prov. 1. 2. discern; Acts 8. 23; 14. 9; 2 Cor. 7. 8. see and seeing; Luke 6. 41. considereth; Mark 12. 28. knowing; John 12. 19. behold; Acts 23. 29. found
PERDITION, John 17. 12. Phil. 1. 28. 2 Thes. 2. 3. 1 Tim. 6. 9. Heb. 10. 39. 2 Pet. 3. 7. Rev. 17. 3, 11.
R. V. 2 Pet. 3. 7. destruction
PERFECT, Deut. 25. 15. Ps. 18. 32.
Gen. 6. 9. Noah was a just man and *p.*
17. 1. walk before me, and be *p.*
Deut. 18. 13. shalt be *p.* with God
32. 4. this work is *p.*, just, and right
2 Sam. 22. 31. his way is *p.*
Job 1. 1. man was *p.* and upright
Ps. 19. 7. law of the Lord is *p.* con.
37. 37. mark the *p.* man and
Ezek. 16. 14. it was *p.* through my
Matt. 5. 48. *p.* as your Father is *p.*
19. 21. if thou wilt be *p.* go and
1 Cor. 2. 6. wisdom among them that are *p.*
2 Cor. 12. 9. strength is made *p.* in
13. 11. be *p.* be of good comfort
Eph. 4. 13. to a *p.* man unto the
Phil. 3. 12. not as though I were already *p.*
15. as many as be *p.* thus minded
Col. 1. 28. present every man *p.*
4. 12. may stand *p.* and complete
2 Tim. 3. 17. man of God may be *p.*
Heb. 2. 10. captain of salvation *p.*
12. 23. spirits of just men made *p.*
13. 21. make you *p.* in every good
Jas. 1. 4. be *p.* and entire
17. *p.* gift
1 Pet. 5. 10. make you *p.* establish
1 John 4. 18. *p.* love casteth out fear
Rev. 3. 2. not found thy works *p.*
2 Cor. 7. 1. *perfecting* holiness in
Eph. 4. 12. for the *p.* of the saints
Job 11. 7. find out the Almighty *perfection*
Ps. 119. 96. have seen end of all *p.*
Luke 8. 14. bring no fruit to *p.*
2 Cor. 13. 9. we wish, even your *p.*
Heb. 6. 1. let us go on unto *p.*
Col. 3. 14. charity the bond of *perfectness*
R. V. Isa. 42. 16. at peace; Acts 22. 3. strict; 24. 22. exact; Eph. 4. 13. full grown; 2 Tim. 3. 17. complete; Job 28. 3. furtherest bound; Isa. 47. 9. full measure
PERFORM, Gen. 26. 3. Ruth 3. 13.
Job 5. 12. hands cannot *p.* their
Ps. 119. 106. I have sworn and I will *p.* it
112. inclined my heart to *p.* thy
Isa. 9. 7. zeal of Lord of hosts will *p.*
44. 28. shall *p.* all my pleasure
Rom. 4. 21. promis., was able to *p.*
7. 18. how to *p.* that which is good
Phil. 1. 6. he will *p.* it unto day of
1 Kings 8. 20. Lord hath *performed*
Neh. 9. 8. hast *p.* thy words
Isa. 10. 12. Lord hath *p.* his whole
Jer. 51. 29. every purpose of Lord shall be *p.*
Ps. 57. 2. God that *performeth* all things
Isa. 44. 26. *p.* counsel of messengers
R. V. Gen. 26. 3; Deut. 9. 5; 1 Kings 6. 12; 8. 20; 12. 15; 2 Chron. 10. 15; Jer. 11. 5. establish, or established; Num. 4. 23. wait upon Deut. 23. 23; Esth. 1. 15; Rom. 7. 18. do or done; 2 Kings 23. 3, 4; Ps. 119. 106. confirm; Num. 15. 38; Luke 2. 39; Rom. 15. 28. accomplish; 2 Cor. 8. 11. complete; Phil. 1. 6. perfect
PERILOUS times, 2 Tim. 3. 1.
PERISH, Gen. 41. 36. Lev. 26. 38.
Num. 17. 12. we die, we *p.* we all *p.*
Esth. 4. 16. I will go in, if I *p.* I *p.*
Ps. 2. 12. ye *p.* from the way, when
119. 92. have *p.* in my affliction
Prov. 29. 18. where no vision is, the people *p.*
Matt. 8. 25. Lord save us, or we *p.*
John 3. 15. believeth should not *p.*
10. 28. I give eternal life, they shall never *p.*
1 Cor. 8. 11. through thy knowledge the weak *p.*
2 Pet. 3. 9. not willing that any *p.*
R. V. Num. 17. 12; Jer. 48. 46. undone; 2 Cor. 4. 16. is decaying
PERJURY condemned, Ex. 20. 16. Lev. 6. 3. & 19. 12. Deut. 5. 20. Ezek. 17. 16. Zech. 5. 4. & 8. 17. 1 Tim. 1. 10.
PERMIT, if Lord, 1 Cor. 16. 7. Heb. 6. 3.
1 Cor. 7. 6. by *permission*, not of commandment
PERNICIOUS ways, 2 Pet. 2. 2.
PERPETUAL, Jer. 50. 5. & 51. 39, 57.
R. V. Ps. 9. 6. forever; Jer. 50. 5; Hab. 3. 6. everlasting
PERPLEXED, 2 Cor. 4. 8. Isa. 22. 5.
PERSECUTE me, Ps. 7. 1. & 31. 15.
Job 19. 22. why *p.* me as God, 28.
Ps. 10. 2. wicked doth *p.* the poor
35. 6 let angel of the Lord *p.* them
71. 11. *p.* and take him; is none
83. 15. *p.* them with thy tempest
Lam. 3. 66. *p.* and destroy them in
Matt. 5. 11. blessed are ye when men *p.* you
44. pray for them that *p.* you
Rom. 12. 14. bless them which *p.*
Ps. 109. 16. *persecuted* the poor and
119. 161. princes *p.* me without
143. 3. the enemy hath *p.* my soul
John 15. 20. if they *p.* me they
Acts 9. 4. why *p.* thou me, 22. 7.
22. 4. I *p.* this way to death, 7. 8.
26. 11. I *p.* them to strange cities
1 Cor. 4. 12. being *p.* we suffer it
15. 9. because I *p.* the church of
2 Cor. 4. 9. *p.* but not forsaken, cast
Gal. 1. 13. beyond measure I *p.* the
4. 29. *p.* him born after the Spirit
1 Thes. 2. 15. have *p.* us and please
1 Tim. 1. 13. who was before a *persecutor*
2 Tim. 3. 12. live godly, shall suffer *persecution*
R. V. Ps. 7. 1, 5; 35. 3, 6; 71. 11; 83. 15; Jer. 29. 18; Lam. 3. 43, 66; 2 Cor. 4. 9. pursue, or pursued; 1 Thes. 2. 15. drave out; Acts 11. 19. tribulation; Neh. 9. 11; Lam. 4. 19. pursuers; Ps. 7. 13. fiery shafts
PERSEVERANCE, watching, Eph. 6. 18.
PERSON, Lev. 19. 15.
Mal. 1. 8. will he accept thy *p.*
Matt. 22. 16. regardest not *p.* of
Acts 10. 34. God is no respecter of

p., Deut. 10. 16. Gal. 2. 6. Eph. 6. 9. Col. 3. 25. 1 Pet. 3. 17.
Heb. 1. 3. express image of his *p.*
12. 16. fornicator or profane *p.* as
2 Pet. 3. 11. what manner of *p.*
Jude 16. men's *p.* in admiration
R. V. Gen. 36. 6; Num. 5. 6. soul; Deut. 15. 22; Ps. 49. 10 —— ; Judg. 9. 4. fellows; Jer. 52. 25. face; Matt. 27. 24. man; Heb. 1. 3. substance

PERSUADE we men, 2 Cor. 5. 11.
Gal. 1. 10. do I *p.* men, or God
Acts 13. 43. *persuaded* them to
21. 14. when we would not be *p.*
Rom. 8. 38. I am *p.* that neither death
Heb. 6. 9. we are *p.* better things
11. 13. having seen them, were *p.*
Acts 26. 28. almost thou *persuadest* me to be a Christian
Gal. 5. 8. this *persuasion* cometh
R. V. 1 Kings 22. 20, 21, 22. entice; 2 Chron. 18. 2. moved; Acts 13. 43. urged; Rom. 4. 21; 14. 5. assumed; Heb. 11. 13. greeted

PERTAIN, Lev. 7. 29. 1 Cor. 6. 3, 4. Rom. 9. 4. Heb. 2. 17. & 5. 1. & 9. 9. 2 Pet. 1. 3.
Acts 1. 3. *pertaining*
R. V. Num. 4. 16. shall be; 31. 43. congregation's half; Josh. 24. 33; 1 Chron. 11. 31. of; 2 Sam. 2. 15. and for; 1 Kings 7. 48. were in; Acts 1. 3. concerning; Rom. 4. 1. according; 9. 4. whose is; Heb. 7. 13. belongeth; 9. 9. touching

PERVERSE, Num. 22. 32. Deut. 32. 5. Job 6. 30. Prov. 4. 24. & 12. 8. & 14. 2. & 17. 20. Isa. 19. 14. Matt. 17. 17. Acts 20. 30. Phil. 2. 15. 1 Tim. 6. 5.
R. V. Job 6. 30. mischievous; Prov. 23. 33. froward; 1 Tim. 6. 5. wranglings

PERVERT judgment, Deut. 24. 17. & 16. 19. 1 Sam. 8. 3. Job 8. 3. & 34. 12. Prov. 17. 23. & 31. 5. Mic. 3. 9.
Acts 13. 10. not cease to *p.* right
Gal. 1. 7. would *p.* Gospel of Christ
Job 33. 27. *perverted* that which
Jer. 3. 21. they have *p.* their way
Prov. 19. 3. foolishness of man *p.*
Luke 23. 2. this fellow *p.* the nation
R. V. Deut. 24. 17; 27. 19. wrest; Prov. 19. 3. subverteth; Eccl. 5. 8. taking away

PESTILENCE, 2 Sam. 24. 15. 1 Kings 8. 37. Ps. 78. 50. & 91. 3. Jer. 14. 12. Ezek. 5. 12. Amos 4. 10. Hab. 3. 5. Matt. 24. 7.
Acts 24. 5. found this man a *pestilent* fellow
R. V. Matt. 24. 7 ——

PETITION, 2 Sam. 1. 17. Esth. 5. 6. Ps. 20. 5. *petitions*, 1 John 5. 15.

PHILOSOPHY, Col. 2. 8.

PHYLACTERIES, Matt. 23. 5.

PHYSICIAN of no value, Job 13. 4.
Jer. 8. 22. is there no *p.* there
Matt. 9. 12. that be whole need not *p.*
Luke 4. 23. say to me, *p.* heal thyself
Col. 4. 14. Luke the beloved *p.*

PIECE of bread. Prov. 6. 26. & 28. 21.
Matt. 9. 16. no man putteth a *p.*
Luke 14. 18. bought a *p.* of ground

PIERCE, Num. 24. 8. 2 Kings 18. 21.
Luke 2. 35. sword shall *p.*
Ps. 22. 16. they *pierced* my hands
Zech. 12. 10. on me whom they *p.*
1 Tim. 6. 10. *p.* themselves through
Rev. 1. 7. they also which *p.* him
Heb. 4. 12. *piercing* even to divid.
R. V. Num. 24. 8. smite; Isa. 27. 1. swift

PIETY at home, 1 Tim. 5. 4.

PILGRIMS, Heb. 11. 13. 1 Pet. 2. 11.
Gen. 47. 9. *pilgrimage*, Ex. 6. 4. Ps. 119. 54.
R. V. Ex. 6. 4. sojournings

PILLAR of salt, Gen. 19. 26.
Ex. 13. 21. by day in *p.* of cloud; and by night in a *p.* of fire, Num. 12. 5. & 14. 14. Deut. 31. 15. Neh. 9. 12. Ps. 99. 7.
Isa. 19. 19. a *p.* at the border
Jer. 1. 18. I have made thee iron *p.*
1 Tim. 3. 15. *p.* and ground of truth
Rev. 3. 12. in temple I will make him a *p.*
Job 9. 6. *pillars* thereof tremble
26. 11. the *p.* of heaven tremble
Ps. 75. 3. I bear up the *p.* of it
Prov. 9. 1. hewn out her seven *p.*
S. of S. 3. 6. *p.* of smoke
5. 15. *p.* of marble
3. 10. *p.* of silver
Rev. 10. 1. *p.* of fire

PILLOW, Gen. 28. 11. Ezek. 13. 18.
R. V. Gen. 28. 11, 18. under his head; Mark 4. 38. cushion

PINE, Lev. 26. 39. Ezek. 24. 23.

PINE TREE, Isa. 41. 19. & 60. 13.

PIPE, Zech. 4. 2, 12. Matt. 11. 17.
R. V. Zech. 4. 12. spouts

PIT, Gen. 14. 10. & 37. 20.
Ex. 21. 33. if a man dig a *p.*, 34.
Num. 16. 30. they go down quick into the *p.*
Job 33. 24. deliver him from going to the *p.*
Ps. 9. 15. sunk in *p.* they had made
28. 1. go down to the *p.*, 30. 3. & 88. 4. & 143. 7. Prov. 1. 12. Isa. 38. 18.
Ps. 40. 2. horrible *p.*
119. 85. proud digged a *p.* for me
Prov. 22. 14. strange wom. a deep *p.*
28. 10. fall into his own *p.*, Eccl. 10. 8.
Isa. 38. 17. delivered it from the *p.*
51. 1. hole of *p.* whence he digged
Jer. 14. 13. come to *p.* and found
Zech. 9. 11. sent prison. out of *p.*
Rev. 9. 1. key of bottomless *p.*, 20. 1.
R. V. Job 6. 27. make merchandise; 17. 16. Sheol; Isa. 30. 4. abyss; Luke 14. 5. well; Rev. 9. 1, 2, 11; 11. 7; 17. 8; 20. 1, 3. abyss

PITY, Deut. 7. 16. & 13. 8. & 19. 13.
Job 6. 14. to the afflicted *p.* should
19. 21. have *p.* on me, have *p.*
Prov. 19. 17. hath *p.* on poor, lend.
Isa. 63. 9. in his *p.* he redeemed
Ezek. 36. 21. I had *p.* for my
Matt. 18. 33. even as I had *p.* on
Ps. 103. 13. as a father *pitieth* his children, so the Lord *p.* them
Jas. 5. 11. *pitiful*, 1 Pet. 3. 8.
R. V. 1 Pet. 3. 8. tenderhearted; Job 6. 14. kindness; Matt. 18. 33. mercy

PLACE, Ex. 3. 5. Deut. 12. 5, 14.
Ps. 26. 8. *p.* where thine honor
32. 7. art my hiding *p.*, 119. 114.
90. 1. hast been our dwelling *p.*
Prov. 15. 3. eyes of the Lord are in every *p.*
Isa. 66. 1. where is the *p.* of my
Hos. 5. 15. go and return to my *p.*
John 8. 37. my word hath no *p.* in
Rom. 12. 19. aven. not, but give *p.*
1 Cor. 4. 11. no certain dwelling *p.*
11. 20. ye come together in one *p.*
Eph. 4. 27. neither give *p.* to devil
2 Pet. 1. 19. a light that shineth in a dark *p.*
Rev. 12. 6. hath *p.* prepared of God
Job 7. 10. neither shall *his place*
Ps. 37. 10. diligently consider —
Isa. 26. 21. Lord cometh out of —
Acts 1. 25. that he might go to —
Ps. 16. 6. lines fallen in pleasant *places*
Isa. 40. 4. rough *p.* shall be made
Eph. 1. 3. in *heavenly p.*, 20. & 2. 6. & 3. 10.
6. 12. *high p.*, Hab. 3. 19. Amos 4. 13. Hos. 10. 8. Prov. 8. 2. & 9. 14.
R. V. Frequent changes, mostly dependent on antecedent and consequent words

PLAGUE, 1 Kings 8. 37, 38. Ps. 89. 23. Hos. 13. 14. *plagues*, Rev. 16. 9. & 18. 4, 8. & 22. 28.
R. V. Ex. 32. 35. smote; Ps. 89. 23. smite

PLAIN man, Jacob was a, Gen. 25. 27.
Ps. 27. 11. lead me in a *p.* path
Prov. 8. 9. words are all *p.* to him
Zech. 4. 7. before Zerubbabel thou shalt become *p.*
John 16. 29. now speakest *plainly*
2 Cor. 3. 12. we use great *plainness*
R. V. Gen. 12. 6; 13. 18; 14. 13; Judg. 4. 11; 9. 6; 1 Sam. 10. 3. oak, or oaks; Obad. 19; Zech. 7. 7. lowland; 2 Sam. 15. 28. fords; Luke 6. 17. level place; 1 Sam. 2. 27. reveal; Heb. 11. 14. make manifest

PLAISTER, Lev. 14. 42. Isa. 38. 21.

PLAIT, Matt. 27. 29. 1 Pet. 3. 3.

PLANT, Gen. 2. 5. Job 14. 9.
Isa. 53. 2. will grow up as a tend. *p.*
Jer. 2. 21. turned into degener. *p.*
24. 6. *p.* them, and not pluck
Ezek. 34. 29. raise for them a *p.*
Ps. 128. 3. children like olive *plants*
1. 3. like a tree *planted* by river
92. 13. *p.* in the house of the Lord
94. 9. that *p.* ear, shall he not hear
Isa. 40. 24. yea, they shall not be *p.*
Jer. 2. 21. I *p.* thee a noble vine
17. 8. as a tree *p.* by the waters
Matt. 15. 13. my Father hath not *p.*
21. 33. *p.* a vine, and let it out
Rom. 6. 5. *p.* together in likeness
1 Cor. 3. 6. I have *p.* Apollos
9. 7. who *planteth* a vineyard
Isa. 60. 21. my *planting*
61. 3. *p.* of the Lord

PLAY, Ex. 32. 6. 2 Sam. 2. 14. & 10. 12. Ezek. 33. 32. 1 Cor. 10. 7.
R. V. S. of S. 4. 13. shoots; Jer. 48. 32. branches; Ezek. 31. 4; 34. 29. plantation; 1 Chron. 4. 23. inhabitants of Netaim

PLEAD for Baal, Judg. 6. 31.
Job 13. 19. who will *p.* with me
16. 21. might *p.* for me with God
23. 6. will he *p.* against me with
Isa. 1. 17. *p.* for the widow
43. 26. let us *p.*
66. 16. by fire and sword will Lord *p.*
Jer. 2. 9. I will *p.* with you and
29. wherefore will ye *p.* with me
25. 31. he will *p.* with all flesh
Hos. 2. 2. *p.* with your mother, *p.*
Joel 3. 2. I will *p.* with them for
R. V. Job 16. 21. maintain right; 23. 6. contend with; Ps. 35. 1. strive; Prov. 31. 9. minister judg.

PLEADING of God with Israel, Isa. 1. & 3. 13. & 43. 26. & Jer. 2-6. & 13. Ezek. 17. 20. & 20. 36. & 22. Hos. 2. &c. Joel 3. 2. Micah 2; of Job with God, Job 9. 19. & 16. 21.

PLEASE, 2 Sam. 7. 29. Job 6. 9.
Ps. 69. 31. this also shall *p.* Lord
Prov. 16. 7. when a man's ways *p.*
Isa. 55. 11. accomp. that which I *p.*
56. 4. choose the things that *p.* me
Rom. 8. 8. that in flesh cannot *p.* God
15. 1. bear with weak and not *p.*
2. let every one *p.* his neighbor
1 Cor. 7. 32. how *p.* the Lord
33. *p.* his wife
10. 33. I *p.* men, in all things
Gal. 1. 10. do I seek to *p.* men
1 Thes. 4. 1. walk, and to *p.* God
Heb. 11. 6. without faith impossible to *p.* God
Ps. 51. 19. thou be *pleased* with sacrifices
115. 3. hath done whatsoever he *p.*
Isa. 42. 21. Lord is well *p.* for his
53. 10. it *p.* the Lord to bruise him
Mic. 6. 7. will the Lord be *p.*
Matt. 3. 17. beloved Son, in whom he is well *p.*, 17. 5.
Rom. 15. 3. Christ *p.* not himself
Col. 1. 19. *p.* the Father that in him

Heb. 13. 16. with such sacrifices God is well *p.*
Eccl. 7. 26. *p.* God, shall escape
8. 3. he doeth whatever *p.* him
Phil. 4. 18. a sacrifice well *pleasing*
Col. 1. 10. worth. of Lord unto all *p.*
3. 20. obey parents is well *p.* to
1 Thes. 2. 4. not as *p.* men, Eph. 6. 6. Col. 3. 22.
Heb. 13. 21. working in you, that is well *p.*
1 John 3. 22. do things *p.* in his
Gen. 2. 9. *pleasant*, 3. 6. Mic. 2. 9.
2 Sam. 1. 23. Saul and Jonathan were *p.*
Ps. 16. 6. lines fallen to me in *p.*
133. 1. how *p.* for brethren to
Prov. 2. 10. knowledge is *p.* to soul
9. 17. bread eaten in secret is *p.*
Eccl. 11. 7. *p.* for eyes to behold
S. of S. 1. 16. thou art fair, yea, *p.*
4. 13. *p.* fruits, 16. & 7. 13.
7. 6. how *p.* art thou, O love
Isa. 5. 7. men of Judah, his *p.* plant
Jer. 31. 20. Ephraim, is he a *p.* child
Dan. 8. 9. *p.* land, Jer. 3. 19. Zech. 7. 14.
Prov. 3. 17. her ways are ways of *pleasantness*
Gen. 18. 12. shall I have *pleasure*
1 Chron. 29. 17. *p.* in uprightness
Ps. 5. 4. not a God that hath *p.* in
35. 27. hath *p.* in prosperity of
51. 18. do good in good *p.* to Zion
102. 14. servants take *p.* in stones
103. 21. ministers that do his *p.*
147. 11. Lord taketh *p.* in them
Prov. 21. 17. he that loveth *p.* shall
Eccl. 5. 4. he hath no *p.* in fools
12. 1. say, I have no *p.* in them
Isa. 44. 28. shall perform all my *p.*
53. 10. *p.* of Lord shall prosper in
58. 13. not finding thy own *p.*
Jer. 22. 28. vessel wherein is no *p.*
Ezek. 18. 32. have no *p.* in death
Mal. 1. 10. I have no *p.* in you
Luke 12. 32. fear not, it is your Father's good *p.*
2 Cor. 12. 10. I take *p.* in infirmi.
Eph. 1. 5. according to the good *p.*
Phil. 2. 13. and to do of his good *p.*
2 Thes. 1. 11. fulfil all good *p.* of
Heb. 10. 38. soul shall have no *p.*
12. 10. chastened us after their *p.*
Rev. 4. 11. for thy *p.* they are cre.
Ps. 16. 11. at thy right hand are *pleasures* evermore
36. 8. drink of the river of thy *p.*
2 Tim. 3. 4. lovers of *p.* more than
Tit. 3. 3. serv. divers lusts and *p.*
Heb. 11. 25. than to enjoy *p.* of sin
R. V. Gen. 3. 6. a delight; S. of S. 4. 13; 7. 13. precious; Dan. 8. 9. glorious; Jer. 23. 10. pastures; Gen. 16. 6. good in eyes; 2 Chron. 3. 4. right in eyes; Ps. 51. 19. delight in; Rom. 15. 26, 27; 1 Cor. 1. 21; Gal. 1. 15; Col. 1. 19. good pleasure; Gal. 1. 10; Heb. 11. 5. pleasing; 1 Cor. 7. 12. content; Acts 15. 22. seemed good; Acts 15. 34——; Job 21. 25. good; Jer. 2. 24; 2 Thes. 1. 11. desire; Acts 24. 27; 25. 9. gain favor; Jas. 5. 5. delicately
PLEDGE, Ex. 22. 26. Deut. 24. 6.
PLEIADES, Job 9. 9. & 38. 31.
PLENTY, Job 37. 23. Prov. 3. 10.
Ps. 86. 5. *plenteous* in mercy, 103. 8.
130. 7. with him is *p.* redemption
Matt. 9. 37. harvest is *p.* but
R. V. Lev. 1. 36. gathering; Job 22. 25. precious; 37. 23. plenteous
PLOUGH, Deut. 22. 10. Prov. 20. 4.
Job 4. 8. they that *p.* iniquity, and
Isa. 28. 24. doth ploughman *p.* all
Luke 9. 62. hav. put his hand to *p.*
Judg. 14. 18. if ye had not *ploughed*
Ps. 129. 3. ploughers *p.* on my back
Jer. 26. 18. Zion shall be *p.* as a
Hos. 10. 13. ye have *p.* wickedness
Prov. 21. 4. *ploughing* of wicked is
1 Cor. 9. 10. *plougheth* should *p.*
Amos 9. 13. *ploughman*, Isa. 61. 5.
Isa. 2. 4. *ploughshares*, Joel 3. 10. Mic. 4. 3.
PLUCK out, Ps. 25. 15. & 52. 5. & 74. 11. Amos 4. 11. Zech. 3. 2. Matt. 5. 29. & 18. 9. John 10. 28, 29. Gal. 4. 15.
2 Chron. 7. 20. *pluck up*, Jer. 12. 17. & 18. 7. & 31. 28, 40. Dan. 11. 4. Jude 12.
Ezra 9. 3. *pluck off*, Job 29. 17. Isa. 50. 6. Ezra 23. 34. Mic. 3. 2.
R. V. Ex. 4. 7. took; Lev. 1. 16. take; Num. 33. 52. demolish; Ruth 4. 7. drew; Ezek. 23. 34. tear; Luke 17. 6. root up; Mark 5. 4. rent; 9. 7. cast; John 10. 28, 29. snatch
PLUMBLINE and plummet, 2 Kings 21. 13. Isa. 28. 17. Amos 7. 8. Zech. 4. 10.
POISON, Deut. 32. 24, 33. Job 6. 4. & 20. 16. Ps. 58. 4. & 140. 3. Rom. 3. 13. Jas. 3. 8.
POLLUTE, Num. 18. 32. Ezek. 7. 21. Mic. 2. 10. Zeph. 3. 1. Mal. 1. 7, 12.
Acts 15. 20. *pollutions*, 2 Pet. 2. 20.
R. V. Jer. 7. 30. defile; Num. 18. 23; Ezek. 7. 21, 22; 13. 19; 20. 39; 39. 7; 44. 7; Dan. 11. 31. profane, or profaned; Isa. 47. 6; 48. 11; Jer. 34. 16; Lam. 2. 2; Ezek. 20. 9, 13, 14, 16, 21, 22, 24. profaned; Ezek. 16. 6, 22. weltering; 2 Kings 23. 16; Jer. 2. 23; Ezek. 14. 11; 36. 18; Acts 21. 28. defiled; Hos. 6. 8. stained; Amos 7. 17. unclean; Mic. 2. 10. uncleanness; 2 Pet. 2. 20. defilements
PONDER path of thy feet, Prov. 4. 26.
Luke 2. 19. *pondered* them in heart
Prov. 5. 21. *pondereth* all his goings
21. 2. Lord *p.* the hearts, 24. 12.
R. V. Prov. 4. 26; 5. 6; 5. 21. level, and make level; 21. 2; 24. 12. weigheth
POOR may eat, Ex. 23. 11.
Ex. 30. 15. the *p.* shall not give less
Lev. 19. 15. not respect person of *p.*
Deut. 15. 4. there shall be no *p.*
1 Sam. 2. 7. Lord maketh *p.* and
8. raiseth *p.* out of dust, Ps. 113. 7.
Job 5. 16. the *p.* hath hope
36. 15. delivereth *p.* in affliction
Ps. 10. 14. *p.* committeth himself
69. 33. the Lord heareth the *p.* and
72. 2. he shall judge thy *p.*, 4. 13.
132. 15. satisfy her *p.* with bread
Prov. 13. 7. there is that maketh himself *p.*
14. 20. *p.* is hated of his neighbor
31. oppresseth *p.* reproacheth
19. 4. the *p.* is separated from
7. all brethren of the *p.* do hate
22. 2. rich and the *p.* meet together
22. rob not the *p.* because he is *p.*
30. 9. lest I be *p.* and steal
Isa. 14. 32. *p.* of his people shall
29. 19. *p.* among men shall rejoice
41. 17. when the *p.* and needy
58. 7. bring *p.* that are cast into
66. 2. that is *p.* and of a contrite
Jer. 5. 4. surely these are *p.* they
Amos 2. 6. sold *p.* for a pair of
Zeph. 3. 12. an afflicted and *p.* peo.
Zech. 11. 11. *p.* of flock waited on
Matt. 5. 3. blessed are the *p.* in spi.
11. 5. *p.* have Gospel preached to
26. 11. have *p.* with you, John 12. 8.
Luke 6. 20. blessed be ye *p.* for
14. 13. call the *p.* maimed and the
2 Cor. 6. 10. as *p.* yet making rich
8. 9. for your sakes he became *p.*
9. 9. he hath given to *p.*, Ps. 112. 9.
Gal. 2. 10. that we should remember the *p.*
Jas. 2. 5. God hath chosen *p.* of
Rev. 3. 17. knowest not that thou art *p.*
R. V. In O. T., frequent changes to needy
PORTION, Deut. 21. 17. & 33. 21.
Deut. 32. 9. Lord's *p.* is his people
2 Kings 2. 9. double *p.* of thy spir.
Job 20. 29. the *p.* of a wicked man
26. 14. how little a *p.* is heard
31. 2. what *p.* of God is there
Ps. 16. 5. the Lord is the *p.* of my
17. 14. have their *p.* in this life
63. 10. shall be a *p.* for foxes
3. 26. God is my *p.* for ever, 119. 57.
142. 5. art my *p.* in land of living
Eccl. 11. 2. give *p.* to seven and to
Isa. 53. 12. divide him a *p.* with the
61. 7. they shall rejoice in their *p.*
Jer. 10. 16. the *p.* of Jacob not
Lam. 3. 24. Lord is my *p.* saith my
Hab. 1. 16. by them their *p.* is fat
Zech. 2. 12. the Lord shall inherit Judah his *p.*
Matt. 24. 51. appoint him his *p.*
Neh. 8. 10. send *portions*, Esth. 9. 19, 22.
R. V. Josh. 17. 14; 19. 9. part; Job 26. 14. whisper; Prov. 31. 15. task; Hos. 5. 7. fields; Ezek. 45. 7; 48. 18——
POSSESS, Gen. 22. 17. Judg. 11. 24.
Job 7. 3. I am made to *p.* months
13. 26. makest *p.* iniquities of
Luke 21. 9. in patience *p.* your souls
1 Thes. 4. 4. know how to *p.* vessel
Ps. 139. 13. hast *possessed* my reins
Prov. 8. 22. Lord *p.* me in beginning
Isa. 63. 18. people of thy holiness *p.*
Dan. 7. 22. saints *p.* kingdom, 18.
1 Cor. 7. 30. as though they *p.* not
2 Cor. 6. 10. having nothing yet *p.* all things
Eph. 1. 14. redemption of purchased *possession*
Gen. 14. 9. God *possessor* of heaven
R. V. Job 13. 26; Zeph. 2. 9; Zech. 8. 12. inherit; Num. 26. 56; Josh. 22. 7. inheritance
POSSIBLE, all things with God, Matt. 19. 26.
Matt. 24. 24. if *p.* shall deceive elect
Mark 9. 23. all things *p.* to him
14. 36. Father, all things are *p.* to
Luke 18. 27. impossible with men, *p.* with God
Rom. 12. 18. if *p.* much as in you
Heb. 10. 4. not *p.* that blood of bulls
POSTERITY, Gen. 45. 7. Ps. 49. 13.
POT, Ex. 16. 33. Ps. 68. 13. & 81. 6. Jer. 1. 13. Zech. 14. 21.
Job 2. 8. *potsherd*, Ps. 22. 15. Prov. 26. 23. Isa. 45. 9. Rev. 2. 27.
Isa. 29. 16. *potter*, 64. 8. Jer. 18. 6. Lam. 4. 2. Rom. 9. 21.
R. V. Lev. 6. 28. vessel; Job 41. 31; Mark 7. 8——; Ps. 68. 13. sheepfolds; 81. 6. basket; Jer. 1. 13. caldron; 35. 5. bowls; Prov. 26. 23. earthen vessel
POTENTATE, blessed, 1 Tim. 6. 15.
POUND, Luke 19. 13. John 19. 39.
POUR, Job 36. 27. Lev. 14. 18, 41.
Ps. 62. 8. *p.* out your heart
79. 6. *p.* out thy wrath on the heathen, 69. 24. Jer. 10. 25. Zeph. 3. 8.
Prov. 1. 23. I will *p.* out my Spirit
Isa. 44. 3. *p.* water on the thirsty; *p.* my Spirit
Joel 2. 28. *p.* my Spirit on all flesh
Job 10. 10. *poured* me out as milk
12. 21. *p.* contempt on princes
16. 20. mine eye *p.* out tears to
30. 16. my soul *p.* out in me
Ps. 45. 2. grace is *p.* into thy lips
S. of S. 1. 3. name is as ointment *p.*
Isa. 26. 16. in trouble *p.* out a pray.
53. 12. *p.* out his soul unto death
Jer. 7. 20. my fury shall be *p.* out, 42. 18. & 44. 6. Isa. 42. 25. Ezek. 7. 8. & 14. 19. & 20. 8, 13, 21. & 30. 15.
Rev. 16. 1-17. *p.* out vials of God's wrath

POVERTY, Gen. 45. 11. Prov. 11. 24.
Prov. 6. 11. so shall thy *p.* come, 24. 34.
10.15. destruction of the poor is *p.*
20. 13. love not sleep lest thou come to *p.*
23. 21. drunkard and glutton shall come to *p.*
30. 8. give me neither *p.* nor rich.
2 Cor. 8. 2. their deep *p.* abounded
9. ye through his *p.* might be rich
Rev. 2. 9. I know thy works and *p.*
R. V. Prov. 11. 24; 28. 22. want
POWDER, Ex. 32. 20. Deut. 28. 24. 2 Kings 23. 15. S. of S. 3. 6. Matt. 21. 44.
R. V. Matt. 21. 44; Luke 20. 18. dust
POWER, with God as a prince, Gen. 32. 28.
Gen. 49. 3. excell. of dignity and *p.*
Lev. 26. 19. I will break the pride of your *p.*
Deut. 8. 18. giveth *p.* to get wealth
2 Sam. 22. 33. God is my strength and *p.*
1 Chron. 29. 11. thine is the *p.* and
Ezra 8. 22. *p.* and wrath is against
Job 26. 2. him that is without *p.*
14. thunder of his *p.* who can
Ps. 62. 11. *p.* belongeth unto God
90. 11. knoweth *p.* of thy anger
Prov. 3. 27. when it is in the *p.* of
18. 21. death and life are in *p.*
Isa. 40. 29. he giveth *p.* to the faint
Eccl. 8. 4. where word of king is there is *p.*
Jer. 10.12. made the earth by his *p.*
Hos. 12. 3. by his strength had *p.*
Mic. 3. 8. I am full of *p.* by the
Hab. 1. 11. imputing his *p.* to God
Zech. 4. 6. not by might, nor by *p.*
Matt. 9. 6. *p.* on earth to forgive
8. glorified God who had given *p.*
22. 29. not knowing the *p.* of God
28. 18. *p.* is given to me in heaven
Mark 9. 1. kingdom of God come with *p.*
Luke 1. 35. *p.* of the Highest
4. 32. astonished, for his word was with *p.*
5. 17. *p.* of the Lord to heal them
22. 53. this is your hour and *p.* of
24. 49. till ye be endued with *p.*
John 1. 12. gave he *p.* to become
10. 18. *p.* to lay it down and *p.*
17. 2. given him *p.* over all flesh
19. 10. *p.* to crucify, *p.* to release
Acts 26. 18. turn them from the *p.*
Rom. 1. 16. Gospel is *p.* of God to
20. his eternal *p.* and Godhead, 4.
9. 22. to make his *p.* known
13. 1. there is no *p.* but of God
1 Cor. 1. 24. Christ, the *p.* of God, 18.
2. 4. demonstra. of Spirit and *p.*
4. 19. speech of them, but the *p.*
5.4. gathered together with the *p.*
9. 4. have we not *p.* to eat and
2 Cor. 4. 7. excellency of *p.* may be
13. 10. according to *p.* Lord
Eph. 1. 19. exceed. greatness of *p.*
2. 2. prince of the *p.* of the air
6. 12. principalities and *p.*, 1. 21.
Phil. 3. 10. know *p.* of his resur.
Col. 1. 11. according to his glorious
13. delivered from *p.* of darkness
1 Thes. 1. 5. Gospel not in word, but in *p.*
2 Thes. 1. 9. the glory of his *p.*
11. fulfil the work of faith with *p.*
2 Tim. 1. 7. Spirit of *p.* and of love
3. 5. form of godliness, deny. *p.*
Heb. 1. 3. upholding all things by word of his *p.*
6. 5. tasted word of God and *p.* of
1 Pet. 1. 5. *p.* of God through faith
2 Pet. 1. 3. his divine *p.* hath given
Rev. 2. 26. to him will I give *p.*
4. 11. worthy to receive *p.*, 5. 13. & 7. 12. & 19. 1. 1 Tim. 6. 16. Jude 25.
Rev. 11. 3. *p.* to my two witnesses
17. taken to thee thy great *p.*
12. 10. now is come *p.* of his Chri.
Rev. 16. 9. had *p.* over these plagues
Ex. 15. 6. *in power*, Job 37. 23. Nah. 1. 3. 1 Cor. 4. 20. & 15. 43. Eph. 6. 10.
Ps. 63. 2. *thy power*, 110. 3. & 145. 11.
29. 4. *powerful*, Heb. 4. 12.
R. V. 1 Sam. 9. 1. valor; Esth. 9. 1. rule; Job 41. 12; Ps. 59. 16; Dan. 11. 6; 2 Cor. 12. 9; Eph. 6. 10. strength; Ps. 66. 7; 71. 8; 2 Thes. 1. 19. might; Hab. 2. 9. hand; Matt. 10. 1; 28. 18; Mark 3. 15; 6. 7; Luke 4. 6, 32; 10. 19; John 17. 2; Acts 1. 7; 1 Cor. 11. 10; 2 Cor. 13. 10; Eph. 1. 21; Rev. 2. 26; 6. 8; 8. 1; 12. 10; 13. 4, 7, 12, 15; 17. 12. authority; Luke 9. 43. majesty; Rom. 9. 21; 1 Cor. 9. 4, 5, 6, 12; 2 Thes. 3. 9. a right; Rev. 5. 13. dominion; Matt. 6. 13; Rev. 11. 3——; 2 Cor. 10. 10. strong; Heb. 4. 12. active
PRAISE, Judg. 5. 3. Ps. 7. 17.
Deut. 10. 21. he is thy *p.* and thy
Neh. 9. 5. above all blessing and *p.*
Ps. 22. 25. my *p.* shall be of thee
33. 1. *p.* is comely for upright
34. 1. his *p.* is continually in
50. 23. who offers *p.* glorifies me
65. 1. *p.* waiteth for thee, O God
109. 1. hold not thy peace, God of my *p.*
Isa. 60.18. walls Salvation, gates *P.*
62. 7. Jerusalem a *p.* in the earth
Jer. 13. 11. for a *p.* and for a glory
17. 14. art my *p.*
26. sacrifice of *p.*
Hab. 3. 3. earth was full of his *p.*
John 12. 43. loved the *p.* of men
Rom. 2. 29. whose *p.* is not of men
2 Cor. 8. 18. whose *p.* is in Gospel
Eph. 1. 6. *p.* of glory of his grace
Phil. 4. 8. if there be any *p.* think
Heb. 13. 15. offer sacrifice of *p.*
1 Pet. 2. 14. *p.* of them that do well
Ex. 15. 11. *praises*, Ps. 22. 3. & 78. 4. & 149. 6. Isa. 60. 6. & 63. 7. 1 Pet. 2. 9.
Ps. 30. 9. shall dust *praise* thee
42. 5. I shall *p.* him for help
63. 3. my lips shall *p.* thee
88. 10. shall the dead arise and *p.*
119. 164. seven times a day will I *p.*
Prov. 27. 2. let another *p.* thee, not
31. 31. let her own works *p.* her
Isa. 38. 18. the grave cannot *p.* thee
19. the living shall *p.* thee as I do
Dan. 2. 23. I thank thee, and *p.* thee
Joel 2. 26. eat in plenty, and *p.* Lord
Ps. 9. 1. *I will praise thee*, 111. 1. & 138. 1. & 35. 18. & 52. 9. & 56. 4. & 118. 21. & 119. 7. & 139. 14. Isa. 12. 1.
2 Sam. 22. 4. worthy to be *praised*
1 Chron. 16. 25. greatly to be *p.*, Ps. 48. 1. & 96. 4. & 145. 3. & 72. 15.
2 Chron. 5. 13. *praising*, Ezra 3. 11. Ps. 34. 4. Luke 2. 13, 20. Acts 2. 46.
R. V. A few changes to thanksgiving. Many changes, especially in Ps., to give thanks
PRATING, Prov. 10. 8, 10. 3 John 10.
PRAY for thee and shalt live, Gen. 20. 7.
1 Sam. 7. 5. I will *p.* for you to
2 Sam. 7. 27. found in heart to *p.*
Job 21. 15. profit have we if we *p.*
42. 8. my servant Job shall *p.* for
Ps. 5. 2. my God, to thee will I *p.*
55. 17. evening and morning and noon I will *p.*
Jer. 7. 16. *p.* not for this people, 11. 14. & 14. 11.
Zech. 8. 22. seek Lord and *p.* before
Matt. 5. 44. *p.* for them that desp.
26. 41. watch and *p.* that ye enter
Mark 11. 24. things ye desire when ye *p.*
13. 33. watch and *p.* ye know not
Luke 11. 1. teach us to *p.* as John
18. 1. men ought always to *p.*
21. 36. watch ye and *p.* always
John 16. 26. I will *p.* the Father for
20. neither *p.* I for these alone
Acts 8. 22. *p.* God, if perhaps the
Acts 8.24. *p.* ye to the Lord for me
10. 9. Peter went on housetop to *p.*
Rom. 8. 26. we know not what we should *p.* for
1 Cor. 14. 15. I will *p.* with Spirit
2 Cor. 5. 20. *p.* you in Christ's stead
Col. 1. 9. do not cease to *p.* for you
1 Thes. 5. 17. *p.* without ceasing
25. *p.* for us, 2 Thes. 3. 1. Heb. 13. 18.
Jas. 5. 13. any afflicted let him *p.*
16. *p.* for one another, Eph. 6. 18.
Luke 22. 32. I have *prayed* for thee
Acts 10. 2. gave alms and *p.* to God
20. 36. Paul *p.* with them all
Jas. 5. 17. he *p.* earnestly that it
Acts 9. 11. behold he *prayeth*
Dan. 9. 20. *praying*, 1 Cor. 11. 4.
1 Thes. 3. 10. night and day *p.* ex.
Jude 20. building up faith, *p.* in
1 Kings 8. 45. hear in heaven their *prayer*
2 Sam. 7. 27. found in his heart to pray this *p.*
1 Kings 8. 28. respect to *p.* of serv.
38. what *p.* and supplication
2 Chron. 30. 27. *p.* came up to God
Neh. 1. 6. mayest hear *p.* of servant
4. 9. we made our *p.* to our God
Job 15. 4. restrainest *p.* before God
Ps. 65. 2. thou that hearest *p.* to
102. 17. he will regard the *p.* of
109. 4. I give myself to *p.*
Prov. 15. 8. *p.* of the upright is his
29. Lord heareth *p.* of righteous
Isa. 26. 16. poured out a *p.* when
56. 7. an house of *p.* for all people
Jer. 7. 16. lift up cry, nor *p.* for
Lam. 3. 44. our *p.* should not pass
Dan. 9. 3. by *p.* and supplication
Matt. 17. 21. not come out but by *p.*
Acts 3. 1. to temple at hour of *p.*
6. 4. give ourselves continu. to *p.*
12. 5. *p.* was made without ceasing
1 Cor. 7. 5. give yourselves to fasting and *p.*
2 Cor. 1. 11. helping together by *p.*
Eph. 6. 18. *praying* alw. with all *p.*
Phil. 4. 6. in every thing by *p.* and
1 Tim. 4. 5. sanctifi. by word and *p.*
Jas. 5. 15. *p.* of faith shall save
16. effectual fervent *p.* of right.
1 Pet. 4. 7. watch unto *p.*, Col. 4. 2.
Luke 6. 12. continued *in prayer*, Acts 1. 14. Rom. 12. 12. Col. 4. 2.
Job 16. 17. *my prayer*, Ps. 5. 3. & 6. 9. & 17. 1. & 35. 13. & 66. 20. & 88. 2. Lam. 3. 8. Jonah 2. 7.
Job 22. 27. *thy prayer*, Isa. 37. 4 Luke 1. 13. Acts 10. 31.
Ps. 72. 20. *prayers* of David ended
Isa. 1. 15. when ye make many *p.*
Matt. 23. 14. make long *p.*
Acts 10. 4. thy *p.* and thine alms
1 Tim. 2. 1. first of all that *p.* and
1 Pet. 3. 7. your *p.* be not hindered
12. his ears are open to their *p.*
Rev. 5. 8. which are *p.* of saints
R. V. But few changes, and mostly to beseech, intreat. Job 15. 4. devotion; Ps. 64. 1. complaint, Luke 1. 13; 2. 37; 5. 33; Rom. 10. 1; 2 Cor. 1. 11; 9. 14; Phil. 1. 4, 19; 2 Tim. 1. 3; Jas. 5. 16; 1 Pet. 3. 12. supplication; Matt. 17. 21; 23 14——
PREACH at Jerusalem, Neh. 6. 7.
Isa. 61. 1. anointed to *p.* good
Jonah 3. 2. *p.* to it preaching I bid
Matt. 4. 17. Jesus began to *p.*
10. 27. what ye hear in ear, *p.* on
Mark 1. 4. *p.* baptism of repent.
Luke 4. 18. *p.* liberty to captives
9. 60. go and *p.* kingdom of God
Acts 10. 42. commanded to *p.* to
Rom. 10. 8. word of faith we *p.*
15. how shall they *p.* except they
1 Cor. 1. 23. we *p.* Christ crucified
15. 11. so we *p.* and so ye believed
2 Cor. 4. 5. we *p.* not ourselves but
Phil. 1. 15. some *p.* Christ of envy
Col. 1. 28. whom we *p.* warning
2 Tim. 4. 2. *p.* the word; be instant
Ps. 40. 9. I *preached* righteousness

Mark 2. 2. he *p.* the word unto them
6. 12. he *p.* that men should rep.
16. 20. *p.* every where, the Lord
Luke 4. 44. he *p.* in the synagogues
24. 47. remission of sins be *p.* in
Acts 8. 5. Philip *p.* Christ, 40.
9. 20. Saul *p.* Christ in synagogues
1 Cor. 9. 27. when I have *p.* to
15. 7. Gospel which I *p.* unto you
2. keep in memory what I *p.*
12. if Christ be *p.* that he rose
2 Cor. 11. 4. *p.* another Jesus whom
Gal. 1. 23. *p.* faith he once destroyed
Eph. 2. 17. *p.* peace to you, which
Col. 1. 23. which was *p.* to every
Heb. 4. 2. the word *p.* did not profit
1 Pet. 3. 19. *p.* to the spirits in
Eccl. 1. 1. *preacher*, 2. 12. & 12. 8, 9.
Rom. 10. 14. how shall they hear without a *p.*
1 Tim. 2. 7. I am ordained a *p.*
2 Pet. 2. 5. saved Noah a *p.* of
Acts 10. 36. *preaching* peace, by
11. 19. *p.* word to none but Jews
1 Cor. 1. 18. *p.* of the cross to them
21. by foolishness of *p.* to save
2. 4. my *p.* was not with enticing
15. 14. then is our *p.* vain, and faith
R. V. Ps. 40. 9; Luke 6. 90. published; Matt. 10. 27; Luke 4. 18, 19; Acts 4. 2; 8. 5; 9. 20; 13. 5, 38; 15. 36; 17. 13; 1 Cor. 9. 14; Phil. 1. 16, 18; Col. 1. 28. proclaim, or proclaimed; Mark 2. 2; Acts 16. 6. speak or spake; Acts 20. 7. discoursed; Acts 11. 19. speaking; 1 Cor. 1.18. word; Tit. 1.3; 2 Tim. 4. 17. message; 2 Cor. 10. 14——

PRECEPTS, Neh. 9. 14. Jer. 35. 18.
Ps. 119. 4. commanded us to keep *p.*
15. I will meditate in thy *p.*, 78.
40. long after thy *p.*
56. I kept thy *p.*, 63, 69, 100, 134.
110. I erred not from thy *p.*
141. I do not forget thy *p.*, 93.
159. I love thy *p.*
173. chosen thy *p.*
Isa. 28. 10. *p.* upon *p.*, *p.* upon *p.*
29. 14. fear is taught by *p.* of men
R. V. Isa. 29. 13; Neh. 9. 14; Mark 10. 5; Heb. 9. 19. commandment

PRECIOUS things, Deut. 33. 13–16.
1 Sam. 3. 1. word of the Lord *p.* in
26. 21. my soul was *p.* in thine eyes
Ps. 49. 8. redemption of soul is *p.*
72. 14. *p.* shall their blood be in
116. 16. p. in sight of the Lord
126. 6. goeth forth, bearing *p.* seed
139. 17. how *p.* are thy thoughts
Eccl. 7. 1. good name is better than *p.* ointment
Isa. 13. 12. a man more *p.* than
28. 16. foundation *p.* corner stone
Jer. 15. 19. if thou take forth *p.*
Lam. 4. 2. *p.* sons of Zion are as
Jas. 5. 7. husbandman waiteth for *p.* fruit
1 Pet. 1. 7. tri. of your faith more *p.*
19. redeemed with *p.* blood of
2. 4. stone chosen of God and *p.*, 6.
7. unto them who believe he is *p.*
2 Pet. 1. 1. obtained the like *p.* faith
4. exceeding great and *p.* promis.
R. V. Ps. 49. 8; Mark 14. 3; 1 Cor. 3. 12. costly; Isa. 13. 12. rare; Dan. 11. 8. goodly

PREDESTINATE, Rom. 8. 29, 30.
Eph. 1. 5. *predestinated*, 11.

PREEMINENCE, man hath no, Eccl. 3. 19. Col. 1. 18. 3 John 9.

PREFER, Ps. 137. 6. John 1. 15, 27, 30.
Rom. 12. 10. *preferring*, 1 Tim. 5. 21.
R. V. Esth. 2. 9. removed; Dan. 6. 3. distinguished; John 1. 15, 30. become; 1 Tim. 5. 21. prejudice

PREMEDITATE not, Mark 13. 11.

PREPARE, Ex. 15. 2. & 16. 5.
1 Sam. 7. 3. *p.* your hearts to Lord
1 Chron. 29. 18. *p.* hearts unto thee
2 Chron. 35. 6. *p.* your brethren
Job 11. 13. if thou *p.* thy heart and
Ps. 10. 17. thou wilt *p.* their heart
Prov. 24. 27. *p.* thy work without
Isa. 40. 3. *p.* ye the way of the Lord
Amos 4. 12. *p.* to meet thy God, O
Mic. 3. 5. they *p.* war against him
Matt. 11. 10. shall *p.* thy way
John 14. 2. I go to *p.* a place for you
2 Chron. 19. 3. hast *prepared* heart
27. 6. *p.* his ways before the Lord
30. 19. every one that *p.*
Ezra 7. 10. Ezra had *p.* his heart to
Neh. 8. 10. for whom nothing is *p.*
Ps. 23. 5. thou hast *p.* a table before
68. 10. *p.* goodness
147. 8. who *p.* rain for the earth
Isa. 64. 4. what God *p.* for, 1 Cor. 2. 9.
Hos. 6. 3. his going forth is *p.*
Matt. 20. 23. given to them for whom it is *p.*
22. 4. I have *p.* my dinner; my
25. 34. inherit the kingdom *p.* for
Luke 1. 17. ready people *p.* for Lord
12. 47. knew Lord's will, and *p.*
Rom. 9. 23. vessels of mercy *p.* to
2 Tim. 2. 21. *p.* to every good work
Heb. 10. 5. a body hast thou *p.* me
11. 7. *p.* ark to save his house
16. God hath *p.* for them a city
Rev. 12. 6. into the wilderness, a place *p.* of God
21. 2. new Jerusalem *p.* as a bride
Prov. 16. 1. *preparations* of heart
Mark 15. 42. it was the *p.* the day
Eph. 6. 15. shod with *p.* of Gospel
R. V. Many changes to make ready, establish, etc.

PRESBYTERY, 1 Tim. 4. 14.

PRESENT help in troub., Ps. 46. 1.
Acts 10. 33. all here *p.* before God
Rom. 7. 18. to will is *p.*
8. 38. nor things *p.* nor, 1 Cor. 3. 22.
1 Cor. 5. 3. absent in body, *p.* in
2 Cor. 5. 8. to be *p.* with the Lord
9. whether *p.* or absent, we may
2 Tim. 4. 10. having loved *p.* world
Heb. 12. 11. chastening for the *p.*
2 Pet. 1. 12. established in *p.* truth
Rom. 12. 1. *p.* your bodies a living
2 Cor. 11. 2. *p.* you as a chaste
Col. 1. 22. to *p.* you holy and
28. *p.* every man perfect in Christ
Jude 24. *p.* you faultless before
Gen. 3. 8. hide themselves from the *presence* of the Lord
4. 16. Cain went from *p.* of Lord
Job 1. 12. & 2. 7. Ps. 114. 7. Jer. 4. 26. Jonah 1. 3, 10. Zech. 1. 7. Jude 24.
Job 23. 15. I am troubled at his *p.*
Ps. 16. 11. in thy *p.* is fulness
31. 20. hide them in secret of thy *p.*
100. 2. before his *p.* with singing
114. 7. tremble, earth, at *p.* of Lord
139. 7. whither shall I flee from *p.*
140. 13. upright shall dwell in thy *p.*
Isa. 63. 9. angel of his *p.* saved
Jer. 5. 22. will ye not tremble at my *p.*
Luke 13. 26. eaten and drunk. in *p.*
Acts 3. 19. blotted out from *p.* of Lord
1 Cor. 1. 29. no flesh glory in his *p.*
2 Cor. 10. 1. in *p.* am base among
2 Thes. 1. 9. punished from *p.* of
Rev. 14. 10. *p.* of holy angels
R. V. Few changes to before; Matt. 21. 19. immediately; 26. 53. even now; Phil. 2. 23. forthwith

PRESERVE, Gen. 45. 7. Ps. 12. 7.
Ps. 16. 1. *p.* me, O God, for I trust
25. 21. let integrity and truth *p.*
32. 7. thou shalt *p.* me from
61. 7. mercy and truth *p.* him
64. 1. *p.* life from fear of enemies
86. 2. *p.* my soul, for I am holy
121. 7. Lord shall *p.* thee from evil
140. 1. *p.* me from the violent man
Prov. 2. 11. discretion shall *p.* thee
Luke 17. 33. will lose his life, *p.* it
2 Tim. 4. 18. will *p.* to his heaven.
Josh. 24. 17. *preserved* us in all the
2 Sam. 8. 6. Lord *p.* David
Job 10. 12. thy visitation *p.* my
1 Thes. 5. 23. soul and body be *p.*
Jude 1. *p.* in Christ Jesus, and
Ps. 36. 6. Lord thou *preservest* man
29. 10. he *preserveth* the souls of
116. 6. Lord *p.* the simple
145. 20. Lord *p.* all that love him
Prov. 2. 8. he *p.* way of his saints
Job 7. 20. O thou *Preserver* of men
R. V. 2 Sam. 8. 6, 14; 1 Chron. 18. 6, 13. gave victory; Job 29. 2; Prov. 2. 11. watch over; Ps. 121. 7. keep; 2 Tim. 4. 18. save; Jude 1. kept; Luke 5. 38——

PRESS, Gen. 40. 11. Judg. 16. 16.
Phil. 3. 14. I *p.* towards the mark
Ps. 38. 2. thy hand *presseth* me sore
Luke 16. 16. kingdom of God every man *p.* unto
Amos 2. 13. *pressed* as a cart is *p.*
Luke 6. 38. good measure, *p.* down
Acts 18. 5. Paul was *p.* in spirit
R. V. Joel 3. 13. winepress; Mark 2. 4; 5. 27, 30; Luke 8. 19; 19. 3. crowd; 8. 45. crush; Gen. 19. 3. urged; Acts 18. 5. constrained; 2 Cor. 1. 8. weighed down; Luke 16. 16. entereth violently

PRESUMPTION of Israelites, Num. 14. 44. Deut. 1. 43; prophets, Deut. 18. 20; builders of Babel, Gen. 11; Korah, &c., Num. 16; Beth-shemites, 1 Sam. 6. 19; Hiel, the Bethelite, 1 Kings 16. 34; Uzzah, 2 Sam. 6. 6; Uzziah, 2 Chron. 26. 16; Jewish exorcists, Acts 19. 13; Diotrephes, 3 John 9.

PRESUMPTUOUS, Ps. 19. 13.
2 Pet. 2. 10. Num. 15. 30. Deut. 17. 12, 13.
R. V. 2 Pet. 2. 10. daring

PRETENCE, Matt. 23. 14. Phil. 1. 18.
R. V. Matt. 23. 14——

PREVAIL, Gen. 7. 20. Judg. 16. 5.
1 Sam. 2. 9. by strength, shall no man *p.*
Ps. 9. 19. O Lord, let not man *p.*
65. 3. iniquities *p.* against me
Eccl. 4. 12. if one *p.* against him
Matt. 16. 18. gates of hell not *p.*
Gen. 32. 28. power with God and hast *prevailed*
Ex. 17. 11. Moses held up hand, Israel *p.*
Hos. 12. 4. pow. over angels, and *p.*
Acts 19. 20. word of God grew, and *p.*
Job 14. 20. thou *prevailest* for ever
R. V. Gen. 47. 20; 2 Kings 25. 3. was sore upon; Job 18. 9. lay hold on; Isa. 42. 13. do mightily; Rev. 5. 5. overcome

PREVENT, Job 3. 12. Ps. 59. 10. & 79. 8. & 88. 13. & 119. 148. Amos 9. 10. 1 Thes. 4. 15.
2 Sam. 22. 6. *prevented*, 19. Job 30. 27. & 41. 11. Ps. 18. 5, 18. & 21. 3. & 119. 147. Isa. 21. 14. Matt. 17. 25.
R. V. Job 3. 12. receive; Ps. 88. 13. come before; 2 Sam. 22. 6, 19; Job 30. 27; Ps. 18. 5, 18. came upon; Matt. 17. 25. spake first to

PREY, Gen. 49. 9, 27. Esth. 9. 15, 16.
Isa. 49. 24. *p.* be taken from mighty
Jer. 21. 9. life for a *p.*, 38. 2 & 39. 18. & 45. 5.
Ps. 124. 6. not given us a *p.* to their
R. V. Judg. 5. 30; 8. 24, 25, Esth. 9. 15, 16; Isa. 10. 2; Jer. 50. 10. spoil; Job 24. 5. meat; Prov. 23. 28. robber

PRICE, Lev. 25. 16. Deut. 23. 18.
Job 28. 13. man knoweth not the *p.*
Ps. 44. 12. not increase wealth, by their *p.*
Prov. 17. 16. a *p.* in the hand of
Isa. 55. 1. wine and milk without *p.*
Matt. 13. 46. pearl of great *p.*
Acts 5. 2. kept back part of the *p.*
1 Cor. 6. 20. bought with a *p.*, 7. 23.
1 Pet. 3. 4. sight of God of great *p.*
R. V. Deut. 23. 18. wages; Zech. 11. 12. hire

PRICKS, kick against, Acts 9. 5. & 26. 14.
Ps. 73. 21. *pricked*, Acts 2. 37.
R. V. Acts 9. 5 —— ; 26. 14. goad
PRIDE of heart, 2 Chron. 32. 26. Ps. 10. 4.
Job 33. 17. he may hide *p.* from
Ps. 10. 2. wicked in *p.* doth per.
31. 20. hide them from *p.* of man
73. 6. *p.* compasseth them about
Prov. 8. 13. *p.* and arrogance I hate
13. 10. by *p.* cometh contention
16. 18. *p.* goeth before destruction
Isa. 23. 9. Lord purposed it, to stain *p.*
Jer. 13. 17. weep in secr. for your *p.*
Ezek. 7. 10. rod hath blossomed, *p.*
16. 49. iniquity of Sodom, *p.* and
Dan. 4. 37. those that walk in *p.*
Hos. 5. 5. *p.* of Israel testify
Obad. 3. *p.* of thy heart deceived
Mark 7. 22. blasphemy, *p.* foolish.
1 Tim. 3. 6. lifted up with *p.* he fall
1 John 2. 16. lust of eyes, *p.* of life
R. V. Ps. 31. 20. plottings; 1 John 2. 16. vainglory. A few other changes due to the context
PRIEST, Gen. 14. 18. Ex. 2. 16. Lev. 6. 20, 26. & 5. 6. & 6. 7. & 12. 8.
Isa. 24. 2. with peop., so with the *p.*
28. 7. *p.* and prophet have erred
Jer. 23. 11. prophet and *p.* profane
Ezek. 7. 26. law shall perish from *p.*
Hos. 4. 4. those that strive with *p.*
9. like people, like *p.*
Mal. 2. 7. *p.* lips should keep
Heb. 5. 6. a *p.* for ever, 7. 17, 21.
Lev. 21. 10. *high priest*, Heb. 2. 17. & 3. 1. & 4. 14, 15. & 5. 1, 10. & 6. 20. & 7. 26. & 8. 1, 3. & 9. 11. & 10. 21.
Ps. 132. 9. let thy *priests* be clothed
16. clothe her *p.* with salvation
Isa. 61. 6. ye be named *p.* of
Jer. 5. 31. *p.* bear rule by their
31. 14. satisfy soul of *p.* with
Ezek. 22. 26. *p.* have violated my
Joel 1. 9. *p.* Lord's ministers, 2. 17.
Mic. 3. 11. the *p.* teach for hire
Matt. 12. 5. *p.* in the temple
Acts 6. 7. company of *p.* obedient
Rev. 1. 6. kings and *p.* to God
Ex. 40. 15. everlasting *priesthood*
Heb. 7. 24. an unchangeable *p.*
1 Pet. 2. 5. ye are a holy *p.*
PRINCE, Gen. 23. 6. & 34. 2.
Gen. 32. 28. as a *p.* hast power with
Ex. 2. 14. who made thee a *p.* over
2 Sam. 3. 38. *p.* and great man
Job 31. 47. as a *p.* would I go
Isa. 9. 6. everlasting Father, *p.* of
Ezek. 34. 24. my servant David, a *p.* among them, 37. 24, 25. & 44. 3. & 45. 7. & 46. 10, 16. Dan. 9. 25.
Dan. 10. 21. Michael your *p.*
Hos. 3. 4. many days without a *p.*
John 12. 31. now shall *p.* of world
14. 30. *p.* of world cometh and
16. 11. *p.* of this world judged
Acts 3. 15. ye killed the *p.* of life
5. 31. to be a *P.* and a Saviour
Eph. 2. 2. *p.* of the power of air
Rev. 1. 5. Jesus *p.* of kings of earth
Job 12. 19. leads *princes* away
21. pours contem. on *p.*, Ps. 107. 40.
Job 34. 18. is it fit to say to *p.*
Ps. 45. 16. thou makest *p.* in earth
82. 7. shall fall like one of the *p.*
118. 9. than to put confidence in *p.*
161. *p.* persecuted me without
146. 3. put not trust in *p.* nor man
Prov. 8. 15. by me *p.* decree jus.
17. 26. not good to strike *p.* for
31. 4. not for *p.* to drink strong
Eccl. 10. 7. seen *p.* walk on earth
Isa. 3. 4. give children to be their *p.*
Hos. 7. 5. *p.* made the king sick
Matt. 20. 25. *p.* of Gentiles exer.
1 Cor. 2. 6. wisdom of *p.* of world
8. none of *p.* of this world knew
Prov. 4. 7. wisdom is the *principal*
Eph. 1. 21. *principality* and power, Col. 2. 10. Jer. 13. 18. Rom. 8. 38. Eph. 6. 12. Col. 2. 15. Tit. 3. 1.
Heb. 5. 12. *principles*, 6. 1.
R. V. Frequent changes in Kings and Chron. to captains; in Dan. to satraps; in N. T. to rulers; Ex. 30. 23; Neh. 11. 17. chief; 2 Kings 25. 19; Jer. 52. 25. captain; Jer. 13. 18. headtires; Eph. 1. 21. rule; Tit. 3. 1. rulers
PRISON, Gen. 39. 20. Eccl. 4. 14.
Isa. 42. 7. bring out prison. from *p.*
58. 8. he was taken from *p.* and
61. 1. opening of the *p.* to them
Matt. 5. 25. and thou be cast into *p.*
18. 30. cast into *p.* till he should
25. 36. I was in *p.* and ye came
1 Pet. 3. 19. preach. to spirits in *p.*
Rev. 2. 10. devil cast some into *p.*
Luke 21. 12. *prisons*, 2 Cor. 11. 23.
Ps. 79. 11. sighing of *prisoner* come
102. 20. to hear the groaning of *p.*
Eph. 4. 1. I the *p.* of the Lord
Job 3. 18. there the *prisoners* rest
Ps. 69. 33. Lord despiseth not his *p.*
146. 7. the Lord looseth the *p.*
Zech. 9. 11. sent forth thy *p.* out
R. V. Gen. 42. 16. bound; Neh. 3. 25; Jer. 32. 2, 8, 12; 33. 1; 37. 21; 38. 6, 13, 28; 39. 14, 15. guard; Isa. 42. 7. dungeon; Acts 12. 7. cell; Num. 21. 1; Isa. 20. 4. captive; Acts 28. 16 ——
PRIVATE, 2 Pet. 1. 20. Gal. 2. 2.
PRIVY, Deut. 23. 1. Acts 5. 2.
Ps. 10. 8. *privily*, 11. 2. & 101. 5. Acts 16. 37. Gal. 2. 4. 2 Pet. 2. 1.
R. V. Ezek. 21. 14 ——; Judg. 9. 31. craftily; Ps. 11. 2. darkness
PRIZE, 1 Cor. 9. 24. Phil. 3. 14.
PROCEED, 2 Sam. 7. 12. Jer. 30. 21.
Job 40. 5. twice spoken; I will *p.*
Isa. 29. 14. I will *p.* to do a marvel.
51. 4. a law shall *p.* from me
Jer. 9. 3. they *p.* from evil to evil.
Matt. 15. 19. out of heart *p.* evil
Eph. 4. 29. no corrupt communication *p.* out of your mouth
2 Tim. 3. 9. they shall *p.* no further
Luke 4. 22. the gracious words that *proceeded* out of his mouth
John 8. 42. I *p.* and came from God
Gen. 24. 50. thing *proceedeth* from
Deut. 8. 3. by every word that *p.*
1 Sam. 24. 13. wickedness *p.* from
Lam. 3. 38. out of the mouth of the Lord *p.* not evil
John 15. 26. Spirit of tru. which *p.*
Jas. 3. 10. out of the same mouth *p.* blessing
Rev. 11. 5. fire *p.* out of their mouth
PROCLAIM, Lev. 23. 2. Deut. 20. 10.
Ex. 33. 19. I will *p.* the name of the Lord, 34. 6.
Prov. 20. 6. most men will *p.* their
Isa. 61. 1. *p.* liberty to the captives
2. to *p.* the acceptable year of Lord
Prov. 12. 23. the heart of fools *proclaimeth* foolishness
PROCURED, Jer. 2. 17. & 4. 18.
R. V. Prov. 11. 27. seeketh; Jer. 26. 19. commit
PRODIGAL son, parable of, Luke 15. 11.
PROFANE not the name of Lord, Lev. 18. 21. & 19. 12. & 20. 3. & 21. 6. & 22. 9, 15.
Neh. 13. 17. *p.* sabbath, Matt. 12. 5.
Ezek. 22. 26. put no difference between holy and *p.*
Amos 2. 7. to *p.* my holy name
1 Tim. 1. 9. law is for unholy and *p.*
4. 7. refuse *p.* and old wives' fa.
Heb. 12. 16. fornicator or *p.* person
Ps. 89. 39. hast *profaned* his crown
Ezek. 22. 8. thou hast *p.* my sabb.
Mal. 1. 11. Judah hath *p.* the holi.
2. 10. by *profaning* the covenant
R. V. Ezek. 21. 25. deadly wounded; 22. 26; 44. 23. common
PROFESS, Deut. 26. 3. Tit. 1. 16.
1 Tim. 6. 12. *profession*, 13. Heb. 3. 1. & 4. 14. & 10. 23.
R. V. 1 Tim. 6. 12. confess; Heb. 3. 1; 4. 14; 10. 23. confession
PROFIT, Prov. 14. 23. Eccl. 7. 11. Jer. 16. 19. 2 Tim. 2. 14. Heb. 12. 10.
1 Sam. 12. 21. *not profit*, Job 33. 27. & 34. 9. Prov. 10. 2. & 11. 4. Isa. 30. 5. & 44. 9, 10. & 57. 12. Jer. 2. 8, 11. & 7. 8. & 23. 32. John 6. 63. 1 Cor. 13. 3. Gal. 5. 2. Heb. 4. 2. Jas. 2. 14.
Job 22. 2. *profitable*, Eccl. 10. 10. Acts 20. 20. 1 Tim. 4. 8. 2 Tim. 3. 16. Tit. 3. 8. Phile. 11.
1 Tim. 4. 15. thy *profiting* appear
PROLONG thy days, Deut. 4. 26, 40. & 5. 16, 33. & 6. 2. & 11. 9. & 17. 20. & 22. 7. & 30. 18. & 32. 47. Prov. 10. 27. & 28. 16. Eccl. 8. 13. Isa. 53. 10.
R. V. Job 6. 11. be patient; Ezek. 12. 25, 28. deferred
PROMISE, Num. 14. 34. Neh. 5. 12
Ps. 77. 8. doth his *p.* fail for ever
105. 42. he remember. his holy *p.*
Luke 24. 49. the *p.* of my Father
Acts 1. 4. wait for *p.* of the Father
2. 39. *p.* is to you, and your child.
Rom. 4. 16. *p.* might be sure to all
9. 8. children of *p.*, 9. Gal. 4. 28.
Eph. 1. 13. holy Spirit of *p.*
2. 12. covenant of *p.* having no
6. 2. commandment with *p.*
1 Tim. 4. 8. *p.* of the life, 2 Tim. 1. 1.
Heb. 4. 1. lest a *p.* being left us of
6. 17. heirs of his *p.*, 11. 9.
9. 15. receive *p.* of eternal life
2 Pet. 3. 4. where is the *p.* of com.
1 John 2. 25. *p.* he *promised* eternal life, Luke 1. 72. Rom. 1. 2. & 4. 21. Tit. 1. 2. Heb. 10. 23. & 11. 11. & 12. 26.
Rom. 9. 4. pertain the *promises*
15. 8. confirm *p.* made to fathers
2 Cor. 1. 20. all *p.* of God are yea
7. 1. having these *p.* let us
Gal. 3. 21. is the law against the *p.*
Heb. 6. 12. patience inherit *p.*
11. 17. he that had received *p.*
2 Pet. 1. 4. great and precious *p.*
R. V. Deut. 10. 9; Josh. 9. 21; 22. 4; 23. 5, 10, 15. spake unto; Luke 1. 72. shew mercy; 22. 6. consented
PROMOTION, Ps. 75. 6. Prov. 3. 35.
PROOF, Acts 1. 3. 2 Cor. 2. 9. & 8. 24.
PROPER, 1 Chron. 29. 3. Heb. 11. 23.
R. V. 1 Cor. 7. 7. own gift from
PROPHECY, 1 Cor. 12. 10. 1 Tim. 4. 14. & 1. 18. 2 Pet. 1. 19, 20. Rev. 1. 3. & 11. 6. & 19. 10. & 22. 7, 10, 18, 19.
1 Kings 22. 8. not *prophesy* good, 18.
Isa. 30. 10. speak smooth things, *p.* deceits
Jer. 14. 14. prophets *p.* lies in my
Joel 2. 28. your sons and your daughters shall *p.*
Amos 2. 12. *p.* not
1 Cor. 13. 9. we *p.* in part
14. 1. but rather that ye may *p.*
39. covet to *p.* and forbid not to
Rev. 10. 11. thou must *p.* again
Num. 11. 25. they *prophesied*
Jer. 23. 21. not spoken yet they *p.*
Matt. 7. 22. we have *p.* in thy
11. 13. the prophets *p.* until John
John 11. 51. *p.* that Jesus should
1 Pet. 1. 10. prophets *p.* of the grace
Jude 14. Enoch also *p.* of these
Ezra 6. 14. *prophesying*, 1 Cor. 11. 4. & 14. 6, 22. 1 Thes. 5. 20.
Gen. 20. 7. he is a *prophet*, and
Ex. 7. 1. Aaron thy brother shall be thy *p.*
Deut. 18. 15. raise up un. thee a *p.*

1 Kings 5. 13. if the *p.* had bid
Ps. 74. 9. there is no more any *p.*
Ezek. 33. 33. then shall they know that a *p.* hath been among them
Hos. 9. 7. *p.* is a fool, spiritual man
12. 13. by a *p.* was he preserved
Amos 7. 14. no *p.* neither a *p.'s* son
Matt. 10. 41. he that receiveth a *p.*
11. 9. see a *p.* and more than a *p.*
13. 57. a *p.* is not without honor
Luke 7. 28. there is not a greater *p.*
24. 19. *p.* mighty in deed and
John 7. 40. this is the *p.*, 1. 21. & 6. 14.
52. out of Galilee ariseth no *p.*
Acts 3. 22. a *p.* shall the Lord raise
23. will not hear that *p.* shall
Tit. 1. 12. a *p.* of their own, said
1 Pet. 2. 16. madness of the *p.*
Num. 11. 29. all the Lord's people *prophets*
1 Sam. 10. 12. is Saul among the *p.*
Ps. 105. 15. do my *p.* no harm
Jer. 5. 13. the *p.* shall become
23. 26. are *p.* of the deceit of
Lam. 2. 14. *p.* have seen vain
Hos. 6. 5. I hewed them by the *p.*
Zeph. 3. 4. her *p.* are treacherous
Zech. 1. 5. *p.* do they live for ever
Matt. 5. 17. not come to destroy law, or the *p.*
7. 12. this is the law and the *p.*
13. 17. many *p.* have desired
22. 40. on these hang all the law and the *p.*
23. 34. I send you *p.* and wise men
Luke 1. 70. spake by mouth of holy *p.*, 2 Pet. 1. 20.
6. 23. so did their fathers to *p.*
16. 29. they have Moses and the *p.*
31. if they hear not Moses and *p.*
24. 25. to believe all that *p.*
John 8. 52. Abraham is dead, and *p.*
Acts 3. 25. ye are children of the *p.*
10. 43. to him give all the *p.*
13. 27. knew not voices of the *p.*
26. 27. believest thou the *p.*
22. things which the *p.* and Moses
Rom. 1. 2. which he had promised afore by his *p.* in Holy Scriptures
1 Cor. 12. 28. God hath set some in the church, first apostles; secondarily *p.*
Eph. 2. 20. are built upon the foundation of the apostles and *p.*
1 Cor. 14. 32. spirit of *p.* sub. to *p.*
1 Thes. 2. 15. who kill. their own *p.*
Heb. 1. 1. God spake to fath. by *p.*
Jas. 5. 10. take *p.* for example
1 Pet. 1. 10. of which salva. the *p.*
Rev. 18. 20. rejoice over her, ye apostles and *p.*
22. 6. Lord God of holy *p.* sent his
9. and of the brethren the *p.*
R. V. Prov. 30. 1. oracle

PROPHETESSES, Anna, Luke 2. 36; Deborah, Judg. 4. 4; Huldah, 2 Kings, 22. 14; Miriam, Ex. 15. 20; Noadiah, Neh. 6. 14.

PROPITIATION, Rom. 3. 25. 1 John 2. 2. & 4. 10.

PROPORTION of faith, Rom. 12. 6.
R. V. 1 Kings 7. 36. space

PROSELYTE, Matt. 23. 15. Acts 2. 10. & 6. 5. & 13. 43.

PROSPER, Gen. 24. 40. Neh. 1. 11.
Gen. 39. 3. Lord made all to *p.*
Deut. 29. 9. may *p.* in all ye do
2 Chron. 20. 20. believe prophets, so shall ye *p.*
Job 12. 6. tabernacles of robbers *p.*
Ps. 1. 3. whatsoever he doeth, it shall *p.*
122. 6. they shall *p.* that love thee
Isa. 53. 10. pleasure of Lord shall *p.*
54. 17. no weapon formed against thee shall *p.*
55. 11. shall *p.* in the thing whereto
Jer. 12. 1. wherefore doth the way of the wicked *p.*
1 Cor. 16. 2. God hath *prospered* him
3 John 2. *p.* as thy soul *prospereth*
Job 36. 11. spend their days in *prosperity*
1 Kings 10. 7. thy wisdom and *p.* exceedeth
Ps. 30. 6. in my *p.* I shall never
73. 3. when I saw *p.* of the wicked
122. 7. *p.* be within thy palaces
Prov. 1. 32. *p.* of fools shall destroy
Eccl. 7. 14. in day of *p.* be joyful
Jer. 22. 21. I spake to thee in thy *p.*
Gen. 24. 21. journey *prosperous*, Josh. 1. 8. Ps. 45. 4. Rom. 1. 10.
R. V. Ps. 73. 12. being at ease; Jer. 20. 11; 23. 5. deal wisely; Jer. 33. 9. peace

PROTEST, Gen. 43. 3. 1 Sam. 8. 9. Jer. 11. 7; Zech. 3. 6. 1 Cor. 15. 31.

PROUD, Job 9. 13. & 26. 12. & 38. 11. & 40. 11, 12. Ps. 12. 3.
Ps. 40. 4. respecteth not the *p.* nor
101. 5. a *p.* heart I will not suffer
Prov. 6. 17. *p.* look and lying tongue
21. 4. high look and *p.* heart
Eccl. 7. 8. patient is better than *p.*
Mal. 3. 15. we call the *p.* happy
Luke 1. 51. the *p.* in imagination
1 Tim. 6. 4. is *p.* knowing nothing
Jas. 4. 6. God resisteth *p.*, 1 Pet. 5. 5.
Ex. 18. 11. wherein dealt *proudly*
1 Sam. 2. 3. no more so exceeding *p.*
Neh. 9. 10. knowest they dealt *p.*, 16.
Ps. 17. 10. they spake *p.*, 31. 18.
Isa. 3. 5. child shall behave *p.* against
R. V. Job 26. 12. Rahab; Ps. 12. 3; Ps. 138. 6; Prov. 6. 17; Hab. 2. 5; Rom. 1. 30; 2 Tim. 3. 2. haughty; 1 Tim. 6. 4. puffed up

PROVE them, Ex. 16. 4. Deut. 8. 16.
Ex. 20. 20. God is come up to *p.* you
Deut. 13. 3. the Lord *p.* you
33. 8. Holy One thou didst *p.* at
1 Kings 10. 1. she came to *p.* him
Job 9. 20. mouth shall *p.* me
Ps. 26. 2. examine me, O Lord, *p.*
Rom. 12. 2. *p.* what is will of God
2 Cor. 8. 8. to *p.* the sincerity of
13. 5. *p.* your own selves, know
Gal. 6. 4. let every man *p.* his work
1 Thes. 5. 21. *p.* all things; hold fast
Ps. 17. 3. thou hast *proved* my heart
66. 10. thou, O God, hast *p.* us as
Acts 9. 22. *proving*, Eph. 5. 10.

PROVERB and a by-word, Deut. 28. 37. 1 Kings 9. 7. Jer. 24. 9. Ezek. 14. 8.
Ps. 69. 11. I became a *p.* to them
Eccl. 12. 9. he set in order many *p.*, 1 Kings 4. 32. Prov. 1. 1. & 10. 1. & 25. 1.
Isa. 14. 4. thou shalt take up this *p.* against, Luke 4. 23.
John 16. 25. I have spoken in *p.*
2 Pet. 2. 22. according to true *p.*
R. V. Isa. 14. 4; Luke 4. 23. parable

PROVIDE, Ex. 18. 21. Acts 23. 24.
Gen. 22. 8. God will *p.* himself a
Ps. 78. 20. can he *p.* flesh for people
Matt. 10. 9. *p.* neither gold nor
Rom. 12. 17. *p.* things honest in
Job 38. 41. *provideth* raven his food
Prov. 6. 8. *p.* her meat in summer
1 Tim. 5. 8. if any *p.* not for his
Ps. 132. 15. *provision*, Rom. 13. 14.
R. V. Ps. 65. 9. prepared; Matt. 10. 9. get you no; Luke 12. 33. make for; Rom. 12. 17; 2 Cor. 8. 21. take thought for

PROVIDENCE of God, Gen. 8. 22. Josh. 7. 14. 1 Sam. 6. 7. Ps. 36. 6. 104. & 136. & 145. & 147. Prov. 16. & 19. & 20. & 33. Matt. 6. 26. & 10. 29, 30. Luke 21. 18. Acts 1. 26. & 17. 26.

PROVOKE him not, Ex. 23. 21.
Num. 14. 11. how long will ye *p.*
Deut. 31. 20. *p.* me, and break my
Job 12. 6. that *p.* God are secure
Ps. 78. 40. how oft did they *p.* him
Isa. 3. 8. to *p.* the eyes of his glory
Jer. 7. 19. do they *p.* me to anger
44. 8. ye *p.* me to wrath with your
Luke 11. 53. to *p.* him to speak of
Rom. 10. 19. *p.* you to jealousy
1 Cor. 10. 22. do we *p.* the Lord to
Eph. 6. 4. fathers *p.* not children
Heb. 3. 16. when they heard did *p.*
10. 24. to *p.* unto love and good
Num. 16. 30. these have *provoked*
14. 23. neither any which *p.* me
Deut. 9. 8. ye *p.* Lord to wrath
1 Sam. 1. 6. adversary *p.* her sore
1 Kings 14. 22. *p.* him to jealousy
2 Kings 23. 26. because Manasseh *p.*
1 Chron. 21. 1. Satan *p.* David to
Ezra 5. 12. our fathers had *p.* God
Ps. 78. 56. and *p.* the Most High
106. 7. *p.* him at the Red sea
Zech. 8. 14. when your fathers *p.*
1 Cor. 13. 5. not easily *p.* thinketh
2 Cor. 9. 2. your zeal hath *p.* many
Deut. 32. 19. *provoking*, 1 Kings 14. 15. & 16. 7. Ps. 78. 17. Gal. 5. 26.
R. V. Num. 14. 11, 23; 16. 30; Deut. 31. 20; Isa. 1. 4. despise; Deut. 32. 16; 1 Chron. 22. 1. moved; Ps. 78. 40, 56. rebel against; Ps. 106. 7, 33, 43. were rebellious; 2 Cor. 9. 2. stirred up

PRUDENT in matters, 1 Sam. 16. 18.
Prov. 12. 16. a *p.* man covereth
23. *p.* man concealeth knowledge
13. 16. every *p.* man dealeth with
14. 8. wisdom of the *p.* is to
15. the *p.* man looketh well to his
15. 5. he that regard. reproof is *p.*
16. 21. wise in heart shall be call. *p.*
18. 15. heart of *p.* getteth knowl.
22. 3. a *p.* man foreseeth the evil
Isa. 5. 21. woe to them that are *p.* in
Jer. 49. 7. is counsel perish. from *p.*
Hos. 14. 9. who is *p.* and he shall
Amos 5. 13. *p.* shall keep silent in
Matt. 11. 25. hid these things from the wise and *p.*
1 Cor. 1. 19. I will bring to nothing the understanding of the *p.*
Isa. 52. 13. my servant shall deal *prudently*
2 Chron. 2. 12. endued with *prudence* and understanding, Prov. 8. 12. Eph. 1. 8.
R. V. 2 Chron. 2. 12. discretion; Prov. 8. 12. subtlety; Isa. 3. 2. diviner; Matt. 11. 25; Luke 10. 21; Acts 13. 7. understanding

PSALM, 1 Chron. 16. 7. Ps. 81. 2. & 98. 5. Acts 13. 33. 1 Cor. 14. 26.
1 Chron. 16. 9. sing *psalms* unto him, Ps. 105. 2.
Ps. 95. 2. a joyful noise with *p.*
Eph. 5. 19. speaking to your. in *p.*
Col. 3. 16. admon. one another in *p.*
Jas. 5. 13. merry, let him sing *p.*
R. V. 1 Chron. 16. 9; Ps. 105. 2; Jas. 5. 13. praises

PSALMODY, singing, service of song, Jewish, Ex. 15. 1. 1 Chron. 6. 31. & 13. 8. 2 Chron. 5. 13. & 20. 22. & 29. 30. Neh. 12. 27; Christian, Matt. 26. 30. Mark 14. 26. Jas. 5. 13; spiritual songs, Eph. 5. 19. Col. 3. 16.

PUBLICAN, Matt. 18. 17; Luke 18. 13.
Matt. 5. 46. even the *p.* the same, 47.
11. 19. a friend of *p.* and sinners
Luke 3. 12. came also *publicans* to
7. 29. the *p.* justified God
R. V. Matt. 5. 47. Gentiles

PUBLISH name of the Lord, Deut. 32. 3.
2 Sam. 1. 20. *p.* it not in the streets
Ps. 26. 7. *p.* with voice of thanks.
Isa. 52. 7. feet of him that *publisheth* peace
Jer. 4. 15. a voice *p.* affliction
Mark 13. 10. the Gospel must first be *published*
Acts 13. 49. word of the Lord was *p.*
R. V. Deut. 32. 3. proclaim; 1 Sam. 31. 9. carry tidings; Ps. 26. 7. make to be heard; Mark 13. 10.

preached; Acts 13. 49. spread abroad
PUFFED up, 1 Cor. 4. 6, 19. & 5. 2. & 8. 1. & 13. 4. Col. 2. 18.
PULL out, Ps. 31. 4. Jer. 12. 3. Matt. 7. 4. Luke 14. 5. Jude 23.
Isa. 22. 19. *pull down*, Jer. 1. 10. & 18. 7. & 24. 6. & 42. 10. Luke 12. 18. 2 Cor. 10. 4.
Lam. 3. 11. *pull in pieces*, Acts 23. 10.
Ezek. 17. 9. *pull up*, Amos 9. 15.
Zech. 7. 11. they *pulled* away the
R. V. Gen. 8. 9; 19. 10. brought; 1 Kings 13. 4; Luke 14. 5. draw; Ps. 31. 4; Amos 9. 15. pluck; Jer. 1. 10; 18. 7. break; Mic. 2. 8. strip; Matt. 7. 4; Luke 6. 42. cast; Acts 23. 10. torn; 2 Cor. 10. 4. casting, Jude 23. snatching.
PULPIT of wood, Neh. 8. 4.
PUNISH, seven times, Lev. 26. 18.
Prov. 17. 26. to *p.* the just is not
Isa. 10. 12. *p.* fruit of the stout
13. 11. I will *p.* the world for their
Jer. 9. 25. *p.* all circumcised with
Hos. 4. 14. I will not *p.* daughters
Ezra 9. 13. *p.* us less than we
2 Thes. 1. 9. be *p.* with destruction
2 Pet. 2. 9. reserve unjust to be *p.*
Gen. 4. 13. my *punishment* is great.
Lev. 26. 41. accept *p.* of their iniq.
Job. 31. 3. a strange *p.* to workers
Lam. 3. 39. complain for *p.* of sins
Amos 1. 3. not turn away the *p.*
Matt. 25. 46. go into everlasting *p.*
2 Cor. 2. 6. suffi. to such is this *p.*
Heb. 10. 29. of how much sorer *p.*
1 Pet. 2. 14. sent by him, for the *p.*
R. V. Ex. 21. 22. fined; Lev. 26. 18. chastise; 26. 24. smite; Prov. 22. 3; 27. 12. suffer for it; Jer. 41. 44. do judgment; Amos 3. 2. visit upon you; Zech. 8. 14. do evil unto; Prov. 19. 19. penalty; Lam. 4. 6; Ezek. 14. 10 —; Ezek. 14. 10. iniquity; Job 31. 3. disaster; 1 Pet. 2. 14. vengeance
PURCHASED, Ps. 74. 2. Acts 8. 20. & 20. 28. Eph. 1. 14. 1 Tim. 3. 13.
R. V. Lev. 25. 33. redeem; Acts 1. 18; 8. 20. obtain
PURCHASES, Gen. 23. Ruth 4. Jer. 32. 6.
PURE, Ex. 27. 20. & 30. 23, 34.
2 Sam. 22. 27. with the *p.* thou wilt
Job 4. 17. can man be more *p.* than
25. 5. stars are not *p.* in his sight
Ps. 12. 6. words of the Lord are *p.*
19. 8. commandment of Lord is *p.*
24. 4. clean hands and a *p.* heart
Prov. 15. 26. words of *p.* are pleas.
30. 5. every word of God is *p.*
12. a generation *p.* in
Zeph. 3. 9. turn to the people a *p.*
Acts 20. 26. I am *p.* from blood of
Rom. 14. 20. all things indeed are *p.*
Phil. 4. 8. whatsoever things are *p.*
1 Tim. 3. 9. mystery of faith in a *p.* conscience
5. 22. of other men's sins keep thyself *p.*
Tit. 1. 15. to the *p.* all things are *p.*
Heb. 10. 22. washed with *p.* water
Jas. 1. 27. *p.* religion and undefiled
3. 17. wis. from above is first *p.*
2 Pet. 3. 1. stir up your *p.* minds
Isa. 1. 25. *purely* purge away dross
Job 22. 30. by *pureness*, 2 Cor. 6. 6.
1 Tim. 4. 12. *purity*, 5. 2.
Hab. 1. 13. of *purer* eyes than to
R. V. Ex. 30. 23. flowing; Ps. 21. 3. fine; Prov. 30. 5. tried; Rom. 14. 20. clean; 2 Pet. 3. 1. sincere; Rev. 22. 1 —
PURGE me with hyssop, Ps. 51. 7.
Ps. 65. 3. our transgressions, thou shalt *p.* them away
79. 9. *p.* away our sins for thy
Mal. 3. 3. purify and *p.* them as
Matt. 3. 12. thoroughly *p.* his floor
1 Cor. 5. 7. *p.* the old leaven
2 Tim. 2. 21. if a man *p.* himself
Heb. 9. 14. *p.* your conscience from
Prov. 16. 6. by mercy iniquity is *purged*
Isa. 6. 7. iniqu. is taken, and sin *p.*
Ezek. 24. 13. because I *p.* thee
Heb. 1. 3. had by himself *p.* our
2 Pet. 1. 9. he was *p.* from sins
John 15. 2. he *purgeth* that it may
R. V. Ezek. 43. 20. make atonement; Dan. 11. 35. purify, Matt. 3. 12; Mark 7. 19; Luke 3. 17; John 15. 2; Heb. 9. 14, 22; 10. 2; 2 Pet. 1. 9. cleanse, cleansed, clean
PURIFY sons of Levi, Mal. 3. 3.
Jas. 4. 8. *p.* your hearts, ye double
Ps. 12. 6. silver *purified* seven
Dan. 12. 10. many shall be *p.*
1 Pet. 1. 22. *p.* your souls in obey.
Mal. 3. 3. sit as *purifier* of silver
1 John 3. 3. *purifieth* himself as he
Acts 15. 9. *purifying* their hearts
Tit. 2. 14. *p.* to himself a peculiar
Heb. 9. 13. sanctifieth to *p.* of flesh
R. V. Job. 41. 25. are beside; Heb. 9. 23. cleansed; Num. 8. 7. expiation, Acts 15. 9. cleansing
PURPOSE, Jer. 6. 20. & 49. 30.
Job 33. 17. withdraw man from *p.*
Prov. 20. 18. every *p.* is established
Eccl. 3. 17. a time to every *p.*, 8. 6.
Isa. 14. 26. the *p.* that is purposed
Jer. 51. 29. *p.* of Lord shall stand
Acts 11. 23. with *p.* of heart cleave
Rom. 8. 28. according to his *p.*
Eph. 1. 11. according to *p.* of him
3. 11. the eternal *p.* which he *p.*
2 Tim. 1. 9. according to his own *p.*
1 John 3. 8. for this *p.* he was
R. V. Acts 26. 18; 1 John 3. 8. to this end, Acts 20. 3. determined
PURSE, Prov. 1. 14. Matt. 10. 9.
PURSUE, Gen. 35. 5. Deut. 28. 22.
Ex. 15. 9. the enemy said, I will *p.*
Job 13. 25. wilt thou *p.* dry stubble
Ps. 34. 14. seek peace and *p.* it
Prov. 11. 19. that *pursueth* evil, *p.* it
28. 1. wicked flee when none *p.*
R. V. Judg. 20. 45. followed; Job 30. 15; Lam. 4. 19. chase
PUT, Gen. 2. 8. & 3. 15, 22.
Neh. 2. 12. what God *p.* in my heart, 7. 5. Ezra 7. 27. Rev. 17. 17.
Neh. 3. 5. nobles *p.* not their necks
Job 4. 18. he *p.* no trust in servants
38. 36. hath *p.* wisdom in inward
Ps. 4. 7. hast *p.* gladness in heart
8. 6. *p.* all things under his feet
Eccl. 10. 10. *p.* to more strength
S. of S. 5. 3. *p.* off my coat, how shall
Isa. 5. 20. woe to them that *p.* dark.
42. 1. I will *p.* my Spirit upon
53. 10. Lord hath *p.* him to grief
63. 11. who *p.* his Holy Spirit in
Jer. 31. 33. *p.* law in inward parts
32. 40. I will *p.* my fear in hearts
Ezek. 11. 19. *p.* a new spirit within
36. 27. I will *p.* my Spirit within
Mic. 7. 5. *p.* not confidence in guide
Matt. 5. 15. *p.* it under a bushel
19. 6. what God joined, let no man *p.* asunder
Luke 1. 52. *p.* down mighty from
Acts 1. 7. which Father *p.* in his
13. 46. seeing you *p.* the Gospel
15. 9. *p.* no difference between us
Eph. 4. 22. *p.* off the old man
2 Pet. 1. 14. I must *p.* off this
Gen. 28. 20. God will give raiment to *put on*
Job 29. 14. I—righteousness and it
Isa. 51. 9. awake, arm of Lord, — strength
59. 15. for he — righteousness as a breastplate
Matt. 6. 25. nor for body what ye—
Rom. 13. 12. — armor of light
14. — Lord Jesus Christ
Gal. 3. 27. baptized into Christ have — Christ
Eph. 4. 24.—the new man, Col. 3. 10.
6. 11. — whole armor of God
Col. 3. 12. — bowels of mercies
1 Chron. 5. 20. *put trust* in, Ps. 4. 5. & 7. 1. & 9. 10. & 56. 4. & 146. 3.
Prov. 28. 25. & 29. 25. Isa. 57. 13. Jer. 39. 18. Hab. 2. 13.
Num. 22. 38. word that God *putteth*
Job 15. 15. he *p.* no trust in saints
Ps. 15. 5. that *p.* not out money
75. 7. God *p.* down one, and set.
S. of S. 2. 13. *p.* forth green figs
Lam. 3. 29. he *p.* his mouth in
Mic. 3. 5. that *p.* not into their
Mal. 2. 16. he hateth *putting* away
Eph. 4. 25. *p.* away lying, speak
Col. 2. 11 in *p.* off the body of sins
1 Thes. 5. 8. *p.* on the breastplate
2 Tim. 1. 6. gift given thee by *p.*
1 Pet. 3. 3. wearing of gold or *p.* on
R. V. Many changes, but chiefly due to context

Q

QUAILS, Ex. 16. 13. Num. 11. 31.
QUAKE, Ex. 19. 18. Matt. 27. 51.
Ezek. 12. 18. *quaking*, Dan. 10. 7.
QUARREL, Lev. 26. 25. Col. 3. 13.
R. V. Lev. 26. 25. execute vengeance, Mark 6. 19. set herself; Col. 3. 13. complain
QUEEN, 1 Kings 10. 1. & 15. 13. Ps. 45. 9. S. of S. 6. 8. Jer. 44. 17, 24. Rev. 18. 7.
Matt. 12. 42. *q.* of the south rise
Isa. 49. 23. *q.* their nursing moth.
R. V. Jer. 13. 18; 29. 12. queen-mother
QUENCH my coal, 2 Sam. 14. 7.
2 Sam. 21. 17. that thou *q.* not
S. of S. 8. 7. waters cannot *q.* love
Isa. 42. 3. flax he will not *q.*
Eph. 6. 15. to *q.* fiery darts of dev.
1 Thes. 5. 19. *q.* not the Spirit
Mark 9. 43. fire that never shall be *quenched*, 44. 46, 48.
R. V. Num. 11. 2. abated; Mark 9. 44, 45, 46 —
QUESTION, Mark 12. 34. 1 Cor. 10. 25.
1 Kings 10. 1. *questions*, Luke 2. 46.
1 Tim. 1. 4. & 6. 4. 2 Tim. 2. 23.
R. V. 1 Tim. 1. 4; 6. 4; 2 Tim. 2. 23; Tit. 3. 9. questionings
QUICK, Num. 16. 30. Ps. 55. 15.
Ps. 124. 3. had swallowed us up *q.*
Isa. 11. 3. of *q.* understanding
Acts 10. 42. Judge of *q.* and dead
2 Tim. 4. 1. who shall judge the *q.*
Ps. 71. 20. *quicken* me again and
80. 18. *q.* us and we will call
119. 25. *q.* me according to word
40. *q.* me in thy righteousness
149. *q.* me according to judgment
Rom. 8. 11. *q.* your mortal bodies
Eph. 2. 5. *q.* us together with
Ps. 119. 50. for thy word hath *quickened* me
Eph. 2. 1. you he *q.* who were
1 Pet. 3. 18. but *q.* by the Spirit
John 5. 21. Son *quickeneth* whom he
1 Cor. 15. 45. last Adam be made a *quickening* Spirit
R. V. Num. 16. 30; Ps. 55. 15; 124. 3. alive; Isa. 11. 3. his delight shall be; Heb. 4. 12. living; 1 Cor. 15. 45. become a life giving
QUICKLY, Ex. 32. 8. Deut. 11. 17.
Eccl. 4. 12. cord is not *q.* broken
Matt. 5. 25. agree with adversary *q.*
Rev. 3. 11. behold I come *q.*, 22. 7.
R. V. Mark 16. 8; Rev. 2. 5 —
QUIET, Judg. 18. 27. Job 3. 13, 26.
Eccl. 9. 17. the words of the wise are heard in *q.*
Isa. 7. 4. take heed and be *q.* fear
33. 20. shall see Jerusalem a *q.*
1 Thes. 4. 11. study to be *q.* and to
1 Tim. 2. 2. lead a *q.* and peaceable
1 Pet. 3. 4. ornament of a meek and *q.* spirit
1 Chron. 22. 9. *quietness*, Job 20. 20.
Job 34. 29. when he giveth *q.* who
Prov. 17. 1. better is dry morsel and *q.*
Eccl. 4. 6. better is a hand. with *q.*

Isa. 30. 15. in *q.* shall be strength
32. 17. the effect of righteousness shall be *q.*
2 Thes. 3. 12. exhort with *q.* they
R. V. Nah. 1. 12. in full strength; Judg. 8. 28. had rest; Acts 24. 2. much peace

QUIT you like men, 1 Sam. 4. 9. 1 Cor. 16. 13.
R. V. Josh. 2. 20. guiltless

QUIVER full of them, Ps. 127. 5.
Isa. 49. 2. in his *q.* hath he hid me
Jer. 5. 16. *q.* is an open sepulchre

R

RABBI, Matt. 23. 7, 8. John 20. 16.
R. V. Matt. 23. 7 —

RACE, Ps. 19. 5. Eccl. 9. 11. 1 Cor. 9. 24. Heb. 12. 1.
R. V. Ps. 19. 5. course

RAGE, 2 Kings 5. 12. 2 Chron. 16. 10.
2 Chron. 28. 9. ye have slain them in a *r.*
Ps. 2. 1. why do the heathen *r.*
Prov. 6. 34. jealousy is *r.* of a man
29. 9. whether he *r.* or laugh is no
Ps. 46. 6. the heathen *raged*
Prov. 14. 16. the fool *rageth*
Ps. 89. 9. rulest the *raging* of sea
Prov. 20. 1. wine is a mocker, strong drink is *r.*
Jude 13. *r.* waves of sea, foaming
R. V. Job 40. 11. overflowings; Prov. 29. 9. be angry; 14. 16. beareth himself insolently; Prov. 20. 1. a brawler

RAGS, Prov. 23. 21. Isa. 64. 6.

RAILER, or drunkard, 1 Cor. 5. 11.
1 Tim. 6. 4. *railing*, 1 Pet. 3. 9.
2 Pet. 2. 11. *r.* accusation, Jude 9.
R. V. 1 Pet. 3. 9. reviling

RAIMENT to put on, Gen. 28. 20.
Ex. 21. 10. food and *r.* not dimin.
Deut. 8. 4. thy *r.* waxed not old
Zech. 3. 4. clothe thee with change of *r.*
Matt. 6. 26. body more than *r.*, 28.
11. 8. man clothed in soft *r.*
17. 2. his *r.* was white as the light
1 Tim. 6. 8. having food and *r.* let
Rev. 3. 5. clothed in white *r.*, 18.
R. V. Ex. 22. 26, 27; Deut. 22. 3; 24. 13; Num. 31. 20; Matt. 17. 2; 27. 31; Mark 9. 3; Luke 23. 34; John 19. 24; Acts 22. 20; Rev. 3. 5, 18; 4. 4. garment or garments; Ps. 45. 14. broidered work; Zech. 3. 4. apparel; 1 Tim. 6. 8. covering; Jas. 2. 2. clothing; Luke 10. 30 —

RAIN in due season, Lev. 26. 4. Deut. 11. 14. & 28. 12.
Deut. 32. 2. my doctrine drop as *r.*
2 Sam. 23. 4. clear shining after *r.*
1 Kings 8. 35. no *r.* because sinned
2 Chron. 7. 13. that there be no *r.*
Job 5. 10. giveth *r.* on the earth
38. 28. hath the *r.* a father
Ps. 68. 9. didst send a plentiful *r.*
72. 6. he shall come down like *r.*
147. 8. who prepareth *r.* for earth
Prov. 16. 15. king's favor is like the latter *r.*
Eccl. 12. 2. nor clouds ret. after *r.*
S. of S. 2. 11. winter is past; *r.* is over
Isa. 4. 6. covert from storm and *r.*
30. 23. shall give the *r.* of thy
55. 10. as *r.* cometh down from
Jer. 5. 24. fear Lord who giveth *r.*
14. 22. vanities of the Gentiles that can *r.*
Amos 4. 7. withholden *r.* from you
Zech. 10. 1. ask of the Lord *r.* in
14. 17. upon them shall be no *r.*
Matt. 5. 45. sendeth *r.* on the just
Heb. 6. 7. earth which drink. in *r.*
Jas. 5. 18. he prayed, and heaven gave *r.*
Job 38. 26. cause it to *r.* on the earth
Ps. 11. 6. on the wicked he shall *r.*
Hos. 10. 12. till he *r.* righteousness
Ps. 78. 27. had *rained* upon them
Ezek. 22. 24. land not cleansed nor *r.* upon
Prov. 27. 15. continual dropping in a *rainy* day

RAISE, Deut. 18. 15, 18. 2 Sam. 12. 11.
Isa. 44. 26. *r.* up decayed places
58. 12. *r.* up foundations of
Hos. 6. 2. third day he will *r.* us
Amos 9. 11. I will *r.* up tabernacle
Luke 1. 69. *r.* up a horn of salva.
John 6. 40. I will *r.* him up at
Ex. 9. 16. I *raised* thee up to show
Matt. 11. 5. deaf hear, dead are *r.*
Rom. 4. 25. *r.* again for justifica.
6. 4. as Christ was *r.* by glory of
1 Cor. 6. 14. God hath *r.* up the
2 Cor. 4. 14. he that *r.* up the
Eph. 2. 6. hath *r.* us up together
1 Sam. 2. 8. he *raiseth* up the poor
Ps. 113. 7. he *r.* up poor out of
145. 14. *r.* up those that be
R. V. Job 3. 8; 14. 12. roused; S. of S. 8. 5. awakened; Job 50. 9; Ezek. 1. 5; Jer. 6. 22; 50. 41; 51. 11; Joel 3. 7; Zech. 9. 13; Acts 13. 50. stir or stirred

RANSOM of life, Ex. 21. 30.
Ex. 30. 12. give every man a *r.* for
Job 33. 24. deliver him, I have found *r.*
36. 18. great *r.* cannot deliver
Ps. 49. 7. nor give to God a *r.* for
Prov. 6. 35. will not regard any *r.*
13. 8. *r.* of man's life are his
21. 18. wicked ar a *r.* for right.
Isa. 43. 3. I gave Egypt for thy *r.*
Hos. 13. 14. *r.* them from power
Matt. 20. 28. to give his life a *r.* for
1 Tim. 2. 6. gave himself a *r.* for
Isa. 35. 10. *ransomed*, 51. 10. Jer. 31. 11.
R. V. Ex. 21. 30. redemption; Isa. 51. 10. redeemed

RASH, Eccl. 5. 2. Isa. 32. 4.

RAVISHED, Prov. 5. 19. S. of S. 4. 9.

REACH, Gen. 11. 4. John 20. 27.
Ps. 36. 5. faithfulness *reacheth* to
Phil. 3. 13. *reaching* forth to those
R. V. Ex. 26. 28. pass through; Phil. 3. 13. stretching forward

READ in audience, Ex. 24. 7.
Deut. 17. 19. *r.* therein all his life
Neh. 13. 1. *r.* in the book of Moses
Luke 4. 16. as his custom was, stood up to *r.*
Acts 15. 21. *r.* in synagogue
2 Cor. 3. 2. known and *r.* of all
Acts 8. 30. understandest thou what thou *readest*
Rev. 1. 3. blessed is he that *readeth*
Neh. 8. 8. *reading*, 1 Tim. 4. 13.

READY to pardon, God, Neh. 9. 17.
Ps. 45. 1. tongue is as a pen of a *r.* writer
86. 5. thou, Lord, art good, and *r.* to forgive
Eccl. 5. 1. more *r.* to hear, than
Matt. 24. 44. be ye also *r.*
Mark 14. 38. spirit is *r.* but the
Acts 21. 13. *r.* not to be bound
1 Tim. 6. 18. do good *r.* to distrib.
2 Tim. 4. 6. now *r.* to be offered
Tit. 3. 1. *r.* to every good work
1 Pet. 5. 2. willingly of a *r.* mind
Rev. 3. 2. strengthen things *r.* to
Acts 17. 11. *readiness*, 2 Cor. 10. 6.
R. V. 2 Chron. 35. 14; 2 Cor. 9. 2, 3. prepared; 1 Chron. 12. 23, 24. armed for; Mark 14. 38. willing; Acts 20. 7. intending; Heb. 8. 13. nigh; Rev. 12. 4. about

REAP, Lev. 19. 9.
Hos. 10. 12. *r.* in mercy
1 Cor. 9. 11. a great thing if we *r.*
Gal. 6. 9. shall *r.* if we faint not
Hos. 10. 13. ploughed wickedness, ye have *reaped* iniquity
Rev. 14. 16. the earth was *r.*, 15.
Matt. 13. 39. *reapers* are angels, 30.
John 4. 36. he that *reapeth* receiv.
R. V. Lev. 23. 22 —; Jas. 5. 4. mowed

REASON, Prov. 26. 16. Dan. 4. 36.
Isa. 41. 21. bring forth your strong *r.*
1 Pet. 3. 15. asketh a *r.* of the hope
Acts 24. 25. as he *reasoned* of
Rom. 12. 1. your *reasonable* service

REBEL not against Lord, Num. 14. 9. Josh. 22. 19.
Job 24. 13. of those that *r.* against
Neh. 9. 26. they *rebelled* against thee
Isa. 63. 10. they *r.* and vexed his
1 Sam. 15. 23. *rebellion*, the sin
Num. 20. 10. hear now, ye *rebels*
Ezek. 20. 38. purge out the *r.* from
Deut. 9. 7. been *rebellious* against
Ps. 68. 18. received gifts for men, for the *r.* also
Isa. 30. 9. this a *r.* people, lying
50. 5. I was not *r.* nor turned
Jer. 4. 17. hath been *r.*
Ezek. 2. 3, 5, 8. *r.* house, 3. 9, 26. & 12. 2, 3. & 17. 12. & 24. 3. & 44. 6.

REBUKE thy neighbor, Lev. 19. 17.
2 Kings 19. 3. a day of *r.*
Ps. 6. 1. *r.* me not in anger, nor
Prov. 9. 8. *r.* a wise man, he will
27. 5. open *r.* is better than secret
Zech. 3. 2. the Lord said to Satan, the Lord *r.* thee
Matt. 16. 22. Peter began to *r.* him
Luke 17. 3. if thy brother trespass, *r.* him
Phil. 2. 15. sons of God without *r.*
1 Tim. 5. 1. *r.* not an elder, entreat
20. them that sin *r.* before all
Tit. 1. 13. *r.* them sharply, that
3. 15. exhort and *r.* with author.
Heb. 12. 5. not faint, when *rebuked*
Prov. 28. 23. he that *rebuked*, shall
Amos 5. 10. hate him that *r.* in
R. V. Phil. 2. 15. blemish; Jer. 15. 15. reproach; Prov. 9. 7, 8; Amos 5. 10; 1 Tim. 5. 20; Tit. 2. 15; Rev. 3. 19. reprove or reproveth

RECEIVE good and not evil, Job 2. 10.
Job 22. 22. *r.* the law from his
Ps. 6. 9. the Lord will *r.* my prayer
73. 24. guide me and afterwards *r.*
75. 2. when I shall *r.* congregation
Hos. 14. 2. take away iniqu., *r.* us
Matt. 10. 41. *r.* a prophet's reward
18. 5. *r.* little child in my name
19. 11. all men cannot *r.* this
21. 22. ask, believing, ye shall *r.*
Mark 4. 16. hear the word, and *r.*
11. 24. believe that ye *r.* and ye
Luke 16. 9. may *r.* into everlast.
John 3. 27. man can *r.* nothing
5. 44. which *r.* honor one of
Acts 2. 38. shall *r.* gift of Holy Ghost
7. 59. Lord Jesus *r.* my spirit
13. 43. he that believeth shall *r.*
20. 35. more bless. to give than *r.*
26. 18. may *r.* forgiveness of sins
Rom. 14. 1. that is weak in faith *r.*
1 Cor. 3. 8. every man *r.* his reward
2 Cor. 5. 10. may *r.* things done
6. 1. *r.* not grace of God in vain
Gal. 3. 14. *r.* promise of the
4. 5. might *r.* the adoption of
Eph. 6. 8. same shall he *r.* of
Col. 3. 24. *r.* reward of inheritance
Jas. 1. 21. *r.* with meekness
3. 1. *r.* greater condemnation
1 Pet. 5. 4. shall *r.* a crown of glory
1 John 3. 22. whatso. we ask, we *r*
2 John 8. look that we *r.* a full
Job 4. 12. mine ear *received* a little
Ps. 68. 18. thou hast *r.* gifts for
Jer. 2. 30. *r.* no correction
Matt. 10. 8. freely ye have *r.* freely
Luke 6. 24. have *r.* your consola.
16. 25. hast *r.* thy good things
John 1. 11. own *r.* him not
16. of his fulness have we all *r.*
Acts 8. 17. they *r.* the Holy Ghost
17. 11. *r.* the word

Acts 20. 24. which I *r.* of Lord
Rom. 5. 11. Christ by whom we have *r.* atonement
14. 3. judge him not, for God hath *r.* him
15. 7. *r.* one anoth. as Christ *r.* us
1 Tim. 3. 16. *r.* up into glory
4. 3. to be *r.* with thanksgiving
Heb. 11. 13. not having *r.* promises
Jer. 7. 28. nor *receiveth* correction
Matt. 7. 8. every one that asketh *r.*
10. 40. he that *r.* you, *r.* me
13. 20. hears the word, and anon *r.*
John 3. 32. no man *r.* his testimony
12. 48. rejecteth me, *r.* not my
1 Cor. 2. 14. natural man *r.* not
Phil. 4. 15. in giving and *receiving*
Heb. 12. 28. we *r.* a kingdom
1 Pet. 1. 9. *r.* the end of your faith
R. V. Ex. 29. 25; 1 Sam. 12. 3; 2 Kings 12. 7, 8; John 16. 14; Heb. 7. 6. take; Hos. 14. 2; Mark 4. 20; 1 Thes. 2. 13. accept; Luke 9. 11; 3 John 8. welcome; many other changes due to context

RECKONED, Ps. 40. 5. Isa. 38. 13. Luke 22. 37. Rom. 4. 4, 9, 10. & 6. 11. & 8. 18.

RECOMPENSE, Prov. 12. 14. Isa. 35. 4.
Deut. 32. 35. to me belongeth *r.*
Job 15. 31. vanity shall be his *r.*
Prov. 20. 22. say not thou I will *r.* evil
Jer. 25. 14. I will *r.* your iniquities
Luke 14. 14. they cannot *r.* thee
Rom. 12. 17. *r.* to no man evil for
Isa. 34. 8. it is the year of *r.* for
66. 6. render *r.* to his enemies
Jer. 51. 56. the Lord God of *r.*
Hos. 9. 7. the days of *r.* are come
Luke 14. 12. lest a *r.* be made thee
Heb. 2. 2. received just *r.* of reward
11. 26. he had respect unto *r.* of
Num. 5. 8. trespass be *recompensed*
2 Sam. 22. 21. according to righteousness he *r.* me
Prov. 11. 31. righteous shall be *r.*
Jer. 18. 20. shall evil be *r.* for good
Rom. 11. 35. it shall be *r.* to him
R. V. Num. 5. 7, 8. restitution; Ezek. 7. 3, 4, 9; 11. 21; 16. 34; 17. 19; 22. 31; 2 Chron. 6. 23; bring or brought; Rom. 12. 17. render

RECONCILE with blood, Lev. 6. 30.
Eph. 2. 16. *r.* both to God into one
Col. 1. 20. to *r.* all things to him.
2 Cor. 5. 19. God in Christ *reconciling* the world
Matt. 5. 24. be *reconciled* to brother
Rom. 5. 10. when enemies we were *r.*
2 Cor. 5. 18. he hath *r.* us to
20. be ye *r.* to God
Lev. 8. 15. to make *reconciliation*, 2 Chron. 29. 24. Ezek. 45. 15, 17. Dan. 8. 24. Heb. 2. 17.
2 Cor. 5. 18. given to us ministry of *r.*
19. committ. to us the word of *r.*
R. V. Lev. 6. 30; Ezek. 45. 20. make atonement; Lev. 8. 15; 16. 20; Ezek. 45. 15, 17. atonement; 2 Chron. 29. 24. sin offering; Heb. 2. 17. propitiation

RECORD my name, Ex. 20. 24.
Deut. 30. 19. I call heaven and earth to *r.* against, 31. 28.
Job 16. 19. my witness and my *r.*
John 1. 32. bare *r.*, 8. 13, 14. & 12. 17. & 19. 35. Rom. 10. 2. Gal. 4. 15.
2 Cor. 1. 23. I call God for a *r.*
1 John 5. 7. three bear *r.* in heaven
11. this is the *r.* God hath given
Rev. 1. 2. bare *r.* of the word of
R. V. Very general change to witness; Deut. 30. 19. witness; 1 Chron. 16. 4. celebrate; Acts 20. 26. testify

RECOVER strength, Ps. 39. 13.
Hos. 2. 9. I will *r.* my wool and
2 Tim. 2. 26. may *r.* themselves
Jer. 8. 22. is not health of my people *recovered*
Luke 4. 18. *recovering* of sight to
R. V. 1 Sam. 30. 19. brought back; Hos. 2. 9. pluck away

RED, Ps. 75. 8. Isa. 1. 18. & 27. 2. & 63. 2. Zech. 1. 8. & 6. 2. Rev. 6. 4. & 12. 3.
R. V. Ps. 75. 8. foameth

RED DRAGON, Rev. 12. 3.

RED HORSE, vision of, Zech. 1. 8. & 6. 2. Rev. 6. 4.

REDEEM with outstretched arm, Ex. 6. 6.
2 Sam. 7. 23. Israel whom God went to *r.*
Job 5. 20. in famine he shall *r.* thee
Ps. 44. 26. *r.* us for thy mercies' sake
130. 8. shall *r.* Israel from
Hos. 13. 14. I will *r.* them from
Tit. 2. 14. might *r.* us from iniquity
Gen. 48. 16. angel which *redeemed*
2 Sam. 4. 9. hath *r.* my soul out
Ps. 136. 24. hath *r.* us from our
Isa. 1. 27. Zion shall be *r.* with
51. 11. *r.* of the Lord shall return
52. 3. shall be *r.* without money
63. 9. in his love and pity he *r.*
Luke 1. 68. visited and *r.* his peo.
24. 21. he that should have *r.*
Gal. 3. 13. Christ hath *r.* us from
1 Pet. 1. 18. not *r.* with corrupti.
Rev. 5. 9. hast *r.* us to God, by
14. 4. these were *r.* from among
Ps. 34. 22. Lord *redeemeth* the soul
103. 4. who *r.* thy life from de.
Eph. 5. 16. *redeeming* the time
Job 19. 25. I know that my *Redeemer* liveth
Ps. 19. 14. my strength and my *R.*
Prov. 23. 11. their *R.* is mighty
Isa. 63. 16. our Father and *R.*
Jer. 50. 34. their *R.* is strong
Lev. 25. 34. *redemption*, Num. 3. 49.
Ps. 49. 8. *r.* of their soul is pre.
130. 7. with him is plenteous *r.*
Luke 2. 38. looked for *r.* in Jerusalem
21. 28. your *r.* draweth nigh
Rom. 3. 24. through *r.* in Christ
8. 23. waiting for the *r.* of our body
1 Cor. 1. 30. made unto us wisdom, and righteousness, and *r.*
Eph. 1. 7. in whom we have *r.*
14. until *r.* of the purchased
4. 30. sealed unto the day of *r.*
Heb. 9. 12. obtain. eternal *r.* for us
R. V. Lev. 25. 29; 27. 27; Isa. 5. 11; Jer. 31. 11. ransom; Lev. 25. 29; Num. 3. 51; Ruth 4. 6. redemption; Ps. 136. 24. delivered; Rev. 5. 9; 14. 3, 4. purchased

REFINE, Isa. 25. 6. & 48. 10. Zech. 13. 9. Mal. 3. 2, 3.

REFORMATION, Heb. 9. 10.

REFRAIN, Prov. 1. 15. 1 Pet. 3. 10.
Prov. 10. 29. he that *refraineth* his lips is wise

REFRESHING, Isa. 28. 12. Acts 3. 19.

REFUGE, Num. 35. 13. Josh. 20. 3.
Deut. 33. 27. eternal God is thy *r.*
Ps. 9. 9. the Lord also will be a *r.* for the oppressed, 14. 6. Isa. 4. 6. & 25. 4.
Ps. 57. 1. God is my *r.* and, 59. 16. & 62. 7. & 71. 7. & 142. 5. Jer. 16. 19.
Ps. 46. 1. God is our *r.*, 7. 11. & 62. 8.
Isa. 28. 15. have made lies our *r.*
Heb. 6. 18. fled for *r.* to lay hold on
R. V. Deut. 33. 27. dwelling place; Ps. 9. 9. high tower

REFUSE, Lam. 3. 45. Amos 8. 6.
Neh. 9. 17. *refused* to obey, neither
Ps. 77. 2. my soul *r.* to be comforted
118. 22. the stone which builders *r.*
Prov. 1. 24. I have called, and ye *r.*
Jer. 31. 15. Rachel *r.* to be com.
Hos. 11. 5. because they *r.* to return
1 Tim. 4. 4. good and noth. to be *r.*
Jer. 3. 3. *refusedst* to be ashamed
15. 18. *refuseth* to be healed
Heb. 12. 25. *r.* not him that speak.
R. V. 1 Sam. 16. 7; Ps. 118. 22; Ezek. 5. 6; 1 Tim. 4. 4. reject or rejected; Prov. 10. 17. forsaketh; Isa. 54. 6. cast off

REGARD not works of the Lord, Ps. 28. 5.
Ps. 66. 18. if I *r.* iniquity in heart
102. 17. will *r.* prayer of destitute
Isa. 5. 12. that *r.* not work of Lord
Prov. 1. 24. no man *regarded*
Ps. 106. 44. he *r.* their affliction
Luke 1. 48. *r.* low estate of his
Heb. 8. 9. not in my covenant I *r.* them not
Deut. 10. 17. God *regardeth* not
Job 34. 19. nor *r.* rich more than
Prov. 12. 10. righteous *r.* life of
15. 5. he that *r.* reproof is prudent
Eccl. 5. 8. he that is higher than the highest *r.*
Rom. 14. 6. he that *r.* the day, *r.* it
Matt. 22. 16. *regardest* not person
R. V. *gave heed*; 2 Sam. 13. 20. take thing to heart; Job 39. 7. heareth; Ps. 94. 7. consider; Prov. 5. 2. preserve; Mal. 1. 9. accept; Luke 1. 48. looked upon; Acts 8. 11. gave heed; Phil. 2. 30. hazarding; Rom. 14. 6; Gal. 6. 4 ——

REGENERATION, Matt. 19. 28. Tit. 3. 5.

REIGN, Gen. 37. 8. Lev. 26. 17.
Ex. 15. 18. Lord shall *r.* for ever, Ps. 146. 10.
Prov. 8. 15. by me kings *r.* and
Isa. 32. 1. a king shall *r.* in right.
Jer. 23. 5. a king shall *r.* and pros.
Luke 19. 14. not have this man to *r.*
Rom. 5. 17. shall *r.* in life by one
1 Cor. 4. 8. would to God ye did *r.*
2 Tim. 2. 12. if we suffer, we shall *r.*
Rev. 5. 10. we shall *r.* on the earth
22. 5. they shall *r.* for ever and
Rom. 5. 14. death *reigned* from
21. that as sin *r.* unto death so
Rev. 20. 4. they lived and *r.* with
1 Chron. 20. 12. thou *reignest* over
Ps. 93. 1. Lord *reigneth*, 97. 1. & 99. 1.
Isa. 52. 7. saith unto Zion, thy God *r.*
Rev. 19. 6. Allelula, Lord God omnipotent *r.*
R. V. Lev. 26. 17; Deut. 15. 6; Josh. 12. 5; Judg. 9. 2; 1 Kings 4. 21; Rom. 15. 12. rule or ruled

REINS, Job 16. 13. & 19. 27.
Ps. 7. 9. God trieth hearts and *r.*, Jer. 17. 10. & 20. 12. Rev. 2. 23.
Ps. 16. 7. my *r.* instruct me in
73. 21. I was pricked in my *r.*
139. 13. thou hast possessed my *r.*
Prov. 23. 16. my *r.* shall rejoice
Jer. 12. 2. thou art far from their *r.*

REJECT, Mark 6. 26. Gal. 4. 14.
Mark 7. 9. ye *r.* command. of God
Tit. 3. 10. after first and second admonition *r.*
1 Sam. 8. 7. have not *rejected* thee
Isa. 53. 3. is despised and *r.* of men
Jer. 2. 37. Lord hath *r.* confidences
6. 30. Lord *r.* them, 7. 29. & 14. 19.
2 Kings 17. 20. Lam. 5. 22.
Jer. 8. 9. *r.* word of the Lord
Hos. 4. 6. hast *r.* knowledge
Luke 7. 30. *r.* the counsel of God
Heb. 12. 17. was *r.* for he found no
John 12. 48. he that *rejecteth* me

REJOICE, Ex. 18. 9. Deut. 12. 7.
Deut. 28. 63. Lord will *r.* over you
1 Sam. 2. 1. because I *r.* in thy
2 Chron. 6. 41. let thy saints *r.* in
20. 27. the Lord made them to *r.*
Neh. 12. 43. God made them *r.* with
Ps. 2. 11. serve God and *r.* with
5. 11. let those that trust in thee *r.*
9. 14. I will *r.* in thy salvation

Ps. 58. 10. righteous will *r.* when he
63. 7. in the shadow of thy wings
I will *r.*
65. 8. thou makest the morning
and the evening to *r.*
68. 3. let righteous *r.* before God
86. 4. *r.* the soul of thy servant
104. 31. Lord shall *r.* in his works
119. 162. I *r.* at thy word as one
Prov. 5. 18. *r.* with wife of thy
24. 17. *r.* not when enemy falleth
Eccl. 11. 9. *r.* O young man, in thy
Isa. 29. 19. poor among men shall *r.*
62. 5. thy God shall *r.* over thee
Jer. 32. 41. I will *r.* over them to do
Zeph. 3. 17. *r.* over thee with joy
Luke 6. 23. *r.* ye in that day; leap
10. 20. rather *r.* that your names
John 5. 35. willing to *r.* in his light
14. 28. if ye loved me ye would *r.*
Rom. 5. 2. *r.* in hope of glory of God
12. 15. *r.* with them that do *r.*
1 Cor. 7. 30. that *r.* as though *r.* not
Phil. 3. 3. worship God and *r.* in
Col. 1. 24. *r.* in my sufferings for
1 Thes. 5. 16. *r.* evermore
Jas. 1. 9. brother of low degree *r.*
1 Pet. 1. 8. *r.* with joy unspeakable
Ps. 33. 1. *rejoice in the Lord*, 97. 12.
Isa. 41. 16. & 61. 10. Joel 2. 23. Hab.
3. 18. Zech. 10. 7. Phil. 3. 1. & 4. 4.
Ps. 119. 14. I have *rejoiced* in way
Luke 1. 47. my spirit *r.* in God my
10. 21. Jesus *r.* in spirit and said
John 8. 56. Abraham *r.* to see my
1 Cor. 7. 30. as though they *r.* not
Ps. 16. 9. my heart is glad, my
glory *rejoiceth*
28. 7. Lord my heart greatly *r.*
Prov. 13. 9. the light of righteous *r.*
Isa. 62. 5. bridegroom *r.* over bride
64. 5. thou meetest him that *r.*
1 Cor. 13. 6. *r.* not in iniquity
Jas. 2. 13. mercy *r.* against
Ps. 19. 8. the statutes of the Lord
rejoicing the heart
119. 111. are the *r.* of my heart
Prov. 8. 31. *r.* in the habitable
Isa. 65. 18. I create Jerusalem a *r.*
Jer. 13. 15, 16. thy word was the *r.*
Acts 5. 41. *r.* that they were
counted
8. 39. eunuch went on his way *r.*
Rom. 12. 12. *r.* in hope, 5. 2, 3.
2 Cor. 1. 12. our *r.* is the testimony
Gal. 6. 4. he shall have *r.* in him.
Heb. 3. 6. *r.* of hope, firm to the
R. V. 1 Sam. 2. 1; 1 Chron. 16. 32;
Ps. 9. 2; 60. 6; 68. 3, 4; 108. 7; Isa.
13. 3. exult; Ps. 20. 5; Prov. 28. 12.
triumph; Ps. 96. 12; 98. 4. sing for
joy; Ps. 96. 11; 107. 42; Prov. 23.
15; Zech. 10. 7; Acts 2. 26. be glad;
Prov. 31. 25. laugheth; Phil. 2. 16;
3. 3; Jas. 1. 9; 2. 13; 4. 16. glory;
Job 8. 21. shouting; Ps. 107. 22.
singing; 126. 6. joy; 1 Cor. 15. 31;
2 Cor. 1. 12, 14; Gal. 6. 4; Phil. 1.
26; 1 Thes. 2. 19; Heb. 3. 6; Jas. 4.
16. glorying

RELEASE, year of, Ex. 21. 2.
Deut. 15. 1. & 31. 10. Jer. 34. 14.

RELIEVE, Lev. 25. 35. Isa. 1. 17.
Ps. 146. 9. Acts 11. 29. 1 Tim. 5. 16.
R. V. Lev. 25. 35; Ps. 146. 9. uphold;
Lam. 1. 11, 16, 19. refresh

RELIGION, Acts 26. 5. Gal. 1. 13,
14. Jas. 1. 26, 27.
Acts 13. 43. *religious*, Jas. 1. 26.

REMAINDER, 1 Thes. 4. 13. Rev.
3. 2. Eccl. 2. 9. Lam. 5. 19. John 1.
33.
John 9. 41. your sin *remaineth*
2 Cor. 9. 9. righteousness *r.* for
Heb. 4. 9. *r.* a rest for people of God
10. 26. there *r.* no more sacrifice
1 John 3. 9. his seed *r.* in him
Ps. 76. 10. *remainder* of wrath
R. V. Several changes, chiefly to
abide, or to a sense of settling,
rest; Lev. 6. 16. is left; Ps. 76. 10.
residue

REMEDY, 2 Chron. 36. 16. Prov. 6.
15. & 29. 1.

REMEMBER, Gen. 40. 23. Neh. 1.
8.
Gen. 9. 16. look upon it that I may *r.*
Ex. 13. 3. *r.* this day ye came out
Deut. 5. 15. *r.* thou wast a servant
8. 8. thou shalt *r.* Lord thy God
9. 7. *r.* and forget not how
32. 7. *r.* days of old, consider
2 Kings 20. 3. *r.* how I walked
Ps. 20. 7. we will *r.* name of Lord
74. 2. *r.* thy congregation, 18.
79. 8. *r.* not against us former, Isa.
64. 9. Jer. 14. 10. Hos. 8. 13.
89. 47. *r.* how short my time is
132. 1. *r.* David and his afflictions
Eccl. 12. 1. *r.* thy Creator in days
S. of S. 1. 4. we will *r.* thy love
Isa. 43. 25. I will not *r.* thy sins
46. 8. *r.* this, show yourselves
Jer. 31. 20. I do earnestly *r.* him
Ezek. 16. 61. shall *r.* thy ways
63. mayest *r.* and be confounded
36. 31. shall *r.* your own evil
Mic. 6. 5. *r.* what Balak consulted
Hab. 3. 2. in wrath *r.* mercy
Luke 1. 72. to *r.* his holy covenant
17. 32. *r.* Lot's wife, Gen. 19. 26.
Gal. 2. 10. that we should *r.* the
Col. 4. 18. *r.* my bonds
Heb. 8. 12. iniquity I will *r.* no
13. 3. *r.* them that are in bonds
Neh. 13. 14. *r.* me, 22. 31. Ps. 25. 7.
& 106. 4. Luke 23. 43.
Ps. 63. 6. *I remember*, 143. 5.
Jer. 2. 2. for—kindness of thy
Lev. 26. 43. *I will remember* my
covenant, 45. Ezek. 16. 60.
Ps. 79. 11—the works of the Lord
Jer. 31. 34.—their sin no more
Gen. 8. 1. God *remembered* Noah
30. 22. God *r.* Rachel, 1 Sam. 1. 19.
Ex. 2. 24. God *r.* his covenant
Num. 10. 9. shall be *r.* before Lord
Ps. 77. 3. I *r.* God and was troubled
78. 39. he *r.* they were but flesh
98. 3. hath *r.* his mercy and truth
119. 52. I *r.* thy judgments of old
136. 23. who *r.* us in our low estate
137. 1. we wept when we *r.* Zion
Matt. 26. 35. Peter *r.* words of
Luke 24. 8. they *r.* his words, and
John 2. 17. his disciples *r.* that it
Rev. 18. 5. God hath *r.* her iniqui.
Ps. 103. 14. he *r.* we are but dust
Lam. 1. 9. she *r.* not her last end
3. 19. *remembering*, 1 Thes. 1. 3.
1 Kings 17. 18. call my sin to *remembrance*
Ps. 6. 5. in death there is no *r.* of
Isa. 26. 8. *r.* of thee
Lam. 3. 20. my soul hath them in *r.*
Mal. 3. 16. in a book of *r.* was
Luke 1. 54. he hath holpen Israel
in *r.* of his mercy
22. 19. this do in *r.* of me
John 14. 26. bring all things to
your *r.*
Acts 10. 31. thy alms are had in *r.*
2 Tim. 1. 6. put in *r.*, 2. 14. 2 Pet. 1.
12. & 3. 1. Jude 5.
Rev. 16. 19. Babylon came in *r.*
R. V. Ps. 20. 7; 77. 11; S. of S. 1. 4;
Hos. 2. 17. mention; Job 32. 12.
memorable sayings; Isa. 57. 8.
memorial; 1 Tim. 4. 6. mind

REMIT sins, they shall, John 20. 23.
Matt. 26. 28. *remission of sins*, Mark
1. 4. Luke 1. 77. & 3. 3. & 24. 47.
Acts 2. 38. & 10. 43. Rom. 3. 25. Heb.
9. 22. & 10. 18.

REMNANT, Lev. 2. 3. Deut. 3. 11.
2 Kings 19. 4. lift up thy prayer
for *r.*
Ezra 9. 8. leave us a *r.* to escape
Isa. 1. 9. Lord left us a small *r.*
10. 21. a *r.* shall return, 22.
Jer. 15. 11. it shall be well with thy
r.
23. 3. I will gather *r.* of my flock
Ezek. 6. 8. yet will I leave a *r.*
Rom. 9. 27. a *r.* shall be saved, 11. 5.
R. V. Lev. 2. 3. which is left; Ex.
2. 12. overhanging part; 2 Kings
25. 11; Jer. 39. 9; Ezek. 23. 25; Mic.
5. 3. residue; Lev. 14. 18; 1 Kings
12. 23; 1 Chron. 6. 70; Ezra 3. 8;
Matt. 22. 6; Rev. 11. 13; 12. 17; 19.
21. rest

REMOVE thy stroke from me, Ps.
39. 10.
Ps. 119. 22. *r.* from me reproach
29. *r.* from me the way of lying
Prov. 4. 27. *r.* thy foot from evil
30. 8. *r.* far from me vanity
Eccl. 11. 10. *r.* sorrow from thy
Matt. 17. 20. *r.* hence, and it shall *r.*
Luke 22. 42. if willing *r.* this cup
Rev. 2. 5. I will *r.* thy candlestick
Ps. 103. 12. so far he *removed* our
Prov. 10. 30. the righteous shall
never be *r.*
Isa. 30. 20. teachers not be *r.*
Ezek. 36. 17. as uncleanness of a *r.*
woman
Gal. 1. 6. so soon *r.* for him that
R. V. Gen. 13. 18; Ps. 104. 5; 125. 1;
Isa. 24. 20. moved; Ex. 20. 18.
trembled; Num. (in all places)
journeyed; 2 Sam. 20. 12; 2 Kings
17. 26; 1 Chron. 8. 6, 7; Isa. 38. 12.
carried; 1 Kings 15. 14; 2 Kings
15. 4, 35. taken away; Job 19. 10;
Isa. 33. 20. plucked up; Isa. 10. 31.
fugitive; Lam. 1. 8; Ezek. 7. 19.
unclean; Deut. 28. 25; Jer. 15. 4;
24. 9; 29. 18; 34. 17; Ezek. 23. 46.
tossed to and fro; Matt. 21. 21;
Mark 11. 23. taken up; other
changes of minor moment

REND heav. and come, Isa. 64. 1.
Joel 2. 13. *r.* hearts and not gar.
Jer. 4. 30. though thou *rendest* face
R. V. Gen. 37. 33; Mark 9. 26. torn;
Jer. 4. 30. enlargest

RENDER vengeance, Deut. 32.
41, 43.
2 Chron. 6. 30. *r.* to every man
Job 33. 26. he will *r.* to man his
34. 11. work of a man shall he *r.* to
Ps. 116. 12. what shall I *r.* to Lord
Prov. 26. 16. men that can *r.* a
Hos. 14. 2. *r.* the calves of our lips
Matt. 22. 21. *r.* to Cesar the things
Rom. 13. 7. *r.* to all their dues
1 Thes. 5. 15. that none *r.* evil, 3. 9.
2 Chron. 30. 25. Hezekiah *rendered*
R. V. Judg. 9. 56, 57. requite; Job
33. 26. restoreth

RENDING the clothes, Gen. 37.
34. 2 Sam. 13. 19. 2 Chron. 34. 27.
Ezra 9. 5. Job 1. 20. & 2. 12. Joel 2.
13; by the high priest, Matt. 26.
65. Mark 14. 63.

RENEW right spirit within me,
Ps. 51. 10.
Isa. 40. 31. wait on Lord shall *r.*
Heb. 6. 6. *r.* them again to repent.
Ps. 103. 5. thy youth is *renewed* like
2 Cor. 4. 16. inward man is *r.* day
Eph. 4. 23. be *r.* in spirit of mind
Col. 3. 10. *r.* in knowledge, image
Ps. 104. 30. *renewest* face of earth
Rom. 12. 2. *renewing*, Tit. 3. 5.

RENOUNCED hidden things of,
1 Cor. 4. 2.

RENOWN, Ezek. 34. 29. & 39. 13.
Isa. 14. 20. *renowned*, Ezek. 23. 23.
R. V. Num. 1. 16. called; Isa. 14.
20. named

REPAIRER of breach., Isa. 58. 12.
R. V. 2 Chron. 24. 27. rebuilding

REPAY, Job 21. 31. & 41. 11.
Deut. 7. 10. he will *r.* him to his
Isa. 59. 18. according to deeds he *r.*
Rom. 12. 19. vengeance is mine, I
will *r.*
Prov. 13. 21. to the righteous good
be *repaid*
R. V. Prov. 13. 21; Rom. 12. 19.
recompense

REPENT of this evil, Ex. 32. 12.
Num. 23. 19. not the son of man
that he should *r.*
Deut. 32. 36. Lord shall *r.* himself
1 Sam. 15. 29. not man that he
should *r.*
1 Kings 8. 47. *r.* and make suppli.
Job 42. 6. I abhor and *r.* in dust

Ps. 90. 13. let it *r.* thee concerning
135. 14. will *r.* himself concerning
Jer. 18. 8. I will *r.* of evil I
Ezek. 14. 6. *r.* and return, 18. 30.
Joel 2. 14. if he will *r.* and
Jonah 3. 9. can tell if God will turn and *r.*
Matt. 3. 2. *r.* for kingdom of
Mark 1. 15. *r.* and believe Gospel
6. 12. preached that men should *r.*
Luke 13. 3. except ye *r.* ye shall
17. 3. if he *r.* forgive him, 4.
Acts 2. 38. *r.* and be baptized
3. 19. *r.* and be converted, that
17. 30. commandeth all men to *r.*
26. 30. should *r.* and turn to God
Rev. 2. 5. rem. whence fall. and *r.*
16. *r.* or I will come unto thee
21. I gave her space to *r.* of her
3. 19. be zealous and *r.*
Gen. 6. 6. *repented* the Lord, Ex. 32. 14. Judg. 2. 18. 2 Sam. 24. 16. Joel 2. 13.
Jer. 8. 6. no man *r.* of his wicked.
Matt. 21. 29. afterward *r.* and went
27. 3. Judas *r.* himself, and
Luke 15. 7. one sin. that *repenteth*
Jer. 15. 6. *repenting*, Hos. 11. 8.
Hos. 13. 14. *repentance* hid from
Matt. 3. 8. fruits meet for *r.*
11. baptiz. you with water unto *r.*
9. 13. not righte. but sinners to *r.*
Mark 1. 4. baptism of *r.*, Luke 3. 3.
Luke 15. 7. just persons need no *r.*
24. 47. that *r.* and remission be
Acts 5. 31. give *r.* to Israel and
11. 18. God to Gentiles granted *r.*
20. 21. testifying *r.* towards God
Rom. 2. 4. goodness of God leadeth thee to *r.*
2 Cor. 7. 10. sorrow worketh *r.*
Heb. 6. 1. not laying foundation of *r.*
12. 17. found no place of *r.*
2 Pet. 3. 9. all should come to *r.*
R. V. 1 Kings 8. 47. turn again; Ezek. 14. 6; 18. 30. return ye; 2 Cor. 7. 8. regret; Matt. 9. 13; Mark 2. 17 —; *compassions;* Hos. 11. 8. my *c.* are kindled together

REPETITIONS, vain, Matt. 6. 7.

REPLIEST against God, Rom. 9. 20.

REPORT, evil, Gen. 37. 2. Num. 13. 32. & 14. 37. Neh. 6. 13.
Ex. 23. 1. should not raise a false *r.*
Prov. 15. 30. good *r.* maketh bones
Isa. 53. 1. who hath believed our *r.*, John 12. 38. Rom. 10. 16.
2 Cor. 6. 8. by evil *r.* and good *r.*
1 Tim. 3. 7. a good *r.* of them who
Heb. 11. 2. obtained a good *r.*
R. V. Isa. 28. 19. message; Jer. 50. 43. fame; Prov. 15. 30. good tidings; 1 Tim. 3. 7. testimony; Heb. 11. 2, 39; 3 John 12. witness; Neh. 6. 19. spake of; 1 Pet. 1. 12. announced; Matt. 28. 15. spread abroad

REPROACH, Josh. 5. 9. Neh. 1. 3. Ps. 69. 7. Prov. 18. 3. Isa. 54. 4. Jer. 31. 19. Heb. 13. 13. Gen. 30. 23. Luke 1. 25.
Job 27. 6. my heart shall not *r.* me
Ps. 15. 3. up a *r.* against neighbor
20. *r.* hath broken my heart
Prov. 14. 34. sin is a *r.* to any peo.
Isa. 51. 7. fear ye not the *r.* of men
Zeph. 3. 18. to whom *r.* of it
Heb. 11. 26. esteeming the *r.* of Christ
Ps. 69. 9. *r.* of them that *reproached*
2 Cor. 12. 10. I take pleasure in *reproaches*
Prov. 14. 31. *reproacheth* his Maker
1 Pet. 4. 14. if *reproached* for name
R. V. Prov. 22. 10. ignominy; Job 20. 3. reproof; 2 Cor. 11. 21. disparagement; 12. 10. injuries; Isa. 43. 28. a reviling; Num. 15. 30. blasphemeth

REPROBATE, Jer. 6. 30. Rom. 1. 28. 1 Cor. 13. 5, 6, 7. 2 Tim. 3. 8. Tit. 1. 16.
R. V. Jer. 6. 30. refuse

REPROOF, astonished at, Job 26. 11.
Prov. 1. 23. turn ye at my *r.* I will
10. 17. he that refuseth *r.* erreth
13. 18. he that regardeth *r.* shall be honored
15. 5. he that regardeth *r.* is
10. he that hateth *r.* shall die
31. heareth *r.* abideth among wise
17. 10. *r.* entereth more into a wise
29. 15. the rod and *r.* give wisdom
2 Tim. 3. 16. Scripture profitable for *r.*
Ps. 38. 14. *reproofs*, Prov. 6. 23.
Ps. 50. 21. I will *reprove* thee, and
Prov. 9. 8. *r.* not a scorner, lest he
Hos. 4. 4. let no man strive nor *r.*
John 16. 8. *r.* world of sin
Eph. 5. 11. works of dark. but *r.*
Ps. 105. 14. he *reproved* kings
Prov. 29. 1. he that being often *r.*
John 3. 20. deeds should be *r.*
Eph. 5. 13. things that are *r.* are
Isa. 29. 21. snare from him that *reproveth* in the gate
Prov. 9. 7. that *r.* a scorner, getteth
15. 12. loveth not one that *r.* him
25. 12. *reprover*, Ezek. 3. 26.
R. V. Job 26. 11; Prov. 17. 10. rebuke; 2 Kings 19. 4; Isa. 37. 4; Jer. 29. 27. rebuke; John 16. 8. convict

REPUTATION, Eccl. 10. 1. Acts 5. 34. Gal. 2. 2. Phil. 2. 7, 29.
R. V. Eccl. 10. 1. outweigh; Acts 5. 34. honor of; Gal. 2. 2. repute; Phil. 2. 7. emptied himself

REQUEST, Ps. 106. 15. Phil. 4. 6.
R. V. Phil. 1. 4. supplication

REQUIRE, Gen. 9. 5. & 42. 22. Ezek. 3. 18, 20. & 33. 8.
Deut. 10. 12. what doth the Lord *r.*
18. 19. speak in my name, I will *r.*
1 Kings 8. 59. maintain as matter shall *r.*
Prov. 30. 7. two things I *required*
Isa. 1. 12. who *r.* this at your
Luke 12. 20. shall thy soul be *r.*
48. of him shall much be *r.*
1 Cor. 4. 2. it is *r.* of stewards to be
R. V. Neh. 5. 18. demanded; Ex. 12. 36; Prov. 30. 7; Luke 23. 23, 25. ask; Ruth 3. 11. sayest; Eccl. 3. 15. seeketh again

REQUITE, Gen. 50. 15. 2 Sam. 16. 12.
Deut. 32. 6. do ye thus *r.* the Lord
1 Tim. 5. 4. learn to *r.* their parents
2 Chron. 6. 23. by *requiting* wicked
R. V. 1 Sam. 25. 21. returned; Ps. 10. 14. take

RERE-WARD, Isa. 52. 12. & 58. 8.

RESERVE, Jer. 50. 20. 2 Pet. 2. 9.
Jer. 3. 5. will he *r.* his anger for ever
Job 21. 30. wicked is *reserved* to
1 Pet. 1. 4. inheritance *r.* in heav.
Jude 6. *r.* in everlasting chains
Jer. 5. 24. he *reserveth* the appoin.
Nah. 1. 2. *r.* wrath for his enemies
R. V. Deut. 33. 21. seated; Judg. 21. 22. took; Ruth 2. 18; Rom. 11. 4. left; Acts 25. 21; Jude 6. kept

RESIDE, Zeph. 2. 9. Matt. 1. 15.

RESIST not evil, Matt. 5. 39.
Zech. 3. 1. Satan at his right hand to *r.* him
Acts 7. 51. ye do always *r.* the Holy
2 Tim. 3. 8. so do these *r.* the truth
Jas. 4. 7. *r.* the devil and he
1 Pet. 5. 9. whom *r.* steadfast in
Rom. 9. 19. who hath *resisted* will
Heb. 12. 4. have not yet *r.* to blood
Rom. 13. 2. that *resisteth* shall
Jas. 4. 6. God *r.* proud, 1 Pet. 5. 5.
R. V. Luke 21. 15; Acts 6. 10; Rom. 9. 19; 13. 2; 2 Tim. 3. 8; 1 Pet. 5. 9. withstand; Zech. 3. 11. be adversary

RESPECT to Abel, Lord had, Gen. 4. 4. Ex. 2. 25. Lev. 26. 9. 2 Kings 13. 23.
Deut. 1. 17. ye shall not *r.* persons
2 Chron. 19. 7. nor *r.* of persons, Rom. 2. 11. Eph. 6. 9. Col. 3. 25. Acts 10. 34. Job 37. 24. 1 Pet. 1. 17.
Ps. 40. 4. *r.* not the proud
119. 6. *r.* to all thy commandments
138. 6. *r.* the lowly
Prov. 24. 23. not good to have *r.* of persons, 28. 21. Lev. 19. 15. Jas. 2. 1, 3, 9.
Heb. 11. 26. he had *r.* to recom.
R. V. Ex. 2. 25. took knowledge; Heb. 11. 26. looked; Jas. 2. 3. regard; Job 37. 24. regardeth

REST, Ex. 16. 23. & 33. 14. Deut. 12. 9.
Ps. 95. 11. not enter into my *r.*
116. 7. return to thy *r.* O my soul
132. 14. this is my *r.* here I will
Isa. 11. 10. his *r.* shall be glorious
28. 12. this is the *r.* and refreshing
62. 7. him no *r.* till he establish
Jer. 6. 16. shall find *r.* for your
Mic. 2. 10. this is not your *r.* it is
Matt. 11. 28, 29. I will give *r.* to
Acts 9. 31. had the churches *r.*
2 Thes. 1. 7. who are troubled *r.*
Heb. 4. 9. *r.* for the people of God
10. enter into his *r.*
11. enter into that *r.* lest any
Rev. 14. 11. they have no *r.* day not
Ps. 16. 9. my flesh shall *r.* in hope
37. 7. *r.* in the Lord and wait
Isa. 57. 2. in peace *r.* on their beds
20. wicked are like the troubled sea when it cannot *r.*
Hab. 3. 16. I might *r.* in the
Zeph. 3. 17. he will *r.* in his love
Rev. 14. 13. dead in the Lord, *r.*
Rom. 2. 17. art a Jew, and *restest*
Prov. 14. 33. wisdom *resteth*
Eccl. 7. 9. anger *r.* in bosom
1 Pet. 4. 14. Spirit of God *r.* upon
Num. 10. 33. *resting place*, 2 Chron. 6. 41. Prov. 24. 15. Isa. 32. 18. Jer. 50. 6.
R. V. Several changes, but none of moment

RESTORE, Ps. 51. 12. & 23. 3. & 69. 4. Isa. 58. 12. Luke 19. 8. Gal. 6. 1.
Ex. 22. 3. *restitution*, Acts 3. 21.
R. V. Job 20. 18. hath gotten; Acts 3. 21. restoration; Ex. 22. 1. pay; Lev. 24. 21. make good; 25. 28. get it back; 2 Chron. 8. 2. given

RESTRAIN, 1 Sam. 3. 13. Job 15. 4. Ps. 76. 10. Isa. 63. 15.
R. V. Gen. 11. 6. withholden

RESURRECTION, Matt. 22. 23, 28, 30. Acts 23. 8. 1 Cor. 15. 12. Heb. 6. 2.
Luke 20. 36. children of God being children of the *r.*
John 5. 29. done good to *r.* of life
11. 25. I am the *r.* and the life
Acts 17. 18. preached Jesus and *r.*
Rom. 6. 5. in likeness of his *r.*
Phil. 3. 10. power of *r.*
11. attain unto the *r.* of the dead
1 Tim. 2. 18. erred, say. that *r.* is
Heb. 11. 35 might obtain better *r.*
Rev. 20. 5. this is the first *r.*, 6.

RETAIN, Job 2. 9. John 20. 23. Prov. 3. 18. & 11. 16. Eccl. 8. 8. Rom. 1. 28.
Mic. 7. 18. *retaineth* not his anger
R. V. Job 2. 9. hold fast; Rom. 1. 28. have; Phile. 13. fain have kept

RETURN to the ground, Gen. 3. 19. *r.* to dust
1 Kings 8. 48. *r.* to thee with all
Job 1. 21. naked shall I *r.* thither
Ps. 73. 10. his people *r.* hither
116. 7. *r.* unto thy rest, O my soul
Eccl. 12. 7. dust shall *r.* to the
S. of S. 6. 13. *r.* *r.* O Shulamite
Isa. 10. 21. remnant shall *r.* to
35. 10. the ransomed of the Lord shall *r.*, 51. 11.
55. 11. my word shall not *r.* void
Jer. 3. 12. *r.* backsliding Israel
4. 1. if thou wilt *r.* *r.* unto me
Hos. 2. 7. *r.* to my first husband
5. 15. I will go and *r.* to my place
7. 16. they *r.* but not to Most High
11. 9. not *r.* to destroy Ephraim

Mal. 3. 7. *r.* to me, and I will *r.* to
Ps. 35. 13. my prayer *returned*
78. 34. they *r.* and inquired early
Amos 4. 6. ye *r.* not to me, 8-11.
1 Pet. 2. 25. are *r.* unto Shepherd
Isa. 30. 15. in *returning* and rest
Jer. 5. 3. they refused to *return*
Deut. 30. 2. *return to the Lord*,
1 Sam. 7. 3. Isa. 55. 7. Hos. 6. 1. &
3. 5. & 7. 10. & 14. 1, 7.
R. V. Several unimportant
changes, chiefly to sense of
turned, came, or bring back
REVEAL, Prov. 11. 13. Dan. 2. 19.
Job 20. 27. heaven shall *r.* his ini.
Gal. 1. 16. pleased God to *r.* his
Phil. 3. 15. God shall *r.* even this
Deut. 29. 29. those things which
are *revealed*
Isa. 22. 14. it was *r.* in mine ears
53. 1. to whom is arm of Lord *r.*
Matt. 10. 26. covered that shall
not be *r.*
11. 25. hid from wise, and *r.*
16. 17. flesh and blood hath not *r.*
Rom. 1. 17. righteous. of God *r.*
1 Cor. 2. 10. God hath *r.* them to
us
2 Thes. 1. 7. when the Lord Jesus
shall be *r.*
2. 3. fall. away, man of sin be *r.*
Prov. 20. 19. a tale-bearer *revealeth*
Amos 3. 7. *r.* his secret to servants
Rom. 2. 5. *revelation*, 16. 25. Gal.
1. 12. Eph. 1. 17. & 3. 3. 1 Pet. 1. 13.
2 Cor. 12. 1. Rev. 1. 1.
R. V. 1 Cor. 14. 30; 2 Thes. 1. 7;
1 Pet. 4. 13. revelation
REVELLINGS, Gal. 5. 21. 1 Pet.
4. 3.
REVENGE, Jer. 15. 15. 2 Cor. 7.
11. & 10. 6. Nah. 1. 2.
Ps. 79. 10. by *revenging* blood
Num. 35. 19. *revenger*, Rom. 13. 4.
R. V. Deut. 32. 42. leaders; 2 Cor.
7. 11. avenging; Jer. 15. 15; 2 Cor.
10. 6. avenge
REVERENCE my sanctuary, Lev.
19. 30.
Ps. 89. 7. to be had in *r.* of all
Eph. 5. 33. see that she *r.* her
Heb. 12. 28. serve God acceptably
with *r.*
Ps. 111. 9. and *reverend* is his name
R. V. 2 Sam. 9. 6; 1 Kings 1. 31.
obeisance; Ps. 89. 7. feared above;
Eph. 5. 33. fear
REVILE, Ex. 22. 28. Matt. 5. 11.
1 Cor. 4. 12. being *reviled* we bless
1 Pet. 2. 23. when he was *r.* *r.* not
1 Cor. 6. 10. nor *revilers* inherit
Isa. 51. 7. *revilings*, Zeph. 2. 8.
R. V. Matt. 27. 39. railed on; Mark
15. 32. reproached
REVIVE us again, Ps. 85. 6.
Isa. 57. 15. to *r.* the spirit of the
Hos. 6. 2. after two days will *r.* us
14. 7. they shall *r.* as the corn
Hab. 3. 2. *r.* thy work in midst of
Rom. 7. 9. sin *revived* and I died
14. 9. Christ died, and rose, and *r.*
Ezra 9. 8. give us a little *reviving*
R. V. Ps. 85. 6. quicken; Rom. 14.
9. lived again
REVOLT more and more, Isa. 1.
5.
Isa. 31. 6. children of Israel have
deeply *revolted*
Jer. 5. 23. this people hath a *revolting heart*
6. 28. *revolters*, Hos. 5. 2. & 9. 5.
REWARD, exceeding great, Gen.
15. 1.
Deut. 10. 17. God taketh not *r.*
Ps. 19. 11. keeping them is great *r.*
58. 11. there is a *r.* for righteous
Prov. 11. 18. that soweth righteousness sure *r.*
Isa. 3. 11. the *r.* of his hands
5. 23. who justify wicked for a *r.*
Mic. 7. 3. the judge asketh for a *r.*
Matt. 5. 12. great is your *r.* in
6. 2. verily they have their *r.*
10. 41. shall receive a prophet's *r.*
Rom. 4. 4. *r.* is not reckoned of
1 Cor. 3. 8. shall receive his own *r.*
Col. 2. 18 man beguile you of *r.*
1 Tim. 5. 18. labor. is worthy of *r.*
Heb. 2. 2. just recompense of *r.*
2 John 8. we may receive a full *r.*
Matt. 6. 4. Father shall *r.* openly
2 Tim. 4. 14. Lord *r.* him accord.
Rev. 22. 12. I come and my *r.* is
with
18. 6. *r.* her as she *rewarded* you
Ps. 103. 10. nor *r.* us according
Isa. 3. 9. *r.* evil unto themselves
Ps. 31. 25. plentifully *rewardeth*
Heb. 11. 6. *rewarder* of them that
R. V. Job 6. 22; Prov. 21. 14; Jer.
40. 5. present; Job 7. 2. wages; Ps.
40. 15; 70. 3. by reason; 94. 2. desert; Ezek. 16. 34; Hos. 2. 12;
9. 1; 1 Tim. 5. 18; 2 Pet. 2. 13;
Jude 11. hire; Obad. 15. dealing;
Col. 2. 18. prize by; 3. 24. recompense; 1 Sam. 24. 17; Matt. 16. 27;
2 Tim. 4. 14; Rev. 18. 6. render;
Deut. 32. 41; Matt. 6. 4, 6, 18. recompense; Ps. 54. 5. requite
RICH, Gen. 13. 2. & 14. 23. Ex. 30. 15.
Prov. 10. 4. hand of diligent maketh *r.*
22. bless. of the Lord maketh *r.*
13. 7. maketh himself *r.* yet
14. 20. *r.* man hath many friends
18. 11. *r.* man's wealth is
23. the *r.* answereth roughly
22. 2. *r.* and poor meet together
23. 4. labor not to be *r.*
28. 11. *r.* man is wise in his
Eccl. 5. 12. abundance of the *r.*
10. 20. curse not the *r.* in thy
Jer. 9. 23. let not *r.* man glory in
Matt. 19. 23. *r.* man hardly enter
Luke 1. 53. *r.* he sent empty away
6. 24. woe unto you that are *r.*
12. 21. layeth up, and is not *r.*
16. 1. certain *r.* man which had
18. 23. sorrow. for he was very *r.*
2 Cor. 6. 10. yet making many *r.*
8. 9. Jesus, though he was *r.*
Eph. 2. 4. God who is *r.* in mercy
1 Tim. 6. 9. they that will be *r.*
18. they that be *r.* in good works
Jas. 2. 5. poor of this world, *r.*
Rev. 2. 9. I know thy poverty, but
thou art *r.*
3. 17. sayest, I am *r.*
18. mayest be *r.*
1 Chron. 29. 12. *riches* and honor
Ps. 39. 6. he heapeth up *r.* and
52. 7. trust. in abundance of his *r.*
62. 10. if *r.* increase, set not
104. 24. the earth is full of thy *r.*
112. 3. wealth and *r.* shall be
119. 14. rejoic. as much as in all *r.*
Prov. 3. 16. in her left hand *r.*
11. 4. *r.* profit not in day of
13. 8. ransom of man's life are
his *r.*
23. 5. *r.* make themselves wings
27. 24. *r.* are not for ever, nor the
30. 8. give me neither pover. nor *r.*
Jer. 17. 11. so he that getteth *r.*
Matt. 13. 22. deceitfulness of *r.*
Luke 16. 11. your trust the true *r.*
Rom. 2. 4. despisest thou *r.* of his
9. 23. known the *r.* of his glory
2 Cor. 8. 2. abounded unto *r.* of
Eph. 1. 7. according to the *r.* of
2. 7. show exceeding *r.* of grace
Phil. 4. 19. according to his *r.* in
Col. 2. 2. unto all *r.* of the full
1 Tim. 6. 17. trust in uncertain *r.*
Heb. 11. 26. the reproach of Christ
greater *r.*
Jas. 5. 2. your *r.* are corrupted
Col. 3. 16. word of God dwell *richly*
1 Tim. 6. 17. giveth us *r.* all things
R. V. Gen. 36. 7; Dan. 11. 13, 24, 28.
substance; Josh. 22. 8; Isa. 61. 6.
wealth; Ps. 37. 16; Jer. 48. 36.
abundance; Prov. 22. 16. gain
RIDE, Ps. 45. 4. & 66. 12. Hab. 3. 8.
Deut. 33. 26. *rideth*, Ps. 68. 4, 33. Isa.
19. 1.
RIGHT, Num. 27. 7. Deut. 21. 17.
Gen. 18. 25. shall not the Judge of
the earth do *r.*
Ezra 8. 21. seek of him a *r.* way for
Job 34. 23. lay on man more than *r.*
Ps. 19. 8. statu. of the Lord are *r.*
51. 10. renew a *r.* spirit within
119. 128. I esteem all thy precepts
to be *r.*
Prov. 4. 11. I have led thee in *r.*
paths
8. 9. all *r.* to them that find
12. 5. thoughts of righteous are *r.*
14. 12. a way which seemeth *r.* to
21. 2. way of man is *r.* in own
Isa. 30. 10. prophesy not unto us *r.*
Ezek. 18. 5. be just and do lawful
and *r.*
Hos. 14. 9. ways of the Lord are *r.*
Amos 3. 10. know not to do *r.*
Mark 5. 15. and in his *r.* mind
Luke 12. 57. jud. ye not what is *r.*
Acts 4. 19. whether it be *r.* in sight
8. 21. thy heart is not *r.* in sight
13. 10. not cease to pervert *r.*
ways
Eph. 6. 1. children obey your
parents; this is *r.*
2 Pet. 2. 15. forsaken the *r.* way
Rev. 22. 14. have *r.* to tree
2 Tim. 2. 15. *rightly* dividing word
Gen. 7. 1. seen thee *righteous* be.
18. 23. wilt thou destroy *r.*
Num. 23. 10. let me die death of *r.*
Deut. 25. 1. justify *r.* and condemn
1 Kings 8. 32. justifying the *r.* to
Job 4. 7. where were the *r.* cut off
17. 9. the *r.* shall hold on his way
Ps. 1. 6. Lord knoweth way of *r.*
5. 12. wilt bless the *r.* with favor
7. 11. God judgeth the *r.*
11. 5. Lord trieth *r.* but wicked
32. 11. rejoice in the Lord ye *r.*
34. 17. *r.* cry, and Lord heareth
37. 17. the Lord upholdeth the *r.*
25. I have not seen the *r.* forsaken
29. the *r.* shall inherit the land
55. 22. shall never suffer the *r.*
58. 11 there is a reward for the *r.*
64. 10. *r.* shall be glad in the Lord
68. 3. let the *r.* be glad and rejoice
92. 12. the *r.* shall flourish like
97. 11. light is sown for the *r.*
112. 6. the *r.* shall be in everlast.
141. 5 let *r.* smite me; it shall be
Ps. 145. 17. Lord is *r.*, Lam. 1. 18.
Dan. 9. 14.
146. 8. the Lord loveth the *r.*
Prov. 3. 22. his secret is with the *r.*
10. 3. will not suffer the soul of *r.*
16. labor of the *r.* tendeth to life
21. the lips of the *r.* feed many
24. desire of the *r.* shall be grant.
25. *r.* is an everlasting foundation
28. the hope of *r.* shall be glad.
30. the *r.* shall never be removed
32. the lips of the *r.* know what
11. 8. *r.* is delivered out of
21. seed of *r.* shall be delivered
28. the *r.* shall flourish as a
30. fruit of the *r.* is a tree of life
12. 3. root of *r.* shall not be
5. the thoughts of the *r.* are *r.*
7. the house of the *r.* shall
10. a *r.* man regardeth life of
12. root of *r.* yieldeth fruit
13. 9. the light of the *r.* rejoiceth
25. *r.* eateth to satisfying of soul
14. 32. *r.* hath hope in his death
15. 6. in house of *r.* is much
29. Lord heareth the prayer of *r.*
18. 10. *r.* runneth into it and is
28. 1. the *r.* are bold as a lion
Eccl. 7. 16. be not *r.* overmuch, nor
Isa. 3. 10. say to *r.* it shall be well
41. 2. raised up *r.* man from east
57. 1. the *r.* perisheth and are
60. 21. thy people also shall be *r.*
Ezek. 3. 20. when a *r.* man turneth
Mal. 3. 18. discern between *r.* and
Matt. 9. 13. not come to call *r.* but
10. 41. shall receive *r.* man's rew.
25. 46. *r.* shall go into life eternal
Luke 1. 6. were both *r.* before God
18. 9. trusted that they were *r.*

Rom. 3. 10. there is none *r.* no not
5. 7. scarcely for a *r.* man will one
19. by the ob. of one many made *r.*
2 Thes. 1. 5. a manifest token of *r.* judgment
1 Tim. 1. 9. law is not made for a *r.*
Jas. 5. 16. fervent prayer of *r.* man
1 Pet. 4. 18. the *r.* scarcely be saved
1 John 3. 7. he that doeth righteousness is *r.* even as he is *r.*
Rev. 22. 11. he that is *r.* let him be *r.*
Tit. 2. 12. live soberly, *righteously*
Deut. 6. 25. it shall be our *righteousness*
33. 19. offer sacrifice of *r.*
Job 29. 14. I put on *r.* and it cloth.
36. 3. I will ascribe *r.* to my Maker
Ps. 11. 7. righteous Lord loveth *r.*
15. 2. walk upright and work. *r.*
97. 2. *r.* and judgment are habita.
106. 3. he that doeth *r.* at all
Prov. 10. 2. *r.* delivereth from
11. 5. *r.* of perfect shall direct way
6. *r.* of upright shall deliver them
18. to him that soweth *r.* a sure
19. *r.* tendeth to life; so evil to
12. 28. in the way of *r.* is life
13. 6. *r.* keepeth the upright in
14. 34. *r.* exalteth a nation, but sin
15. 9. he loveth him that followeth after *r.*
16. 8. better is a little with *r.* than
12. his throne is established by *r.*
Isa. 11. 5. *r.* shall be girdle of his
26. 9. inhabitants of the world will learn *r.*
28. 17. judgment to line and *r.* to
32. 17. work of *r.* shall be peace
45. 24. in the Lord have I *r.* and
46. 12. far from *r.*
13. I bring near my *r.*
54. 17. their *r.* is of me, saith Lord
61. 3. trees of *r.* planting of Lord
10. covered me with robes of *r.*
62. 1. till the *r.* thereof go forth
64. 5. that rejoiceth and work. *r.*
Jer. 23. 6. be called Lord our *r.*
Dan. 4. 27. break off thy sins by *r.*
9. 7. O Lord *r.* belongeth unto thee
12. 3. that turn many to *r.* shine
Zeph. 2. 3. seek *r.* seek meekness
Mal. 4. 2. Sun of *r.* arise with
Matt. 3. 15. it becom. to fulfil all *r.*
5. 6. hunger and thirst after *r.*
20. except your *r.* exceed the *r.* of
21. 32. John came in the way of *r.*
Luke 1. 75. in holiness and *r.* before
John 16. 8. reprove world of sin, *r.*
Acts 10. 35. he that worketh *r.* is
13. 10. thou enemy of all *r.*
24. 25. as he reasoned of *r.*
Rom. 1. 17. therein is the *r.* of God
3. 22. even *r.* of God by faith
4. 6. man to whom God imput. *r.*
11. a seal of the *r.* of faith
5. 18. by *r.* of one free gift came
21. grace reign through *r.* unto
6. 13. membe. as instruments of *r.*
18. servants of *r.* to holiness, 19.
8. 4. that the *r.* of the law might
9. 30. Gentiles who followed not after *r.* have attained to *r.* even *r.* of faith, 31.
10. 3. ignorant of *r.* of God, establish their own *r.* have not submitted to *r.* of God
5. *r.* of law
6. *r.* which is of faith
9, 10. with the heart man beli. to *r.*
14. 17. kingdom of God is *r.* peace
1 Cor. 1. 30. made unto us wisdom and *r.*
15. 34. awake to *r.* and sin not
2 Cor. 5. 21. the *r.* of God in him
6. 7. armor of *r.*
14. what fellowship hath *r.*
9. 10. increase the fruits of your *r.*
11. 15. ministers as ministers of *r.*
Gal. 2. 21. if *r.* come by the law
Eph. 6. 14. having on the breastplate of *r.*
Phil. 1. 11. being filled with fruits of *r.*
3. 6. touching *r.* of law blameless

1 Tim. 6. 11. follow *r.*, 2 Tim. 2. 22.
Tit. 3. 5. not by works of *r.* we
Heb. 12. 11. peaceable fruits of *r.*
Jas. 1. 20. man worketh not the *r.* of God
3. 18. fruit of *r.* is sown in peace
1 Pet. 3. 14. if ye suffer for *r.* happy
2 Pet. 1. 1. through the *r.* of God
2. 5. Noah a preacher of *r.*
3. 13. wherein dwelleth *r.*
1 John 2. 29. that doeth *r.* is born
3. 7. he that doeth *r.* is righteous
Rev. 19. 8. fine linen is the *r.* of saints
Gen. 15. 6. counted to him for *righteousness*, Ps. 106. 31. Rom. 4. 3, 5, 9, 22. Gal. 3. 6.
1 Kings 8. 32. *his righteousness*, Job 33. 26. Ps. 50. 6. Ezek. 3. 20. Matt. 6. 33. Rom. 3. 25. 2 Cor. 9. 9.
Ps. 17. 15. *in righteousness*, Hos. 10. 12. Acts 17. 31. Ps. 96. 13. & 98. 9. Eph. 4. 24. Rev. 19. 11.
Deut. 9. 5. *thy righteousness*, Job 35. 8. Ps. 35. 28. & 40. 10. & 51. 14. & 89. 16. & 119. 142. Isa. 57. 12. & 58. 8. & 62. 2.
Isa. 64. 6. *all our righteousness*, Ezek. 33. 13. Dan. 9. 18.
R. V. Many changes, chiefly due to context. Many changes in Job, Ps., and Prov. to upright; Ps. 67. 4; 96. 10. with equity; Rom. 2. 26; 8. 4. ordinance; Rom. 9. 28; 10. 3 —

RIGOR, Ex. 1. 13. Lev. 25. 43, 53.

RIOT, Tit. 1. 6. 1 Pet. 4. 4.
2 Pet. 2. 13. *rioting*, Rom. 13. 13.
Prov. 23. 20. *riotous*, 28. 7. Luke 15. 13.
R. V. Rom. 13. 13. revelling; 2 Pet. 2. 13. revel; Prov. 23. 20; 28. 7. gluttonous

RIPE fruit, Ex. 22. 29. Num. 18. 13. Mic. 7. 1. Jer. 24. 2; *r.* figs, Hos. 9. 10. Nah. 3. 12.
Gen. 40. 10. *ripe grapes*, Num. 13. 20.
Joel 3. 13. harvest is *r.*, Rev. 14. 15.

RISE, S. of S. 3. 2. Isa. 14. 21. & 24. 20. & 26. 14. & 33. 10. & 43. 17. & 54. 17. & 58. 10. 1 Thes. 4. 16.
Prov. 30. 31. *rising*, Luke 2. 34.
R. V. Many changes to arise; oth. frequent but suiting context

RIVER, Ex. 1. 22. & 4. 9. Job 40. 23. Ps. 36. 8. & 46. 4. & 65. 9. Isa. 48. 18. & 66. 12. Rev. 22. 1, 2.
Job 20. 17. *rivers*, 29. 9. Ps. 119. 136. Prov. 5. 16. & 21. 1. Isa. 32. 2. & 33. 21. Mic. 6. 7. John 7. 38.
R. V. Num. 34. 5; Deut. 10. 7; Josh. 15. 4, 47; 16. 8; 17. 9; 19. 11; 1 Kings 8. 65; 2 Kings 24. 7; 2 Chron. 7. 8; S. of S. 5. 12; Ezek. 47. 19; Amos 6. 14; Joel 3. 18. brook or brooks; Ezek. 6. 3; 31. 12; 32. 6; 34. 13; 35. 8; 36. 4, 6; Prov. 21. 1. water courses; Deut. 2. 24, 36; 3. 8, 12; 4. 48; Josh. 12. 1, 2; 13. 9, 16; 2 Sam. 24. 5; 2 Kings 10. 33. valley; Ex. 8. 5; Ps. 1. 3. streams; Isa. 23. 3, 10; Zech. 10. 11. Nile; Job 28. 10; Ezek. 31. 4. channels

ROAR, Isa. 42. 13. Jer. 25. 30. Hos. 11. 10. Joel 3. 16. Amos 1. 2.
R. V. Isa. 42. 13. shout aloud

ROB, Lev. 19. 13. Prov. 22. 22.
Mal. 3. 8. will a man *r.* God
Isa. 42. 22. a people *robbed* and
2 Cor. 11. 8. I *r.* other churches
Job 5. 5. the *robber* swalloweth up
John 10. 1. that climbeth up is a thief and a *r.*
Ps. 62. 10. *robbery*, Prov. 21. 7. Isa. 61. 8. Amos 3. 10. Phil. 2. 6.
R. V. Ps. 119. 61. wrapped me round; Job 5. 5; 18. 9. snare; Dan. 11. 14. children of the violent; Prov. 21. 7. violence; Nah. 3. 1. rapine

ROBE, Isa. 61. 10. Rev. 7. 9, 13, 14.
R. V. Luke 23. 11. apparel; John 19. 2. garment; Rev. 22. 14. do his commandments

ROCK, Ex. 17. 6. Num. 20. 8, 11. Deut. 32. 4, 13, 15, 18, 30, 31.
Ps. 18. 2. Lord is my *r.* and, 92. 15.
31. 3. thou art my *r.* and fortress
61. 2. lead me to the *r.* higher
62. 2. he only is my *r.* and, 6.
71. 3. thou art my *r.* and fortress
89. 26. my Father and *r.* of my
94. 22. God is the *r.* of my refuge
Matt. 7. 24. wise man built his house on a *r.*
16. 18. on this *r.* will I build
1 Cor. 10. 4. that *r.* was Christ
Rev. 6. 16. said to *rocks*, fall on us
R. V. Judg. 6. 26. stronghold; 1 Sam. 14. 4. crag; Isa. 42. 11. Sela; Luke 6. 48. well builded; Acts 27. 29. rocky ground

ROD, Ex. 4. 4, 20. Num. 17. 2, 8.
Ps. 23. 4. thy *r.* and staff comfort
125. 3. *r.* of wicked shall not rest
Prov. 13. 24. spareth *r.* hateth his
22. 15. *r.* of correction shall drive
29. 15. *r.* and reproof give wisdom
Isa. 10. 5. *r.* of my anger, staff of
Ezek. 20. 37. cause to pass under *r.*
Mic. 6. 9. hear the *r.*
Rev. 12. 5. rule with *r.* of iron, 19.
R. V. Ps. 125. 3. sceptre; Isa. 11. 1. shoot; Jer. 10. 16; 51. 19. tribe

ROOM, Prov. 18. 6. Luke 14. 22.
R. V. 2 Kings 15. 25; 1 Chron. 4. 41. stead; Ps. 31. 8; Luke 14. 9, 10; 20. 46; 1 Cor. 14. 16. place; Matt. 23. 6; Mark 12. 39. chief place; Luke 14. 7. 8. chief seat; Acts 1. 13. chamber

ROOT, Job 5. 3. & 31. 12. Ps. 52. 5.
Deut. 29. 18. a *r.* that beareth gall
Job 19. 28. seeing *r.* of the matter
Prov. 12. 3. *r.* of the righteous
Isa. 11. 10. there shall be *r.*
Matt. 3. 10. axe is laid to *r.* of tree
13. 6. because it had no *r.* it
Rom. 11. 16. if *r.* be holy, so are
1 Tim. 6. 10. love of money is *r.* of
Heb. 12. 15. lest *r.* of bitterness
Matt. 15. 13. plant Father hath not planted shall be *rooted* up
Eph. 3. 17. being *r.* and grounded
Col. 2. 7. *r.* and built up in him

ROSE, S. of S. 2. 1. Isa. 35. 1.

ROYAL diadem in hand of God, Isa. 62. 3.
Jas. 2. 8. if ye fulfil *r.* law
1 Pet. 2. 9. ye are a *r.* priesthood

RUBIES, price of wisdom is above, Job 28. 18. Prov. 3. 15. & 8. 11. & 31. 10.

RUDDY, S. of. S. 5. 10. Lam. 4. 7.

RUDIMENTS, Col. 2. 8, 20.

RULE, Esth. 9. 1. Prov. 17. 2.
Prov. 25. 28. no *r.* over own spirit
Gal. 6. 16. walk according to this *r.*
Phil. 3. 16. let us walk by same *r.*
Heb. 13. 7. which have *r.* over you
Col. 3. 15. let the peace of God *r.*
1 Tim. 3. 5. how to *r.* his own house
5. 17. let the elders that *r.*
Rev. 12. 5. man child was to *r.* all
2 Sam. 23. 3. *ruleth* over men
Ps. 103. 19. his kingdom *r.* over all
Prov. 16. 32. he that *r.* his spirit
Hos. 11. 12. Judah yet *r.* with God
Mic. 5. 2. is to be *ruler* in Israel
Matt. 25. 21. make thee *r.* over
Acts 23. 5. not speak evil of *r.*
Rom. 13. 3. *rulers* are not a terror
Eph. 6. 12. *r.* of darkness of world
R. V. 1 Kings 22. 31. command; Prov. 25. 26. restraint; Isa. 44. 13. line; 2 Cor. 10. 13, 15. province; Ezek. 22. 33. be king; Matt. 2. 6. be shepherd; Ruth 1. 1. judged; Gen. 43. 16. steward; Num. 13. 2; 1 Sam. 25. 30; 2 Sam. 6. 21; 7. 8; 1 Kings 1. 35; 1 Chron. 2. 12; 5. 2; 11. 2; 17. 7; 28. 4; 2 Chron. 6. 5; 11. 22; 29. 20; Ezra 10. 14; Neh. 11. 1; Esth. 3. 12; 8. 9; 9. 3. prince or princes; 1 Kings 11. 28; Neh. 7. 2. charge; 2 Kings 25. 22; Mark 13. 9; Luke 21. 12. governor; 2 Chron. 26. 11. officer; 2 Sam. 8. 18; 20. 26. priest; Gen. 41. 43; Matt. 24. 45, 47; 25. 21.

23. set; Deut. 1. 13; Isa. 29. 10. heads; 1 Chron. 26. 32. overseers; Jer. 51. 23, 28, 57. deputies
RUN, Gen. 49. 22. Lev. 15. 3. 1 Sam. 8. 11. Ps. 19. 5. Eccl. 1. 7. Heb. 6. 20.
2 Chron. 16. 9. eyes of the Lord *r*.
Ps. 119. 32. I will *r*. in way
S. of S. 1. 4. draw me, we will *r*.
Isa. 40. 31. shall *r*. and not be
Dan. 12. 4. many shall *r*. to and
1 Cor. 9. 24. *r*. so that we may
Gal. 2. 2. *r*. in vain
5. 7. did *r*. well
Heb. 12. 1. *r*. with patience the race
1 Pet. 4. 4. *r*. not to same excess of
Ps. 23. 5. my cup *runneth* over
Prov. 18. 10. righteous *r*. into it
Rom. 9. 16. it is not of him that *r*.
R. V. Judg. 18. 25. fall; 1 Sam. 17. 17. carry quickly; Amos 5. 24. roll; Joel 2. 9. leap upon; Matt. 9. 17. is spilled

S

SABBATH holy, Ex. 16. 23, 29. & 20. 8–11. & 31. 14. Acts 13. 42. & 18. 4.
Lev. 23. 3. seventh day is *s*. of rest
Neh. 9. 14. madest known thy *s*.
13. 18. bring wrath by profan. *s*.
Isa. 56. 2. keepeth *s*. from pollut.
58. 13. call *s*. a delight, holy
Matt. 12. 5. priests profane *s*. and
28. 1. end of *s*. as it began to dawn
Lev. 19. 3. *my sabbaths*, 30. & 26. 2. Isa. 56. 4. Ezek. 20. 12, 13. & 22. 8, 26. & 23. 38. & 44. 24. & 46. 3.
Deut. 5. 12. *sabbath day*, Neh. 13. 22. Jer. 17. 21. Acts 15. 21. Col. 2. 16.
R. V. Lev. 23. 24, 39. solemn rest; Lam. 1. 7. desolations
SACKCLOTH, Gen. 37. 34. Job 16. 15. Ps. 30. 11. & 35. 13. Isa. 22. 12. Rev. 11. 3.
SACRIFICE, Gen. 31. 54. Ex. 8. 25.
1 Sam. 2. 29. wherefore kick ye at my *s*.
3. 14. Eli's house not purg. with *s*.
15. 22. to obey is better than *s*.
Ps. 4. 5. offer *s*. of righteousness
40. 6. *s*. and offering thou
51. 16. desirest not *s*. else I would
17. *s*. of God are a broken spirit
107. 22. *s*. the *s*. of thanksgiving
141. 2. lifting up hands as even. *s*.
Prov. 15. 8. *s*. of wicked is abomination
21. 3. to do justice more acceptable than *s*.
Eccl. 5. 1. than to give *s*. of fools
Dan. 8. 11. daily *s*. was taken away
9. 27. cause *s*. and oblation to cease
11. 31. take away daily *s*., 12. 11.
Hos. 6. 6. mercy and not *s*.
Mark 9. 49. every *s*. be salted
Rom. 12. 1. present bodies a liv. *s*.
1 Cor. 5. 7. Christ our passover is *s*.
Eph. 5. 2. *s*. to God for a sweet
Phil. 2. 17. offered on *s*. of your
4. 18. a *s*. acceptable to God
Heb. 9. 26. put away sin by *s*. of
13. 15. *s*. of praise
1 Pet. 2. 5. priesthood to offer spiritual *s*.
R. V. In O. T. frequent changes to offering, oblation
SACRILEGE, commit, Rom. 2. 22.
SAD, 1 Sam. 1. 18. Ezek. 13. 22. Mark 10. 22.
Eccl. 7. 3. by *sadness* the heart is
R. V. Ezek. 13. 22. grieved; Mark 10. 22. countenance fell
SAFE, Ps. 119. 117. Prov. 18. 10. & 29. 25.
Job 5. 4. *safety*, 11. Ps. 4. 8. & 12. 5. & 33. 17. Prov. 11. 14. & 21. 31.
R. V. Ezek. 34. 27. secure; 2 Sam. 18. 29, 32. well with; Job 3. 26. ease; 24. 23. security; Prov. 21. 31. victory
SAINTS, Ps. 52. 9. & 79. 2. & 89. 5. Deut. 33. 2. came with ten thousands of *s*., Jude 14.
Deut. 33. 3. all his *s*. are in thy
1 Sam. 2. 9. keep feet of his *s*.
2 Chron. 6. 41. let thy *s*. rejoice
Job 15. 15. he putteth no trust in *s*.
Ps. 16. 3. goodness extendeth to *s*.
37. 28. Lord forsaketh not his *s*.
50. 5. gather my *s*. together
97. 10. Lord preserveth souls of *s*.
106. 16. envied Aaron *s*. of Lord
116. 15. precious in the sight of the Lord is death of *s*.
149. 9. this honor have all his *s*.
Prov. 2. 8. preserv. way of his *s*.
Hos. 11. 12. Judah is faith. with *s*.
Zech. 14. 5. shall come and all *s*.
Rom. 1. 7. called to be *s*., 1 Cor. 1. 2. 2 Cor. 1. 1. Eph. 1. 1. Col. 1. 2, 4, 12, 26.
Rom. 8. 27. intercession for *s*.
12. 13. necessity of *s*.
15. 25. minister to *s*., 26. 31. 1 Cor. 16. 1. 2 Cor. 8. 4. & 9. 1. Heb. 6. 10.
1 Cor. 6. 2. *s*. shall judge the world
Eph. 3. 8. less than the least of all *s*.
4. 12. for perfecting the *s*. for
1 Thes. 3. 13. coming of Jesus with all his *s*.
2 Thes. 1. 10. come to be glorified in his *s*.
Rev. 5. 8. prayers of the *s*., 8. 3, 4.
11. 18. reward of *s*.
14. 11. patience of *s*.
15. 3. King of *s*.
16. 16. blood of *s*., 17. 6. & 18. 24.
19. 8. righteousness of *s*.
R. V. Deut. 33. 2; 1 Sam. 2. 9; Job 5. 11; 15. 15; Ps. 89. 5, 7; Dan. 8. 13; Hos. 11. 12; Zech. 14. 5; Jude 14. holy one, or ones; Rev. 15. 3. ages
SALT, Gen. 19. 26. Lev. 2. 13. Matt. 5. 13. Mark 9. 49, 50. Col. 4. 6.
R. V. Mark 9. 49 ——
SALVATION, Ps. 14. 7. & 53. 6.
Ex. 14. 13. stand still and see the *s*.
Ps. 3. 8. *s*. belongeth only to Lord
50. 23. I will show him the *s*. of
68. 20. God is the God of *s*., 65. 5.
85. 9. his *s*. is nigh them that
98. 2. made known his *s*.
119. 155. *s*. is far from the wicked
149. 4. Lord will beautify the meek with *s*.
Isa. 25. 9. we will rejoice in his *s*.
26. 1. *s*. will God appoint for walls
33. 2. our *s*. also in the
46. 13. I will place *s*. in Zion for
52. 7. him that publisheth *s*.
59. 16. arm brought *s*. unto me
17. for a helmet of *s*., Eph. 6. 17.
Ps. 60. 18. call thy walls *s*. thy
62. 1 *s*. as a lamp
Jer. 3. 23. in vain is *s*. hoped for
Lam. 3. 26. quietly wait for *s*.
Jonah 2. 9. *s*. is of the Lord
Hab. 3. 8. ride on thy char. of *s*.
Zech. 9. 9. king cometh having *s*.
Luke 19. 9. *s*. is come to thy house
John 4. 22. *s*. is of the Jews
Acts 4. 12. neither is there *s*. in
13. 26. word of *s*. sent
Rom. 1. 16. Gospel is the power of God to *s*.
11. 11. through their fall *s*. is come
2 Cor. 1. 6. for your *s*.
Eph. 1. 13. the Gospel of your *s*.
Phil. 2. 12. work out your own *s*.
1 Thes. 5. 8. hope of *s*.
2 Thes. 2. 13. hath chosen you to *s*.
2 Tim. 2 10. to obtain *s*. with eter.
3. 15. scriptures able to make wise unto *s*.
Tit. 2. 11. grace of God bringeth *s*.
Heb. 1. 14. who shall be heirs of *s*.
2. 3. how escape if we neglect so great *s*.
10. make Captain of our *s*. perfect
6. 9. things that accompany *s*.
9. 28. appear without sin unto *s*.
1 Pet. 1. 5. kept through faith to *s*.
Jude 3. write unto you of com. *s*.
Rev. 7. 10. *s*. to our God, 12. 10. & 19. 1.
Ex. 15. 2. God is become *my salvation*, Job 13. 16. Ps. 18. 2. & 25. 5. & 27. 1. & 38. 22. & 51. 14. & 62. 7. & 88. 1. & 118. 14. Isa. 12. 2. Mic. 7. 7. Hab. 3. 18.
Ps. 89. 26. rock of —
140. 7. strength of —
2 Sam. 23. 5. thy covenant is all —
Isa. 46. 13. — shall not tarry, 49. 6. & 51. 5, 6, 8. & 56. 1.
Gen. 49. 18. *thy salvation*, 1 Sam. 2. 1. Ps. 9. 14. & 13. 5. & 20. 5. & 18. 35. & 21. 1, 5. & 35. 3. & 40. 10, 16. & 51. 12. & 69. 13, 29. & 70. 4. & 71. 15. & 85. 7. & 106. 4. & 119. 41, 81, 123, 166, 174. Isa. 17. 10. & 62. 11. Luke 2. 30.
R. V. 1 Sam. 11. 13; 2 Sam. 22. 51; Ps. 68. 20. deliverance; 1 Sam. 19. 5. victory; Jer. 3. 23. help; 2 Cor. 1. 6 ——
SAME, Ps. 102. 27. Heb. 13. 8. Rom. 10. 2. 1 Cor. 12. 4, 5, 6. Eph. 4. 10.
SANCTIFY, Ex. 13. 2. & 19. 10.
Ex. 31. 13. I am Lord that doth *s*.
Lev. 20. 7. *s*. yourselves and be holy
Num. 20. 12. believed me not, to *s*.
Isa. 8. 13. *s*. the Lord of hosts
Ezek. 28. 23. I will *s*. myself
Joel 1. 14. *s*. a fast
John 17. 17. *s*. them through truth
19. for their sakes I *s*. myself
Eph. 5. 26. might *s*. and cleanse it
1 Thes. 5. 23. God of peace *s*. you
Heb. 13. 12. that he might *s*. people
1 Pet. 3. 15. *s*. the Lord God in
Gen. 2. 3. blessed the seventh day and *sanctified* it
Lev. 10. 3. I will be *s*. in them
Deut. 32. 51. ye *s*. me not in midst
Job 1. 5. Job sent and *s*. them
Isa. 5. 16. God that is holy shall be *s*.
13. 3. commanded my *s*. ones
Jer. 1. 5. before thou camest I *s*.
Ezek. 20. 41. be *s*. in you before the heathen, 28. 22, 25. & 38. 16. & 39. 27.
John 10. 36. whom Father hath *s*.
Acts 20. 32. inheritance among all them which are *s*., 26. 18.
Rom. 15. 16. offering of Gent. *s*.
1 Cor. 1. 2. *s*. in Christ Jesus
7. 14. unbelieving husband is *s*.
1 Tim. 4. 5. *s*. by word and
2 Tim. 2. 21. *s*. and meet for mas.
Heb. 2. 11. they who are *s*. all
Matt. 23. 17. temple that *sanctifieth*
1 Cor. 1. 30. *sanctification*, 1 Thes. 4. 3, 4. 2 Thes. 2. 13. 1 Pet. 1. 2.
R. V. Gen. 2. 3; 2 Chron. 7. 16, 20. hallowed: Deut. 5. 12. keep it holy; 1 Sam. 21. 5. be holy; Isa. 13. 3. consecrated; Jude 1. beloved
SANCTUARY, Ps. 63. 2. & 73. 17. Isa. 8. 14. Ezek. 11. 16. Dan. 9. 17. Heb. 9. 2.
R. V. Ezek. 45. 2; Heb. 9. 2; 13. 11. holy place
SAND, Gen. 22. 17. & 32. 12. Job 6. 3. & 29. 18. Isa. 10. 22. Matt. 7. 26.
SATAN provoked David, 1 Chron. 21. 1.
Job 1. 6. *s*. came also among
Ps. 109. 6. let *s*. stand at his right
Matt. 4. 10. get thee hence *s*.
Luke 10. 18. I beheld *s*. as light.
22. 31. *s*. hath desired to

Acts 26. 18. turn from power of *s*.
Rom. 16. 20. God shall bruise *s*.
1 Cor. 5. 5. deliver such a one to *s*.
7. 5. that *s*. tempt you not for
2 Cor. 2. 11. let *s*. get advantage
11. 14. *s*. is transformed into angel
12. 7. messenger of *s*. to
1 Tim. 1. 20. I have delivered to *s*.
Rev. 2. 9. synagogue of *s*.
24. depth of *s*.
SATIATE, Jer. 31. 14, 25. & 46. 10.
SATISFY, Job 38. 27. Prov. 6. 30.
Ps. 90. 14. O *s*. us early with mercy
91. 16. with long life I will *s*. him
103. 5. who *s*. thy mouth with
107. 9. he *s*. the longing soul
132. 15. will *s*. her poor with
Prov. 5. 19. breasts *s*. thee at all
Isa. 55. 2. that which *s*. not
Ps. 17. 15. *satisfied* with thy like.
22. 26. meek shall eat and be *s*.
63. 5. soul shall be *s*. as with
65. 4. *s*. with goodness of house
Prov. 14. 14. good man *s*. from
27. 20. eyes of man are never *s*.
30. 15. are three things never *s*.
Eccl. 5. 10. that loveth silver shall not be *s*.
Isa. 9. 20. shall eat and not be *s*.
66. 11. be *s*. with breasts of her
Jer. 31. 14. my people be *s*. with
Ezek. 16. 28. couldest not be *s*.
Amos 4. 8. they were not *s*.
Hab. 2. 5. his desire cannot be *s*.
Num. 35. 31. shall take no *satisfaction*, 32.
R. V. Prov. 12. 11. have plenty; 18. 20. filled
SAVE your lives, preserve and, Gen. 45. 7.
Gen. 50. 20. for good to *s*. much
Job 22. 29. he shall *s*. the humble
Ps. 18. 27. wilt *s*. afflicted people
28. 9. *s*. thy people and lift them
69. 35. God will *s*. Zion
72. 4. *s*. children of needy
13. *s*. souls of needy
86. 2. *s*. thy servant
109. 31. poor to *s*. him
118. 25. *s*. now; send prosperity
Prov. 20. 22. he shall *s*. thee
Isa. 35. 4. God will come and *s*.
45. 20. cannot *s*., 59. 1. Jer. 9. 14.
Isa. 49. 25. I will *s*. thy children
Ezek. 18. 27. shall *s*. his soul
36. 29. I will *s*. from all unclean.
Hos. 1. 7. I will *s*. them by Lord
Zeph. 3. 17. he will *s*.
19. *s*. her that halteth
Zech. 8. 7. I will *s*. my people
Matt. 1. 21. *s*. his people from sins
16. 25. who will *s*. his life shall
8. 11. Son of man is come to *s*. that which was lost, Luke 19. 10.
Mark 3. 4. is it lawful to *s*. life or
John 12. 47. not to judge but to *s*.
Acts 2. 40. *s*. yourselves from this
1 Cor. 1. 21. by foolishness of preaching to *s*.
9. 22. became all, that I might *s*.
1 Tim. 1. 15. to *s*. sinners, of whom
Heb. 7. 25. able to *s*. to the utter.
Jas. 1. 21. word able to *s*.
2. 14. faith *s*.
5. 15. faith shall *s*. sick
20. converts a sinner shall *s*. soul
Jude 23. others *s*. with fear
Ps. 6. 4. *save me*, 55. 16. & 57. 3. & 119. 94. Jer. 17. 14. John 12. 27.
Isa. 25. 9. *save us*, 33. 22. & 37. 20. Hos. 14. 3. Matt. 8. 25. 1 Pet. 3. 21.
Ps. 44. 7. thou hast *saved* us from
106. 8. *s*. them for his name's sake
Isa. 45. 22. look . . and be ye *s*.
Jer. 4. 14. mayest be *s*.
8. 20. we are not *s*.
Matt. 19. 25. who then can be *s*., Luke 18. 29.
Luke 1. 71. be *s*. from our enemies
7. 50. thy faith hath *s*. thee
13. 23. are few *s*.
23. 35. he *s*. others
John 3. 17. through him be *s*.
Acts 2. 47. added to church such as should be *s*.
4. 12. name whereby be *s*.
16. 30. what must I do to be *s*.
Rom. 8. 24. we are *s*. by hope
10. 1. prayer for Israel that they may be *s*.
1 Cor. 1. 18. to us who are *s*. it is
Eph. 2. 5. by grace ye are *s*., 8.
1 Tim. 2. 4. all men to be *s*.
Tit. 3. 5. according to his mercy *s*.
1 Pet. 4. 18. righteous scarcely be *s*.
Rev. 21. 24. nations which are *s*.
Ps. 80. 3. *shall be saved*, 7. 19. Isa. 45. 17. & 64. 5. Jer. 23. 6. & 30. 7. Matt. 10. 22. & 24. 13. Mark 16. 16. Acts 16. 31. Rom. 5. 10, 11, 26. 1 Tim. 2. 15.
2 Sam. 22. 3. God my refuge and my *Saviour*
2 Kings 13. 5. Lord gave Israel a *S*.
Ps. 106. 21. forgat God their *S*.
Isa. 43. 3. I am thy *S*., 49. 26.
11. besides me is no *S*., Hos. 13. 4.
45. 15. of Israel, the *S*., Jer. 14. 8.
Obad. 21. *S*. shall come up on
Luke 1. 47. rejoiced in God my *S*.
2. 11. to you is born a *S*. which is
Acts 5. 31. him hath God exalted to be a *S*.
Eph. 5. 23. Christ is head and *S*.
1 Tim. 4. 10. who is the *S*. of all men, 1. 1; God our *S*., Tit. 1. 4. & 2. 10, 13. & 3. 4, 6. 2 Pet. 1. 1, 11. Jude 25.
2 Pet. 2. 20. knowledge of our *S*.
SAVOR, sweet, Gen. 8. 21. Ex. 29. 18. Lev. 1. 9. & 2. 9. & 3. 16.
S. of S. 1. 3. of *s*. of thy good oint.
2 Cor. 2. 14. the *s*. of his knowledge
15. are to God a sweet *s*. of Christ
16. to one *s*. of death
Eph. 5. 2. sacrifice to God of sweet smelling *s*.
Matt. 16. 23. *savorest* not things of God
SAY, Matt. 3. 9. & 5. 22, 28, 32, 34, 39, 44. & 7. 22. & 23. 3. 1 Cor. 12. 3.
R. V. Frequent changes to speak, tell, etc.
SCAB, Lev. 13. 1; Deut. 28. 27; Isa. 3. 17.
SCARCELY, Rom. 5. 7. 1 Pet. 4. 18.
SCATTER them in Israel, Gen. 49. 7.
Num. 10. 35. let thine enemies be *scattered*
Matt. 9. 36. *s*. abroad as sheep
Luke 1. 51. *s*. proud in imagination
Prov. 11. 21. that *scattereth* and yet
SCEPTRE not depart from Judah, Gen. 49. 10.
Num. 24. 17. a *s*. shall rise out of
Ps. 45. 6. the *s*. of thy kingdom is
Zech. 10. 11. *s*. of Egypt shall de.
R. V. 2 Sam. 18. 8; Job 37. 1. spread; Ps. 60. 1. broken down; Prov. 20. 26. winnoweth; Isa. 18. 2. tall; 30. 30. a blast; Dan. 12. 7. breaking in pieces; Ezek. 12. 15; Acts 5. 36. disperse; Jas. 1. 1; 1 Pet. 1. 1. the Dispersion
SCHISM, 1 Cor. 1. 10. &. 12. 25.
SCHOLAR, 1 Chron. 25. 8. Mal. 2. 12.
Gal. 3. 24. the law was our *schoolmaster*
R. V. Mal. 2. 12. that answereth
SCOFFERS, Hab. 1. 10. 2 Pet. 3. 3.
R. V. Mal. 2. 12. that answereth
SCORN, Job 16. 20. Ps. 44. 13.
Prov. 9. 8. reprove not a *scorner*
14. 6. a *s*. seeketh wisdom and
1. 22. *scorners* delight in scorning
3. 34. he *scorneth* the *s*. but giveth
9. 12. if thou *scornest* thou
Ps. 1. 1. *scornful*, Prov. 29. 8. Isa. 28. 14.
R. V. Job 12. 4. laughing-stock; Hab. 1. 10. derision; Prov. 19. 28. mocketh at
SCORPIONS, 2 Chron. 10. 11. Ezek. 2. 6.
SCOURGE of the tongue, Job 5. 21.
Isa. 28. 15. overflowing *s*., 18.
Heb. 12. 6. Lord *scourgeth* every
R. V. Lev. 19. 20. punished
SCRIPTURE of truth, Dan. 10. 21.
Matt. 22. 29. err, not knowing *s*.
John 5. 39. search *s*., Acts 17. 11. & 18. 24.
Rom. 15. 4. through comfort of *s*.
2 Tim. 3. 15. from a child known *s*.
16. all *s*. is given by inspiration
2 Pet. 1. 20. no prophecy of *s*. is of private interpretation
R. V. Dan. 10. 21. writing; 2 Tim 3. 15. holy writing; Mark 15. 28 ——
SCROLL, the heavens compared to, Isa. 34. 4; Rev. 6. 14.
SEA, Ps. 35. 7. & 72. 8. Prov. 8 29. Isa. 48. 18. & 57. 20. Zech. 9. 10. Rev. 4. 6. & 10. 2. & 15. 2. & 21. 1.
SEAL upon thine heart, S. of S. 8. 6.
John 3. 33. set to his *s*. that God is
Rom. 4. 11. *s*. of the righteousness
1 Cor. 9. 2. *s*. of my apostleship
2 Tim. 2. 19. having *s*. Lord know.
Rev. 7. 2. angel having *s*. of living
Deut. 32. 34. *sealed* up among
Job 14. 17. my transgression is *s*.
S. of S. 4. 12. spring shut up, fountain *s*.
John 6. 27. hath God the Father *s*.
2 Cor. 1. 22. who hath *s*. us and
Eph. 1. 13. ye were *s*. with the
Rev. 5. 1. a book *s*. with seven
7. 3. *s*. the servants of our God
4. were *s*. a hundred and forty
R. V. Rev. 7. 5-8 ——
SEARCH out resting place, Num. 10. 33.
Ps. 139. 23. *s*. me, O God, and
Prov. 25. 27. men to *s*. own glory
Jer. 17. 10. I the Lord *s*. the heart
29. 13. when ye shall *s*. with me
Lam. 3. 40. *s*. and try our ways
Zeph. 1. 12. *s*. Jerusalem with
Acts 17. 11. *s*. Scriptures, John 5. 39.
1 Chron. 28. 9. the Lord *searcheth* all hearts
1 Cor. 2. 10. Spirit *s*. deep things
Rev. 2. 23. I am he that *s*. the
Job 10. 6. that *searchest* after my
Prov. 2. 4. *s*. for her as for hidden
Judg. 5. 16. great *searchings* of
R. V. Job 38. 16. recesses; Gen. 31. 34, 37. felt about; Num. 10. 33; Deut. 1. 33. seek; Num. 13. 2, 21, 32; 14. 6, 7, 34, 36, 38; Deut. 1. 24. spy or spied out; Acts 17. 11. examining; Num. 13. 25. spying out
SEARED, with hot iron, 1 Tim. 4. 2.
SEASON, Gen. 40. 4. Ex. 13. 10.
Ps. 1. 3. bring. forth fruit in his *s*.
Eccl. 3. 1. to . . thing there is a *s*.
Isa. 50. 4. to speak a word in *s*.
Luke 4. 13. depart. from him for *s*.
John 5. 35. willing for a *s*. to re.
Acts 1. 7. know the times and *s*.
14. 17. gave us rain and fruitful *s*.
1 Thes. 5. 1. of times and *s*. ye
2 Tim. 4. 2. instant in *s*. and out
Heb. 11. 25. pleasures of sin for a *s*.
1 Pet. 1. 6. for a *s*. ye are in heav.
Col. 4. 6. let speech be *seasoned*
R. V. Josh. 24. 7. days; 1 Chron. 21. 29; Luke 23. 8; Acts 20. 18; Rev. 6. 11; 20. 3. time; Acts 19. 22; 1 Pet. 1. 6. while; John 5. 4 ——
SECOND COMING, Christ's, Acts 1. 11.
SECOND DEATH, Rev. 20. 14.
SECRET, Gen. 49. 6. Job 40. 13.
Job 11. 6. show thee *s*. of wisdom
29. 4. *s*. of God on my tabernacle
Ps. 25. 14. *s*. of Lord is with them
31. 20. hide them in *s*. presence
Prov. 3. 32. his *s*. is with righteous
9. 17. bread eaten in *s*. is pleasant
11. 13. talebearer revealeth *s*.
25. 9. discover not *s*. to another
Dan. 2. 28. a God that revealeth *s*.
Amos 3. 7. revealeth his *s*. unto
Matt. 6. 4. alms in *s*. Father seeth in *s*.

John 18. 20. in *s*. have I said no.
19. 38. *secretly* for fear of Jews
Rom. 2. 16. when God shall judge *secrets* of men
R. V. Gen. 49. 6. council; Judg. 13. 18. wonderful; Job 40. 13; Ps. 19. 12; Prov. 27. 5; Eccl. 12. 14; Matt. 13. 35. hidden; Ps. 10. 8; 27. 5; 31. 20; S. of S. 2. 14. covert; Ps. 18. 11. hiding; Job 20. 26. treasures; Matt. 24. 26. inner; Luke 11. 33. cellar; 1 Sam. 23. 9——; Ps. 10. 9. the covert
SECT, Acts 24. 5. & 26. 5. & 28. 22.
SEDITION, Gal. 5. 20; 2 Pet. 2. 19.
SEDUCE, Ezek. 13. 10. Mark 13. 22. 2 Tim. 3. 13. *seducers*, 1 Tim. 4. 1.
R. V. Isa. 19. 13; Mark 13. 22; 1 John 2. 26. go or lead astray
SEE, Ps. 34. 8. Matt. 5. 8. John 16. 22. 1 John 3. 2. Rev. 1. 7. & 22. 4.
Matt. 6. 1. before men to be *seen* of
13. 17. to see and have not *s*.
23. 5. their works to be *s*.
John 1. 18. no man hath *s*. God
14. 9. he that hath *s*. me hath *s*. the Father
20. 29. thou hast *s*. and believed
2 Cor. 4. 18. look not at things *s*.
1 Tim. 6. 16. no man hath *s*.
Heb. 11. 1. evidence of things not *s*.
1 Pet. 1. 8. having not *s*. ye love
1 John 1. 1. that which we have *s*.
12. no man hath *s*. God at any
Job 10. 4. seest thou as man *seeth*
John 12. 17. because it *s*. him not
12. 45. he that *s*. me, *s*. him that
SEED, Gen. 1. 11. & 17. 7. & 38. 9.
Ps. 126. 6. bearing precious *s*.
Eccl. 11. 6. in morning sow thy *s*
Isa. 55. 10. give *s*. to the sower
Matt. 13. 38. good *s*. are children
Luke 8. 11. good *s*. is word of God
1 Pet. 1. 23. born again not of corruptible *s*.
1 John 3. 9. his *s*. remaineth in
Ps. 37. 28. *s*. of wicked shall be
69. 36. *s*. of his servants
Prov. 11. 21. *s*. of righteous
Isa. 1. 4. sinful nation *s*. of evil
14. 20. the *s*. of evil doers
45. 5. all *s*. of Israel be justified
Mal. 2. 15. might seek a godly *s*.
Rom. 9. 8. children are count. for *s*.
Gal. 3. 16. not to *seeds* but to thy *s*.
SEEK, Ezra 8. 21. Job 5. 8. Ps. 10. 15.
Deut. 4. 29. if thou *s*. him with all the heart, 1 Chron. 28. 9. 2 Chron. 15. 2. Jer. 29. 13.
2 Chron. 19. 3. prepare heart to *s*. God, 30. 19.
Ezra 8. 22. them for good that *s*.
Ps. 9. 10. forsake them that *s*.
63. 1. God, early will I *s*. thee
69. 32. heart. live that *s*. God
119. 2. bless. are they that *s*. him
Prov. 8. 17. that *s*. me early
S. of S. 3. 2. *s*. him whom soul lov.
Isa. 26. 9. my spirit will I *s*. thee
45. 19. I said not *s*. me in vain
Jer. 29. 13. he shall *s*. me and
Amos 5. 4. *s*. me and ye shall live
Zeph. 2. 3. *s*. Lord, *s*. righteous.
Mal. 2. 7. *s*. the law
Matt. 6. 33. *s*. first kingdom of God
7. 7. *s*. and ye shall find
Luke 13. 24. many will *s*. to enter
19. 10. to *s*. and to save that which is lost, Matt. 18. 11.
John 8. 21. shall *s*. me and not
Rom. 2. 7. *s*. for glory, honor
1 Cor. 10. 24. let no man *s*. own
13. 5. charity *s*. not her own
Phil. 2. 21. all *s*. their own, not
Col. 3. 1. *s*. things which are above
1 Pet. 3. 11. *s*. peace and ensue it
Lam. 3. 25. to soul that *seeketh*
John 4. 23. the Father *s*. such
1 Pet. 5. 8. *seeking* whom he may
SEEM, Gen. 27. 12. Deut. 25. 3.
1 Cor. 11. 16. if any man *s*. conten.
Heb. 4. 1. lest any *s*. to come short
Jas. 1. 26. if any *s*. to be religious
Luke 8. 18. taken that he *seemeth*
1 Cor. 3. 18. if any man *s*. wise
Heb. 12. 11. no chastening *s*. joyous
SELF-DENIAL, Prov. 23. 2. Jer. 35. Luke 3. 11. & 14. 33. Acts 2. 45. Rom. 6. 12. & 8. 13. & 14. 20. & 15. 1. 1 Cor. 10. 23. & 13. 5. & 24. 33. Gal. 5. 24. Phil. 2. 4. Tit. 2. 12. 1 Pet. 2. 11.
Christ an example of, Matt. 4. 8. & 8. 20. Rom. 15. 3. Phil. 2. 6.
incumbent on His followers, Matt. 10. 38. & 16. 24. Mark 8. 34. Luke 9. 23.
SELF-EXAMINATION enjoined, Lam. 3. 40. Ps. 4. 4. 1 Cor. 11. 28. 2 Cor. 13. 5.
SELFISHNESS, Isa. 56. 11. Rom. 15. 1. 1 Cor. 10. 24. 2 Cor. 5. 15. Phil. 2. 4, 21. 2 Tim. 3. 2. Jas. 2. 8.
SELF-WILL, Ps. 75. 5. Tit. 1. 7. 2 Pet. 2. 10.
SELL me thy birthright, Gen. 25. 31.
Prov. 23. 23. buy truth and *s*. it
Matt. 19. 21. go *s*. that thou hast
25. 9. go to them that *s*. and buy
13. 44. he *selleth* all and buyeth
R. V. Jas. 4. 13. trade
SENATORS, Ps. 105. 22.
SEND help from the sanctuary, Ps. 20. 2.
Ps. 43. 3. O *s*. out thy light and
57. 3. he shall *s*. from heaven
Matt. 9. 38. *s*. forth laborers into
John 14. 26. the Father will *s*.
16. 7. if I depart I will *s*. him
2 Thes. 2. 11. *s*. them strong delus.
R. V. Gen. 12. 20. brought; Judg. 5. 15. rushed forth; other changes of slight moment, and chiefly dependent on antecedent or consequent word
SENSE, Neh. 8. 8. Heb. 5. 14.
Jas. 3. 15. *sensual*, Jude 19.
SENTENCE, Deut. 17. 9. Da[illegible] 12.
Prov. 16. 10. a divine *s*. is in lips
2 Cor. 1. 9. we had *s*. of death in
R. V. Jer. 4. 12; Acts 15. 19. judgment
SEPARATE, Gen. 13. 9. Ex. 33. 16.
Gen. 49. 6. head of him that was *s*. from his brethren, Deut. 33. 16.
Deut. 29. 21. Lord shall *s*. him
Isa. 59. 2. iniquities have *separated*
Acts 13. 2. *s*. me Saul and Barna.
19. 9. departed and *s*. the disciples
Rom. 8. 35. who *s*. us from Christ
2 Cor. 6. 17. come out, be ye *s*.
Gal. 1. 15. who *s*. me from moth.
Heb. 7. 26. holy, harmless, *s*. from
R. V. Num. 6. 2. make special; Jer. 37. 12. receive his portion; Hos. 4. 14. go apart; 9. 10. consecrated
SERAPHIMS, Isa. 6. 2, 6.
SERMON on the mount, Matt. 5–7. Luke 6. 20. *See* CHRIST.
SERPENT, Gen. 3. 1, 13. & 49. 17.
Num. 21. 6. Lord sent fiery *s*., 8. 9.
Prov. 23. 32. it biteth like a *s*.
Eccl. 10. 11. *s*. will bite without
Matt. 7. 10. will he give him a *s*.
10. 16. be wise as *s*. harmless as
John 3. 14. as Moses lifted up *s*.
2 Cor. 11. 3. as the *s*. beguiled Eve
Rev. 12. 9. that old *s*. called devil
R. V. Deut. 32. 24. crawling things; Jas. 3. 7. creeping things
SERVE the Lord with all thy heart, Deut. 10. 12, 20. & 11. 13. Josh. 22. 5. 1 Sam. 12. 20.
Deut. 13. 4. shall *s*. him, and cleave
Josh. 24. 14. fear the Lord, *s*. him
15. choose this day whom ye will *s*. . . . me and my house, we will *s*. the Lord
1 Sam. 12. 24. fear the Lord, *s*. him
Job 21. 15. what is the Almighty that we should *s*. him
Ps. 2. 11. *s*. Lord with fear, rejoice
Isa. 43. 24. made me to *s*. with sins
Matt. 6. 24. no man can *s*. two masters; ye cannot *s*. God and mam.
Luke 1. 74. *s*. him in holiness
12. 37. will come forth and *s*.
John 12. 26. if any man *s*. me let
Acts 6. 2. leave word of God and *s*. tables
27. 23. whose I am, and whom I *s*.
Rom. 1. 9. whom I *s*. with my spirit
6. 6. henceforth should not *s*. sin
7. 25. *s*. law of God
Col. 3. 24. *s*. Lord Jesus Christ
Gal. 5. 13. by love *s*. one another
1 Thes. 1. 9. to *s*. living God
Heb. 12. 28. may *s*. God accept.
Rev. 7. 15. *s*. him day and night
Prov. 29. 19. a *servant* will not be
Isa. 24. 2. with *s*. so with his mas.
42. 1. behold my *s*., 49. 3. & 52. 13.
Matt. 20. 27. be chief, let him be *s*.
25. 21. well done, good and faithful *s*., 23.
John 8. 34. committeth sin is *s*.
13. 16. *s*. is not greater than his
1 Cor. 7. 21. called, being a *s*.
9. 19. I made myself *s*. to
Gal. 1. 10. pleased men, not *s*.
Phil. 2. 7. took on him form of a *s*.
2 Tim. 2. 24. *s*. of Lord must not
Ezra 5. 11. *servants* of the God of heaven, Dan. 3. 26. Acts 16. 17. 1 Pet. 2. 16. Rev. 7. 3.
Rom. 6. 16. yield yourselves *s*. to obey, his *s*. ye are, whom ye obey
19. members *s*. to uncleanness
1 Cor. 7. 23. ye the *s*. of men
Phil. 1. 1. *s*. of Christ
2 Pet. 2. 19. *s*. of corruption
Rev. 22. 3. his *s*. shall serve him
Rom. 12. 1. reasonable *service*
Luke 10. 40. cumbered about much *serving*
Acts 20. 19. *s*. Lord with all humil.
26. 7. tribes instantly *s*. God
Rom. 12. 11. fervent in spirit *s*. Lord
Tit. 3. 3. *s*. divers lusts and pleas.
R. V. Gen. 26. 14. household; 44. 10, 16, 17. bondmen; Gen. 14. 14. 1 Sam. 24. 7. men; 1 Sam. 16. 18; 25. 19; 2 Sam. 21. 2. young men; Ex. 33. 11; Num. 11. 28; Mark 9. 35. minister; Deut. 15. 18. hireling; 2 Kings 10. 19. worshippers; Ezra 2. 65; Eccl. 2. 7. menservants; Matt. 26. 58; Mark 14. 54. officers; John 8. 34, 35; 1 Cor. 7. 21, 22, 23; Gal. 4. 1, 7; 1 Pet. 2. 16; 2 Pet. 2. 19. bondservant; Gen. 39. 4; 40. 4; 2 Chron. 29. 11; Esth. 1. 10; Ps. 101. 6, Isa. 56. 6. minister; 19. 23. worship; Jer. 40. 10; 52. 12. stand before; Ezek. 48. 18, 19. labor in; Ex. 35. 19; 39. 1, 41; 1 Chron. 9. 28. ministering; Num. 4. 47, & 24. work; Rom. 15. 31. ministration; Gal. 4. 8. bondage; Rev. 2. 19. ministry; 2 Cor. 11. 8. minister unto
SERVILE work forbidden on holy days, Lev. 23. 7. Num. 28. 18 & 29. 1.
SET, Ps. 2. 6. & 4. 3. & 12. 5. & 16. 8. & 54. 8. & 75. 7. & 113. 8. Prov. 1. 25. S. of S. 8. 6. Rom. 3. 25. Col. 3. 2.
R. V. Frequent changes, chiefly due to antecedent and consequent words
SETTLE, Luke 21. 14. 1 Pet. 5. 10.
Col. 1. 23. if ye continue in faith, *settled*
R. V. Ezek. 36. 11. cause to be inhabited; 1 Pet. 5. 10——
SEVENTY elders, the, Ex. 18. 25. Num. 11. 16.
years' captivity foretold, Jer. 25. 11.
weeks, Daniel's prophecy concerning, Dan. 9. 24.
disciples, Christ's charge to, Luke 10.
SEVERITY, goodness and, Rom. 11. 22.
SHADE, Lord is thy, Ps. 121. 5.

SHADOW, our days are as a, 1 Chron. 29. 15. Eccl. 8. 13. & 6. 12. Job 8. 9. Ps. 107. 11. & 109. 23. & 144. 4.
Ps. 17. 8. hide me under the *s.* of thy wings, 36. 7. & 57. 1. & 63. 7.
S. of S. 2. 3. I sat under his *s.*
Isa. 4. 6. for a *s.* from heat
49. 2. in *s.* of his hand hath he
Jer. 6. 4. *s.* of evening are stretch.
Acts 5. 15. *s.* of Peter might
Col. 2. 17. *s.* of things to come
Jas. 1. 17. no variableness nor *s.*

SHAKE heaven and earth, Hag. 2. 6, 21.
Hag. 2. 7. I will *s.* all nations
Matt. 10. 14. *s.* off the dust of feet
11. 7. a reed *shaken* with the wind
Luke 6. 38. good measure *s.* toget.
2 Thes. 2. 2. be not soon *s.* in mind
Ps. 44. 14. *shaking*, Isa. 17. 6. & 24. 13. & 30. 32. Ezek. 37. 7. & 38. 19.
R. V. Lev. 26. 36. driven; Job 16. 12. dashed; Isa. 13. 13; Heb. 12. 26. make tremble; Matt. 28. 4. quake; Job 41. 29. rushing; Ezek. 37. 7. an earthquake

SHAME, 1 Sam. 20. 34. 2 Sam. 13. 13.
Ps. 119. 31. put me not to *s.*, 69. 7.
Prov. 3. 35. *s.* shall be the promotion of fools, 9. 7. & 10. 5. & 11. 2. & 13. 5, 18. & 14. 35. & 17. 2. & 18. 13. & 19. 26. & 25. 8. & 29. 15. Isa. 22. 18.
Isa. 50. 6. hid not my face from *s.*
Dan. 12. 2. some to life, some to *s.*
Hos. 4. 7. change glory into *s.*
Zeph. 3. 5. unjust knoweth no *s.*
Acts 5. 41. worthy to suffer *s.* for
Phil. 3. 19. glory is in their *s.*
Heb. 12. 2. endured the cross, despising the *s.*
Rev. 3. 18. *s.* of thy nakedness
1 Tim. 2. 9. *shamefacedness*
R. V. Ex. 32. 25. derision; Ps. 4. 2; 35. 4; 40. 14; 44. 9; 109. 29; Acts 5. 41; 1 Cor. 11. 14. dishonor; Ps. 83. 16. confusion; 83. 17. confounded; Prov. 25. 10. revile; Jer. 3. 24; Hos. 9. 10; 1 Cor. 14. 35. shameful; Mic. 2. 6. reproaches

SHAPE, Luke 3. 22. John 5. 37. Ps. 51. 5.
R. V. Luke 3. 22; John 5. 37. form

SHARP, Isa. 41. 15. & 49. 2. Rev. 1. 16.
Job 16. 9. *sharpeneth*, Prov. 27. 17.
Mic. 7. 4. *sharper* than, Heb. 4. 12.
Judg. 8. 1. *sharply*, Tit. 1. 13.
2 Cor. 13. 10. should use *sharpness*
R. V. Josh. 5. 2, 3. flint; 1 Sam. 14. 4. rocky; Job 41. 30. threshing wain; Ex. 4. 25 ——; Mic. 7. 4. worse

SHEARING sheep, rejoicing at, 1 Sam. 25. 4. 2 Sam. 13. 23.

SHEAVES of corn, Joseph's dream, Gen. 37. 7.
sheaf of the firstfruits of harvest, Lev. 23. 10-12.
forgotten, to be left in the field, Deut. 24. 19. Job 24. 10.
typical, Ps. 126. 6. Mic. 4. 12. Matt. 13. 30.

SHED for many, for remission, Matt. 26. 28.
Rom. 5. 5. love of God is *s.* abroad
Tit. 3. 6. Holy Ghost be *s.* on us
R. V. Ex. 22. 2, 3; 1 Sam. 25. 26, 33. bloodguiltiness; Ezek. 35. 5. given over to; Ezek. 36. 18; Luke 22. 20; Acts 2. 33; Tit. 3. 6; Rev. 16. 6. poured out

SHEEP, Ps. 49. 14. & 74. 1. & 78. 52.
Ps. 44. 22, 23. *s.* for the slaughter
79. 13. *s.* of thy pasture, 100. 3.
119. 176. gone astray like lost *s.*
Isa. 53. 6. like *s.* have gone astray
Ezek. 34. 12. *s.* that are scattered
Matt. 9. 36. as *s.* having no shep.
10. 6. to lost *s.* of house of
18. 12. hundred *s.* and one of
25. 32. divideth the *s.* from goats
John 10. 2-7. the *s.*
27. my *s.*
21. 15-17. feed lambs, feed my *s.*
1 Pet. 2. 25. were as *s.* going astray
R. V. Gen. 34. 28; Ex. 9. 3; Lev. 22. 21; Num. 31. 28; Deut. 7. 13; 15. 19; 28. 4, 18, 51; 1 Sam. 8. 17; Ps. 49. 17. flock or flocks; S. of S. 4. 2; 6. 6. ewes; John 10. 4. his own; 10. 14. mine own

SHEPHERD, Gen. 46. 34. & 49. 24. Ex. 2. 17, 19.
Num. 17. 17. sheep that have no *s.*, 1 Kings 22. 17. Mark 6. 34.
Ps. 23. 1. the Lord is my *s.*
S. of S. 1. 8. feed thy kids before the *s.* tents
Ezek. 34. 2. prophesy against *s.*, woe to the *s.*
5. scattered because no *s.*
12. *s.* seeketh out his flock
23. set up one *s.* even David
37. 24. all shall have one *s.*
Mic. 5. 5. against him seven *s.*
John 10. 11. I am the good *s.*
16. one fold and one *s.*, Eccl. 12. 11.
Heb. 13. 20. Jesus, that great *s.*
1 Pet. 2. 25. returned to *s.* of souls
5. 4. when the chief *s.* shall ap.

SHIELD and great reward, Gen. 15. 1.
Deut. 33. 29. Lord the *s.* of thy help
Ps. 3. 3. Lord is a *s.* for me, 28. 7.
33. 20. Lord our *s.*, 59. 11. & 84. 9.
84. 11. God is a sun and a *s.*
115. 9. their help and their *s.*
Prov. 30. 5. a *s.* unto them that
Eph. 6. 16. taking the *s.* of faith

SHINE, Job 22. 28. & 36. 32. & 37. 15.
Num. 6. 25. make his face to *s.*
Job 10. 3. *s.* on counsel of wicked
Ps. 31. 16. thy face to *s.* on thy
Eccl. 8. 1. man's wisdom maketh his face *s.*
Dan. 12. 3. wise shall *s.* as firma.
Matt. 5. 16. let your light so *s.*
13. 43. righteous *s.* forth as the
2 Cor. 4. 6. commanded light to *s.*
Phil. 2. 15. among whom ye *s.* as
R. V. Matt. 24. 27. is seen; Job 25. 25. no brightness

SHIPWRECK, 1 Tim. 1. 19.

SHORT, is the Lord's hand waxed, Num. 11. 23.
Ps. 89. 47. remember how *s.* time
Rom. 3. 23. and come *s.* of glory
Ps. 102. 23. he *shortened* my days
Isa. 50. 2. is my hand *s.*, 59. 1.
Matt. 24. 22. except the days be *s.*

SHOUT, Num. 23. 21. Isa. 12. 6. & 42. 11. & 44. 23. Zeph. 3. 14. Zech. 9. 9.
Ps. 47. 5. God is gone up with a *s.*
1 Thes. 4. 16. the Lord shall descend with a *s.*

SHOW, Ps. 39. 6. Luke 20. 47. Col. 2. 23.
Ps. 4. 6. who will *s.* us any good
16. 11. wilt *s.* me path of life
91. 16. I will *s.* him my salvation
1 Cor. 11. 26. *s.* forth Lord's death
Tit. 2. 7. *s.* thyself a pattern
1 Pet. 2. 9. *s.* forth the praise
Rev. 22. 6. sent his angel to *s.*
John 5. 20. loved Son, and *showeth*
R. V. frequent changes, chiefly to tell, declare, manifest, etc.

SHRINES, Acts 19. 24.

SHUT up or left, Deut. 32. 36.
Matt. 23. 13. ye *s.* up the kingdom
Gal. 3. 23. *s.* up to the faith which
Rev. 3. 7. that openeth, and no man *shutteth*, Isa. 22. 22.
R. V. Deut. 32. 30. delivered

SICK of love, S. of S. 2. 5. & 5. 8.
Isa. 1. 5. whole head is *s.* and
John 11. 1. a certain man was *s.*
Jas. 5. 14. is any *s.* call the
15. faith shall save the *s.*
1 Cor. 11. 30. are weak and *sickly*
Ps. 41. 3. make his bed in *sickness*
Ex. 23. 25. I will take *s.* away
Matt. 8. 17. bare our *sicknesses*
R. V. Prov. 23. 35. hurt; Mic. 6. 13. wound; Luke 7. 10 ——; 5. 24; Acts 9. 33. palsied; Matt. 8. 17. diseases; Mark 3. 15 ——

SIFT, Isa. 30. 28. Amos 9. 9. Luke 22. 31.

SIGHT, Ex. 3. 3. 2 Cor. 5. 7.
R. V. Many changes to eyes, presence, appearance, etc.

SIGN, Gen. 9. 12, 13. & 17. 11. Ex. 4. 17. Isa. 8. 18. Rom. 15. 19.
Rom. 4. 11. received the *s.* of cir.
Jer. 22. 24. *signet*, Hag. 2. 23.

SILENT in darkness, 1 Sam. 2. 9.
Ps. 21. 1. be not *s.* to me, 30. 12.
Zech. 2. 13. be *s.* O all flesh before
Ps. 31. 18. *silence*, 32. 3. & 35. 22. & 50. 3. 21. & 83. 1. & 94. 17. Jer. 8. 14. Amos 5. 13. & 8. 3. 1 Cor. 14. 34. 1 Tim. 2. 11, 12. 1 Pet. 2. 15. Rev. 8. 1.
R. V. Ps. 31. 18. dumb; Isa. 15. 1. nought; 62. 6. take no rest; Acts 22. 2. quiet; 1 Tim. 2. 11, 12. quietness; Ps. 28. 1. deaf unto

SILLY, Job 5. 2. 2 Tim. 3. 6.

SIMPLE, Prov. 1. 4, 22, 32. & 7. 7 & 8. 5. & 9. 4, 13. & 19. 25. & 21. 11.
Ps. 19. 7. testimony sure, making wise the *s.*
116. 16. Lord preserveth the *s.*
119. 130. understanding to the *s.*
Prov. 14. 15. the *s.* believeth
22. 3. *s.* pass on and are punished
Rom. 16. 19. but *s.* concerning evil
R. V. Rom. 16. 18. innocent

SIN lieth at the door, Gen. 4. 7.
Job 10. 6. searchest after my *s.*
Ps. 4. 4. stand in awe and *s.* not
32. 1. blessed is he whose *s.* is covered
38. 18. I will be sorry for my *s.*
51. 3. my *s.* is ever before me
119. 11. that I might not *s.* against
Prov. 14. 34. *s.* is a reproach to
Isa. 30. 1. counsel to add *s.* to *s.*
53. 10. offering for *s.*
John 1. 29. take. away *s.* of world
5. 14. *s.* no more lest a worse
Rom. 5. 12. by one *s.* entered
6. 14. *s.* shall not have dominion
7. 13. *s.* might appear *s.*
17. *s.* that dwelleth in me
8. 2. free from the law of *s.*
1 Cor. 15. 34. awake to righteousness and *s.* not
2 Cor. 5. 21. made *s.* for us, who
Eph. 4. 26. be angry, and *s.* not
Jas. 1. 15. lust bringeth forth *s.* and *s.* death
1 Pet. 2. 22. who did no *s.* neither
1 John 1. 8. say we have no *s.*
2. 1. ye *s.* not; if any man *s.* we have an advocate
5. 16. there is a *s.* unto death
Ps. 19. 13. keep me from presumptuous *sins*
Isa. 43. 25. not remember *s.*
Ezek. 33. 16. none of his *s.* shall
Dan. 9. 24. transgression, make end of *s.*
1 Tim. 5. 22. partaker of other men's *s.*
2 Tim. 3. 6. women laden with *s.*
1 John 2. 2. propitiation for *s.* of
Ps. 69. 5. *my sins*, 51. 9. Isa. 38. 17. 79. 9. *our sins*, 90. 8. & 103. 10. Isa. 59. 12. Dan. 9. 16. Gal. 1. 4. 1 Cor. 15. 3. Heb. 1. 3. 1 Pet. 2. 24. Rev. 1. 5.
Matt. 1. 21. *their sins*, Rom. 11. 27. Heb. 8. 12. & 10. 17. Num. 16. 26.
Isa. 59. 2. *your sins*, Jer. 5. 25. John 8. 21. 1 Cor. 15. 17. Josh. 24. 19.
Ex. 32. 33. who hath *sinned*, I
Job 1. 22. in all this Job *s.* not
Lam. 1. 8. Jerusalem grievously *s.*
Rom. 2. 12. many as *s.* without
3. 23. all have *s.* and come short
1 John 1. 10. say we have not *s.*
Ex. 9. 27. *I have sinned*, Num 22. 34. Josh. 7. 20. 1 Sam. 15. 24, 30. 2 Sam. 12. 13. & 24. 10. Job 7. 20. &

33. 27. Ps. 41. 4. & 51. 4. Mic. 7. 9.
Matt. 27. 4. Luke 15. 18, 21.
Judg. 10. 10. *we have sinned*, 1 Sam. 7. 6. Ps. 106. 6. Isa. 42. 24. & 64. 5. Jer. 3. 25. & 8. 14. & 14. 7, 20. Lam. 5. 16. Dan. 9. 5, 8, 11, 15.
1 Kings 8. 46. man that *sinneth*
Prov. 8. 36. *s*. against me wrong
Eccl. 7. 20. doeth good, and *s*. not
Ezek. 18. 4. soul that *s*. it shall die
1 John 5. 18. is born of God *s*. not
Eccl. 7. 26. the *sinner* shall be
9. 18. *s*. destroyeth much good
Isa. 65. 20. *s*. a hundred years
Luke 15. 7. joy over one *s*. that repenteth
18. 13. be merciful to me a *s*.
Jas. 5. 20. convert a *s*. from
1 Pet. 4. 18. where shall *s*. appear
Gen. 13. 13. *sinners* before the
Ps. 1. 1. standeth in way of *s*.
51. 13. *s*. shall be converted to thee
Isa. 33. 14. *s*. in Zion are afraid
Matt. 9. 13. call *s*. to repentance
John 9. 31. God heareth not *s*.
Rom. 5. 8. that while we were yet *s*. Christ died for us
19. by disobedi. many made *s*.
Gal. 2. 15. are Jews and not *s*.
1 Tim. 1. 15. Jesus came to save *s*.
Heb. 7. 26. holy, separate from *s*.
Jude 15. ungodly *s*. have spoken
Num. 32. 14. *sinful*, Isa. 1. 4. Luke 5. 8. Rom. 7. 13. & 8. 3.
R. V. Prov. 10. 12, 19; 28. 13. transgression; 14. 9. Jer. 51. 5. guilt; 2 Chron. 28. 10; Eph. 1. 7; 2. 5; Col. 1. 13. trespasses; Col. 2. 11; 1 John 2. 2 —; Lev. 4. 13. err

SINCERE, Phil. 1. 10, 16. 1 Pet. 2. 2.
Josh. 24. 14. serve him in *sincerity*
1 Cor. 5. 8. unleavened bread of *s*.
2 Cor. 1. 12. in godly *s*. we have
2. 17. as of *s*. in the sight of God
8. 8. prove the *s*. of your love
Eph. 6. 24. love Lord Jesus in *s*.
Tit. 2. 7. showing gravity, *s*.
R. V. 1 Pet. 2. 2. spiritual; Eph. 6. 24. uncorruptness; Tit. 2. 7 —

SINEW, Isa. 48. 4. Job 10. 11.
R. V. Job 30. 17. gnaw

SING to the Lord, Ex. 15. 21. 1 Chron. 16. 23. Ps. 30. 4. & 68. 32. & 81. 1. & 95. 1. & 96. 1, 2. & 98. 1. & 147. 7. & 149. 1. Isa. 12. 5. & 52. 9. Eph. 5. 19.
Ex. 15. 1. I will *s*., Judg. 5. 3. Ps. 13. 6. & 57. 7, 9. & 59. 16, 17. & 101. 1. & 104. 33. & 144. 9. Isa. 5. 1. 1 Cor. 14. 15.
Job 29. 13. *s*. for joy, Isa. 65. 14.
Ps. 9. 11. *s*. praise, 18. 49. & 27. 6. & 30. 12. & 47. 6, 7. & 68. 4. & 75. 9. & 92. 1. & 108. 1, 3. & 135. 3. & 146. 2. & 147. 1. & 149. 3.
Ps. 145. 7. *s*. of thy righteousness
Prov. 29. 6. righteous doth *s*.
Isa. 35. 6. shall tongue of dumb *s*.
1 Cor. 14. 15. I will *s*. with the spirit
R. V. Ps. 30. 4; 33. 2; 57. 9; 71. 22, 23; 98. 5; 101. 1. sing praises; Isa. 24. 14. shout; Hos. 2. 15. make answer

SINGLE eye, Matt. 6. 22. Luke 11. 34.
Acts 2. 46. *singleness* of heart, Eph. 6. 5. Col. 3. 22.

SINK, Ps. 69. 2, 14. Luke 9. 44.

SISTER, S. of S. 4. 9. & 5. 1. & 8. 8.
R. V. 1 Chron. 7. 15; 1 Cor. 9. 15. wife; Col. 4. 10. cousin

SITUATION, 2 Kings 2. 19. Ps. 48. 2.
R. V. Ps. 48. 2. elevation

SKIN for skin, Job 2. 4. & 10. 11. & 19. 26. Jer. 13. 23. Heb. 11. 37.
R. V. Ex. 16. 10; 36. 19; Num. 4. 6, 8, 10, 11, 12, 14, 25; Ezek. 16. 10. sealskin; Job 18. 13. body; Ps. 102. 5. flesh; Mark 1. 6. leathern girdle

SKIP, Ps. 29. 6. & 114. 4. S. of S. 2. 8.
R. V. Jer. 48. 27. waggest the head

SLACK, Deut. 7. 10. Prov. 10. 4. Hab. 1. 4. Zeph. 3. 16. 2 Pet. 3. 9.

SLANDER, Ex. 23. 1; Ps. 15. 3; 31. 13; 34. 13. (1 Pet. 3. 10.); 50. 20; 64. 3; 101. 5; Prov. 10. 18; Jer. 6. 28; 9. 4; Eph. 4. 31; Tit. 3. 2.
effects of, and conduct under, Prov. 16. 28; 17. 9; 18. 8; 26. 20, 22; Jer. 38. 4; Ezek. 22. 9; Matt. 5. 11; 26. 59; Acts 6. 11; 17. 7; 24. 5; 1 Cor. 4. 12.

SLANDEROUSLY reported, Rom. 3. 8.

SLAY, Job 13. 15. Ps. 139. 19. Lev. 14. 13.
Eph. 2. 16. having *slain* the enmi.
Rev. 5. 9. wast *s*. and hast redeem.
6. 9. were *s*. for word of God
13. 8. Lamb *s*. from foundation
R. V. Lev. 26. 17; Deut. 1. 1. smitten. Many changes to kill, smote, put to death, etc.

SLAYING unpremeditatedly, Num. 35. 11. Deut. 4. 42. & 19. 3. Josh. 20. 3.

SLEEP, deep, Gen. 2. 21. & 15. 12. 1 Sam. 26. 12. Job 4. 13. Ps. 76. 6. Prov. 19. 15. Isa. 29. 10.
Ps. 90. 5. as a *s*. in morning
127. 2. he giveth his beloved *s*.
Prov. 3. 24. thy *s*. shall be sweet
6. 10. a little *s*. a little slumber
20. 13. love not *s*. lest thou
Eccl. 5. 12. *s*. of a laboring man
Jer. 31. 26. my *s*. was sweet to me
Luke 9. 32. were heavy with *s*.
Rom. 13. 11. time to wake out of *s*.
Esth. 6. 1. night king could not *s*.
Eccl. 5. 12. the abundance of the rich will not suffer him to *s*.
S. of S. 5. 2. I *s*. but my heart wak.
1 Cor. 11. 30. for this cause many *s*.
15. 51. we shall not all *s*. but
1 Thes. 4. 14. them which *s*. in Jesus
5. 6. let us not *s*. as others; but
Ps. 3. 5. laid me down and *slept*
76. 5. they have *s*. their sleep
1 Cor. 15. 20. the firstfruits of them that *s*.
Eph. 5. 14. awake, thou that *sleepest*
R. V. Isa. 56. 10. dreaming

SLIDE, Deut. 32. 35. Ps. 26. 1. & 37. 31. Jer. 8. 5. Hos. 4. 16.
R. V. Ps. 26. 1. without wavering; Hos. 4. 16. behaved stubbornly

SLIGHTLY, Jer. 6. 14. & 8. 11.

SLING, 1 Sam. 25. 29. Jer. 10. 18.

SLIP, Ps. 17. 5. & 18. 36. & 38. 16. & 94. 18. Heb. 2. 1.
Ps. 35. 6. *slippery*, 73. 18. Jer. 23. 12.
R. V Heb. 2. 1. drift away

SLOTHFUL are under tribute, Prov. 12. 24.
Prov. 12. 27. *s*. roasteth not which
18. 9. *s*. is brother to great waster
19. 24. *s*. hideth hand in bosom
24. 30. by the field of the *s*.
26. 14. door on hinges so doth *s*.
Rom. 12. 11. not *s*. in business
Heb. 6. 12. be not *s*. but followers
Prov. 19. 15. *slothfulness* casteth in a deep sleep
R. V. Prov. 15. 19; 19. 24; 22. 13; 26. 13, 14, 15. sluggard; 18. 9. slack; Heb. 6. 12. sluggish

SLOW to anger, Neh. 9. 17.
Luke 24. 25. fools, *s*. of heart to
Jas. 1. 19. *s*. to speak, *s*. to wrath, Prov. 14. 29.
R. V. Tit. 1. 12. idle

SLUGGARD, go to ant, Prov. 6. 6.
Prov. 6. 9. how long wilt sleep, O *s*.
20. 4. *s*. will not plough by reason
26. 16. *s*. is wiser in his own conceit

SLUMBER, Ps. 132. 4. Rom. 11. 8.
Ps. 121. 3. he that keepeth thee will not *s*., 4.
Matt. 25. 5. they all *slumbered* and
2 Pet. 2. 3. their damnation *slumbereth* not
R. V. Rom. 11. 8. stupor

SMITE, Lord shall, Deut. 28. 22.
Ps. 141. 5. let the righteous *s*. me
Zech. 13. 7. *s*. the shepherd
Matt. 5. 39. *s*. thee on thy right
John 18. 23. why *smitest* thou me
Isa. 53. 4. him *smitten* of God
Hos. 6. 1. hath *s*. and he will bind
R. V. 1 Sam. 23. 5. slew; 2 Sam. 10. 15, 19. put to the worse; 2 Chron 22. 5. wounded; Matt. 24 49; Luke 12. 63. beat; Matt. 26. 51; Luke 22 64; John 18. 10; 19. 3. struck

SMOKE, Gen. 19. 28. Ex. 19. 18.
Deut. 29. 20. anger of Lord shall *s*.
Ps. 74. 1. why doth thy anger *s*.
102. 3. as *s*., Prov. 10. 26. Isa. 65. 5
Rev. 14. 11. *s*. of torment ascend.
Isa. 42 3. *smoking* flax, Matt. 12. 20.

SMOOTH, Gen. 27. 11, 16. Isa. 30. 10.
Ps. 55. 21. *smoother*, Prov. 5. 3.

SNARE, Ex. 23. 33. Judg. 2. 3.
Ps. 69. 22. table become a *s*.
91. 3. deliver thee from the *s*.
119. 110. wicked laid a *s*. for me
Prov. 29. 25. fear of man bringeth a *s*.
1 Tim. 6. 9. they that will be rich fall into a *s*.
2 Tim. 2. 26. out of the *s*. of devil
Ps. 11. 6. on the wicked he will rain *snares*
Prov. 13. 14. depart from *s*. of dea.
Ps. 9. 16. *snared*, Prov. 6. 2. & 12. 13. Eccl. 9. 12. Isa. 8. 15. & 28. 13. & 42. 22.
R. V. Job 18. 8. toils; 18. 10. noose; Prov. 29. 8. flame; Lam. 3. 47. pit; Jer. 5. 26. lie in wait

SNOW, as, Ps. 51. 7. & 68. 14. Isa. 1. 18. Dan. 7. 9. Matt. 28. 3. Rev. 1. 14.

SNUFFED, Mal. 1. 13. Jer. 2. 24.

SOAP, Jer. 2. 22. Mal. 3. 2.

SOBER for your cause, 2 Cor. 5. 13.
1 Thes. 5. 6. watch and be *s*.
1 Tim. 3. 2. bishop must be vigilant, *s*.
11. wives not slanderers, *s*.
Tit. 1. 8. *s*. just, holy, temperate
2. 4. teach young women to be *s*
1 Pet. 1. 13. gird up your loins, be *s*.
4. 7. be *s*. and watch unto prayer
5. 8. be *s*. be vigilant, for your
Rom. 12. 3. not to think highly, but *soberly*
Tit. 2. 12. teaching us to live *s*.
Acts 26. 25. words of *soberness*
1 Tim. 2. 9. *sobriety*, 15.
R. V. 2 Cor. 5. 13; 2 Tim. 3. 2; Tit. 1. 8. soberminded; 1 Tim. 3. 11; Tit. 2. 2. temperate; 1 Pet. 4. 7. of sound mind; Tit. 2. 4 —

SOFT, God maketh my heart, Job 23. 16.
Prov. 15. 1. *s*. answer turneth
25. 15. *s*. tongue breaketh the
Matt. 11. 8. man clothed in *s*. rai.
R. V. Job 23. 16. faint

SOJOURN, Gen. 12. 10. Ps. 120. 5.
Lev. 25. 23. *sojourners* with me, 1 Chron. 29. 15. Ps. 39. 12.
Ex. 12. 40. *sojourning*, 1 Pet. 1. 17.

SOLD thyself to work evil, 1 Kings 21. 20.
Rom. 7. 14. I am carnal, *s*. under sin

SOLDIER of Jesus Christ, 2 Tim. 2. 3, 4.
R. V. 1 Chron. 7. 4. host; 2 Chron 25. 13; Isa. 15. 4. men; 1 Chron. 7. 11; Matt. 27. 27 —

SON, 2 Sam. 18. 33. & 19. 4.
Ps. 2. 12. kiss the *S*. lest he be
Prov. 10. 1. a wise *s*. maketh a glad father, 15. 20.
Mal. 3. 17. as a man spareth his *s*.
Matt. 11. 27. no man know. the *S*.
17. 5. this is my beloved *S*. 3. 17.

Luke 10. 6. if *s*. of peace be there
John 1. 18. only begotten *S*., 3. 16.
5. 21. *S*. quickeneth whom he will
8. 35. *S*. abideth ever
36. the *S*. maketh free
Rom. 8. 3. sent his own *S*. in the
Gal. 4. 7. if *s*. then an heir of God
2 Thes. 2. 3. man of sin, *s*. of per.
Heb. 5. 8. though a *S*. yet learned
1 John 2. 22. denieth the *S*. denieth
5. 12. that hath *S*. hath life
Matt. 21. 37. *his son*, Acts 3. 13. Rom. 1. 3, 9. & 5. 10. & 8. 29, 32. 1 Cor. 1. 9. Gal. 1. 16. & 4. 4, 6. 1 Thes. 1. 10. Heb. 1. 2. 1 John 1. 7. & 2. 23. & 3. 23. & 4. 9, 10, 14. & 5. 9, 10, 11, 20.
Luke 15. 19. *thy son*, John 17. 1. & 19. 26.
Dan. 3. 25. *the son of God*, Matt. 4. 3. & 16. 16. and forty-one other places
Num. 23. 19. *Son of man*, Job 25. 6. Ps. 8. 4. & 80. 17. & 144. 3. Dan. 7. 13. Ezekiel is so called about ninety and Christ about eighty-four times
Ps. 144. 12. that our *sons* may be as
S. of S. 2. 3. is my beloved among *s*.
Isa. 60. 10. *s*. of strangers, 61. 5. & 62. 8.
Mal. 3. 3. purify *s*. of Levi
Mark 3. 17. Boanerges, *s*. of thun.
1 Cor. 4. 14. as my beloved *s*. I
Gal. 4. 6. because ye are *s*. God sent forth the Spirit of his Son
Heb. 2. 10. bring many *s*. to glory
12. 7. God dealeth with you as *s*.
Gen. 6. 2. *sons of God*, Job 1. 6. & 2. 1. & 38. 7. Hos. 1. 10. John 1. 12. Rom. 8. 14, 19. Phil. 2. 15. 1 John 3. 1, 2.
R. V. Gen. 23. 3, 16, 20; 25. 10; 32. 22; Num. 2. 14, 18, 22; Deut. 4. 1; 2 Chron. 21. 7; Mark 13. 12; John 1. 12; 1 Cor. 4. 14, 17; Col. 3. 6; Phil. 2. 15, 22; 1 Tim. 1. 18; 2 Tim. 1. 2; 2. 1; Tit. 1. 4; Phile. 10; 1 John 3. 1, 2. child or children; Num. 1. 20; 26. 5. firstborn; 2 Sam. 23. 6. ungodly; Acts 3. 13, 26. Servant; Col. 4. 10. cousin; Gen. 36. 15; Isa. 56. 3, 6; Matt. 18. 11; 24. 36; 25. 13; Luke 9. 56; John 12. 4; Acts 8. 37; 1 John 5. 13——

SONG to the Lord, Ex. 15. 1. Num. 21. 17.
Ex. 15. 2. Lord is my *s*., Ps. 118. 14. Isa. 12. 2.
Job 30. 9. I am their *s*., Ps. 69. 12.
35. 10. giveth *s*. in the night, Ps. 42. 8. & 77. 6. Isa. 30. 29.
Ps. 32. 7. compass with *s*. of deliv.
119. 54. *s*. in house of pilgrimage
Ezek. 33. 32. as a very lovely *s*.
Eph. 5. 19. speak to yourselves in spiritual *s*.
Rev. 14. 3. could learn that *s*.
15. 3. sing *s*. of Moses and of Lamb
Ps. 33. 3. sing a *new song*, 40. 3. & 96. 1. & 144. 9. & 149. 1. Isa. 42. 10. Rev. 5. 9.
R. V. 1 Chron. 25. 7; Isa. 35. 10. singing

SOON as they be born, Ps. 58. 3.
Ps. 106. 13. *s*. forget his works
Prov. 14. 17. *s*. angry dealeth fool.
Gal. 1. 6. *s*. removed to another
R. V. Ps. 68. 31. haste to; Matt. 21. 20. immediately; Gal. 1. 6; 2 Thes. 2. 2. quickly; Josh. 3. 13; 2 Sam. 6. 18; Mark 14. 45; Luke 1. 44; 15. 30; 23. 7; John 16. 21; Acts 10. 29; Rev. 10. 10; 12. 4. when

SORCERER, Acts 13. 6, 8. & 8. 9, 11.
Jer. 27. 9. *sorcerers*, Mal. 3. 5. Rev. 21. 8.

SORE, 2 Chron. 6. 28. Job 5. 18.
Heb. 10. 29. much *sorer* punish.
Isa. 1. 6. and putrefying *sores*
R. V. Lev. 13. 42, 43; 2 Chron. 6. 28, 29; Ps. 38. 11. plague

SORRY, Ps. 38. 18. 2 Cor. 2. 2. & 7. 8.
Ps. 90. 10. labor and *sorrow*
Prov. 15. 13. by *s*. of heart the
Eccl. 1. 18. knowledge increaseth *s*.
7. 3. *s*. is better than laughter
Isa. 35. 10. *s*. and sighing flee, 51. 11.
Lam. 1. 12. be any *s*. like unto my
John 16. 6. *s*. hath filled your
20. *s*. shall be turned into joy
2 Cor. 7. 10. godly *s*. worketh repentance to salvation, but *s*. of world, 9.
Phil. 2. 27. should have *s*. upon *s*.
1 Thes. 4. 13. *s*. not as others
Rev. 21. 4. no more death, neither *s*.
Ps. 18. 5. the *s*. of hell
116. 3. the *s*. of death
Isa. 53. 3. man of *s*.
4. carried our *s*.
Matt. 24. 8. beginning of *sorrows*
1 Tim. 6. 10. pierced through with many *s*.
2 Cor. 7. 9. *sorrowed*, Jer. 31. 12.
1 Sam. 1. 15. woman of *sorrowful* spirit
Prov. 14. 13. in laughter heart is *s*.
Jer. 31. 25. replenished *s*. soul
Matt. 19. 22. man went away *s*.
26. 22, 38. my soul is exceeding *s*.
2 Cor. 6. 10. *s*. yet always rejoicing
Luke 2. 48. *sorrowing*, Acts 20. 38.
R. V. Gen. 3. 17; Ps. 127. 2. toil; Ex. 15. 14. pangs; Deut. 28. 65. pining; Job 3. 10. trouble; 41. 22. terror; Job 6. 10; Jer. 30. 15; 45. 3; 51. 29; Rom. 9. 2. pain; 2 Sam. 22. 6; Ps. 18. 4, 5; 116. 3. cords; Ps. 55. 10. mischief; Isa. 5. 30. distress; Isa. 29. 2. lamentation; Matt. 24. 8; Mark 13. 8. travail; Rev. 18. 7; 21. 4. mourning; Neh. 8. 10; Matt. 14. 9. grieved; Isa. 51. 19. bemoaned

SORT, 2 Cor. 7. 11. 3 John 6.
R. V. Deut. 22. 11. mingled stuff; Ps. 78. 45; 105. 31. swarms; Dan. 1. 10. own age; Acts 17. 5. rabble; Rom. 15. 15. measure

SOUGHT the Lord, Ex. 33. 7. 2 Chron. 14. 7.
Ps. 34. 4. I *s*. Lord, and he heard
119. 10. with my whole heart I *s*.
Eccl. 7. 29. *s*. out many inventions
Isa. 62. 12. be called *s*. out, a city
65. 1. found of them that *s*. me
Rom. 9. 32. *s*. it not by faith, but
Heb. 12. 17. though he *s*. it care.
2 Chron. 16. 12. *s*. not Lord
1 Chron. 15. 13. *sought him*, 2 Chron. 14. 7. & 15. 4. Ps. 78. 34. S. of S. 3. 1, 2. & 5. 6. Jer. 8. 2. & 26. 21.

SOUL abhor my judgments, Lev. 26. 15, 43.
Gen. 2. 7. man became a living *s*.
Deut. 11. 13. serve him with all *s*.
13. 3. love the Lord with all thy *s*., Josh. 22. 5. 1 Kings 2. 4. Mark 12. 33.
1 Sam. 18. 1. *s*. of Jonathan knit
1 Kings 8. 48. with all their *s*.
1 Chron. 22. 19. set your *s*. to seek
Job 16. 4. if your *s*. were in my *s*.'s stead
Ps. 19. 7. law is perfect, convert. *s*.
49. 8. redemption of *s*. is precious
107. 9. filleth the hungry *s*. with
Prov. 10. 3. not suffer *s*. of right.
18. 2. *s*. be without knowledge
27. 17. full *s*. loatheth honey-comb
Isa. 55. 2. let your *s* delight
58. 10. I will satisfy the afflicted *s*.
Jer. 31. 25. have satiated weary *s*.
38. 16. the Lord made us this *s*.
Ezek. 18. 4. *s*. that sinneth, it
Matt. 10. 28. are not able to kill *s*.
Rom. 13. 1. let every *s*. be subject
1 Thes. 5. 23. spirit, *s*. and body
Heb. 4. 12. piercing to divid. of *s*.
10. 39. believe to saving of the *s*.
Ex. 30. 12. ransom for *his soul*
Judg. 10. 16. — was grieved for
2 Kings 23. 25. turned to Lord with all —
Job 27. 8. God taketh away —
Hab. 2. 4. — lifted up, is not
Matt. 16. 26. lose —; what in exchange for —
Ps. 16. 10. not leave *my soul* in
35. 3. say to — I am thy salvation
42. 5, 11. why cast down, O —
62. 1. — waiteth upon God, 5.
63. 1. — thirsteth for thee, my flesh
Isa. 26. 9. with — have I desired thee, 8.
61. 10. shall be joyful in my God
Luke 1. 46. — doth magnify the
John 12. 27. now is — troubled, Matt. 26. 38.
Ps. 33. 20. *our soul*, 44. 25. & 66. 9. & 123. 4. & 124. 4. Isa. 26. 8.
Deut. 13. 6. *own soul*, 1 Sam. 18. 1. & 20. 17. Ps. 22. 29. Prov. 8. 36. & 11. 17. & 15. 32. & 19. 8, 16. & 6. 32. & 20. 2. & 29. 24. Mark 8. 36. Luke 2. 35.
Deut. 4. 9. *with all thy soul*, 6. 5. & 10. 12. & 30. 6. Matt. 22. 37.
Ezek. 3. 19. deliver *thy soul*, 21. & 33. 9.
Luke 12. 20. this night — shall be required of thee
3 John 2. prosper — as prospereth
Ps. 72. 13. save *souls* of the
Prov. 11. 36. winneth *s*. is wise
Isa. 57. 16. spirit fail, and *s*.
Ezek. 14. 14. should but deliver *s*.
1 Pet. 3. 20. few, i. e. eight *s*. saved
2 Pet. 2. 14. beguiling unstable *s*.
Rev. 6. 9. *s*. of slain and behead.
Luke 21. 19. *your souls*, Josh. 23. 14. Jer. 6. 16. & 26. 19. Matt. 11. 29. Heb. 13. 17. 1 Pet. 1. 9, 22. & 2. 25.
R. V. Lev. 17. 11; Num. 16. 38; 1 Sam. 26. 21; Job 31. 30; Prov. 22. 23; Matt. 16. 26; Mark 8. 36, 37. life or lives; Lev. 4. 2; 5. 1, 2, 4, 15, 17 6. 2; 7. 21. any one; Num. 15. 27. one person; Job 30. 15. honor; Prov. 19. 18. heart; Hos. 9. 4. appetite; Ps. 16. 2; Jer. 5. 41; Mark 12. 23——

SOUND, dreadful, Job 15. 21.
Ps. 47. 5. God is gone up with *s*.
119. 80. let my heart be *s*.
Prov. 2. 7. *s*. wisdom, 3. 21.
Eccl. 12. 4. *s*. of the grinding is
Amos 6. 5, that chant to *s*. of viol
Rom. 10. 18. *s*. went into all the
1 Tim. 1. 10. contrary to *s*. doc.
2 Tim. 1. 7. *s*. mind
13. of *s*. words
Tit. 1. 9. *s*. doctrine, *s*. in faith
2. 8. *s*. speech that cannot
Isa. 63. 15. *sounding* of bowels, 16. 11.
Ps. 38. 3, 7. no *soundness*, Isa. 1. 6.
R. V. Job 39. 24; John 3. 8; 1 Cor. 14. 7, 8; Rev. 1. 15; 18. 22. voice; Ps. 119. 80. perfect; 2 Tim. 1. 7. discipline; Isa. 63. 15. yearning; Ezek. 7. 7. joyful shouting

SOUR GRAPES, proverb concerning, Jer. 31. 29. Ezek. 18. 2.

SOUTH, the king of, Dan. 11.
— queen of, Matt. 12. 42.

SOW that was washed, 2 Pet. 2. 22.

SOW wickedness reap the same, Job 4. 8.
Ps. 126. 5. *s*. in tears, reap in joy
Isa. 32. 20. blessed that *s*. beside
Jer. 4. 3. *s*. not among thorns
Hos. 10. 12. *s*. in righteousness
Mic. 6. 15. thou shalt *s*. and not
Matt. 13. 3. sower went out to *s*.
Luke 12. 24. the ravens neither *s*.
Ps. 97. 11. light is *sown* for right.
Hos. 8. 7. *s*. wind, reap whirlwind
1 Cor. 9. 11. have *s*. to you spiritual
15. 42. it is *s*. in corruption
2 Cor. 9. 10. multiply your seed *s*.
Jas. 3. 18. fruit of righteousness is *s*. in peace
Prov. 11. 18. that *soweth* righteous
22. 8. *s*. iniquity, shall reap van.
John 4. 37. one *s*. another reapeth
2 Cor. 9. 6. *s*. sparingly, *s*. bounti.
Gal. 6. 7. what a man *s*. that shall
Isa. 55. 10. seed to *sower*, 2 Cor. 9. 10.
R. V. Prov. 16. 28. scattereth

SPARE all the place, Gen. 18. 16.
Neh. 13. 22. *s*. me according to

Ps. 39. 13. *s.* me that I may
Prov. 19. 18. let not thy soul *s.* for
Joel 2. 17. *s.* thy people and give
Mal. 3. 17. I will *s.* them, as
Rom. 8. 32. *spared* not his own Son
11. 21. if God *s.* not the natural
2 Pet. 2. 4. God *s.* not angels that
Prov. 13. 24. he that *spareth* rod
R. V. Ps. 72. 13; Jonah 4. 11. have pity on; Prov. 21. 26. withholdeth
SPARKS, Job 5. 7. Isa. 50. 11.
R. V. Isa. 50. 11. firebrands
SPARROW, Ps. 102. 7. Matt. 10. 29.
SPEAK against Moses, Num. 12. 8.
Gen. 18. 27. taken on me to *s.*
Ex. 4. 14. Aaron thy brother can *s.*
34. 35. went in to *s.* to the Lord
1 Sam. 3. 9. *s.* Lord, thy servant
Ps. 85. 8. Lord will *s.* peace to peo.
Isa. 8. 20. if *s.* not according to
Jer. 18. 7. at what instant I *s.*, 9.
Hab. 2. 3. at end it shall *s.* and
Matt. 10. 19. what ye shall *s.*
Luke 6. 26. when all men *s.* well
John 3. 11. we *s.* that we do know
Acts 4. 20. cannot but *s.* things
1 Cor. 1. 10. ye all *s.* the same
Tit. 3. 2. to *s.* evil of no man
Jas. 1. 19. swift to hear, slow to *s.*
2 Pet. 2. 10. *s.* evil of dignities
Jude 10. *s.* evil of things which
Matt. 12. 32. *speaketh* against Son
34. out of the abundance of the heart the mouth *s.*
Heb. 11. 4. he being dead yet *s.*
12. 24. *s.* better things than
1 Pet. 2. 12. *s.* against you as evil
Isa. 45. 19. *I speak*, 63. 1. John 4. 26. & 7. 17. & 8. 26, 28, 38. & 12. 50. Rom. 3. 5. & 6. 19. 1 Tim. 2. 7.
Isa. 58. 13. nor *speaking* own
65. 24. while they are *s.* I will
Dan. 9. 20. while I was *s.* and
Matt. 6. 7. heard for much *s.*
Eph. 4. 15. *s.* the truth in love
31. evil *s.* be put away
5. 19. *s.* to yourselves in psalms
1 Tim. 4. 2. *s.* lies in hypocrisy
Rev. 13. 5. a mouth *s.* great
Gen. 11. 1. earth was of one *speech*
Deut. 32. 2. my *s.* shall distil
Matt. 26. 73. thy *s.* bewrayeth
1 Cor. 2. 1. with excellency of *s.*
2 Cor. 3. 12. great plainness of *s.*
Col. 4. 6. let your *s.* be with grace
Tit. 2. 8. sound *s.* that cannot
Jude 15. all their hard *speeches*
Rom. 16. 18. by fair *s.* deceive
Matt. 22. 12. he was *speechless*
R. V. Many changes, chiefly to say, said, answered, spoken, utter; 2 Sam. 14. 20. matter; 2 Chron. 32. 18. language; S. of S. 4. 3. mouth; Ezek. 1. 24. tumult; Hab. 3. 2. report; 1 Cor. 4. 19. word; Jude 15. things; Luke 1. 22. dumb
SPECTACLE to angels, 1 Cor. 4. 9.
SPEED, Gen. 24. 12. 2 John 10. 11.
Ezra 7. 21. *speedily*, 26. Ps. 31. 2. & 79. 8. Ex. 8. 11. Luke 18. 8.
R. V. Ezek. 6. 12. all diligence; 2 John 10. 11. greeting; Gen. 44. 11. hasted; 2 Sam. 17. 16. in any wise; 2 Chron. 35. 13. quickly; Ezek. 6. 13; 7. 17, 21, 26. with diligence; Ps. 143. 7. make haste
SPEND their days in wealth, Job 21. 13.
Ps. 90. 9. *s.* our years as a tale
Isa. 55. 2. *s.* money for that is
49. 4. have *spent* my strength
Rom. 13. 12. night is far *s.* day
2 Cor. 12. 15. spend and be *s.*
R. V. Ps. 90. 9. bring to an end; Prov. 21. 20. swalloweth; 29. 3. wasteth
SPICES, S. of S. 4. 10, 14, 16. & 8. 14.
R. V. Gen. 43. 11. spicery; 1 Kings 10. 15 ——; Ezek. 24. 10. make thick the broth
SPIDER, Prov. 30. 28. Job 8. 14. Isa. 59. 5.
Prov. 30. 28. *s.* take hold with hands
R. V. *lizard*
SPIES sent into Canaan by Moses, Num. 13. 3, 17, 26. & 14. 36. Deut. 1. 22. Heb. 3. 17.
sent to Jericho by Joshua, Josh. 2. 1, 4, 17, 23. & 6. 17, 23.
SPIKENARD, S. of S. 1. 12. & 4. 13, 14.
SPIRIT made willing, Ex. 35. 21.
Num. 11. 17. take of *s.* which is
2 Kings 2. 9. portion of thy *s.*
Ezra 1. 5. whose *s.* God raised
Neh. 9. 20. gavest good *s.* to instr.
Job 26. 13. by his *s.* he garnished
Ps. 31. 5. into thy hand I commit *s.*
32. 2. in whose *s.* there is no guile
51. 10. renew a right *s.* within me
12. uphold me with thy free *s.*
17. a broken *s.* and contrite, 34. 18. Prov. 15. 13. & 17. 22. Isa. 57. 15. & 66. 2.
Ps. 76. 12. will cut off *s.* of princes
104. 30. sendest forth thy *s.*
139. 7. whither should I go from *s.*
142. 3. my *s.* was overwhelmed
143. 7. *s.* faileth
10. thy *s.* is good
Prov. 14. 29. hasty of *s.* exalteth
15. 13. sorrow of heart the *s.*
16. 18. a haughty *s.* before a fall
18. 14. a wounded *s.* who can bear
Eccl. 3. 21. who knoweth *s.* of man
8. 8. no power over *s.* to retain *s.*
12. 7. the *s.* shall return to God
Isa. 32. 15. until *s.* be poured on us
Mic. 2. 11. walking in *s.* and false.
Zech. 12. 1. formeth *s.* of man within
Mal. 2. 15. take heed to your *s.*
Matt. 22. 43. doth David in *s.* call
26. 41. *s.* is willing, but flesh
Luke 1. 80. John waxed strong in *s.*
8. 55. *s.* came again and she arose
9. 55. what kind of *s.* ye are
24. 39. *s.* hath not flesh and
John 3. 5. born of water and of *s.*
34. God giveth not *s.* by measure
4. 24. God is a *s.* worship him
6. 63. it is the *s.* that quickeneth
Acts 6. 10. not able to resist the *s.*
16. 7. the *s.* suffered them not
17. 16. Paul's *s.* was stirred in
Rom. 8. 1. not after flesh, but *s.*
2. *s.* of life in Christ Jesus made
9. if any have not *s.* of Christ
8. 13. if ye through *s.* mortify
26. the *s.* helpeth our infirmi.
1 Cor. 2. 10. *s.* searcheth all things
5. 3. present in *s.*
5. *s.* may be saved
6. 17. joined unto the Lord is one *s.*, 12. 13.
2 Cor. 3. 3. written with *s.* of liv.
17. *s.* of Lord is, there is liberty
Gal. 3. 3. begun in *s.* are now per.
4. 6. sent forth *s.* of Son into
5. 16. walk in the *s.*
18. if led by *s.* are not under law
22. fruit of *s.* is love, joy, peace
25. if we live in the *s.* let us walk
6. 18. grace be with your *s.*
Eph. 1. 13. with holy *s.* of promise
4. 4. one body and one *s.*
23. renewed in *s.* of your mind
5. 9. fruit of *s.* is in all godliness
Col. 2. 5. I am with you in the *s.*
1 Thes. 5. 23. whole *s.* soul and
Heb. 4. 12. dividing asunder of soul and *s.*
9. 14. through eternal *s.* offered
Jas. 4. 5. *s.* that dwelleth in us
1 Pet. 3. 4. ornament of a meek and quiet *s.*
4. 6. live according to God in the *s.*
1 John 4. 1. believe not every *s.* but try *s.*
Rev. 1. 10. I was in *s.* on Lord's
11. 11. *s.* of life from God entered
14. 13. yea, saith the *s.* that they
Gen. 6. 3. *my spirit*, Job 10. 12. Ps. 31. 5. & 77. 6. Isa. 38. 16. Ezek. 36. 27. Zech. 4. 6. Luke 1. 47. & 23. 46. Acts 7. 59. Rom. 1. 9. 1 Cor. 14. 14.
Gen. 1. 2. *Spirit of God*, Ex. 31. 3. 2 Chron. 15. 1. Job 33. 4. Ezek. 11. 24. Matt. 3. 16. & 12. 28. Rom. 8. 9, 14. & 15. 19. 1 Cor. 2. 11, 14. & 3. 16. & 6. 11. & 12. 3. 2 Cor. 3. 3. Eph. 4. 30. 1 Pet. 4. 14. 1 John 4. 2.
Isa. 11. 2. *s.* of wisdom, Eph. 1. 17.
Zech. 13. 2. unclean *s.*, Matt. 12. 43.
Ps. 104. 4. maketh angels *spirits*
Prov. 16. 2. Lord weigheth the *s.*
Matt. 10. 1. *unclean spirits*, Acts 5. 16. & 8. 7. Rev. 16. 13, 14.
Luke 10. 20. the *s.* are subject
1 Cor. 14. 32. *s.* of the prophets
Heb. 12. 23. to *s.* of just men made
1 Pet. 3. 19. preached to *s.* in prison
1 John 4. 1. try *s.* whether they be
Hos. 9. 7. the *spiritual* man is mad
Rom. 1. 11. impart some *s.* gift
7. 14. law is *s.* but I am carnal
15. 27. partakers of their *s.* things
1 Cor. 2. 13. comparing *s.* things
15. he that is *s.* judgeth all things
9. 11. sown to you *s.* things
10. 3. eat *s.* meat
15. 44. it is raised a *s.* body
Gal. 6. 1. ye which are *s.* restore
Eph. 1. 3. blessed us with *s.* bless.
5. 19. speaking in *s.* songs
6. 12. wrestle against *s.* wicked.
Col. 1. 9. filled with *s.* understand.
1 Pet. 2. 5. built us *s.* house; offer
Rom. 8. 6. to be *spiritually* minded
1 Cor. 2. 14. because *s.* discerned
Rev. 11. 8. *s.* is called Sodom and
R. V. Ps. 104. 4; Eccl. 1. 14, 17; 2. 11, 17, 26; 4. 4, 6, 16; 6. 9; 11. 5; Zech. 6. 5; Heb. 1. 7. wind or winds; Isa. 40. 7; 59. 19; 2 Thes. 2. 8; Rev. 11. 1. breath; Matt. 14. 26; Mark 6. 49. apparition; Acts 18. 5. by word; Eph. 5. 9. light; Luke 2. 40; 9. 55; Rom. 8. 1; 1 Cor. 6. 20; 1 Tim. 4. 12; 1 Pet. 1. 22——
SPITE, Ps. 10. 14. Matt. 22. 6.
SPITTING, Isa. 50. 6. Luke 18. 32.
SPOIL, Gen. 49. 27. Ps. 68. 12.
Ps. 119. 162. that finds great *s.*
Matt. 12. 29. he will *s.* his house
Col. 2. 8. lest any *s.* you through
Ex. 12. 36. *spoiled* the Egyptians
Col. 2. 15. having *s.* principalities
Heb. 10. 34. took joyfully *spoiling*
R. V. Num. 31. 53; 2 Chron. 14. 13. booty; Job 29. 17. prey; Prov. 31. 11. gain; Isa. 25. 11. craft; Hab. 2. 17. destruction; Ps. 35. 12. bereaving
SPOT, without, Num. 19. 2. & 28. 3, 9. Job 11. 15. 2 Tim. 6. 14. Heb. 9. 14. 1 Pet. 1. 19. 2 Pet. 3. 14.
S. of S. 4. 7. there is no *s.* in thee
Eph. 5. 27. not having *s.* or wrinkle
Jer. 13. 23. *spots*, Jude 12, 23.
R. V. Num. 28. 3, 9, 11; 29. 17, 26; Deut. 32. 5; Heb. 9. 14. blemish; Lev. 13. 39. tetter; Jude 12. hidden rocks
SPREAD, Job 9. 8. Isa. 25. 11. & 37. 14. Jer. 4. 3. Lam. 1. 17. Ezek. 16. 8.
R. V. 2 Sam. 17. 19. strewed; 1 Chron. 14. 9. made raid; Job 9. 8. stretcheth; Mark 1. 28. went out; 6. 14. become known; 1 Thes. 1. 8. gone forth
SPRING, Ps. 85. 11. Matt. 13. 5, 7.
Ps. 65. 10. *springing*, John 4. 14. Heb. 12. 15.
Ps. 87. 7. all my *springs* are in thee
R. V. Deut. 4. 49; Josh. 10. 40; 12. 8. slopes; Ps. 87. 7; Jer. 51. 36. fountains; Lev. 13. 42. breaking out; Matt. 13. 7; Luke 8. 6, 7, 8. grew; Mark 4. 8. growing
SPRINKLE, Lev. 14. 7. & 16. 14.
Isa. 52. 15. he shall *s.* many nations
Ezek. 36. 25. I will *s.* clean water
Heb. 10. 22. having hearts *sprinkled* from an evil conscience
12. 24. to blood of *sprinkling*
1 Pet. 1. 2. through *s.* of the blood
SPUE thee out of my mouth, Rev.

3. 16. Hab. 2. 16. Lev. 18. 28. Jer. 25. 27.
R. V. Lev. 18. 28; 20. 22. vomit
SPY, Num. 13. 16. Josh. 2. 1. Gal. 2. 4.
STABILITY of times, Isa. 33. 6.
STAFF, Gen. 32. 10. Zech. 11. 10.
Ps. 23. 4. thy rod and *s.* comfort
Isa. 3. 1. stay and *s.* of bread
10. 5. *s.* in their hand is my
STAGGER, Ps. 107. 27. Rom. 4. 20.
STAIN, Isa. 23. 9. & 63. 3.
R. V. Job 3. 5. claim it
STAKES, Isa. 33. 20. & 54. 2.
STAMMER, Isa. 28. 11. & 33. 19. & 32. 4.
STAND, Ezek. 29. 7. Ex. 9. 11.
Job 19. 25. *s.* at latter day on earth
Ps. 76. 7. who may *s.* in thy sight
130. 3. if Lord mark iniquities who shall *s.*
Isa. 46. 10. my counsel shall *s.*
Mal. 3. 2. who shall *s.* when he
Matt. 12. 25. house divided against itself shall not *s.*
Rom. 5. 2. this grace wherein we *s.*
14. 4. God is able to make him *s.*
2 Cor. 1. 24. by faith ye *s.*
Eph. 6. 13. having done all to *s.*
1 Pet. 5. 12. grace of God wherein ye *s.*
Rev. 3. 20. I *s.* at the door and
Nah. 1. 6. *stand before*, 1 Sam. 6. 20. Luke 21. 36. Rom. 14. 10. Rev. 20. 12.
1 Cor. 16. 13. *stand fast* in the faith
Gal. 5. 1. — in the liberty where.
Phil. 1. 27. — in one spirit
4. 1. — in the Lord
1 Thes. 3. 8. live, if ye — in Lord
2 Thes. 2. 15. — and hold traditions
Ps. 1. 5. *stand in*, 4. 4. & 24. 3.
Ex. 14. 13. *stand still*, see salvation, 2 Chron. 20. 17. Josh. 10. 12. Zech. 11. 16.
Ps. 1. 1. *standeth*, 26. 12. & 33. 11. Prov. 8. 2. S. of S. 2. 9. Isa. 3. 13.
Ps. 119. 161. my heart *s.* in awe of
1 Cor. 10. 12. thinketh he *s.* take
2 Tim. 2. 19. foundation of God *s.*
Jas. 5. 9. the Judge *s.* at the door
R. V. Several changes, but chiefly due to words before and after
STAR, Num. 24. 17. Matt. 2. 2.
Judg. 5. 20. *stars* in their courses
Job 25. 5. *s.* are not pure in his
Dan. 12. 3. shall shine as *s.* for
Jude 13. wandering *s.* to whom is
Rev. 12. 1. a crown of twelve *s.*
R. V. Amos 5. 8. Pleiades
STATURE, Matt. 6. 27. Eph. 4. 13.
STATUTES and laws, Neh. 9. 14.
Ps. 19. 8. *s.* of the Lord are right
Ezek. 20. 25. *s.* not good
Ex. 15. 26. *his statutes*, Deut. 6. 17. 2 Kings 17. 15. Ps. 18. 22. & 105. 45.
1 Chron. 29. 19. *thy statutes*, Ps. 119. 12, 16, 23, 26, 33, 54, 64, 68, 71, 117.
STAVES for the tabernacle, Ex. 25. 13. & 37. 15. & 40. 20. Num. 4. 6.
STAY, Ps. 18. 18. S. of S. 2. 5. Isa. 10. 20. & 26. 3. & 27. 8. & 48. 2. & 50. 10.
R. V. 1 Sam. 24. 7. checked; Job 38. 37. pour out
STEAD, Gen. 4. 25. & 22. 13.
Job 16. 4. if your soul were in my soul's *s.*
2 Cor. 5. 20. pray you in Christ's *s.*
R. V. Phile. 13. behalf
STEADFAST, Job 11. 15. Dan. 6. 26.
Ps. 78. 8. spirit not *s.* with God
Acts 2. 42. continued *s.* in apos.
1 Cor. 15. 58. be ye *s.*, immovable
Heb. 3. 14. hold confidence *s.* to
Col. 2. 5. *steadfastness*, 2 Pet. 3. 17.
R. V. Ps. 78. 37. faithful; Heb. 3. 14. firm
STEAL, Ex. 20. 15. Lev. 19. 11.
Prov. 6. 30. if he *s.* to satisfy his
30. 9. lest I be poor and *s.* and
Matt. 6. 19. thieves break through and *s.*
Matt. 27. 64. disciples come by night and *s.* him away
Eph. 4. 28. that *stole*, steal no more
Prov. 9. 17. *stolen* waters are sweet
STEALING, Ex. 20. 15. & 21. 16. Lev. 19. 11. Deut. 5. 19. & 24. 7. Ps. 50. 18. Zech. 5. 4. Matt. 19. 18. Rom. 13. 9. Eph. 4. 28. 1 Pet. 4. 15.
restoration inculcated, Ex. 22. 1. Lev. 6. 4. Prov. 6. 30, 31.
STEPS, Ex. 20. 26. Ps. 18. 36.
Ps. 37. 23. *s.* of good men ordered
44. 18. neither our *s.* declined
Prov. 16. 9. Lord directeth his *s.*
Jer. 10. 23. man to direct his *s.*
Rom. 4. 12. walk in *s.* of that faith
1 Pet. 2. 21. should follow his *s.*
R. V. Ps. 27. 23. goings; 85. 13. footsteps
STEWARD, Luke 12. 42. & 16. 2. 1 Cor. 4. 1. Tit. 1. 7. 1 Pet. 4. 10.
R. V. 1 Chron. 28. 1. rulers
STIFF neck, Deut. 31. 27. Jer. 17. 23.
Ex. 32. 9. *stiff-necked* people, 33. 3, 5. & 34. 9. Deut. 9. 6, 13. & 10. 16.
Acts 7. 51. — ye do always resist
2 Chron. 36. 13. he *stiffened* his neck
STILL, Ex. 15. 16. Ps. 8. 2. & 139. 18.
Ps. 4. 4. be *s.*, Jer. 47. 6. Mark 4. 39.
46. 10. be *s.* and know that I am
Isa. 30. 7. their strength is to sit *s.*
Rev. 22. 11. unjust *s.* filthy *s.*
Ps. 65. 7. *stilleth* noise of the sea, 89. 9.
STING, 1 Cor. 15. 55, 56. Rev. 9. 10.
Prov. 23. 32. it *stings* like an adder
STINK, Ps. 38. 5. Isa. 3. 24.
R. V. Isa. 3. 24. rottenness
STIR up, Num. 24. 9. Job 17. 8.
Ps. 35. 23. *s.* up thyself, awake
78. 38. did not *s.* up all his wrath
S. of S. 2. 7. that ye *s.* not up
2 Tim. 1. 6. *s.* up gift of God that
2 Pet. 1. 13. think it meet to *s.* you
R. V. Isa. 22. 2. shoutings; Num. 24. 9. rouse; 1 Kings 11. 14, 23. raised; Dan. 11. 10. war; Acts 13. 50. urged on; 17. 16. provoked
STONE of Israel, Gen. 49. 24.
Ps. 118. 22. *s.* which the builders refused
Isa. 8. 14. a *s.* of stumbling
28. 16. a tried *s.* a precious cor. *s.*
Hab. 2. 11. *s.* shall cry out of wall
Matt. 3. 9. of *s.* to raise up children unto Abraham
7. 9. bread, will he give him *s.*
1 Pet. 2. 4. as unto a living *s.*
6. lay in Sion a chief corner *s.*
Ezek. 11. 19. *stony*, Matt. 13. 5.
R. V. Ex. 4. 25. flint; Job 40. 17. thighs; Ps. 137. 9. rock; Isa. 34. 11. plummet; Mark 12. 4. —; John 1. 42. Peter; Matt. 13. 5, 20; Mark 4. 5, 16. rocky
STOOP, Job 9. 13. Prov. 12. 25. Mark 1. 7.
R. V. 1 Sam. 24. 8; 28. 14. bowed
STORE, 1 Cor. 16. 2. 1 Tim. 6. 19.
Luke 12. 24. *storehouse*, Ps. 33. 7.
R. V. Deut. 28. 5, 17. kneading-trough
STORM, Ps. 55. 8. & 83. 15.
Ps. 107. 29. maketh the *s.* a calm
Isa. 4. 6. covert from the *s.*
Mark 4. 37. a great *s.*, Luke 8. 23.
Ps. 148. 8. *stormy* wind fulfilling
R. V. Isa. 29. 6. whirlwind
STOUT hearted, Ps. 76. 5. Isa. 46. 12.
Isa. 10. 12. punish fruit of *s.* heart
Mal. 3. 13. words have been *s.*
Isa. 9. 9. say to pride and *stoutness*
STRAIGHT, Josh. 6. 5. Jer. 31. 9.
Ps. 5. 8. thy way *s.* before my
Isa. 40. 3. make *s.* a highway
4. crooked he made *s.*, 43. 16. Luke 3. 5.
Luke 3. 4. way of the Lord, make his paths *s.*
Heb. 12. 13. make *s.* paths for feet
R. V. Isa. 45. 2. plain
STRAIN at a gnat, Matt. 23. 24.
STRAIT, 2 Sam. 24. 14. Job 20. 22. & 36. 16. Isa. 49. 20. Phil. 1. 23.
Matt. 7. 13. enter in at the *s.* gate
Job 18. 7. steps *straitened*
Mic. 2. 7. spirit of the Lord *s.*
Luke 12. 50. how am I *s.* till it be
2 Cor. 6. 12. not *s.* in us, *s.* in your
R. V. Job 36. 16. distress; Matt. 7. 13, 14; Luke 13. 24. narrow
STRANGE, Ex. 21. 8. & 30. 9. Lev. 10. 1. Ps. 81. 9. Jer. 2. 21. Luke 5. 26. Heb. 11. 9. 1 Pet. 4. 12. Jude 7.
Job 31. 3. is not a *s.* punishment
Isa. 28. 21. do his *s.* work bring
Hos. 8. 12. counted as a *s.* thing
Zeph. 1. 8. clothed with *s.* apparel
Heb. 13. 9. about with *s.* doctrines
Judg. 11. 2. *strange women*, Prov. 2. 16. & 5. 3, 20. & 6. 24. & 20. 16. & 23. 27. & 27. 13. Ezra 10. 2, 11.
Gen. 23. 4. *stranger* and sojourner, Ps. 39. 12. & 119. 19. 1 Chron. 29. 15.
Prov. 14. 10. a *s.* doth not meddle
Jer. 14. 8. should. thou be as a *s.*
Matt. 25. 35. I was a *s.* and ye
Luke 17. 18. to give God glory save this *s.*
John 10. 5. a *s.* will they not follow
Ps. 105. 12. very few and *strangers*
146. 9. Lord preserveth the *s.*
Eph. 2. 12. *s.* from the covenant
Heb. 11. 13. confessed they were *s.*
13. 2. not forgetful to entertain *s.*
1 Pet. 2. 11. beseech you as *s.*
R. V. Job 31. 3. disaster; 19. 13. hardly with; Prov. 21. 8. crooked; Judg. 11. 2. another; Zeph. 1. 8; Acts 26. 11. foreign; Heb. 11. 9. not his own; Gen. 17. 8; 28. 4; 36. 7; 37. 1. sojournings; Ex. 12. 43; Prov. 5. 10; Ezek. 44. 7, 9. alien; Ex. 2. 22; 12. 19; Lev. 25. 47; 1 Chron. 16. 19; Ps. 105. 12; 119. 19; Jer. 14. 8; Acts 2. 10; 7. 29; 1 Pet. 2. 11. sojourner; Deut. 17. 15; 23. 20; 29. 22. foreigner; Isa. 5. 17. wanderers; 29. 5. foes; Obad. 12. of his disaster
STRANGLED, Acts 15. 20, 29. & 21. 25.
Job 7. 15. soul chooseth *strangling*
STREAM, Isa. 30. 33. & 66. 12. Dan. 7. 10. Amos 5. 24. Luke 6. 48.
Ps. 46. 4. *streams*, 126. 4. S. of S. 4. 15. Isa. 30. 25. & 33. 21. & 35. 6.
R. V. Ex. 7. 19; 8. 5. rivers; Num. 21. 15. slope; Job 6. 15. channel; Isa. 27. 12. brook; 57. 6. valley
STREET, Rev. 11. 8. & 21. 21. & 22. 2.
Prov. 1. 20. *streets*, S. of S. 3. 2. Luke 14. 21.
R. V. 2 Chron. 29. 4; 32. 6; Ezra 10. 9; Neh. 8. 1, 3, 16; Esth. 4. 6; Prov. 1. 20; 7. 12; Isa. 15. 3; Amos 5. 16. broad place or way; Ps. 144. 13. fields; Mark 6. 56. market place
STRENGTH, Gen. 49. 24. Ex. 13. 3.
Ex. 15. 2. the Lord is my *s.* and my song, Ps. 18. 2. & 28. 7. & 118. 14. Isa. 12. 2.
Judg. 5. 21. soul thou hast trodden down *s.*
1 Sam. 2. 9. by *s.* shall no man
Job 9. 19. if I speak of *s.* lo, he
Ps. 18. 32. girded me with *s.*, 39.
27. 1. the Lord is the *s.* of my life
29. 11. Lord will give *s.* to his
33. 16. mighty not delivered by *s.*
39. 13. spare me that I recover *s.*
46. 1. God is our refuge and *s.*
73. 26. God is *s.* of my heart
84. 5. blessed whose *s.* is in thee
93. 1. the Lord is clothed with *s.*
96. 6. *s.* and beauty are in his
140. 7. Lord, the *s.* of my salvation
Prov. 10. 29. Lord is *s.* to the up.
Eccl. 9. 16. wisd. is better than *s.*
Isa. 25. 4. *s.* to poor and *s.* to needy
26. 4. in Jehovah is everlasting *s.*
Joel 3. 16. Lord is the *s.* of child.
Luke 1. 51. shewed *s.* with his

Rom. 5. 6. we were without *s.*
1 Cor. 15. 56. *s.* of sin is the law
Rev. 3. 8. thou hast a little *s.* and
5. 12. worthy is the Lamb to receive *s.*
17. 13. give their *s.* to beast
1 Chron. 16. 11. *his strength,* Ps. 33. 17. Isa. 61. 1. Hos. 7. 9. & 12. 3.
Gen. 49. 24. *in strength,* Job 9. 4. & 36. 5. Ps. 71. 16. & 103. 20. & 147. 10. Isa. 33. 6.
Gen. 49. 3. *my strength,* Ex. 15. 2. 2 Sam. 22. 33. Job 6. 12. Ps. 8. 1, 2. & 19. 14. & 28. 7. & 38. 10. & 43. 2. & 59. 17. & 62. 7. & 71. 9. & 99. 4. & 102. 23. & 118. 14. & 144. 1. Isa. 12. 2. & 27. 5. & 49. 4, 5. Jer. 16. 19. Hab. 3. 19. 2 Cor. 12. 9.
Ps. 37. 39. *their strength,* 89. 17. Prov. 20. 29. Isa. 30. 7. & 40. 31.
Ps. 8. 2. *thy strength,* 86. 16. & 110. 2. Prov. 24. 10. & 31. 3. Isa. 17. 10. & 63. 15. Mark 14. 32. Deut. 33. 25.
Neh. 8. 10. *your strength,* Isa. 23. 14. & 30. 15. Ezek. 24. 21. Lev. 26. 20.
Ps. 20. 2. Lord *strengthen* thee
27. 14. the Lord, he shall *s.* your
31. 24. he shall *s.* your heart
41. 3. *s.* him on bed of languish.
Isa. 35. 3. *s.* ye the weak hands
Dan. 11. 1. stood to confirm and *s.*
Zech. 10. 12. I will *s.* them in Lord
Luke 22. 32. when converted *s.* thy brethren
Rev. 3. 2. *s.* the things that rema.
1 Sam. 23. 16. *strengthened* his hand in God
Ezek. 34. 4. diseased have ye not *s.*
Eph. 3. 16. *s.* with might, Col. 1. 11.
2 Tim. 4. 17. the Lord stood with me and *s.* me
Ps. 138. 3. *s.* me with *s.* in my soul
104. 15. bread which *strengtheneth*
Phil. 4. 13. Christ who *s.* me
R. V. Job 12. 13; 39. 19; Ps. 80. 2; Prov. 8. 14; 24. 5; Rev. 5. 12. might; Ps. 18. 2; 144. 1; Isa. 26. 4. rock; Ps. 60. 7; 108. 8. defence; Ps. 31. 4; 37. 39; Prov. 10. 29; Isa. 23. 4, 14; 25. 4; Ezek. 30. 15; Nah. 3. 11. strong hold; Ps. 33. 17; Ezek. 24. 21; 30. 18; 33. 28; 1 Cor. 15. 56; 2 Cor. 12. 9; Heb. 11. 11; Rev. 3. 8; 12. 10. power; Ps. 41. 3. support; Ezek. 30. 25. hold up; Luke 22. 32; Acts 18. 23; Rev. 3. 2. stablish

STRETCH thy hands, Job 11. 13.
Amos 6. 4. *s.* themselves on couch.
Matt. 12. 13. *s.* forth thy hand
John 21. 18. thou shalt *s.* forth
Gen. 22. 10. *stretched* forth his
1 Kings 17. 21. *s.* himself upon
1 Chron. 21. 16. drawn sword *s.*
Isa. 5. 25. hand is *s.* out still
Job 15. 25. he *stretcheth* out hand
Prov. 31. 20. she *s.* out hand to
Isa. 40. 22. *s.* out the heavens as a curtain, 42. 5. & 44. 24. & 45. 12. & 51. 13. Jer. 10. 12. & 51. 15. Zech. 12. 1.
R. V. Ex. 3. 20; 9. 15; 1 Sam. 24. 6; 26. 9, 11, 23; 2 Sam. 1. 14; Job 30. 24; Acts 12. 1. put; Ex. 25. 20; Ps. 44. 20; 88. 9; 136. 6; 143. 6; Prov. 31. 20; Isa. 16. 8; Rom. 10. 21. spread, or spread forth

STRIFE between me, Gen. 13. 8.
Ps. 80. 6. us a *s.* to our neighbors
Prov. 10. 12. hatred stirreth up *s.*
16. 28. froward man soweth *s.*
20. 3. an honor to cease from *s.*
28. 25. proud heart stirreth up *s.*
Isa. 58. 4. ye fast for *s.* and debate
Luke 22. 24. was a *s.* among them
Rom. 13. 13. not in *s.* and envying
Gal. 5. 20. wrath, *s.*, sedition
Phil. 1. 15. preach Christ of *s.* and
2 Tim. 2. 23. gender *s.*, 2 Cor. 12. 20.
Jas. 3. 14. bitter envying and *s.* 16.
R. V. Ps. 106. 32. Meribah; Prov. 15. 18; 26. 20; Luke 22. 24. contention; 2 Cor. 12. 20; Gal. 5. 20; Phil. 2. 3; Jas. 3. 14, 16. faction: 1 Tim. 6. 4. disputes

STRIKE hands, Job 17. 3. Prov. 6. 1.
Prov. 17. 26. *s.* princes for equity
Isa. 1. 5. why be *stricken* any more
53. 4. esteem him *s.* of God
1 Tim. 3. 3. a bishop, no *striker*
R. V. Ex. 12. 7. put; Deut. 21. 4. break; 2 Kings 5. 11. wave; Hab. 3. 14. pierce; Mark 14. 65. received blows; 2 Chron. 13. 20; Matt. 26. 51. smote; Luke 22. 64 ——

STRIPES, Isa. 53. 5. 1 Pet. 2. 24. Prov. 17. 10. & 20. 30. Luke 12. 47, 48.
R. V. Prov. 20. 30. strokes

STRIVE, Ex. 21. 18, 22. Job 33. 13.
Gen. 6. 3. Spirit shall not alw. *s.*
Prov. 3. 30. *s.* not without cause
Hos. 4. 4. let no man *s.* nor reprove
Matt. 12. 19. he shall not *s.* nor
Luke 13. 24. *s.* to enter in at strait
Isa. 45. 9. that *striveth* with Maker
Phil. 1. 27. *striving* together for
Heb. 12. 4. resisted unto blood *s.*
R. V. Ex. 21. 18; 2 Tim. 2. 5. contend; Rom. 15. 20. making it my aim

STRONG this day, Josh. 14. 11.
Ps. 24 8. Lord is *s.* and mighty
30. 7. made mountain to stand *s.*
31. 2. be thou my *s.* rock
71. 7. thou art my *s.* refuge, 3.
Prov. 10. 15. rich man's wealth is his *s.* city
18. 10. name of Lord is a *s.* tower
24. 5. a wise man is *s.* and
Eccl. 9. 11. battle is not to the *s.*
S. of S. 8. 6. love is *s.* as death
Isa. 1. 31. *s.* shall be as tow and
35. 4. be *s.* fear not, behold your
53. 12. divide the spoil with *s.*
Jer. 50. 34. their Redeemer is *s.*
Joel 3. 10. the weak say I am *s.*
Luke 11. 21. *s.* man armed keepeth
Rom. 4. 20. *s.* in faith, giving glory
15. 1. we that are *s* ought to bear the infirmities of the weak
Heb. 11. 34. weakness made *s.*
1 John 2. 14. because ye are *s.*
Isa. 35. 4. *be strong,* Hag. 2. 4. 1 Cor. 16. 13. Eph. 6. 10. 2 Tim. 2. 1.
1 Cor. 1. 25. *stronger* than men
Job 17. 9. clean hands shall be *s.*
Jer. 20. 7. thou art *s.* than I
R. V. Few changes to mighty, valiant, etc.

STUBBLE, Job 13. 25. & 21. 18. Ps. 83. 13. Isa. 33. 11. Mal. 4. 1. 1 Cor. 3. 12.

STUBBORN, Deut. 21. 18. Ps. 78. 8.
1 Sam. 15. 23. *stubbornness,* Deut. 9. 27.
R. V. Prov. 7. 11. wilful

STUDY, Eccl. 12. 12. 1 Thes. 4. 11. 2 Tim. 2. 15. Prov. 15. 28. & 24. 2.
R. V. 2 Tim. 2. 15. give diligence

STUMBLE, foot shall not, Prov. 3. 23.
Prov. 4. 12. runnest, shalt not *s.*
Isa. 5. 27. shall be weary nor *s.*
8. 15. many shall *s.* and fall
Mal. 2. 8. cause many to *s.* at law
1 Pet. 2. 8. which *s.* at the word
Rom. 9. 32. they *stumbled* at that
John 11. 9. day he *stumbleth* not
Rom. 14. 21. whereby thy brother *s.*
Isa. 8. 14. *stumbling,* 1 John 2. 10.
Lev. 19. 14. *stumbling-block,* Isa. 8. 14. & 57. 14. Jer. 6. 21. Ezek. 3. 20. & 7. 19. & 14. 3, 4, 7. Rom. 9. 32, 33. & 11. 9. & 14. 13. 1 Cor. 1. 23. & 8. 9. Rev. 2. 14.
R. V. Prov. 24. 17. is overthrown

SUBDUE our iniquities, Mic. 7. 9.
Ps. 81. 14. soon *s.* their enemies
Phil. 3. 21. able to *s.* all things
Heb. 11. 33. through faith *subdued*
R. V. Deut. 20. 20. fall; Dan. 7. 24. put down; Mic. 7. 19. tread under foot; Zech. 9. 15. tread down; 1 Cor. 15. 28; Phil. 3. 21. subject

SUBJECT, devils are, Luke 10. 17, 20.
Rom. 8. 7. not *s.* to law of God
13. 1. every soul be *s.* to higher
1 Cor. 14. 32. spirit of prophets *s.*
15. 28. Son shall be *s.* to him that
Eph. 5. 24. as church is *s.* to Christ
Tit. 3. 1. to be *s.* to principalities
Heb. 2. 15. all lifetime *s.* to bond.
Jas. 5. 17. Elias, a man *s.* to
1 Pet. 2. 18. servants be *s.* to mas.
3. 22. angels and powers made *s.*
5. 5. all ye be *s.* one to another
1 Cor. 9. 27. *subjection,* 1 Tim. 2. 11. & 3. 4. Heb. 2. 5, 8. & 12. 9. 1 Pet. 3. 1, 5.
R. V. Rom. 13. 5; Tit. 3. 1; 1 Pet. 2. 18. in subjection; 1 Cor. 9. 27. bondage; 2 Cor. 9. 13. obedience

SUBMIT, Gen. 16. 9. Ps. 18. 44. & 66. 3. & 68. 30. & 81. 15.
1 Cor. 16. 16. *submit yourselves,* Eph. 5. 21, 22. Col. 3. 18. Heb. 13. 17. Jas. 4. 7. 1 Pet. 2. 13. & 5. 5.
Rom. 10. 3. have not *submitted* to righteousness
R. V. Rom. 10. 3; Eph. 5. 21, 22; 1 Cor. 16. 16; Col. 3. 18; Jas. 4. 7; 1 Pet. 2. 13; 5. 5. be subject or subjection

SUBSCRIBE, Isa. 44. 5. Jer. 32. 44.

SUBSTANCE, Gen. 7. 4. & 15. 14.
Deut. 33. 11. bless Lord, his *s.*
Job 30. 22. thou dissolvest my *s*
Ps. 139. 15. my *s.* was not hid
Prov. 3. 9. honor Lord with thy *s.*
Hos. 12. 8. I have found me out *s.*
Luke 8. 3. ministered to him of *s.*
Heb. 10. 34. a more enduring *s.*
11. 1. faith is *s.* of things hoped
R. V. Gen. 7. 4. thing; Deut. 11. 6. living thing; Gen. 36. 6; Heb. 10. 34. possession; Ps. 139. 15. frame; Prov. 10. 3. desire; Isa. 6. 13. stock; Hos. 12. 8. wealth; Heb. 11. 1. assurance

SUBTIL, Gen. 3. 1. Prov. 7. 10.
Acts 13. 10. *subtilty,* 2 Cor. 11. 3. Prov. 1. 4.
R. V. Prov. 7. 10. wily

SUBVERT, Lam. 3. 36. Tit. 1. 11. & 3. 11.
Acts 13. 24. *subverting* souls, 2 Tim. 2. 14.
R. V. Tit. 1. 11. overthrow; 3. 11. perverted

SUCK, Gen. 21. 7. Deut. 32. 13. & 33. 19.
Job 20. 16. *s.* poison of asps and
Isa. 60. 16. *s.* milk of Gentiles
66. 11. *s.* and be satisfied, 12.
Matt. 24. 19. to them that give *s.*
Luke 23. 29. blessed are paps which never gave *s.*
11. 27. blessed are paps thou hast *sucked*
Isa. 11. 8. *sucking* child, 49. 15.
Ps. 8. 2. *suckling,* Lam. 2. 11. & 4. 4.
R. V. Ezek. 23. 34. drain

SUDDEN, Prov. 3. 25. 1 Thes. 5. 3.

SUFFER, Ex. 12. 23. Lev. 19. 17.
Ps. 55. 22. never *s.* righteous
89. 33. nor *s.* my faithfulness
121. 3. *s.* thy foot to be moved
Prov. 10. 3. *s.* soul of righteous
Matt. 16. 21. must *s.* many things
17. 17. how long shall I *s.* you
19. 14. *s.* little children to come
1 Cor. 4. 12. being persecuted, we *s.*
Phil. 1. 29. also to *s.* for his sake
2 Tim. 2. 12. if we *s.* we shall reign
Heb. 11. 25. rather to *s.* affliction
13. 3. them who *s.* adversity
1 Pet. 4. 15. none *s.* as a murderer
Ps. 105. 14. he *suffered* no man
Acts 14. 16. *s.* all to walk in his
16. 7. the Spirit *s.* them not
Phil. 3. 8. for whom I *s.* loss of all
Heb. 5. 8. learned obedience by the things he *s.*
1 Pet. 2. 21. *s.* for us leaving us
3. 18. Christ hath *s.* once for sins

Matt. 11. 12. *suffereth*, 1 Cor. 13. 4.
Rom. 8. 18. *sufferings*, 2 Cor. 1. 5, 6. Phil. 3. 10. Col. 1. 24. Heb. 2. 10. 1 Pet. 1. 11. & 4. 13. & 5. 1.
R. V. Lev. 22. 16. cause; Lev. 19. 17; Prov. 19. 19; Matt. 17. 17; Mark 9. 19; Luke 9. 41; 1 Cor. 9. 12; 2 Cor. 11. 19, 20; Heb. 13. 22. bear, or bear with; Luke 8. 32. give leave; 12. 39. left; 1 Cor. 4. 12; 2 Tim. 2. 12. endure; 1 Tim. 2. 12. permit; 4. 10. strive
SUFFICE, 1 Pet. 4. 3. John 14. 8.
Matt. 6. 34. *sufficient* to-day is evil
2 Cor. 2. 16. who is *s*. for these
3. 5. we are not *s*. of ourselves
12. 9. my grace is *s*. for thee
Job 20. 22. *sufficiency*, 2 Cor. 3. 5. & 9. 8.
SUM, Ps. 139. 17. Ezek. 28. 12. Heb. 8. 1.
R. V. Ex. 21. 30. ransom; Acts 7. 16. price; Heb. 8. 1. chief point
SUMMER and winter not cease, Gen. 8. 22.
Ps. 74. 17. hast made *s*. and winter
Prov. 6. 8. provideth her meat in *s*.
10. 5. gathereth in *s*. is a wise
Isa. 18. 6. fowls shall *s*. and winter
Jer. 8. 20. harvest past and *s*. ended
Zech. 14. 3. living waters in *s*.
SUMPTUOUSLY, fared, Luke 16. 19.
SUN, stand thou still, Josh. 10. 12.
Ps. 19. 4. he set a tabernacle for *s*.
104. 19. *s*. knoweth his going
121. 6. *s*. not smite thee by day
136. 8. *s*. to rule day, Gen. 1. 16.
Eccl. 12. 2. while *s*. or stars be not darkened
S. of S. 1. 6. because the *s*. hath
Isa. 30. 26. light of the *s*. shall
66. 19. *s*. no more thy light by
Jer. 31. 35. giveth *s*. for a light by
Mal. 4. 2. *S*. of righteousness arise
Matt. 5. 45. his *s*. to rise on evil
13. 43. shine as *s*. in the kingdom
1 Cor. 15. 41. there is one glory of *s*.
Eph. 4. 26. let not *s*. go down on
Rev. 7. 16. neither *s*. light on them
10. 1. his face as *s*., 1. 16.
21. 23. city had no need of the *s*., 22. 5.
SUP, Luke 17. 8. Rev. 3. 20. Hab. 1. 9.
Luke 14. 16. certain man made a great *supper*
1 Cor. 11. 20. to eat Lord's *s*., Luke 22. 20.
Rev. 19. 9. to marriage *s*.
R. V. Hab. 1. 9. set eagerly
SUPERFLUITY of naughtiness, Jas. 1. 21.
SUPERSTITION, Acts 25. 19. & 17. 22.
SUPPLICATION, 1 Kings 8. 28. & 9. 3. Job 8. 5. & 9. 15. Ps. 6. 9. & 30. 8. & 55. 1. & 142. 1. & 119. 170. Dan. 6. 11. & 9. 20. Hos. 12. 4. Zech. 12. 10. Eph. 6. 18. Phil. 4. 6. 1 Tim. 2. 1. & 5. 5. Heb. 5. 7.
SUPPLY spirit of Jesus Christ, Phil. 1. 19.
Phil. 4. 19. God shall *s*. all need
2 Cor. 9. 12. *supplieth*, Eph. 4. 16.
R. V. 2 Cor. 9. 12. filleth measure
SUPPORT the weak, Acts 20. 35.
1 Thes. 5. 14.
R. V. Acts 20. 35. help
SUPREME, 1 Pet. 2. 13.
SURE, Gen. 23. 17. 1 Sam. 25. 28.
Neh. 9. 38. we make a *s*. covenant
Ps. 19. 7. testimo. of the Lord is *s*.
111. 7. his commandments are *s*.
Prov. 11. 15. hateth suretiship is *s*.
18. righteous. shall be *s*. reward
Isa. 22. 23, 25. *s*. place
28. 16. *s*. foundation
55. 3. *s*. mercies of David
John 6. 69. we believe and are *s*.
Rom. 4. 16. promise might be *s*.
2 Tim. 2. 19. the foundation of God standeth *s*.

2 Pet. 1. 10. calling and election *s*.
R. V. Prov. 6. 3. importune; Ex. 3. 19; 1 Sam. 20. 7; Luke 10. 11; John 6. 69; 16. 30; Rom. 2. 2; 15. 29. know; 2 Tim. 2. 19. firm
SURETY for servant, Ps. 119. 122.
Heb. 7. 22. Jesus made *s*. of better
R. V. Acts 12. 11. truth
SURETYSHIP, evils of, Prov. 6. 1. & 11. 15. & 17. 18. & 20. 16. & 22. 26. & 27. 13.
SURFEITING and drunkenness, Luke 21. 34.
SURPRISED hypocrites, Isa. 33. 14.
SUSTAIN, Ps. 55. 22. Prov. 18. 14.
Ps. 3. 5. *sustained*, Isa. 59. 16.
R. V. Isa. 59. 16. upheld
SWALLOW, Ps. 84. 3. Jer. 8. 7.
Isa. 25. 8. will *s*. up death in vic.
Matt. 23. 24. gnat, and *s*. a camel
Ex. 15. 12. earth *swallowed* them
Ps. 124. 3. they had *s*. us up quick
2 Cor. 2. 7. be *s*. up with overmuch sorrow
5. 4. mortality be *s*. up of life
R. V. Job 5. 5. gapeth for; Hab. 1. 13. devoureth
SWEAR, Num. 30. 2. Deut. 6. 13.
Isa. 45. 23. every tongue shall *s*.
65. 16. shall *s*. by the God of truth
Jer. 4. 2. shalt *s*. Lord liveth in
Zeph. 1. 5. *s*. by Lord, and *s*.
Matt. 5. 34. *s*. not at all
Ps. 15. 4. *sweareth* to his own hurt
Eccl. 9. 2. *s*. as he that feareth
Zech. 5. 3. every one that *s*. shall
Jer. 23. 10. because of *swearing*
Hos. 4. 2. by *s*. and lying they
10. 4. *s*. falsely in making a cov.
Mal. 3. 5. I will be a witness against false *s*.
R. V. Ex. 6. 8. lifted up my hand; Lev. 5. 1. adjuration
SWEAT, Gen. 3. 19. Luke 22. 44.
SWEET, Job 20. 12. Ps. 55. 14.
Ps. 104. 34. meditation of him be *s*.
119. 103. how *s*. thy words to my
Prov. 3. 24. thy sleep shall be *s*.
9. 17. stolen waters are *s*.
27. 7. to hungry bitter thing is *s*.
Eccl. 5. 12. sleep of labor. man *s*.
S. of S. 2. 8. his fruit was *s*. to my
14. *s*. is thy voice and thy counte.
Isa. 5. 20. put bitter for *s*. and *s*.
Phil. 4. 18. odor of a *s*. smell
Rev. 10. 9. in thy mouth *s*. as hon.
Ps. 19. 10. *sweeter* than honey
Judg. 14. 14. *sweetness*, Prov. 16. 21. & 27. 9.
R. V. Jer. 6. 20. pleasing; Mark 16. 1 —
SWELLING, Jer. 12. 5. 2 Pet. 2. 18.
R. V. Jer. 12. 5; 49. 19; 50. 44. pride
SWIFT, Deut. 28. 49. Job 9. 26.
Eccl. 9. 11. race is not to the *s*.
Rom. 3. 15. feet are *s*. to shed
Jas. 1. 19. *s*. to hear, slow to
2 Pet. 2. 1. bring on themselves *s*. destruction
Job 7. 6. days *swifter* than a shut.
Ps. 147. 15. *swiftly*, Joel 3. 4.
SWIM, 2 Kings 6. 6. Ps. 6. 6. Ezek. 47. 5.
SWORD, Ex. 32. 27. Lev. 26. 24.
Deut. 32. 29. *s*. of thy excellency
Judg. 7. 20. *s*. of Lord and Gideon
2 Sam. 12. 10. *s*. shall never depart
Ps. 17. 13. wicked which is thy *s*.
149. 6. two-edged *s*. in their hands
S. of S. 3. 8. man hath his *s*. on
Jer. 9. 16. send a *s*. after them
Ezek. 21. 13. if *s*. contemn rod
Zech. 11. 17. *s*. shall be upon his
13. 7. awake, O *s*., against shep.
Matt. 10. 34. not send peace, but *s*.
Luke 2. 35. a *s*. shall pierce through
Rom. 13. 4. beareth not *s*. in vain
Eph. 6. 17. *s*. of the Spirit, which
Heb. 4. 12. word is sharper than any two-edged *s*.
Rev. 1. 16. a sharp two-edged *s*.
Ps. 55. 21. *swords*, 59. 7. Prov. 30. 14.
Isa. 2. 4. Ezek. 32. 27. Joel 3. 10.

R. V. Job 2. 25. point; Joel 2. 8. weapons
SWORN by myself, Gen. 22. 16.
Ps. 24. 4. that hath not *s*. deceit.
119. 106. I have *s*. and will per.
SYNAGOGUE, Ps. 74. 8. Matt. 6. 5. & 23. 6. Luke 7. 5. John 9. 22. & 18. 20. Acts 15. 21. Rev. 2. 9. & 3. 9.
R. V. Acts 13. 42 —

T

TABERNACLE, Ex. 26. 1. & 29. 43.
Job 5. 24. thy *t*. shall be in peace
Ps. 15. 1. who shall abide in thy *t*.
27. 5. in secret of his *t*. shall hide
Prov. 14. 11. *t*. of the upright shall
Isa. 33. 20. a *t*. shall not be taken
Amos 9. 11. raise up *t*. of David
2 Cor. 5. 1. earthly house of this *t*.
Heb. 8. 2. minister of the true *t*.
2 Pet. 1. 13. I am in this *t*.
Rev. 21. 3. *t*. of God is with men
Job 12. 6. *tabernacles* of robbers
Ps. 84. 1. how amiable are thy *t*.
118. 15. salvation is in the *t*. of the
Heb. 11. 9. dwell in *t*. with Isaac
R. V. In O. T. nearly always tent or tents; Luke 16. 9; Acts 7. 46. habitation
TABLE, Ex. 25. 23. Job 36. 16.
Ps. 23. 5. prepared a *t*. before me
69. 22. let their *t*. become a snare
Prov. 3. 3. write them on *t*. of heart
S. of S. 1. 12. king sitteth at his *t*.
Mal. 1. 7. *t*. of Lord is contempt.
Matt. 15. 27. crumbs from mast. *t*.
1 Cor. 10. 21. partakers of Lord's *t*.
Deut. 10. 4. *tables*, 5. Heb. 9. 4. 2 Chron. 4. 8, 19. Isa. 28. 8. Ezek. 40. 41.
Hab. 2. 2. make it plain upon *t*.
Acts 6. 2. leave . . God and serve *t*.
2 Cor. 3. 3. not in *t*. of stone, but
R. V. Isa. 30. 8; Luke 1. 63. tablet; Mark 7. 4 —; John 12. 2. meat
TAKE you for a people, Ex. 6. 7
Ex. 20. 7. not *t*. name of the Lord
34. 9. *t*. us for thine inheritance
Ps. 27. 12. the Lord will *t*. me up
116. 12. I will *t*. cup of salvation
119. 43. *t*. not the word of truth
Hos. 14. 2. *t*. with you words; say *t*.
Matt. 16. 24. *t*. up his cross and
18. 16. *t*. with thee one or two
20. 14. *t*. that thine is, and go thy
26. 26. said *t*. eat, this is my body, 1 Cor. 11. 24.
Luke 12. 19. *t*. thine ease, eat
Eph. 6. 13. *t*. the whole armor of
Rev. 3. 11. no man *t*. thy crown
Ex. 23. 25. *take away*, Josh. 7. 13. 2 Sam. 24. 10. 1 Chron. 17. 13. Job 7. 21. & 32. 22. & 36. 1. Ps. 58. 9. Isa. 58. 9. Jer. 15. 15. Hos. 1. 6. & 4. 11. & 14. 2. Amos 4. 2. Mal. 2. 3. Luke 17. 31. John 1. 29. 1 John 3. 5. Rev. 22. 19.
Deut. 4. 9. *take heed*, 11. 16. & 27. 9. 2 Chron. 19. 6. Ps. 39. 1. Isa. 7. 4. Mal. 2. 15. Matt. 6. 1. & 16. 6. & 18. 10. & 24. 4. Mark 4. 24. & 13. 33. Luke 8. 18. & 12. 15. 1 Cor. 10. 12. Col. 4. 17. Heb. 3. 12. 2 Pet. 1. 19.
Deut. 32. 41. *take hold*, Ps. 69. 24. Isa. 27. 5. & 56. 4. & 64. 7. Zech. 1. 6.
Ps. 83. 3. *taken* crafty counsel
119. 111. testimony have I *t*.
Isa. 53. 8. he was *t*. from prison
Lam. 4. 20. the anointed was *t*. in
Matt. 21. 43. kingdom of God *t*.
24. 40. one shall be *t*. the other
Mark 4. 25. be *t*. that which he hath
Acts 1. 9. *t*. up into heaven
2 Tim. 2. 26. *t*. captive by him
Isa. 6. 7. thy iniquity is *taken away*
57. 1. merciful men are —
Luke 10. 42. good part not be—from
2 Cor. 3. 16. return to Lord, veil —
Ps. 40. 12. my iniquities *taken hold*
Prov. 1. 19. *taketh away*, John 1. 29 & 10. 18. & 15. 2; *taketh from*. 16. 22

Ps. 119. 9. by *taking* heed thereto
Matt. 6. 27. who by *t.* thought can
Rom. 7. 8. sin *t.* occasion deceived
Eph. 6. 16. above all *t.* shield of
R. V. The frequent changes are mostly due to context; as, Matt. 6. 25. take no thought, becomes, be not anxious, etc.

TALE, Ps. 90. 9. Ezek. 22. 29. Luke 24. 11.
Lev. 19. 16. *tale-bearer*, Prov. 11. 13. & 18. 8. & 20. 19. & 26. 20, 22.
R. V. Luke 24. 11. talk

TALENTS, Matt. 18. 24. & 25. 15, 25.

TALK of them when thou sittest, Deut. 6. 7.
1 Sam. 2. 3. *t.* no more so proudly
Job. 13. 7. and *t.* deceitfully for
Ps. 71. 24. my tongue shall *t.*
77. 12. I will *t.* of thy doings
105. 2. *t.* ye of his wondrous works
145. 11. speak of glory and *t.* of
Jer. 12. 1. *t.* with thee of judgment
John 14. 30. I will not *t.* much
Ps. 37. 30. his tongue *talketh* of
Eph. 5. 4. nor foolish *talking*
Tit. 1. 10. unruly and vain *talkers*
R. V. Several changes and nearly all to speak or spake; 1 Kings 18. 27. musing

TAME, Mark 5. 4. Jas. 3. 7, 8.

TARRY, 1 Chron. 19. 5. 2 Kings 14. 10.
Prov. 23. 30. that *t.* long at wine
Isa. 46. 13. my salvation shall not *t.*
Hab. 2. 3. though it *t.* wait for it
Matt. 26. 38. *t.* ye here and watch
John 21. 22. that he *t.* till I come
1 Cor. 11. 33. come to eat *t.* for one
Ps. 68. 12. she that *tarried* at home
Matt. 25. 5. the bridegroom *t.* all
Luke 2. 43. child Jesus *t.* behind in
Acts 22. 16. why *tarriest* thou
Ps. 40. 17. make no *tarrying*, 70. 5.
R. V. Lev. 14. 8. dwell; 1 Sam. 14. 2; 2 Sam. 15. 29; 2 Kings 14. 10; Matt. 26. 38; Mark 14. 34; Luke 24. 29; John 4. 40; Acts 9. 43; 18. 20. abide or abode; Ps. 101. 7. be established; Hab. 2. 3. delay; Acts 20. 5; 27. 33; 1 Cor. 11. 38. wait or waiting, Acts 15. 33. spent time; Acts 20. 15 —

TASKMASTERS, Ex. 1. 11. & 5. 6.

TASTE, Ex. 16. 31. 1 Sam. 14. 43.
Job 6. 6. *t.* in white of an egg
Ps. 34. 8. *t.* and see Lord is good
119. 103. sweet are thy words to *t.*
S. of S. 2. 3. fruit was sweet to *t.*
Jer. 48. 11. *t.* remained in him
Matt. 16. 28. not *t.* of death
Luke 14. 24. *t.* of my supper
John 8. 52. keep my saying, never *t.* death
Col. 2. 21. touch not, *t.* not, handle
Heb. 2. 9. *t.* death for every man
6. 4. *t.* heavenly gift
5. *t.* good word of God
1 Pet. 2. 3. if ye have *tasted* that

TATTLERS, 1 Tim. 5. 13.

TAXATION of all the world, under Cæsar Augustus, Luke 2. 1.

TEACH, Ex. 4. 12. Lev. 10. 11.
Deut. 4. 9. *t.* them thy sons, 6. 7.
33. 10. shall *t.* Jacob thy judg.
1 Sam. 12. 23. *t.* good way
2 Chron. 17. 7. to *t.* in cities of
Job 21. 22. shall any *t.* God
Ps. 25. 8. *t.* sinners in the way
34. 11. *t.* you fear of Lord
51. 13. *t.* transgressors thy way
90. 12. *t.* us to number our days
Isa. 2. 3. he will *t.* us of his ways
Jer. 31. 34. *t.* no more every man
Matt. 28. 19. go and *t.* all nations
John 9. 34. dost thou *t.* us
14. 26. Holy Ghost shall *t.* you all
1 Cor. 4. 17. as I *t.* in every church
1 Tim. 3. 2. given to hospitality, apt to *t.*
2 Tim. 2. 2. faithful men able to *t.*
Heb. 5. 12. need that one *t.* you
Job 34. 32. what I see not, *teach me*
Ps. 25. 4. — thy paths, 5. & 27. 11. — thy way, 86. 11. & 119. 12. — thy statutes, 26. 64, 66, 68, 124, 135. — good judgment, 108. — thy judgments, 143. 10. — to do thy will
2 Chron. 32. 22. *taught* good knowl.
Ps. 71. 17. hast *t.* me from my
119. 171. hast *t.* me thy statutes
Eccl. 12. 9. he *t.* people knowledge
Isa. 29. 13. *t.* by precepts of men
John 6. 45. shall be all *t.* of God
Acts 20. 20. *t.* you publicly and
Gal. 6. 6. let him that is *t.* in word
1 Thes. 4. 9. yourselves are *t.* of God
Ps. 94. 12. *teachest* him out of law
Matt. 22. 16. *t.* way of God in
Rom. 2. 21. *t.* another, *t.* not thy.
Job 36. 22. who *teacheth* like him
Ps. 18. 34. *t.* my hands to war
94. 10. he that *t.* man knowledge
Isa. 48. 17. Lord thy God *t.* thee to
1 Cor. 2. 13. words which man's wisdom *t.* but which the Holy Ghost *t.*
1 John 2. 27. anointing *t.* you
Hab. 2. 18. *teacher*, John 3. 2. Rom. 2. 20. 1 Tim. 2. 7. 2 Tim. 1. 11.
Ps. 119. 99. *teachers*, Isa. 30. 20.
2 Tim. 4. 3. heap to themselves *t.*
Tit. 2. 3. be *t.* of good things
Heb. 5. 12. ought to be *t.* ye have
2 Chron. 15. 3. a *teaching* priest
Matt. 15. 9. *t.* for doctrines the
28. 20. *t.* them to observe all things
Col. 1. 28. *t.* every man in all wis.
Tit. 2. 12. *t.* us that denying
R. V. 1 Sam. 12. 23; Ps. 25. 8, 12; Acts 22. 3; 1 Cor. 14. 19. instruct; Jer. 28. 16; 29. 32. spoken; Matt. 28. 19. make disciples; Acts 16. 21. set forth; Tit. 2. 4. train; Isa. 43. 27. interpreters

TEAR, Ps. 50. 22. Hos. 5. 14. Job 16. 9.
R. V. 2 Sam. 13. 31. rent; Jer. 16. 17. break bread; Mark 9. 18. dasheth down; Isa. 5. 25. refuse; Mal. 1. 13. taken by violence

TEARS, Job 16. 20. Ps. 6. 6. Isa. 38. 5.
Ps. 56. 8. put *t.* in thy bottle
126. 5. they that sow in *t.* shall
Isa. 25. 8. wipe away all *t.* from off
Jer. 9. 1. eyes were a fountain of *t.*
Luke 7. 38. to wash his feet with *t.*
Acts 20. 19. *t.* and temptations, 31.
2 Cor. 2. 4. wrote with many *t.*
2 Tim. 1. 4. being mindful of thy *t.*
Heb. 5. 7. with strong crying and *t.*
Rev. 7. 17. wipe all *t.* from their
R. V. Mark 9. 24 —

TEATS, Isa. 32. 12. Ezek. 23. 3, 21.

TEETH white with milk, Gen. 49. 12.
Job 4. 10. *t.* broken, Ps. 3. 7. & 58. 6.
S. of S. 4. 2. *t.* are like a flock of
Jer. 31. 29. children's *t.* set on
Amos 4. 6. cleanness of *t.* in all
Matt. 8. 12. weeping and gnashing of *t.*, 22. 13. & 24. 51. & 25. 30. Ps. 112. 10.

TEKEL, Dan. 5. 25.

TELL it not in Gath, 2 Sam. 1. 20.
Ps. 48. 13. *t.* it to the generation
Prov. 30. 4. name, if thou canst *t.*
Matt. 8. 4. see thou *t.* no man
18. 15. *t.* him his fault
John 3. 8. not *t.* whence it cometh
4. 25. he is come he will *t.*
8. 14. ye cannot *t.* whence I come
2 Cor. 12. 2. out of body I cannot *t.*
Gal. 4. 16. I *t.* you the truth
Phil. 3. 18. *t.* you even weeping
Ps. 56. 8. *tellest* all my wanderings
R. V. Frequent changes to speak, say, shew, etc.

TEMPERANCE, Acts 24. 25. Gal. 5. 23. 2 Pet. 1. 6.
1 Cor. 9. 25. *temperate*, Tit. 1. 8. & 2. 2.

TEMPLE, 1 Sam. 1. 9. 1 Kings 6. 5.
Ps. 29. 9. in *t.* doth every one speak
Jer. 7. 4. *t.* of the Lord, *t.* of Lord
Mal. 3. 1. suddenly come to his *t.*
Matt. 12. 6. greater than the *t.* is
John 2. 19. destroy this *t.* and in
21. he spake of the *t.* of his body
1 Cor. 3. 16. ye are the *t.* of God
6. 19. body is *t.* of Holy Ghost
2 Cor. 6. 16. what agreement hath the *t.* of God with idols, for ye are the *t.* of the living God
Rev. 7. 15. serve him in his *t.*
11. 19. *t.* of God was opened in
S. of S. 4. 3. thy *temples*, 6. 7.
Acts 7. 48. Most High dwel. not in *t.*
R. V. 1 Kings 11. 10, 11, 13; 1 Chron. 6. 10; 10. 10; 2 Chron. 23. 10; Acts 7. 48. house or houses; Hos. 8. 14. palaces; Matt. 23. 35; 27. 5; Luke 11. 51. sanctuary

TEMPORAL, 2 Cor. 4. 18.

TEMPT Abraham, God did, Gen. 22. 1.
Ex. 17. 2. wherefore do ye *t.* Lord
Deut. 6. 16. shall not *t.* the Lord
Isa. 7. 12. ask, nor will I *t.* Lord
Matt. 4. 7. shalt not *t.* the Lord
22. 18. why *t.* ye me, show
Acts 5. 9. agreed together to *t.*
1 Cor. 7. 5. that Satan *t.* you not
Ex. 17. 7. they *tempted* Lord
Num. 14. 22. *t.* me now ten times
Ps. 78. 18. *t.* God in their heart
95. 9. when your fathers *t.* me
Matt. 4. 1. wilderness, to be *t.*
Luke 10. 25. lawyer *t.* him, saying
1 Cor. 10. 13. suffer you to be *t.*
Gal. 6. 1. lest thou also be *t.*
Heb. 2. 18. he is able to succor them that are *t.*
4. 15. in all points *t.* as we are
Jas. 1. 13. I am *t.* of God
14. every man is *t.* when drawn
Matt. 16. 1. *tempting* him, 19. 3. & 22. 35. Luke 11. 16. John 8. 6.
Ps. 95. 8. as in day of *temptation*
Matt. 6. 13. lead us not into *t.*
Luke 4. 13. devil had ended all *t.*
8. 13. in time of *t.* fall away
1 Cor. 10. 13. no *t.* taken you
Gal. 4. 14. my *t.* in flesh despised
1 Tim. 6. 9. rich fall into *t.* and
Heb. 3. 8. in day of *t.* in wilderness
Jas. 1. 12. blessed is he that endureth *t.*
Deut. 4. 34. *temptations*, 7. 19. Luke 22. 28. Acts 20. 19. Jas. 1. 2. 1 Pet. 1. 6. 2 Pet. 2. 9.
Matt. 4. 3. *tempter*, 1 Thes. 3. 5.
R. V. Luke 20. 23 —; Ps. 95. 8. Massah; Acts 20. 19; Rev. 3. 10. trial

TENDER, thy heart was, 2 Kings 22. 19. Eph. 4. 32.
Luke 1. 78. *t.* mercy, Jas. 5. 11.
R. V. S. of S. 2. 13, 15; 7. 12. in blossom; Dan. 1. 9. compassion; Jas. 5. 11. merciful

TENDETH, Prov. 10. 16. & 11. 19. & 19. 23. & 11. 24. & 14. 23. & 21. 5.

TENTS of Shem, dwell in, Gen. 9. 27.
1 Kings 12. 16. to your *t.* O Israel, 2 Sam. 20. 1.
Ps. 84. 10. dwell in *t.* of wickedness
S. of S. 1. 8. kids besi. shepherds' *t.*
R. V. Gen. 26. 17; 33. 18; Num. 9. 17, 18, 20–23; Ezra 8. 15. encamped; Num. 25. 8. pavilion; Num. 13. 19; 1 Sam. 17. 53; 2 Kings 7. 16; 2 Chron. 31. 2. camp or camps; 2 Sam. 11. 11. booths

TERRESTRIAL, 1 Cor. 15. 40.

TERRIBLE, Ex. 34. 10. Deut. 1. 19.
Deut. 7. 21. a mighty God and *t.*, 10. 17. Neh. 1. 5. & 4. 14. & 9. 32. Jer. 20. 11.
Deut. 10. 21. done *t.* things
Job 37. 22. with God is *t.* majesty
Ps. 45. 4. hand shall teach *t.*
47. 2. Lord most high is *t.*
65. 5. *t.* things wilt thou answer
66. 3. how *t.* art thou in thy
76. 12. he is *t.* to kings of the
99. 3. praise thy great and *t.*
S. of S. 6. 4. *t.* as army with ban.
Isa. 64. 3. *t.* things we looked not
Joel 2. 11. day of the Lord is *t.*
Zeph. 2. 11.
Heb. 12. 21. so *t.* was the sight

1 Chron. 17. 21. *terribleness*, Jer. 49. 16.
Job 7. 14. *terrifiest*, Phil. 1. 28.
R. V. Lam. 5. 10. burning; Dan. 7. 7. powerful; Heb. 12. 21. fearful
TERROR, Gen. 35. 5. Deut. 32. 25.
Job 31. 23. destr. from God was a *t.*
Isa. 33. 18. heart shall meditate *t.*
Jer. 17. 17. be not a *t.* unto me
20. 4. a *t.* to thyself, and all
Rom. 13. 3. rulers are not a *t.* to
2 Cor. 5. 11. know. *t.* of the Lord
1 Pet. 3. 14. be not afraid of their *t.*
Job 6. 4. *terrors*, 18. 11, 14. & 27. 20.
Ps. 55. 4. & 73. 19. & 88. 15, 16.
R. V. 2 Cor. 5, 11; 1 Pet. 3. 14. fear
TESTAMENT, Matt. 26. 28. Luke 22. 20. 1 Cor. 11. 25. 2 Cor. 3. 6, 14. Gal. 3. 15. Heb. 7. 22. & 9. 15, 16, 17, 18. Rev. 11. 19.
Heb. 9. 16. death of the *testator*
TESTIFY, Deut. 8. 19. & 32. 46. Neh. 9. 26, 34. Ps. 50. 7. & 81. 8.
Num. 35. 30. witness shall not *t.*
Isa. 59. 12. our sins *t.* against us
Hos. 5. 5. pride of Israel *t.* to his
John 3. 11. *t.* that we have seen
5. 39. search the Scriptures, they *t.* of me, 15. 26.
Acts 20. 24. *t.* the Gospel of grace
1 John 4. 14. *t.* that the Father
2 Chron. 24. 19. *testified*, Neh. 13. 15. Acts 23. 11. 1 Tim. 2. 6. 1 John 5. 9.
Heb. 11. 4. *testifying*, 1 Pet. 5. 12.
2 Kings 11. 12. gave him the *testimony*
Ps. 78. 5. established a *t.* in Jacob
Isa. 8. 16. bind up the *t.*, seal the law
Matt. 10. 18. for a *t.* against them
John 3. 32. no man receiveth his *t.*
Acts 14. 3. *t.* to word of his grace
2 Cor. 1. 12. the *t.* of our conscience
Rev. 1. 9. *t.* of Jesus Christ
11. 7. have finished their *t.*
Ps. 25. 10. keep his *testimonies*, 93. 5; *thy testimonies*, 119. 14, 24, 31, 46, 59, 95, 111, 129, 144.
R. V. John 2. 25; 3. 11, 39; 5. 39; 15. 26; 21. 24; Heb. 11. 14; 1 John 4. bear witness; 1 Cor. 15. 15; Heb. 7. 17. witnessed; Ruth 4. 7. attestation; John 3. 32, 33; 8. 17; 21. 24. witness; Acts 13. 22; 14. 3; Heb. 11. 5. bear witness; 1 Cor. 2. 1. mystery
THANK, 1 Chron. 16. 4. & 29. 13. Matt. 11. 25, 26. Luke 6. 32, 33. & 17. 9. & 18. 11. John 11. 41. Rom. 1. 8. & 7. 25. 1 Cor. 1. 4. 2 Thes. 2. 13. 1 Tim. 1. 12.
Ps. 100. 4. be *thankful*, Acts 24. 3. Rom. 1. 21. Col. 3. 15.
1 Pet. 2. 19. this is *thankworthy*
Dan. 6. 10. gave *thanks*, Matt. 26. 27. Mark 8. 6. Luke 22. 17. Rom. 14. 6.
2 Cor. 9. 15. *t.* to God for his unspeakable gift, 2. 14. & 8. 16. 1 Cor. 15. 57.
Eph. 5. 4. *giving of thanks*, 20. 1. Tit. 2. 1. Heb. 13. 15.
1 Thes. 3. 9. what *t.* can we render
Lev. 7. 12. *thanksgiving*, Neh. 11. 17. Ps. 26. 7. & 50. 14. & 100. 4. & 107. 22. & 116. 17. Isa. 51. 3. Phil. 4. 6. 1 Tim. 4. 3. Rev. 7. 12.
R. V. Heb. 13. 15. confession; Ps. 100. 4; Rom. 1. 21. give thanks
THEATRE, Acts 19. 29.
THINE is the day and night, Ps. 74. 16.
Ps. 119. 94. I am *t.*, save me
Isa. 63. 19. we are *t.* thou never
Matt. 20. 14. take that *t.* is and go
John 17. 6. *t.* they were, and thou
10. all mine are *t.* and *t.* are mine
R. V. Many changes to thy
THINGS devoted, Lev. 27. Num. 18. 14. Ezek. 44. 29; not to be redeemed, Lev. 27. 33; abuse of (Corban), Matt. 15. 5. Mark 7. 11.
THINK on me for good, Neh. 5. 19.
Job 31. 1. should I *t.* on a maid
Jer. 29. 11. I know that I *t.* toward
Rom. 12. 3. not to *t.* more highly
1 Cor. 8. 2. if any *t.* that he know.
Gal. 6. 3. *t.* himself to be some.
Eph. 3. 20. above all we ask or *t.*
Phil. 4. 8. *t.* on these things
Gen. 50. 20. *thought* evil against
Ps. 48. 9. we have *t.* of thy loving
119. 59. I *t.* on my ways and
Matt. 3. 16. that *t.* on his name
Mark 14. 72. he *t.* thereon wept
1 Cor. 13. 11. I *t.* as a child, spake
Phil. 2. 6. *t.* it not robbery to be
Ps. 139. 2. understandest my *t.*
Prov. 24. 9. the *t.* of foolishness
Eccl. 10. 20. curse not king in thy *t.*
Matt. 6. 25. take no *t.* for life
6. 34. take no *t.* for the morrow
Mark 13. 11. take no *t.* beforehand
2 Cor. 10. 5. every *t.* into captivity
Ps. 50. 21. thou *thoughtest* I was
Gen. 6. 5. imagination of *thoughts*
Judg. 5. 15. were great *t.* of heart
Ps. 10. 4. God is not in all his *t.*
33. 11. the *t.* of his heart to all
94. 11. Lord know. the *t.* of man
19. in multitude of my *t.* within
119. 113. hate vain *t.* but thy law
139. 17. how precious are thy *t.*
139. 23. try me and know my *t.*
Prov. 12. 5. *t.* of righte. are right
15. 26. the *t.* of the wicked are
16. 3. thy *t.* shall be established
Isa. 55. 7. let the unrighteous man forsake his *t.*
8. my *t.* are not your *t.*
Jer. 4. 14. how long shall vain *t.*
29. 11. *t.* I think toward you are *t.*
Mic. 4. 12. know not *t.* of the Lord
Matt. 15. 19. out of the heart proceed evil *t.*
Luke 2. 35. the *t.* of many hearts
24. 38. do *t.* arise in your hearts
Rom. 2. 15. their *t.* accusing, or
1 Cor. 3. 20. Lord knoweth the *t.*
Heb. 4. 12. a discerner of the *t.*
Jas. 2. 4. become judges of evil *t.*
R. V. Gen. 50. 10. meant; Ex. 32. 14; Esth. 6. 6. said; 2 Sam. 14. 13; Ezek. 38. 10. devise; 2 Chron. 11. 32. was minded; Neh. 5. 19. remember; Job 31. 1. look; 42. 2. purpose; Ezek. 38. 10. device; Luke 9. 47; 12. 7. reasoned; Luke 19. 11; Acts 13. 25. suppose; Acts 26. 8; Heb. 10. 29. judged; Rom. 2. 3. reckon; 2 Cor. 3. 5; 12. 16. account; 10. 7. consider; 10. 11. reckon
THIRST, Deut. 28. 48. & 29. 19.
Isa. 49. 10. shall not hunger nor *t.*
Matt. 5. 6. blessed are they which hunger and *t.* after righteousness
John 4. 14. shall never *t.*, 6. 35.
7. 37. if any *t.* let him come
Rom. 12. 20. if he *t.* give him drink
Rev. 7. 16. hunger nor *t.* any more
Ps. 42. 2. my soul *thirsteth* for God
Isa. 55. 1. ho, every one that *t.*
THORNS in your sides, Num. 33. 55. Judg. 2. 3. Gen. 3. 18.
Josh. 23. 13. be *t.* in your eyes
2 Sam. 23. 6. as *t.* thrust away
Jer. 4. 3. sow not among *t.*
Hos. 2. 6. hedge up thy way with *t.*
Matt. 7. 16. gather grapes of *t.*
13. 7. some fell among *t.*, 22.
Heb. 6. 8. that which beareth *t.*
R. V. 2 Chron. 33. 11. in chains; Job 41. 2. hook
THREATENING, Eph. 6. 9. Acts 4. 29. & 9. 1. 1 Pet. 2. 23.
THREE, 2 Sam. 24. 12. Prov. 30. 15, 18, 21, 29. Amos 1. 3, 13. & 2. 1. 1 Cor. 14. 27. 1 John 5. 7, 8. Rev. 16. 13.
THRESH, Isa. 21. 10. & 41. 15. Jer. 51. 33. Mic. 4. 13 Hab. 3. 12. 1 Cor. 9. 10.
Lev. 26. 5. and your *threshing* shall reach unto the vintage
2 Sam. 24. 18. *threshing-floor*, 21. 24.
R. V. Judg. 6. 11. beating out; Jer. 51. 33. trodden
THROAT is an open sepulchre, Ps. 5. 9.
Ps. 69. 3. weary of crying, my *t.*
Prov. 23. 2. put a knife to thy *t.*
THRONE, Lord is in heaven, Ps. 11. 4.
Ps. 94. 20. *t.* of iniquity have fel.
Prov. 25. 5. *t.* is established by
Isa. 66. 1. heaven is my *t.*
Jer. 14. 21. not disgrace *t.* of glory
Lam. 5. 19. *t.* from generation to
Dan. 7. 9. *t.* was like fiery flame
Matt. 19. 28. sit in *t.* of his glory, ye shall sit on twelve *thrones*
Col. 1. 16. whether they be *t.* or
Heb. 4. 16. boldly to the *t.* of grace
Rev. 3. 21. sit on my *t.* with my Father on his *t.*
22. 3. *t.* of God and Lamb shall be
Job 26. 9. *his throne*, Ps. 89. 14, 29, 44. & 97. 2. & 103. 19. Prov. 20. 28. & 25. 5. Dan. 7. 9. Zech. 6. 13.
Ps. 45. 6. *thy throne*, 99. 4. Heb. 1. 8.
Isa. 22. 33. *glorious throne*, Jer. 17. 12.
THRUST, Ex. 11. 1. Job 32. 13. Luke 13. 28. John 20. 25. Acts 16. 37.
R. V. Deut. 13. 5, 10. draw; Judg. 6. 38. pressed; 9. 41; 11. 2. drave; Job 32. 13. vanquished; 1 Sam. 11. 2; Luke 5. 3; John 20. 25, 27. put; Luke 4. 29; Acts 16. 24, 37; Rev. 14. 19. cast; Luke 10. 15. brought; Acts 27. 39. drive; Heb. 12. 20——; Rev. 14. 15, 18. send forth
THUNDER, Job 26. 14. & 40. 9. Ps. 29. 3. & 81. 7. Mark 3. 17.
Rev. 4. 5. *thunderings*, 8. 5. & 10. 3. & 11. 19. & 16. 18. & 19. 6.
R. V. Job 39. 19. quivering mane
TIDINGS, evil, Ex. 33. 4. Ps. 112. 7.
Luke 1. 19. show the glad *t.*, 8. 1. Acts 13. 32. Rom. 10. 15.
R. V. 1 Sam. 11. 4, 5, 6. word; Acts 11. 22. report
TIME when thou mayest be found, Ps. 32. 6.
Ps. 37. 19. evil *t.*
41. 1. *t.* of trouble
69. 13. acceptable *t.*, Isa. 49. 8. 2 Cor. 6. 2.
Ps. 89. 47. how short my *t.*
Eccl. 3. 1-8. *a time* to every purpose—to be born—to die—to plant—to pluck up—to love—to hate—of war—of peace
9. 11. *t.* and chance happen.
Ezek. 16. 8. *t.* was the *t.* of love
Dan. 7. 25. till a *t.* and times, div.
Amos 5. 13. evil *t.*, Mic. 2. 3.
Luke 19. 44. knew. not *t.* of thy
John 7. 6. my *t.* is not yet come
Acts 17. 21. spent *t.* in nothing
Rom. 13. 11. high *t.* to awake out
1 Cor. 7. 29. the *t.* is short, it rem.
2 Cor. 6. 2. accepted *t.* the day of
Eph. 5. 16. redeeming the *t.*
1 Pet. 1. 17. past *t.* of your sojourn.
Rev. 10. 6. *t.* shall be no longer
Ps. 31. 15. my *times* are in thy
Luke 21. 24. till *t.* of the Gentiles
Acts 1. 7. for you to know the *t.*
17. 26. determined the *t.* before
1 Tim. 4. 1. in latter *t.* some shall
2 Tim. 3. 1. in last days perilous *t.*
Ps. 34. 1. bless the Lord *at all times*
106. 3. blessed is he that doeth righteousness—
Prov. 5. 19. her breasts satisfy—
17. 17. a friend loveth—
R. V. Many changes to day, season, hour. So, many to suit context, as Matt. 4. 6. at any time to haply
TIN, Num. 31. 22. Isa. 1. 25. Ezek. 22. 18.
TITHES, Gen. 14. 20. Mal. 3. 8. Amos 4. 4. Matt. 23. 23. Luke 18. 12.
TITTLE or jot pass from the law, Matt. 5. 18.
R. V. 2 Kings 23. 17. monument
TOGETHER, Ps. 2. 2. Prov. 22. 2.
Rom. 8. 28. all things work *t.* for
1 Cor. 3. 9. laborers *t.* with God

2 Cor. 6. 1. as workers *t.* with him
Eph. 2. 5. quickened us *t.* with
6. raised us up *t.* made us sit *t.*
TOKEN of covenant, Gen. 9. 12, 13.
& 17. 11.
Ps. 86. 17. show me a *t.* for good
Phil. 1. 28. evident *t.* of perdition
2 Thes. 1. 5. manifest *t.* of right.
Job 21. 29. not know their *tokens*
Ps. 65. 8. they are afraid at thy *t.*
135. 9. who sent *t.* and wonders
Isa. 44. 25. frustrated the *t.* of liars
R. V. Ex. 13. 16; Ps. 135. 9. sign
TONGUE, Ex. 11. 7. Josh. 10. 21.
Job 5. 21. hid from scourge of *t.*
Ps. 34. 13. keep thy *t.* from evil
Prov. 10. 20. *t.* of the just is as
12. 18. *t.* of wise is health
15. 4. wholesome *t.* is a tree of
21. 6. get. treasure by a lying *t.*
25. 15. soft *t.* breaketh the bone
Isa. 30. 27. *t.* as a devouring fire
Jer. 9. 5. taught their *t.* to speak
18. 18. smite him with the *t.*
Jas. 1. 26. be religious and bridleth not his *t.*
3. 8. the *t.* can no man tame, 5.
1 Pet. 3. 10. refrain his *t.* from evil
1 John 3. 18. love in *t.* but deed
Ps. 35. 28. *my tongue*, 39. 1. & 45. 1.
& 51. 14. & 71. 24. & 119. 172. & 137.
6. & 139. 4. Acts 2. 26.
Ps. 31. 26. *tongues*, 55. 9. Mark 16. 17.
Acts 19. 6. 1 Cor. 12. 10, 28. & 14. 23.
TOOK out of the womb, Ps. 22. 9.
Phil. 2. 7. *t.* on him form of ser.
Heb. 10. 34. *t.* joyfully the spoiling
R. V. Ezra 4. 17; Esth. 7. 4; Job 6.
24; 13. 19; Amos 6. 10. peace;
Acts 2. 8; 21. 40; 22. 2; 26. 14. language; Rev. 9. 11; 16. 16 ——
TOPHET, Isa. 30. 33. Jer. 7. 31, 32.
TORCH, Zech. 12. 6. Nah. 2. 3, 4.
R. V. Nah. 2. 3. flash with steel
TORMENT us before the time,
Matt. 8. 29.
Luke 16. 28. to this place of *t.*
Rev. 18. 7. so much *t.* and sorrow
Luke 16. 24. am *tormented* in this
25. he is comforted, thou art *t.*
Heb. 11. 37. destitute, afflicted, *t.*
R. V. 1 John 4. 18. punishment;
Luke 16. 24, 25. in anguish; Heb.
11. 37. evil entreated
TORN, Hos. 6. 1. Mal. 1. 13. Mark
1. 26.
TOSS, Isa. 22. 18. Jer. 5. 22. Jas. 1. 6.
Ps. 109. 23. I am *tossed* up and
Isa. 54. 11. *t.* with a tempest
Eph. 4. 14. children *t.* to and fro
R. V. Prov. 21. 6. driven; Matt. 14.
24. distressed; Acts 27. 18. labored
TOUCH not mine anointed, Ps.
105. 15.
Job 5. 19. in seven shall no evil *t.*
Isa. 52. 11. *t.* no unclean thing
Matt. 9. 21. but *t.* his garment
14. 36. only *t.* hem of his garment
Mark 10. 13. chil. that he should *t.*
Luke 11. 46. *t.* not the burdens
John 20. 17. *t.* me not, for I am
2 Cor. 6. 17. *t.* not the unclean
Col. 2. 21. *t.* not, taste not, handle
1 Sam. 10. 26. whose heart God
had *touched*
Job 19. 21. hand of God hath *t.*
Luke 8. 45. who *t.* me
Zech. 2. 8. *toucheth* you, *t.* apple
1 John 5. 18. wicked one *t.* him
TOWER, God is a high, Ps. 18. 2.
& 144. 2.
Ps. 61. 3. strong *t.*, Prov. 18. 10.
S. of S. 4. 4. *t.* of David
7. 4. *t.* of ivory; *t.* of Lebanon
Isa. 5. 2. built a *t.*, Matt. 21. 33.
R. V. 2 Kings 5. 24. hill; Zeph. 1.
16; 3. 6. battlements
TRADERS in Tyre, Ezek. 27.
TRADITION, Matt. 15. 3. Gal. 1.
14. Col. 2. 8. 2 Thes. 2. 15. & 3. 6.
1 Pet. 1. 18.
R. V. 1 Pet. 1. 18. handed down
TRAIN, Prov. 22. 6. Isa. 6. 1.

TRAITOR, Luke 6. 16. 2 Tim. 3. 4.
TRAMPLE, Isa. 63. 3. Matt. 7. 6.
TRANCE, Num. 24. 4. Acts 10. 10.
& 11. 5. & 22. 17.
R. V. Num. 24. 4, 16. down
TRANQUILLITY, Dan. 4. 27.
TRANSFIGURED, Matt. 17. 2.
Mark 9. 2.
TRANSFORMED, Rom. 12. 2.
2 Cor. 11. 14, 15.
R. V. 2 Cor. 11. 13, 14, 15. fashion
TRANSGRESS the commandment of the Lord, Num. 14. 41.
1 Sam. 2. 24. ye make the Lord's
people to *t.*
2 Chron. 24. 20. why *t.* ye the
Neh. 1. 8. if ye *t.* I will scatter
Ps. 17. 3. mouth shall not *t.*
25. 3. ashamed that *t.* without
Prov. 28. 21. for piece of bread
man will *t.*
Amos 4. 4. come to Bethel and *t.*
Matt. 15. 2. why do thy disciples *t.*
3. why do ye *t.* the command.
Rom. 2. 27. by circumcision dost *t.*
Deut. 26. 13. not *transgressed* thy
Josh. 7. 11. have *t.* my covenant
Isa. 43. 27. teachers have *t.* against
Jer. 2. 8. pastors also *t.* against
Lam. 3. 42. have *t.* and rebelled
Ezek. 2. 3. and their fathers *t.*
Dan. 9. 11. all Israel have *t.* thy
Hos. 6. 7. men have *t.* the covenant
Hab. 2. 5. *transgresseth* by wine
1 John 3. 4. committeth sin, *t.*
Ex. 34. 7. forgiving iniquity,
transgression, and sin, Num. 14.
18.
1 Chron. 10. 13. Saul died for his *t.*
Ezra 10. 6. mourned because of *t.*
Job 13. 23. make me to know my *t.*
Ps. 32. 1. blessed is he whose *t.* is
forgiven
89. 32. visit their *t.* with rod
Prov. 17. 9. he that covereth *t.* seek.
Isa. 53. 8. for *t.* of my people
58. 1. show my people their *t.*
Dan. 9. 24. to finish *t.* and make
Amos 4. 4. at Gilgal multiply *t.*
Mic. 3. 8. declare to Jacob his *t.*
Rom. 4. 15. no law is, there is no
t.
1 John 3. 4. sin is the *t.* of the
Ex. 23. 21. pardon *transgressions*
Lev. 16. 21. all their *t.* in all their
Josh. 24. 19. not forgive your *t.*
Job 31. 33. covered my *t.* as Adam
Ps. 25. 7. remember not my *t.*
39. 8. deliver me from all my *t.*
51. 1. blot out my *t.*
65. 3. our *t.* thou shalt purge
103. 12. so far removed our *t.*
Isa. 43. 25. he that blotteth out *t.*
44. 22. out as a thick cloud, thy *t.*
53. 5. he was wounded for our *t.*
Ezek. 18. 31. cast away all your *t.*
Heb. 9. 15. the redemption of *t.*
Isa. 48. 8. wast a *transgressor* from
Jas. 2. 11. if thou kill, thou art become a *t.* of the law
Ps. 51. 13. teach *transgressors* thy
59. 5. be not merciful to wicked *t.*
119. 158. I beheld the *t.* and
Prov. 13. 15. the way of *t.* is hard
Isa. 53. 12. was numbered with *t.*
and made intercession for *t.*,
Mark 15. 28.
Hos. 14. 9. the *t.* shall fall therein
R. V. 1 Chron. 2. 7; 5. 25; 2 Chron.
12. 2; 26. 16; 28. 19; 36. 14; Ezra 10.
10; Neh. 1. 8; 13. 27; Hos. 7. 13.
trespass; 1 Sam. 14. 33; Ps. 25. 3;
Hab. 2. 5. deal treacherously;
Jer. 2. 20. serve; 1 John 3. 4. doeth
lawlessness; 2 John 9. goeth onward; Josh. 22. 22; 1 Chron. 10. 13;
Ezra 9. 14; 10. 6; 2 Chron. 29. 19.
trespass; 1 John 3. 4. lawlessness;
Prov. 2. 22; 11. 3, 6; 13. 2, 15; 21.
18; 22. 12; 23. 28. treacherous;
26. 10. that pass by
TRANSLATION, of Enoch, Gen.
5. 24. Heb. 11. 5; of Elijah, 2 Kings
2.

TRAVAIL, Isa. 53. 11. Gal. 4. 19, 27.
Job 15. 20. the wicked *travaileth*
Ps. 7. 14. he *t.* with iniquity
Isa. 66. 7. before she *travailed*, 8.
42. 14. *travailing* woman, Hos. 13.
13. Isa. 13. 8. & 21. 3. Jer. 31. 8.
Rev. 12. 2.
R. V. Eccl. 4. 4. labor; 5. 14. adventure
TRAVEL, Eccl. 1. 13. & 2. 23, 26.
& 4. 4, 6, 8. & 5. 14. 2 Thes. 3. 8.
Job 15. 20. *travelleth*, Prov. 6. 11. &
24. 34.
Isa. 21. 13. *travelling*, 63. 1.
R. V. Prov. 6. 11; 24. 34. a robber;
Isa. 63. 1. marching; Matt. 25. 14.
going
TREACHEROUS, Isa. 21. 2. & 24.
16.
Jer. 9. 2. an assembly of *t.* men
Isa. 21. 2. *treacherously*, 24. 16. &
33. 1.
48. 8. knew thou wouldst deal *t.*
Jer. 3. 20. as a wife *t.* departeth
12. 1. all happy that deal *t.*
Hos. 5. 7. dealt *t.* against Lord
Mal. 2. 15. none deal *t.* against
TREACHERY, instances of, Gen.
34. 13. Judg. 9. 1 Sam. 21. 7. & 22.
9. (Ps. 52.) 2 Sam. 3. 27. & 11. 14. & 16.
& 20. 9. 1 Kings 21. 5. 2 Kings 10. 18.
Esth. 3. Matt. 26. 47. Mark 14. 43.
Luke 22. 47. John 18. 3.
TREAD down wicked in place,
Job 40. 12.
Ps. 7. 5. let him *t.* down my life
Isa. 1. 12. required this to *t.* my
63. 3. *t.* them in mine anger, 6.
Hos. 10. 11. Ephraim loveth to *t.*
Rev. 11. 2. city shall be *t.* under
Deut. 25. 4. not muzzle the ox that
treadeth out the corn, 1 Cor. 9. 9.
1 Tim. 5. 18.
Isa. 22. 5. *treading*, Amos 5. 11.
R. V. Isa. 1. 12; Amos 5. 11. trample
TREASON, instances, 2 Sam. 15-
18. & 20. 1 Kings 1. & 16. 10. 2 Kings
11. & 15. 10. 2 Chron. 22. 10. Esth. 2.
21.
TREASURE, Prov. 15. 6, 16. & 21.
20.
Ex. 19. 5. peculiar *t.*, Ps. 135. 4.
Isa. 33. 6. fear of the Lord is his *t.*
Matt. 6. 21. where your *t.* is there
12. 35. good man out of good *t.*
13. 52. bringeth forth out of his *t.*
19. 21. shalt have *t.* in heaven
Luke 12. 21. layeth up *t.* for him.
2 Cor. 4. 7. this *t.* in earthen ves.
Deut. 32. 34. sealed up among my
treasures
Ps. 17. 14. fillest with thy hid *t.*
Prov. 2. 4. search. for her as hid *t.*
10. 2. *t.* of wickedness profit no.
Matt. 6. 19. lay not up *t.* on earth
20. lay up for yourselves *t.* in
Col. 2. 3. in whom are hid all the
t. of wisdom
Rom. 2. 5. *treasurest* up unto thy.
R. V. 1 Chron. 26. 20, 22, 24, 26; 27. 25;
Job 38. 22; Prov. 8. 21; Jer. 10. 3;
51. 16. treasuries; Jer. 41. 8. stores
hidden
TREE, Gen. 2. 16, 17. & 3. 22.
Ps. 1. 3. like a *t.* planted by rivers
52. 8. I am like a green olive *t.*
Prov. 3. 18. she is a *t.* of life to
11. 30. fruit of righteous. is *t.* of
Isa. 6. 13. be eaten as a teil *t.*
56. 3. eunuch say, I am a dry *t.*
Jer. 17. 8. a *t.* planted by the wat.
Matt. 3. 10. *t.* that bringeth not
7. 17. good *t.* bringeth forth
12. 33. make the *t.* good; or else
1 Pet. 2. 24. in his own body on *t.*
Rev. 2. 7. give to eat of *t.* of life
22. 2. midst of city was *t.* of life
14. have right to the *t.* of life
Ps. 104. 16. the *trees* of the Lord
Isa. 61. 3. called *t.* of righteous.
Ezek. 47. 12. grow all *t.* for meat
Mark 8. 24. I see men as *t.* walk.
Jude 12. *t.* whose fruit withereth

TREMBLE at the commandment of our God, Ezra 10. 3.
Ps. 99. 1. Lord reign., let people *t.*
Isa. 66. 5. ye that *t.* at his word
Jer. 5. 22. not *t.* at my presence
10. 10. at his wrath earth shall *t.*
Dan. 6. 26. men *t.* before the God
Jas. 2. 19. devils believe and *t.*
1 Sam. 4. 13. heart *trembled* for ark
Ezra 9. 4. every one that *t.* at
Acts 24. 25. he reasoned, Felix *t.*
Job 37. 1. *trembleth*, Ps. 119. 120. Isa. 66. 2.
1 Sam. 13. 7. followed *trembling*
Deut. 28. 65. give thee a *t.* heart
Ezra 10. 9. people sat *t.* because
Ps. 2. 11. serve God and rejoice *t.*
Ezek. 12. 18. drink thy water with *t.*, 26. 16.
Hos. 13. 1. Ephraim spake *t.*
1 Cor. 2. 3. fear and in much *t.*
Eph. 6. 5. fear and *t.* in singleness
Phil. 2. 12. work out your sal. with *t.*
R. V. Hab. 3. 10. were afraid; Acts 24. 25. was terrified; Job 21. 6. horror; Isa. 51. 17, 22. staggering; Zech. 12. 2. reeling

TRESPASS, Lev. 26. 40. Ezra 9. 6. 1 Kings 8. 31. Matt. 18. 15. Luke 17. 3.
Ezra 9. 15. *trespasses*, Ezek. 39. 26.
Ps. 68. 21. goeth on still in his *t.*
Matt. 6. 14. forgive men their *t.*
18. 35. if ye forgive not every one his brother their *t.*
Eph. 2. 1. dead in *t.* and sins
Col. 2. 13. forgiven you all *t.*
R. V. Gen. 50. 17. transgression; Num. 5. 7, 8; Lev. 6. 5; 22. 16; 1 Chron. 21. 3; 2 Chron. 19. 10; Ezra 9. 7, 13; 10. 10, 19. guilt or guilty; 2 Chron. 24. 18; Ezra 6. 15; 9. 6, 15; Ps. 68. 21. guiltiness; Matt. 8.35; Mark 11. 26 ——; 2 Chron. 19. 10. be guilty; 1 Kings 8. 31; Matt. 18. 5; Luke 17. 3, 4. sin

TRIAL, Job 9. 23. Ezek. 21. 13. 2 Cor. 8. 2. Heb. 11. 36. 1 Pet. 1. 7. & 4. 12.
R. V. 2 Cor. 8. 2; 1 Pet. 1. 7. proof

TRIBES, Num. 24. 2.
Ps. 105. 37. one feeble among *t.*
122. 4. whither *t.* go up, *t.* of
Matt. 24. 30. all the *t.* of earth
Acts 26. 7. promise our twelve *t.*

TRIBULATION, art in, Deut. 4. 30.
Judg. 10. 14. deliver you in *t.*
Matt. 13. 21. when *t.* or persecu.
24. 21. then shall be great *t.* such
29. immediately after the *t.*
John 16. 33. ye shall have *t.*
Acts 14. 22. through much *t.*
Rom. 2. 9. *t.* and anguish on every
5. 3. knowing *t.* worketh patience
12. 12. in hope, patient in *t.*
2 Cor. 1. 4. comfort. us in all our *t.*
1 Thes. 3. 4. we should suffer *t.*
2 Thes. 1. 6. to recompense *t.* to
Rev. 1. 9. and companion in *t.*
2. 9. I know thy works and *t.*
22. cast into great *t.* except
7. 14. have come out of great *t.*
Rom. 5. 3. glory in *tribulations*
1 Sam. 10. 19. save. you out of all *t.*
Eph. 3. 13. faint not at my *t.* for
2 Thes. 1. 4. patience in all *t.*
R. V. Judg. 10. 14; 1 Sam. 10. 19. distress; 2 Cor. 1. 4; 7. 4; 1 Thes. 1. 4; 3. 4; 2 Thes. 1. 6. affliction

TRIBUTE, Gen. 49. 15. Num. 31. 28.
Matt. 17. 24. doth not your Master pay *t.*
22. 17. is it lawful to give *t.* to Cæsar
Rom. 13. 7. *t.* to whom *t.* is due
R. V. Gen. 49. 15; Josh. 16. 10; 17. 13; Judg. 1. 28; Prov. 12. 24. task work; 1 Kings 4. 6; 9. 21; 12. 18; 2 Chron. 10. 18. levy; 2 Chron. 8. 8. bond servants; Matt. 17. 24. half shekel

TRIMMED, Jer. 2. 33. Matt. 25. 7.

TRIUMPH, 2 Sam. 1. 20. Ps. 25. 2.
Ps. 92. 4. *t.* in works of thy hands
2 Cor. 2. 14. always cause. us to *t.*
Ex. 15. 1. *triumphed* gloriously
Job 20. 5. *triumphing*, Col. 2. 15.
R. V. Ps. 60. 8; 108. 9. shout

TRODDEN down strength, Judg. 5. 21.
Ps. 119. 118. *t.* down all them
Isa. 63. 3. have *t.* winepress alone
Luke 21. 24. Jerusalem shall be *t.*
Heb. 10. 29. *t.* under foot Son of

TROUBLE, 2 Chron. 15. 4. Neh. 9. 32.
Job 5. 6. neither doth *t.* spring
14. 1. man is of few days and full of *t.*
Ps. 9. 9. refuge in times of *t.*
22. 11. *t.* is near; there is none
27. 5. in time of *t.* he shall hide
46. 1. God is a present help in *t.*
91. 15. I will be with him in *t.*
143. 11. bring my soul out of *t.*
Prov. 11. 8. the righteous is delivered out of *t.*
Isa. 26. 16. Lord. in *t.* have they
33. 2. our salvation in time of *t.*
Jer. 8. 15. looked for health, and behold *t.*
14. 8. and Saviour in time of *t.*
Dan. 12. 1. shall be a time of *t.*
Cor. 7. 28. have *t.* in the flesh
Ps. 25. 17. the *troubles* of my heart
34. 17. deliver them out of all *t.*
88. 3. my soul is full of *t.*
Ex. 14. 24. Lord *troubled* the host
Ps. 30. 7. and I was *t.*
Isa. 57. 20. wic. are like the *t.* sea
John 12. 27. now is my soul *t.*
14. 1. let not your hearts be *t.*
2 Cor. 4. 8. *t.* on every side, 7. 5.
2 Thes. 1. 7. to you who are *t.* rest
Job 23. 16. Almighty *troubleth* me
1 Kings 18. 17. he that *t.* Israel
Prov. 11. 17. cruel *t.* his own flesh
29. he that *t.* his own house
Luke 18. 5. because this widow *t.*
Gal. 5. 10. he that *t.* you shall
Job 3. 17. *troubling*, John 5. 4.
R. V. 1 Chron. 22. 14; Ps. 9. 13; 31. 7, 9; 2 Cor. 1. 4, 8. affliction; 2 Chron. 15.4; Job 15. 24; Ps. 59. 16; 66. 14, 17; 102. 2; Isa. 8. 22. distress; 2 Chron. 29. 8. tossed to and fro; Neh. 9. 32. travail; Job 34. 29. condemn; Ps. 41. 1. evil; Ps. 78. 33; Isa. 17. 14. terror; Ps. 3. 1; 13. 4; 60. 11. adversaries; Isa. 22. 5. discomfiture; 65. 23. calamity; Jer. 8. 15; 14. 19. dismay; Ezek. 7. 7. tumult; Acts 20. 10. make no ado; 1 Cor. 7. 28. tribulation; 2 Tim. 2. 9. hardship; Mark 13. 8 ——; Ex. 14. 24. discomfited; Job 34. 20. shaken; Ps. 38. 5. pained; 77. 3. disquieted; 77. 16. trembled; 48. 5; 83. 17; Ezek. 26. 18. dismayed; Zech. 10. 2; 2 Thes. 1. 7. afflicted; John 5. 4 ——

TRUCE breakers, 2 Tim. 3. 3.

TRUE, Gen. 42. 11. 2 Sam. 7. 28.
Ps. 19. 9. judgments of Lord are *t.*
119. 160. thy word is *t.*
Prov. 14. 25. *t.* witness delivereth
Jer. 42. 5. be *t.* and faithful wit.
Ezek. 18. 8. *t.* judgment, Zech. 7. 9.
Matt. 22. 16. we know thou art *t.*
Luke 16. 11. *t.* riches
John 1. 9. *t.* light
4. 23. *t.* worshippers
6. 32. *t.* bread from heaven
15. 1. I am the *t.* vine
2 Cor. 1. 18. as God is *t.* our word
6. 8. as deceivers and yet *t.*
Phil. 4. 8. what. things are *t.*
1 John 5. 20. know him that is *t.*
Rev. 3. 7. saith he that is *t.*
19. 11. was called faithful and *t.*
R. V. 2 Cor. 1. 18; 1 Tim. 3. 1. faithful

TRUMP, 1 Cor. 15. 52. 1 Thes. 16. 4.

TRUMPET, Ex. 19. 16. Ps. 81. 3.
Isa. 27. 13. great *t.* shall be blown
Isa. 58. 1. lift up thy voice like a *t.*
Matt. 6. 2. not sound a *t.* before
Num. 10. 2. *trumpets*, Josh. 6. 4. Ps. 98. 6. Rev. 8. 9.

TRUST in him, 1 Chron. 5. 20.
Job 4. 10. put no *t.* in servants
8. 14. his *t.* is a spider's web
Ps. 4. 5. put your *t.* in the Lord
40. 4. maketh the Lord his *t.*
71. 5. art my *t.* from my youth
Prov. 22. 19. thy *t.* may be in Lord
Job 13. 15. though he slay me I will *t.*
Ps. 37. 3. *t.* in Lord, and do good
5. *t.* in him; he will bring it to
55. 23. I will *t.* in thee
62. 8. *t.* in him at all times, ye
115. 8, 9, 10, 11. *t.* in the Lord
118. 8. it is better to *t.* in Lord, 9.
119. 42. for I *t.* in thy word
Prov. 3. 5. *t.* in the Lord with all
Isa. 26. 4. *t.* ye in the Lord for ever
Jer. 7. 4. *t.* not in lying words
9. 4. *t.* not in any brother
Mic. 7. 5. *t.* ye not in a friend
Mark 10. 24. them that *t.* in riches
2 Cor. 1. 9. not *t.* in ourselves
Phil. 3. 4. whereof to *t.* in flesh
1 Tim. 6. 20. committed to thy *t.*
Ps. 22. 4. our fathers *trusted* in
52. 7. *t.* in abundance of his
Luke 18. 9. *t.* in themselves
Eph. 1. 12. who first *t.* in Christ
Ps. 32. 10. *trusteth* in Lord's
34. 8. blessed is man that *t.* in
86. 2. save servant that *t.* in thee
Jer. 17. 5. cursed be the man that *t.* in man
1 Tim. 5. 5. desolate *t.* in God
Ps. 112. 7. heart is fixed *trusting*
R. V. Ruth 2. 12; Ps. 36. 7; 37. 40; 61. 4; 91. 4; Isa. 14. 32. take refuge; Matt. 12. 21; Luke 24. 21; Rom. 15. 12, 24; 1 Cor. 16. 7; 2 Cor. 1. 10, 13; 5. 11; 13. 6; Eph. 1. 12; Phil. 2. 19; 1 Tim. 4. 10; 6. 17; Phile. 22; 2 John 12; 3 John 14. hope or hoped; 2 Cor. 3. 4; Phil. 3. 4. confidence; Heb. 13. 18. persuaded

TRUTH, Gen. 24. 27. Ex. 18. 21.
Deut. 34. 4. a God of *t.* and with.
Ps. 15. 2. speaketh *t.* in his heart
25. 10. the paths of the Lord are mercy and *t.*
91. 4. his *t.* shall be thy shield
117. 2. his *t.* endureth for ever
119. 30. chosen the way of *t.*
Prov. 12. 19. lip of *t.* shall be
16. 6. by mercy and *t.* iniquity
23. 23. buy the *t.* and sell it not
Isa. 59. 14. *t.* is fallen in the streets
Jer. 4. 2. swear Lord liveth in *t.*
Dan. 4. 37. all whose ways are *t.*
Zech. 8. 16. speak every man *t.* to his neighbor
Mal. 2. 6. law of *t.* was in his mouth
John 1. 14. full of grace and *t.*
8. 32. know the *t.* and the *t.* shall make you free
14. 6. the way, the *t.* and life
17. 17. sanctify them through *t.*
18. 37. bear witness to *t.*
Acts 20. 25. words of *t.* and sober.
Rom. 1. 18. hold *t.* in unrighteous.
2. 2. judg. of God is accord. to *t.*
1 Cor. 5. 8. the unleavened bread of sincerity and *t.*
2 Cor. 13. 8. do nothing against *t.*
Gal. 3. 1. should not obey the *t.*
Eph. 4. 15. speaking *t.* in love
5. 9. fruit of the Spirit is in all *t.*
6. 14. loins girt about with *t.*
2 Thes. 2. 10. receiv. not love of *t.*
1 Tim. 3. 15. pillar and ground of *t.*
6. 5. corrupt, destitute of the *t.*
2 Tim. 2. 18. who concerning the *t.*
25. acknowledging of the *t.*
3. 7. come to the knowl. of the *t.*
4. 4. turn away their ears from *t.*
Jas. 3. 14. nor lie against *t.*
2 Pet. 1. 12. establish. in present *t.*
1 John 1. 8. *t.* is not in us
5. 6. Spirit is *t.*

Josh. 24. 14. *in truth*, 1 Sam. 12. 24. Ps. 145. 18. Jer. 4. 2. John 4. 24. 1 Thes. 2. 13. 1 John 3. 18. 2 John 4.
Ps. 25. 5. *thy truth*, 26. 3. & 43. 3. & 108. 4. John 17. 17.
R. V. Deut. 32. 4; Ps. 33. 4; 89. 49; 98. 3; 119. 30. faithfulness
TRY, Judg. 7. 4. Job 12. 11. Jer. 6. 27.
2 Chron. 32. 31. God left him to *t.*
Job 7. 18. visit him and *t.* him
Ps. 11. 4. eyelids *t.* the children
26. 2. *t.* my reins and my heart
Jer. 9. 7. melt them, and *t.* them
Lam. 3. 40. search and *t.* our ways
Dan. 11. 35. shall fall to *t.* them
Zech. 13. 9. *t.* them as gold is tried
1 Cor. 3. 13. fire shall *t.* every
1 Pet. 4. 12. fiery trial which is to *t.*
1 John 4. 1. *t.* the spirits whether
Rev. 3. 10. to *t.* them that dwell
2 Sam. 22. 31. word of Lord is *tried*, Ps. 18. 30.
Ps. 12. 6. word is pure as silver *t.*
66. 10. *t.* us as silver is *t.*
105. 19. word of the Lord *t.* him
Jer. 12. 3. *t.* mine heart towards
Dan. 12. 10. be purified and *t.*
Jas. 1. 12. when he is *t.* he shall receive the crown of life
Rev. 2. 2. hast *t.* them and found
3. 18. buy of me gold, *t.* in the
1 Chron. 29. 17. I know thou *triest*
Jer. 11. 20. that *t.* the reins and
20. 12. thou that *t.* the righteous
Ps. 7. 9. the righteous God *trieth*
11. 5. the Lord *t.* the righteous
1 Thes. 2. 4. pleasing God, who *t.*
Jas. 1. 3. *trying* of your faith
R. V. Dan. 11. 35. refine; 1 Cor. 3. 13; 1 Pet. 4. 12; 1 John 4. 1. prove
TUMULT, Ps. 65. 7. 2 Cor. 12. 20.
R. V. 2 Kings 19. 28; Isa. 37. 29. arrogancy; Acts 21. 34. uproar
TURN, from their sin, 1 Kings 8. 35.
2 Kings 17. 13. *t.* from your evil
Job 23. 13. who can *t.* him
Prov. 1. 23. *t.* you at my reproof
S. of S. 2. 17. *t.* my belov., be thou
Isa. 31. 6. *t.* ye unto him, from
Jer. 18. 8. if *t.* from their evil; I
31. 18. *t.* thou me and I shall
Lam. 5. 21. *t.* us unto thee, O Lord
Ezek. 3. 19. *t.* not from his wicked.
18. 30. *t.* yourselves from your
32. *t.* yourselves and live, 33. 9. Hos. 12. 6. Joel 2. 12. Zech. 9. 12.
Zech. 1. 3. *t.* to me, and I will *t.*
Mal. 4. 6. *t.* hearts of fathers to
Acts 26. 18. *t.* them from darkness
20. should repent, and *t.* to God
2 Pet. 2. 21. to *t.* from holy com.
2 Chron. 30. 6. *turn again*, Ps. 60. 1. & 80. 3, 7, 19. & 85. 8. Lam. 3. 40. Mic. 7. 19. Zech. 10. 9. Gal. 4. 9.
1 Sam. 12. 20. *turn aside*, Ps. 40. 4. Isa. 30. 11. Lam. 3. 35. Amos 2. 7. & 5. 12.
Ps. 119. 37. *turn away*, 39. S. of S. 6. 5. Isa. 58. 13. 1 Tim. 3. 5. Heb. 12. 25.
Deut. 4. 20. *turn to the Lord*, 20. 10. 2 Chron. 15. 4. Ps. 4. 22, 27. Lam. 3. 40. Hos. 14. 2. Joel 2. 13. Luke 1. 16. 2 Cor. 3. 16.
Ps. 9. 17. wicked shall be *turned*
30. 11. *t.* my mourning into danc.
119. 5. *t.* my feet to thy testimo.
Isa. 53. 6. *t.* every one to own
63. 10. was *t.* to be their enemy
Jer. 2. 27. *t.* their back to me
8. 6. every one *t.* to his own
Hos. 7. 8. Ephraim is a cake not *t.*
John 6. 20. sorrow shall be *t.* to
1 Thes. 1. 9. *t.* to God from idols
Jas. 4. 9. laughter be *t.* to mourn.
2 Pet. 2. 22. dog is *t.* to his vomit
Deut. 9. 12. *turned aside*, Ps. 78. 57. Isa. 44. 20. 2 Tim. 1. 6. & 5 15.
1 Kings 11. 3. *turned away*, Ps. 66. 20. & 78. 38. Isa. 5. 25. & 9. 12. & 10. 4. Jer. 5. 25.
Ps. 44. 18. *turned back*, 78. 9, 41. Isa. 42. 17. Jer. 4. 8. Zeph. 1. 6.
Job 15. 13. *turnest*, Ps. 90. 3.
Ps. 146. 9. wicked he *turneth*
Prov. 15. 1. soft answer *t.* away
21. 1. he *t.* it whithersoever he
Isa. 9. 13. the people *t.* not unto
Jer. 14. 8. *t.* aside to tarry for a
Jas. 1. 17. no shadow of *turning*
Jude 4. *t.* grace of God into
R. V. Changes are chiefly to return, change, and other words dependent on context
TURTLE, Lev. 1. 14. & 5. 7, 11. & 12. 6. Ps. 74. 19. S. of S. 2. 12. Jer. 8. 7.
TUTORS, Gal. 4. 2.
TWAIN, Matt. 5. 41. & 19. 5. Eph. 2. 15.
TWELVE, the, ordained, Mark 3. 14.
TWICE, Gen. 41. 32. Ex. 16. 22. Num. 20. 11. 1 Kings 11. 9. Job 33. 14. & 40. 5. Ps. 62. 11. Mark 14. 30. Luke 18. 12. *t.* dead, Jude 12.
TWINKLING, 1 Cor. 15. 52.
TYPES of Christ. *See* CHRIST
TYRANNY, instances of, Ex. 1. & 5. 1 Sam. 22. 9. 1 Kings 12. 4. & 21. Jer. 26. 20. Matt. 2. Acts 12.

U

UNACCUSTOMED, Jer. 31. 18.
UNADVISEDLY, Ps. 106. 33.
UNAWARES, Deut. 4. 42. Ps. 35. 8. Luke 21. 34. Heb. 13. 2. Jude 4.
R. V. Num. 35. 11, 15; Josh. 20. 3, 9. unwittingly; Luke 21. 34. suddenly; Gal. 2. 4; Jude 4. privily
UNBELIEF, did not many mighty works there bec. of, Matt. 13. 58.
Mark 6. 6. marvelled because of *u.*
9. 24. help thou mine *u.*
Rom. 4. 20. stagger. not through *u.*
11. 20. because of *u.* were broken
1 Tim. 1. 13. ignorantly in *u.*
Heb. 3. 12. an evil heart of *u.*
19. not enter in because of *u.*
R. V. Matt. 17. 20. little faith; Rom. 11. 30, 32; Heb. 4. 6, 11. disobedience; Rom. 3. 3. want of faith
UNBELIEVERS, Luke 12. 46. 2 Cor. 6. 14.
R. V. Luke 12. 46. unfaithful
UNBELIEVING, Acts 14. 2. 1 Cor. 7. 14, 15. Tit. 1. 15. Rev. 21. 8.
R. V. Acts 14. 2. disobedient
UNBLAMABLE, Col. 1. 22. 1 Thes. 3. 13.
1 Thes. 2. 10. *unblamably* behaving
R. V. Col. 1. 22. without blemish
UNCERTAIN, 1 Cor. 14. 8. 1 Tim. 6. 17.
UNCIRCUMCISED, Ex. 6. 12, 30. Jer. 6. 10. & 9. 25, 26. Acts 7. 51.
UNCIRCUMCISION, Rom. 2. 25, 26, 27. & 3. 30. & 4. 10. 1 Cor. 7. 18, 19. Gal. 2. 7. & 5. 6. & 6. 15. Col. 2. 13. & 3. 11.
UNCLEAN, Lev. 5. 11, 13, 15. Num. 19. 19.
Lev. 10. 10. difference between *u.*
Isa. 6. 5. I am a man of *u.* lips
Lam. 4. 15. depart ye; it is *u.*
Ezek. 44. 23. discern between *u.*
Hag. 2. 13. if one *u.* touch
Acts 10. 28. not call any man common or *u.*, 14.
Rom. 14. 14. is nothing *u.* of itself
1 Cor. 7. 14. else were children *u.*
Eph. 5. 5. nor *u.* person hath any
Num. 5. 19. *uncleanness*, Ezra 9. 11.
Zech. 13. 1. fountain for sin and *u.*
Matt. 23. 27. are with. full of all *u.*
Eph. 4. 19. all *u.* with greediness
5. 3. all *u.* let it not once be
1 Thes. 4. 7. not called us to *u.*
Ezek. 36. 29. save you from all *u.*
R. V. 2 Pet. 2. 10. defilement
UNCLEAN SPIRITS, Matt. 10. 1. & 12. 43, 45. Acts 5. 16. Rev. 16. 13.
—animals, Lev. 11. & 20. 25. Deut. 14. 3.
UNCLOTHED, 2 Cor. 5. 4.
UNCOMELY, 1 Cor. 7. 36. & 12. 23.
UNCONDEMNED, Acts 16. 37. & 22. 25.
UNCORRUPTNESS, Tit. 2. 7.
UNCOVER, Lev. 18. 18. 1 Cor. 11. 5, 13.
R. V. Lev. 21. 6, 10; Num. 5. 18. let hair go loose; Isa. 47. 2. remove; Hab. 2. 16. circumcised; Zeph. 2. 14. laid bare; 1 Cor. 11. 5, 13. unveiled
UNCTION, 1 John 2. 20, 27.
UNDEFILED in way, Ps. 119. 1.
S. of S. 5. 2. my dove, my *u.*, 6. 9.
Heb. 7. 26. holy, harmless, *u.*
Jas. 1. 27. pure religion and *u.*
R. V. Ps. 119. 1. perfect
UNDER their God, Hos. 4. 12.
Rom. 3. 9. all *u.* sin, 7. 14. Gal. 3. 22; *u.* law, Rom. 6. 15. 1 Cor. 9. 20. Gal. 3. 23. & 4. 4.
1 Cor. 9. 27. I keep *u.* my body
UNDERSTAND not, one another's speech, Gen. 11. 7.
Neh. 8. 7. caused people to *u.*
Ps. 19. 12. who can *u.* his errors
107. 43. shall *u.* loving kindness
119. 100. I *u.* more than ancients
Prov. 2. 5. shalt thou *u.* fear of
8. 5. *u.* wisdom
19. 25. *u.* knowledge
Isa. 32. 4. heart of the rash shall *u.*
1 Cor. 13. 2. to *u.* all mysteries
Ps. 139. 2. thou *understandest* my thoughts
Acts 8. 30. *u.* thou what thou
1 Chron. 28. 9. *understandeth* all the imaginations
Ps. 49. 20. man that *u.* not, is like
Prov. 8. 9. plain to him that *u.*
Jer. 9. 24. glory in this, that he *u.*
Matt. 13. 19. hear. word and *u.* not
Ex. 31. 3. wis. and *understanding*
Deut. 4. 6. is your wisdom and *u.*
1 Kings 3. 11. asked for thyself *u.*
4. 29. Solomon wisdom and *u.*
7. 14. filled with wisdom and *u.*
1 Chron. 12. 32. men that had *u.* of
Job 12. 13. he hath counsel and *u.*
17. 4. hid their heart from *u.*
28. 12. where is the place of *u.*
28. to depart from evil is *u.*
38. 36. who hath given *u.* to heart
Ps. 47. 7. sing ye praise with *u.*
49. 3. the meditations of my heart shall be of *u.*
119. 34. give me *u.* and I shall keep
130. giveth *u.* unto the simple
147. 5. his *u.* is infinite
Prov. 2. 2. apply thine heart to *u.*
11. *u.* shall keep thee; to deliver
3. 5. lean not to thine own *u.*
13. the man that getteth *u.*
8. 1. doth not *u.* cry
9. 6. go in the way of *u.*
14. 29. slow to wrath is of great *u.*
19. 8. keepeth *u.* shall find good
21. 30. no *u.* nor counsel against
23. 23. buy truth, wisdom and *u.*
30. 2. I have not the *u.* of a man
Eccl. 9. 11. nor riches to men of *u.*
Isa. 11. 2. spirit of wisdom and *u.*
3. make him of quick *u.* in the
27. 11. it is a people of no *u.*
Jer. 51. 15. stretched out heaven by his *u.*
Matt. 15. 16. also without *u.*
Mark 12. 33. love him with all the heart and with all the *u.*
Luke 2. 47. astonished at his *u.*
Rom. 1. 31. without *u.* unthankful
1 Cor. 1. 19. bring to nothing the *u.* of the prudent
14. 14. my *u.* unfruitful
15. pray with the *u.* also
Eph. 1. 18. eyes of *u.* enlightened
4. 18. having the *u.* darkened
Phil. 4. 7. the peace of God, which passeth all *u.*

Col. 1. 9. filled with all spiritual *u.*
2 Tim. 2. 7. give thee *u.* in all
1 John 5. 20. given us *u.* to know
Ps. 111. 10. *good understanding*, Prov. 3. 4. & 13. 15.
Prov. 1. 5. *a man of understanding*, 10. 23. & 11. 12. & 15. 21. & 17. 27.
Deut. 32. 29. O that they *understood*
Ps. 73. 17. then *u.* I their end
Dan. 9. 2. *u.* by books number
Matt. 13. 51. have ye *u.* all these
John 12. 16. these things *u.* not
1 Cor. 13. 11. when a child I *u.*
2 Pet. 3. 16. things hard to be *u.*
R. V. Gen. 41. 15. hearest; Deut. 9. 3, 6. know; Neh. 8. 13. give attention; Ps. 19. 12; Dan. 9. 25. discern; 11. 33. be wise; Ps. 73. 17; 94. 8; 107 43; Isa. 44. 18. consider; Ps. 81. 5; 1 Cor. 13. 2; Phil. 1. 12. know or knew; Matt. 15. 17; 26. 10; John 8. 27; 12. 40; Rom. 1. 20; Eph. 3. 14. perceive; Acts 23. 27. learned; 1 Cor. 13. 11. felt; Ezra 8. 16. teachers; 8. 18. discretion; Prov. 17. 28. prudent; 10. 13. discernment; Dan. 11. 35. wise; Luke 1. 3. accurately; 24. 45; 1 Cor. 14. 20. mind; Eph. 1. 18. heart

UNDERTAKE for me, Isa. 38. 14.
R. V. Isa. 38. 14. be surety

UNDONE, Isa. 6. 5. Matt. 23. 23.

UNEQUAL, your ways are, Ezek. 18. 25.
2 Cor. 6. 14. not *unequally* yoked

UNFAITHFUL, Prov. 25. 19. Ps. 78. 57.
R. V. Ps. 78. 57. treacherously

UNFEIGNED, 2 Cor. 6. 6. 1 Tim. 1. 5. 2 Tim. 1. 5. 1 Pet. 1. 22.

UNFRUITFUL, Matt. 13. 22. 1 Cor. 14. 14. Eph. 5. 11. Tit. 3. 14. 2 Pet. 1. 8.

UNGODLY men, 2 Sam. 22. 5.
2 Chron. 19. 2. should. help the *u.*
Job 16. 11. delivered me to the *u.*
34. 18. say to princes ye are *u.*
Ps. 1. 1. walketh not in counsel of *u.*
6. way of *u.* men shall perish
3. 7. hast broken the teeth of *u.*
73. 12. these are *u.* that prosper
Prov. 16. 27. *u.* man diggeth up
19. 28. an *u.* witness scorneth
Rom. 4. 5. God that justifi. the *u.*
5. 6. in due time Christ died for *u.*
1 Tim. 1. 9. law not for righteous, but for the *u.*
1 Pet. 4. 18. where shall *u.* appear
2 Pet. 2. 5. bring a flood on world of the *u.*
3. 7. day of perdition of *u.* men
Jude 4. *u.* men turning grace
15. convince all that are *u.* of
18. mockers walk after *u.* lusts
Rom. 1. 18. wrath revealed against *ungodliness*
2 Tim. 2. 16. increase to more *u.*
Tit. 2. 12. denying *u.* and worldly
R. V. Prov. 16. 27; 19. 28. worthless; 2 Chron. 19. 2; Job 34. 18; Ps. 1. 1, 4, 5, 6; 3. 7; 78. 12. wicked

UNHOLY, Lev. 10. 10. 1 Tim. 1 9. 2 Tim. 3. 2. Heb. 10. 29.
R. V. Lev. 10. 10. the common

UNION in worship and prayer, Ps. 34. 3. & 55. & 14. & 122. Rom. 15. 30. 2 Cor. 1. 11. Eph. 6. 18. Col. 1. 3. & 3. 16. Heb. 10. 25.

UNITE, Ps. 86. 11. Gen. 49. 6.
Ps. 133. 1. brethren to dwell together in *unity*
Eph. 4. 3. keep the *u.* of the Spirit
13. till we all come in *u.* of faith

UNJUST, deliver from, Ps. 43 1.
Prov. 11. 7. hope of the *u.* perish.
29. 27. *u.* man is abomination
Zeph. 3. 5. the *u.* knoweth no
Matt. 5. 45. rain on the just and *u.*
Luke 16. 8. Lord commended the *u.* steward
10. he that is *u.* in least, is
18. 6. hear what the *u.* judge
Acts 24. 15. resurrection both of just and *u.*
1 Cor. 6. 1. go to law before the *u.*
1 Pet. 3. 18. suffered, just for *u.*
2 Pet. 2. 9. reserve the *u.* to day
Rev. 22. 11. that is *u.* let him be *u.*
Ps. 82. 2. will ye judge *unjustly*
Isa. 26. 10. will he deal *u.*
R. V. Prov. 28. 8 —; 11. 7. iniquity; Luke 16. 8, 10; 18. 6; 1 Cor. 6. 1; 1 Pet. 3. 18; 2 Pet. 2. 9; Rev. 22. 11. unrighteous

UNKNOWN God, Acts 17. 23. Gal. 1. 22.
1 Cor. 14. 2. speak in an *u.* tongue, 4. 27.
2 Cor. 6. 9. as *u.* and yet well

UNLAWFUL, Acts 10. 28. 2 Pet. 2. 8.
R. V. 2 Pet. 2. 8. lawless

UNLEARNED, Acts 4. 13. 1 Cor. 14. 16, 23, 24. 2 Tim. 2. 23. 2 Pet. 3. 16.
R. V. 2 Tim. 2. 23; 2 Pet. 3. 16. ignorant

UNLEAVENED, Ex. 12. 39. 1 Cor. 5. 7.

UNMARRIED (virgins), Paul's exhortation to, 1 Cor. 7. 8, 11, 25, 32.

UNMERCIFUL, Rom. 1. 31.

UNMINDFUL, Deut. 32. 8.

UNMOVABLE, 1 Cor. 15. 58.

UNPERFECT, Ps. 139. 16.

UNPREPARED, 2 Cor. 9. 4.

UNPROFITABLE talk, Job 15. 3.
Matt. 25. 30. cast the *u.* servant
Luke 17. 10. are all *u.* servants
Rom. 3. 12. altogether become *u.*
Tit. 3. 9. they are *u.* and vain
Phile. 11. was to thee *u.* but
Heb. 13. 17. for that is *u.* for you

UNPUNISHED, Prov. 11. 21. & 16. 5. & 17. 5. & 19. 5, 9. Jer. 25. 29. & 30. 11. & 46. 28. & 49. 12.

UNQUENCHABLE, Matt. 3. 12. Luke 3. 17.

UNREASONABLE, Acts 25. 27. 2 Thes. 3. 2.

UNREBUKABLE, 1 Tim. 6. 14.

UNREPROVABLE, Col. 1. 22.

UNRIGHTEOUS decrees, Isa. 10. 1.
Isa. 55. 7. *u.* man forsake his
Rom. 3. 5. is God *u.* who taketh
1 Cor. 6. 9. *u.* shall not inherit
Heb. 6. 10. God is not *u.* to forget
Lev. 19. 15. do no *unrighteousness*
Ps. 92. 15. there is no *u.* in him
Luke 16. 9. mammon of *u.*
John 7. 18. true, and no *u.* in him
Rom. 1. 18. hold the truth in *u.*
6. 13. members instruments of *u.*
9. 14. is there *u.* with God? God
2 Cor. 6. 14. fellowship hath righteousness with *u.*
2 Thes. 2. 10. all deceivable. of *u.*
Heb. 8. 12. be merciful to their *u.*
1 John 1. 9. cleanse us from all *u.*
5. 17. all *u.* is sin
R. V. 2 Cor. 6. 14; Heb. 8. 12. iniquity; 2 Pet. 2. 13, 15. wrong doing

UNRULY, 1 Thes. 5. 14. Tit. 1. 6, 10. Jas. 3. 8.
R. V. 1 Thes. 5. 14. disorderly; Jas. 3. 8. restless

UNSAVORY, Job 6. 6. Jer. 23. 13.

UNSEARCHABLE things, Job 5. 9.
Ps. 145. 3. his greatness is *u.*
Prov. 25. 3. heart of kings is *u.*
Rom. 11. 33. *u.* are his judgments
Eph. 3. 8. preach *u.* riches of

UNSEEMLY, Rom. 1. 27. 1 Cor. 13. 5.

UNSKILFUL in word, Heb. 5. 13.

UNSPEAKABLE, 2 Cor. 9. 15. & 12. 4. 1 Pet. 1. 8.

UNSPOTTED, Jas. 1. 27.

UNSTABLE, Gen. 49. 4. Jas. 1. 8.
2 Pet. 2. 14. *u.* souls
3. 16. unlearned and *u.*
R. V. 2 Pet. 2. 14; 3. 16. unstedfast

UNTHANKFUL, Luke 6. 35. 2 Tim. 3. 2.

UNTOWARD, Acts 2. 40.

UNWASHEN, Matt. 15. 20. Mark 7. 2, 5.
R. V. Mark 7. 5. defiled

UNWISE, Deut. 32. 6. Hos. 13. 13. Rom. 1. 14. Eph. 5. 17.
R. V. Rom. 1. 14. Eph. 5. 17. foolish

UNWORTHY, Acts 13. 46. 1 Cor 6. 2.
1 Cor. 11. 27. drinketh *unworthily*

UPBRAID, Judg. 18. 15. Matt. 11. 20. Mark 16. 14. Jas. 1. 5.

UPHOLD me with thy Spirit, Ps. 51. 12.
Ps. 119. 116. *u.* me according to
Prov. 29. 23. honor shall *u.* humble
Isa. 41. 10. I will *u.* thee with the right hand of my righteousness
42. 1. my servant whom I *u.*
63. 5. my fury it *upheld* me
57. 17. Lord *upholdeth* righteous
145. 14. Lord *u.* all that fall
41. 12. thou *upholdest* me in
Heb. 1. 3. *upholding* all by word

UPRIGHT in heart, Ps. 7. 10.
Ps. 11. 7. his countenance doth behold the *u.*
18. 23. I was also *u.* before him
25. with *u.* wilt show thyself *u.*
25. 8. good and *u.* is the Lord
37. 37. mark the perfect man and behold the *u.*
64. 10. all *u.* in heart shall glory
112. 4. to *u.* light ariseth in dark.
140. 13. the *u.* shall dwell in
Prov. 2. 21. *u.* shall dwell in the
11. 3. integrity of *u.* shall guide
20. *u.* in their way, are his de.
12. 6. mouth of *u.* shall deliver
13. 6. righteous. keepeth the *u.*
15. 8. prayer of *u.* is his delight
21. 18. the transgressor for the *u.*
28. 10. *u.* shall have good things
Eccl. 7. 29. God hath made man *u.*
S. of S. 1. 4. the *u.* love thee
Hab. 2. 4. his soul is not *u.* in him
Ps. 15. 2. that walketh *uprightly*, 84. 11. Prov. 2. 7. & 10. 9. & 15. 21. & 29. 18. Mic. 2. 7. Gal. 2. 14.
Ps. 58. 1. do ye judge *u.*, 75. 2.
Isa. 33. 15. he that speaketh *u.*
Deut. 9. 5. not for the *uprightness* of thy heart
Job 33. 23. to show unto man his *u.*
Ps. 25. 21. let integrity and *u.* preserve me
Isa. 26. 7. way of the just is *u.*
10. land of *u.* will he deal unjustly
R. V. 2 Sam. 22. 24, 26; Job 12. 4; Ps. 18. 23, 25; 19. 13; 37. 18; Prov. 11. 20; 28. 10; 29. 10. perfect; Prov. 2. 7; Job 4. 6; Prov. 28. 6. integrity

URIM and Thummin, Ex. 28. 30. Lev. 88. Num. 27. 21. 1 Sam. 28. 6. Ezra 2. 63. Neh. 7. 65.

US, Gen. 1. 26. & 3. 22. & 11. 7. Isa. 6. 8. & 9. 6. Rom. 4. 24. 2 Cor. 5. 21. Gal. 3. 13. 1 Thes. 5. 10. Heb. 6. 20. 1 Pet. 2. 21. & 4. 1. 1 John 5. 11.

USE, Rom. 1. 26. Eph. 4. 29. Heb. 5. 14.
1 Cor. 7. 31. *u.* world as not abus.
Gal. 5. 13. *u.* not liberty for occa.
1 Tim. 1. 8. law is good if a man *u.*
1 Cor. 9. 15. I have *used* none of
Jer. 22. 13. *useth* his neighbor's
Tit. 3. 14. learn good works for necessary *uses*
Ps. 119. 132. as thou *usest* to do to
Col. 2. 22. *using*, 1 Pet. 2. 16.
R. V. 2 Sam. 1. 18. song

USURP, 1 Tim. 2. 12.

USURY, Ex. 22. 25. Lev. 25. 36, 37. Deut. 23. 19, 20. Neh. 5. 7, 10. Ps. 15. 5. Prov. 28. 8. Isa. 24. 2. Jer. 15. 10. Ezek. 18. 8, 13, 17. & 22. 12. Matt. 25. 27. Luke 19. 23.
R. V. Matt. 25. 27; Luke 19. 23. interest

UTTER, Ps. 78. 2. & 94. 4.

Ps. 106. 2. who can *u.* mighty acts
2 Cor. 12. 4. lawful for a man to *u.*
Rom. 8. 26. groanings that cannot be *uttered*
Heb. 5. 11. things hard to be *u.*
Ps. 19. 2. day unto day *uttereth*
Acts 2. 4. as the spirit gave them *utterance*
Eph. 6. 19. that *u.* may be given
Deut. 7. 2. *utterly*, Ps. 89. 33. & 119. 8, 43. S. of S. 8. 7. Jer. 14. 9.
1 Thes. 2. 16. *uttermost*, Heb. 7. 25.
R. V. *outer*, Ezek. 40. 31. arches were toward *u.* court; 42. 1; 44. 19; 46. 20; 47. 2; Ex. 26. 4; 36. 11, 17; 2 Kings 7. 5, 8. outmost; Deut. 11. 24. hinder; Josh. 15. 5. end; Matt. 5. 26. last

V

VAIL (of women), Gen. 24. 65. Ruth 3. 15. 1 Cor. 11. 10.
of Moses, Ex. 34. 33. 2 Cor. 3. 13.
of the tabernacle and temple, Ex. 26. 31. & 36. 35. 2 Cor. 3. 14. *See* Heb. 6. 19. & 9. 3. & 10. 20.
of temple rent at crucifixion, Matt. 27. 51. Mark 15. 38. Luke 23. 45.
VAIN, Ex. 5. 9. & 20. 7.
Deut. 32. 47. it is not a *v.* thing
1 Sam. 12. 21. turn not after *v.*
Ps. 39. 6. every man walketh in a *v.* shew, and they are disquiet. in *v.*
Job 11. 12. *v.* man would be wise
Ps. 60. 11. *v.* is help of man
119. 113. I hate *v.* thoughts, but
Jer. 4. 14. long shall *v.* thoughts
Mal. 3. 14. it is *v.* to serve God
Matt. 6. 7. use not *v.* repetitions
Rom. 1. 21. they glorified not God, but became *v.* in their imagina.
1 Cor. 3. 20. thoughts of wise are *v.*
Eph. 5. 6. deceive you with *v.*
Col. 2. 8. through *v.* philosophy
1 Pet. 1. 18. from *v.* conversation
Ps. 73. 13. cleansed my heart *in vain*
89. 47. why hast thou made all men —
127. 1. labor —; walketh —
Isa. 45. 19. seek ye me —
Jer. 3. 23 — is salvation hoped
Matt. 15. 9.— do they worship me
Rom. 13. 4. bear not the sword —
1 Cor. 15. 58. your labor is not —
2 Cor. 6. 1. receive not grace of God —
Phil. 2. 16. not run — nor labored —
2 Kings 17. 15. followed *vanity*
Job 7. 3. possess months of *v.*
16. let me alone; my days are *v.*
Ps. 12. 2. speak *v.* every one
24. 4. nor lifted up his soul to *v.*
11. surely every man is *v.*
62. 9. men of low degree are *v.*
119. 37. turn mine eyes from beholding *v.*
Prov. 22. 8. that soweth iniquity shall reap *v.*
Eccl. 1. 2. *v.* of vanities, all is *v.*, 14. & 3. 19. & 2. 1. & 4. 8. & 12. 8.
Isa. 5. 18. iniquity with cords of *v.*
40. 17. less than nothing and *v.*
Hab. 2. 13. weary themselves for *v.*
Rom. 8. 20. the creature was made subject to *v.*
Eph. 4. 17. walk in *v.* of their
2 Pet. 2. 18. swelling words of *v.*
Ps. 31. 6. I hate them that regard lying *vanities*
Jer. 10. 8. a doctrine of *v.*
Jonah 2. 8. that observe lying *v.*
Acts 14. 15. turn from these *v.*
R. V. Ex. 5. 9. lying; Job 35. 16; Ps. 89. 47; Isa. 49. 4; Jer. 10. 3; 23. 15; 51. 58; Lam. 2. 14; Isa. 49. 4. vanity; Jer. 4. 14. evil; Isa. 45. 18. waste; Eph. 5. 6. empty; Gal. 2. 21. nought; 1 Tim. 6. 20; 2 Tim. 2. 16 —
VALIANT, S. of S. 3. 7. Isa. 10. 13.
Jer. 9. 3. not *v.* for the truth
Heb. 11. 34. faith waxed *v.*
Ps. 60. 12. *valiantly*, 108. 13. & 118. 15, 16. Num. 24. 18.
R. V. 1 Kings 1. 42; 1 Chron. 7. 2, 5; 11. 26; 28. 1; S. of S. 3. 7; Heb. 11. 34. mighty; Jer. 46. 15. strong
VALUE, Job 13. 4. Matt. 10. 31.
VAPOR, Jer. 10. 13. Jas. 4. 14.
VARIABLENESS, Jas. 1. 17.
VARIANCE, Matt. 10. 35. Gal. 5. 20.
R. V. Gal. 5. 20. strife
VAUNT, Judg. 7. 2. 1 Cor. 13. 4.
VEHEMENT, S. of S. 8. 6. 2 Cor. 7. 11.
R. V. 2 Cor. 7. 11 —
VEIL, Gen. 24. 65. S. of S. 5. 7.
Isa. 25. 7. destroy the *v.* spread
Matt. 27. 51. *v.* was rent from top
2 Cor. 3. 13. Moses put a *v.* over
15. *v.* is upon their heart
Heb. 6. 19. into that within *v.*
VENGEANCE taken, Gen 4. 15.
Deut. 32. 35. to me belongeth *v.*, Ps. 94. 1. Rom. 12. 19. Heb. 10. 30.
Ps. 58. 10. rejoice when he seeth *v.*
99. 8. tookest *v.* of their inven.
Isa. 34. 8. day of the Lord's *v.*
Jer. 11. 20. let me see thy *v.*
51. 6. time of the Lord's *v.*, 11.
Luke 21. 22. these be days of *v.*
2 Thes. 1. 8. fire taking *v.*
Jude 7. suffering *v.* of eternal fire
R. V. Acts 28. 4. justice; Jude 7. punishment
VENISON, Gen. 25. 28. & 27. 3.
VERILY, Gen. 42. 21. Jer. 15. 11. It is often used by Christ, as well as *verily, verily*, John 1. 51. & 3. 3, 5, 11. & 5. 19, 24, 25. & 6. 26.
VERITY, Ps. 111. 7. 1 Tim. 2. 7.
VERY, Prov. 17. 9. Matt. 24. 24. John 7. 26. & 14. 11. 1 Thes. 5. 23.
VESSEL, Ps. 2. 9. & 31. 12. Jer. 18. 4.
Jer. 22. 28. *v.* wherein is no pleas.
48. 11. emptied from *v.* to *v.*
Acts 9. 15. he is a chosen *v.* unto
Rom. 9. 21. one *v.* to honor and
1 Thes. 4. 4. possess his *v.* in sanc.
2 Tim. 2. 21. be a *v.* unto honor
1 Pet. 3. 7. honor to wife as the weaker *v.*
Rom. 9. 21. *vessels* of wrath fitted
2 Cor. 4. 7. treasure in earthen *v.*
R. V. Ex. 27. 19; 39. 40; Num. 3. 36. instruments; Ex. 40. 9; Num. 1. 50; 4. 15, 16; 1 Chron. 9. 29. furniture
VESTURE, lots cast for Christ's, Matt. 27. 35; John 19. 24. *See* Ps. 22. 18. Rev. 19. 13.
VEXED, Job 27. 2. Ps. 6. 2, 3, 10.
Isa. 63. 10. and *v.* his Holy Spirit
2 Pet. 2. 7. Lot *v.* with filthy con.
R. V. Neh. 9. 27; 2 Pet. 2. 7. distressed; Isa. 63. 10. grieved; Ezek. 22. 7. wronged; Luke 6. 18. troubled
VIAL, Rev. 5. 8. & 16. 1. & 21. 9.
R. V. In Rev. bowl or bowls
VICTORY is thine, O Lord, 1 Chron. 29. 11.
Ps. 98. 1. hand and arm gotten him the *v.*
Isa. 25. 8. swallow up death in *v.*
Matt. 20. 12. judgment unto *v.*
1 Cor. 15. 54. death is swallowed up in *v.*
55. O grave, where is thy *v.*
57. God who giveth us *v.*
1 John 5. 4. *v.* that overcometh
VIGILANT, 1 Tim. 3. 2. 1 Pet. 5. 8.
R. V. 1 Tim. 3. 2. temperate; 1 Pet. 5. 8. watchful
VILE, thy brother seem, Deut. 25. 3.
1 Sam. 3. 13. made themselves *v.*
2 Sam. 6. 22. I will yet be more *v.*
Job 40. 4. I am *v.*; what shall I an.
Ps. 15. 4. whose eyes a *v.* person
Isa. 32. 6. *v.* person will speak vill.
Rom. 1. 26. up to *v.* affections
Phil. 3. 21. change our *v.* body
R. V. Judg. 19. 24. folly; Job 18. 3. unclean; 40. 4. small account; Ps. 15. 4. reprobate; Dan. 11. 21. contemptible; Phil. 3. 21. humiliation
VINE, 1 Kings 4. 25. Mic. 4. 4.
Deut. 32. 32. *v.* is the *v.* of Sodom
Ps. 128. 3. thy wife shall be as a fruitful *v.*
Jer. 2. 21. planted thee a noble *v.*
Hos. 10. 1. Israel is an empty *v.*
14. 7. they shall grow as the *v.*
Matt. 26. 29. drink of fruit of *v.*
John 15. 1. I am the true *v.* and my Father is the husbandman
5. I am the *v.* ye are the branch.
Ps. 80. 15. *vineyard*, Prov. 24. 30. S of S. 1. 6. Isa. 5. 1, 7. Matt. 20. 1. & 21. 33. Luke 13. 6. 1 Cor. 9. 7. S. of S. 8. 11, 12.
R. V. Rev. 14. 19. vintage
VIOLENCE, Lev. 6. 2. 2 Sam. 22. 3.
Gen. 6. 11. earth was filled with *v.*
Hab. 1. 2. cry out unto thee of *v.*
Matt. 11. 12. the kingdom of heaven suffereth *v.*
Luke 3. 14. do *v.* to no man, and
Heb. 11. 34. quenched the *v.* of
R. V. Lev. 6. 2. robbery; Mic. 2. 2. seize; Acts 24. 7 —; Heb. 11. 34. power; Rev. 18. 21. mighty fall
VIRGIN, Isa. 7. 14. 2 Cor. 11. 2. S. of S. 1. 3. *virgins*, Rev. 14. 4.
VIRTUE, Mark 5. 30. Luke 6. 19.
2 Pet. 1. 3. call. us to glory and *v.*
5. to faith *v.* and to *v.* knowledge
Phil. 4. 8. if there be any *v.* think
Prov. 12. 4. *virtuous* woman, 31. 10.
R. V. Mark 5. 30; Luke 6. 19; 8. 46. power
VISAGE, Isa. 52. 14. Lam. 4. 8.
VISIBLE and invisible, Col. 1. 16.
VISION, 1 Sam. 3. 1. Ps. 89. 19. Matt. 17. 9. Acts 10. 19. & 16. 9.
Hab. 2. 2. write the *v.*
3. the *v.* is for a time
Ezek. 13. 16. see *visions* of peace
Hos. 12. 10. I have multiplied *v.*
Joel 2. 28. young men shall see *v.*
2 Cor. 12. 1. I will come to *v.* and
R. V. Ezek. 8. 4. appearance; Acts 9. 12 —
VISIT you, Gen. 50. 24, 25. Ex. 13. 19.
Job 7. 18. shouldest *v.* him every
Ps. 106. 4. *v.* me with thy salvation
Jer. 5. 9. shall I not *v.* you for
Lam. 4. 22. *v.* iniquity, Jer. 14. 10. & 23. 2. Hos. 2. 13. & 8. 13.
Acts 7. 23. *v.* his brethren, 15. 36.
15. 14. God did *v.* the Gentiles
Jas. 1. 27. to *v.* the fatherless
Ex. 3. 16. I have surely *visited*
Ps. 17. 3. thou hast *v.* me in night
Isa. 26. 16. in trouble have they *v.*
Matt. 25. 36. I was sick and ye *v.*
Luke 1. 68. *v.* and redeem. people
Ps. 8. 4. *visitest*, 65. 9. Heb. 2. 6.
Ex. 20. 5. *visiting* the iniquity of the fathers upon the children, 34. 7.
VOCATION, worthy of, Eph. 4. 1.
VOICE is *v.* of Jacob, Gen. 27. 22.
Gen. 4. 10. *v.* of brother's blood
Ex. 5. 2. who is the Lord that I should obey his *v.*
Ps. 5. 3. my *v.* shalt thou hear
18. 13. the Highest gave his *v.*
95. 7. to-day, if ye will hear his *v.*
Eccl. 12. 4. rise up at the *v.* of
S. of S. 2. 14. let me hear thy *v.*
Isa. 30. 19. gracious at *v.* of thy
Ezek. 33. 32. hath a pleasant *v.*
John 5. 25. dead shall hear the *v.*
10. 3. sheep hear his *v.*, 4. 16, 27.
Gal. 4. 20. I desire to change my *v.*
1 Thes. 4. 16. with *v.* of archangel
Rev. 3. 20. if any man hear my *v.*
Acts 13. 27. *voices*, Rev. 4. 5. & 11. 19.

VOID of counsel, Deut. 32. 28.
Ps. 30. 39. made *v.* the covenant
Isa. 55. 11. shall not return *v.*
Acts 24. 16. conscience *v.* of offence
Rom. 3. 31. do we make *v.* the law
1 Cor. 9. 15. make my glorying *v.*
VOLUME, Ps. 40. 7. Heb. 10. 17.
VOMIT, Job 20. 15. Prov. 23. 8. & 26. 11. Isa. 19. 14. 2 Pet. 2. 22.
VOW, Jacob vowed a, Gen. 28. 20. & 31. 13. Num. 6. 2. & 21. 2. & 30. 1 Sam. 1. 11. 2 Sam. 15. 7, 8.
Ps. 65. 1. to thee shall the *v.* be
76. 11. *v.* and pay unto the
Eccl. 5. 4. a *v.* defer not to pay, 5.
Isa. 19. 21. shall *v.* a *v.* to the Lord
Jonah 2. 9. pay that I have *vowed*
Job 22. 27. shall pay thy *vows*
Ps. 22. 25. I will pay my *v.* before
56. 12. thy *v.* O God are upon
61. 5. heard my *v.*
Prov. 20. 25. after *v.* to make enqu.
31. 2. son of my *v.*, 1 Sam. 1. 11.
Jonah 1. 16. offer. sacri. and made *v.*
VOYAGE, Paul's, Acts 27. & 28.

W

WAGES, Lev. 19. 13. Ezek. 29. 18.
Jer. 22. 13. neighbor's service without *w.*
Hag. 1. 6. earneth *w.* to put it
Mal. 3. 5. oppress hirel. in his *w.*
Luke 3. 14. be conte. with your *w.*
Rom. 6. 23. the *w.* of sin is death
R. V. 2 Pet. 2. 15. hire
WAIT till my change come, Job 14. 14.
Ps. 25. 5. on thee do I *w.* all the day
27. 14. *w.* on the Lord; *w.* I say
37. 34. *w.* on the Lord and keep
62. 5. *w.* thou only upon God
130. 5. I *w.* for the Lord, my
145. 15. eyes of all *w.* upon thee
Prov. 20. 22. *w.* on the Lord and
Isa. 8. 17. I will *w.* upon the Lord
30. 18. will the Lord *w.* blessed
40. 31. that *w.* on the Lord shall renew their strength
Lam. 3. 25. good to them that *w.*
26. quietly *w.* for salvation of
Hos. 12. 6. *w.* on thy God contin.
Mic. 7. 7. I will *w.* for God of my
Hab. 2. 3. *w.* for it, it will surely
Zeph. 3. 8. *w.* ye on me, I will rise
Luke 12. 36. men that *w.* for their
Gal. 5. 5. through the Spirit *w.*
1 Thes. 1. 10. *w.* for his Son from
Gen. 49. 18. *waited* for thy salva.
Ps. 40. 1. I *w.* patiently for the
Isa. 25. 9. our God, we have *w.* for
Zech. 11. 11. poor of flock that *w.*
Mark 15. 43. *w.* for kingdom of God
1 Pet. 3. 20. long suffering of God *w.*
Ps. 33. 20. our soul *waiteth* for
65. 1. praise *w.* for thee, in Zion
130. 6. my soul *w.* for Lord more
Isa. 64. 4. prepared for him that *w.*
Prov. 8. 34. *waiting* at the posts
Luke 2. 25. *w.* for the consolation
Rom. 8. 23. *w.* for the adoption
1 Cor. 1. 7. *w.* for coming of Lord
2 Thes. 3. 5. to a patient *w.* for
R. V. Job 17. 13; Isa. 59. 9; Ps. 128. 2; Luke 12. 36. look; Ps. 71. 10; Jer. 5. 26. watch; Judg. 9. 35. ambush
WAKETH, Ps. 127. 1. S. of S. 5. 2.
Ps. 77. 4. holdest my eyes *waking*
Isa. 50. 4. *wakeneth*, Joel 3. 12.
WALK in my law, Ex. 16. 4.
Gen. 17. 1. *w.* before me and be per.
24. 40. before whom I *w.*
Lev. 26. 12. I will *w.* among
24. will I *w.* contrary unto you
Deut. 5. 33. *w.* in the ways of the Lord, 8. 6. & 10. 12. & 11. 22. & 13. 5. & 28. 9.
13. 4. shall *w.* after the Lord
Ps. 23. 4. though I *w.* through valley of death
Ps. 84. 11. no good thing from them that *w.* uprightly
Eccl. 11. 9. *w.* in way of thy heart
Isa. 2. 3. will *w.* in his paths
30. 21. this is the way, *w.* ye in
40. 31. shall *w.* and not faint
Dan. 4. 37. that *w.* in pride he is
Hos. 14. 9. just shall *w.* in them
Mic. 6. 8. *w.* humbly with thy
Amos 3. 3. how can two *w.* to.
Zech. 10. 12. *w.* up and down in
Luke 13. 33. I must *w.* to-day and
John 8. 12. followeth me, not *w.*
11. 9. *w.* in day, he stumbleth not
Rom. 4. 12. *w.* in steps of that faith
8. 1. *w.* not after the flesh, 4.
2 Cor. 5. 7. we *w.* by faith, not
10. 3. though *w.* in the flesh, we
Gal. 6. 16. as many as *w.* accord.
Eph. 2. 10. ordained that we *w.*
5. 15. *w.* circumspectly, not as
Phil. 3. 17. mark them who *w.* so
Col. 1. 10. that ye might *w.* worthy
1 Thes. 2. 12. ye would *w.* worthy
4. 1. how ought ye to *w.* and
1 John 1. 7. if we *w.* in the light
2. 6. ought so to *w.* as he walked
Rev. 3. 4. *w.* with me in white
16. 15. lest he *w.* naked and see
21. 24. nations shall *w.* in light
John 12. 35. *w.* in light while ye
Rom. 13. 13. let us *w.* honestly as
Gal. 5. 16. *w.* in Spirit, and not ful.
25. if we live in Spirit, let us *w.*
Eph. 5. 2. *w.* in love as Christ
8. *w.* as children of light
Phil. 3. 16. let us *w.* by the same
Gen. 6. 9. Noah *walked* with God
5. 22. Enoch *w.* with God, 24.
Ps. 55. 14. we *w.* unto the house
81. 12. *w.* in their own counsels
Isa. 9. 2. people that *w.* in darkness
2 Cor. 10. 2. as if we *w.* accord.
12. 18. *w.* we not in same spirit
Gal. 2. 14. they *w.* not uprightly
Eph. 2. 2. in time past we *w.*
1 Pet. 4. 3. we *w.* in lasciviousness
Isa. 43. 2. when thou *walkest* through the fire
Rom. 14. 15. *w.* thou not charitably
Ps. 15. 2. he that *walketh* uprightly
39. 6. every man *w.* in a vain
Prov. 10. 9. he that *w.* uprightly
13. 20. *w.* with wise men shall
Isa. 50. 10. *w.* in darkness, and
Jer. 10. 23. not in man that *w.* to direct his steps
Mic. 2. 7. him that *w.* uprightly
2 Thes. 3. 6. from brother that *w.* disorderly
1 Pet. 5. 8. *w.* about seeking
Rev. 2. 1. *w.* in midst of the
Gen. 3. 8. voice of Lord *walking* in
Isa. 57. 2. *w.* in his own upright.
Jer. 6. 28. revolters *w.* with sland.
Mic. 2. 11. if man *w.* in falsehood
Luke 1. 6. *w.* in all command.
Acts 9. 31. *w.* in the fear of the
2 Cor. 4. 2. not *w.* in craftiness
2 Pet. 3. 3. *w.* after their own
2 John 4. thy children *w.* in truth
WALL, Ps. 62. 3. Prov. 18. 11. S. of S. 2. 9. & 8. 9, 10. Isa. 26. 1. & 60. 18.
R. V. Gen. 49. 6. ox; Num. 13. 28; 22. 24; Deut. 1. 28; Isa. 5. 5; Hos. 2. 6. fence or fenced; 1 Kings 21. 23. rampart
WANDER, Num. 14. 33. Ps. 119. 10.
Lam. 4. 14. *wandered*, Heb. 11. 37.
Prov. 21. 16. *wandereth*, 27. 8.
1 Tim. 5. 13. *wandering*, Jude 13.
Ps. 56. 8. tellest my *wanderings*
WANT, Deut. 28. 48. Job 31. 19.
Ps. 23. 1. the Lord is my shepherd, I shall not *w.*
34. 9. no *w.* to them that fear
Prov. 6. 11. thy *w.* come as an
2 Cor. 8. 14. a supply for your *w.*
Phil. 4. 11. speak in respect of *w.*
Jas. 1. 4. perfect and entire, *wanting*
R. V. Prov. 10. 21. lack; Phil. 2. 25 need; Prov. 28. 16; Eccl. 6. 2; Jas. 1. 4. lack or lacking
WANTONNESS, Rom. 13. 13. 2 Pet. 2. 18.
R. V. 2 Pet. 2. 18. lasciviousness
WAR, Ex. 13. 17. & 17. 16. Ps. 27. 3.
Job 10. 17. changes and *w.* are
Ps. 18. 34. teacheth my hands to *w.*
120. 7. I am for peace, they for *w.*
Prov. 20. 18. good advice make *w.*
Eccl. 8. 8. discharge in this *w.*
Isa. 2. 4. not learn *w.* any more
Mic. 3. 5. prepare *w.* against him
2 Cor. 10. 3. do not *w.* after flesh
1 Tim. 1. 18. mightest *w.* a good warfare
Rev. 11. 7. beast shall make *w.*
12. 7. there was *w.* in heaven
Num. 21. 14. in the book of the *wars* of the Lord
Ps. 46. 9. he maketh *w.* to cease
Matt. 24. 6. hear of *w.* and rumors of *w.*
Jas. 4. 1. whence come *w.* and
2 Tim. 2. 4. no man that *warreth*
Isa. 37. 8. *warring*, Rom. 7. 23.
R. V. Deut. 21. 10; Judg. 21. 22; 2 Chron. 6. 34; Jer. 6. 23. battle
WARFARE, Isa. 40. 2. 1 Cor. 9. 7. 2 Cor. 10. 4. 1 Tim. 1. 18.
WARN, 2 Chron. 19. 10. Acts 10. 22.
Ezek. 3. 19. if thou *w.* the wicked
33. 3. blow the trumpet and *w.*
Acts 20. 31. I ceased not to *w.* every one night and day
1 Cor. 4. 14. my beloved sons I *w.*
1 Thes. 5. 14. *w.* them that are un.
Ps. 19. 11. by them is thy servant *warned*
Matt. 3. 7. who hath *w.* you to flee
Heb. 11. 7. Noah being *w.* of God
Jer. 6. 10. to whom I give *warning*
Col. 1. 28. teaching every man, *w.*
R. V. Acts 20. 31; 1 Cor. 4. 14; 1 Thes. 5. 14. admonish
WASH, Lev. 6. 27. & 14. 15, 16.
Job 9. 30. if I *w.* myself in snow
Ps. 26. 6. *w.* my hands in innocen.
51. 7. *w.* me and I shall be whiter
58. 10. shall *w.* his feet in blood
Isa. 1. 16. *w.* you, make you clean
Jer. 2. 22. *w.* thee with nitre
Luke 7. 8. *w.* his feet with tears
John 13. 5. *w.* disciples' feet
8. I *w.* thee not, thou hast no
14. *w.* one another's feet
Acts 22. 16. baptized and *w.* away
Job 29. 6. I *washed* my steps
S. of S. 5. 3. I have *w.* my feet
Isa. 4. 4. *w.* away the filth
Ezek. 16. 4. neither wast thou *w.*
16. 9. I thoroughly *w.* away blood
1 Cor. 6. 11. we are *w.* justified
Heb. 10. 22. *w.* with pure water
Rev. 1. 5. *w.* us from sins in his
7. 14. *w.* robes, and made white in
Eph. 5. 26. *washing*, Tit. 3. 5.
R. V. Ex. 2. 5; Lev. 14. 8, 9; 15. 16 16. 4, 24; 22. 6; Deut. 23. 11; 2 Sam. 11. 2; John 13. 10. bathe; Luke 7. 38, 44. wet; Rev. 1. 5. loosed
WASTE, Ps. 80. 13. Matt. 26. 8.
Luke 15. 11. *wasted*, 36. 1. Gal. 1. 13.
Job 14. 10. *wasteth*, Prov. 19. 26.
Prov. 18. 9. *waster*, Isa. 54. 16.
Isa. 59. 7. *wasting* and destruction, 60. 18.
R. V. Prov. 18. 9. destroyer
WATCH, Neh. 4. 9. Job 7. 12.
Job 14. 15. dost thou not *w.* over
Ps. 102. 7. I *w.* and am as a sparrow
141. 3. set a *w.* before my mouth
Jer. 44. 27. *w.* over them for evil
Matt. 24. 42. *w.* for ye know not
26. 41. *w.* and pray that ye enter
Mark 13. 33. take heed, *w.* and
1 Cor. 16. 13. *w.* ye, stand fast in
1 Thes. 5. 6. let us *w.* and be sober
2 Tim. 4. 5. *w.* thou in all things
Heb. 13. 17. they *w.* for your souls
1 Pet. 4. 7. be sober, *w.* unto prayer

Jer. 31. 28. like as I *watched* over
Matt. 24. 43. he would have *w*.
Ps. 37. 32. the wicked *watcheth*
Ezek. 7. 6. the end is come; it *w*.
Rev. 16. 15. blessed is he that *w*.
Dan. 4. 13. a *watcher* and holy
Ps. 63. 6. *watches*, 119. 148. Lam. 2. 19.
Rev. 3. 2. be *watchful*
Prov. 8. 34. *watching* daily at gates
Luke 12. 37. blessed whom the Lord shall find *w*.
2 Cor. 6. 5. in *watchings*, 11. 27.
Isa. 21. 11. *watchman*, Ezek. 3. 17. & 33. 7.
S. of S. 3. 3. *watchmen*, 5. 7. Isa. 52. 8. & 56. 10. & 62. 6. Jer. 31. 6.
WATER, Gen. 49. 4. Ex. 12. 9. & 17. 6.
2 Sam. 14. 14. we are as *w*. spilt
Job 15. 16. drink. iniquity like *w*.
Ps. 22. 14. I am poured out like *w*.
Isa. 12. 3. draw *w*. out of the wells of salvation
30. 20. give you *w*. of affliction
58. 11. shalt be like a spring of *w*.
Lam. 1. 16. mine eye runneth down with *w*., 3. 48.
Ezek. 36. 25. sprinkle clean *w*. on
Amos 8. 11. nor a thirst for *w*.
Matt. 3. 11. I baptize you with *w*.
10. 42. cup of cold *w*. in name of
Luke 16. 24. tip of his finger in *w*.
John 3. 5. man be born of *w*.
4. 14. shall be in him a well of *w*.
7. 38. flow rivers of living *w*.
19. 34. there out blood and *w*.
Acts 8. 38. went down into the *w*.
Eph. 5. 26. cleanse it with the washing of *w*.
1 John 5. 6. he that came by *w*.
8. three bear witness, Spirit, *w*.
Jude 12. clouds they are without *w*.
Rev. 7. 17. lead them to living fountains of *w*.
21. 6. fountain of *w*. of life
22. 17. take the *w*. of life freely
Ps. 23. 2. leadeth me beside the still *waters*
Prov. 5. 15. drink *w*. out of thine
9. 17. stolen *w*. are sweet
Eccl. 11. 1. cast thy bread upon *w*.
S. of S. 4. 15. a well of living *w*.
Isa. 32. 20. blessed are ye that sow beside all *w*.
35. 6. in wilderness shall *w*. break
55. 1. come ye to *w*. buy and eat
58. 11. whose *w*. fail not
Jer 2. 13. fountain of living *w*.
9. 1. O that my head were *w*.
Hab. 2. 14. as *w*. cover the sea
Zech. 14. 8. living *w*. shall go out
Rev. 1. 15. his voice as the sound of many *w*., 14. 2. & 19. 6.
Prov. 11. 25. he that *watereth* shall be *watered*
Isa. 58. 11. be like a *w*. garden
1 Cor. 3. 6. I planted, Apollos *w*.
Ps. 42. 7. noise of thy *waterspouts*
WAVERING, Heb. 10. 23. Jas. 1. 6.
R.V. Jas. 1. 6. doubteth
WAX, Ex. 32. 10, 11, 22. Ps. 22. 14. & 68. 2. & 97. 5. Matt. 24. 12. Luke 12. 33. 1 Tim. 5. 11. 2 Tim. 3. 13.
R. V. Gen. 41. 56; Josh. 23. 1. was; Acts 13. 46. spake out
WAY, Ex. 13. 21. & 23. 20. & 32. 8.
1 Sam. 12. 23. teach you good and right *w*.
1 Kings 2. 2. *w*. of all the earth
Ezra 8. 21. seek of him a right *w*.
Ps. 1. 6. the Lord knoweth the *w*. of the righteous
49. 13. their *w*. is their folly
67. 2. thy *w*. may be known
119. 30. chosen *w*. of truth
104. I hate every false *w*.
Prov. 2. 8. Lord preserveth the *w*. of his saints
10. 29. *w*. of the Lord is strength
14. 12. a *w*. that seemeth right
Eccl. 11. 5. thou knowest not what is the *w*. of the spirit
Isa. 26. 7. *w*. of just is uprightness.
30. 21. this is the *w*. walk ye in
35. 8. a high *w*. and a *w*. called
40. 3. prepare the *w*. of the
43. 19. a *w*. in the wilderness
59. 8. *w*. of peace they know not
Jer. 6. 16. where is a good *w*. and
21. 8. set before you the *w*. of life
32. 39. give them one heart and *w*.
Amos 2. 7. turn aside *w*. of the
Mal. 3. 1. prepare the *w*. before
Matt. 7. 13. broad is *w*. to destruc.
14. narrow is *w*. that leadeth to
22. 16. teacheth *w*. of God in
John 1. 23. straight the *w*. of Lord
14. 4. *w*. ye know
6. I am the *w*.
Acts 16. 17. which show unto us the *w*. of salvation
1 Cor. 10. 13. make a *w*. to escape
12. 31. show you more excellent *w*.
2 Pet. 2. 2. the *w*. of truth be evil
1 Kings 8. 32. bring *his way* on his head
Job 17. 9. right. shall hold on —
Ps. 18. 30. as for God — is perfect
37. 23. delight in —
34. and keep —
119. 9. young man cleanse —
Prov. 14. 8. prudent to understand —
Isa. 55. 7. let the wicked forsake —
Ps. 25. 8. teach sinners *in the way*
119. 14. I rejoiced — of testimo.
139. 24. lead me — everlasting
Isa. 26. 8. — of thy judgments we
Matt. 5. 25. agree with adversary —
21. 32. John came — of righteous.
Luke 1. 79. guide your feet —
Job 40. 19. he is chief of *ways* of
Ps. 84. 5. in whose heart are *w*.
Prov. 3. 17. *w*. are *w*. of pleasant.
5. 21. *w*. of man are before Lord
16. 7. a man's *w*. please
Jer. 7. 3. amend your *w*. and doings
Lam. 1. 4. the *w*. of Zion do mourn
Deut. 32. 4. *his ways*, Ps. 145. 17. Isa. 2. 3. Mic. 4. 2. Rom. 11. 33.
Ps. 119. 5. *my ways*, 15. 26, 59, 168. & 139. 3. & 39. 1. Prov. 23. 26. Isa. 55. 8. & 49. 11.
Prov. 14. 14. *own ways*, Isa. 53. 6. & 58. 13. & 66. 3. Ezek. 36. 31, 32.
Job 21. 14. *thy ways*, Ps. 25. 4. & 91. 11. Prov. 3. 6. & 4. 26. Isa. 63. 17. Ezek. 16. 61. Dan. 5. 23. Rev. 15. 3.
Isa. 35. 8. *wayfaring*, Jer. 14. 8.
WEAK, 2 Chron. 15. 7. Job 4. 3. Ps. 6. 2.
Isa. 35. 3. strengthen ye *w*. hands
Ezek. 16. 30. how *w*. is thy heart
Matt. 26. 41. spirit is willing but the flesh is *w*.
Rom. 4. 19. not *w*. in faith
14. 1. him that is *w*. in faith receive
1 Cor. 4. 10. we are *w*. but ye
2 Cor. 11. 29. who is *w*. and I not *w*.
12. 10. I am *w*. then am I strong
1 Thes. 5. 13. support the *w*. be
Isa. 14. 12. *weaken*, Ps. 102. 23. Job 12. 21.
2 Sam. 3. 1. *weaker*, 1 Pet. 3. 7.
1 Cor. 1. 25. *weakness*, 2. 3. & 15. 43. 2 Cor. 12. 9. & 13. 4. Heb. 11. 34.
R. V. Job 12. 21. looseth; Isa. 14. 12. lay low
WEALTH, Gen. 34. 29. Deut. 8. 17.
Deut. 8. 18. give. power to get *w*.
Job. 21. 13. spend their days in *w*.
Ps. 49. 6. that trust in their *w*.
112. 3. *w*. and riches are in his
Prov. 10. 15. the rich man's *w*. is
13. 11. *w*. gotten by vanity
22. *w*. of sinners is laid up for
19. 4. *w*. maketh many friends
1 Cor. 10. 24. seek another's *w*.
R. V. Ezra 9. 12; Job 21. 13. prosperity; Esth. 10. 3; 1 Cor. 10. 24. good; Prov. 5. 10. strength
WEANED, Ps. 131. 2. Isa. 11. 8. & 28. 9.
WEAPON, Isa. 13. 5. & 54. 17. 2 Cor. 10. 4.
WEAR, Deut. 22. 5, 11. Dan. 7. 25. Matt. 11. 8. Jas. 2. 3. 1 Pet. 3. 3.
WEARY of my life, Gen. 27. 46.
Job 3. 17. there the *w*. be at rest
10. 1. soul is *w*. of life, Jer. 4. 31.
Prov. 3. 11. neither be *w*. of his
Isa. 7. 13. *w*. men, but will ye *w*.
40. 31. shall run and not be *w*.
43. 22. hast been *w*. of me, O
Jer. 6. 11. *w*. with holding in
9. 5. *w*. themselves to commit
15. 6. I am *w*. with repenting
Gal. 6. 9. *w*. in well doing
Isa. 43. 24. *wearied*, 57. 10. Jer. 12. 5. Ezek. 24. 12. Mic. 6. 3. Mal. 2. 17. John 4. 7. Heb. 12. 3.
Eccl. 12. 12. *weariness*, Mal. 1. 13.
Job 7. 3. *wearisome* nights
R. V. Job 37. 11. ladeth
WEB, Job 8. 14. Isa. 59. 5, 6.
WEDDING, Matt. 22. 3, 8, 11. Luke 14. 8.
WEEK, Dan. 9. 27. Matt. 28. 1. Luke 18. 12. Acts 20. 7. 1 Cor. 16. 2.
Jer. 5. 24. *weeks*, Dan. 9. 24-26. & 10. 2.
WEEP, Job 30. 25. Isa. 30. 19. & 33. 7. Jer. 9. 1. & 13. 17. Joel 2. 17.
Luke 6. 21. blessed are ye that *w*.
Acts 21. 13. what mean ye to *w*.
Rom. 12. 15. *w*. with them that *w*.
1 Cor. 7. 30. that *w*. as though *wept*
Jas. 5. 1. rich men *w*. and howl
Ps. 126. 6. *weepeth*, Lam. 1. 2.
1 Sam. 1. 8. why *weepest*, John 20. 13, 15.
Ps. 30. 5. *weeping* may endure for
Isa. 22. 12. Lord call to *w*. and
Jer. 31. 9. they shall come with *w*.
Joel 2. 12. turn to me with *w*.
Matt. 8. 12. *w*. and gnashing of teeth, 22. 13. & 24. 51. & 25. 30.
WEIGH the paths of the just, Isa. 26. 7.
Prov. 16. 2. Lord *weigheth* spirits
Job 31. 6. me be *weighed* in balances
Dan. 5. 27. art *w*. in the balances
Prov. 11. 1. just *weight* is his de.
2 Cor. 4. 17. eternal *w*. of glory
Heb. 12. 1. laying aside every *w*.
Lev. 19. 36. just *weights*
Deut. 55. 13. divers *w*., Prov. 20. 10, 23.
Matt. 23. 23. omit *weightier* matters
WELL, Ps. 84. 6. Prov. 5. 15. & 10. 11. S. of S. 4. 15. Isa. 12. 3. John 4. 14. 2 Pet. 2. 17.
Gen. 4. 7. if thou doest *well*, shalt
Ex. 1. 20. God dealt *w*. with mid.
Ps. 119. 65. hast dealt *w*. with thy
Eccl. 8. 12. it shall be *w*. with them
Isa. 3. 10. shall be *w*. with him
Rom. 2. 7. *well doing*, Gal. 6. 9. 2 Thes. 3. 13. 1 Pet. 2. 15. & 3. 17. & 4. 19.
R. V. Gen. 24. 13, 16, 29, 30, 42, 43; 49. 22; Josh. 18. 15; 2 Kings 3. 19, 25; Prov. 10. 11. fountain or fountains; Ex. 15. 27; Judg. 7. 1; Ps. 84. 6; 2 Pet. 2. 17. spring or springs; Deut. 6. 11; 2 Kings 26. 10; Neh. 9. 25. cisterns
WENT, Ps. 42. 4. & 119. 67. Matt. 21. 30.
WEPT, Neh. 1. 4. Ps. 69. 10. Hos. 12. 4. Matt. 26. 75. Luke 19. 41. John 11. 35.
WHEAT, Ps. 81. 16. Prov. 27. 22. S. of S. 7. 2.
Jer. 12. 13. have sown *w*. but reap
23. 28. what is the chaff to the *w*.
Matt. 3. 12. gather his *w*. into the
Luke 22. 31. may sift you as *w*.
John 12. 24. except a corn of *w*. fall
R. V. Num. 18. 12. corn; Prov. 27. 22. bruised corn
WHEEL, Ps. 83. 13. Prov. 20. 26.
Ezek. 1. 16. a *w*. in the midst of a *w*.
Ex. 14. 25. *wheels*, Judg. 5. 28. Dan. 7. 9. Nah. 3. 2.
R. V. Ps. 83. 13. whirling dust; Ezek. 23. 24; 26. 10. wagons
WHELPS (lions'), parable of, Ezek. 19. Nah. 2. 12.

WHET, Deut. 32. 41. Ps. 7. 12. & 64. 3.
WHISPERER, Prov. 16. 28.
WHIT, John 7. 23. & 12. 10. 2 Cor. 11. 5.
WHITE, Lev. 13. 3, 4. Num. 12. 10.
Job 6. 6. in the *w.* of an egg
Ps. 68. 14. *w.* as snow, Dan. 7. 9.
Eccl. 9. 8. garments be always *w.*
S. of S. 5. 10. my beloved is *w.* and
Isa. 1. 18. sins shall be *w.* as snow
Dan. 11. 35. fall.. to make them *w.*
Matt. 17. 2. his raiment was *w.*
Rev. 2. 17. gave him a *w.* stone
3. 4. walk with me in *w.* raiment, 5. 18. & 4. 4. & 7. 9, 13. & 15. 16. & 19. 8, 14.
Matt. 23. 27. *whited,* Acts 23. 3.
Ps. 51. 7. *whiter* than snow
WHITE HORSE, Rev. 6. 2. & 19. 11; cloud, Rev. 14. 14.
WHITE THRONE, Rev. 20. 11.
WHOLE, Ps. 9. 1. & 119. 10. Isa. 54. 5. Mic. 4. 13. Zech. 4. 14. Matt. 6. 26. Eph. 6. 11. 1 John 2. 2. & 5. 19.
Job 5. 18. his hands make *w.*
Matt. 9. 12. those that are *w.* need not a physician, Luke 5. 31.
Mark 5. 34. faith hath made thee *w.*, 10. 52. Luke 8. 48. & 17. 19.
John 5. 4. *w.* of whatsoever dis.
Acts 9. 34. Christ maketh thee *w.*
Jer. 46. 28. *wholly,* 1 Thes. 5. 23. 1 Tim. 4. 15.
Prov. 15. 4. *wholesome,* 1 Tim. 6. 3.
WHORE, Lev. 19. 29. & 21. 7, 9. Deut. 22. 21. & 23. 17, 18. Prov. 23. 27. Ezek. 16. 28. Rev. 17. 1, 16.
Jer. 3. 9. *whoredom,* Ezek. 16. Hos. 2. 2, 4. & 4. 11, 12. & 5. 3, 4.
Eph. 5. 5. *whoremonger,* 1 Tim. 1. 10. Heb. 13. 4. Rev. 21. 8. & 22. 15.
R. V. Lev. 19. 29; 21. 7, 9; Deut. 22. 21; 23. 17; Judg. 19. 2; Ezek. 16. 28, 33; Rev. 17. 1, 15, 16; 19. 2. harlot
WICKED, Ex. 23. 7. Deut. 15. 9. & 25. 1.
Gen. 18. 25. destroy right. with *w.*
1 Sam. 2. 9. *w.* shall be silent
Job 21. 30. *w.* is reserved till the
34. 18. is it fit to say to king thou art *w.*
Ps. 7. 11. God is angry with the *w.*
9. 17. *w.* shall be turned into
11. 6. on *w.* he will rain snares
119. 155. salvation is far from *w.*
145. 20. all the *w.* shall he destroy
Prov. 11. 5. *w.* shall fall by his
21. *w.* shall not be unpunished
21. 12. God overthroweth the *w.*
28. 1. the *w.* flee when no man
Eccl. 7. 17. be not overmuch *w.*
Isa. 55. 7. let the *w.* forsake his
57. 20. *w.* are like the troubled
Jer. 17. 9. heart is desperately *w.*
Ezek. 3. 18. warn the *w.*, 33. 8, 9.
Dan. 12. 10. *w.* shall do *wickedly*
Gen. 19. 7. do not so *w.*, Neh. 9. 33.
1 Sam. 12. 25. if ye shall do *w.*
Job 13. 7. will ye speak *w.* for God
Ps. 18. 21. have not *w.* departed
Gen. 6. 5. God saw that *wickedness*
39. 9. how can I do this great *w.*
1 Sam. 24. 13. *w.* proceedeth from
Job 4. 8. that sow *w.* shall reap
Ps. 7. 9. *w.* of wicked come to end
Prov. 8. 7. *w.* is abomination to
13. 6. *w.* overthroweth sinners
Eccl. 8. 8. neither shall *w.* deliver
Isa. 9. 18. *w.* burneth as the fire
Jer. 2. 19. thine own *w.* shall cor.
14. 20. we acknowledge our *w.*
Hos. 10. 13. ye have ploughed *w.*
Acts 8. 22. repent of this thy *w.*
1 John 5. 19. world lieth in *w.*
R. V. Frequent changes to evil, unrighteous, etc.
WIDE, Deut. 15. 8, 11. Ps. 35. 2. & 81. 10. Prov. 13. 3. Matt. 7. 13.
WIDOW, Mark 12. 42. 1 Tim. 5. 5. Deut. 10. 18. Ps. 146. 9. Luke 18. 3, 5.
Ps. 68. 5. *widows,* Jer. 49. 11. Matt. 23. 14. 1 Tim. 5. 3. Jas. 1. 27.

WIFE, Ex. 20. 17. Lev. 21. 13.
Prov. 5. 18. rejoice with *w.* of
18. 22. findeth a *w.* findeth a good
Eccl. 9. 9. live joyfully with thy *w.*
Hos. 12. 12. Israel served for a *w.*
Mal. 2. 15. against *w.* of thy youth
Luke 17. 32. remember Lot's *w.*
Eph. 5. 33. every man love his *w.*
Rev. 19. 7. his *w.* made herself
21. 9. the bride, the Lamb's *w.*
1 Cor. 7. 29. *wives,* Eph. 5. 25, 28, 33. Col. 3. 18, 19. 1 Tim. 3. 11. 1 Pet. 3. 1, 7.
R. V. Ex. 19. 15; Lev. 21. 7; Judg. 21. 14; Ezra 10. 2, 10, 11, 14, 17, 18; Neh. 12. 43; 13. 23, 27; 1 Tim. 3. 11; 1 Pet. 3. 7. woman or women; Matt. 19. 29; 22. 25; Mark 10. 29; Luke 17. 27; 20. 30 —
WILDERNESS, Deut. 32. 10. Prov. 21. 19. S. of S. 3. 6. & 8. 5. Isa. 35. 1, 6. & 41. 18, 19. & 42. 11. & 43. 19, 20. Rev. 12. 6.
R. V. Job 30. 3. dry ground; Ps. 107. 40. waste; Amos 6. 14. Arabah; Ps. 78. 17; Prov. 21. 19; Isa. 33. 9; Jer. 51. 43; Matt. 15. 43; Mark 8. 14; Luke 5. 16; 8. 29. desert, or desert place
WILES, Num. 25. 18. Eph. 6. 11.
WILL, Lev. 1. 3. & 19. 5. & 22. 19.
Deut 33. 16. the good *w.* of him that dwelt in the bush
Matt. 7. 21. doeth *w.* of my Father
Luke 2. 14. good *w.* towards men
John 1. 13. *w.* of flesh, nor
3. 34. my meat is to do *w.* of him
6. 40. this is the *w.* of him that
Acts 21. 14. *w.* of the Lord be done
Eph. 5. 17. understandeth what the *w.* of the Lord is
Acts 22. 14. *his will,* John 7. 17. Rom. 2. 18. Eph. 1. 5, 9. Col. 1. 9. 2 Tim. 2. 26. Heb. 13. 21. 1 John 5. 14. Rev. 17. 17.
Luke 22. 42. *my will,* Acts 13. 22.
John 5. 30. *own will,* 6. 38. Eph. 1. 11. Heb. 2. 4. Jas. 1. 18.
Ps. 40. 8. *thy will,* 143. 10. Matt. 6. 10. & 26. 42. Heb. 10. 7, 9.
Ezra 7. 18. *will of God,* Mark 3. 35. Rom. 1. 10. & 8. 27. & 12. 2. 1 Cor. 1. 1. 2 Cor. 8. 5. Gal. 1. 4. Eph. 1. 1. & 6. 6. Col. 1. 1. & 4. 12. 1 Thes. 4. 3. Heb. 10. 36. 1 Pet. 4. 2, 19. 1 John 2. 17.
Matt. 26. 39. not as *I will,* but as
John 15. 7. ask what ye *w.* and it
17. 24. I *w.* that those thou hast
Rom. 7. 18. to *w.* is present with
Phil. 2. 13. worketh to *w.* and to
Rev. 22. 17. whosoever *w.* let him
Rom. 9. 16. of him that *willeth*
Heb. 10. 26. if we sin *wilfully*
Ex. 35. 5. whoso is of a *willing* heart
1 Chron. 28. 9. with a perfect heart and *w.* mind
Ps. 110. 3. people shall be *w.* in the
Isa. 1. 19. be *w.* and obedient
Matt. 26. 41. Spirit is *w.* but the
Luke 22. 42. if thou be *w.* remove
John 5. 35. *w.* for a season to rej.
2 Cor. 5. 8. *w.* rather to be absent
1 Tim. 6. 18. be *w.* to communicate
Heb. 13. 18. *w.* in all things to
2 Pet. 3. 9. not *w.* any should per.
Judg. 5. 2. *willingly* offered them.
1 Chron. 29. 9. heart offered *w.*
Lam. 3. 33. Lord doth not afflict *w.*
Hos. 5. 11. he *w.* walked after the
Col. 2. 23. wisdom in *will worship*
R. V. Changes of the pure auxiliary are to would, should, shall, etc. Ex. 35. 29. free will; Job 39. 9. content; Mark 15. 15; 2 Pet. 3. 9. wishing; Luke 10. 29; 23. 20; Acts 24. 27; 25. 9; 27. 43; Heb. 13. 18. desiring; 1 Thes. 2. 8. well pleased; Heb. 6. 17. being minded
WILLOWS, Lev. 23. 40. Isa. 44. 4.
WIN, Phil. 3. 8.
Prov. 11. 30. *winneth*
R. V. Phil. 3. 8. gain

WIND, Job 7. 7. & 30. 15. Ps. 103. 16.
Prov. 11. 29. inherit *w.*
30. 4. gathereth the *w.*
Eccl. 11. 4. that observeth the *w.*
Isa. 26. 18. have brought forth *w.*
Jer. 5. 13. prophets shall become *w.*
10. 13. bring *w.* out of his treas.
Hos. 8. 7. sown *w.*
John 3. 8. *w.* bloweth where it
Eph. 4. 14. about with every *w.*
2 Kings 2. 11. *whirlwind,* Prov. 1. 27. & 10. 25. Isa. 66. 15. Hos. 8. 7. & 13. 3. Nah. 1. 3. Hab. 3. 14. Zech. 7. 14. & 9. 14.
Ezek. 37. 9. *winds,* Matt. 8. 26. Luke 8. 25.
R. V. Isa. 27. 8. blast; Jer. 14. 6. air; Hos. 13. 15. breath; Ezek. 41. 7. encompass
WINDOWS, Gen. 7. 11. Eccl. 12. 3. S. of S. 2. 9. Isa. 60. 8. Jer. 9. 21.
R. V. Gen. 6. 16. light; 1 Kings 7. 4, 5. prospects; Isa. 54. 12. pinnacles
WINE maketh glad the heart, Ps. 104. 15.
Prov. 20. 1. *w.* is a mocker
21. 17. loveth *w.* and oil shall
23. 30. that tarry long at *w.* that
31. look not upon *w.* when it is
S. of S. 1. 2. love is better than *w.*
Isa. 5. 11. till *w.* inflame them
25. 6. *w.* on the lees well refined
55. 1. buy *w.* and milk
Hos. 2. 9. take away my *w.* in
4. 11. *w.* take away the heart
Hab. 2. 5. transgresseth by *w.*
Eph. 5. 18. not drunk with *w.*
1 Tim. 3. 3. not given to *w.*, 8.
5. 23. a little *w.* for stomach's
Prov. 23. 20. *wine-bibber,* Matt. 11. 19.
R. V. Num. 18. 12; Mic. 6. 15. vintage; Num. 28. 7. drink; 2 Sam. 6. 19; 1 Chron. 16. 3; Hos. 3. 1. raisins
WINGS of the God of Israel, Ruth 2. 12.
Ps. 17. 8. hide under shadow of *w.*, 36. 7. & 57. 1. & 61. 4. & 91. 4.
18. 10. on *w.* of the wind, 2 Sam. 22. 11.
Prov. 23. 5. riches make themselves *w.* and fly away
Isa. 6. 2. seraphims; each had six *w.*
Mal. 4. 2. with healing in his *w.*
R. V. Deut. 32. 11. pinions
WINK, Job 15. 12. Ps. 35. 19. Prov. 6. 13. & 10. 10. Acts 17. 30.
R. V. *overlook,* Acts 17. 30. ignorance God *w.* at
WINTER, S. of S. 2. 11. Zech. 14. 8.
WIPE, 2 Kings 21. 13. Neh. 13. 14. Prov. 6. 33. Isa. 25. 8. Rev. 7. 17. & 21. 4.
WISE, Gen. 41. 39. Ex. 23. 8. Deut. 16. 19.
Deut. 4. 6. this great nation is a *w.* people
Job 5. 13. taketh the *w.* in their
11. 12. vain man would be *w.*
32. 9. great men are not always *w.*
Ps. 2. 10. be *w.* O kings, be taught
29. 7. making the simple *w.*
Prov. 3. 7. be not *w.* in own eyes
35. the *w.* shall inherit glory
26. 12. a man *w.* in his own conceit
Eccl. 7. 4. heart of *w.* in house
9. 1. the *w.* are in the hand of God
Isa. 5. 21. are *w.* in their own eyes
Jer. 4. 22. they are *w.* to do evil
Dan. 12. 3. *w.* shall shine as stars
Hos. 14. 9. who is *w.* and he shall
Matt. 10. 16. be ye *w.* as serpents
Rom. 1. 22. professing themselves to be *w.*
16. 19. be *w.* to that which is good
1 Cor. 3. 18. seem. *w.* in this world
4. 10. but ye are *w.* in Christ
Eph. 5. 15. not as fools but as *w.*
2 Tim. 3. 15. is able to make thee *w.*

Matt. 10. 42. *in no wise* lose his
Luke 18. 17. shall—enter therein
John 6. 37. cometh, I will—cast out
Rev. 21. 27. shall—enter into it
Deut. 4. 6. this is your *wisdom*
1 Kings 4. 29. God gave Solomon *w.*, 5. 12.
Job 28. 28. fear of Lord, that is *w.*
Prov. 4. 5. get *w.* get understand.
7. *w.* is the principal thing, 8.
16. 16. better to get *w.* than gold
19. 8. he that getteth *w.* loveth his own soul
Eccl. 1. 18. in much *w.* is much grief
8. 1. a man's *w.* maketh his face
Matt. 11. 19. *w.* is justified of her
1 Cor. 1. 30. who of God is made unto us *w.*
2. 6. we speak *w.* among perfect
3. 19. *w.* of this world is foolish.
2 Cor. 1. 12. not with fleshly *w.*
Col. 1. 9. might be filled with all *w.*
4. 5. walk in *w.* towards them that
Jas. 1. 5. if any lack *w.* ask it of
3. 17. *w.* from above is pure
Rev. 5. 12. worthy is the Lamb to receive *w.*
13. 18. here is *w.* let him that hath, 17. 9.
Ps. 111. 10. *of wisdom*, Prov. 9. 10. & 10. 21. Mic. 6. 9. Col. 2. 3. Jas. 3. 13.
64. 9. *wisely*, 101. 2. Eccl. 7. 10.
1 Kings 4. 31. *wiser*, Job 35. 11. Ps. 119. 98. Luke 16. 8. 1 Cor. 1. 25.
R. V. 1 Chron. 26. 14. discreet; Prov. 1. 5. sound; 1 Tim. 1. 17; Jude 25——; Lev. 19. 17; Deut. 21. 23. surely; Rom. 10. 6. thus; 1 Chron. 22. 12. discretion; Job 36. 5; Ps. 136. 5; Prov. 10. 21; Eccl. 10. 3. understanding; Prov. 1. 3. wise dealing; 8. 5. subtilty; 8. 14. knowledge; Dan. 2. 14. prudence
WITCH, Ex. 22. 18. Deut. 18. 10.
1 Sam. 15. 23. *witchcraft*, Gal. 5. 20.
WITHDRAW, Job 9. 13. & 33. 17. Prov. 25. 17. S. of S. 5. 6. 2 Thes. 3. 6. 1 Tim. 6. 5.
WITHERED hand of Jeroboam healed, 1 Kings 13.
——hand healed by Christ, Matt. 12. 10. Mark 3. Luke 6. 6.
WITHHOLD not thy mercies, Ps. 40. 11.
Ps. 84. 11. no good thing will he *w.*
Prov. 3. 27. *w.* not good from them
23. 13. *w.* not correction from child
Gen. 20. 6. *withheld*, 22. 12. Job 31. 16.
Job 42. 2. *withholden*, Jer. 5. 25.
Prov. 11. 24. *withholdeth*, 26. 2 Thes. 2. 6.
R. V. Job 42. 2; 2 Thes. 2. 6. restrain
WITHIN, Ps. 40. 8. & 45. 13. Matt. 3. 9. & 23. 26. Mark 7. 21. 2 Cor. 7. 5. Rev. 5. 1.
WITHOUT, Prov. 1. 20. & 24. 27. 1 Cor. 5. 12. 2 Cor. 7. 5. Col. 4. 5. Rev. 22. 15.
WITHSTAND, Eccl. 4. 12. Eph. 6. 13.
Acts 11. 17. what was I, that I could *w.* God
Gal. 2. 11. *withstood*, 2 Tim. 4. 15.
WITNESS, Gen. 31. 44, 48. Lev. 5. 1.
Num. 35. 30. one *w.* shall not testify against him, Deut. 17. 6. & 19. 15. 2 Cor. 13. 1.
Judg. 11. 10. Lord be *w.*, 1 Sam. 12. 5. Jer. 42. 5. & 29. 23. Mic. 1. 2.
Ps. 89. 37. as a faithful *w.* in heaven
Prov. 14. 5. a faithful *w.* will not lie
Isa. 55. 4. him for a *w.* to the people
Mal. 3. 5. I will be a swift *w.* again.
John 3. 11. ye receive not our *w.*
Acts 14. 17. left not himself without *w.*
1 John 5. 10. believeth him hath *w.*
Rev. 1. 5. is the faithful *w.*, 3. 14.
20. 4. beheaded for *w.* of Jesus
Deut. 17. 6. two or three *witnesses*, 19. 15. 2 Cor. 13. 1. Matt. 18. 16. Heb. 10. 28. 1 Tim. 5. 19. Num. 35. 30.
Josh. 24. 22. ye are *w.* against
Isa. 43. 10. ye are my *w.* saith the Lord, 12. & 44. 8.
1 Thes. 2. 10. ye are *w.* and God
6. 12. before many *w.*
Heb. 12. 1. so great a cloud of *w.*
Rev. 11. 3. power unto my two *w.*
WIVES, their duties to husbands, Gen. 3. 16. Ex. 20. 14. Rom. 7. 2. 1 Cor. 7. 3. & 14. 34. Eph. 5. 22, 33. Tit. 2. 4. 1 Pet. 3. 1.
good, Prov. 12. 4. & 18. 22. & 19. 14. & 31. 10.
Levitical laws concerning, Ex. 21. 3, 22. & 22. 16. Num. 5. 12. & 30. Deut. 21. 10, 15. & 24. 1. Jer. 3. 1. Matt. 19. 3.
the wife a type of the church, Eph. 5. 23. Rev. 19. 7. & 21. 9.
WIZARDS, Lev. 19. 31. & 20. 6. Isa. 8. 19.
WOES against wickedness, etc., Isa. 5. 8. & 10. 1. & 29. 15. & 31. 1. & 45. 9. Jer. 22. 13. Amos 6. 1. Mic. 2. 1. Hab. 2. 6. Zeph. 3. 1. Zech. 11. 17. Matt. 26. 24. Luke 6. 24. Jude 11. Rev. 8. 13. & 9. 12. & 11. 14.
against unbelief, Matt. 11. 21. & 23. 13. Luke 10. 13. & 11. 42.
WOLF, Isa. 11. 6. & 65. 25. Jer. 5. 6. Ezek. 22. 27. *wolves*, Hab. 1. 8. Zeph. 3. 3. Matt. 7. 15. & 10. 16. Acts 20. 29.
WOMAN, Gen. 2. 23. & 3. 15. Lev. 18. 22, 23. & 20. 13. Num. 30. 3.
Prov. 11. 16. gracious *w.* retaineth honor
Ps. 48. 6. pain as of a *w.* in travail
Prov. 12. 4. a virtuous *w.* is a crown
14. 1. every wise *w.* buildeth her
31. 10. a virtuous *w.* who can find
30. *w.* that feareth the Lord shall
Eccl. 7. 26. *w.* whose heart is snares
28. *w.* among all I have not found
Isa. 49. 15. can a *w.* forget her suckl-
54. 6. called thee as a *w.* forsaken
Jer. 31. 22. *w.* shall compass a man
Matt. 5. 28. looketh on a *w.* to lust
15. 28. O *w.* great is thy faith
John 2. 4. *w.* what have I to do with
8. 3. brought *w.* taken in adultery
19. 26. *w.* behold thy son
Rom. 1. 27. the natural use of *w.*
1 Cor. 11. 7. *w.* is the glory of man
Gal. 4. 4. sent his Son made of a *w.*
1 Tim. 2. 12. I suffer not *w.* to teach
14. *w.* being deceived was in the
Rev. 12. 1. *w.* clothed with the sun, 6. 16.
17. 18. *w.* thou sawest is that city
Judg. 5. 24. blessed above *women* shall Jael be
Prov. 31. 3. give not thy strength to *w.*
S. of S. 1. 8. fairest among *w.*, 5. 9. & 6. 1.
Jer. 9. 17. call for the mourning *w.*
Lam. 4. 10. *w.* had sodden children
Matt. 11. 11. among them born of *w.*
Luke 1. 28. blessed art thou among *w.*
Rom. 1. 26. *w.* did change their
1 Cor. 14. 34. let *w.* keep silence
1 Tim. 2. 9. let *w.* adorn themselves
11. let *w.* learn in silence with
5. 14. that the younger *w.* marry
1 Pet. 3. 5. after this manner holy *w.*
Rev. 14. 4. are not defiled with *w.*
WOMB, Gen. 25. 23. & 29. 31.
Gen. 49. 25. blessings of the *w.* and
1 Sam. 1. 5. Lord hath shut her *w.*
Ps. 22. 9. took me out of the *w.*
10. I was cast upon thee from *w.*
139. 13. covered me in mother's *w.*
Eccl. 11. 5. how bones grow in *w.*
Isa. 44. 2. the Lord that formed thee from the *w.*
Hos. 9. 14. give them miscarrying *w.*
Luke 1. 42. blessed is fruit of thy *w.*
11. 27. blessed is *w.* that bare thee
23. 29. blessed are *w.* that never
R. V. Deut. 7. 13. body
WONDER, Deut. 13. 1. & 28. 46. Ps. 71. 7. Isa. 29. 14. Rev. 12. 1.
Acts 13. 41. *w.* and perish, Hab. 1. 5.
Ex. 3. 20. *wonders*, 7. 3. & 15. 11.
1 Chron. 16. 12. remember his *w.*, Ps. 105. 5.
Job 9. 10. God doeth *w.*, Ps. 77. 11, 14.
Ps. 88. 11. wilt thou show *w.* to the dead
Dan. 12. 6. how long to the end of these *w.*
John 4. 48. except they see signs and *w.*
Acts 2. 43. many *w.* were done, 6. 8.
Rom. 15. 19. mighty signs and *w.*
2 Thes. 2. 9. and signs and lying *w.*
Rev. 13. 13. he doeth great *w.*
Zech. 3. 8. they are men *wondered*
Isa. 59. 16. *w.* there was no inter.
Luke 4. 22. *w.* at the gracious words
Rev. 13. 3. all the world *w.* after
17. 6. I *w.* with great admiration
Job 37. 14. *wondrous* works, Ps. 26. 7. & 75. 1. & 105. 2. & 119. 27. & 145. 5. & 71. 17. & 78. 32. & 106. 22.
Ps. 72. 18. *w.* things, 86. 10. & 119. 18.
Judg. 13. 19. *wondrously*, Joel 2. 26.
Deut. 28. 59. thy plagues *wonderful*
Ps. 119. 129. thy testimonies are *w.*
Prov. 30. 18. three things too *w.* for
Isa. 9. 6. his name shall be called *W.*
Jer. 5. 30. a *w.* thing is committed
Ps. 139. 14. *wonderfully*, Lam. 1. 9.
R. V. Rev. 12. 1, 3. sign; Gen. 24. 21. looked stedfastly; Mark 6. 51. ——; Luke 8. 25; 11. 14. marvelled; Acts 8. 13. amazed; Ps. 78. 4. wondrous; Matt. 7. 22; Acts 2. 21. mighty; 1 Chron. 16. 9; Ps. 105. 2. marvellous
WOOD, hay, stubble, 1 Cor. 3. 12.
2 Tim. 2. 20. also vessels of *w.* and
R. V. Deut. 19. 5; Josh. 17. 18; 1 Sam. 14. 25, 26; Ps. 83. 14; Eccl. 2. 6; Isa. 7. 2; Mic. 7. 14. forest; 1 Chron. 22. 4. trees; Ex. 26. 32, 37; 36. 36; Ps. 141. 7——
WORD, Num. 23. 5. Deut. 4. 2.
Deut. 8. 3. every *w.* of God, Matt. 4. 4.
30. 14. *w.* is very nigh, Rom. 10. 8.
Ps. 68. 11. the Lord gave the *w.*
Prov. 15. 23. *w.* spoken in due season
25. 11. a *w.* fitly spoken is like apples of gold
Isa. 29. 21. man an offender for a *w.*
50. 4. how to speak a *w.* in season
Jer. 5. 13. the *w.* is not in them
Matt. 8. 8. speak the *w.* only and my servant shall be healed
12. 36. every idle *w.* that men
Luke 4. 36. what a *w.* is this
John 1. 1. in the beginning was the *W.* and the *W.* was with God
14. the *W.* was made flesh
15. 3. ye are clean through the *w.*
Acts 13. 15. any *w.* of exhortation
26. to you is *w.* of salvation sent
17. 11. the *w.* with all readiness
20. 32. and to the *w.* of his grace
1 Cor. 4. 20. kingdom of God is not in *w.*
Gal. 6. 6. taught in *w.* communicate
Eph. 5. 26. washing of water by *w.*
Col. 3. 16. let *w.* of Christ dwell in
17. whatsoever ye do in *w.* or deed
1 Thes. 1. 5. Gospel came not in *w.*
2 Thes. 2. 17. stablish you in every good *w.*
3. 14. if any obey not our *w.* note
1 Tim. 5. 17. labor in *w.* and
2 Tim. 4. 2. preach *w.* be instant in
Tit. 1. 9. holding fast the faithful *w.*
Heb. 4. 2. the *w.* preached did not
5. 13. is unskilful in *w.* of right.
13. 22. suffer the *w.* of exhortation
Jas. 1. 21. receive the engrafted *w.*
22. be doers of the *w.*
3. 2. offend not in *w.*
1 Pet. 3. 1. if any obey not the *w.*
2 Pet. 1. 19. sure *w.* of prophecy
1 John 1. 1. hands handled of the *w.*

1 John 5. 7. Father, *W.* and Holy Ghost
Rev. 3. 10. kept *w.* of my patience
12. 11. overcame by *w.* of their testimony
Ps. 130. 5. in *his word* do I hope, 119. 81.
Jer. 20. 9.—was in my heart as fire
John 5. 38. have not—abiding in you
Acts 2. 41. that gladly received—were baptized
John 8. 37. *my word*, 43. Rev. 3. 8.
Isa. 8. 20. *this word*, Rom. 9. 9.
Ps. 119. 11. *thy word* have I hid in mine heart
105.—is a lamp unto my feet
140.—is very pure
160.—is true from the beginning
Jer. 15. 16.—was unto me joy and
John 17. 6. I kept—
17.—is truth
Prov. 30. 5. *word of God*, Isa. 40. 8. Mark 7. 13. Rom. 10. 17. 1 Thes. 2. 13. Heb. 4. 12. & 6. 5. 1 Pet. 1. 23. Rev. 19. 13.
2 Kings 20. 19. *word of the Lord*, Ps. 18. 30. & 33. 4. 2 Thes. 3. 1. 1 Pet. 1. 25.
Ps. 119. 43. *word of truth*, 2 Cor. 6. 7. Eph. 1. 13. Col. 1. 5. 2 Tim. 2. 15. Jas. 1. 18.
Job 23. 12. esteemed *words* of
Prov. 15. 26. *w.* of pure are pleas.
22. 17. bow down thine ear, hear *w.*
Eccl. 10. 12. the *w.* of a wise man
11. *w.* of the wise are as goads
Jer. 7. 4. trust ye not in lying *w.*
Dan. 7. 25. speak great *w.* against
Hos. 6. 5. slain by *w.* of my mouth
Zech. 1. 13. good *w.* comfortable *w.*
Matt. 26. 44. prayed, saying same *w.*
Luke 4. 22. the gracious *w.* that
John 6. 63. *w.* I speak are Spirit and
68. thou hast the *w.* of eternal life
17. 8. given unto them *w.* which
Acts 7. 22. Moses mighty in *w.* and
15. 24. troubled you with *w.*, 18. 15.
20. 35. remember the *w.* of Lord
26. 25. speak the *w.* of truth and
1 Cor. 2. 4. not with enticing *w.* of
2 Tim. 1. 13. hold fast the form of sound *w.*
2. 14. strive not about *w.* to no
Rev. 1. 3. hear *w.* of this prophecy, 22. 18.
Ps. 50. 17. *my words*, Isa. 51. 16. & 59. 21. Jer. 5. 14. Mic. 2. 7. Mark 8. 38. & 13. 31. John 5. 47. & 15. 7.
1 Thes. 4. 18. *these words*, Rev. 21. 5.
Ps. 119. 103. *thy words*, 130. & 139. Prov. 23. 8. Eccl. 5. 2. Ezek. 33. 31. Matt. 12. 37.
R. V. Num. 4. 45; Josh. 19. 50; 22. 9. commandment; Deut. 8. 3; 2 Kings 23. 16; John 7. 9; 8. 30; 9. 22, 40; 17. 1. thing; 2 Sam. 19. 14; 1 Kings 2. 42; Luke 20. 26; John 12. 47, 48. saying; 1 Kings 13. 26. mouth; 1 Chron. 21. 12. answer; Jonah 3. 6. tidings; Matt. 2. 13. tell; Luke 4. 4; Acts 28. 29; 1 John 5. 7 ——

WORK, Gen. 2. 3. Ex. 20. 10. & 31. 14.
Deut. 33. 11. accept *w.* of his hands
Job 1. 10. thou hast blessed the *w.*
10. 3. despise the *w.* of thy hands
36. 9. he showeth them their *w.*
Ps. 19. 1. the firmament sheweth his handy-*w.*
101. 3. I hate the *w.* of them that
143. 5. muse on *w.* of thy hands
Eccl. 8. 14. according to *w.* of wicked
17. I beheld all the *w.* of God
12. 14. God shall bring every *w.* into judgment
Isa. 16. 12. performed his whole *w.*
64. 8. we are called *w.* of thy hands
Jer. 10. 15. vanity and *w.* of error
18. 3. potter wrought a *w.* on the
Hab. 1. 5. a *w.* in your days, Acts 13. 41.
Mark 6. 5. could do no mighty *w.*
John 17. 4. finished *w.* thou gavest
Acts 5. 38. if this *w.* be of men
13. 2. for the *w.* whereto I called
Rom. 2. 15. show *w.* of law written
11. 6. otherwise *w.* is no more *w.*
1 Cor. 3. 13. every man's *w.* made
9. 1. are not ye my *w.* in the Lord
Eph. 4. 12. for *w.* of the ministry
2 Thes. 1. 11. *w.* of faith with pow.
2. 17. stablish you in every good *w.*
2 Tim. 4. 5. do *w.* of an evangelist
Jas. 1. 4. let patience have perfect *w.*
25. doer of the *w.* shall be blessed
1 Pet. 1. 17. judgeth every man's *w.*
Ps. 104. 23. *his work*, 62. 12. & 111. 3. Prov. 24. 29. Isa. 40. 10. Job 36. 24.
Ps. 90. 16. *thy work*, 92. 4. Prov. 24. 27. Jer. 31. 16. Hab. 3. 2.
Ex. 32. 16. *work of God*, Ps. 64. 9. Eccl. 7. 13. & 8. 17. John 6. 29. Rom. 14. 20.
Ps. 28. 5. *work of the Lord*, Isa. 5. 12. Jer. 48. 10. 1 Cor. 15. 58. & 16. 10.
Ps. 17. 4. concerning *works* of men
92. 4. triumph in *w.* of thy hands
138. 8. forsake not *w.* of thy hands
Prov. 31. 31. let her own *w.* praise
Isa. 26. 12. wrought all our *w.* in us
Dan. 4. 37. all whose *w.* are truth
John 5. 20. show him greater *w.*
10. 32. of those *w.* do ye stone me
38. believe the *w.* that I do
Acts 26. 20. *w.* meet for repent.
Rom. 3. 27. by what law? of *w.*
4. 6. God imputeth righteousness without *w.*
9. 32. sought it as by *w.* of the law
11. 6. then it is no more of *w.*
13. 12. us cast off *w.* of darkness
Gal. 2. 16. by *w.* of law no flesh be
3. 2. received ye spirit by *w.* of law
10. as many as are *w.* of the law
5. 19. *w.* of the flesh are manifest
Eph. 2. 9. not of *w.*
10. to good *w.* which God
5. 11. unfruitful *w.* of darkness
Col. 1. 21. enemies in mind by wicked *w.*
1 Thes. 5. 13. love them for their *w.*
2 Tim. 1. 9. not according to our *w.*
Tit. 1. 16. in *w.* they deny him
3. 5. not by *w.* of righteousness
Heb. 6. 1. repentance from dead *w.*
9. 14. conscience from dead *w.*
Jas. 2. 14. and have not *w.* can
20. faith without *w.* is dead, 17. 26.
21. justified by *w.*, 24. 25.
22. by *w.* was faith made perfect
1 John 3. 8. he might destroy *w.* of
Rev. 9. 20. repented not of the *w.* of
18. 6. according to her *w.*, 20. 12, 13.
Ps. 33. 4. *his works*, 78. 11. & 103. 22. 104. 31. & 106. 13. & 107. 22. & 145. 9, 17. Dan. 9. 14. Acts 15. 18. Heb. 4. 10.
Ps. 106. 35. *their works*, Isa. 66. 18. Jonah 3. 10. Matt. 23. 3, 5. 2 Cor. 11. 15. Rev. 14. 13. & 20. 12, 13.
Deut. 15. 10. *thy works*, Ps. 66. 3. & 73. 28. & 92. 5. & 104. 24. & 143. 5. Prov. 16. 3. Eccl. 9. 7. Rev. 2. 3.
Ps. 40. 5. *wonderful works*, 78. 4. & 107. 8. & 111. 4. Matt. 7. 22. Acts 2. 11.
Job 37. 14. *works of God*, Ps. 66. 5. & 78. 7. Eccl. 11. 5. John 6. 28. & 9. 3.
Ps. 46. 8. *w.* of the Lord, 111. 2.
1 Sam. 14. 6. may be the Lord will *work* for us
Isa. 43. 13. I will *w.* and who
Matt. 7. 23. depart from me ye that *w.* iniquity
John 6. 28. might *w.* works of God
9. 4. I must *w.* the works of him
Phil. 2. 12. *w.* out your salvation
2 Thes. 2. 7. iniquity doth already *w.*
3. 10. if any *w.* not, neither should
Prov. 11. 18. the wicked *worketh* a deceitful *w.*
Isa. 64. 5. meet. him that *w.* right.
John 5. 17. my Father *w.* and I *w.*
Acts 10. 35. that *w.* righteousness is accepted
2 Cor. 4. 17. *w.* for us a far more
Gal. 5. 6. faith which *w.* by love
Phil. 2. 13. it is God that *w.* in you
1 Thes. 2. 13. effectually *w.* in you
Mark 16. 20. the Lord *w.* with them
Rom. 7. 13. sin *w.* death in me
Eph. 1. 10. accord. to *w.* of mighty
3. 7. by effectual *w.* of his power
4. 28. *w.* with his hands the thing
Phil. 3. 21. accord. to *w.* whereby
2 Thes. 3. 11. *w.* not at all, but are
Heb. 13. 21. *w.* in you that which
2 Cor. 6. 1. *workers*, 11. 13. Phil. 3. 2.
Job 31. 3. *workers of iniquity*, 34. 8, 22. Ps. 5. 5. & 6. 8. & 28. 3. & 125. 5. & 141. 9. Prov. 10. 29. & 21. 15.
Matt. 10. 10. *workman*, 2 Tim. 2. 15.
Ex. 31. 3. *workmanship*, Eph. 2. 10.
R. V. Ex. 35. 33, 35. workmanship; Prov. 11. 18. wages; Isa. 40. 10; 49. 4; 61. 8; 62. 11. recompense; Ps. 77. 11; 141. 4; Matt. 16. 27. deeds; Rom. 11. 6. grace; Heb. 13. 21. thing

WORLD, 1 Sam. 2. 8. 1 Chron. 16. 30.
Ps. 17. 14. from men of the *w.*
24. 1. *w.* is the Lord's, 9. 8. Nah. 1. 5.
Ps. 50. 12. *w.* is mine and the ful.
Eccl. 3. 11. hath set *w.* in his heart
Isa. 26. 9. the inhabitants of the *w.* learn righteousness
Jer. 10. 12. established the *w.* by his wisdom, 51. 15. Ps. 93. 1. & 96. 10.
Matt. 16. 26. what is a man profited if he shall gain the whole *w.* and lose his own soul, Mark 8. 36.
18. 7. woe to the *w.* because
Mark 16. 15. go into all the *w.* and
Luke 20. 35. worthy to obtain that *w.*
John 1. 10. *w.* was made by him, and *w.* knew him not
29. Lamb of God taketh away sin of the *w.*
3. 16. God so loved the *w.* he gave
17. *w.* through him might be saved
7. 7. the *w.* cannot hate you, but
14. 17. whom *w.* cannot receive
19. *w.* seeth me no more; but ye
15. 18. if the *w.* hate you
19. chosen you out of the *w.* therefore the *w.* hateth you
17. 9. I pray not for the *w.*
11. I am no more in the *w.*
16. not of *w.* even as I am not of *w*
23. *w.* may know thou hast sent
Rom. 3. 19. all the *w.* become guilty
1 Cor. 1. 21. *w.* by wisdom knew not
Gal. 6. 14. *w.* is crucified unto me
Col. 1. 6. as in all *w.* and bringeth
Tit. 1. 2. promised before *w.* began
Heb. 2. 5. *w.* to come, 6. 5.
11. 38. the *w.* was not worthy
1 John 2. 2. a propitiation for sins of the whole *w.*
2. 15. love not the *w.* nor things in the *w.*
16. all that is in the *w.* is of the *w.*
3. 1. the *w.* knoweth us not
4. 5. they are of the *w.* they speak of the *w.* and the *w.* heareth them
Rev. 3. 10. temptation come on all *w.*
13. 3. all *w.* wondered after beast
Matt. 12. 32. *this world*, John 8. 32. & 13. 36. Rom. 12. 2. 1 Tim. 6. 7.
Heb. 1. 2. he made the *worlds*
11. 3. the *w.* were framed by him

R. V. Ps. 22. 27; Isa. 62. 11; Rev. 13. 13. earth; 1 Cor. 10. 11; Eph. 3. 9; Heb. 6. 5; 9. 26. age or ages; Isa. 60. 4. of old; Matt. 12. 32. that which is; Rom. 16. 25; 2 Tim. 1. 9; Tit. 1. 2. time eternal; John 17. 12 ——

WORM, Ex. 16. 20. Isa. 51. 8.
Job 25. 6. man that is a *w.*
Isa. 41. 14. fear not, thou *w.* Jacob
66. 24. their *w.* shall not die, Mark 9. 44, 48.
Job 19. 26. *worms* destroy my body, Acts 12. 23.
Deut. 29. 18. *wormwood*, Prov. 5. 4. Lam. 3. 15, 19. Amos 5. 7. Rev. 8. 11.
R. V. Mic. 7. 17. crawling thing; Job 19. 26; Mark 9. 44, 46 ——

WORSE, Matt. 12. 45. John 5. 14. 1 Cor. 8. 8. & 11. 17. 2 Tim. 3. 13. 2 Pet. 2. 20.

WORSHIP the Lord in beauty of holiness, 1 Chron. 16. 29. Ps. 29. 2. & 66. 4. & 96. 9. & 45. 11. & 95. 6. & 99. 5. Matt. 4. 10.
Matt. 15. 9. in vain do they *w.* me
John 4. 24. *w.* him must *w.* in truth
Acts 17. 23. whom ye ignorantly *w.*
24. 14. so *w.* I the God of my
Rev. 3. 9. *w.* before thy feet
19. 10. to *w.* God, 22. 9.
Ex. 4. 31. *worshipped*, 32. 8. Jer. 1. 16. 1 Chron. 29. 20. Rom. 1. 25. 2 Thes. 2. 4. Rev. 5. 14. & 7. 11. & 11. 16. & 13. 4.
R. V. 2 Kings 17. 36. bow; Luke 14. 10. glory; Acts 7. 42; 17. 25; 24. 14. serve

WORTH, Job 24. 25. Prov. 10. 20.
Gen. 32. 10. I am not *worthy* of least
Matt. 8. 8. I am not *w.* thou shouldest
10. 10. workman is *w.* of his meat
13. if house be *w.* let your peace
22. 8. that were bidden were not *w.*
Luke 3. 8. fruits *w.* of repentance
7. 4. *w.* for whom he should do this
10. 7. laborer is *w.* of his hire
15. 19. no more *w.* to be called
Acts 5. 41. counted *w.* to suffer
Rom. 8. 18. not *w.* to be compared
Eph. 4. 1. walk *w.* of the vocation
Col. 1. 10. walk *w.* of the Lord being
1 Thes. 2. 12. walk *w.* of God who
2 Thes. 1. 5. be counted *w.* of the
11. God count you *w.* of this calling
1 Tim. 1. 15. *w.* of all acceptation, 4. 9.
5. 17. elders *w.* of double honor
18. laborer is *w.* of reward
6. 1. counted masters *w.* of honor
Heb. 11. 38. of whom world was not *w.*
Rev. 3. 4. walk in white, they are *w.*
5. 12. *w.* is the Lamb that was slain
16. 6. blood to drink; for they are *w.*

WOULD God, Ex. 16. 3. Num. 11. 29. Acts 26. 29. 1 Cor. 4. 8. 2 Cor. 11. 1.
Neh. 9. 30. *would not*, Isa. 30. 15. Matt. 18. 30. & 23. 30, 37. Rom. 11. 25.
Prov. 1. 25. *w.* none of my reproof
30. they *w.* none of my counsel
Matt. 7. 12. whatsoever ye *w.* that men should do unto you
Rev. 3. 15. I *w.* thou wert cold or hot
R. V. Many changes to did, could, may, should, might, etc.

WOUND, Ex. 21. 25. Prov. 6. 33. Jer. 10. 19. & 15. 18. & 30. 12, 14. Mic. 1. 9.
Prov. 27. 6. *wounds*, Isa. 1. 6. Jer. 30. 17.
Deut. 32. 39. I *wound* and I heal
1 Cor. 8. 12. *w.* their weak conscience
Rev. 13. 3. his deadly *w.* was healed, 14.
Ps. 69. 26. *wounded*, 109. 22. S. of S. 5. 7.
Prov. 18. 14. a *w.* spirit who can bear
Isa. 53. 5. *w.* for our transgressions
Job 5. 18. he *woundeth* and his hands
R. V. Prov. 18. 8; 26. 22. dainty morsels; Obad. 7. snare; Rev. 13. 3, 12. death stroke; 2 Sam. 22. 39; Ps. 18. 38; 32. 39; 110. 6; Rev. 13. 13. smite or smitten through; 1 Sam. 31. 3; 1 Chron. 10. 3. distressed; Isa. 51. 9. pierced; Luke 10. 30. beat

WRATH, Gen. 49. 7. Ex. 32. 10, 11.
Num. 16. 46. *w.* gone out from
Deut. 32. 27. feared *w.* of the enemy
Neh. 13. 18. bring more *w.* on Israel
Job 5. 2. *w.* killeth the foolish man
Prov. 16. 14. *w.* of a king is as mes.
Isa. 54. 8. in a little *w.* I hid my face
Matt. 3. 7. flee from *w.* to come
Rom. 2. 5. treasure up *w.* against
5. 9. saved from *w.* through him
12. 19. give place unto *w.*
Eph. 2. 3. by nature children of *w.*
4. 26. let not the sun go down on your *w.*
1 Thes. 1. 10. delivered from the *w.*
2. 16. *w.* is come on them to the
1 Tim. 2. 8. holy hands without *w.*
Heb. 11. 27. not fearing *w.* of king
Jas. 1. 19. slow to speak, slow to *w.*
20. *w.* of man worketh not right.
Rev. 6. 16. from *w.* of the Lamb
12. 12. having great *w.* because
14. 8. wine of *w.* of her fornication, 18. 3.
Ezra 8. 22. *his wrath*, Ps. 2. 5, 12. & 78. 38. Jer. 7. 29. & 10. 10. Rev. 6. 17.
Num. 25. 11. *my wrath*, Ps. 95. 11. Isa. 10. 6. & 60. 10. Ezek. 7. 14. Hos. 5. 10.
Ps. 38. 1. *thy wrath*, 85. 3. & 88. 7, 16. & 9. 46. & 90. 9, 11. & 102. 10. 89. 38. *wroth*, Isa. 54. 9. & 57. 17.
R. V. Num. 11. 33; Deut. 11. 17; 2 Chron. 29. 10; 30. 8; Job 36. 13; 40. 11; Ps. 55. 3; 78. 31; Prov. 14. 29; Jer. 44. 8. anger; Deut. 32. 27. provocation; Job 5. 2; Prov. 12. 16; 27. 3. vexation; Ps. 58. 9. burning

WREST, Ex. 23. 2. 2 Pet. 3. 16.

WRESTLE, Gen. 32. 24, 25. Eph. 6. 12.

WRETCHED, Rom. 7. 24. Rev. 3. 17.

WRINKLE, Job 16. 8. Eph. 5. 27.

WRITE, Ex. 34. 1, 27. Deut. 27. 3. Isa. 3. 8. Jer. 30. 2. Hab. 2. 2.
Deut. 6. 9. *w.* them upon the posts
Prov. 3. 3. *w.* them on the table of thine heart, 7. 3.
Jer. 31. 33. I will *w.* it in their hearts
Ps. 102. 18. be *written* for the generation
Prov. 22. 20. have not I *w.* to thee
Eccl. 12. 10. that which was *w.*
Dan. 12. 1. shall be found *w.* in book
1 Cor. 10. 11. *w.* for our admonition
2 Cor. 3. 3. ministered by us, *w.* not with ink, but with the Spirit
Heb. 12. 23. are *w.* in heaven, Luke 10. 20.
R. V. Few changes, and chiefly to wrote

WRONG, Ps. 105. 14. Jer. 22. 3, 13.
Matt. 20. 13. I do thee no *w.* didst
1 Cor. 6. 7. why not rather take *w.*, 8.
Col. 3. 25. that doeth *w.* shall receive
2 Cor. 7. 2. *wronged*, Phile. 18.
Prov. 8. 36. *wrongeth* his own soul
R. V. Jer. 22. 13. injustice; Hab. 1. 4. perverted

WROUGHT, 1 Sam. 6. 6. & 14. 45.
Ps. 139. 15. curiously *w.* in lowest
Ezek. 20. 9. I *w.* for my name's sake, 22.
John 3. 21. his works are *w.* in God
2 Cor. 5. 5. that hath *w.* us for the selfsame thing is God
Eph. 1. 20. which he *w.* in Christ
1 Pet. 4. 3. have *w.* will of Gentiles
R. V. Ex. 26. 36; 27. 16; 36. 1. work; Deut. 17. 2. doeth; 1 Kings 16. 25; 2 Kings 3. 2; 2 Chron. 21. 6; 34. 13. did; 2 Sam. 18. 13. dealt; Jonah 1. 11. grow; Ps. 78. 43. set; Matt. 20. 12. spent; 2 Thes. 3. 8. working

Y

YARN, Solomon brought out of East, 1 Kings 10. 28.
2 Chron. 1. 16. merchants received linen *y.*
R. V. 1 Kings 10. 28; 2 Chron. 1. 16. droves

YE, wherefore look so sadly, Gen. 40. 7.
Matt. 5. 13. *y.* are the salt of earth

YEA, yea, nay, nay, Matt. 5. 37.
2 Cor. 1. 18. *y.* and nay
20. *y.* and amen

YEAR, Gen. 1. 14. & 47. 9.
Ex. 7. 7. Moses was fourscore *y.* old
Lev. 12. 6. sh. bring lamb of first *y.*
Num. 1. 3. from twenty *y.* old and upward
Deut. 8. 2. God led thee forty *y.* in
Josh. 5. 6. chil. of Is. walk. forty *y.*
Judg. 3. 11. land had rest forty *y.*
Ruth 1. 1. dwelt there about ten *y.*
1 Sam. 1. 7. he did so *y.* by *y.* when
2 Sam. 14. 28. A. dw. two *y.* in Jer.
1 Kings 5. 11. Solomon gave to Hiram *y.* by *y.*
2 Kings 1. 17. in second *y.* of Jehoram
1 Chron. 21. 12. either three *y.* famine, or
2 Chron. 8. 13. three times in *y.*; or
Ezra 1. 1. in first *y.* of Cyrus of Persia
Neh. 1. 1. twent *y.*, I was in Shus.
Esth. 1. 3. third *y.* he ma. a decree
Job 10. 5. are thy *y.* as man's days
Ps. 90. 4. thousand *y.* in thy sight are but as yesterday
10. our *y.* are threescore and
Prov. 10. 27. *y.* of the wicked shall be shortened
Eccl. 6. 3. so that his *y.* be many
Isa. 6. 1. In *y.* Uz. died I saw Lord
Jer. 17. 8. not care. in *y.* of drought
Ezek. 1. 2. fifth *y.* of King Jehoiac.
Dan. 1. 5. so nourish. them three *y.*
Joel 2. 2. ev. to *y.* of many genera.
Amos 1. 1. two *y.* before the earth.
Mic. 6. 6. come with calves of a *y.* old?
Hab. 3. 2. thy work in midst of *y.*
Hag. 1. 1. in second *y.* of Da. came
Zech. 14. 16. go up *y.* to *y.* to wor.
Mal. 3. 4. offerings, as in former *y.*
Matt. 9. 20. an issue of bl. twenty *y.*
Mark 5. 42. she was age of twelve *y.*
Luke 4. 19. to preach accep. *y.* of Lord
John 2. 20. forty and six *y.* was the temple in building
Acts 4. 22. the man was ab. fort. *y.*
Rom. 15. 23. hav. gr. desire many *y.*
2 Cor. 8. 10. but to be forward a *y.*
Gal. 1. 18. aft. three *y.* went to Jer.
1 Tim. 5. 9. to num. und. threesc. *y.*

Heb. 1. 12. and thy *y.* shall not fail
2 Pet. 3. 8. and thous. *y.* as one day
Rev. 20. 2. Sa., bound him thous. *y.*
YESTERDAY, Job 8. 9. Hab. 13. 8.
YIELD, fruit after his kind, Gen. 1. 11.
Lev. 25. 19. land shall *y.* her fr., and
Num. 17. 8. rod of Aa. *y.* almonds
Deut. 11. 17. land *y.* not her fruit
2 Chron. 30. 8. *y.* yourselves unto Lord
Neh. 9. 37. it *y.* increase to kings
Ps. 67. 6. shall earth *y.* her increase
Prov. 12. 12. root of right. *y.* fruit
Eccl. 10. 4. *y.* pacifi. great offences
Isa. 5. 10. ten acres sh. *y.* one bath
Jer. 17. 8. nei. shall cease fr. *y.* fruit
Ezek. 34. 27. earth sh. *y.* her incre.
Hos. 8. 7. the bud shall *y.* no meal
Joel 2. 22. fig tree and vi. *y.* stren.
Hab. 3. 17. altho. fields *y.* no meat
Matt. 27. 50. Jesus *y.* up the ghost
Mark 4. 7. choked it, it *y.* no fruit
Acts 23. 21. do not thou *y.* to them
Rom. 6. 13. but *y.* yourselves unto God
Heb. 12. 11. it *y.* peaceable fruit
Jas. 3. 12. no fount. bo. *y.* salt wat.
Rev. 22. 2. tree of life *y.* her fruit
R. V. Num. 17. 8. bare; Acts 5. 10. gave; Rom. 16. 19. presented
YOKE, break from thy neck, Gen. 27. 40.
Lev. 26. 13. brok. bands of your *y.*
Num. 19. 2. on which nev. came *y.*
Deut. 28. 48. put *y.* of iron on thy n.
1 Sam. 11. 7. they took a *y.* of oxen
14. 14. a *y.* of oxen might plow
1 Kings 12. 4. thy father made our *y.* grievous
2 Chron. 10. 11. I will put more to your *y.*
Job 1. 3. J. had fiv. hun. *y.* of oxen
Isa. 9. 4. hast brok. *y.* of his burd.
Jer. 2. 20. of old I ha. broken thy *y.*
Lam. 1. 14. *y.* of my trans. is bound
Ezek. 30. 18. break there *y.* of Egy.
Hos. 11. 4. as they had taken off *y.*
Nah. 1. 13. now will I break his *y.*
Matt. 11. 30. for my *y.* is easy, and
Luke 14. 19. I bought five *y.* of oxen
Acts 15. 10. put *y.* on disciples' neck
Gal. 5. 1. be not entangled with *y.*
1 Tim. 6. 1. as many as under *y.*
R. V. Jer. 27. 2; 28. 10, 12, 13. bar or bars; 1 Sam. 14. 14 —
YOU only have I known, Amos 3. 2.
Luke 10. 16. heareth *y.* heareth me
13. 28. and *y.* yourselves thrust out
2 Cor. 12. 14. I seek not *yours* but *y.*
Eph. 2. 1. *y.* hath he quickened
Col. 1. 21. *y.* that were sometime
Luke 6. 20. *y.* is the kingdom of God
1 Cor. 3. 22. all are *y.* and ye are Christ's, 23.
YOUNG, I have been, Ps. 37. 25.
Isa. 40. 11. gently lead those with *y.*
1 Tim. 5. 1. entreat the *younger*
14. I will that *y.* women marry
1 Pet. 5. 5. ye *y.* submit to elder
Gen. 8. 21. the imagination of man is evil from his *youth*
1 Kings 18. 12. the Lord from my *y.*
Job 13. 26. possess iniquities of my *y.*
Ps. 25. 7. sins of my *y.*
103. 5. thy *y.* is renewed as eagle's
Eccl. 11. 9. O young man, in thy *y.*
10. childhood and *y.* are vanity
Jer. 2. 2. the kindness of thy *y.*
1 Tim. 4. 12. man despise thy *y.*
Prov. 7. 7. *youths*, Isa. 40. 30.
2 Tim. 2. 22. flee *youthful* lusts
R. V. 1 Sam. 20. 22. boy; Mark 7. 25; 10. 13. little; Acts 20. 12. lad; Job 29. 4. ripeness; 30. 12. rabble

Z

ZEAL for Lord, 2 Kings 10. 16.
Ps. 69. 9. the *z.* of thine house hath
119. 139. my *z.* hath consumed me
Isa. 9. 7. *z.* of the Lord will perform
59. 17. I was clad with *z.* as a cloak
63. 15. where is thy *z.* and stren.
Rom. 10. 2. they have a *z.* for God
2 Cor. 7. 11. *z.* yea, what revenge
Phil. 3. 6. concerning *z.* persecut.
Num. 25. 13. was *zealous* for his God
Acts 22. 3. I was *z.* towards God as
Tit. 2. 14. people *z.* of good works
Rev. 3. 19. therefore be *z.* and repent
Gal. 4. 18. good to be *zealously* affected in a good thing
R. V. Num. 25. 11, 13. jealous
ZION, 2 Sam. 5. 7. 1 Kings 8. 1. for Jerusalem, temple, or church, 2 Kings 19. 31. Ps. 2. 6. & 9. 11. & 14. 7. & 48. 2, 11, 12. & 146. 10. & 147. 12. Isa. 1. 27. & 2. 3. & 60. 14. & 62. 1. and in about seventy other places

---

CURIOUS FACTS AND INTERESTING INFORMATION ABOUT THE BIBLE

The 66 Books or sub-divisions comprising the Old and New Testaments contain: 1,189 Chapters, 31,093 Verses, 773,692 Words, 3,586,489 Letters.

The Shortest Verse in the Bible is the 35th in the 11th Chapter of St. John.
The Longest Verse in the Bible is the 9th in the 8th Chapter of Esther.
The Middle Verse in the Bible is the 8th in the 118th Chapter of Psalms.

The 21st Verse of the 7th Chapter of Ezra contains all the letters of the Alphabet except "j."
The 8th, 15th, 21st, and 31st Verses of the 107th Psalm are alike.

Every Verse in the 136th Psalm has the same ending.
The Longest Chapter is the 119th Psalm.
The Shortest Chapter is the 117th Psalm.

The word "Lord" occurs 7736 times in the Old and New Testaments.
The word "God" occurs 4370 times in the Old and New Testaments.
The words "Boy" and "Boys" are mentioned 3 times as follows: Gen. 25. 27; Joel 3. 3; Zech. 8. 5.
The words "Girl" and "Girls" are mentioned 2 times as follows: Joel 3. 3; Zech. 8. 5.
The name of "God" is not mentioned in the Book of Esther, or in the Song of Solomon (A. V.).
The 19th Chapter of II. Kings and the 37th Chapter of Isaiah are practically alike.